An Integrated Language Perspective in the Elementary School

An Action Approach

THIRD EDITION

Christine C. Pappas
University of Illinois at Chicago

Barbara Z. Kiefer
Teachers College, Columbia University

Linda S. Levstik
University of Kentucky

 LONGMAN

An imprint of Addison Wesley Longman, Inc.

New York • Reading, Massachusetts • Menlo Park, California • Harlow, England
Don Mills, Ontario • Sydney • Mexico City • Madrid • Amsterdam

Acquisitions Editor: Virginia L. Blanford
Marketing Manager: Renée Ortbals
Project Coordination and Text Design: Electronic Publishing Services, Inc., NYC
Cover Designer/Manager: Nancy Danahy
Cover Photo: PhotoDisc, Inc.
Full Service Production Manager: Valerie L. Zaborski
Print Buyer: Denise Sandler
Electronic Page Makeup: Electronic Publishing Services Inc., NYC
Printer and Binder: Courier/Westford, Inc.
Cover Printer: Phoenix Color Corp.

For permission to use copyrighted material, grateful acknowledgment is made to the copyright
holders on p. iv, which are hereby made part of this copyright page.

Library of Congress Cataloging-in-Publication Data
Pappas, Christine.
    An integrated language perspective in the elementary school : an action approach /
Christine C. Pappas, Barbara Z. Kiefer, Linda S. Levstik. — 3rd. ed.
        p.   cm.
    Rev. ed. of: An integrated language perspective in the elementary school. 2nd ed. c1995.
    Includes bibliographical references and index.
    ISBN 0-8013-3055-6 (pbk.)
    1. English language—Study and teaching (Elementary) 2. Language arts (Elementary)—
Curricula. I. Pappas, Christine. Integrated language perspective in the elementary school.
II. Kiefer, Barbara Zulandt, 1944– . III. Levstik, Linda S. IV. Title.
LB1576.P257   1988
372.6'043—DC21   98-28989
                                                                          CIP
                                                                          Rev.

Please visit our website at http://longman.awl.com

ISBN 0-8013-3055-6

12345678910—CRW—01009998

To our children, with love
Christina and Sara, Jon, Jennifer and Jeremy

Acknowledgments

We want to acknowledge some important people for their help and support during the process of writing this third edition. First, we want once again to thank one another. This is a fully co-written book that required immense collaboration. We are good friends and valuable co-critics. We always learn a lot from each other as we share our respective expertise.

We also had a lot of fun writing this third edition, mostly because this edition has given us the opportunity to incorporate what we have learned from students and teachers with whom we worked since the previous edition. We thank them immensely. Chris Pappas thanks the urban teachers at Andersen and Jungman in Chicago with whom she has collaborated over several years as they have attempted to develop culturally and linguistically responsive pedagogy. Barbara Kiefer thanks the preservice and inservice teachers at Teachers College, and particularly Valerie Bang-Jensen, who shared her experience with the deaf to shape the SOUNDS ALL AROUND thematic unit. Linda Levstik thanks the preservice and inservice teachers and graduate students with whom she has worked since the last edition of this book. Their questions and insightful comments have helped shape the revisions in this edition. In addition, we are especially grateful for Karen Beeman's bilingual ROOTS thematic unit. We hope we have captured all the teachers' spirit, commitment, expertise, and delight in teaching elementary-age children.

Finally, we thank our editor, Ginny Blanford, and the reviewers of this edition:

    Helen R. Abadiano, Central Connecticut State University
    John G. Barnitz, University of New Orleans
    Maria Ceprano, Buffalo State College
    Karl Matz, Mankato State University
    Jacqueline K. Peck, Cleveland State University
    Ivan J. Quandt, Temple University

Their feedback was valuable in our journey in crafting the book.

Credits

Dialogues on pp. 9 & 11 from Gordon Wells, *Learning Through Interaction: The Study of Language Development*. New York: Cambridge University Press, 1981. Reprinted by permission.

Figure 1.4 from Brian Wildsmith, *The Owl and the Woodpecker*. Oxford, England: Oxford University Press, 1971. Reprinted by permission.

Figure 1.5 from Brian Wildsmith, *Squirrels*. Oxford, England: Oxford University Press, 1974. Reprinted by permission.

Figure 1.6 from Donald Holdaway, *Foundations of Literacy*. Sydney: Ashton Scholastic, 1979. Reprinted by permission.

Figure 6.1 from *Mouse*, text copyright © 1985 by Sara Bonnett Stein, illustration copyright © 1985 by Manuel Garcia. Reprinted by permission of Harcourt Brace & Company.

Figure 6.1 from *Panda* by Susan Bonners. Copyright © 1978 by Susan Bonners. Used by permission of Dell Books, a division of Bantam Doubleday Dell Publishing Group, Inc.

Excerpt on p. 234 from *Mojave* by Diane Siebert. Illustrated by Wendell Minor (Crowell). Text copyright © 1988 by Diane Siebert. Illustrations copyright © 1988 by Wendell Minor. All selections by permission of HarperCollins Publishers, Inc.

Excerpt on p. 235 from *The See-Through Zoo: How Glass Animals Are Made*, by Suzanne Haldane. Text and photographs copyright © 1984 by Suzanne Haldane. Reprinted by permission of Pantheon Books, a division of Random House, Inc.

Excerpt on p. 238 from *Child of the Owl*, by Laurence Yep. Text copyright © 1977 by Laurence Yep. Selection by permission of HarperCollins Publishers, Inc.

Table 6.3 from Susan L. Lytle and Morton Botel, PCRP II: *Reading, Writing and Talking Across the Curriculum*. Harrisburg, PA: Pennsylvania Department of Education, 1988. Reprinted by permission of the authors.

Tables 6.4, 6.5, 6.6, 6.7 adapted from *Towards a Reading-Writing Classroom* by Andrea Butler and Jan Turbill. Published 1985 by Heinemann. Reprinted with the permission of the Primary English Teaching Association, Australia.

Figure 7.2 from "Constructing Knowledge Together: Classrooms as Centers of Inquiry and Literacy" in Sharon, *Cooperative Learning, Theory and Research*, 1990, Praeger Publishers, an imprint of Greenwood Publishing Group, Inc., Westport, CT. Reprinted by permission.

Figure 7.4 "Slave Narrative" courtesy of the Ohio Historical Society, Columbus, Ohio.

Figure 7.5 Photograph of a 1930s sorghum mill worked by a mule courtesy of the Kentucky Department for the Libraries and Archives, Frankfort, Kentucky.

Figure 7.20 from *Children's Literature in the Elementary School*, 1997, by Charlotte S. Huck, Susan Hepler, Janet Hickman, & Barbara Z. Kiefer, Brown & Benchmark, Madison, WI. Reprinted by permission.

Figure 8.19 adapted from *Childwatching at Playgroup and Nursery School*, 1980, by Kathy Sylva, Carolyn Roy, and Marjorie Painter. Reprinted by permission of Blackwell Publishers, Oxford, England.

Contents

7 More How-To: Action Approaches in Integrated Language Classrooms 252

Introduction

A Brief Sketch of the Integrated Language Perspective

Teachers who work from an integrated language perspective "own"—with their students—their curriculum. Teachers plan and develop long-range units of study—called *thematic units*—so that their students have ample opportunities to use language for many meaningful purposes. In these classrooms, speaking, listening, reading, and writing are not separate subjects or ends in and of themselves, but tools that are used together for learning worthwhile and interesting content, ideas, and information. In the process, students learn both the content and the language. Activities and projects span the curriculum so that there is enough time for children to engage in systematic and reflective inquiry on a range of topics. As children use language to learn, teachers collaborate, respond, facilitate, and support their efforts. These roles engage teachers in their own inquiry into teaching and learning.

Authentic, integrated language is promoted.

Many topics or domains are explored by children.

Teachers use a collaborative style of teaching.

This is our third edition—a *fully co-written* book—that outlines our best and latest ideas about an integrated language perspective on teaching and learning in the elementary school. It is an action approach to implement theory and practice in educating students for a democratic, multicultural society.

We believe that teachers who foster children's using their own language (listening, speaking, reading, and writing) for authentic purposes across the curriculum (in social studies, science, math, art, and music) have always existed, though perhaps their approaches were labeled something else, and may not have been based on *current* research, which we try to provide here. Also, there are current views that share the integrated language principles we address in this book but that may be called something else. For example, the whole-language perspective depicts language and learning in ways that are similar to ours. Thus, although we have used the term *integrated language* to name our perspective, we want to de-emphasize the label and instead stress the importance of the *principles* of the approach. Too frequently, important educational reforms have not lasted because people have taken on only the label without understanding the substance—the principles—that the new approach may have represented. We invite you to adopt—with a critical eye—the principles that the integrated language perspective provides and implies; we will leave you with the choice as to what you want to call your perspective and yourself as a teacher.

Willinsky (1990) uses "New Literacy" as an umbrella term to cover these approaches, which have two common features: (1) they shift control of literacy from the teacher to students; and (2) they focus on language as a social process that extends students' meanings and connections.

The principles of an integrated language perspective are now more acceptable and widely known than when our first edition was published in 1990, as well as the second edition in 1995. However, students who are learning to become teachers and those who are already practicing teachers still have difficulty in seeing how these principles of the perspectives might be realized in actual classrooms. This is because traditional, transmission-oriented curriculum and teaching and learning continue to be strongly felt in many schools. In fact, in some settings, this old view—frequently called as a cry for a "back to basics" approach—has constituted a "backlash" to teachers' and schools' efforts in developing an integrated language perspective (as well as whole-language and other similar approaches) in classrooms. These are political times.

Many teachers are not used to speaking out and being professional decision makers; many students learning to become teachers just want to find the right "methods" and want to avoid anything that might seem to be controversial. Nevertheless, because too many voices in and out of the profession of teaching are demanding to tell teachers how and what to teach, we feel we have to address these and other issues. These have been implicit in the preceding editions, but we are more explicit about them in this third edition. That is, *we* feel that we have to *speak out*, because the political climate of the times requires that teachers must be willing to *speak out*. Teachers' voices must be heard because they have special expertise to bring to the conversation of what good education entails. We believe this book provides the "good news" of teachers who have created successful thematic units and who have striven to do better through self-critique and inquiry. It also provides useful information about the various political issues that surround these efforts.

Speaking Out: Major Critical Concepts and Issues Emphasized in This Book

The five major interrelated emphases in this edition are:

A Social, Functional View of Language and Language Learning: A Genre Approach. Most human activities involve the use of language, and the nature of the language employed in these activities is determined on social grounds. A social, functional view of language considers two major questions: (1) how do people use language? or, what do people *do* with language? and (2) how is language structured for use? We will use the term *text* to stress this functional role of language doing some job in some *context*. Based on contextual factors, language users make different linguistic choices, which in turn, result in different wording patterns or different structures of text.

Because there are recurring situations in the culture in which people interact and enact social activities, this contextual regularity gives rise to regularities in texts. These similar kinds, types, or classes of communicative events/texts are what is meant by *genres*. That is, genres reflect patterns of textual and social regularity. By examining the nature and use of genres, we better understand what texts do and how they do it. And, this understanding helps teachers see how best to create experiences in the classroom for students to use and learn the genres of our society.

This approach is frequently very different from how various materials and commercially-produced programs are used in schools. These materials are rarely text- or genre-based. For example, reading materials are frequently used that focus solely on phonics or letter-sound relationships in words in "isolation" of real texts. Or these materials may be texts, but ones that are "contrived for decoding" and therefore poor examples of written language. "Formal" grammar that stresses "rules" at the sentence level only is still taught even though there has been lots of research indicating that it does not improve children's writing of various genres.

We believe that children learn to read and write by their engaging in a range of genres of high-quality children's literature. We think that although children's literature authors write *for* children, attempting to craft books that children will find interesting and exciting to read, these authors also use the typical linguistic patterns of adult genres and therefore better prepare students in literacy learning.

All of our thematic units are composed of children's literature. We explain the nature of texts and genres in several chapters (especially in Chapters 1 and 6) and how to use them throughout the book. We have also included two topics—"Phonics in Context" and "Grammar in Context" (in Chapter 7)—as well as what to do when teachers are also "stuck" with commercially-produced materials (Chapter 10). We describe and illustrate how teachers *immerse* children in reading and writing experiences

Routman (1996).

Because of the current political climate, all educators must be prepared to "speak out."

Eggins (1994)

A social, functional approach emphasizes: how people use language and how language is structured for use.

See Chapter 1 for more on "text" and "context."

"Genres," both oral and written, are classes of texts that are reoccurring because they are doing similar jobs in the world.

High-quality children's literature provides excellent examples of a range of genres to learn from.

New London Group (1996)

and how they provide more explicit, *overt* instruction about particular features of texts or genres.

Ideology. No matter what genres we are using or are involved in, our use of language is influenced by our values or *ideology*. Ideology refers to the belief systems we hold, and the biases and perspectives we possess. Ideology is embedded throughout our use of language. Sometimes it is very noticeable and easy to spot, but most frequently it is very subtle and unconscious, and therefore hard to detect. Thus, the social, functional view of language we present in the book means that we must examine how ideological dimensions are also expressed in genres, and especially how genres enable privileged interests to establish and maintain unequal power relations in our multicultural society.

Eggins (1994); Fairclough (1989, 1992); Lemke (1995)

All language reflects values and is therefore ideological.

Schools can help students to have conversations about differences having to do with race, class, gender, and ideology. Differences make things complicated. But dealing with complexity prepares students for becoming good citizens and being able to participate in a democratic life. Thus, this focus on ideology requires that we consider how we select the books we include in thematic units; how we make sure science and math get taught so that *all* children learn these subject areas and are able to examine the genres that these disciplines employ; how we create opportunities for student-directed inquiries where children can explore the different perspectives of authors they read and reflect on their own perspectives as they write up their findings, and so forth. In fact, our being more explicit about "speaking out" in this edition has led to our including this whole section so you have a better sense of *our* ideology in the very beginning.

Meier (1995)

Our speaking out has required that we point out our ideology early in this book.

Important Content Should Be Included in Thematic Units. Thematic units are ways for teachers to develop dynamic, long-term curriculum planning. But they are more than that. They enable teachers to organize interesting, worthwhile curriculum—content that "counts." Because knowledge in every discipline grows continuously, and because there is constant pressure to add more and more to the curriculum (without taking anything away!), teachers have to make decisions about *what content* to include in their teaching. They will have various school, district, state, and national guidelines to think about and demands to "cover the curriculum." Thematic units, as we depict them in this book, reflect the philosophy that "less is more" because it is only by limiting the amount that we teach, can students learn the important things well and be able to investigate topics in depth. These ideas have always been included in our approach. However, we make it more explicit in this new edition. In Chapters 3 and 4, which cover planning thematic units and then illustrating them, we discuss why it is important for teachers to think more clearly about the content of units. What concepts and strategies they want students to remember and be able to apply in the future (for instance, after a year when they have forgotten most of the details). In the WEBS, the graphic organizers that show the books, resources, and activities of particular units, we have highlighted what various teachers have considered to be the crucial concepts and the central questions of content. These, then, serve as frameworks for student inquiry.

Fried (1995); Meier (1995)

The "less is more" approach enables teachers to create opportunities for students to study topics in-depth.

Student-Inquiry Is the Core of Children's Learning. We believe that *all* children—all humans—are active, constructive meaning makers. Children learn best when they are participating and engaging in the pursuit of essential questions and ideas about content connected to the world outside school. They are given opportunities to make choices about what and how to explore content; they collaborate with other students and the teacher in their study; and they are responsible about their own learning. This has always been a critical facet of the integrated language perspective and we underscore it again in this edition. Inquiry projects provide students with authentic purposes for reading and writing a range of genres.

This is in contrast to a behaviorist, back-to-basics view, where children learn by passively practicing skills and facts from prepackaged materials.

A major reason for developing thematic units is to plan and organize curriculum as a blueprint for student-directed inquiry. Our emphasis in this edition on the essential questions and major concepts in the thematic units we talk about and illustrate in the book will make this feature of the perspective more evident.

Fried (1995)

Important concepts and essential questions are stressed in thematic units.

Bartolome (1994); Fried (1995); Willinsky (1990)

Integrated Language Teachers Are Passionate, Collaborative, Reflective Teachers. Passionate teaching involves a love of ideas, mutual respect for students and their capabilities, and taking on collaborative styles of teaching. There is no magic formula for teaching, but we believe that for it to be successful and meaningful in the learning and the lives of children, teachers must be ready to collaborate with the children in their classrooms. This is the only way that teachers can provide a multicultural education and develop culturally and linguistically responsive pedagogy. The purpose of this book is to try to help you be that kind of teacher.

This notion of passion in teaching was implicit in our previous editions, but we want to highlight it in this edition. One of the major ways that teachers become passionate teachers is by taking risks, by being reflective about the teaching and learning in their classroom, school, and community. Passionate teachers are excited about content knowledge; they are challenged and captivated by how their students think about it and make connections of these content ideas in units to their life experiences. Thus, there are important parallels between teacher inquiry and student inquiry. Teacher research was especially emphasized in the second edition. In the current edition, we extend the topic even more by including "Guidelines for Teacher Inquiry" at the end of the book. We cover strategies and possibilities for both the already practicing teacher, as well as the student teacher.

Teacher inquiry promotes and supports passionate teaching.

Reflective teachers raise questions about teaching-learning and study them in systematic ways, learning how to collect data as an integral part of their teaching. They develop ways of evaluating student learning in an ongoing manner; they create innovative performance-based assessment on how students apply what they have learned in their projects-of-inquiry. Besides being better and passionate teachers, we believe that teacher researchers are better prepared to "speak out" about the issues in their profession.

Cochran-Smith & Lytle (1993)

Power (1996)

An Overview of the Book

Descriptions of the book's chapters

As its subtitle suggests, this book is an action approach that deals with the theory and practice of the integrated language perspective. The plan of the book is first to provide you with the big picture in the first several chapters, and then in subsequent chapters to "go in close" by filling in with more detailed, specific information. *Chapter 1* provides the theory and general principles of the integrated language perspective and introduces the concept of ideology. *Chapter 2* describes the characteristics of the participants in the integrated language classroom—children and teachers—followed by the nature of classroom discourse that realizes a collaborative approach to teaching and learning. *Chapter 3* shows how to plan thematic units. *Chapter 4* then demonstrates how to implement the units in the classroom and how to conduct teacher inquiry as an integral part of these thematic units. Eight prototypes in action (actually, there are nine—the CHANGES prototype includes two versions) at various grade levels and in various school settings are provided. *Chapter 5* goes into more detail about how to integrate language across various curricular areas—social studies, science, math, and art and music. *Chapter 6* returns to the theory of the perspective introduced in Chapter 1, emphasizing important aspects of literacy. It provides a model of written genres, issues of ideology, and explains more about the reading and writing processes. *Chapter 7* discusses in much greater detail many of the activities and routines mentioned in Chapters 3 and 4 (as well as in other chapters). *Chapter 8* covers a range of "kid-watching" procedures and techniques. *Chapter 9* deals with evaluation and accountability. *Chapter 10* provides suggestions for changing current programs in elementary schools along the integrated language perspective. Finally, the *Guidelines for Teacher Inquiry* sets forth ideas for in-service and student teachers to *do* teacher research in fieldwork settings. Thus, these chapters are "integrated" in certain ways—Figure I.1 depicts how the major threads of ideas and themes in the various chapters and the Guidelines are interrelated in the book.

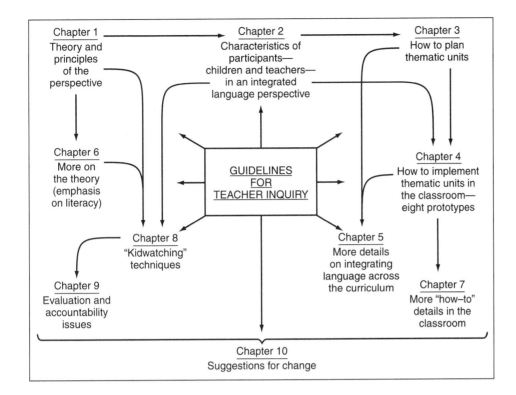

Figure I.1
INTERRELATED THREADS
OF THIS BOOK

Explanations of the book's features

In addition, four features have been incorporated to help you use this book more easily and effectively. The first feature is marginal notations, as you have already noted in reading this Introduction. Four types of notations are used throughout the book: (1) to cite the persons whose work and ideas we have drawn on in writing the book; (2) to refer to sources for possible further exploration of a topic, idea, or concept; (3) to highlight a specific concept, idea, or topic covered in the text; and (4) to provide a shorter definition or explanation of an important concept, idea, or topic discussed in the text.

The second feature is a variety of activities that are found in Chapters 1, 2, and 6. Chapters 1 and 6 are heavy-duty theory chapters, and these activities are suggested to help you get a better understanding of the critical ideas about oral and written language that are discussed. Chapter 2 specifically covers the type of classroom discourse that is realized when teachers share power and authority with their students and take on a collaborative style of teaching. The activities offered in this chapter help you examine this crucial dimension of the integrated language perspective.

The third feature is the inclusion of bibliographic information for cited references. References are provided at the end of each chapter in two lists (when applicable): one provides the scholarly and professional works we have cited, listed alphabetically by author; the other gives the children's literature books we have mentioned, listed alphabetically by title.

The fourth feature is identifying routines, activities, or experiences that might be unfamiliar to you that integrated language teachers employ in implementing their thematic units. Thus, throughout the book, any time we mention these routines, such as Sustained Silent Reading (SSR)*, Comparison Charts*, Big Books*, Literature Response Groups*, we have marked them with an asterisk. You can find a more detailed explanation of these routines in Chapter 7, the how-to chapter. Another convention to note is that all the titles of the thematic units we mention or discuss are in capital letters for easy recognition.

REFERENCES

Bartolome, L. I. (1994). Beyond the methods fetish: Towards a humanizing pedagogy. *Harvard Educational Review, 64,* 173-194.

Cochran-Smith, M., & Lytle, S. (1993). *Inside/outside: Teacher research and knowledge.* New York: Teachers College Press.

Eggins, S. (1994). *An introduction to systematic functional linguistics.* London: Pinter.

Fairclough, N. (1989). *Language and power.* London: Longman.

Fairclough, N. (1992). *Discourse and social change.* Cambridge: Polity Press.

Fried, R. L. (1995). *The passionate teacher: A practical guide.* Boston: Beacon Press.

Lemke, J. L. (1995). *Textual politics: Discourse and social dynamics.* London: Taylor & Francis.

Meier, D. (1995). *The power of their ideas: Lessons for America from a small school in Harlem.* Boston: Beacon Press.

New London Group, The. (1996). A pedagogy of multiliteracies: Designing social futures. *Harvard Educational Review, 66,* 60-92.

Power, B. M. (1996). *Taking note: Improvising your observational notetaking.* York, ME: Stenhouse.

Routman, R. (1996). *Literacy at the crossroads.* Heinemann, NH: Portsmouth.

Willinsky, J. (1990). *The New Literacy: Redefining reading and writing in the schools.* New York: Routledge.

The Theory of the Integrated Language Perspective

The integrated language perspective is based on three major interrelated principles:

- Children are constructive learners. They are active meaning makers. They are continuously interpreting and making sense of their world based on what they have already learned, on what they have already constructed and reconstructed.

- Language is the major system by which meanings are communicated and expressed in our social world. Because language is used for various purposes our meanings are expressed in various ways, by various language patterns. Thus, language cannot be understood, interpreted, or evaluated unless it is related to the social contexts in which it is being used. Moreover, language and its patterns are learned through actual use, as part of human activity for various purposes in various social contexts.

- Knowledge is in the minds of individuals. It is organized and constructed through social interaction. It is built-up mental representations that are based on our individual experiences and is constantly changing over our lives. Thus, it is always being modified; it is tentative and provisional. Knowledge is not a static, absolute, "out-there" object but a process of knowing or coming to know. Because we are social beings, our knowledge is always affected by our culture, existing social circumstances, the historical moment, and so forth.

Children are active, constructive learners.

Language is used for many social purposes that are expressed by many language patterns.

Knowledge is organized and constructed by individual learners through social interaction.

In this chapter we examine these principles in more detail, and then extend and elaborate on them throughout the book. We begin by considering how children learn to use oral, or spoken, language.

How Do Children Learn Spoken Language?

Regardless of race, class, or family background, children learn their native language during infancy and the preschool years with ease and success. Without special tutoring or formal instruction they learn not only the structure of language but also how to use it for numerous communicative purposes. They learn language within a natural environment of language use. An integrated language perspective applies to the classroom principles operating in early language acquisition. Therefore, the first question we must address is: What are the characteristics of a natural environment of language use? Infants, who initially do not know what a language is or what it is for, discover both by *interacting* with their immediate family and other members of their community. The medium of these interactions is *conversation*. Thus, our first step is to examine what goes on in our everyday face-to-face conversations.

Spoken language is learned within a natural environment of language use.

What is the nature of conversation? How are conversations organized? Try to envision a normal conversation between two adults (a male and a female in this example). Consider the pattern of a typical conversation: First, the speaker expresses or translates the meaning of his experience, intentions, and ideas through a conventionally agreed-

General organization of conversations

upon communication system so that these experiences, intentions, and ideas can then be shared with the listener, who is also an active meaning maker. The listener uses this coded message offered by the speaker and other cues provided in the situation to construct the meaning that she believes the speaker to have intended. She then signals in some way—by gesture or what she says next—that the meaning of the speaker has been understood. This exchange between a speaker and listener (who take turns as speaker and listener) is what linguists and psychologists call *intersubjectivity*. It means that I (the speaker) know that you (the listener) know what I mean, and you know that I know that you know. For any conversation to have any success at all, speakers and listeners have to be sure that they are talking about the same thing — referring to the same meanings. An integral part of these meanings that are being considered in this intersubjectively are the values or *ideologies* that each participant expresses through language.

Actually, this account of a typical conversation is too simplistic. It sounds as if the speaker's meanings are totally unknown to the listener until that speaker has completed his linguistic utterances during his turn in the conversation (and vice versa, for the listener's turn as speaker). In fact, at the very point of utterance, at the very beginning of a conversation, meanings are created for both participants. This is because, based on the situation or circumstances of the conversation, the listener usually has a good idea of what the speaker is going to say, the speaker can also predict what the listener will say next, and so forth. Most of these predictions are subconscious, operating below the level of awareness, and they account for most of what is understood in conversations. The ideologies the two members of the conversation may bring to the conversation are also subconscious, perhaps in this case because they are of a different gender and may see the topic from different perspectives.

This example also characterizes intersubjectivity in conversations as an all-or-nothing affair. That is not the case, rather, the intersubjectivity achieved by participants in conversations is always a matter of degree. We can all recall an extreme case, a conversation in which we felt that we and our conversational partner were not talking about the same thing at all. Nevertheless, most conversations are successful because most of the time intersubjectivity has been established.

Thus, an important aspect of a typical conversation is that it is a *collaborative* activity between participants who take turns offering, modifying, extending, and sustaining a meaning that is coconstructed by their joint efforts. In any conversation, participants must *negotiate* the meanings that are expressed. Again, it's done subconsciously—because each person has different ideas, experiences, and values. Also, each person has different purposes and expectations about what the conversation is to achieve. As with intersubjectivity, these processes of collaboration and negotiation are a matter of degree. However, in most typical conversation interactions, each participant subconsciously makes constant adjustments to take account of the perspective of the other.

How do these ideas of intersubjectivity, collaboration, and negotiation function in learning spoken language? The following is a conversation between Mark, aged twenty-three months, and his mother (taken from Wells's longitudinal study of language development). This conversation occurred in the kitchen after breakfast while Mark's mother was involved in domestic tasks. Helen, Mark's nine-month-old sister, was also there, seated in her high chair. The conversation begins with Mark's discovery that when he looks into a mirror, he can see both himself and his mother. (See Figure 1.1.)

Even though Mark has limited linguistic resources—he uses one- or two-word utterances, and there is much repetition—it is clear that he is an active participant in a coherent conversation. His remarks are full of meaning and his mother is able to pick up that meaning and respond to it. They negotiate and collaborate to construct this meaning. Intersubjectivity occurs through his mother's responses in units 5 and 9 of Figure 1.1. It is lost later when she introduces a new topic (that Helen has fallen asleep) in units 17 and 18, but by unit 23, intersubjectivity has been achieved again. Now, Mark can add information to his topic (*Jubs bread*) and his mother can take the meaning and reply with more information about the topic he has initiated.

Intersubjectivity is understanding another's perspective so that meanings—which includes ideologies or values—can be shared.

Eggins (1994); Fairclough (1989, 1992); Lemke (1995); Luke, 1996

Bakhtin (1986); Hasan (1995)

Conversations require collaboration and negotiation.

Wells (1981)

Even very young children actively participate in conversations.

```
 1   Mark: Mummy(v)                                                    [Mark is look-
 2         Mummy                                                        ing in a
 3                              Mother: What?                           mirror and
 4   Mark: There, there Mark                                           sees reflec-
 5                              Mother: Is that Mark?                   tion of
 6   Mark: Mummy                                                       himself and
 7                              Mother: Mm                             his mother]
 8   Mark: Mummy
 9                              Mother: Yes that's Mummy
10   Mark: *
11         Mummy
12         Mummy(v)
13                              Mother: Mm
14   Mark: There Mummy
15         Mummy(v)
16         There, Mark there
17                              Mother:Look at Helen
18                                     She's going to sleep
                                       (long pause)
19   Mark: [e ə æ](=look at that)                                      [Mark can see
20         Birds Mummy(v)                                              birds in the
21                              Mother: Mm                             garden]
22   Mark: Jubs (=birds)
23                              Mother: What are they doing?
24   Mark: Jubs bread
25                              Mother: Oh look
26                                     They're eating the
                                       berries aren't they?
27   Mark: Yeh
28                              Mother: That's their food
29                                     They have berries
                                       for dinner
30   Mark: Oh
```

Figure 1.1

Source: Wells, 1981, p. 102

Thus, this conversation between Mark and his mother is like an ordinary conversation. Turn-taking is well established, topics are sustained over turns, and both participants seem to understand each other's contributions. This successful interaction did not happen overnight. Its roots can be found in the time when Mark was a tiny baby.

Early Communication Developments

The past thirty years of research have indicated that intersubjectivity can be seen very early in infancy. Children have an innate ability to know another human being. Researchers have carefully studied the behavior of two-month-old babies and their mothers on videotape. They have been able to analyze how the babies move their whole bodies—how they move their mouths and faces, their hands and legs—along with those of the mothers' movements, and they have demonstrated that strong reciprocal, highly synchronized, interactional patterns exist between participants. The mother (or father, or another important caregiver) may talk to or smile at the young baby, who in turn may gurgle and move mouth and face (and other body parts) in such a way that researchers have termed the interaction a primitive conversation, or protoconversation. Thus, at the very beginning of life the infant's reciprocal behavior shows an ability to take account of another's perspective. These early interpersonal relations constitute a *primary intersubjectivity* and provide the initial communication framework by which children learn their language and how to make meaning in their culture.

The past several decades of research have shown that young babies also appear to know much more about the properties of objects than was earlier thought. Very young babies are endowed with an ability to hypothesize about how objects "work" in their world. At approximately six months, infants begin to interact with objects in a different way. As a result, a new kind of intersubjectivity is ushered in that influences language development in important ways. Before six months, a baby interacts with ob-

See Bates (1976) & Trevarthan (1979a, 1980) for more information on early infant communication.

Learning language and learning one's culture evolve out of early interpersonal communication.

Bower (1974, 1978); Kagan (1972); Stern (1985); Trevarthan (1979a, 1980); Trevarthan & Hubley (1978)

Trevarthan (1979a, 1979b, 1980); Trevarthan & Hubley (1978)

Secondary intersubjectivity

jects *or* humans, but not with objects and people *simultaneously*. At this new stage, objects begin to be incorporated into the earlier, purely interpersonal intersubjectivity to form a new type of intersubjectivity called *secondary intersubjectivity*. As parent and baby interact with objects in everyday activities the baby gains important understandings about action schemes involving objects. For example, the parent as an actor acts on an object such as a ball or cup, and the baby serves as recipient of this action. Then the roles of participants get reversed as the baby becomes the agent of the action on the ball (giving the ball back, for example), so that now the parent is the beneficiary of the action.

Bruner (1975a, 1975b, 1983, 1990)

Another important aspect of language has its roots in this secondary intersubjectivity stage. Babies develop an understanding with their caregiver that they can share a focus on an object or person—a topic—that can then be commented on. That is, Baby, Mommy, or ball can serve as a topic about which something can be said: it can go or be up or pretty. Therefore, in the middle of the first year the young infant is already discovering two important universal features of language: that these basic relationships between agents (persons), actions, and objects can be encoded or expressed in language, and that an object in the world can serve as a *joint* topic, a focus that the baby can share *with* another person and that can subsequently be commented on. Much of what young children learn about the properties of objects is mediated by conversations about various everyday physical activities, and is therefore largely constructed in social interaction.

Babies learn important universal properties of language through social interaction.

The example of Mark's conversation shows how his present turn-taking, conversational exchanges with his mother have been supported by earlier reciprocity in routines of activity and vocalizations with another person. That is, Mark's language system has built on and extended these earlier understandings. His mother's showing that she values what he says in general, as well as the specific meanings he has expressed, is also present at the early beginnings of Mark's development of speech.

Halliday (1975, 1993)

Mark also has clearly moved beyond what is called the *protolanguage* stage of language development that has been described by linguist Michael Halliday. Protolanguage typically begins at the end of a child's first year or the beginning of the second year before conventional words, or vocabulary, and grammar develop. Protolanguage emerges when the child pairs certain sounds with certain meanings, or functions, in a regularized, systematic way. Mark's utterance in unit 19 of Figure 1.1 is a remnant of his protolanguage. That is, a particular set of sounds is used by Mark to mean "look at that." Babies can do things with language with such a system, although usually only immediate family members and caregivers can understand and interpret their communication efforts. One-year-olds, for example, can use their own sound-meaning constructions to give commands, get something, ask about something, or express a "we-ness" with another.

Protolanguage is a baby's system of regularized sound-meaning constructions.

Before adultlike grammar and vocabulary emerge, protolanguage provides a set of functions through which to communicate.

Back to Mark

Mark's language has developed from a protolanguage sound-meaning system to a rudimentary level of organization that relates meaning and sounds in a different and more complex way. Here are the beginnings of a *grammar*, a structural language system that allows him to mean two things at once. For example, Mark's *Jubs bread* (unit 24) enables him to express the meaning relationship of an agent, *Jubs* (his word for "birds"), and an object, *bread*, and at the same time express the pragmatic meaning of indicating this aspect of his experience (the birds and bread) to his mother.

Grammar: Language both classifies experience into categories and expresses that experience to others.

This primitive grammar will be gradually expanded and developed as Mark has more conversations about his everyday experiences. The next conversation (Figure 1.2) between Mark and his mother occurred two months later and gives us an idea of how children increase their mastery of the language system. Here Mark (now twenty-five months old) is looking out of the window. Earlier he had been watching a neighbor working in his garden and now the man has disappeared. Look how Mark has progressed in only two months! His utterances are longer and more complex (see units

Wells (1981)

```
1    Mark: Where man gone?                                              [Mark has seen
2          Where man gone?                                              a man work-
3                              Mother: I don't know                     ing in his
4                                      I expect he's gone               garden]
                                       inside because
                                       it's snowing
5    Mark: Where man gone?
6                              Mother: In the house
7    Mark: Uh?
8                              Mother: Into his house
9    Mark: No
10         No
11         Gone to shop Mummy(v)                                        [The local shop
12                             Mother: Gone where?                      is close to
13   Mark: Gone shop                                                    Mark's
                                                                        house]
14                             Mother: To the shop?
15   Mark: Yeh
16                             Mother: What's he going to buy?
17   Mark: Er–biscuits
18                             Mother: Biscuits mm
19   Mark: Uh?
20                             Mother: Mm
21                                     What else?
22   Mark: Er–meat
23                             Mother: Mm
24   Mark: Meat
25         Er–sweeties
26         Buy a big bag sweets
27                             Mother: Buy sweets?
28   Mark: Yeh
29         M–er–man–buy
           the man buy
           sweets
30                             Mother: Will he?
31   Mark: Yeh
32         Daddy buy sweets
33         Daddy buy sweets
34                             Mother: Why?
35   Mark: Oh er–[ə] shop
36   Mark: Mark do buy some–
             sweet–sweeties
37           Mark buy some–um–
38           Mark buy some–um–
39           I did
```

Figure 1.2

Source: Wells, 1981, p. 107

11, 26, and 36 especially). He is a better respondent when his mother asks for information (units 17 and 22). Moreover, most of his talk deals with persons and events that are not present in the here and now but recalled or imagined. Here is evidence of Mark's developing understanding of a certain *script* in his culture; a knowledge of what typically happens at shops. A script, sometimes also called a *schema*, represents what Mark has generalized about the events that he has observed at the local shop and perhaps at others like it that he has visited. Mark's mother's behavior is critical in supporting this "story" about the shop. She provides a reasonable explanation for his question about where the man has gone. In units 9 and 10 Mark rejects it and provides in unit 11 an alternative—*gone to shop*. She checks this meaning in units 12 to 14 and then joins his game, again also giving him a message about how she values this kind of fun through language

Scripts specify obligatory and optional actors, actions, and props or objects relevant to particular goals and circumstances. Mark's mother helps him by suggesting the action of buying (unit 16) and then urges him to come up with different props. Mark

Nelson (1986); Swales (1990)

Scripts, or schemas, are generalized event knowledge.

tries out three actors as customers for the services obtained at the shop (the goal and circumstances of the script). First, the man (the disappearing neighbor), then his daddy, and finally Mark himself buy certain props. Mark tries out several props for the man to buy, but only Daddy and Mark buy sweets, obviously a favorite of Mark's.

These two conversations illustrate how children's participation in everyday conversations enables them to learn language *and* learn through language. In fact, these two types of learning are almost indistinguishable in the natural environment of language use. Notice how skillful the mother is in supporting this learning. She is "teaching" but not directing language lessons on sounds, words, or sentences, or lessons on birds or shops. She "leads from behind" by being "contingently responsive" to Mark's efforts. That is, she tracks and pays attention to what Mark is trying to express about what he already knows and what he is attempting to know. By addressing his meanings—which include his values and beliefs—about the world, she expresses her values and helps Mark acquire a system of language structure to express or realize these meanings.

Spoken Communication

People express meanings in both oral and written language through text. We do not speak or write isolated words or sentences. Instead, we speak and write through connected discourse or text. Individual words and sentences in a text can be understood only when they are related to other words, sentences, or the text as a whole. However, oral and written texts are different because they serve different purposes in our culture. This section examines the nature of oral language texts so that they can be contrasted with written language texts and the reading and writing processes in a later section.

What Is a Text?

A text, either spoken or written, is a social exchange of meanings—a semantic unit. *A text is both a product and a process.* It is a product in that it is an output of a particular social interaction that can be recorded and studied. The two conversations between Mark and his mother in the preceding section were texts in this sense. In fact, every language example in this textbook is such a product (although no oral language texts could ever be duplicated exactly in print, of course).

It is the second sense of text that we want to emphasize, however. A text is also a process in that it represents a *continuous process of semantic choice* based on factors that are operating in a particular context of situation. For any context of situation, we can ask three general questions: (1) *What's happening?* What is the setting or subject matter? What are the topics being discussed? (2) *Who is taking part?* What is the personal relationship of the participants? (3) *What role is the language playing?* What do the participants expect their language to do for them in the situation? What is the purpose of the language being used?

On the basis of these three contextual factors, participants select certain wordings or expressions to relate their meanings. Consequently, Mark's and his mother's linguistic contributions were choices made because of particular factors operating in each conversational setting. And we couldn't have evaluated or even understood their wordings unless we also considered this situational information.

Language is a meaning potential or resource, and drawing on this resource, speakers make certain linguistic choices on the basis of what's going on in a situation. Different situations result in different linguistic choices, different wording patterns. For example, a college student's discussion of homework with a roommate in a dormitory would be different from this same student's conversation with a blind date while en route to a movie, which, in turn, would be different from the student's talk when meeting with the college dean over some academic issue. Our language varies depending on the context in which it is used. Language variation that exists in varying contexts is called *register*.

Both learning language and learning through language are fostered in conversations.

Halliday (1975, 1982, 1993); Wells (1986, 1994)

Bruner (1983); Wells (1981, 1994); Wells & Chang-Wells (1992)

All language is communicated through texts.

A text is a social exchange of meaning.

Halliday (1996); Halliday & Hasan (1985); Hasan (1995)

A text represents a process of semantic choices.

A text always relates to a context of situation.

Context of situation: (1) What's happening? (2) Who is taking part? (3) What role is language playing?

Language is a resource used to express meanings to others.

Register is language variation.

Typical Oral Language Registers

The participants' utterances in the following excerpts were all overheard at a place that is well known in our culture. Read through each numbered excerpt as though it were a clue, and see if you can guess where the language occurred:

1. *A:* How far do you want to go?   *B:* [Shrugs shoulders]
2. *A:* I want to sit in the first one.   *B:* Okay.
3. *A:* Right here.   *B:* Go ahead.
4. *A:* Ah, it's nice and cold in here.   *B:* Brrr! I'll say.
5. *A:* Did you forget your glasses?   *B:* Nah. [Pats glasses in shirt pocket]
6. *A:* Why are you sitting here?   *B:* 'Cause Joe is already sitting here.
7. *A:* Do I have a choice?   *B:* Sure.
8. *A:* Here's a seat.   *B:* Get in front.   *C:* Not too far.

Could you figure out where the texts were produced? Some people are puzzled until they read text 8. Many others continue to be perplexed, but then they all nod with understanding once the answer is given: a movie theater. All these excerpts, as you have probably already concluded, were gathered while people were finding their seats before the movie began. We can imagine the kind of language that would have been used in the lobby while people bought their tickets and refreshments. After the movie, the language would probably have been centered on the content of the movie. This language would be more difficult for us to predict because it would be so directly related to the specific movie being seen, but we could imagine what would most likely be discussed. For example, people would probably use evaluative language to report whether they liked the movie—their ideologies may be even very evident as they share or even debate about how they valued aspects of it. Perhaps they would also include in their conversations information about other movies of the same type or other movies made by the same actors, directors, and producers.

We want to make two important points about the language in the foregoing excerpts. First, the language is typical oral language that accompanies action—in this case, finding a seat at a movie during the summer (where there is air-conditioning in the theater, hence the remarks in text 4). Attention is focused only partially on what is said. Nonverbal gestures and other perceptual cues, such as specific objects present or the emphasis or tone of a participant's voice, contribute and support the meanings expressed in the actual situational setting. In conversations such as these, words fit the world. Short responses, such as *okay*, *sure*, and *go ahead*, as well as nonverbal gestures, such as shrugging one's shoulders, are typical in such contexts. Terms such as *the first one* and *here*, referring to a row, a seat, or the theater itself, that may have seemed ambiguous to you are easily interpreted by participants in the conversations.

The second point is that once you found out about the social situation, the language appeared to be familiar. This is because you already have a script, a schema, a mental representation about the events that typically occur at a movie theater. Along with this event knowledge, you also know about the kind of language (the type of linguistic register) that is likely to be used to express the meanings at a particular instance of this script. You can even predict or consider variations of this script. For example, if you have been to an opera or symphony concert, you know that open seating is unlikely. Tickets for particular seats must be purchased ahead of time, and an usher probably helps you find your seat. In contrast, seeing a rented movie on VCR equipment in your own home presents a related but very different variation of the going to the movies script.

During the preschool years, children acquire considerable event knowledge or scripts about a variety of familiar experiences (getting dressed scripts, baking cookies scripts, birthday party scripts, or going to restaurants scripts) and a range of oral lan-

Spoken language usually accompanies action.

Halliday (1977, 1996); Hasan (1984a, 1996)

In typical oral language, words fit in the world.

Donaldson (1978); Wells (1986)

Language is predictable.

Nelson (1986); Swales (1990)

Communicative competence is knowing how to use language appropriately on the basis of context.

Newkirk (1989)

Children are adept semioticians—they have the social abilities to make sense of their culture.

Children's sparse language is rarely due to anything wrong with them, but due to the particulars in the social setting.

Hasan, (1996); Heath (1983, 1996); McCollum (1991); Nieto (1996)

guage registers to express meanings in these contexts. Children learn to adjust their linguistic choices to meet the features of particular social contexts in their culture—the setting, the participants, and the specific task at hand. By the time children begin kindergarten they have remarkable oral *communicative competence*; they know how to use language appropriately in many social contexts. They are already expert "semioticians" in that they can "read" situations—that is, assign meanings to them—and act in suitable ways. They have also acquired a considerable vocabulary and internalized the fundamental aspects of grammar.

Unfortunately, we do not always appreciate children's already developed control of language. If a child says very little (one- or two-word utterances) to our questions in the classroom, we frequently believe that the child has impoverished language skills. Teachers do not always consider that the child's short answers may actually be appropriate in the social setting operating at that time. Nor are teachers always aware that in a particular context, children's language would reflect their distinctive "ways with words," which they have learned to assign meanings and use language competently in similar social circumstances in their communities.

What are questions and answers like in everyday social contexts? Two examples follow. Example A illustrates a typical exchange between a parent and a teenager.

Example A

1. *Q:* Have you finished your homework?   *A:* Yes.
2. *Q:* Even your math?   *A:* Well, no.
3. *Q:* Cleaned up the kitchen?   *A:* No.
4. *Q:* When are you going to?   *A:* Soon.
5. *Q:* Promise?   *A:* Yes.

Questions and answers in the real world are frequently short.

Except for question 1, all the questions in Example A are abbreviated, and all the answers are short. Yet you were able to understand the exchanges. These abbreviations are grammatically appropriate as well. They are what linguists call *elliptical constructions*: they presuppose or rely on other information already given. For example, in answer 1, it is understood that the *yes* is an affirmative response to the question about whether the teenager had finished the homework. The one-word response does not indicate the teenager's linguistic incompetence; instead, *yes* demonstrates that the teenager understood both the *content* and *form* of the question. In this context, *yes* is enough of an answer. The parent's questions 2 and 3 are also enough. *You* (the teenager) and *finished* in question 1 are meanings presumed in these questions; they need not be expressed again. The remaining questions and answers are likewise adequate.

Now read through Example B, where all the presupposed understandings are included.

Example B

1. *Q:* Have you finished your homework?   *A:* Yes, I have finished my homework.

2. *Q:* Have you even finished your math?   *A:* Well, no. I haven't finished my math.

3. *Q:* Have you cleaned up the kitchen?   *A:* No. I haven't cleaned up the kitchen.

4. *Q:* When are you going to finish your homework and clean up the kitchen?   *A:* I am going to finish my homework and clean up the kitchen soon.

5. *Q:* Do you promise to finish your homework and clean up the kitchen soon?   *A:* I promise to finish my homework and clean up the kitchen soon.

Example B sounds unnatural because it is not typical of everyday conversations. This example, however, represents the kind of questions and answers that are promoted in many language textbooks and programs (especially for nonmainstream, culturally and linguistically different students). Teachers following the routines in these programs may ask children questions such as "How are you feeling?" or, pointing to a picture of a cat in a tree, "Where is the cat?" Answers such as "fine" or "in the tree" are not acceptable responses according to these programs. Instead, children are required to answer, "I am feeling fine," or "The cat is in the tree." They are admonished to say it in a "whole sentence," presumably because talking this way will teach them language skills. If they talked like this anywhere else, however, their speech would be considered odd.

Another feature of the questions in Example A is that they are genuine and authentic. The parent actually wants to know if the teenager has finished the homework and cleaned up the kitchen. Or perhaps, depending on the history between the parent and teenager about homework and household duties, the parent is also attempting to remind the teenager about these responsibilities. Various family ideologies about the teenager's need to do household tasks and homework (as well as the teenager's resistance to them) may also be operating here, too. At any rate, very few questions in traditional classrooms are like those in Example A. Relying on questions from basal readers, language, social studies, and science textbooks, and so forth, teachers tend to look for answers that they themselves already know. These materials frequently list questions the teachers should ask as well as the "right answers" to these questions. In a story about a boy whose dog has run away, the teacher's manual of a basal reader may tell teachers to ask questions such as "What ran away?" "How did the boy feel?" "What was the color of the dog?" Next to these questions, the answers "the dog," "sad," and "black" may be found. Because teachers always ask the questions and because they already have the answers, children are always in a respondent position to provide answers that indicate the possession of certain information and vocabulary. In reading lessons and in the other lessons in other school subjects, children are given few opportunities to take an initiating role in asking their own questions. They are rarely asked about their own plans, thoughts, or feelings concerning their activities.

Questions and answers in the real world are authentic.

Teachers obviously know about the nature of spoken language because they use language appropriately in a range of communicative contexts. However, their knowledge may be subconscious or tacit. Unless this tacit understanding becomes more of an explicit awareness on the part of the teachers, several things will happen. First, if they are not sensitive to various typical oral language registers or culturally different discourse styles, teachers will be confused about the "correctness" of children's spoken language. They will mistake appropriate children's language behavior as deficits. Second, without an understanding of how spoken texts are created and used, teachers will not be able to provide opportunities for children to employ a range of oral language registers in the classroom, nor will they be able to accommodate children's diverse "ways with words," the ways that children have learned to participate successfully in conversations in their communities. Finally, unless teachers recognize how spoken language differs from written language, teachers cannot support children in learning to use written language effectively. (Activity 1 at the end of this chapter can help you explore more about spoken language registers.)

See Activity 1

Written Communication

As discussed in the previous section, we also communicate in written language through texts. Written texts are structured differently than typical spoken texts because we use them in our culture to serve different communicative functions. One of the most obvious differences between a spoken text and a written one is that a typical spoken text is constructed collaboratively by the participants in a conversation. In contrast, a reader's or writer's use of a written text is more of a solo enterprise. Readers and writers, usually unknown to each other, communicate across space and time. Consequently, written texts require a disembedded quality. Wordings must be organized in a different way and different language registers must be employed to accomplish this type of communication.

Written texts are different from spoken texts.

Halliday (1985, 1987, 1993, 1996); Nystrand & Wiemelt (1991); Smith (1982a, 1982b); Tannen (1985); Wells (1981, 1985, 1986, 1994); Wells & Chang-Wells (1992)

Written texts serve many various communicative functions.

Written texts are expressed by many various language registers.

As will be noted in more detail later, even if a written text is usually used alone in a physical sense, a reader and writer can still "collaborate" with each other because each has internalized the conventions of language registers. Each has an idea of the kinds of interpretations that are likely, based on the ways the language patterns of the written text are expressed.

Typical Written Language Registers

What are typical written language registers? How are they different from spoken texts? It is not the channel of communication alone—oral or written—that distinguishes written from spoken texts. Written phone messages can look like oral texts; oral presentations or lectures can be like written registers. Instead, it is the entire context in which the language is used and all factors (the setting, location, participants, and purpose) operating in that context that determine how particular language patterns are organized. Important differences between oral and written texts exist, but these differences do not represent a dichotomy based solely on whether a text is oral or written.

To clarify some of these differences, let's start by considering the following text. Can you interpret it?

You got a big *one* today.
It's got *lots. It*'s got *more* than *the other one.*
Can *I do it* ?

The reason you are having trouble figuring out this text is that it is the beginning of a typical conversation. Although it was completely appropriate and understood in the context in which it was uttered, only information about the situation will enable you to decipher it.

Context

A six-year-old child is getting ready to dictate an original story, and a visiting teacher is preparing to take down the child's dictation. The story will be tape-recorded as it is being dictated, and this is a familiar routine for both participants. A new tape recorder has been brought to school today and is the focus of shared attention. The child is touching the buttons on the new recorder as she speaks the words above.

Now it is easy to figure out what the italicized words mean. *You* and *I* refer to the teacher and the child, the two participants in the conversation. The words *one* and *it* refer to the new tape recorder and *the other one* to the tape recorder that had been used in the past. *Lots* and *more* are easily understood as "lots of buttons" and "more buttons" (than the old tape recorder had). Finally, *do it* means "push the buttons."

The foregoing italicized words are *implicit* linguistic devices. They are called implicit because their interpretation must be found by reference to some other source. The question is: Where is that interpretative source? We have argued that a strong relationship exists between context and text structure, or the ways words are organized or patterned in texts. Thus, for any linguistic unit on which we want to focus, there are two environments: (1) the extralinguistic environment or actual situation (i.e., the context) related to the total text, and (2) the linguistic environment (i.e., the co-text), the actual language accompanying or surrounding that linguistic unit. Consequently, implicit devices could either be co-textual or purely contextual. In the foregoing conversation about the tape recorder, the source of interpretation for these implicit devices is contextual. The implicit devices are called *exophoric* because the source of their interpretation lies outside the co-text; they can be understood only through an examination of the immediate context of situation. Figure 1.3 depicts aspects of the situation that provide the interpretative sources for the exophoric implicit devices used in the conversation about the tape recorder. (Activity 2 will help you explore more about exophoric implicit wordings.)

The use of exophoric implicit wordings is typical in spoken language. Although the oral text example we have included is perhaps an extreme case with respect to its density of exophoric implicit wordings, it is a useful illustration to demonstrate that in con-

Implicit wordings

Halliday & Hasan (1976, 1985)

Two interpretative sources: situational environment, or context; and linguistic environment, or co-text.

Exophoric implicit devices point outward to the immediate situational context.

See Activity 2

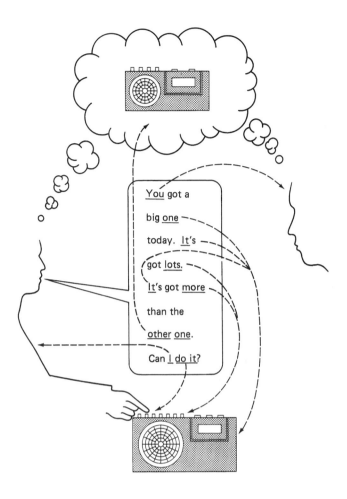

Figure 1.3

versations, words fit in the world. In written language, however, words create a world in that implicit and other types of wordings are chosen so that the text stands on its own. The typical written text creates its own context of situation, and the source of interpretation of implicit devices lies within the co-text, not the immediate surroundings in which a text is being used.

We will discuss excerpts from two written texts to help you better understand these differences of language variation that characterize linguistic registers of written communication.

Two Examples of Written Texts

Figure 1.4 contains the first six sentences of *The Owl and the Woodpecker*, a story written by Brian Wildsmith. Let's look first at how the author used implicit devices. In the first sentence *a Woodpecker* is introduced. This woodpecker then becomes the source with which to interpret subsequent implicit devices. The definite article *the* plus *Woodpecker* are used (in sentences 2, 4, and 6) to refer back to the woodpecker. Other pronouns, *he, his, you, my,* and *I,* are also used to refer to the woodpecker and are thereby easily understood. The same kind of use of implicit devices is employed by Wildsmith with respect to the other main character and the woodpecker's tree. *An Owl* is presented in the third sentence and serves as the interpretative source to understand *the Owl* (in sentences 4 and 5) and *I* (in 5), and *there* (in 5) and *it* (in 6) through earlier mention of tree (in 2 and 6).

You can see that the implicit devices in this example of written language are very different from those we have seen in conversations. Rather than being exophoric, referring to items outside the text, these implicit devices in typical written language are *endophoric.* They refer to items inside the text for their interpretation. This doesn't

Wells (1986)

Words create a world in written language use.

Wildsmith (1971)

Halliday & Hasan (1976, 1985)

Endophoric implicit devices point into the text.

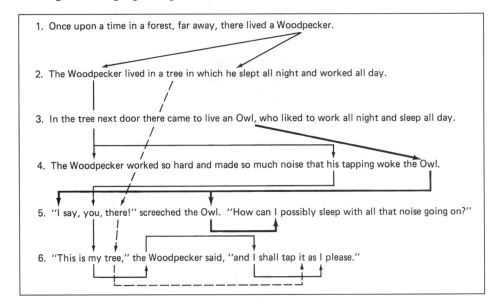

1. Once upon a time in a forest, far away, there lived a Woodpecker.

2. The Woodpecker lived in a tree in which he slept all night and worked all day.

3. In the tree next door there came to live an Owl, who liked to work all night and sleep all day.

4. The Woodpecker worked so hard and made so much noise that his tapping woke the Owl.

5. "I say, you, there!" screeched the Owl. "How can I possibly sleep with all that noise going on?"

6. "This is my tree," the Woodpecker said, "and I shall tap it as I please."

Figure 1.4

THE OWL AND THE WOODPECKER

Source: Wildsmith, 1971

Endophoric implicit wordings form threads or chains within the text.

Pappas (1993); Hasan (1984b)

Chafe (1985); Chafe & Danielewicz (1987); Halliday (1985, 1987, 1996)

Written texts are also related to social contexts in our culture.

Bakhtin (1986); Halliday (1985, 1993, 1996); Halliday & Hasan (1985); Swales (1990)

Wildsmith (1974)

Information texts are expressed by different registers from stories.

Identity chains versus classification chains

Martin (1985, 1993); Martin & Peters (1985); Pappas (1991a, 1991b, 1993, in press)

---

mean that exophoric implicit wordings can be found only in spoken language and that endophoric implicit ones exist only in written language. Oral language also contains a lot of endophoric implicit wordings—for example, the elliptical constructions illustrated in the conversation about homework (page 13) were endophoric. Moreover, certain exophoric implicit wordings may also occur in written language. It is a matter of degree: Exophoric implicit wordings are typically found in spoken language because spoken language accompanies action; endophoric implicit wordings are usually present in written language because written language is used for more "disembedded" communication.

In written texts, the use of endophoric implicit wordings creates "threads" or "chains" of meaning. These threads or chains, illustrated for the woodpecker, owl, and the woodpecker's tree in Figure 1.4, run throughout the text. The chains help the text "hang together"; they contribute to the text's coherence. Because written texts, like stories, can be read at any time or place, they have to be more explicit than spoken text. Because written texts sustain continuous messages that do not rely *directly* on particular sets of circumstances for understanding them, implicit devices are usually used endophorically, and lexical, or content, wordings—nouns, verbs, adjectives, and adverbs—are employed to a much larger extent. In addition, lexical items, or vocabulary, are frequently more formal and less colloquial. (Chapter 6 discusses these aspects of written language in more detail.)

The fact that typical written texts possess a disembedded quality and cannot be seen as having a direct relation between their message and the immediate surroundings in which they are being used does not mean they are not related to some context but that they are related to a context of our social system in a more complicated, indirect way. Written texts serve various purposes in our culture. Storybooks such as *The Owl and the Woodpecker* create imaginative worlds and are used to entertain young children in our culture. Other written texts—for example, the information book *Squirrels*—also written by Wildsmith—play a different role in our culture. They attempt to explain and describe humans, animals, objects, places, and happenings in the world to young children. Variation in purpose and context in our culture means variation of language. Consequently, other registers and linguistic patterns are found in information books, as revealed by the first few sentences of *Squirrels* in Figure 1.5.

Consider the implicit pronoun devices first. *He* is used three times, and *his* twice, all referring to *a squirrel* in the first sentence. Also, there is an *it* (in 5) that refers to *coat* (in 4). Thus, as in *The Owl and the Woodpecker*, the implicit devices used in *Squirrels* are endophoric. They refer to aspects of the co-text for their interpretation.

However, take another look at the *Squirrels* excerpt. Note that the threads or chains created are different in a subtle but important way. In *The Owl and the Wood-*

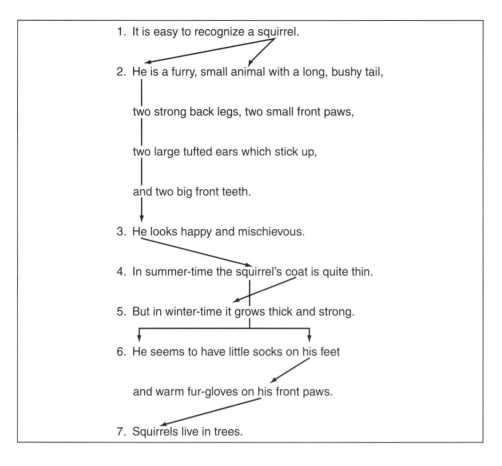

1. It is easy to recognize a squirrel.

2. He is a furry, small animal with a long, bushy tail,

   two strong back legs, two small front paws,

   two large tufted ears which stick up,

   and two big front teeth.

3. He looks happy and mischievous.

4. In summer-time the squirrel's coat is quite thin.

5. But in winter-time it grows thick and strong.

6. He seems to have little socks on his feet

   and warm fur-gloves on his front paws.

7. Squirrels live in trees.

Figure 1.5

SQUIRRELS

Source: Wildsmith, 1974

pecker the threads involved the same individual or animal (woodpecker and owl) or object (tree). In contrast, in *Squirrels* the threads depict a class of animals (squirrel) and object or part of a squirrel (coat). For example, if you trace the squirrel chain (illustrated with a single line) in Figure 1.5, you will discover that it does not refer to the same individual squirrel but to the same animal class, that is, all squirrels. This is why it is possible to include in this chain the plural form of the class, namely *squirrels* in the last sentence. Thus, although Wildsmith used the same forms (*a woodpecker* and *a squirrel*) in the first sentence of each book, as well as the same implicit device *the* (plus *woodpecker* and *squirrel*) in both books, these forms are functioning quite differently in each book.

Most information books are similar to *Squirrels*. For example, they don't identify particular persons as characters, and then follow their conflicts, motives, reactions, and exploits as stories do. Instead, information books make general statements about animals, objects, places, or people. Other linguistic features contribute to the general nature of information books that can be illustrated in *Squirrels*. Information books use the present tense; for example, *is, looks, seems to have.* (Storybooks are usually in the past tense, except in quoted dialogue.) Information books contain a lot of descriptive constructions (e.g., "*[a squirrel] is a furry, small animal . . .*"). (Of course, storybooks also contain descriptions but not nearly as many as information books.)

These are only some examples of the wording patterns found in information books. Again, just as teachers have a subconscious awareness of various types of spoken language registers, they also have a tacit understanding of various written language registers. They subconsciously know that meanings are expressed in imaginative, fictional narrative through wording patterns different from those expressed in nonfictional expository texts. However, unless these tacit understandings become more explicit, teachers will not be able to expose children to representative examples of the written genres used in our culture or to support children's efforts to read and write these genres on their own. (Activities 3 and 4 can help you explore more about dif-

See Activities 3 and 4

ferences between oral and written registers and about the differences between typical storybooks and information books.)

Examining Ideologies in the Two Written Texts

Different kinds of ideologies, values, perspectives, or biases are also expressed in different genres by various authors. Let's look at each of the Wildsmith books to examine the possibilities. In *The Owl and the Woodpecker*, the two main characters, the owl and the woodpecker, as well as all of the other animal characters, are male. The major conflict in the book involves how the woodpecker's pecking is keeping the owl awake all day. The owl becomes more and more irritable, causing strife in the forest. There is a meeting of the animals about this problem but no useful strategies come from it. It is only when a crisis of a great storm occurs and the woodpecker saves the owl's life by pecking next to his ear to wake him up, thereby saving his life, that a solution to the problem gets developed.

So what perspectives might be examined here? First, the fact that all the characters are male is something that might be considered, as well as whether this maleness might have been seen by Wildsmith as necessary for creating the conflict in his story. That is, would the author have had to come up with a quite different conflict if his main characters had been female, or if they had been of different genders? What "hidden" messages are given by the all-male cast, the failure of conflict resolution by the animals in the forest, or the characterization of the owl as a bully towards the smaller animals?

In the *Squirrels* book, Wildsmith also used masculine pronouns (*he*, *his*, *him*—instead of *it*) every time he referred to the singular form of the squirrel class. The only exception is the small section in which the female squirrel is mentioned and the birth of baby squirrels is covered. Can an informational book like this be giving a subtle message about gender? What is it? Also, does some of the vocabulary words in this book reflect the ideological claim that factual information about squirrels for young children should be written differently from factual writing about that topic for adults? That is, if the audience were adults, would a squirrel be described as "happy and mischievous" or as having "little socks on his feet"?

All texts/genres reflect ideologies.

Our use of language is influenced by our values, or ideology, no matter what genres we are involved in. Sometimes the perspectives or biases embedded in language are easy to spot. However, most of the time these values are very subtle and unconscious, and therefore hard to detect. Because the vocabulary and the grammatical patterns realized in texts (as well as the illustrations used in books) are integrally related to ideological issues, a critical stance has to be present in teaching reading and writing. However, for reasons that are themselves ideological, few of us have been educated to identify or examine ideology in texts. Instead, we have learned to read texts as kinds of "*natural* representations of reality," and we have never considered what values or biases we might be expressing when we write texts. Thus, understanding the ideological features of texts and other related issues of education is a major challenge for integrated language teachers who want to help their students develop this critical view in literacy learning.

Eggins (1994)

Exploring the ideological features of texts fosters a critical stance to literacy learning.

Emergent Literacy

How do children learn how to use written texts? The research of the last few decades on early literacy has indicated that our previous belief that learning to read and write begins only when children are instructed in elementary school has to be questioned. Like talking and listening, the roots of reading and writing reach back into infancy. Early literacy begins when children encounter books and other written texts in their own social, cultural environments. Beginning understandings of written language are also learned within an environment of language use. Children learn that written texts, too, can be used to get things done. They learn what books and other written texts are, in what circumstances they are employed, and what is in reading and writing for them.

Early literacy understandings are also learned within an environment of language use.

Goodman & Goodman (1979); Harste, Woodward, & Burke (1984); Holdaway (1979); Pontecorvo, et al. (1996); Teale & Sulzby (1986); Sulzby & Teale (1991)

This early awareness of the purpose of written language in the environment of their homes and communities is called *emergent literacy.*

Two major traditional assumptions are questioned in this new view of literacy. First, the mastery of oral language is no longer a prerequisite to the development of written language. Oral and written language develop simultaneously, each facilitating and supporting a child's understanding of the other. Second, literacy learning need not be tutored in specific ways. Instead of direct, formal instruction, children learn written language by interacting with adults or older children in reading and writing situations, by exploring print on their own, and by observing significant adults, especially their parents, actually using written language for their communicative ends. In other words, they learn literacy understandings similar to the way they learned their spoken language, that is, in the manner illustrated by Mark's oral language development. Thus, children's early, emergent efforts to read and write consist of their own inventions or approximations of adult written forms, just like those that Mark had constructed (e.g., *Jubs bread*) in developing his spoken language.

The term *emergent literacy* is used to emphasize the continuities and discontinuities in becoming literate, how young children develop early concepts and skills that precede and lead to conventional reading and writing. All children have acquired some of these understandings because our culture is a literate one. Individual children's knowledge about literacy, however, differs as a result of the manner and extent to which written language has been shared with them.

A major element contributing to young children's understanding of typical written registers and the ways they differ from typical spoken ones is adults' practice of reading storybooks and other types of written texts to children during the preschool years. Extensive and repetitive experiences with a range of favorite books enable young children to learn about these written registers. As a result, they develop a *literacy set.* Holdaway describes literacy set in terms of four factors: motivational, linguistic, operational, and orthographic. *Motivational* factors consist of children's seeking out, enjoying, and reenacting reading and writing events. *Linguistic* factors involve the ways in which children learn about the nature of written dialect or "book language"; for example, the ways they approximate the grammatical and lexical features of written texts as they "pretend read" a book that has been read to them. *Operational* factors relate to the imaginative, predictive, or self-correcting strategies that they develop for handling the disembedded qualities of written language. Finally, the *orthographic* factors pertain to children's early understandings of the conventions of print—directionality of written language, concepts of letters and words, the phonetic principle (that the spelling of words reflect letter-sound relationships). Figure 1.6 describes these factors of Holdaway's literacy set in more detail.

An integrated language perspective fosters and further builds on this initial literate behavior. Learning to read and write is seen as children's extending the potential, or resource, of language for new ways to understand and express meanings. Reading and writing are not considered ends in and of themselves but tools of learning by which to communicate for various purposes. Let's examine this type of communication more. How do readers and writers, the participants in the use of written texts, manage this kind of social interaction?

Reader-Writer Contract

We have noted how written texts have a disembedded quality because in written communication readers and writers are frequently unknown to each other and they are rarely communicating in the same place in time and space. However, that does not mean that readers and writers are not related or involved with each other. A writer must always keep the reader in view in composing or constructing a text, otherwise, the reader would never be able to interpret the writer's message. And the reader must constantly construct in reading what he or she believes to be the writer's message. Both readers and writers construct written texts; both are involved in problem-solving processes as they create meanings for some purpose. With any use of a written text,

---

Emergent literacy

Schickedanz (1986); Sulzby (1996)

Written language develops along with oral language development.

Literacy learning doesn't require special tutoring.

Reading to children is a crucial factor in fostering understanding of written language registers.

Cambourne (1981); Krashen (1993); Smith (1997); Wells (1985, 1986)

Literacy set

Holdaway (1979)

Motivational factors focus on children's wanting experiences with print.

Linguistic factors concern children's developing a familiarity with "book language."

Operational factors have to do with children's developing essential strategies for handling written language.

Orthographic factors involve children's learning the conventions of the medium of written language.

Halliday (1978)

Literacy is an extension of the potential of language to express meanings.

Written texts have a disembedded quality.

Cazden (1992); Wells (1985, 1986); Wells & Chang-Wells (1992)

Both reading and writing consist of the construction of texts.

Rosebery et al. (1989); Smith (1982b, 1997); Tierney & Pearson (1984)

A reader-writer contract exists when written texts are used.

A. **Motivational Factors** (High expectations of print)

Enjoys books and stories—appreciates the special rewards of print.

Has had extensive, repetitive experience of a wide range of favorite books.

Seeks book experiences–asks for stories, goes to books independently.

Is curious about all aspects of print, e.g., signs, labels, advertisements.

Experiments with producing written language.

B. **Linguistic Factors** (Familiarity with written dialect in oral form)

Has built extensive models for the special features of written dialect.

Syntax—grammatical structures learned through meaningful use, e.g., full forms of contractions
    such as "I'm" or "What's"; structures which imply consequence "if . . .then . . ."

Vocabulary—words not normally used in conversation, e.g., "however," "dine," "ogre."

Intonation Patterns—appropriate intonations for literary or non-conversational English, e.g., "Fat, indeed!
    The very idea of it!"

Idioms—special usage contrary to normal grammatical or semantic rules, e.g., same example as for into-
    nation—illustrates that idiom often works with special intonation.

C. **Operational Factors** (Essential strategies for handling written language)

Self-monitoring operations: Self-correction and confirmation.

Predictive operations: Ability to "use the context" to fill particular language slots.

Structural operations: Ability to follow plot, temporal and causal sequences, logical arrangements, etc.

Non-situational operations: Ability to understand language without the help of immediate sensory
context.

Imaginative operations: Ability to create images which have not been experienced or represented in
sensory reality, and apply metaphorical meanings.

D. **Orthographic Factors** (Knowledge of the conventions of print)

Note: Few pre-schoolers would have grasped more than a few of the orthographic principles.

Story comes from print, not from pictures.

Directional conventions—a complex progression:

    Front of book has spine on left

    Story begins where print begins

    Left hand page comes before right hand

    Move from top to bottom of page

    Begin left along line to right

    Return to next line on left margin

Print components—clear concept of "words," "spaces," "letters."

Letter-form generalizations—same letter may be written in upper and lower case, and in different
print styles.

Punctuation conventions.

Phonetic principle—letters have some relationship to speech sounds.

Consistency principle—same word always has same spelling.

Figure 1.6

LITERACY SET
Source: Holdaway, 1979

there is a reader-writer contract by which particular readers and writers achieve inter-subjectivity in written communication.

As do speakers and listeners, writers (during the composing process) and readers (during the comprehension process) rely on their mental representation of the world to communicate. Researchers call these mental representations by different terms—*scripts, cognitive structures,* or *schemas*. In this book, although we may at times use any one of these terms, most of the time we use schemas to designate individual mental representations. The next section covers schemas in detail, but some general remarks about them are necessary now to clarify these reader-writer relationships.

Schemas are our individual organizations of what we know. They consist of what we know of our world—persons and personal relationships, the properties and features of objects, and the way language works to express understandings and values. Our knowledge of conventions or registers of written language is crucial in the reader-writer contract, as shown in Figure 1.7.

Schemas are our organized mental representations of our knowledge of the world.

Schemas include our people world, our object world, and our language world.

Karmiloff-Smith (1979)

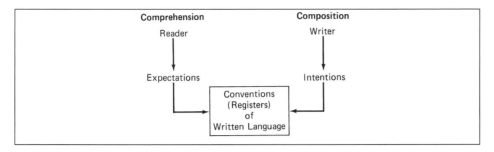

Figure 1.7
READER-WRITER CONTRACT

From a writer's side of the contract, a particular written text is the result of a writer's intentions to communicate meanings. Those meanings, drawn from the writer's schemas, are expressed through the conventions of written language. The text represents a blueprint, or a set of cues, that a reader uses to evoke the particular schemas needed to comprehend the writer's message. From the reader's view, expectations about what the conventions express or stand for enable the reader to predict, according to his or her perceptions, what the writer has communicated. Using the cues provided by the writer to spark the appropriate schemas, the reader constructs the perceived textual world the writer has envisioned. Both readers and writers bring meaning (based on their schemas) to texts.

Writer's intentions

Reader's expectations

Rabinowitz (1987); Rosenblatt (1978); Smith (1997); Swales (1990)

Schemas: Our Mental Representations of Knowledge

We are learning all the time. What we learn at any time is always based on what we already know. Knowledge of the world is not picked up by osmosis like a sponge but actively *constructed* by individual minds. It is a "theory of the world in the head" developed over a lifetime of experiences.

Knowledge is constructed by individual learners.

Smith (1982a, 1982b, 1997); Wells (1986); Wells & Chang-Wells (1992)

Jean Piaget, an influential proponent of this constructive view of learning and knowledge, described learning as a process of continuous modification of our schemas or cognitive structures in our mind. Through two simultaneous processes—assimilation and accommodation—children develop new information about the world to their schemas to adapt to their environment. *Assimilation* is the process by which knowledge is restructured by being integrated into existing schemas. In contrast, *accommodation* is the process by which knowledge is restructured by making modifications in existing schemas. In Piaget's theory, development is explained in terms of *global* knowledge restructuring. Children go through four broad, qualitatively different stages of development corresponding to age: sensorimotor stage (birth to two years), preoperational stage (two to seven years), concrete-operational stage (seven to eleven years), and formal-operational stage (beyond the eleventh year). Children's thinking processes are constrained and determined by what stage they are in. Children's logical processes are different from adults' in Piaget's view.

Piaget (1926, 1969a, 1969b, 1975)

Piaget's theory of development is one of global knowledge restructuring.

More recent research in both cognitive and developmental psychology has extended many Piagetian ideas about development, learning, and knowledge. Some aspects of his theory have been modified and reinterpreted. Whereas Piaget for the most part studied how children's schemas developed through interactions with objects in the physical world, more recent views emphasize how this knowledge is mediated and influenced through social interaction. As illustrated in earlier sections, children act on objects and play with toys on their own, but most of their activities with objects are immersed in a sea of conversation with others. Individual schemas constructed by individual learners are not developed in a void; schemas are influenced by social and cultural interactions and practices.

Bruner (1986); Donaldson (1978); Dunn (1988); Vygotsky (1962, 1978); Wells & Chang-Wells (1992); Wertsch (1985, 1989, 1991)

Current views emphasize the social aspects of acquiring knowledge.

Another feature of Piaget's theory has also been challenged. Piaget characterized preschoolers' thought as *egocentric*. That is, young children are not able to take the point of view of another. However, this cannot be true, as noted when we discussed *intersubjectivity*. Through their reciprocal interactions with their parents, even two-

Current views question Piaget's concept of egocentrism.

month-olds demonstrate that they are sensitive to another's behavior. Babies are affected by the smile or other facial gestures and verbalizations of the adult, *and* their facial expressions, gurgles, and body movements affect the adult's movements, and articulations. Babies are already taking account of another person and adapting their behavior to respond. In fact, children could never learn language at all if they were as egocentric as Piaget suggested. Recall Mark and how hard he worked to achieve intersubjectivity with his mother—how he made sure that his mother understood what he was trying to tell her.

Finally, questions about Piaget's theory of how knowledge is reconstructed have been raised. In his view, restructuring of knowledge is global. Children in a particular stage of development apply the same kind of thinking processes no matter what the area or topic is. The procedures or routines that children employ in each stage are independent of the content of the knowledge they operate on because it is assumed that their schemas vary little across domains. Consequently, the process of learning is affected only slightly, or not at all, by the concepts contained in a learner's schemas in each domain. The procedures and routines used by children change only when they enter a new stage in which these general or global structures are modified.

Carey (1985, 1988, 1991); Gelman & Baillargeon (1983); Keil (1984, 1991); Mandler (1983); Vosniadou & Brewer (1987)

In the more recent views of development, the area, topic, or conceptual domain that the learner is involved with or trying to figure out *is* significant. Properties or concepts in particular domains affect the thinking processes, routines, strategies, and procedures that children apply in their experiences. In this way, children's thinking and learning processes are similar to those of adults. Young children can learn things in particular domains much earlier in development than was previously thought *and* learning in those domains takes a much longer time during development than was previously realized. In this domain-specific knowledge restructuring view, inferences made by a learner at any time are based more on what and how concepts are structured and organized in particular domains, or specific content, than on the age of the learner. For example, if children have many experiences with clay—perhaps because their parents are potters, or they live and play where the ground is claylike, or they regularly play with leftover pie dough—then they may come to understand that a particular ball of clay is the same amount when it is rolled into a long "snake." In Piagetian terms, these children can conserve mass: They realize that the quantity of the clay is the same despite its transformation in shape. The reason these children can acquire these understandings at age four or five (instead of seven or eight, according to Piaget's theory) is that they have a schema in the particular domain of clay and its properties and transformations. In this view, children can be "experts" in a particular area in which adults may function as novices. How many five-year-old dinosaur experts do you know? How about eight-year-old *Star Wars* masters or space whizzes? Teenage computer hackers? These are all cases of children who have knowledge in a specific topic or domain, a domain that many adults may know little about.

Newer developmental theories emphasize knowledge restructuring in specific domains.

Children are constructive learners.

Children generate and test hypotheses.

Foreman & Kushner (1983)

Cognitive conflict leads to changes in children's schemas.

The importance of social interaction on knowledge restructuring

Bruner (1986); Lindfors (1987); Vygotsky (1978); Wells & Chang-Wells (1992)

The importance of knowledge restructuring in specific domains

In this book, certain important Piagetian notions are emphasized. Children are seen as active, constructive learners as they continuously generate and test hypotheses about aspects of their environment. Like Piaget, we stress the importance of cognitive conflict in children's development—that children learn when their theories are questioned. Conflict inducement leads to modification of their schemas.

However, we expand on these Piagetian views in two major ways. First, we emphasize the role of social interaction with others as an important source of cognitive conflict. Having to collaborate and cooperate with others about an area of interest promotes the restructuring of children's knowledge. With the assistance of others, children can go beyond their limits to solve problems through interaction. Second, we emphasize the importance of content or concepts in specific domains in development and learning. Traditional elementary schools frequently concentrate on basic skills, especially at the early grades, so that children can deal with content parceled out in later grades. An integrated language perspective, in contrast, insists that skills go hand-in-hand with content. Children comprehend and learn how to do things on the basis of their knowledge structures of specific content of particular topics, fields, or domains. Let's look further at how this domain-specific knowledge is organized and how it is developed.

The Organization of Schemas

Schemas are not random bits of information stored in any haphazard way. Instead, schemas are organized, coherent category systems consisting of three major components: (1) categories or concepts of knowledge; (2) features, attributes, characteristics, or rules for determining what constitutes a category or concept—that is, rules of category membership; and (3) a network of connections and interrelationships between categories or concepts, which includes how concepts are incorporated in social, cultural interactional procedures or routines. Thus, schemas can be conceived of as dynamic, always changing, structured mental representations of what we know. Each experience we have is interpreted in terms of the knowledge we have acquired, stored, and organized, and this knowledge is modified and reorganized (restructured) as a result of each experience.

Schemas are organized.

Nelson (1986); Rumelhart (1980); Smith (1982a, 1982b, 1997); Swales (1990)

Our knowledge is restructured as a result of our experience.

Schemas As Semantic Maps of Domains

A good way to visualize schemas is to see them as *semantic maps*—that is, maps of concepts or meanings. Semantic maps are diagrams of what researchers think schemas in our minds are like. Although schemas or maps are related to each other in ways we do not quite understand, they are coherent units, or wholes, in different areas, or domains. Domains themselves are best seen as a continuum from general, broad fields, or areas of knowledge to more specific topics or concepts. For example, curricular areas or academic disciplines, such as biology or history, can be seen as illustrations of broad, general domains, whereas cats, dogs, and dinosaurs exemplify concepts at the specific end of the continuum. Similarly, mathematics, art, music, and language can be thought of as general symbolic domains. Then, within each of these general domains, more narrow domains can be considered, for example, geometry and algebra in mathematics, drawing and sculpture in art, symphonies and rock songs in music, stories and information books in written language, and so forth. Domain-specific knowledge restructuring can be conceived of as occurring at various levels of generality in development. However, it is distinguished from global knowledge restructuring in that schemas are not overarching structures developed in the same way over all domains. Children may be able to conserve a substance like clay but unable to conserve number. For example, they may not realize that there is the same number of beads in two rows when the beads in the shorter row are placed next to each other and the beads in the longer row are placed with spaces between them. Children who have played marbles with their parents and siblings may be able to conserve number but not substance. Some children may be already competent at reading stories when they begin school because their family has always read lots of stories to them; other children may enter school understanding many number concepts because their family has played a lot of board and card games requiring counting. Various communities offer different cultural "funds of knowledge" for their children to develop. In sum, knowledge structures are developed with more or less elaboration and differentiation in particular domains.

Semantic maps are diagrams depicting our concepts in domains.

Johnson & Pearson (1984); Pearson & Johnson (1978)

Domains are areas of knowledge.

Schemas are developed in specific domains.

Moll (1992)

The Development of Schemas

How do people develop these domain-specific schemas? Children and adults alike learn by inventing new categories or concepts and by constructing and making new and different connections and relationships between these concepts. Although people have many similar experiences and therefore possess common knowledge, each individual has unique experiences and therefore develops unique schemas (unique categories, rules, and interrelationships).

    To better understand how this development of a schema may occur, let's follow Sara as she learns about or constructs a schema in the domain of spiders. We begin our story when Sara is six or seven months old. Perhaps her first construction is the result of her observations of her parents' enactment of the cleaning the house script or

Schemas are unique and individualized.

The construction of a schema in the domain of spiders

Semantic map of Sara's initial spider schema

schema. Sitting in her high chair, she notices how a spider, which has crawled out from a chair Mommy or Daddy has moved, is vacuumed up with all the other dirt that had accumulated since the last time the room was cleaned. Figure 1.8 is a semantic map depicting Sara's initial, rudimentary spider schema.

Because Sara has noted that the spider actively moves across the floor, she categorizes the creature as a type of animal. Also, both the action of "cleans up" and the agent (Mommy or Daddy) of that action are somehow part of her conception of spider. She develops certain characteristics of spider: that a spider has legs, crawls, and is small. She may also include a feature of "dirt" for the spider because the spider has been so much a part of the dirt that is usually cleaned up. Similarly, she develops the idea that the concept of spider can be found at a certain location, namely, "inside the house," because this is where the events of cleaning up the spider have occurred.

Second semantic map of Sara's spider schema

About two months later, Sara's parents begin to play the "itsy-bitsy spider went up the waterspout" game with her. Therefore, modifications in her spider schema evolve. Figure 1.9 is a semantic map showing this restructuring. She develops new connections to her spider concept. As a result of repeated instances of the itsy-bitsy spider family routine, her schema includes Sara and her parents, as agents, pretending to be a spider. In the game, fingers are like spider legs, so that idea is incorporated. Some idea that spiders may also possess fingers may be constructed in her schema as well. Another place that spiders can be found—in a waterspout—is added, although what a waterspout is Sara does not really understand. Similarly, she develops some preliminary notion that rain washes out spiders. Notice how a two-way mapping process that relates concepts and language is being evolved. Schemas provide clues to word meanings that people use, and others' word meanings embedded in everyday routines and conversations help modify one's own old schemas. This is a consistent pattern that continues throughout development.

Third semantic map of Sara's spider schema

Over the years, Sara's spider schema becomes more and more elaborated, modified, reorganized, and restructured. Figures 1.10, 1.11, and 1.12 attempt to depict some of these changes. There isn't enough space to show all possible changes, so only the more salient ones are included.

As the semantic map in Figure 1.10 indicates, "spider," along with "fly," "ant," and "bee," has become part of a class of "bugs" in Sara's schema. The earlier dirt and fingers relationships have been dropped and new characteristics of spiders have been added—that they eat other bugs, lay eggs, and make webs. A new location connection—"outside"—has been incorporated and differentiated. Sara now understands that spiders can also be found outside in parks and gardens. She has also noted that people have varying degrees of liking for spiders.

Fourth semantic map of Sara's spider schema

White (1952)

As the result of hearing *Charlotte's Web* by E. B. White read aloud, and of later reading on her own, Sara's schema on spiders (Figure 1.11) again shows modification. Although *Charlotte's Web* is a fantasy, it provides useful information about spiders that induces Sara to elaborate on her "lays eggs" and "outside" connections. Of course, "make believe" connections (marked by asterisks) are also added—Charlotte, the spider in this delightful book, talks and spells words, thereby saving Wilbur the pig from slaughter.

Fifth semantic map of Sara's spider schema

Subsequently, Sara's spider becomes even more restructured (see Figure 1.12). As a result of a school project on spiders, the earlier "bugs" classification drops altogether, and Sara begins to differentiate between the class of "insects" and that of "arachnids," of which spiders are members. She learns that insects and arachnids have certain distinguishing features: insects have six legs and three body parts, whereas arachnids have eight legs and two body parts. As Sara incorporates this distinction into her schema, she includes members of the insect class, noting that there are members of the arachnid class other than spiders. She also realizes that there are many kinds of spiders, including the largest tarantulas, as well as the poisonous Black Widow spiders. Sara has relied on the use of several information books in her study of spiders. However, an integral part of her inquiry has been an investigation of several African folktales that involve Anansi (or Ananse) the spider. As she read the Arkhurst "why" tales of how the

Arkhurst (1964)

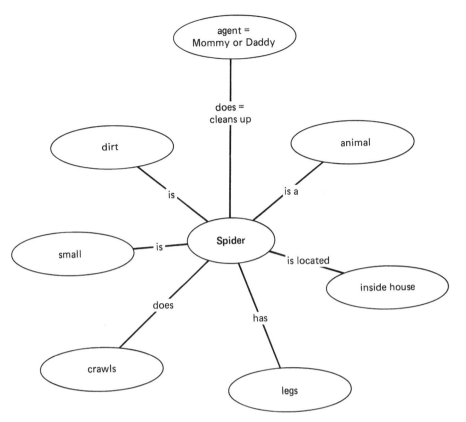

Figure 1.8

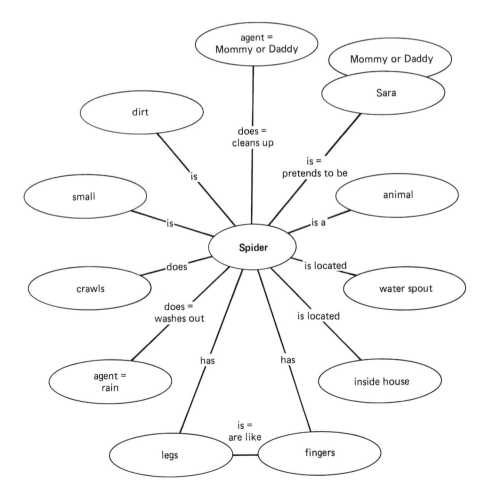

Figure 1.9

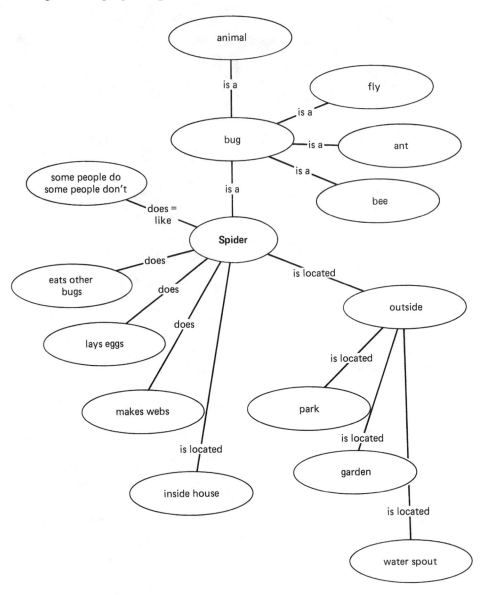

Figure 1.10

McDermott (1972)

Chocolate (1993a, 1993b)

spider got his "bald head" and "thin waist," these spider characteristics became included in her schemas. From other books—*Anansi the Spider* by McDermott and *Spider and the Sky God* and *Talk Talk: An Ashanti Legend*, both written by Deborah Chocolate—she relates how the spider Anansi has become an "African folk hero" having human qualities. He is a lovable "mischief maker" and "trickster," who can be shrewd in order to "triumph over larger foes."

Of course, our account of Sara's development of the spider schema is much too simplistic of how children actually construct and reconstruct their schemas. Networks of particular schemas overlap with and link to many other schemas, all of which are unique. For example, the spider schemas for an avid gardener, a biologist, an entomologist, and an expert in Anansi and other folktales are most likely to be very different from yours. As children learn, existing categories and connections are enlarged and restructured and new categories are created and modified in many particular domains. These schemas develop on the basis of individual experiences and interests.

Another schema example is shown in Figure 1.13, which illustrates a seven-year-old child's schema of "living things," a more general domain than that of Sara's spider domain. The child was given a new large tablet by his mother and was told that he could write whatever he wanted in it. One of his earliest efforts was this list of living

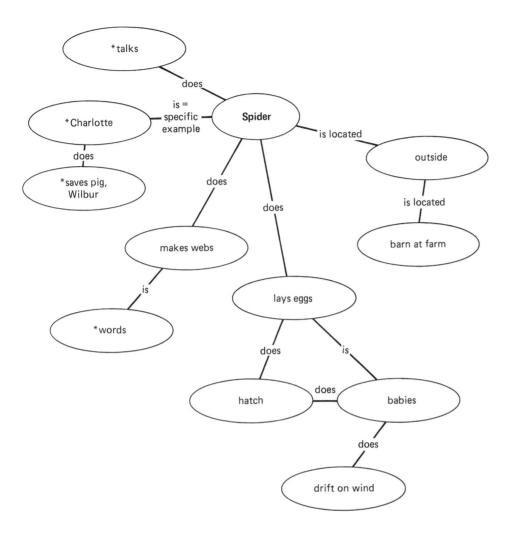

Figure 1.11

things. Although his list is a linear display, it is easy to imagine offshoots of subdomains and perhaps even to infer connections and relationships of distinguishing properties for these more specific subdomains. Many of his entries are amusing, but they are organized. His list reflects both some of the concepts he has already learned in this domain and his ability to express these concepts in language.

SUMMARY

This chapter started by addressing the way language develops in conversation and what conversation is. Then it moved into considering differences between oral and written language. Following that, it went into schemas and their development. In development, a dynamic, two-way mapping process occurs relating concepts and language. Children's existing conceptual schemas provide them with clues to the meanings of the wordings used by others in various contexts, and the language that children experience in a range of contexts leads to modification and restructuring of their schemas.

Children do not sit on the sidelines during this process. They are active participants in the process, constantly charging into the fray. They continually learn how they can use the potential of language to communicate their meanings, ideologies, and perspectives to others in their culture.

These developing language abilities reflect children's evolving understandings of how language relates to context. Table 1.1 summarizes some of the factors, characteristics, and circumstances that exist in typical oral and written communicative contexts. They are organized around the three questions regarding oral and written contexts that we have already covered: What's happening? Who's participating? What

A two-way mapping process that relates concepts and language occurs in development.

Hubbard (1996); Lindfors (1987); Wells (1981)

Contexts for oral and written communication

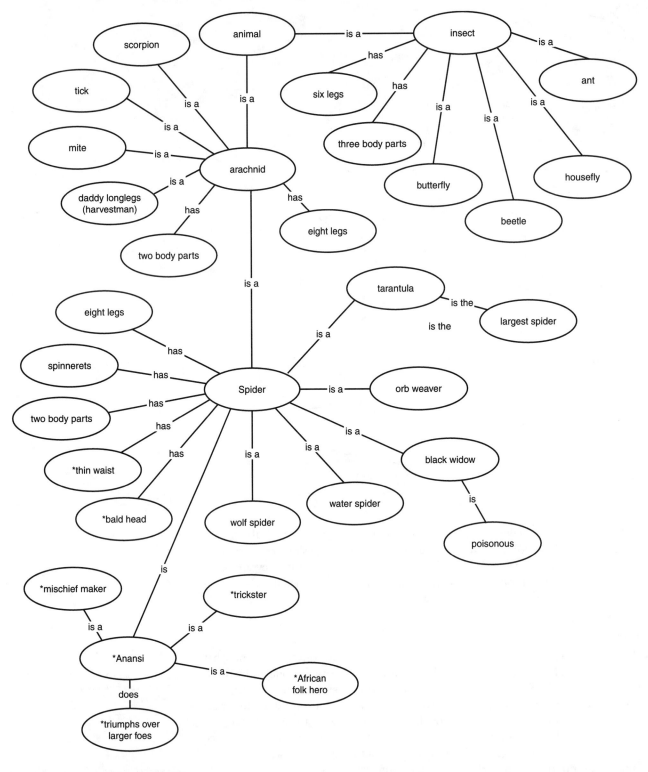

Figure 1.12

role is language playing? Varying factors and circumstances correspond to varying language registers—how language is used and how language patterns are employed.

The circumstances or factors given in Table 1.1 are only broad distinctions, and in many ways they are too simplistic. For example, a letter to your grandmother, although it is written communication, may be very like a spoken conversation in many ways. Because you and your grandmother share many past experiences, you may refer

Living things

aligaters   ground hogs
stingray   moles
birds   ants
reatiles   bees
dad   flise
peoplle   parets
mankeys   hous keeper
lice   termites
flees   golefer
dinodsors   tigers
mom   woodpers
kids   chigmunks
baybeis   tertils
lions   trees
kpords   flowers
mountin lions   dogs
worms   cats

Figure 1.13

Table 1.1 ORAL AND WRITTEN CONTEXTS

Situational Context for Oral Communication	Textual Context for Written Communication
What's Happening	
• the topic of conversation frequently, spontaneous purpose	• the topic of composition frequently, preplanned purpose
• the objects/persons/actions in the situation are mostly referred to exophorically	• the objects/persons/actions in the text are mostly referred to endophorically
• the actual time and place in which the communication occurs are usually pertinent and relevant	• the textual communication occurs across space and time so that the actual space-time in which it occurs is usually not relevant
Who Is Taking Part?	
• the people present their role, status, etc. frequently known to each other need at least a speaker and listener (who take turns)	• reader-writer contract their role, status, etc. usually unknown to each other reader/writer usually alone
• relates to what was just said dialogue, turn taking collaborative construction of meaning	• relates to what was just "said" monologue, continuous text solo construction of meaning (but with reader or writer in mind)
What Role Is Language Playing?	
• the task or purpose that the communication is to accomplish usually accompanies overt physical action	• the task or purpose that the communication is to accomplish usually the act of reading/writing is the only action

to persons, objects, places, and so on exophorically, and your grandmother will understand what you mean. Moreover, the relationship you have with your grandmother might influence your linguistic choices by reflecting certain common family values. Or perhaps your wordings may express ideas that show an intergenerational resistance to these family perspectives on your part.

Retelling a story to someone unfamiliar with it is an example of oral communication. Because such a listener is "naive," the story monologue must be linguistically complete for the listener to understand it, and thus it is very similar to a typical written text. Various ideologies may be expressed in these retelling renditions as well. People might stress certain wordings or put in various elaborations in their retellings, indicating their own stance or perspective towards the meanings expressed in the text, or perhaps what they believe listeners may think about these meanings.

Thus, typical oral or written communication is best seen as one of the two ends of a continuum of language use and this use always reflects various values and perspectives. Especially in the classroom, conversations and written texts can interact in complex ways. The use of a written text can be surrounded by, related to, or discussed through conversation where different points of views and interpretations are shared and examined.

An integrated language perspective stands for real, authentic language use in the classroom because that is how children learn language before they enter school. It requires that the classroom provide many opportunities for children to use language for a range of purposes. Children participate in a broad range of experiences of their choice to help them develop the sustained and deliberate attention to particular topics across the curriculum that makes systematic learning possible. In doing so, they begin to see that the various disciplines are all different ways of knowing, from history and social studies to arithmetic and other domains of mathematics. Disciplines, or content areas, represent particular cultural frames, or ways of sense-making. Members participating in these distinctive domains have constructed certain types of vocabulary, discourse, and ideologies by which to express their meanings to others involved in the various disciplines. Making and understanding these distinctions is at the root of rich interdisciplinary and integrated teaching and learning.

Making and dealing with distinctions also undergirds a multicultural perspective where children can explore and affirm the diversity of people's sense-making from various communities and worlds, as well as the various discourses these people use to communicate their points of view about the world. Thus, questioning and fostering a consciousness of differences makes it possible for children to see that people from various cultures can have a reciprocal impact on each other.

In this view, speaking, listening, reading, and writing are the tools and means to support such learning, not ends in and of themselves. Speaking, listening, reading, and writing are integrated in this perspective because they are integrated in real language use.

An integrated language perspective stands for authentic language use in the classroom.

Dyson (1989); Edelsky (1986, 1991); Fried (1995); Lindfors (1987); Geertz (1983)

Disciplines are domains that are cultural frames.

Disciplines have certain types of discourses or genres and perspectives related to them.

Cope & Kalantzis (1993); Kress (1993); Levstik & Pappas (1992); Pappas (1997); Schryer (1994)

Nieto (1996)

An integrated language perspective affirms diversity.

Speaking, listening, reading, and writing are tools for learning.

SUGGESTED ACTIVITIES

1. To enhance and help make explicit your understanding of spoken registers, collect some samples of typical conversations. With the help of other students in your class, try to tape-record people talking in different contexts of situation: buying doughnuts at a bakery, conversing over lunch, playing on the playground, and so forth. You may want to gather some samples in the classroom too. For each sample, be sure you can answer all three questions about the context of situation: What's happening? Who's participating? What role is language playing? Transcribe as much as you can of your samples so that you can share them with others. Now analyze and compare the linguistic patterns of your and your classmates' samples. How are these patterns the same? How are they different? How is the language being used related to the factors or features of the context of situation? What ideologies or values are expressed in the language samples?

2. To better understand exophoric implicit wordings, go over the spoken language samples you have already collected (or obtain some new ones). Can you identify exophoric devices whose source is not the co-text, but that are understood because of some factor operating in the actual situation in which the conversation took place? Typical implicit devices that can be exophoric include the following:

   a. Pronouns: *I, you, me, he, she, him, her, his, it, they, them,* and so on, including the use of *the, this, that, those, here, there,* and the like.
   b. Substitutions that refer to a class of objects (e.g., *one, ones, the same*) or to actions in a general way (e.g., *do, be, have, do it/that*).
   c. Elliptical constructions in which only part of a phrase or sentence can be completed unless some aspect in the situation is considered. (*Lots* and *more* in the conversation about the new tape recorder are elliptical because we need a feature of the tape recorder—namely, "buttons"—to complete our understanding. (See Figure 1.3.)

   Did participants seem to understand these exophoric wordings in the samples? If not, what did they do to better understand each other?

3. To better understand endophoric implicit wordings, review a range of different types of written text. Can you identify endophoric implicit devices, or wordings whose interpretative source is part of the co-text? Refer to the list of implicit devices in Activity 2; they can be endophoric implicit wordings too. Can you find threads or chains of meanings throughout the texts? Be careful to select children's literature and other books, magazines, newspapers, and other texts found in stores and libraries. (Avoid basals or textbooks, because many of these do not contain typical or good examples of written language.)

4. To better enhance and help make more explicit your understanding of different registers of written language, look at a sample of storybooks and information books. Are there different language patterns? Are there some examples that seem to be "fuzzy," that is, are there some information books that have some storybooklike features? Are there some storybooks that have incorporated informationlike properties? (More will be said about this in Chapter 6.) Are there certain ideologies or values being expressed in the books?

See Halliday & Hasan (1976) for a more detailed discussion of implicit devices.

REFERENCES

Bakhtin, M. M. (1986). *Speech genres and other late essays* (C. Emerson & M. Holquist, Eds., and V. M. McGee, Trans.). Austin: University of Texas Press.

Bates, E. (1976). *Language and context: The acquisition of pragmatics.* New York: Academic Press.

Bower, T. G. R. (1974). *Development in infancy.* San Francisco: Freeman.

Bower, T. G. K. (1978). Perceptual development: Object and space. In E. C. Carterette & M. P. Friedman (Eds.), *Handbook of perception.* (Vol. 8, pp. 83–102). New York: Academic Press.

Bruner, J. S. (1975a). The ontogenesis of speech acts. *Journal of Child Language, 2,* 1–19.

Bruner, J. S. (1975b). From communication to language: A psychological perspective. *Cognition, 3,* 255–287.

Bruner, J. S. (1983). *Child's talk: Learning to use language.* New York: Norton.

Bruner, J. S. (1986). *Actual minds, possible worlds.* Cambridge, MA: Harvard University Press.

Bruner, J. (1990). *Acts of meaning.* Cambridge, MA: Harvard University Press.

Cambourne, B. (1981). Oral and written relationships: A reading perspective. In B. M. Kroll & R. J. Vann (Eds.), *Exploring speaking-writing relationships: Connections and contrasts.* (pp. 82–98). Urbana, IL: National Council of Teachers of English.

Carey, S. (1985). *Conceptual change in childhood.* Cambridge, MA: MIT Press.

Carey, S. (1988). Reorganization of knowledge in the course of acquisition. In S. Strauss (Ed.), *Ontogeny, phylogeny, and historical development: Human development.* (Vol. 2, pp. 1–37). Norwood, NJ: Ablex.

Carey, S. (1991). Knowledge acquisition: Enrichment or conceptual change? In S. Carey & R. Gelman (Eds.), *The epigenesis of mind: Essays on biology and cognition.* (pp. 257–291). Hillsdale, NJ: Erlbaum.

Cazden, C. B. (1992). *Whole language plus: Essays on literacy in the United States and New Zealand.* New York: Teachers College Press.

Chafe, W. L. (1985). Linguistic differences produced by differences between speaking and writing. In D. K. Olson, N. Torrence, & A. Hildyard (Eds.), *Literacy, language, and learning: The nature and consequences of reading and writing.* (pp. 105–123). Cambridge: Cambridge University Press.

Chafe, W. L., & Danielwicz, J. (1987). Properties of spoken and written language. In R. Horowitz & S. J. Samuels (Eds.), *Comprehending oral and written language.* (pp. 83–113). San Diego: Academic Press.

Cope, B., & Kalantzis, M. (Eds.) (1993). *The powers of literacy: A genre approach to teaching writing.* Pittsburgh, PA: University of Pittsburgh Press.

Donaldson, M. (1978). *Children's minds.* Glasgow: William Collins Sons.

Dunn, J. (1988). *The beginnings of social understandings.* Cambridge, MA: Harvard University Press.

Dyson, A. H. (Ed.). (1989). *Collaboration through writing and reading: Exploring possibilities.* Urbana, IL: National Council of Teachers of English.

Edelsky, C. (1986). *Writing in a bilingual program: Habia una vez.* Norwood, NJ: Ablex.

Edelsky, C. (1991). *With literacy and justice for all: Rethinking the social in language and education.* London: Falmer Press.

Eggins, S. (1994). *An introduction to systemic functional linguistics.* London: Pinter.

Fairclough, N. (1989). *Language and power.* London: Longman.

Fairclough, N. (1992). *Discourse and social change.* Cambridge: Polity Press.

Foreman, G. E., & Kushner, D. S. (1983). *The construction of knowledge: Piaget for teaching children.* Washington, D. C.: National Association for the Education of Young Children.

Fried, R. L. (1995). *The passionate teacher.* Boston: Beacon.

Geertz, C. (1983). *Local knowledge: Further essays in interpretive anthropology.* New York: Basic Books.

Gelman, R., & Baillargeon, R. (1983). A review of some Piagetian concepts. In J. H. Flavell & E. M. Markman (Eds.), P. H. Mussen (Gen. Ed.), *Handbook of child psychology: Vol. 3. Cognitive development* (pp. 167–230). New York: Wiley.

Goodman, K. S., & Goodman, Y. M. (1979). Learning to read is natural. In L. B. Resnick & P. A. Weaver (Eds.), *Theory and practice of early reading* (Vol. 1, pp. 137–154). Hillsdale, NJ: Erlbaum.

Halliday, M. A. K. (1975). *Learning how to mean: Explorations in the development of language.* London: Edward Arnold.

Halliday, M. A. K. (1977). Text as semantic choice in social contexts. In T. van Dijk & J. S. Petofi (Eds.), *Grammars and descriptions* (pp. 176–225). Berlin: de Gruyter.

Halliday, M. A. K. (1978). *Language as a social semiotic: The social interpretation of language and meaning.* London: Longman.

Halliday, M. A. K. (1982). Three aspects of children's language development: Learning language, learning through language, and learning about language. In Y. Goodman, M. Haussler, & D. Strickland (Eds.), *Oral and written language development research: Impact on the schools* (pp. 7–19). Urbana, IL: National Council of Teachers of English.

Halliday, M. A. K. (1985). *Spoken and written language.* Victoria, Australia: Deakin University Press.

Halliday, M. A. K. (1987). Spoken and written modes of meaning. In R. Horowitz & S. J. Samuels (Eds.), *Comprehending oral and written language* (pp. 55–82). San Diego: Academic Press.

Halliday, M. A. K. (1993). Towards a language-based theory of learning. *Linguistics and Education, 5,* 93–126.

Halliday, M. A. K. (1996). Literacy and linguistics: A functional perspective. In R. Hasan & G. Williams (Eds.). *Literacy in society* (pp. 339–376). London: Addison Wesley Longman.

Halliday, M. A. K., & Hasan, R. (1976). *Cohesion in English.* White Plains, NY: Longman.

Halliday, M. A. K., & Hasan, R. (1985). *Language, context, and text: Aspects of language in a social-semiotic perspective.* Victoria, Australia: Deakin University Press.

Harste, J. C., Woodward, V. A., & Burke, C. L. (1984). *Language stories and literacy lessons.* Portsmouth, NH: Heinemann.

Hasan, R. (1984a). The nursery tale as a genre. *Nottingham Linguistic Circular, 13,* 71–102.

Hasan, R. (1984b). Coherence and cohesive harmony. In J. Flood (Ed.), *Understanding reading comprehension: Cognition, language, and the structure of prose* (pp. 181–219). Newark, DE: International Reading Association.

Hasan, R. (1995). The conception of context in text. In P. H. Fries & M. Gregory (Eds.), *Discourse in society: Systemic functional perspectives* (pp. 183–283). Norwood, NJ: Ablex.

Hasan, R. (1996). *Ways of saying: Ways of meaning.* C. Cloran, D. Butt, & G. Williams (Eds.). London: Cassell.

Heath, S. B. (1983). *Ways with words: Language, life, and work in communities and classrooms.* Cambridge: Cambridge University Press.

Heath, S. B. (1996). A lot of talk about nothing. In B. M. Power & R. S. Hubbard (Eds.), *Language development: A reader for teachers* (pp. 55–60). Englewood Cliffs, NJ: Prentice-Hall.

Holdaway, D. (1979). *Foundations of literacy.* Sydney, Australia: Ashton Scholastic.

Hubbard, R. S. (1996). Invitations to reflect on our practice: A conversation with Gordon Wells. In B. S. Power & R. S. Hubbard (Eds.), *Language development: A reader for teachers* (pp. 169–180). Englewood Cliffs, NJ: Prentice-Hall.

Johnson, D. D., and Pearson, P. D. (1984). *Teaching reading vocabulary.* New York: Holt, Rinehart & Winston.

Kagan, J. (1972). Do infants think? *Scientific American, 226,* 74–82.

Karmiloff-Smith, A. (1979). *A functional approach to child language: A study of determiners and reference.* Cambridge: Cambridge University Press.

Keil, F. C. (1984). Mechanisms of cognitive development and the structure of knowledge. In R. J. Sternberg (Ed.), *Mechanisms of cognitive change* (pp. 81–99). New York: Freeman.

Keil, F. C. (1991). The emergence of theoretical beliefs as constraints on concepts. In S. Carey & R. Gelman (Eds.), *The epigenesis of mind: Essays on biology and cognition* (pp. 237–256). Hillsdale, NJ: Erlbaum.

Krashen, S. (1993). *The power of reading: Insights from the research.* Englewood, CO: Libraries Unlimited.

Kress, G. (1993). Genre as social process. In B. Cope & M. Kalantzis (Eds.), *The powers of literacy: A genre approach to teaching writing* (pp. 22–37). Pittsburgh, PA: University of Pittsburgh Press.

Lemke, J. L. (1995). *Textual politics: Discourse and social dynamics.* London: Taylor & Francis.

Levstik, L. S., & Pappas, C. C. (1992). New directions for studying historical understanding. *Theory and Research in Social Education, 20,* 369–385.

Lindfors, J. W. (1987). *Children's language and learning*. Englewood Cliffs, NJ: Prentice-Hall.

Luke, A. (1996). Genres of power? Literacy education and the production of capital. In R. Hasan & G. Williams (Eds.), *Literacy in society* (pp. 308–338). London: Addison Wesley Longman.

Mandler, J. M. (1983). Representation. In J. H. Flavell & E. M. Markman (Eds.), P. H. Mussen (Gen. Ed.), *Handbook of child psychology: Vol. 3. Cognitive development* (pp. 420–494). New York: Wiley.

Martin, J. R. (1985). *Factual writing: Exploring and challenging social reality*. Victoria, Australia: Deakin University Press.

Martin, J. R., & Peters, P. (1985). On the analysis of exposition. In R. Hasan (Ed.), *Discourse on discourse* (pp. 61–92). Wollongong: Applied Linguistics Association of Australia.

McCollum, P. (1991). Cross-cultural perspectives on classroom discourse and literacy. In E. H. Hiebert (Ed.), *Literacy for a diverse society: Perspectives, practices, and policies* (pp. 108–121). New York: Teachers College Press.

Moll, L. C. (1992). Literacy research in community and classrooms: A sociocultural approach. In R. Beach, J. L. Green, M. L. Kamil, & T. Shanahan (Eds.), *Multidisciplinary perspectives in literacy research* (pp. 211–244). Urbana, IL: National Conference on Research in English.

Nelson, K. (1986). *Event knowledge: Structure and function in development*. Hillsdale, NJ: Erlbaum.

Newkirk, T. (1989). *More than stories: The range of children's writing*. Portsmouth, NH: Heinemann.

Nieto, S. (1996). *Affirming diversity: The sociopolitical context of multicultural education*. White Plains, NY: Longman.

Nystrand, M., & Wiemelt, J. (1991). When is a text explicit? Formalist and dialogical conceptions. *Text, 11*, 25–41.

Pappas, C. C. (1991a). Young children's strategies in learning the "book language" of information books. *Discourse Processes, 14*, 203–225.

Pappas, C. C. (1991b). Fostering full access to literacy by including information books. *Language Arts, 68*, 449–462.

Pappas, C. C. (1993). Is narrative primary? Some insights from kindergartners' pretend readings of stories and information books. *JRB: A Journal of Literacy, 25*, 97–129.

Pappas, C. C. (1997). Reading instruction in an integrated language perspective: Collaborative interaction in classroom curriculum genres. In S. A. Stahl & D. A. Hayes (Eds.), *Instructional models in reading*. Mahwah, NJ: Lawrence Erlbaum.

Pappas, C. C. (in press). *Learning written language: Genre from a social-semiotic perspective*. Cresskill, NJ: Hampton Press.

Pearson, P. D., & Johnson, D. D. (1978). *Teaching reading comprehension*. New York: Holt, Rinehart & Winston.

Piaget, J. (1926). *The language and thought of the child*. London: Routledge & Kegan Paul.

Piaget, J. (1969a). *The child's conception of the world*. Paterson, NJ: Littlefield, Adams.

Piaget, J. (1969b). *The psychology of intelligence*. Paterson, NJ: Littlefield, Adams.

Piaget, J. (1975). *The development of thought: Equilibration of cognitive structures*. New York: Viking.

Pontecorvo, C., Orsolini, M., Burge, B., & Resnick, L. B. (Eds.). (1996). *Children's early text construction*. Mahwah, NJ: Lawrence Erlbaum.

Rabinowitz, P. J. (1987). *Before reading: Narrative conventions and the politics of interpretation*. Ithaca, NY: Cornell University Press.

Rosebery, A. S., Flower, L., Warren, B., Bowen, B., Bruce, B., Kantz, M., & Penrose, A. M. (1989). The problem-solving processes of writers and readers. In A. Dyson (Ed.), *Collaboration through writing and reading: Exploring possibilities* (pp. 136–163). Urbana, IL: National Council of Teachers of English.

Rosenblatt, L. M. (1978). *The reader, the text, the poem: The transactional theory of the literary work*. Carbondale: Southern Illinois University Press.

Rumelhart, D. E. (1980). Schemata: The building blocks of cognition. In R. J. Spiro, B. C. Bruce, & W. F. Brewer (Eds.), *Theoretical issues in reading comprehension: Perspectives from cognitive psychology, linguistics, artificial intelligence, and education* (pp. 33–58). Hillsdale, NJ: Erlbaum.

Schickedanz, J. A. (1986). *More than the ABCs: The early stages of reading and writing*. Washington, D.C.: National Association for the Education of Young Children.

Schreyer, C. F. (1994). The lab vs. the clinic: Sites of competing genres. In A. Freedman and P. Medway (Eds.), *Genre and the new rhetoric.* (pp. 105–124). London: Taylor & Francis.

Smith, F. (1982a). *Understanding reading* (3rd ed.). New York: Holt, Rinehart & Winston.

Smith, F. (1982b). *Writing and the writer*. New York: Holt, Rinehart & Winston.

Smith, F. (1997). *Reading without nonsense*. New York: Teachers College Press.

Stern, D. N. (1985). *The interpersonal world of the child*. New York: Basic Books.

Sulzby, E. (1996). Roles of oral and written language as children approach conventional literacy. In C. Pontecorvo, M. Orsolini, B. Burge, & L. B. Resnick (Eds.), *Children's early text construction* (pp. 25–46). Mahwah, NJ: Lawrence Erlbaum.

Sulzby, E., & Teale, W. (1991). Emergent literacy. In R. Barr, M. L. Kamil, P. B. Mosenthal, & P. D. Pearson (Eds.), *Handbook of reading research* (Vol. 2, pp. 727–757). White Plains, NY: Longman.

Swales, J. M. (1990). *Genre analysis: English in academic and research settings*. Cambridge: Cambridge University Press.

Tannen, D. (1985). Relative focus on involvement in oral and written discourse. In D. R. Olson, N. Torrence, & A. Hildyard (Eds.), *Literacy, language, and learning: The nature and consequences of reading and writing* (pp. 124–147). Cambridge: Cambridge University Press.

Teale, W. H., & Sulzby, E. (1986). *Emergent literacy: Writing and reading*. Norwood, NJ: Ablex.

Tierney, R. J., & Pearson, P. D. (1984). Toward a composing model of reading. In J. M. Jensen (Ed.), *Composing and comprehending* (pp. 33–45). Urbana, IL: National Conference on Research in English.

Trevarthan, C. (1979a). Descriptive analyses of infant communication behaviour. In H. R. Schaffer (Ed.), *Studies in mother-infant interaction* (pp. 227–270). London: Academic Press.

Trevarthan, C. (1979b). Instincts for human understanding and for cultural cooperation: Their development in infancy. In M. vanCranach, K. Foppa, W. Lepenies, & D. Ploog (Eds.), *Human ethology: Claims and limits of a new discipline* (pp. 530–571). Cambridge: Cambridge University Press.

Trevarthan, C. (1980). The foundations of intersubjectivity: Development of interpersonal and cooperative understanding in infants. In D. R. Olson (Ed.), *The social foundations of language and thought: Essays in honor of Jerome S. Bruner* (pp. 316–342). New York: Norton.

Trevarthan, C., & Hubley, P. (1978). Secondary intersubjectivity: Confidence, confiding and acts of meaning in the first year. In A. Lock (Ed.), *Action, gesture and symbol: The emergence of language* (pp. 183–229). London: Academic Press.

Vosniadou, S., & Brewer, W. F. (1987). Theories of knowledge restructuring in development. *Review of Educational Research, 57,* 51–67.

Vygotsky, L. S. (1962). *Thought and language.* Cambridge, MA: MIT Press.

Vygotsky, L. S. (1978). *Mind in society: The development of higher psychological processes.* Cambridge, MA: Harvard University Press.

Wells, G. (1981). *Learning through interaction: The study of language development.* Cambridge: Cambridge University Press.

Wells, G. (1985). Preschool literacy-related activities and success in school. In D. R. Olson, N. Torrence, & A. Hildyard (Eds.), *Literacy, language, and learning: The nature and consequences of reading and writing* (pp. 229–255). Cambridge: Cambridge University Press.

Wells, G. (1986). *The meaning makers: Children learning language and using language to learn.* Portsmouth, NH: Heinemann.

Wells, G., & Chang-Wells, G. L. (1992). *Constructing knowledge together: Classrooms as centers of inquiry and literacy.* Portsmouth, NH: Heinemann.

Wells, G. (1994). The complimentary contributions of Halliday and Vygoysky to a "language-based theory of learning." *Linguistics and Education, 6,* 41–90.

Wertsch, J. V. (1985). *Vygotsky and the social formation of mind.* Cambridge: Cambridge University Press.

Wertsch, J. V. (1989). A sociocultural approach to mind. In W. Damon (Ed.), *Child development today and tomorrow* (pp. 14–33). San Francisco: Jossey-Bass.

Wertsch, J. V. (1991). *Voices of the mind: A sociocultural approach to mediated action.* Cambridge, MA: Harvard University Press.

CHILDREN'S LITERATURE

The Adventures of Spider: West African Folk Tales by J. C. Arkhurst. Illustrated by J. Pinkney. Little, Brown, 1964.

Anansi the Spider by G. McDermott. Holt, Rinehart, and Winston, 1972.

Charlotte's Web by E. B. White. Illustrated by G. Williams. Harper & Row, 1952.

The Owl and the Woodpecker by B. Wildsmith. Oxford University Press, 1971.

Spider and the Sky God by D. M. N. Chocolate. Illustrated by D. Albers. Troll, 1993.

Squirrels by B. Wildsmith. Oxford University Press, 1974.

Talk Talk: An Ashanti Legend by D. M. N. Chocolate. Illustrated by D. Albers. Troll, 1993.

Children and Teachers in an Integrated Language Classroom

In an integrated language perspective, the classroom represents an environment of authentic language use; it is a culture in which language is used to learn. What are the participants—children and teachers—like in such a classroom culture? In this chapter, we further refine and extend the ideas about learners, language, and knowledge covered in Chapter 1 by summarizing and highlighting characteristic attributes and activities of these participants in the classroom. Chapters 3, 4, and 5 then show how to plan and implement thematic units so that the activities of classroom participants can be realized.

An integrated language perspective is child-centered in that teachers are committed to having students have a voice in their learning. Thus, we first cover what children are like, and then because of these characteristics of children, consider the roles of teachers. It will be clear that having a "child-centered" emphasis does not preclude teacher expertise and input in teaching and learning. Teachers decide on the essential questions and understandings that children are to examine and study; they provide the broad structure of routines students are to engage in; they choose the materials and books children will use; they serve as guides or facilitators to support students' ongoing efforts in learning.

Two major features will be apparent in our discussion about children and teachers in an integrated language perspective: (1) the importance of student-directed inquiry, that is, opportunities for individual knowers to have ownership in activities and projects that enable them to construct and reconstruct knowledge based on what they already know, and (2) how this inquiry is very much a social process. We will be emphasizing *collaborative learning* and the fact that teachers have a *collaborative style of teaching*. Much of this collaborative nature of teaching and learning is revealed through classroom discourse, so later in this chapter we examine more specifically the conversational interactions between students and teachers. The root of collaboration, we will argue, involves teachers sharing authority and power with their students. Thus, collaboration has to do with notions of control, and using some examples of classroom talk we show how collaboration is realized in the culture of the integrated language classroom.

Children

Although we discuss individually the characteristics of children in the context of an integrated language perspective, these characteristics are not separate categories but are fundamentally connected and interrelated because children learn language, learn through language, and learn about language in the integrated language classroom.

Children Generate and Test Hypotheses

Children are meaning makers or semioticians, always trying to make sense of their world. Because they are active, constructive learners, they are constantly solving problems and generating and testing hypotheses. Because their hypotheses may be con-

Meaning makers learn by generating and testing hypotheses about the world.

37

Smith (1982, 1997); Wells (1986)

firmed or disconfirmed at any time, risk taking is inherent in the process of learning. Moreover, their hypotheses are about specific content, domain of knowledge, or problem space. Hypotheses are not content free. What children already know—their schemas on a particular topic—is the basis on which their questions arise. Learning is always the result of "the having of wonderful ideas" to try out in an activity or project. Remember how Sara's earlier knowledge of spiders (in Chapter 1) became extended and differentiated as a result of the opportunity to study spiders in depth at school. The more ideas children already have on a topic—the more there is something to think about—the more ideas are generated, and the more complicated and developed their schemas become.

Duckworth (1987)

Children Are Responsible for Their Own Learning

Children are responsible for what and how they learn.

Donaldson (1978)

The fact that children create and construct their knowledge means that they are responsible for their own learning. Babies are born with a fundamental human urge to make sense of their world and to bring it under their control—to be effective and competent—to act with skill. From the beginning of life, children want to know and do, and their intellectual autonomy is nurtured, encouraged, and supported by informed others.

Dunn (1988); Fried (1995); Lindfors (1987); Wells (1986, 1994); Wells & Chang-Wells (1992)

A child's system of knowledge is self-governed and self-regulated; it is based on the child's own questions and interpretations. Children mediate between their own schemas in their minds and the information available in their environment. Because children construct unique schemas and ask different questions, they follow different routes in learning for which they themselves are responsible. For example, the questions that Sara might ask about spiders (in Chapter 1) would likely be very different from those asked by one of her classmates who hadn't engaged in a systematic study of the topic. Thus, a novice about spiders would not initially ask questions about arachnids, because the child might be still classifying spiders as "bugs."

Children's Language and Learning Reflect Approximations

Approximations are inherent in the learning process.

Cambourne (1984); Fisher (1995); Holdaway (1979); Wells (1986); Wells & Chang-Wells (1992)

Lindfors (1987)

Children are always modifying the ideas and concepts in their schemas. Their present theories are tentative and approximate adult (or expert) views regarding a topic. Their language also includes approximations that reflect their current understanding of the conventions of language to express their ideas. Approximations are the natural consequences of learning. They are intrinsic to the ways in which children construct their knowledge. Approximations are creative constructions. They reflect the linguistic and cultural diversity that children bring to their communication and approaches to learning. Consequently, in this book we do not refer to children's hypotheses about the world or language with negative terms such as *errors* or *mistakes*.

Wells (1981, 1986)

Parents accept and actually reward spoken language approximations during the preschool years. They accept their baby's protolanguage and idiosyncratic constructions (remember Mark's *jubs*, an approximation of the conventional word *birds*) and their child's designation of "doggie" for all four-legged, furry animals and their attempts to regularize all plurals and past tenses with "mouses" and "goed." Thus, although approximations, especially in reading and writing, may not be tolerated in most traditional classrooms, they are welcomed and encouraged in an integrated language classroom because they are considered great indicators of a child's thinking and understanding at a particular time, on a particular topic, and in a particular context. Meaning makers always produce approximations.

Children Use Authentic Language for Meaningful Purposes

Language is learned through authentic use.
Edelsky (1991); Genishi (1985); Halliday (1975)

From the beginning of life, children are immersed in authentic, meaningful spoken language. Even as babies, they are invited to be participants in communication. They do not first learn about oral language and then learn how to use it. They learn oral language and how to use it simultaneously; they learn spoken language for real, functional purposes.

Research in emergent literacy has indicated that young children who come to school already reading and writing also learned this literate behavior in this authentic, meaningful way. Parents of these children shared and discussed books with them and encouraged them to write their own messages and notes. Parents pointed out aspects of print to their children in everyday activities and responded to their children's comments and questions that arose in purposeful, communicative events. When the conditions are right, children can learn to read and write as easily as they learn to talk and listen. Thus, in integrated language classrooms, children use authentic language for meaningful purposes: to write a report on their study of chicks they have seen hatch, to converse with group members about the play they are planning to give, or to read books for a project they are working on.

Cambourne (1984); Holdaway (1979); Jaggar (1985); Newman (1985a)

Authentic language is holistic. Thus, isolated drills or practice on only one part or subsystem of language (e.g., practicing phonics rules on certain letter-sound relationships, copying over and over the spelling words of the week, or underlining nouns in sentences from the language arts textbook) are not used. Instead, children learn letter-sound relationships (or graphophonemic cues) by reading real books and writing their own stories or information books; they learn how to spell through exposure to words in their reading and by trying out their invented spellings to express their own ideas in writing; they understand how nouns work by encountering those employed by authors and by using those they need in their own writing. (This learning, of course, is also supported by explicit teaching by teachers in the context of these experiences—see the prototypes in Chapter 4 and Phonics in Context*, Grammar in Context*, and Focus Lessons* in Chapter 7.)

Edelsky (1986); Goodman & Goodman (1990); Newman (1985b, 1991)

Fisher (1995); Routman (1996); Weaver (1996)

It is through this kind of genuine language use that children also learn about language. At the same time that they are learning language (i.e., constructing the language system or figuring out how symbols represent meanings in oral and written form) and learning through language (i.e., discovering how the world works in conversations with others), they are also learning about language itself (i.e., becoming aware of language as an object that has elements, forms, and functions). Although they are largely tacit or subconscious, these three aspects of language development simultaneously interact and facilitate one another. They are social processes, learned in authentic, meaningful communication with others.

Halliday (1982, 1993); Jaggar (1985)

Children Integrate Speaking, Listening, Reading, and Writing in Their Activities/Projects

In an integrated language classroom, there are no separate speaking, listening, reading, and writing activities. The fact that children use authentic language in the classroom means that their use of language is integrated. Their activities and projects are surrounded by conversation. These projects require reading; writing is needed to share the outcomes or findings of their projects. For example, a small group of children may study slugs. As they observe the slugs, they chat among themselves about what they see, what they have read about slugs, and so forth. They take notes on their observations and about the information they have gleaned in their reading. They individually present their findings; one writing a story about slugs (titled "Sluggo"), another a more informational piece on slugs, and another a pictorial depiction (with captions) of the behavior of slugs. Or, they may examine "changing viewpoints" as part of a CHANGES thematic unit (see Chapter 4). Here, small groups read various books (and primary sources*) on historical events or topics during which they critically discuss the different perspectives and ideologies that the historical participants in these events might have held *and* how the authors of these texts are representing these participants' viewpoints. Subsequently, each group writes and performs a play that reflects the views or biases students have revealed, after which the whole class may further discuss how events have been represented by historical participants, authors of the books or

Language is integrated.

Dyson (1989); Harste & Short (1988); King (1985); Lytle & Botel (1988); Shanahan (1990); Wells (1986); Wells & Chang-Wells (1992)

other historical sources they used in their inquiries, and they themselves as authors of the plays.

Much is learned through use of integrated language. Children learn about reading and writing by listening to books read to them. They also learn about reading and writing by listening and talking to their peers and teacher when they discuss the books they have read or share their writing. They gain insights about writing from reading; they learn to write like a reader. And they acquire knowledge about reading by writing; they learn to read like a writer.

Children Have Choices and Ownership in What They Do

Having choices fosters ownership and autonomy.

During the preschool years, children choose activities that interest them. Their purposes sustain their attention in projects and guide their motivation to understand. By owning what they do and following their own questions about topics, they are able to create new concepts and make new connections in their schemas. Children in an integrated language classroom are also provided with opportunities to initiate their own activities. They select and take on projects; they make their projects their own, thereby making their knowledge their own. It is this ownership that fosters the intellectual autonomy that we discussed earlier. "Owning" an activity, task, or project leads to knowing how, why, and what to do. As a result, children behave responsibly.

Graves (1983); Calkins (1986, 1991); Fried (1995); Wells (1986); Willinsky (1990)

Children Collaborate and Interact with Peers and Teacher about Learning Activities/Projects

Children learn through collaboration with others.

Bayer (1990); King (1985); Newman, Griffin, & Cole (1989); Newman (1985b); Wells (1986); Wells & Chang-Wells (1992)

Just as children use others as resources in learning about the world and language during the preschool years, children in an integrated language classroom are supported through their interactions with their peers and teacher. Rather than hours of individual "seat work" where talk is forbidden, purposeful conversation among children is encouraged. For example, several children in a small group may collaborate with their group members in an activity. Perhaps they are going to do a survey regarding litter in the community. Some children will be responsible for drawing up a rough draft of the questions they will ask, others may be busy brainstorming to decide whom they should ask, and so forth. Decisions about their individual contributions to the project require negotiation. They must decide among themselves who will be doing that task. Or perhaps a problem or issue may be posed by the teacher and then examined by children in the classroom. The teacher may also ask them to consider if they think they have enough categories of people or enough questions to make the results of their survey representative. Children bring their own knowledge to bear on the problem to come up with an answer that is constructed by a group or the class as a whole.

To understand and be understood is the basis of communication and of learning in general. Individual children have had varying experiences and therefore may possess very different knowledge schemas on a particular topic. Thus, individual children offer different contributions to, and have different interpretations of, what is being studied. In addition, children have unique personal characteristics and come from a variety of cultural backgrounds. Such cultural and linguistic diversity means that children also bring their own complex customs or styles of interaction to their activities or projects. Children from different cultural backgrounds have different rules for communication. Because their "ways with words" may not be like those of the other children or of the teacher, collaboration is crucial. Children from different cultural communities bring different ideologies or values about life that are embedded within their ways of expressing themselves through language. Negotiation is the only means by which classroom participants—children and teacher alike—can deal with their various ways of participating or interacting. This is how intersubjectivity is achieved and understanding is accomplished.

Foster (1992); Heath (1983); Lindfors (1987); McCollum (1991)

Distinctive ideologies are "inscribed" within the discourse of children's various cultural groups.

Fairclough (1989, 1992); Stephens (1992)

Children Use Feedback from Peers and Teacher to Self-Regulate Their Use of Language and Modify Their Theories

When children collaborate and negotiate with other classroom participants, they are provided with countless opportunities to reconsider, reevaluate, and reformulate how and what they mean. They present their ideas (orally and in writing) on the basis of their schemas, and they take note of their peers' or teacher's responses or ideas: "That's a great idea! How about . . .?", "I don't understand that.", "What do you mean?", or "Why do you think so?" This feedback extends their ideas, urges them on, and requires them to clarify and justify their views. Listening to a fellow student's report or presentation on a particular topic, or a partner's ideas about how to explore and report on their project, sparks new questions and ideas. This self-regulation, fostered through social interaction, leads to knowledge restructuring and modification of their schemas.

Feedback from others develops children's schemas.

Calkins (1986, 1991, 1994); Cambourne (1984); Wells (1986, 1994); Wells & Chang-Wells (1992)

Self-regulation also promotes children's *metacognitive awareness*, that is, an awareness of their own thinking. They begin to reflect on the thinking processes of communication, what they do when they talk, read, or write, how their interpretations may affect others, and how others' interpretations may influence their own. This is the *literate* thinking that empowers children because they not only learn to take advantage of the potential of language to express their own ideas and thought processes but also because they realize how these thought processes themselves can be seen as an object that can be critically reexamined further.

Children Use and Learn Language across the Curriculum

The understanding of language is increased and intensified when children use integrated language across the curriculum. They speak, listen, read, and write as they conduct a science experiment, consider problems and discover patterns in math, engage in an inquiry in social studies, or reflect on some art project. Because the content of these disciplines (or curricular domains) is different, children discover that different registers of language (both oral and written) must be employed in their projects. Communicative competence is fostered in complex, sophisticated ways. Metalinguistic and metacognitive awareness, the ability to learn about language, the ability to consider language as an object of study in and of itself, the ability to ponder about their own thinking processes, the ability to examine their own strategies in solving or approaching certain problems in science, math, or social studies, are facilitated when children recognize in a more explicit way how linguistic choices are expressed by different genres. They are also facilitated when children realize how various disciplines, as cultural frames, reflect various ways of knowing and ideologies or values. When children can integrate information or knowledge from various curricular domains by using these disciplines' discourse genres (or practices) in undertaking their student-initiated inquiries*, they begin to appreciate the distinctive contributions of various disciplines in present and future inquiries. They also become more adept in deciding which genres are appropriate for sharing the findings of their inquiries. (Subsequent chapters, especially Chapters 5 and 6, cover these differences of disciplines and genres in more detail.)

Language is used across the curriculum.

King (1985); Lytle & Botel (1988); Wells (1986, 1993, 1994); Wells & Chang-Wells (1992)

Britton (1989); Levstik & Pappas (1992); Pappas (1997); Pappas & Pettegrew (1998)

Children Have Sustained Time for Systematic and Reflective Inquiry on a Range of Topics

Children's learning during the preschool years is developed in contexts in which they focus on topics and things that interest them. By engaging in activities with others who sustain and extend these interests, children acquire amazing linguistic, cognitive, and social abilities. Schooling should therefore plan and provide for more of these contexts of concentrated effort. However, in most traditional classrooms the entire school day is fragmented into small time slots during which teachers and children alike are on a treadmill to get it done and move along. Rather than this "cha-cha-cha curriculum," children in an integrated language classroom have ample blocks of time to explore and

Reflective inquiry requires sustained time.

Fried (1995); Wells (1986); Wells & Chang-Wells (1992)

Donald Graves is responsible for the apt term "cha-cha-cha curriculum" (according to Calkins, 1986).

think and change their minds, to consider and evaluate different points of view, to decide on their questions and how to resolve them, to read and reread, and to write and revise. Thus, they have opportunities to study a range of topics in depth and their inquiries are systematic and reflective.

Teachers

The characteristics that we have described for children can be realized in the classroom only when teachers take on certain roles. Thus, it is necessary to examine what these roles are and show how they are related to the characteristics of children as learners in an integrated language classroom. As it was for the children's categories, the teacher categories or roles are not mutually exclusive. You will notice that they are quite interrelated and connected.

Teachers Use a Collaborative Style of Teaching

A collaborative teaching style is used.

Because collaborative meaning making is so successful and efficient in the development of children's learning in the preschool years, it is critical to find ways to achieve such an approach in the classroom. Thus, probably the most important teacher characteristic from an integrated language perspective is a collaborative style of teaching. Remember that individual children's present understandings are based on their existing schemas; consequently, interactions with children must be based on where they are now.

Wells (1986, 1993, 1994); Wells & Chang-Wells (1992)

Recall that learning language and learning through language go hand-in-hand. Conversation is also an important medium for instruction in the classroom. Collaborative talk especially facilitates children's learning—their construction of knowledge—for it makes possible teachers' contributions to be *contingently responsive* to a learner's present needs. Wells provides four general recommendations for teachers to guide them in engaging in the type of talk with children in which contingent responsiveness enables and empowers learning:

Wells offers four guidelines for teachers to promote contingently responsive talk with children.

1. Assume that children attempt to communicate because they have something important to say; that is, take their ways of questioning, commenting, and explaining seriously. Moreover, treat these attempts as an indication of their best efforts to solve a particular problem on their own, without the aid of others.
2. Before responding, try to listen carefully to children's accounts and ask for any needed clarifications from them to understand accurately what children are trying to relate.
3. When responding, confirm or check children's meanings first—that is, attempt to achieve intersubjectivity—and then either extend or develop their accounts, or encourage children to do so themselves.
4. Try to have your contributions at or just beyond children's current understandings. That is, formulate your contributions with *both* children's present abilities and your pedagogical intentions in mind, but always be ready to modify your agenda in light of the feedback that children provide in their responses.

Vygoysky (1978)

ZPDs enable children to learn things with others that they could not learn alone.

These recommendations reflect ideas from Vygoysky, a psychologist who argued that the best kind of social interaction and talk for learning was one in which a *zone of proximal development* (ZPD) is created. That is, "good learning" occurs *in* children when they are interacting *with* teachers (and in cooperation with peers).

Heath (1983); Ladson-Billings (1994); Lindfors (1987); Nieto (199?)

Teachers must keep these principles from Wells in mind especially when teaching children who come from a variety of linguistic and cultural backgrounds. An appreciation of children's different "ways with words" enables teachers to capitalize on children's individual approaches to communicating (in both oral and written form) and to learning in general. For example, children may have different ways or styles of storying. In telling of a personal experience, some may express a series of implicitly associated topics, whereas others may focus on a single, more explicit topic. Or, depending

Cazden (1988); Michaels (1981)

on the customs of their culture, children may have different ideas about what is meant by staying on the subject (due to different rules for relevance) or waiting their turn to talk (due to different expectations regarding the signals for when it's okay to talk), or different orientations to public performance in the classroom (due to different personal and cultural factors that influence whether children are eager or uncomfortable in performing verbally in front of a group). Teachers must accept a wide range of language behaviors as appropriate and must be open and eager to understand children's approaches to mean.

In the traditional classroom, the teacher-controlled initiate-respond-evaluate (IRE) pattern characterizes much of the classroom discourse interactions. When using the IRE pattern, the teacher *initiates* a sequence by calling a child to answer, then the nominated child *responds* to the initiation or questions posed by the teacher, and then the teacher *evaluates* what the child has said before calling on the next child. The IRE pattern is not a structure in which teachers can be sensitive to student-directed work and inquiry. It doesn't regard learners' conceptions of their tasks and the ways they plan to proceed on them so that children can be guided by the teacher to more mature understanding. Thus, the IRE interactional pattern is used sparingly in integrated language classrooms; its purpose is usually employed to promote make possible the range of participation structures that better enable collaboration and negotiation. (IRE and alternative non-IRE patterns will be discussed more later in the chapter.)

Too many whole-group, teacher-led situations tend to constrain flexibility and reduce opportunities for teachers to interact with individual children. In integrated language classrooms, children work individually, in pairs, or in small groups, and consequently the teacher can engage in more face-to-face encounters with the children. Inherent in a collaborative style of teaching is the teacher's capacity to decenter—to take the child's perspective. While children are busy in their activities or projects, the teacher is careful to ask and respond to authentic questions in order to be informed about, and helpful in, children's endeavors and to better address their concerns and difficulties. The intent of the teacher's questions is not to check if children's ideas conform with the teacher's knowledge. The more a teacher knows a domain, the greater is the risk of behaving egocentrically in relation to that knowledge. Egocentricity is more of a problem for the teacher than for children in classrooms. A collaborative style, therefore, bridges the gap between teacher's and children's schemas so that children can create their own concepts and relationships.

Teachers Foster Problem Solving and Risk Taking

As has been noted, children's schemas develop through generating and testing hypotheses about language and the world and by trying to figure out their own problems on a range of topics. For learning to continue in the classroom, the teacher has to provide a climate that will further foster these children's natural learning inclinations. Rather than stress that children discover the "correct" or "right" answer in the textbook or in the teacher's head, the teacher in an integrated language classroom attempts to enhance the probability of children's own discoveries. Such an atmosphere makes children comfortable enough to put their ideas on the line so that risk taking is not cut off. It is okay for them to offer their own interpretation of a story, although it may be different from those of their teacher or their peers; it is all right to use invented spelling to express their good ideas when they don't know the conventional spelling of words. Because risk taking aims at going beyond the status quo, the modification of children's schemas and learning is more likely.

Teachers Demonstrate and Encourage Authentic Language for Meaningful Purposes

Authentic language is a social activity; it is language used for meaningful purposes. For speaking, listening, reading, and writing to be tools for learning instead of ends in and of themselves, teachers demonstrate how something is actually done by using language in integrated language classrooms. They use real books that would be found in homes,

See Cazden (1986, 1988), Lindfors (1987), and Nieto (1996) for the more accounts of various "ways with words."

Cazden (1986, 1988); Edwards & Mercer (1987); Mercer (1995); Young (1992)

The IRE discourse pattern has the teacher dominating all the classroom talk.

Goodman & Goodman (1990); Wells (1986, 1994); Wells & Chang-Wells (1992); Young (1992)

A climate conducive to taking risks is required.

Cambourne (1984); Lindfors (1987); Wells (1986); Wells & Chang-Wells (1992)

Authentic language is used and demonstrated by the teacher.

Calkins (1986, 1994); Newman (1985a, 1985c); Harste & Short (1988)

libraries, and bookstores, and they suggest ways that particular books may be useful for particular activities or projects. When they share these books with children, they read with interest, get children to predict what will happen next, and wonder about an author's choice of words. During sustained silent reading (SSR)* time, they themselves read their own books, and then they frequently share with their students the funny or sad parts. They let children in on strategies that they themselves use in reading—for example, skip what they don't know, read more of the surrounding text to figure out or clarify an unknown word, substitute words that maintain meaning for parts of a text, reread a passage, or when they can't understand a text, even drop it altogether and get another book on the same topic.

Lindfors (1987); Mercer (1995); Wells & Chang-Wells (1992); Young (1992)

They write letters, notes, and messages to children, parents, and colleagues. They write reminders to themselves; they label articles and places in the classroom so it is easy for all to use available resources. They are genuine responders—they acknowledge when they don't understand something children have said or written so that children are given opportunities to rephrase or revise to make their intentions clearer. In sum, teachers use authentic language, and in doing so they encourage children to see how things are done with language. Authentic language fosters children's learning about its various registers and ideologies and their awareness of how language can be used for their own purposes to learn about the world.

Teachers Provide Activities and Projects So That Children Can Integrate Speaking, Listening, Reading, and Writing

Activities are provided so that the integration of language is possible.

Church (1985); Kwak & Newman (1985); Newman (1985d)

Authentic language is language that is integrated. Its use occurs naturally when children have many contexts in which to explore and study a range of topics and many activities and projects to engage in. For example, when a teacher provides several animals for observation and study in the classroom, children in small groups have to work together on their projects. The teacher may initially provide a range of Activity Cards* listing open-ended questions for them to consider regarding these animals. (Activity Cards* are discussed in more detail in Chapter 7.) These initial observations serve as grist for the students to pose their own questions and areas of Student-Initiated Inquiries*. The teacher may also place a broad spectrum of books regarding these animals near the animal centers to support the children's investigations.

Goodman & Goodman (1990); Hyde & Bizar (1989); Wells (1986, 1993, 1994); Wells & Chang-Wells (1992)

Because the teacher offers activities that are centered on or guided by children, the teacher is then available to provide specific feedback to children regarding aspects of their projects. Children may follow up on a question or comment the teacher has made in their journals by reading several books and then discussing them with the teacher. The teacher is also free to facilitate interaction between the children and can guide them to consider their peers as sources of help and support in deciding if their organization of material on their topic seems to be clear and interesting to others. In such situations, therefore, children have many opportunities to take turns offering and listening to each other's ideas about what needs to be done and how to do it. When a child writes a report on a particular subtopic related to a topic another child has chosen, the children become interested conversational partners. They share their resources, pointing out parts of books they have come across in their own research that may be useful for their peers on their projects. When teachers offer meaningful activities and projects, the need for integrated language—the use of authentic language—naturally arises.

Teachers Expect and Understand Children's Approximations in Language and Learning

Approximations help teachers understand children's hypotheses or schemas about the world.

Because teachers view children as active learners who have constructed their own knowledge, they expect children's approximations in their theories about the world and about the rules of language use. Approximations are the result of risk taking and children's current hypotheses and conceptions. These approximations are reflected in everything they do—how they think a machine works, why people acted the way they did years ago, what they believe an author means, how to express and revise the information they found on a topic in their research reports, how to spell a word, or how to figure out a word they encounter in their reading. Because approximations are based on their existing schemas and are important indicators of children's present understandings, teachers in an integrated language classroom are careful observers of how children make sense of language and the world so they know what, why, and how to teach next.

Integrated language teachers are kid-watchers and evaluate children's learning while the children are actually using language in their activities and projects. Approximations are guideposts by which teachers can assess individual children's strategies and knowledge. Teachers realize that the logic by which children learn may not be the same logic as that used by adults. Consequently, they monitor children's approximations so that they know how to respond to children to further foster, sustain, and extend their present efforts. Thus, teachers are involved in an ongoing interplay between assessment and instruction. They document children's approximations made in various contexts and across time, their instructional responses to these approximations, and children's development to more mature understanding and control of conventions so that they have a valid means of accountability regarding children's learning.

Goodman (1985); Goodman & Goodman (1990); King (1985); Newman (1985a); Wilde (1997)

Anthony, Johnson, Mickelson, & Preece (1991); Barrs, Ellis, Hister, & Thomas (1988); Powers (1996)

Teachers Foster Children's Choices and Ownership of Their Activities and Projects and Promote Children's Autonomy and Control of Their Learning

Inherent in the collaborative approach is a certain management style. Rather than control everything done in the classroom, teachers in an integrated language classroom attempt to share with their students control of what happens. They do that by providing many choices—by letting children decide what topic to pursue within a thematic unit, what questions to pose and resolve, and what ways to relate what they have learned. By accepting children's approximations, they help children represent problems to themselves, and they foster children's intellectual autonomy. Thus, the challenge of learning and education in general—children's construction of knowledge by seeking connections that will integrate different areas and by developing strategies to exploit present understandings to maximum effect—is promoted.

When teachers allow children to control their learning and own their activities and projects, children's feelings of self-respect are developed and they become confident in what they know. They are encouraged to be independent, self-motivated learners. The model that teachers have provided means that children learn to treat and respect their peers, who may come from a different social class or ethnolinguistic cultural group, in the same way.

Providing choices is critical to fostering ownership.

Harste & Short (1988); Newman (1985a, 1991); Hyde & Bizar (1989); Kohn (1993); Wells (1986); Wells & Chang-Wells (1992); Willinsky (1990); Young (1992)

Teachers Provide Feedback That Facilitates Children's Self-Regulation of Their Schemas

A collaborative style of teaching gives teachers many opportunities to provide critical feedback to children as they engage in activities and projects. Teachers go in close and listen to understand. They take children's problems seriously and attempt to address their intentions. Their questions and suggestions are related to these intentions—are contingently responsive to students' current efforts—and then children are left on their own to consider these possibilities. Teachers lead from behind; they track what children are trying to do and then provide the support that enables children to stretch and go beyond their own limits, to do on their own what they initially could not do unaided. These ZPD interactions provide the kind of assistance children need to modify their theories and self-regulate their schemas so that they internalize their teachers' response modes and discourse practices and begin to interact with their peers in a similar manner. Children become coaches, asking for and giving useful feedback to one another.

Some of the instructional contexts that teachers provide may be teacher-directed Focus Lessons* for the whole class a particular group (see Chapter 7). Some of these may be pre-planned to launch and support a thematic unit's exploration but many oc-

Useful feedback helps children develop existing schemas.

Bruner (1983, 1986); Goodman (1985); Halliday (1982); Lindfors (1987); Vygotsky (1978); Wells & Chang-Wells (1992); Wertsch (1990)

Teachers create ZPDs (zones of proximal development) to promote children's learning.

Routman (1996)

cur as teachers provide explicit instruction in an ongoing fashion, based on their observation of students' difficulties, misunderstandings, or approximations.

Teachers Provide Opportunities to Integrate Language across the Curriculum

Various curricular areas and disciplines deal with content and domains that are expressed by a number of language patterns and registers. Consequently, providing opportunities to use language across the curriculum fosters communicative competence in a natural way yet at a sophisticated level. Disciplines are cultural frames; they are best seen as certain kinds of social activities conducted by certain communities of scholars, where novelists, mathematicians, historians, geologists, chemists, and biologists participate in particular modes of engagement with life.

Integrated work provides many challenges. It is one thing to know mathematical facts, but how should these data be reported in a survey or expressed in a report on an experiment? Or if information about the Aztecs has been obtained through reading nonfictional history texts and some stories in which Aztecs are characters, how should this information about the Aztecs and their values or ideologies be presented to the class? Should it be expressed by a piece of historical fiction or by an informational report? Maybe poetry should be considered. What is best? What are the advantages and disadvantages of selecting one form over the others? Should art work be included to illustrate the findings? What questions should be considered in terms of representation and accuracy in these pictures?

When children are given opportunities to use language across the curriculum, the choices abound and the decisions to be made seem endless. However, in the process, children learn about the distinctive disciplinary modes of thinking and how these areas of intellectual thought are expressed in recognized linguistic modes or genres. Also, in drawing on knowledge from various disciplines in a particular inquiry, children are encouraged to check and compare information they have gleaned from these resources. This helps them consider the tentative nature of knowledge in various domains and discover that while genres are inherited social forms, they can change and merge. Hence, through integrated inquiries, children become aware of the generative, creative potential of language.

Teachers Can Plan and Implement Thematic Units So That Children Have Sustained Time for Systematic and Reflective Inquiry on a Range of Topics

The use of thematic units has many advantages. It provides both depth and breadth. (Many thematic units are illustrated throughout this book, especially in Chapters 3, 4, and 5.) A thematic unit has a central theme or concept that provides overall coherence. At the same time, it provides opportunities for children to explore specific topics and domains in-depth. Because these individual and group projects are related to the theme, however, many more connections are made. Learning has a richness and a significance rarely seen when basals and textbooks determine the course of study. Thus, a thematic unit approach reflects a "less is more" philosophy by addressing the problems inherent in "teaching for coverage" that is found in traditional classrooms where students are exposed to many topics "at a clip." Through thematic units, teachers do consider various guidelines and standards at the local, state, and national level, but they do this by posing interesting and essential questions about content and setting up a framework for inquiry in which students can examine these central concepts and questions across the curriculum.

Thematic units also allow for children's choice. Moreover, they provide the sustained time children need to pursue their topics of study. Teachers and peers can better interact and support children in their activities and projects. Having time for systematic inquiry on topics of one's choice leads to reflective thinking. There is a constant relating of what one already knows to something new. Because the children know what's familiar and what's new, new routines and connections evolve and become ap-

Many ways to use language across the curriculum are provided.

Britton (1989); Hyde & Bizar (1989); Lytle & Botel (1988); Tierney, Caplan, Ehri, Healy, & Hurdlow (1989)

Geertz (1983); Levstik & Pappas (1992); Pappas (1997)

Halliday (1978, 1993); Wells (1993, 1994)

Thematic units provide sustained time for projects and inquiries.

Gamberg, Kwak, Hutchings, & Altheim (1988); Pappas (1997); Wells (1986)

Fried (1995)

Thematic units promote in-depth, not superficial "at a clip," learning.

Wells & Chang-Wells (1992)

parent. Children actually become more consciously aware of these new interpretations. They move into what are called *disembedded modes of thought*. That is, they are able to reflect on their language and thinking in abstraction; they can take a critical stance to their learning. This is the metalinguistic and metacognitive awareness discussed in an earlier section of this chapter.

Donaldson (1978); Hyde & Bizar (1989)

Teachers Are Learners and Committed Professionals

Teachers in an integrated language classroom see themselves as learners. As children construct their knowledge, teachers learn about their own discoveries. Children become experts on particular topics and share their knowledge with the teacher. Teachers collaborate with children who have different ways with words and learn about the ethnic and cultural complexity of our world. When teachers include books and materials to implement their thematic units, some resources may be unfamiliar to them or known only in a superficial way. Consequently, teachers learn more about content and how that content is expressed in written language. Teachers then see themselves as researchers of their own practice.

Teachers are learners and researchers of their own practice.

Bartolome (1994); Cochran-Smith & Lytle (1993); Goswami & Stillman (1987); Routman (1996)

Unlike teachers in traditional classrooms who believe their job is to implement others' programs and curricula, teachers in integrated language classrooms see themselves as professionals who own and develop their programs. Children operate from their own schemas and, consequently, travel different routes in learning. Thus, a curriculum is not considered very useful when it is in some prepackaged form that has been broken down into small steps or pieces and arranged in a linear sequence to be followed by *every* child. Such a program has been made for *unidirectional transmission*, where bits or "facts" from the material are delivered *one way* straight to the presumably empty mind of the child who is considered to have no influence in learning. Instead, teachers view knowledge in integrated language classrooms as an active reconstruction that is constantly being negotiated. What happens in the classroom must therefore be done in a collaborative way.

Hyde & Bizar (1989); Wells (1986); Wells & Chang-Wells (1992)

As developers of their own programs and curricula, teachers here use their own interpretative frameworks to generate knowledge about teaching and learning. They engage in teacher research—the systematic, intentional inquiry done by them about their own classroom work. This research is *systematic* because teachers gather and record information or document certain experiences in the classroom. It is *intentional* in that the research activity is a planned endeavor, although, of course, teachers gain insights all the time about their teaching as they teach. Finally, teacher research is *inquiry* in that it stems from or generates questions to make sense of classroom life. Because of this, teachers set about their teacher research or inquiry in ways that are parallel to those they support for their students. Like their students, they engage in inquiry that is fundamentally social and constructive, for it enables teachers both to reflect on new information and to interpret the knowledge that they already have. More importantly, though teacher research is an important intellectual heuristic to individual teachers, it also plays a critical role in the formation of the growing knowledge base for teaching that can be useful to the teaching profession at large. Teacher research enables teachers to take charge of their own professional development and learning. It also equips and prepares teachers to enter the public debate at the local and national level about the kind of education that is needed for the 21st century. (More will be said about teacher research in Chapters 3, 4, 9, 10, and the Guidelines for Teacher Inquiry at the end of the book.)

Teacher research is systematic, intentional inquiry.

Cochran-Smith & Lytle (1993)

Pappas & Oyler (1993); Pappas & Zecker (in press a, in press b)

Teacher inquiry is like Student-Initiated Inquiry*.

Sharing Power in Collaboration: Developing Alternative, Non-IRE Classroom Discourse Patterns

We have already argued that taking a collaborative style of teaching involves teachers sharing power and authority with children and that teaching and learning in traditional classrooms reflect a different stance about power and control. In traditional classrooms, the teacher is in control of what is to be learned, when, and how. Knowledge is seen

A collaborative approach to teaching involves sharing power with students.

Cummins (1994); Oyler (1996); Wells & Chang-Wells (1992)

to be the possession of the teacher to be transmitted to students. Thus, it is assumed in this transmission model of teaching that what is learned is a direct reproduction of what is taught because children are not viewed as having their own theories, prior knowledge, or schemas about any particular topic under consideration.

Talk or classroom discourse in a traditional classroom therefore reflects such power and control. Teachers not only do most of the talking, but they also control how much children talk as well as the nature of their talk. Below is an example of discourse in a first-grade classroom. You will note that the structure of the talk follows the typical IRE pattern: the teacher *initiates* the talk—usually by asking questions to which he or she knows the answers—then the child *responds*, and then the teacher *evaluates* the child's response as to its correctness. Let's see how it works.

A small group of first-grade children has been sorting some pieces of plastic food that have been placed in the middle of a small table. The task the teacher has asked the children to accomplish involves having them place each plastic food item next to one of four pictures, each of which depicts one of four food groups: fruit and vegetables, meat, dairy products, bread products. The teacher, who had been working with other small groups in the classroom, has now come to this table, chosen one of the pieces of plastic food, and handed it to Stevie.

> T: What is it?
> S: [Stevie shrugs his shoulders]
> T: Have another look and tell me what it is.
> S: It's [inaudible]. [Other children talk and teacher doesn't hear Stevie]
> T: What's it look like to you?
> S: Eggs.
> T: Eggs?
> S: Scrambled eggs.
> T: It isn't eggs, scrambled eggs. I want you to take another look.
> S: It's yellow.
> T: Yes, it's yellow. What food is yellow?
> S: Corn? [Stevie simultaneously shaking his head indicating "no."]
> T: Does that look like corn?
> S: No.
> T: What is yellow and would be round like this if it were put on a plate ready to eat?
> S: [Stevie shrugs his shoulders]
> T: Well, this is pasta. You know, noodles. So where should you put this pasta? Next to what picture?

You can see how much the teacher was in control of the conversation. She asked all of the questions, even though Stevie had no idea what this plastic object was supposed to represent. She kept trying to ask questions to "help" Stevie discover the "right" answer or make better guesses, and at times the teacher even seemed to lead him to an answer—for example, corn—that he himself felt to be unlikely or "stupid." Finally, she had to tell him what it was.

There were no opportunities for *Stevie* to ask the teacher what *he* thought the plastic item might be, which probably would have been a more appropriate scenario, because the plastic pasta item did not in fact look like pasta or noodles. As the remainder of the conversation (which is not provided here) proceeded, the teacher asked even more questions to get Stevie to place the pasta next to the right food group picture (bread products). Stevie initially put it near the dairy products picture, which was the wrong answer according to the teacher. Stevie mentioned eggs and butter (which, of course, may be used in making some kinds of pasta or noodles), but that was not considered a possibility because in the teaching materials she had relied on in setting up the sorting task, pasta was listed (and shown on the picture) under the bread food group.

The point of the teacher's task and her conversation with her students was to assess what individual children had learned about the four food groups in the nutrition

Cazden (1986, 1988); Edwards & Mercer (1987); Mercer (1995); Young (1992)

In the IRE talk structure, teachers' major purpose is to "test" students' knowledge.

lessons they had covered in preceding days. (We will not consider whether the four food groups is a worthy, interesting, or challenging topic for first-grade children to learn or study.) Even though the children worked in small groups (which the teacher had been trying out in the classroom since attending some workshops on cooperative group learning), the task was just another means of transmitting the teacher's knowledge (or the textbook information) on nutrition to the children in a direct, specified way. Children's ideas or questions were not considered here; the fact that the plastic item wasn't very realistic or that noodles are sometimes made out of eggs and butter, and therefore might be categorized under dairy products, were not problems to be examined. There is no Reflective Inquiry* here—no opportunities even for the teacher to try to understand the learner's conception of the task that the teacher set up. And there was certainly no Student-Initiated Inquiry* where Stevie could have initiated his own task based on his own questions. Thus, the IRE pattern expresses certain notions about knowledge—namely, that children do not have their own theories or knowledge of their own—and as a result teachers must transmit the knowledge or information to students.

The IRE discourse pattern is found in a transmission-oriented curriculum.

Moll (1990); Wells (1993, 1994); Wells & Chang-Wells (1992)

Because teachers in integrated language classrooms have a different view of knowledge—that children construct their own knowledge—teachers take on different roles in teaching so that they can better collaborate with children to assist their learning. In doing so, they develop *alternative* interactional discourse structures that are different from the traditional IRE pattern.

Alternative non-IRE discourse structures are developed in integrated language classrooms.

The examples below involve discourse around classroom sessions where two teachers are reading aloud to their young primary-age children. In the left-hand excerpt, the teacher—we'll refer to her as Teacher A—has finished reading *Bear Shadow* by Frank Asch and is beginning a whole class discussion on the book. On the right, Teacher B has begun to read aloud *Chickens Aren't the Only Ones* by Ruth Heller.

Asch (1985)
Oyler (1996); Oyler & Barry (1992)
Heller (1981)

Teacher A

T: What was the first thing the bear did to get rid of his shadow?
C1: Ran. (T does not respond)
C2: Hid behind a tree.
T: Right. He hid behind a tree. Did it work?
Cs: No.
T: Why?
C2: Because when he left the tree, the shadow was still there.
T: Uhhuh. What was the second thing he did? C3 [child's name]?
C3: Climbed the rocks.
T: Okay, rocks, but the rocks were called . . . C4 [child's name]?
C4: Cliff.
T: And did that work?
Cs: No.
T: Then what did the bear do?
C5: He went home to get his nails and hammer.
T: Okay, but what did he do with the hammer and nails, C5 [child's name]?
C5: He hammered his shadow.
T: Did it work?
Cs: No.
T: Then what did he do? . . .

Teacher B

T: The title page again. The cover, the title page, the author . . . MY SPECIAL THANKS TO, and then the name is Margaret Bradberry Ph.D.—that means she's called doctor. She's the professor of biology at a big university, San Fran—
C1: —cisco.
T: Okay, we're all set.
C2: I hope we begin.
T: CHICKENS LAY THE EGGS YOU BUY, THE EGGS YOU BOIL OR FRY OR . . .
C3: Oil
T: DYE!
C4: They die like that?
T: OR LEAVE ALONE SO YOU CAN SEE WHAT GREW INSIDE NATURALLY.
C2: Eggs.
C1: A real chick. Baby birds are called chicks.
C5: Does that really happen?
C1: Yeah, that really happens. 'Cause I had a little bird and he laid a egg and then it opened.
T: What other bird did we learn about this winter that hatches? In the Antarctic—I'll give you a big hint.
C: Penguin.
T: Penguins! Do they come from eggs?
Cs: Yes.
T: Are they a bird?
Cs: Yes.
C1: The odd bird.
T: We're going to find that out. . . .

Teacher A uses the IRE discourse pattern of interaction.

Wells & Chang-Wells (1992)

Barnes (1976); Barnes & Todd (1995)

Teacher B uses an alternative, non-IRE discourse pattern of interaction.

Student initiations abound in collaborative talk.

Cross discussion is talk between students without teacher mediation.

Cazden (1988); Lemke (1990)

Burbules (1993); Mercer (1995); Wells (1993, 1994); Wells & Chang-Wells (1992); Willinsky (1990); Young (1992)

Collaborative transaction, not transmission

Both student and teacher agendas are considered in a collaborative style of teaching.

Bartolome (1994); Cummins (1994); Oyler (1996); Pappas & Oyler (1993)

See Pappas & Zecker (in press a, in press b) for more examples of urban teachers taking on collaborative styles in teaching.

You can see from these excerpts that Teacher A has followed a fairly strict IRE pattern in her discussion of the book she has read. She initiated all of the turns through her questions that attempted to get at information to be correctly recalled from the text. Her agenda was to "check students' comprehension" of the text, to make sure that children get the sequence of Bear's actions "right." As a result, students' responses indicate the degree to which children dutifully conform to the teacher's agenda. There is no room for considering the affective aspects of the book, for example, the humor that children apparently found in Bear's actions as they laughed and giggled during Teacher A's reading of the book, or the exploratory talk that might have emerged about the relationship of the sun and shadows and why Bear's actions were so funny. That is, there were no opportunities for children to express *their own* reactions to the book and therefore no opportunities for the teacher to assess what their understanding was so that she could then extend it through guided, collaborative participation.

Teacher B shows an alternative approach to reading a book with her children. The most notable difference in the discourse pattern is that students had opportunities to initiate their own responses to the book. In her response—"oil"—C3 tries to predict upcoming text to be read; in his question, C4 queries his interpretation of the DYE of the book to mean "die." Subsequently, C1 comments on the illustration that shows a baby chick standing next to a broken eggshell. C5 wants to know if chicks really come from hatched eggs, to which C1 answers. Here, then, is another aspect of the alternative discourse approach—namely, that children feel free to talk to each other, not just to the teacher. Following this student "cross discussion," Teacher B enters the discussion by trying to link what students had learned about a hatching bird (penguins) earlier in the year with the present opportunity to find out more about the topic. These several turns of teacher-initiated discussion are similar to the traditional IRE pattern, but note that here, in contrast to those noted in Teacher A's excerpt, the interaction follows the *children's* lead—*their* agenda. She then accepts the child's comment that the penguin is "the odd bird" and sets up a real purpose for reading the rest of the book by remarking, "We're going to find that out."

There are many other points to make about these two excerpts. First, the fact that a teacher uses children's literature rather than a basal or textbook passage does not ensure more collaborative, non-IRE discourse interactions. Both Teachers A and B used good literature, but with different results. The difference is that integrated language teachers discover and employ more viable alternatives to a transmission-oriented curriculum. Because they trust in their students' abilities and dispositions to make sense of their experiences, the teachers conceptualize the teaching-learning process in terms of collaborative transaction rather than transmission.

Second, the fact that teachers respect and encourage children's inquiry and their own responses to books does not mean that teachers have a laissez-faire attitude in teaching, that they never share their expertise and knowledge with their students, or never directly tell their students some information on a topic that students may want or need. A collaborative style of teaching takes into account both students' and teachers' agendas. There is no simple teaching formula or techniques to accomplish collaborative learning. Instead, such learning requires vigilant reflection on the part of teachers regarding their interactions with their students. Integrated language teachers are always posing important, challenging questions for themselves: How do I share my expertise or knowledge at the same time I encourage and foster my students' own construction of knowledge and expertise? How do I hear the voices of students who may come from a range of ethnolinguistic, cultural backgrounds, as well as enable them to hear my voice and thus mediate the mainstream culture at large? These kinds of questions are at the core of what it means for teachers to share power and authority with their students; they are basic to successful multicultural education.

In such a teaching approach, using or not using IRE or alternative non-IRE discourse patterns is not an all-or-nothing phenomenon, and although the examples we have provided here came from first-grade classrooms, each discourse type can occur in any grade. More traditional, teacher-directed IRE patterns may and do occur in integrated language classrooms. For example, they are likely to happen when certain procedures are being set up by teachers, such as when a teacher wants students to follow specific practices as they work on small-group projects during integrated work time. Or, they may be employed when teachers develop various short focus lessons* to go over some aspect of students' understandings—perhaps a mathematical or scientific concept, or how to use contractions in their writing, or how to employ a particular reading strategy in doing research for a particular project. These more IRE-like interactions are used when the teacher wants to set up certain rules or routines in the classroom that will enable other, more collaborative ventures with students or to instruct students more explicitly on some specific skill that has been noticed as being problematic in the teacher's ongoing observations of students' work. Thus, when and how to share their teacher expertise in student-centered and -initiated activities and inquiries always involves the "search for the best fit." There is always a *continuum* about how various discourse patterns are realized because these patterns are related to various purposes of teaching and learning. However, more often alternative, collaborative talk (an alternative non-IRE structure) occurs in integrated language classrooms because teachers are attempting to foster students' reflective inquiry and their construction of knowledge; they are promoting independent, self-motivated learners. And for peer groups as well, there will be many occasions where collaborative talk and action are accomplished. In sum, collaborative learning and a collaborative style of teaching entail constant consideration of both teacher and student agendas. (The activities at the end of the chapter can help you become more aware of how various classroom discourse patterns between teachers and students and among students in peer groups reflect issues of power, control, and knowledge.)

Traditional IRE patterns can occur in integrated language classrooms in certain circumstances.

Reyes (1991)

Collaborative talk fosters students' construction of knowledge.

See Activities 1 and 2

The Culture of the Classroom

What does it mean to say that each classroom represents a culture of its own? It means that norms are established regarding cooperation for the use of space and time, for the use of resources, and for valuing and behaving in certain ways. At the beginning of this century, Dewey wrote: "From the standpoint of the child, the great waste in school comes from his inability to utilize the experiences he gets outside of school in any complete and free way; while, on the other hand, he is unable to apply in daily life what he is learning at school" (p. 75). Unfortunately, this description still characterizes many of our schools. In an integrated language classroom, norms are developed and realized in such a way that life in school is not so different from life out of school. Children can readily apply in school what they have learned at home, and what they have learned in school can also be used at home.

Dewey (1956)

Fried (1995)

As you have seen in this chapter, the nature of learners, language, and knowledge when viewed from this perspective means that teachers have certain roles. However, the agendas of teachers and children alike are considered and negotiated. The classroom culture is one in which teaching and learning are a collaborative enterprise.

How can such a classroom culture be realized? How are the norms or behavior patterns in such a classroom culture established? What exactly are thematic units? How can teachers develop plans around themes that provide choices for children that foster the use of integrated, authentic language across the curriculum? How are thematic units implemented on a day-by-day basis? Chapters 3, 4, and 5 will address these kinds of basic questions so that you can better visualize how these ideas can be translated into the classroom.

SUGGESTED ACTIVITIES

1. To become more aware of how various discourse patterns reflect the ways power and knowledge might or might not be shared and constructed between classroom participants, collect some examples of classroom discourse. With the help of

your classmates try to obtain a range of classroom contexts—ones that are whole-class or small-group teacher-led, ones that involve talk among a few students, or ones in which a teacher is talking to just one or a few students. Remember that all talk occurs in a certain context of situation, so you will need to jot down the relevant contextual information for each sample—see Activity 1 at the end of Chapter 1.

Transcribe as much as you can of your samples so you can share them with others in your class. Now analyze and compare yours and your classmates' samples of how the discourse patterns realized the extent to which collaborative talk occurred. In all of your examples, be sure that you consider the *purposes* of the interactions that were realized by the talk and whether there were inconsistencies between the purpose and resulting discourse. Which ones followed the IRE pattern? Which ones were alternative and non-IRE in nature? In what ways was the teacher in control of the students' opportunities to talk? Did students have to follow the teacher agenda or were students able to initiate topics of their own? What was the content of these initiations? To what extent did the teacher follow up, extend, or sustain these student initiations? Was the talk different when the teacher talked to one or a few students as opposed to the whole class or a larger group? What was the peer discourse like—more collaborative or not? How were the structures of the discourse related to the *purposes* of the various interactions?

2. To better understand your own use of various discourse patterns, tape-record your own discussions with students in an elementary classroom. Pick interactions or activities or routines that will likely give you discourse examples across the continuum from teacher-directed to collaborative. For example, select interactional contexts in which you will be following *your own* agenda, offering mostly your knowledge on a topic, or where you outline certain procedures you want students to follow in doing an experiment or in discussing a particular set of books a group has read. These are likely to be more IRE-like in nature. Choose a couple of other activities or interactions in which you hope to share your power and expertise so that students can offer their own knowledge, and which therefore will likely reflect more collaborative talk or be alternative to IRE-like discourse. These might be discussions with a group of students who may be studying particular aspects of a topic, or perhaps content conferences you might have with individual students over their written drafts. Or it might even be a whole-class, teacher-led read-aloud where you are hoping to have students offer *their own* interpretations or responses on a book. Transcribe these interactions and analyze them in the ways suggested in Activity 1 above. How did they go? Did you do a good job in explaining your expertise or agenda in the teacher-directed activity or experience? Did your goals or purposes to share power and knowledge in collaboration get accomplished? Why? Why not?

REFERENCES

Anthony, R. J., Johnson, T. D., Mickelson, N. I., & Preece, A. (1991). *Evaluating literacy: A perspective for change.* Portsmouth, NH: Heinemann.

Barnes, D. (1976). *From communication to curriculum.* London: Penguin.

Barnes, D., & Todd, F. (1995). *Communication and learning revisited: Making meaning through talk.* Portsmouth, NH: Boynton/Cook.

Barrs, M., Ellis, S., Hester, H., & Thomas, A. (1988). *The primary language record: Handbook for teachers.* Portsmouth, NH: Heinemann.

Bartolome, L. I. (1994). Beyond the methods fetish: Toward a humanizing pedagogy. *Harvard Educational Review, 64,* 173–194.

Bayer, A. S. (1990). *Collaborative-apprenticeship learning: Language and thinking across the curriculum, K–12.* Mountain View, CA: Mayfield.

Britton, J. (1989). Writing-and-reading in the classroom. In A. H. Dyson (Ed.), *Collaboration through writing and reading* (pp. 217–246). Urbana, IL: National Council of Teachers of English.

Bruner, J. S. (1983). *Child's talk: Learning to use language.* New York: Norton.

Bruner, J. S. (1986). *Actual minds, possible worlds.* Cambridge, MA: Harvard University Press.

Burbules, N. C. (1993). *Dialogue in teaching: Theory and practice.* New York: Teachers College Press.

Calkins, L. M. (1986). *The art of teaching writing.* Portsmouth, NH: Heinemann.

Calkins, L. M. (1994). *The art of teaching writing.* Portsmouth, NH: Heinemann.

Calkins, L. M., with Harwayne, S. (1991). *Living between the lines.* Portsmouth, NH: Heinemann.

Cambourne, B. (1984). Language, learning and literacy. In A. Butler & J. Turbill, *Towards a reading-writing classroom* (pp. 5–10). Portsmouth, NH: Heinemann.

Cazden, C. B. (1986). Classroom discourse. In M. C. Wittrock (Ed.), *Handbook of research on teaching* (3rd ed., pp. 432–463). New York: Macmillan.

Cazden, C. B. (1988). *Classroom discourse: The language of teaching and learning.* Portsmouth, NH: Heinemann.

Church, S. (1985). The war of the words. In J. M. Newman (Ed.), *Whole language: Theory in use* (pp. 153–162). Portsmouth, NH: Heinemann.

Cochran-Smith, M., & Lytle, S. L. (1993). *Inside/Outside: Teacher research and knowledge.* New York: Teachers College Press.

Cummins, J. (1994). From coercive to collaborative relations of power in the teaching of literacy. In B. M. Ferdman, R. M. Weber, & A.G. Ramírez (Eds.), *Literacy across languages and cultures* (pp. 295-331). Albany: State University of New York Press.

Dewey, J. (1956). *The child and the curriculum and the school and society* (comb. ed.). Chicago: University of Chicago Press.

Donaldson, M. (1978). *Children's minds.* Glasgow: William Collins Sons.

Duckworth, E. (1987). *The having of wonderful ideas and other essays on teaching and learning.* New York: Teachers College Press.

Dunn, J. (1988). *The beginnings of social understandings.* Cambridge, MA: Harvard University Press.

Dyson, A. H. (Ed.). (1989). *Collaboration through writing and reading: Exploring possibilities.* Urbana, IL: National Council of Teachers of English.

Edelsky, C. (1986). *Writing in a bilingual program: Habia una vez.* Norwood, NJ: Ablex.

Edelsky, C. (1991). *With literacy and justice for all: Rethinking the social in language and education.* London: Falmer Press.

Edwards, D., & Mercer, N. (1987). *Common knowledge: The development of understanding in the classroom.* London: Routledge.

Fairclough, N. (1989). *Language and power.* London: Longman.

Fairclough, N. (1992). *Discourse and social change.* Cambridge, MA: Polity Press.

Fisher, B. (1995). *Thinking and learning together: Curriculum and community in a primary classroom.* Portsmouth, NH: Heinemann.

Foster, M. (1992). Sociolinguistics and the African-American community: Implications for literacy. *Theory Into Practice, 32,* 303–311.

Fried, R. L. (1995). *The passionate teacher: A practical guide.* Boston: Beacon Press.

Gamberg, R., Kwak, W., Hutchings, M., & Altheim, J. (1988). *Learning and loving it: Theme studies in the classroom.* Portsmouth, NH: Heinemann.

Geertz, C. (1983). *Local knowledge: Further essays in interpretive anthropology.* New York: Basic Books.

Genishi, C. (1985). Observing communicative performance in young children. In A. Jaggar & M. T. Smith-Burke (Eds.), *Observing the language learner* (pp. 131–143). Newark, DE: International Reading Association.

Goodman, Y. M. (1985). Kidwatching: Observing children in the classroom. In A. Jaggar & M. T. Smith-Burke (Eds.), *Observing the language learner* (pp. 9–18). Newark, DE: International Reading Association.

Goodman, Y., & Goodman, K. S. (1990). Vygotsky in a whole-language perspective. In L. C. Moll (Ed.), *Vygotsky and education: Instructional implications and applications of sociohistorical psychology* (pp. 223–250). Cambridge, MA: Cambridge University Press.

Goswami, D., & Stillman, P. R. (1987). *Reclaiming the classroom: Teacher research as an agency for change.* Portsmouth, NH: Boynton/Cook.

Graves, D. (1983). *Writing: Teachers and children at work.* Portsmouth, NH: Heinemann.

Halliday, M. A. K. (1975). *Learning how to mean: Explorations in the development of language.* London: Edward Arnold.

Halliday, M. A. K. (1978). *Language as a social semiotic: The social interpretation of language and meaning.* London: Longman.

Halliday, M. A. K. (1982). Three aspects of children's language development: Learning language, learning through language, and learning about language. In Y. Goodman, M. Haussler, & D. Strickland (Eds.), *Oral and written language development research: Impact on the schools* (pp. 7–19). Urbana, IL: National Council of Teachers of English.

Halliday, M. A. K. (1993). Towards a language-based theory of learning. *Linguistics and Education, 5,* 93–126.

Harste, J. C., & Short, K. G. (1988). *Creating classrooms for authors: The reading-writing connection.* Portsmouth, NH: Heinemann.

Harste, J. C., Woodward, V. A., & Burke, C. L. (1984). *Language stories and literacy lessons.* Portsmouth, NH: Heinemann.

Heath, S. B. (1983). *Ways with words: Language, life, and work in communities and classrooms.* Cambridge: Cambridge University Press.

Holdaway, D. (1979). *Foundations of literacy.* Sydney, Australia: Ashton Scholastic.

Hyde, A. A., & Bizar, M. (1989). *Thinking in context: Teaching cognitive processes across the elementary school curriculum.* White Plains, NY: Longman.

Jaggar, A. M. (1985). On observing the language learner: Introduction and overview. In A. Jaggar & M. T. Smith-Burke (Eds.), *Observing the language learner* (pp. 1–7). Newark, DE: International Reading Association.

King, M. L. (1985). Language and language learning for child watchers. In A. Jaggar & M. T. Smith-Burke (Eds.), *Observing the language learner* (pp. 19–38). Newark, DE: International Reading Association.

Kohn, A. (1993). Choices for children: Why and how to let students decide. *Phi Delta Kappan, 75,* 8–20.

Kwak, W., & Newman, J. M. (1985). Activity cards. In J. M. Newman (Ed.), *Whole language: Theory in use* (pp. 137–144). Portsmouth, NH: Heinemann.

Ladson-Billings, G. (1994). *The dreamkeepers: Successful teachers of African-American children.* San Francisco: Jossey-Bass.

Lemke, J. L. (1990). *Talking science: Language, learning, and values.* Norwood, NJ: Ablex.

Levstik, L. S., & Pappas, C. C. (1992). New directions for studying historical understanding. *Theory and Research in Social Education. 20,* 368–384.

Lindfors, J. W. (1987). *Children's language and learning.* Englewood Cliffs, NJ: Prentice-Hall.

Lytle, S. L., & Botel, M. (1988). *PCRP II: Reading, writing and talking across the curriculum.* Harrisburg, PA: Pennsylvania Department of Education.

Michaels, S. (1981). "Sharing time": Children's narrative styles and differential access to literacy. *Language in Society, 10,* 423–442.

McCollum, P. (1991). Cross-cultural perspectives on classroom discourse and literacy. In E. H. Hiebert (Ed.), *Literacy for a diverse society: Perspectives, practices and policies* (pp. 108–121). New York: Teachers College Press.

Mercer, N. (1995). *The guided construction of knowledge: Talk amongst teachers and learning.* Clevedon: Multilingual Matters.

Moll, L. C. (1990). Introduction. In L. C. Moll (Ed.), *Vygotsky and education: Instructional implications and applications of sociohistorical psychology* (pp. 1–27). Cambridge, MA: Cambridge University Press.

Newman, D., Griffin, P., & Cole, M. (1989). *The construction zone: Working for cognitive change in school.* Cambridge, MA: Cambridge University Press.

Newman, J. M. (1985a). Insights from recent reading and writing research and their implications for developing whole language curriculum. In J. M. Newman (Ed.), *Whole language: Theory in use* (pp. 7–36). Portsmouth, NH: Heinemann.

Newman, J. M. (1985b). Introduction. In J. M. Newman (Ed.), *Whole language: Theory in use* (pp. 1–6). Portsmouth, NH: Heinemann.

Newman, J. M. (1985c). Using children's books to teach reading. In J. M. Newman (Ed.), *Whole language: Theory in use* (pp. 55–64). Portsmouth, NH: Heinemann.

Newman, J. M. (1985d). Mealworms: Learning about written language through science activities. In J. M. Newman (Ed.*),* *Whole language: Theory in use* (pp. 145–152). Portsmouth, NH: Heinemann.

Newman, J. M. (1991). Learning to teach by uncovering our assumptions. In D. Booth & C. Thornley-Hall (Eds.), *The talk curriculum.* Portsmouth, NH: Heinemann.

Nieto, S. (1996). *Affirming diversity: The sociopolitical context of multicultural education.* White Plains, NY: Longman.

Oyler, C. (1996). *Making room for students in an urban first grade: Sharing authority in Room 104.* New York: Teachers College Press.

Oyler, C., & Barry, A. (1992, December). *Shared authority during teacher-led read alouds: Alternatives to the IRE pattern.* Paper presented at National Reading Conference, San Antonio, TX.

Pappas, C. C. (1997). Reading instruction in an integrated language perspective: Collaborative interaction in classroom curriculum genres. In S. A. Stahl & D. A. Hayes (Eds.), *Instructional models in reading* (pp. 283–310). Mahwah, NJ: Lawrence Erlbaum.

Pappas, C. C., & Oyler, C., with Barry A., & Rassel, M. (1993). Focus on research: Collaborating with teachers developing integrated language arts programs in urban schools. *Language Arts, 70,* 297–303.

Pappas, C. C., & Pettegrew, B. S. (1998). The role of genre in the psycholinguistic guessing game of reading. *Language Arts, 75,* 36–44.

Pappas, C. C., & Zecker, L. B. (in press a). *Working with teacher researchers in urban classrooms: Transforming literacy curriculum genres.* Mahwah, NJ: Lawrence Erlbaum.

Pappas, C. C., & Zecker, L. B. (in press b). *Teacher inquiries in literacy teaching-learning: Learning to collaborate in urban elementary classrooms.* Mahwah, NJ: Lawrence Erlbaum.

Powers, B. M. (1996). *Taking note: Improving your observational notetaking.* York, ME: Stenhouse.

Reyes, M. de la Luz. (1991). A process approach to literacy instruction for Spanish-speaking students: In search of a best fit. In E. F. Hiebert (Ed.), *Literacy for a diverse society: Perspectives, practices, and policies* (pp. 157–171). New York: Teachers College Press.

Routman, R. (1996). *Literacy at the crossroads.* Portsmouth, NH: Heinemann

Shanahan, T. (Ed.). (1990). *Reading and writing together: New perspectives for the classroom.* Norwood, MA: Christopher-Gordon.

Smith, F. (1982). *Understanding reading* (3rd ed). New York: Holt, Rinehart, & Winston.

Smith, F. (1997). *Reading without nonsense.* New York: Teachers College Press.

Stephens, J. (1992). *Language and ideology in children's fiction.* London: Longman.

Tierney, R., Caplan, R., Ehri, L., Healy, M. K., & Hurdlow, M. (1989). Writing and reading working together. In A. H. Dyson (Ed.), *Collaboration through writing and reading: Exploring possibilities* (pp. 169–209). Urbana, IL: National Council of Teachers of English.

Vygotsky L. S. (1978). *Mind in society: The development of higher psychological processes.* Cambridge, MA: Cambridge University Press.

Weaver, C. (1996). *Teaching grammar in context.* Portsmouth, NH: Boynton/Cook.

Wells, G. (1981). *Learning through interaction: The study of language development.* Cambridge, MA: Cambridge University Press.

Wells, G. (1986). *The meaning makers: Children learning language and using language to learn.* Portsmouth, NH: Heinemann.

Wells, G. (1993). Reevaluating the IRF sequence: A proposal for the articulation of theories of activity and discourse for the analysis of teaching and learning in the classroom. *Linguistics and Education, 5,* 1–37.

Wells, G. (1994). The complimentary contributions of Halliday and Vygotsky to a "language-based theory of learning." *Linguistics and Education, 6,* 41–90.

Wells, G., & Chang-Wells, G. L. (1992). *Constructing knowledge together: Classrooms as centers of inquiry and literacy.* Portsmouth, NH: Heinemann.

Wertsch, J. V. (1990). The voice of rationality in a sociocultural approach to mind. In L. C. Moll (Ed.) *Vygotsky and education: Instructional implications and applications of sociohistorical psychology* (pp. 111–126). Cambridge, MA: Cambridge University Press.

Wilde, S. (1997). *What's a schwa sound anyway? A holistic guide to phonetics, phonics, and spelling.* Portsmouth, NH: Heinemann.

Willinsky, J. (1990). *The new literacy: Redefining reading and writing in the schools.* New York: Routledge.

Young, R. (1992). *Critical theory and classroom talk.* Clevedon, England: Multilingual Matters.

Children's Literature

Bear Shadow by F. Asch. Prentice-Hall, 1985.
Chickens Aren't the Only Ones by R. Heller. Scholastic, 1981.

Planning Thematic Units

The preceding chapters have shown how children are active constructors of knowledge. In the years before entering school, children tackle tremendously complex cultural processes not only with determination but also with enthusiasm. This learning occurs in many social contexts when the child uses language for a variety of purposes to express and communicate a variety of ideas and feelings. Once children enter school, learning should build on these same foundations, regardless of their cultural background.

Thematic units reflect patterns of thinking, goals, and concepts common to bodies of knowledge. They link together content from many areas of the curriculum and depict the connections that exist across disciplines. Thematic units provide a framework for a community of learners in which all children can continue to learn language and to construct knowledge. Moreover they provide a context for examining and reflecting on the way meaning is constructed within cultures and across cultures.

The topics chosen for thematic units are broadly based to take advantage of different ways of knowing that individual children bring to the classroom. Thematic units also provide children with many choices about how to pursue their learning. They come to feel a powerful sense of ownership as they initiate some activities and engage in others suggested by their teachers. Moreover, as children work alone or in groups, sharing, and discussing their work and the results of their inquiries, the classroom becomes a community of learners—a classroom culture—that shares ownership of a body of knowledge and understanding that has been jointly created. Teachers, too, are part of this community as they reflect on their teaching and their students' learning within this unique culture.

Such a classroom culture is created by identifying important themes or topics that are worth spending time on and that may be common to many or all subject areas. The theme of HOUSES AND HOMES developed for younger children, for example, could include information about houses in the community as well as houses around the world, imaginary houses, animal houses, or even environments for microorganisms. It could also extend to the concept of home in many cultures and an examination of the problems of homelessness in the local community. A theme of JOURNEYS might involve older children in a study of the age of exploration or the American westward movement. They could also learn about the "journeys" of molecules or nutrients at the same time that they think about journeys in their own lives, or in the lives of characters in their books. They could examine the ways in which political, social, economic, and other forces can cause people to undertake journeys. In both themes, language, the arts, mathematics, science, and the social studies become vehicles for thorough exploration.

Thematic units also take advantage of the cultural diversity (the ways in which people are defined by and find identity in a certain place, region, or culture) and cultural universals (elements of culture common to all nations and people) inherent in American society. When children enter schools, they should enter a cultural "intersection"

See Jacobs, (1989); Lipson, Valencia, Wixson, & Peters, (1993); Neilsen, (1989); Short & Harste (1995); & Stevenson & Carr (1993) for additional views of integrated curriculum.

Teachers and children are part of a community of learners.

Themes provide a central focus for linking many subject areas.

56

where value is placed on what each child brings to the environment. Themes should foster a more inclusive reality by helping children become familiar with, cope with, and benefit from diversity. This means that all themes are multi-cultural and cross-cultural. Thus a STRUCTURES thematic unit might consider the relationship of housing to both environmental and cultural values (such as extended families or notions of privacy) and a PATTERNS theme might include looking at patterns in art both multi-culturally (diversity within a country or culture) and cross-culturally (diversity between countries or cultures). Chapter 5 includes more detailed ideas on making the curriculum more inclusive. In addition, the prototypes in Chapter 4 include specific references to multi-cultural and cross-cultural content.

Thematic units allow for important exploration of points of view.

Hartoonian (1992)

In this book we focus on broadly-based thematic units that may last for many weeks, perhaps a whole grading period. However, thematic units may include topical studies with a more concentrated focus—for example, a section on cumulative stories or on information books on a particular topic, a country, a specific kind of literature such as poetry, the works of one author or illustrator, or even a single book. Whatever the topic or length of study, the aim of any thematic unit is to choose a topic that's worth knowing about, and that will provide a supportive context for meaning-making—that is, one that reflects important concepts or essential questions for students to examine in depth.

Thematic units can be planned to last for several days, for many weeks, or for a whole grading period.

Jorgensen (1994)

Choosing a Theme

There is no single "right" way to develop or plan a thematic unit. We present here methods for planning that can be adapted to individual teachers, classrooms, and children. These methods are guides and suggestions to be tried and modified just as a good cook learns to improve combinations of ingredients to improve the flavor of a dish.

Thematic units evolve in a variety of ways.

The topic of thematic units can be chosen in a variety of ways. You will want to build units around critical questions that will engage children with important ideas and multiple points of view. You will also need to consider areas of study that link content as called for in district and state curriculum guidelines. In addition to considering critical questions and the content of the year's instruction, however, think of children as partners in the learning that is to come, and plan with their interests and enthusiasms in mind, and with their active participation.

Topics come from important questions in the curriculum, yet consider children's interests.

You may want to begin the year by taking full responsibility for choosing and organizing the themes, and then allowing children a more active role in planning as the year progresses and you get to know the needs and interests of your particular students. However, even from the beginning, be open to the ways in which you can tie in concepts to be taught with your students' natural curiosity and excitement about the world around them. For example, a fifth-grade teacher developed a unit on CHANGES when one of his students brought in an article from the local newspaper describing a shopping center planned for nearby wetlands. The teacher channeled the children's outrage into researching questions about the local environment and about possible legal challenges. They organized a petition drive and successfully challenged the developer before the local county planning commission. Another teacher had wanted to explore water and water systems with her third and fourth graders. She wasn't sure how to organize the unit until one of her students reported that his house was being remodeled. "They're tearing out the walls, and there's all these pipes!" he exclaimed. The unit then proceeded with the children studying WATER SYSTEMS in the school and neighborhood, diagramming cross sections of water fountains and fire hydrants, studying physical properties of flush toilets and water wheels, mapping the school's water systems, interviewing roofing (and gutter) and municipal water companies, and completing research reports on a water system. (See Figure 3.1.)

Children's experiences help to shape the direction of the unit.

Levstik & Barton (1997)

In choosing a topic for a thematic unit, pick one that is broad enough to incorporate many types of books, resources, and activities but not so broad that children lose sight of the connections that exist among areas to be explored. The topic of nutrition, for example, is likely to be required at many grade levels. However, it is too narrow

Topics should allow the use of many types of resources.

Figure 3.1

for a good thematic unit. There are few, if any, works of good fiction that would fit that topic, and much as we might hope otherwise, few children would leap to study such a topic. Nutrition may, on the other hand, be explored as part of a unit of health, but health is such a broad area that it would be difficult to cover the vast amount of material in a way that builds strong schemas or domains of knowledge related to the topic. We would prefer to choose a theme like FOOD or EATING, such as the one described in Chapter 4. This topic has considerable child appeal, but it does not ignore critical questions or sacrifice intellectual content.

Webbing

Choosing a topic is the first step in planning thematic units. What follows is a multi-faceted method of planning. There is no one "correct" way to proceed or one single avenue of exploration. Figure 3.2 is an overview of the major components involved in planning and developing a thematic unit. Notice that the planning is a dynamic process. As the first top "diamond" of Figure 3.2 suggests, generating key or essential questions and considering the viewpoints that you want to include will help you select materials and/or choose activities. This process often influences the nature of the theme itself. Recasting the theme may then lead to changes in materials and activities, and so forth. Once begun, the process develops as indicated by the figure, and components may be reshaped or changed as the theme is refined and executed.

Huck, Hepler, Hickman, & Kiefer (1997)

Webbing is a schematic technique, the realization of a brainstorming process. A WEB is a Semantic Map*, a mental representation of concepts and relationships. Webbing allows you to extend a theme in many meaningful directions, fleshing out the topic by choosing meaningful categories and subcategories that relate to questions essential to children's understanding of the theme. Essential questions deal with the most important issues related to a theme and help children understand the nature and purpose of their investigation. In addition, the WEB provides a picture of the possibilities of a given theme and allows you to visualize the many books, props, resources, and activities that are possible avenues of exploration for the theme.

Brainstorm topics with colleagues and /or children.

To get the webbing process started you may want to do some free-associating and simply list everything that comes to mind in connection with a chosen theme. Doing this with a colleague or with children opens up alternative possibilities and prevents you from becoming locked into traditional ideas. As you generate lists or ideas, you will begin to see how many ideas can be grouped together in related categories that represent significant questions you want children to explore. From these, other categories

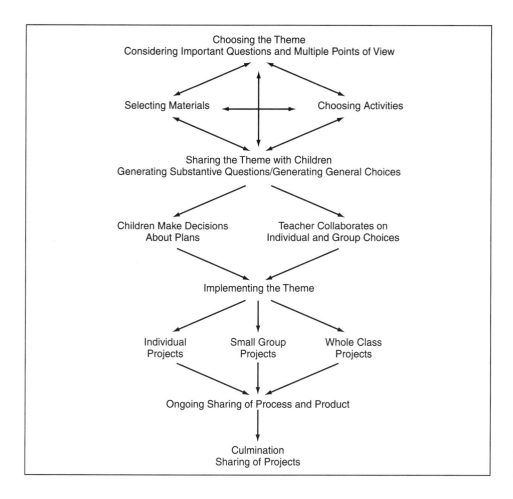

Figure 3.2
PLANNING FOR THEMATIC UNITS

Consider how children can investigate concepts through Reflective Inquiry.

or topics begin to emerge. As you brainstorm, think about ways that Reflective, Disciplined Inquiry* can help children to investigate the theme. You might want to use some of the content standards developed by organizations such as the National Council for the Social Studies, The National Council of Mathematics, and the National Council of Teachers of English to help you think about what big ideas and essential questions children might want to investigate. Also try to keep in mind titles of books and other print resources with which you are familiar, props or manipulatable materials that could give children hands-on experience with the theme, and community resources or resources in the arts that could be incorporated.

The SPACES AND PLACES web that follows began with a group of upper-elementary teachers who wanted to develop an interdisciplinary curriculum that met state curriculum requirements. (See Chapter 4 for a similar theme developed for primary age children.) The state social studies program, for example, called for the study of local communities, and the ways in which social, geographic, and economic factors affect communities. The science syllabus for this age group highlighted the study of ecosystems and the ways in which environmental conditions determine the types and sizes of populations of plants and animals within a community and affect the way the population interacts. Knowing of their students' interest in survival stories the teachers listed some of their favorite titles as a way of pursuing important questions about the interaction of people with their environment. They then listed these questions and other general concepts that children might explore as part of a unit they called "surroundings," sketching out a preliminary web that included activities and books that they knew they wanted to include. Figure 3.3 represents some of the preliminary planning involved in the unit. For example, one teacher had been involved in an overnight field trip to an environmental science center at his previous school and wanted children to experience some sort of outdoor activity. The school media specialist suggested in-

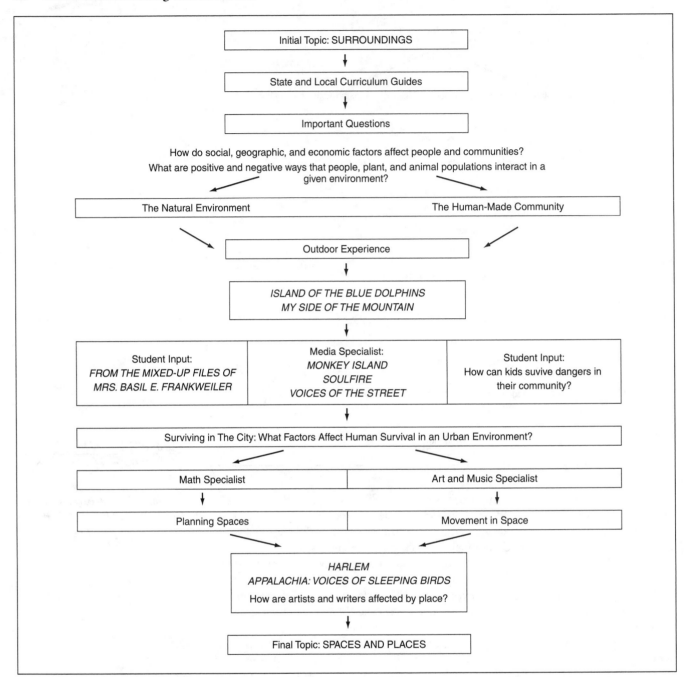

Figure 3.3

Paulsen (1987); O'Dell (1960)

Sutton (1997); Miller-Lachman (1992)

*The first WEB is a sketch that changes
as the unit progresses.*

cluding survival stories like *Hatchet* and *Island of the Blue Dolphins*, and she brought in several indexes of children's literature, *Adventuring with Books* and *Our Family, Our Friends, Our World* to help teachers choose other fiction, poetry, and information books. The initial web was hung in the teachers room as team members consulted with their students and began to flesh out the topic with other activities and books.

As the ideas "incubated" over subsequent days, a child mentioned the empty lot down the street that was full of trash. She wanted to know why the police let people dump garbage there. Another child suggested that the lot could be dangerous to the little kids walking home from the school. Their teacher suggested that this might make a good inquiry project and that they could begin by contacting someone on the city council who knew about city ordinances and planning.

In another class one girl wanted to include a favorite survival story, *From the Mixed Up Files of Mrs. Basil E. Frankweiler,* about two children surviving in The Metropolitan Museum of Art in New York City. Her teacher realized other city survival books such as *Slake's Limbo* and *Scorpions* provided an ideal way to explore diverse points of view. Consultation with the media specialist turned up other books about city survival. Several focused on the homeless, a novel, *Monkey Island,* a picture book, *Fly Away Home,* and an information book, *No Place to Be: Voices of Homeless Children.* Other books featured urban children facing peer pressure and gang violence, two novels, *Soulfire* and *Junebug* and an information book, *Voices from the Street.* Thus the question, "What factors affect human survival in an urban environment?" became an important sub-theme of the unit.

Konigsburg (1969)

Holman (1974); Meyers (1988)

Fox (1991); Bunting (1991); Berck (1992)

Hewett (1996); Mead (1995); Atkin (1996)

A new essential question for the unit emerged.

Consultations with content specialists helped expand the web in additional directions. The district math coordinator suggested that the topic of surroundings seemed to be an ideal way to incorporate geometry or spatial concepts and that the team might want to think about city planning as a way of dividing up space using geometric shapes. The art teacher tied into these concepts with the artist's use of space, from the use of shape as an element of two- and three-dimensional space to the teaching of two-point and three-point perspective. This in turn led to questions about planning for human needs. The P.E. teacher also contributed to the idea of exploring spatial surroundings through movement activities, gymnastics, and dance. Both of the art and music teachers also suggested looking at artistic and musical interpretation's of surroundings through landscape painting and musical compositions such as "Slaughter on Tenth Avenue" or "The Grand Canyon Suite." Exploring the artist's point of view brought to mind the Harlem Renaissance and many artists and musicians affected by their cultural and physical surroundings. Here the media specialist suggested the books, *Harlem* and *Appalachia: Voices of Sleeping Birds,* which talk about this topic. Thus, another essential question emerged: "How are artists and writers affected by place?"

Collaboration of teachers with different expertise can help strengthen the unit.

Myers (1996); Rylant (1991)

Once again, another essential question for the unit developed.

Gradually the initial topic of surroundings grew in many directions and was reshaped into a theme that they called SPACES AND PLACES. (See Figure 3.4.) This figure, although more complex than the first sketch, only captures the possibilities of the topic at a single moment in time. The topic of SPACES AND PLACES will continue to change and to be reshaped as children and teachers encounter issues and find additional interests in the world around them. Note the essential questions under various subtopics of the theme. See Chapter 4 for more information about the role of these key questions in the prototype thematic unit WEBS.

The unit plan will continue to evolve.

The SPACES AND PLACES example reflects a team approach to planning thematic units, but there is no "one" way to develop themes. People tend to start in different ways. Many teachers like to involve students in the planning from the very beginning. For example, you might give children copies of a thematic web that you have generated with only the subcategories of the topic listed. Let the children look at the web and circle topics they are interested in. Then give them index cards and ask them to write down things that are not on the web that they think of as connected to the theme and that they think would be interesting topics and questions they have about topics to pursue. Use the webs and cards to refine the original web and then work with the children to gather resources and plan activities that they think would be important to their inquiries. (See Figure 3.5 on page 64.)

Many teachers elicit input from students early on in developing units.

Some teachers like to begin to think of the theme by planning topics according to more traditional areas like math, science, art, poetry, or writing. As long as these curricula categories allow for valid exploration and inquiry of the theme by children this type of planning may be more comfortable for some, particularly beginners. However they are planned, thematic units that explore ideas worth knowing and essential questions that connect and relate ideas in important ways will likely incorporate traditional content areas in ways that mirror children's learning in the outside-the-school world. In whatever ways teachers use to develop webs it is important to see that a particular unit does cover tra-

Themes should focus on ideas and concepts that are worth spending time on.

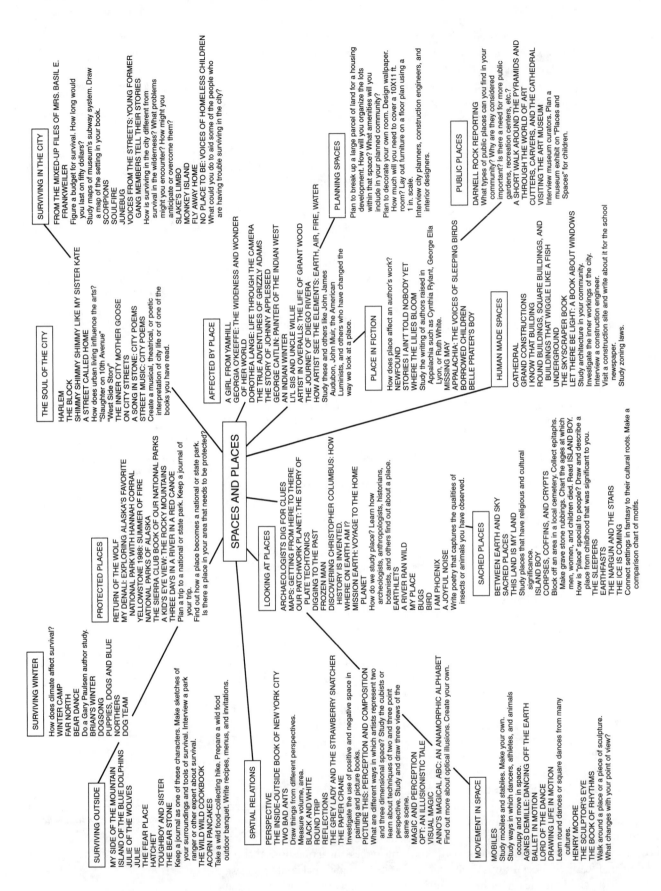

Figure 3.4

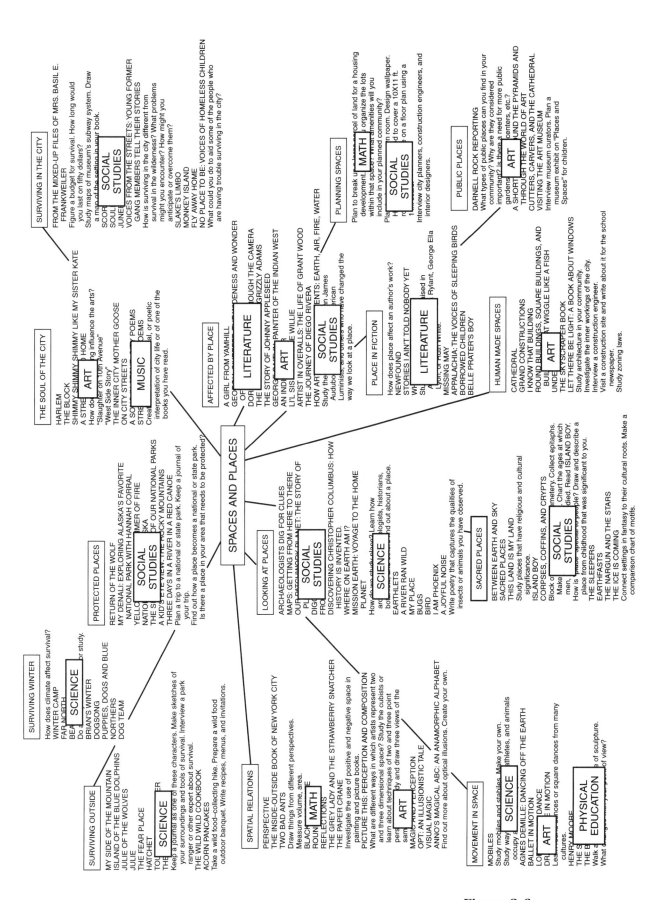

Figure 3.6

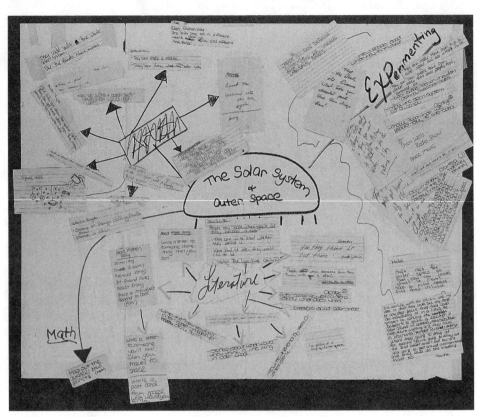

Figure 3.5

ditional areas of the curriculum. The diagram in Figure 3.6 shows how understandings from traditional content areas are represented on the web of SPACES AND PLACES.

Selecting Resources

Resources should be chosen to allow children to explore many cultural perspectives.

One of the aims of a thematic unit is to provide children with wide experience with a range of resources for learning. This broad range is particularly important for exploring different cultural perspectives because not all cultural viewpoints are represented in readily available books. Three major types of resources are incorporated in units. First, a thematic unit includes a variety of genres of children's literature, as well as other sources of printed information—newspapers and magazines, diaries, letters, and other primary sources. Second, thematic units employ many manipulatable materials—artifacts, props, equipment, and so forth. Third, units use resources from the community and the wider world: people, animals, and places that contribute to children's understanding of a theme. The arts can also contribute to the theme through the use of paintings, sculpture, crafts, music, the theater, films, and other media.

Printed Resources

Choose printed resources for their quality and their relevance to the theme.

Books and other printed resources that will be explored in thematic units are best chosen for their literary qualities and for their relationship to the theme. This does not preclude the use of textbooks but it does allow the teacher to make selective use of these materials and to include many of the excellent works of fiction, information books, and periodicals published for children. These resources not only allow for more critical reading on a subject but also accommodate the many reading abilities found in a heterogeneous classroom. In addition, these well-written works provide children with excellent models for their own writing.

The next steps in planning a thematic unit may then be those that lead to the school or municipal library or archives. One of the best sources of information for gathering materials is the librarian or media specialist. These professionals are familiar with good children's books, periodicals, primary source materials, and other printed resources, including computer programs and simulations. They can also direct you to the many good indexes to children's materials, to archival materials, and to other data sources.

Many indexes survey children's literature and other materials. (See Table 3.1.) In addition, up-to-date resources have been made available for selecting multi-cultural titles; the authors and editors of these titles have been careful to select titles that provide an authentic view of particular cultures, books that have been written from the point of view of an insider who knows and understands that culture well.

A broad range of resources can meet the needs of diverse cultural backgrounds.

While some indexes group titles together thematically or are themselves organized around a theme many of these indexes do not. For this reason, it is a good idea to first consult subject headings in making use of these sources, but it may also be helpful to skim through the list of titles and annotations to find materials that could help children explore a theme in unusual ways. In planning a theme of FOOD, for example, a logical place to start would be in the table of contents in a book such as *Adventuring with Books,* in which you can consult the subsection under "Social Studies" titled "Food, Clothing, and Shelter," or the section on "Crafts and Hobbies" (for cookbooks), and the subsection of the "Sciences" titled "Human Development." In addition, consult the subject guide listings under food and cooking. Finally, skim through the list of titles and annotations in the fiction section where you will find books such as *People of Corn: A Mayan Story* or *Dumpling Soup.* Notice that these titles are listed under the subheadings of "Folktales and Fairy Tales" and "Realistic fiction: Human Relationships" than "food" in the table of contents. You would not have found them through the usual research techniques. Therefore, finding titles often requires some digging beneath the surface of indexes or tables of content.

Sutton (1997)

Gerson (1995); Rattigan (1993)

Because we want to make more children be critical readers and to foster their learning in the various registers of written language, it is best to try to include a balance of fiction and nonfiction materials in a thematic unit. If, as you begin collecting titles, you find that there are not enough types of material to provide for a broad range of reading abilities and interests in your class, you may want to broaden the topic of your unit. For example, research on a topic of MACHINES may reveal a limited amount of suitable literature. If the topic was expanded to INVENTIONS AND INVENTORS, the scope is also expanded to include the technology of machines and other inventions, studies of the lives and struggles of inventors, research into the effects of inventions on people and communities, and the imaginary inventions of characters like Professor William Waterman Sherman in *The Twenty-One Balloons.* The change in focus assures that a wealth of materials can be found and that important relationships can be studied.

duBois (1947)

On the other hand, if you find yourself overwhelmed by titles, you may have chosen a topic that will not allow children to explore important concepts beyond a very superficial level. A theme of FEELINGS may be too general; feelings are part of our daily life experience and hard to isolate for meaningful study. In contrast, a theme of WHO AM I, CONFLICTS or CHANGES would focus on important curricular concepts and also allow children to reflect on a variety of feelings as part of the larger topic. If you have chosen a topic like JOURNEYS or CHANGES that could cover a very broad area you may want to let the subcategories limit areas of inquiry, keeping in mind the students you have and making the unit more relevant to their cultural background.

As you plan a thematic unit, you may wonder how many titles are enough. We like to think that, as with chocolate, you can never have enough. Many teachers who have been teaching through thematic units for many years work with between four and five hundred books and other printed materials; their classroom libraries are supplemented by school and municipal collections. We suggest that rather than setting a specific number of titles, you plan to collect the following types of materials:

Materials to Read Aloud

Reading aloud gives teachers the opportunity to share the best works of children's literature with their students. You may also choose materials that children might not

Choose the best works of literature to read aloud.

Table 3.1 SELECTING BOOKS AND MEDIA FOR CHILDREN

A to Zoo—Subject Access to Children's Picture Books (4th ed.) by C. W. Lima (Ed.). Ann Arbor, MI: Bowker, 1993.

Adventuring with Books: A Booklist for Pre-K to Grade 6 (11th ed.) by W. K. Sutton (Ed.). Urbana, IL: National Council of Teachers of English, 1997.

American History for Children and Young Adults: An Annotated Bibliographic Index by V. VanMeter (Ed.). Littleton, CO: Libraries Unlimited, 1990.

Basic Collection of Children's Books in Spanish by I. Schon (Ed.). Metuchen, NJ: Scarecrow Press, 1986.

Best Science Books and AV Materials for Children by S. M. O'Connell et al. (Eds.). Washington, DC: American Association for the Advancement of Science, 1988.

The Black Experience in Children's Books by B. Rollock (Selector). New York: New York Public Library, 1989.

The Bookfinder: Vol. 5. When Kids Need Books by S. S. Dreyer. Circle Pines, MN: American Guidance Service, 1994.

Book Links: Connecting Books, Libraries, and Classrooms (Bimonthly periodical. Available from the American Library Association, 50 E. Huron St., Chicago, IL 60611)

Booklist Magazine (Periodical. Available from the American Library Association, 50 E. Huron St., Chicago, IL 60611)

Choices: A Core Collection for Young Reluctant Readers (Vol. 3) by S. Salluzo & P. Glisson (Eds.). Evanston, IL: John Gordon Burke, 1994.

E for Environment: An Annotated Bibliography of Children's Books with Environmental Themes by P. Sinclair. New York: Bowker, 1992.

Educational Media Yearbook (Annual) by J. W. Brown & S. N. Brown (Eds.). Littleton, CO: Libraries Unlimited.

Exploring the United States Through Literature by K. Latrobe. Phoenix, AZ: Oryx, 1994.

A Hispanic Heritage: A Guide to Juvenile Books about Hispanic People and Cultures (Series 3) by I. Schon. Metuchen, NJ: Scarecrow Press, 1998.

The Horn Book (Periodical. Available from 31 St. James Ave., Boston, MA 02108)

The Horn Book Guide (Published twice yearly. Available from 31 St. James Ave., Boston, MA 02108)

---

initially read on their own. Poetry, information books, biography or autobiography, picture books, periodicals, and primary source materials should be considered for all ages while chapter books and longer information books can be chosen where they are developmentally appropriate.

"Read alouds" allow teachers to demonstrate the full range of responses readers might make to print. During the read-aloud time teachers can share their own and their students' emotional responses to a work, identify and respond to questions or puzzles that arise from the work, or reflect on the artistry of the writing. In addition, these read-alouds may be works that call for careful and sensitive discussion on important issues to be explored within the theme. They may also have intricacies of plot or characterization that demand careful guidance from an adult, or the shared construction of meaning that comes through group discussion or repeated readings.

For the SPACES AND PLACES theme, in addition to collecting poetry and other printed resources to read-aloud, teachers chose four novels (*Scorpions, Julie of the Wolves, Monkey Island,* and *Dogsong*) and four information books (*No Place to Be: Voices of Homeless Children, An Indian Winter, A Short Walk around the Pyramids and through the World of Art, Corpses, Coffins, and Crypts: A History Of Burial*) that they felt were good candidates for reading aloud. They also identified a list of picture books and poetry such as *Harlem* and *Sacred Places* that would provide good connections to important questions they wanted to explore with the students. All these met the criteria of good literature, provided a range of cultural views of the topic, and opened up possibilities for further explorations of issues and ideas.

See Huck, Hepler, Hickman, & Kiefer (1997) for criteria for choosing books for children.

Meyers (1988); George (1972); Fox (1991); Paulsen (1985)

Berck (1992); Freedman (1992); Isaacson (1993); Coleman (1997)

Myers (1997); Yolen (1996)

Table 3.1 (CONTINUED)

Kaleidoscope: A Multicultural Booklist for Grades K-8 by R. Barrera, V. Thompson, & M. Dressman (Eds.) Urbana, IL: National Council of Teachers of English, 1997.

The Museum of Science and Industry Basic List of Children's Science Books by B. Richter. Chicago: American Library Association, 1985.

Our Family, Our Friends, Our World: An Annotated Guide to Significant Multicultural Books for Children and Teenagers by L. Miller-Lachman. New York: Bowker, 1992.

Portraying Persons With Disabilities: An Annotated Bibliography of Fiction for Children by D. Robertson. (Ed.). New York: Bowker, 1991.

Portraying Persons With Disabilities: An Annotated Bibliography of Non-Fiction for Children by J. Brest, Friedberg, J. B. Mullins, and A. W. Sukiennik. (Eds.). New York: Bowker, 1991.

Read Any Good Math Lately? Children's Books for Mathematical Learning by D. J. Whitin & S. Wilde. Portsmouth, NH: Heinemann, 1992.

Reading for Young People Series: The Great Plains; Kentucky, Tennessee, West Virginia; The Middle Atlantic; The Northwest; The Rocky Mountains; The Southeast; The Upper Midwest. Chicago: American Library Association, 1979–1985.

Recreating the Past: A Guide to American and World Historical Fiction for Children and Young Adults by L. G. Adamson. Westport, CT: Greenwood Press, 1994.

Science and Technology in Fact and Fiction: A Guide to Children's Books by P. F. Beilke & F. J. Sciara. Hamden, CT: Shoestring Press, 1990.

Subject Guide to Children's Books in Print (Annual). Ann Arbor, MI: Bowker.

Tried and True: 500 Nonfiction Books Children Want to Read by G. Wilson & J. Moss. New York: Bowker, 1992.

Using Poetry Across the Curriculum: A Whole Language Approach by B. Chatton. Phoenix, AZ: Oryx, 1993.

Venture Into Cultures: A Resource Book of Multicultural Materials and Programs by C. Hayden. Chicago, IL: American Library Association, 1994.

World History for Children and Young Adults by V. VanMeter. Littleton, CO: Libraries Unlimited, 1991.

Your Reading: A Booklist for Junior High and Middle School by B. G. Samuels & G. K. Beers (Eds.). Urbana, IL: National Council of Teachers of English, 1996.

Materials for Group Activities

If these materials are books, you should choose them with literary qualities in mind, but they should also be good candidates for Literature Response Groups* and small group activities that don't require your direct attention. It is important that these materials be rich in possibilities for further inquiry. We want children to deal with the book as an aesthetic event and to find reasons to return to the book to explore it more deeply. We also want the book to raise critical questions about the ideologies or values that are expressed in the text, which will lead children beyond the book to make sense of alternative points of view and to make careful judgments about the wider world.

You can often find multiple copies of paperbacks that fit your theme. For the SPACES AND PLACES unit teachers and children identified five books which they could obtain in paperback sets, *From the Mixed-up Files of Mrs. Basil E. Frankweiler, Slake's Limbo, Toughboy and Sister, Hatchet,* and *Island of the Blue Dolphins.* In addition, teachers developed text sets, individual titles and printed materials grouped together by topics such as "place in fiction" "human made places," and "sacred places." These materials allowed for a wide range of interests and ability levels among the children and provided broad coverage of diverse points of view and concepts important to the theme. Jackdaws*, or collections of primary source materials, which could include such printed sources as journals, letters, maps, old newspapers or advertisements, and photographs, could provide another focus for group work (see Chapter 7 for further information on Reader Literature Response Groups* and assembling jackdaw-like packets).

Konigsburg (1969); Holman (1974); Hill (1990); Paulsen (1987); O'Dell (1960)

See Short & Harste (1995)

Additional Reading Materials for Personal Exploration

Reading interests of individual children in any classroom vary and should be catered to by including many other titles that may be chosen for personal enjoyment or individual research. These materials should be fun to read and may spark an interest in a special child. They can be made available for reading during sustained silent reading time and can give children the time and space to read for pleasure without having to do anything more with the book (unless, of course, they want to). Some children involved in the SPACES AND PLACES theme might choose to read about haunted places in books or periodicals or to explore mysterious places like the Bermuda Triangle. Another child might enjoy reading articles related to the theme in current newspapers and compiling a collection for other students.

Include enough resources to allow for individual interests.

Primary Source* Materials

Primary source* materials include originals, copies, or facsimiles of such printed resources as letters, journals, maps, photographs, newspapers, magazines, advertisements, ledgers, account books, mail-order catalogs, and any other artifacts that give us firsthand information about real people who lived in other times or other places, or about the community of which we are a part today. Primary source material also includes notes of observations, transcriptions of interviews, and the like. In the SPACES AND PLACES theme, in addition to the materials mentioned above, teachers helped children collect maps, blueprints, city planning documents, and aerial photographs of their own community to study city planning and public spaces.

Primary Source materials can foster important inquiries.*

Hands-on Resources: Artifacts, Equipment, and Props

Objects that are products of human culture—tools, machinery, and so on—or natural objects and other materials can be useful features of thematic units. These hands-on resources can provide a focus for wondering, speculating, hypothesizing, or reconstructing events concerning people's lives, both past and present. Consider how old pottery shards, Indian arrowheads, ceremonial masks, costumes, toys, and household items could serve as an entry into another time or another culture. Plan to collect headgear, footwear, and other items of clothing; shells, seeds, rocks, and other natural objects; clocks, watches, irons, toasters, pipes, hammers, beakers, test tubes, and other equipment such as tools and simple machines as a means of extending and exploring the theme. Among the equipment collected by teachers for the SPACES AND PLACES theme were wilderness survival kits, a variety of implements for measuring two- and three-dimensional space, and microscopes and magnifying glasses. Any of these could be included as props in creative dramatics, as objects for ongoing investigations, or as a springboard for focused inquiry.

Hands-on resources inspire dramatics, investigation, and inquiry.

Community Resources

Learning is not confined within the walls of the classroom but extends into the community. When children are involved in a thematic unit, they just naturally connect events and experiences in their lives outside the classroom to things that are happening in school. In addition, plan specifically to make full use of community resources—people, places, animals, and other living things—that can help strengthen children's understanding of the theme and provide access to cultural information that may not be available from printed resources. This is the time to consider the human points of view that may not be represented in printed material and to seek out people who can provide the missing voices that broaden children's understanding. The children themselves are sometimes the best source of information on a topic. Some may have had experiences that can broaden other children's awareness. Others may have unique viewpoints or understandings that shed new light on familiar ideas. Parents and other family members may also have much to contribute in the way of experience, cultural knowledge, or expertise. Plan also to include professionals, specialists, businesspeople, and others in the community who could contribute through classroom visits, inter-

Bring the community into the classroom.

Children and their families are important resources.

views, or field trips. Animals and other living things are sources of information that seem to be especially appealing to children. Many thematic units can include small animals, fish, reptiles, or insects as part of the classroom environment for short periods without harm. Plants also make excellent classroom resources. Zoos, aquariums, farms, arboretums, and other such facilities, as well as the natural environments of forest, park, tidal pools, ponds, or even playgrounds, can provide the children with a wealth of learning experiences and activities. Places in the community can become classrooms as part of the thematic unit. Museums of all types and historical sites often have organized presentations and special exhibits that can be part of, or even trigger, a thematic unit. The city streets, country village, even a cemetery can provide less formal, but no less exciting, learning possibilities.

The theme of SPACES AND PLACES particularly lends itself to exploration outside classroom walls and to the use of a variety of community resources. It is ideal for urban, suburban, or rural settings and lends itself to understanding the complex factors that interact within community places. Or consider how Sara's schema of spiders and insects (discussed in Chapter 1) could have been further extended during a thematic unit on BUGS or SMALL WORLDS. Children could collect insects from home and neighborhood in "bug" jars. Various insects are sketched in different positions and, with a detailed written description, placed in a classroom display. Other children keep a daily journal of their observations of caterpillars that have spun cocoons and have been placed in a see-through box to await their metamorphosis to butterflies. You can invite several persons from the community who have an interest in insects to speak to the class. These could include one child's grandparent who collects butterflies, a local beekeeper who brings honey for the children to taste, an exterminator who arrives in a truck with a model of a huge roach perched on the top, and a local farmer who talks about the ways in which insects can help or hinder crops. The children take notes in their journals and later write up these visits in the class newspaper or use the information in research reports they are writing. Children then elect to do follow-up interviews. Some ask family members about interests or hobbies concerning insects. Others interview farmers about their favorite and least favorite insects. Still others call local pest control companies to find out the biggest pest control problem. Results of these interviews are then written up and displayed on bar graphs. The children visit a special exhibit on insects at the museum of natural history where an entomologist conducts a special hands-on tour. While in the museum, they have some time to do some Thought Ramblings* in a field trip booklet (that leads to their writing a variety of poetry and short descriptive pieces), as well as interview other professional staff. Finally, as a culminating event of the unit, the children present research reports on insects to the rest of the class. Sara, or course, has chosen to do hers on arachnids.

The Arts

Another category of resources for use in thematic units involves the arts—painting, sculpture, or architecture; the decorative arts; the graphic arts; crafts; musical arts; theater, television, and film. These arts provide important visual, auditory, tactile, and kinesthetic experiences that can give rise to important understandings about a theme. The arts of other times and diverse cultures are also rich sources of information that may be especially powerful to children of this generation. (Chapter 5 provides a wider discussion of art and music in thematic units.)

The SPACES AND PLACES theme was particularly suited to involving the arts of painting, photography, sculpture, dance, architecture, and music. The arts were rich sources of information about many American and world cultures. In addition to surveying these arts in many cultural contexts, teachers planned to make use of works by painters and photographers such as Georgia O'Keeffe, Ansel Adams (the American West) and Charles Johnson (Harlem and the rural American South of the twenties and thirties), which were inspired by their creators' intense involvement with a specific place. They looked for musical forms like jazz and rap which grew out of a cultural place. They found such musical compositions as Debussy's "La Mer" or Ferd Groffe's

Include the arts as resources and as vehicles for exploring themes.

See Levstik & Barton (1997)

"Grand Canyon Suite," and paintings by Chinese artists and the American Lumninists, which were inspired by a desire to interpret space. They included works by Ben Shan, Dorothea Lange, and Diego Rivera who brought social commentary to their depictions of place. They found that the mobiles and stabiles of Alexander Calder as well as the dances of Agnes DeMille and Alvin Ailey were developed around the idea of movement in space.

Experiencing the theme of spaces and places through these various art forms can lead children to use the arts to further explore the theme themselves or to use the arts to report back on the outcomes of their exploration of the theme. They may want to create their own mobiles or sculpture, compose a musical or theatrical presentation, choreograph a dance, or make a photo or videotaped record of their inquiries into the theme.

Planning Activities

Reflective, Disciplined Inquiry*

When you collect books and other materials for the thematic unit, consider also the many types of activities and projects from which children can choose to explore the theme. In particular, consider the kinds of activities that will raise questions that call out to be investigated, activities that will motivate children to be genuine seekers after knowledge and understanding. The discovery of a problem to solve that leads students to create and test hypotheses, explore variations on an initial problem, and think about the consequences of answers, leads to the kind of in-depth study that is the lifeblood of a thematic unit. *Reflective, disciplined inquiry* is the term given to this process. Reflective inquiry is more than the acquisition of knowledge and skill—they are the *tools* of inquiry. Reflective inquiry involves the following:

Reflective, Disciplined Inquiry* gives children the tools to seek knowledge.

1. The ability to encode information—that is, to understand what information is relevant or irrelevant to solving a problem.
2. The ability to combine pieces of information, even though those pieces may at first seem unrelated.
3. The ability to compare the problem with problems previously encountered and to use those skills and concepts previously employed.

Ryan & Ellis (1974)

Ryan and Ellis describe the process of inquiry as recognizing a problem, selecting appropriate data sources, processing the data, and making inferences from the data. One teacher begins with a black-box problem. He asks students to watch carefully as he places a black cardboard box with tripod legs on a desk. There are several buckets immediately below the desk, and a jar of clear liquid is next to the box. The box itself has a rubber spigot spouting from the bottom front and a funnel in the center top. A student is asked to pour the liquid from the jar into the funnel, while another student monitors the spigot end. As the liquid pours into the funnel, red liquid begins to pour from the spigot—and pours, and pours—until the bucket and part of another on the floor are full.

Before discussion begins, the teacher asks students to think carefully about what they have seen, and then to draw a picture of what they think is in the black box. Over the next several days, students bring pictures to share and set up possible systems to test, which are all displayed in a center with a sign that reads "How Does It Work?" Another center has reference books about the "insides" of all sorts of machines. Some students ask to build their own black boxes and set them up for their peers to figure out. Stories of inventions are shared, new inventions are proposed, and all are used to spark student writing.

In sum, an initial problem provided the catalyst for a wide variety of learning experiences that might have been less effective if students had simply been assigned the text reading on machines. The inquiry into the problem and sufficient time to reflect on possible solutions, to discuss them, and to test hypotheses also presented a model for problem-solving. So did the teacher's refusal to open the black box. Throughout the year, even after the unit was over, students continued to construct possible machines to make the box work. Their continued reflection would have been shut off if the teacher had revealed a single "right" answer. Instead, he encouraged a form of speculation similar to that used by scholars investigating all manner of "black boxes"—human cognition, prehistory, and quarks, for example.

In the foregoing example, the teacher introduced the problem and provided some of the data sources that students examined. The students then reflected on that data through discussion and the generation and testing of hypotheses. Such teacher-generated problems encourage students to engage in a wide variety of investigations that might not arise naturally in the classroom. It is important to note, however, that inquiry need not begin with a contrived problem. Students can use an inquiry approach to deal with a variety of problems. In one primary classroom, a classmate's playground accident led children to pose their own question: "How can we make a safer playground?" They decided what data they would need, organized to gather it, and worked together to interpret the results of their study. Finally, they presented a plan to the principal and worked on an implementation committee.

Inquiries should focus on the processes of investigation.

In the SPACES AND PLACES unit children noticed a vacant lot near the school that was full of trash and quite an eyesore. As they became involved in a project to clean up the lot, they interviewed residents, spoke with city council members, and involved parents and other school and community members in a joint project that resulted in transforming the lot into a vegetable and flower farm. Students and residents worked jointly to clean up, cultivate, and harvest vegetables and flowers that were then distributed to elderly residents and to a soup kitchen for the homeless.

All types of disciplined reflective inquiry encourage student interaction and can generate ideas for activities. They have the additional advantage of also providing a model that can be used in seeking solutions to other problems. These activities will, in turn, suggest other books and materials; the unit may seem to be taking on a life of its own. In planning for these experiences, consider not only language but also math, social studies, the sciences, and the arts as vehicles for exploring the ideas and concepts within the scope of the thematic unit. The prototypes in Chapter 4 illustrate the kinds of projects that can be planned to include these curricular domains. In addition, Chapter 5 covers important ideas and concepts in these different curricular areas in more detail and provides further support for integrating languages across the curriculum.

Reflective, Disciplined Inquiry* can give children firsthand experience with problem solving.

Purposeful Language Activities

As you consider the many experiences that could be part of a thematic unit, you will note that language will be an important component of any activity. It is, of course, important to ensure that children extend their communicative competence to the fullest extent possible. During their development as competent communicators in their preschool years, children used language for many purposes in learning how to mean. They desired, demanded, socialized, personalized, wondered, imagined, and informed. If they are to continue to grow beyond the confines of their neighborhood into the context of the wider world, these activities must encompass the many situations in which oral language is used in the world and extend across cultures and into the world of print as well. A strong curriculum, therefore, must allow children to continue to express their own personal ideas. It has to provide many opportunities for children to participate in collaborative talk, in *alternative* non-IRE discourse structures (see Chapter 2).

Halliday (1975)

As you select books and other resources for the theme and the WEB begins to take shape, make sure that topics are explored through a variety of purposeful oral and written activities. A balance of these and a balance of materials are more likely to develop competent communicators and critical thinkers. These experiences help children to relate their own views and feelings through discussion, journals, editorials, reviews, and debates; to interact through letters and interviews; to inform through directions, descriptions, records, and reports; to wonder and hypothesize through experiments, observations, and theses; and to imagine through drama, poetry, and story.

Activities should provide opportunities for collaborative discussion among children and teachers.

Planning for activities such as these can occur in several ways. Activities can serve as springboards that lead children to books and other resources. At other times, a book can serve as the focus for meaningful activities, some that lead children back to the book and others that connect to other books or experiences that are part of the thematic unit. Although we illustrate this kind of planning in Chapter 4, it is helpful at this point to provide an example of how teachers might plan activities that will deepen children's response to individual books as well as to broaden their understandings of issues and concepts relating to the theme.

Planning for Response to Literature

Plan discussion and activities that lead children back into the book.

Teachers in integrated classrooms are cognizant of the importance of developing a life-long enthusiasm for reading as well as developing the abilities necessary for strategic and fluent reading. They will thus include time for sustained reading in class and to give students time to reflect on their reading through response journals. Recognizing the social nature of response to literature and the need for joint meaning making, they will provide time for the informal sharing of books and peer-peer and peer-teacher discussion groups. (See Literature Response Groups* in Chapter 7.) They will want children to become aware of the linguistic aspects of all genres, and they will want to plan activities that lead children back to a fictional book, for example, to re-experience characters, settings, themes, and events they have encountered there, or to reflect on the major ways that questions, data, and arguments are explored in information books. In addition, they will want to help children reexamine books they have read to identify connections to the larger theme, to identify possibilities for further inquiry, or to consider the perspective or ideologies or values from which authors have looked at a particular topic, for example.

Take time to develop children's literary responses.

However, sometimes it is difficult to know how to help children get the most out of their literature experiences without ruining the book. Or in our efforts to integrate the curriculum sometimes we may "use" a book to *cover* curricular requirements without allowing time for aesthetic or emotional response. Moreover, there has been some debate about what characterizes authentic responses to literature. Having wrestled with these questions we would like to consider the ways in which children and adults have responded to books outside of classroom contexts. Young children take naturally to exploring their world through play and often very idiosyncratic ways. We know of a four-year-old, for example, who rarely attempted two-dimensional crayon pictures. Instead she symbolized her experiences through paper sculptures and shoe box and matchbox pictures; her parents had to keep a steady supply of scotch tape and glue on hand for her. One of our friends remembers using the white space at the beginning of chapters to create illustrations for the novels she read as a middle-grade student; another recalls directing neighborhood productions of favorite books. These various ways of responding to books can be found among adults as well. Those of us who love to read know the pleasure of passing on the title of a favorite book to a friend or of discussing responses to books that are particularly thought-provoking. In addition, some adults use other vehicles to explore their responses to oral and written literature. Documentaries, editorials, drama, and art are common forms in which adults respond to information and events in their world. Drama and dance are two forms in which story has long been transformed, while art museums of all cultures are filled with paintings and sculptures that are responses to stories. Satirists in the written and pictorial arts delight in manipulating both fiction and nonfiction. We can find humorous commentary; parodies, sequels, and prequels; updated versions; or another character's viewpoint—for example in the pages of *New Yorker* magazine or the widely popular (among adults as well as children) *The Stinky Cheese Man and other Fairly Stupid Tales.* Dressing up as characters, writing recipes, and creating maps and diagrams are also ways in which adults have chosen to respond to well-loved stories or important events. A PBS series called "Time Line" placed a T.V. news team at important historical episodes and included commercials for products invented during that time period. One only has to attend an annual Star Trek convention or read *The Dragon Lovers Guide to Pern,* a book

Each child should be able to choose from a wide range of possible responses to a book.

Scieszka (1992)

published in response to Anne McCaffrey's "Dragon Riders of Pern" series to find similar adult reactions to fiction.

Nye (1989)

Therefore, we suggest that the keys to deepening a child's response to a book will include time to respond to it in a way each reader finds rewarding. In addition, teachers will want to help children identify connections or questions raised by books that will lead to a broader understanding of the theme. Teachers and children should agree together on the most appropriate ways to respond to a book and ways that book can contribute a topic of inquiry. These experiences should allow children to use many reading strategies (comparing and contrasting, sequencing, recalling details, and making inferences about characters), involve them in writing, speaking, and listening for many purposes, and engage them in the reflective problem-solving as well.

Activities should fully engage a child with a book and deepen the child's understanding of that particular book.

Finally, as these activities are developed, teachers will want to consider the focus of their own classroom research and to include activities that will help them focus systematically on teaching and learning. Teachers might, for example, choose to study children's responses to cultural aspects of the theme, their responses to particular types of book, the variations in children's reading strategies, or gender differences in children's learning. In each case, teachers will want to plan specific activities that could be revealing of patterns and processes in children's learning and in their own teaching. (Examples of such activities will be highlighted in the prototypes in Chapter 4. See also "Guidelines for Teacher Inquiry.")

Activities should give teachers opportunities to learn more about their own teaching and their students' learning.

Organizing the Classroom for Complex Instruction

Because the thematic unit presents children with many possibilities for exploring the theme and asks that you play many roles, it is important that the physical setup of the classroom facilitates the implementation of the unit and supports inquiry and group cooperation. Whether you find yourself in a self-contained or an open classroom, whether you take responsibility for the whole day or are in a departmentalized program, your use of space can ease implementation and organization of the unit. Take time with students at the beginning of the year to discuss the setup of the classroom and how to use the space effectively and comfortably. This might, in fact, be an appropriate initiating activity for a theme of SPACES AND PLACES. Children should be made to feel ownership of the classroom and should take responsibility for its uses as well as contribute suggestions concerning its organization. However that organization finally evolves in your classroom, some features we consider important to the integrated language program in general and thematic units in particular are discussed in the following pages. Amenities such as sinks are not available in many classrooms, but the other factors such as centers can be achieved with minimum outlay as long as desks and furniture can be moved around. Moreover, involving children in the collection of supplies, materials and in finding solutions to room layout, storage and display problems creates an important community feeling. A group of fifth graders, for example, hung fish nets from the ceiling to display their work and invented a system of pulleys and buckets to hold art supplies, their solution to a lack of display and storage space.

The classroom layout can facilitate learning and orchestrate group interaction.

Cohen (1994)

Materials and Equipment

We have already mentioned the importance of an extensive classroom library supplemented by volumes from the school or municipal library as new themes are planned. In addition, the thematic unit determines the many other types of resources that are collected and displayed within the classroom at any given time. A variety of materials for writing and art activities are always desirable. These need not eat up the supply budget but can be culled from community or family sources. We have seen books created by children on the backs of wallpaper samples or used computer printouts. Beautiful collages and sculpture have been created from scrap paper, fabric scraps, feathers, sequins, beans, macaroni, paper-towel tubes, and other "found" or recycled materials. Desks, chairs, and tables should be movable so that centers can be reorganized

Donations of furniture and materials can come from parents and other community members.

according to the demands of a particular unit or activity. Comfortable chairs, pillows, and an old couch or area rugs can further define space and indicate quiet corners. (One lucky teacher found an old porcelain bathtub. Filled with throw pillows, it became the focal point of the reading center.) Easels, walls, and movable bulletin boards on which children's work can be displayed are essential. Rooms should be filled with children's writing, art, and other projects. Bookcases, including the type that can display books cover forward, along with storage cabinets for art supplies, science equipment, math manipulables, and other materials are also important features. Additional materials and equipment can be added according to the needs of each unit and the realities of the school budget.

Organization of Space

Both permanent and temporary centers are created in the classroom.

Once furniture and equipment are gathered, they can be arranged into areas that suit the needs of a particular unit. Consideration should be given to the need for quiet places for individual activities such as reading, writing, teacher-child conferencing, and for centers where activities might result in more bustle. Space should be kept clear for large group gatherings and creative dramatics or movement. Some areas are permanent. The classroom library, the reading center, the listening post, the writing center where paper, writing implements, and other materials for publishing are stored, and the art center where art supplies are found and used remain unchanged across thematic units during the whole year. Other places will need to be established for ongoing inquiries; these have a temporary life. Tables are moved to certain places in the room so that children have access to the specific resources to be used and explored during a particular thematic unit. For example, places are set up where animals, insects, or plants can be observed and studied, where equipment to conduct experiments is situated, where a classroom restaurant or museum can be established, and so forth. These areas are not centers in the traditional sense and don't require a lot of teacher made materials. When an individual thematic unit is over, much of what had been found in these temporary centers is dismantled and new centers begun to support the activity and exploration of the next thematic unit.

Implementing the Unit

Agreements serve to help organize and facilitate the ongoing work of the unit.

Whether planning for the unit with children from the beginning or presenting children with a WEB that is more completely planned, teachers should make children aware of their choices regarding activities and also of the contributions they might make early on. Once you begin implementing the unit, ensure that children have the opportunity to explore the theme in ways that will expand domains of knowledge. That is, a thematic unit is a tentative and flexible framework. Changes can be easily made as children's own ideas for projects and activities evolve. Part of this flexibility is accepting even a child's tangential interest. To this end, an initial agreement about what projects are to be carried out as part of the thematic unit is a useful planning and organizing tool. These agreements, which can be realized in many different ways, are means by which children and teacher are able to keep track of what children are doing and are part of the ongoing assessment and evaluation in integrated classrooms. They can provide valuable information about children's processes of learning and serve as sources for accountability. They also help make clear for children what their responsibilities are regarding completion of work and can serve as one focus for self-evaluation. (See Chapters 8 and 9.)

Initial expectations about children's work should be general in nature. Specific projects and dates are then negotiated and become more clearly defined as children have the opportunity to engage in a variety of activities that require reading and writing in a range of genres, that require using language to discuss and organize learning in various areas of the curriculum, and that require participation in various ways of knowing. It is important that children or the teacher have the opportunity to re-negotiate agreements. Perhaps a child becomes excited about a particular topic and wants to do additional research. One of the other activities can be dropped to allow the time needed. Or, if a topic or an assigned book has proven too difficult, a more suitable one can be substituted. This flexibility encourages children to take risks but also to become aware of their capabilities a feature too of the self-evaluation process.

At the outset of each unit, you may decide on several activities that could be major avenues for introducing and exploring the theme. Each child would be expected to choose one of these projects and to choose whether to work alone or with a small group. There may need to be some negotiation here as well. If you want children to work in groups you might introduce children to projects and books and then give them time to browse through collected materials for several days. Then the children can be asked to list their top three topic and book choices. You can then form groups, attempting to give children their first or second choice. If too many children want to read the same book, you might ask for volunteers to move to other groups or promise children who ended up with their third choice a first-place slot next time. You might also consider the child's previous work and suggest options to ensure that, throughout the year, all children have the opportunity to use language for a variety of purposes while engaged with a wide range of resources. This type of planning is particularly well suited to accommodating the interests and abilities of **all** children. Grouping according to interest in a particular topic or project rather than according to so-called reading levels ensures that children will have the opportunity to work with many of their classmates during the year and that the expectations and outcomes of their learning will be a good match with their needs and enthusiasms.

Organizing the unit will involve negotiation as well as choice.

Thematic units can provide many ways to group children.

Agreements can be designed to help you and students plan and to help children know what is expected of them. Due dates can be placed on the agreement to help children become self-monitoring and to aid you in pacing. There may be times when you want children to move through activities at approximately the same pace so that all children are introduced to some aspect of the theme at the same time, or so that everyone is working on a research project at the same time. At other times this may not be crucial, and children can decide which activity to complete first.

Below are some specific agreements that you might make with children in the course of a SPACES AND PLACES theme. To introduce the theme, for example, you might want to plan activities that help children think about the scope of the unit at the same time that you help them begin thinking about important questions for their disciplined inquiries. Notice that the activities are designed to get children immediately involved in their community and to offer them opportunities to understand how a historian, poet, geographer, botanist, artist, or anthropologist might each have a unique view or method of studying a place. These understandings can be built on throughout the course of the unit.

1. Read *My Place*. Share some of the special features of your own neighborhood. Take a walk and draw a map of the neighborhood you find yourself in. Then draw a second map or picture, imagining the neighborhood you've chosen at some point in the past, indicating what year you've chosen. Try to imagine the way the place might have looked before humans came on the scene. Include pictures of natural or human artifacts that are native or authentic to the place.

Wheatley (1992)

2. Read *Island Boy*. Visit a local cemetery. Take a few minutes to sit quietly and listen to the sounds of the place. Choose one of the names on a marker and speculate about that person's life. Make a survey of people by sex, and age when they died. Graph your findings. Compare an older part of the cemetery with a newer part. Make a graph comparing the average age of death from each section. Are there years in which more deaths occurred than others? Why? How has the cemetery been maintained as a special place? What other sacred places can you find out about? How do people from different cultures experience and maintain the sacred qualities of a place?

Cooney (1988)

Willis (1988)

3. Read *Earthlets: As Explained by Professor Xargle*. Observe the behavior of other "earthlings" in your environment as if you were from Professor Xargle's planet. Note the behavior in a field notebook. Include sketches. What might you conclude about the "culture" you have studied based on your observations? Publish your findings or create a museum exhibit.

4. Take a walk. Find a bird or bug to observe. Write a detailed description and note behavior in a field notebook. Share your findings. Read through the Paul Fleischman's *I Am Phoenix* or *A Joyful Noise* and choose several of the poems to read chorally. Try to capture the features you observed with the sounds of language. Write your own poem for two or three voices. Share with the class.

Fleischman (1985, 1988)

D'Alelio (1989)

5. Read *I Know that Building*. Take a walk and sketch architectural features you find in your neighborhood. Draw a composite picture which includes some of the features you found. Write an architectural guide to your neighborhood.

6. Find a place outdoors and study it from three perspectives, your own, a worm's, and a bird's. Draw pictures or construct a model of your findings. Write about the scene from different points-of-view.

As children have time to consider the scope of the theme through such introductory activities and as they chose additional activities and resources from the WEB to explore you can guide them toward student-initiated topics and projects that will involve long-term inquiry such as the following:

1. Study the layout of your community. How has the use of land been planned wisely or unwisely? Research community and urban planning and design a new community in existing space, parceling land according to perceived needs. What aspect of your ideal community could be implemented now and how will you achieve this?

2. Study organizations like Habitat for Humanity that build low-income housing for people. Are there homes (for the elderly) or places (a children's hospital) that need sprucing up? Plan a campaign to raise funds and redecorate one of these places. Interview an interior decorator about interior design. Include plans to paint a mural and wallpaper a room so that you learn how to change scale or measure a repeated pattern.

Myers, (1994)

3. Read *Darnell Rock Reporting*. Is there a place in your community that has been neglected and could be changed for the public good? Create a mural showing the changes. What steps can you take to change this place?

4. In many of the books chosen for the theme, characters struggle to survive against a variety of odds. What are the factors that make living in different places difficult? In what ways can the climactic, geographic, economic, social, and political factors of a place influence people's lives? What is the human response to these factors? Identify someone in your community who is having difficulty surviving and the factors that make this so. What can you do to resolve some of the problems you have identified?

Finally, additional choices can be made available that meet interests and enthusiasms of individual children. The ideas presented here represent only a few of the many additional experiences that are possible as part of a theme and that individual children can select as part of their agreements:

1. Plan creative dramatics or a Reader's Theater* in response to a story or informational book.

2. Visit the art museum and make a list of its sculptures. Observe your favorite sculpture from different perspectives noting changes in light and shadow. Sketch the sculpture and write about it.

3. Interview classmates about favorite places. Write results for class newspaper.

4. Compare settings or locations in books you are reading. Make a graffiti wall* of phrases and words that authors use to describe their setting. Construct a

comparison chart* that looks at how the authors deal with features like physical description, or mood, and use of time in their stories and information books. How do these contribute to your enjoyment of the book? How might your understanding of the book's ideas be influenced by the authors depiction of the setting?

5. Do a thought rambling* in your journal while listening to music that interprets a physical place.

6. Study small spaces through a microscope. Conduct daily observations and note changes in sketches and field notebook.

7. Do a study of the works of illustrators or photographers who use space in unusual ways. Find out about these people and make a display of their works, telling something about their life and explaining their ideas.

In implementing the unit teachers will want to consider how they can most effectively and efficiently carry out their own research. They may want to develop an observational form or checklist for recording the responses and understandings of individual children. They may also need to plan for materials they will use that may include simple things like journals and yellow sticky pads or more complex equipment like audio or videotape recorders or audio-tape transcribing machines. Teachers may want to plan regular times for collecting data and set aside a daily period to reflecting on that data. Perhaps an informal agreement with self would be a helpful reminder to find some time each day for that kind of personal reflection. (See "Guidelines for Teacher Inquiry" at the end of the book.)

Teachers should plan for their own inquiries as well as their students'.

Conclusions

Through the course of a unit, children have many opportunities to share process and products concerning ongoing activities with other classmates (and with the wider community). This collaboration happens in the course of daily discussions as graphic organizers visualizing processes of investigations are developed, criteria for inquiries are discussed, and children's work is presented, published, and displayed. As knowledge is constructed and expanded, integrated language classrooms truly become communities of learning. Children not only pursue their own projects with enthusiasm, but they are also aware of and interested in the projects of their classmates. When the thematic unit culminates in the sharing of final projects, children can be encouraged to look back and reflect on their own learning and also consider the ways in which the classroom culture constructed a body of knowledge together (see the role of Learning Portfolios in this process in Chapter 9). This joining of effort and understanding is the essence of collaboration and is perhaps the most satisfying and enriching aspect of teaching and learning through thematic units. It may seem that thematic units require an inordinate amount of work. You need to remember, however, that all teaching takes time; the integrated language/thematic unit approach only means that time is used differently. Implementing any new approach takes additional time initially, but eventually teaching this way becomes second nature. In her delightful book, *A House Is a House for Me,* poet Mary Anne Hoberman begins with the simple idea of a house and then reshapes the concept of houses into new and unusual configurations. Repeated through the book is the refrain, "Once you get started in thinking this way. . . ." We believe that once you start thinking in terms of thematic units, it's likely that whatever you see in the curriculum you will see in terms of meaningful connections. However you approach thematic units, the goal is to open for children the many possibilities that exist in even the simplest of ideas such as "houses" and to help move them to new and exciting insights and understandings.

Hoberman (1978)

Chapter 4 describes eight prototype thematic units to illustrate in more detail how theory from this approach gets put into action in the classroom. You will visit teachers who use this perspective at various grade levels in the elementary school and who will demonstrate how the integrated language approach can become not just another way of teaching but an exciting and enriching way of living in the world.

REFERENCES

Cohen, E. G. (1994). *Designing groupwork: Strategies for heterogeneous classrooms.* New York: Teachers College Press.

Halliday, M. A. K. (1975). *Learning how to mean: Explorations in the development of language.* London: Edward Arnold.

Hartoonian, H. M. (1992). *A guide to curriculum planning in global studies.* Wisconsin Department of Education.

Huck, C. S., Hepler, S., Hickman, J., & Kiefer, B. (1997). *Children's literature in the elementary school.* Madison, WI: Brown & Benchmark.

Jacobs, H. (Ed.). (1989). *Interdisciplinary curriculum: Design and Implementation.* Alexandria, VA: Association for Supervision and Curriculum Development.

Jorgensen, C. (1994). Creating questions that all students can answer: A key to developing inclusive curriculum. *Equity and Excellence, 2,* 1.

Kobrin, B. (1988). *Eye openers!: How to choose and use children's books about real people, places and things.* New York: Penguin Books.

Levstik, L. S., & Barton, K. C. (1997). *Doing history: Investigating with children in elementary and middle schools.* Mahwah, NJ: Lawrence Erlbaum.

Lipson, M., Valencia, S., Wixson, K., & Peters, C. (1993). Integration and thematic teaching: Integration to improve teaching and learning. *Language Arts, 70,* 251–263.

Miller-Lachman, L. (1992). *Our family, our friends, our world: An annotated guide to significant multicultural literature for children.* New York: R. R. Bowker.

Nielsen, M. E. (1989). Integrative learning for young children: A thematic approach. *Educational Horizons, 68 (1),* 18–24.

Nye, J. L. (1989). *The dragonlovers guide to Pern.* New York: Ballantine Books.

Ryan, F., & Ellis, A. (1974). *Instructional implications of inquiry.* Englewood Cliffs, NJ: Prentice-Hall.

Short, K. G., & Harste, J. C. (1995). *Creating classrooms for authors and inquirers.* Portsmouth, NH: Heinemann.

Stevenson, C., & Carr, J. F. (1993). *Integrated studies in the middle grades: Dancing through walls.* New York: Teachers College Press.

Sutton, W. K. (Ed.). (1997). *Adventuring with books: A booklist for pre-K through grade 6.* Urbana, IL: National Council of Teachers of English.

CHILDREN'S LITERATURE

Acorn Pancakes, Dandelion Salad, and 38 Other Wild Recipes by J. George. Illustrated by P. Mirocha. HarperCollins, 1995.

Agnes De Mille: Dancing off the Earth by B. Gherman. Atheneum, 1990.

Anno's Magical ABC: An Anamorphic Alphabet by M. Anno & M. Anno. Philomel, 1980.

Another Shore by N. Bond. McElderry, 1988.

Appalachia: The Voices of Sleeping Birds by C. Rylant. Illustrated by B. Moser. Harcourt, 1991.

Archeologists Dig for Clues by K. Duke. HarperCollins, 1997.

Artist in Overalls: The Life of Grant Wood by J. Duggleby. Chronicle Books, 1996.

Ballet in Motion: A Three-Dimensional Guide to Ballet for Young People by C. Dodd & S. Soar. Lippincott, 1988.

Bear Dance by W. Hobbs. Atheneum, 1993.

The Bear Stone by W. Hobbs. Atheneum, 1989.

Belle Prater's Boy by R. White. Farrar, Straus, & Giroux, 1996.

Between Earth and Sky: Legends of Native American Sacred Places by J. Bruchac. Illustrated by T. Locker. Harcourt, 1996.

Bird by D. Burnie. Photographs by P. Chadwick. Knopf, 1988.

Black and White by D. Macaulay. Houghton Mifflin, 1990.

The Block by L. Hughes. Illustrated by R. Beardon. Viking, 1995.

The Book of Rhythms by L. Hughes. Illustrated by M. Wawiorka. Oxford, 1995.

Borrowed Children by G. E. Lyon. Orchard, 1988.

Brian's Winter by G. Paulsen. Delacorte, 1996.

Bugs by N. W. Parker & J. R. Wright. Illustrated by N. W. Parker. Greenwillow, 1987.

Cathedral by D. Macaulay. Houghton Mifflin, 1973.

Corpses, Coffins, and Crypts: A History of Burial by P. Colman. Holt, 1996.

Cutters, Carvers, and the Cathedral by G. Ancona. Lothrop, 1995.

Darnell Rock Reporting by W. D. Myers. Delacorte, 1994.

Digging to the Past: Excavations in Ancient Lands by W. J. Hackwell. Scribners, 1986.

Discovering Christopher Columbus: How History Is Invented by K. Pelta. Lerner, 1991.

Dog Team by G. Paulsen. Illustrated by R. W. Paulsen. Delacorte, 1993.

Dogsong by G. Paulsen. Viking, 1985.

Dorothea Lange: Life through the Camera by M. Milton. Illustrated by D. Diamond. Viking, 1985.

Drawing Life in Motion by J. Arnosky. Lothrop, 1984.

Dumpling Soup by J. K. Rattigan. Illustrated by H. Flanders. Little, Brown, 1993.

Earthfasts by W. Mayne. Dutton, 1967.

Earthlets: As Explained by Professor Xargle by J. Willis. Illustrated by T. Ross. Dutton, 1988.

Far North by W. Hobbs. Morrow, 1996.

The Fear Place by P. R. Naylor. Atheneum, 1994.

Fly Away Home by E. Bunting. Illustrated by R. Himler. Clarion, 1991.

From the Mixed-Up Files of Mrs. Basil E. Frankweiler by E. L. Konigsburg. Atheneum, 1969.

Frozen Man by Getz. David Holt, 1994.

George Catlin: Painter of the Indian West, by M. Sufrin. Atheneum, 1991.

Georgia O'Keefe: The Wideness and Wonder of Her World by R. M. Turner. Little, Brown, 1991.

A Girl from Yamhill by B. Cleary. Morrow, 1988.

Grand Constructions by P. Ventura & G. P. Ceserani. Putnam, 1983.

The Grey Lady and the Strawberry Snatcher by M. Bang. Four Winds, 1980.

Harlem by W. D. Myers. Illustrated by C. Myers. Scholastic, 1996.

Hatchet by G. Paulsen. Bradbury, 1987.

Henry Moore: From Bones and Stones to Sketches and Sculptures by J. M. Gardner. Four Winds, 1993.

A House Is a House for Me by M. A. Hoberman. Illustrated by B. Fraser. Viking, 1982.

How Artists See the Elements: Earth, Air, Fire, Water by C. Carroll. Abbeville, 1996.

I Am Phoenix: Poems for Two Voices by P. Fleischman. Illustrated by K. Nutt. Harper, 1985.

I Know That Building! Discovering Architecture with Activities and Games by J. D'Alelio. The Preservation Press, 1989.

The Ice Is Coming by P. Wrightson. Ballantine, 1977.

An Indian Winter by R. Freedman. Illustrated by K. Bodmer. Holiday House, 1992.

The Inner City Mother Goose by E. Merriam. Simon, 1996.

The Inside-Outside Book of New York City by R. Munro. Putnam, 1985.

Island Boy by B. Cooney. Viking, 1988.

Island of the Blue Dolphins by S. O'Dell. Houghton Mifflin, 1960.

The Journey of Diego Rivera by E. Goldstein. Lerner, 1996.

A Joyful Noise: Poems for Two Voices by P. Fleischman. Illustrated by E. Beddows. Harper, 1988.

Julie by J. George. Illustrated by W. Minor. HarperCollins, 1994.

Julie of the Wolves by J. C. George. Illustrated by J. Schoenherr. Harper, 1972.

Junebug by A. Mead. Farrar, Straus, & Giroux, 1995.

A Kid's Eye View: The Rocky Mountains by C. Fisher. Starwood, 1988.

Let There Be Light: A Book about Windows by J. C. Giblin. Crowell, 1988.

Li'l Sis and Uncle Willie by G. Everett. Rizzoli, 1991.

Lord of the Dance: An African Retelling by V. Tadjo. Lippincott, 1988.

Magic and Perception: The Art and Science of Fooling the Senses by B. Friedhoffer & L. Eisenberg. Watts, 1997.

Maps: Getting from Here to There by H. Weiss. Houghton Mifflin, 1991.

Missing May by C. Rylant. Orchard, 1992.

Mission Earth: Voyage to the Home Planet by J. A. English & T. D. Jones. Scholastic, 1996.

Mobiles by B. Zubrowski. Illustrated by R. Doty. Morrow, 1993.

Monkey Island by P. Fox. Orchard, 1991.

My Denali: Exploring Alaska's Favorite National Park with Hannah Corral by K. Corral & H. Corral. Alaska, 1996.

My Place by N. Wheatley. Kane/Miller, 1992.

My Side of the Mountain by J. George. Dutton, 1959.

The Nargun and the Stars by P. Wrightson. Viking, 1970.

National Parks of Alaska by M. Dunmire. Pegasus, 1991.

Newfound by J. W. Miller. Orchard, 1989.

No Place to Be: Voices of Homeless Children by J. Berck. Houghton Mifflin, 1992.

On City Streets by N. Larrick. M. Evans, 1968.

Opt: An Illusionary Tale by A. Baum and J. Baum. Viking, 1987.

Our Patchwork Planet: The Story of Plate Tektonics by H. R. Sattler. Illustrated by G. Maestro. Lothrop, 1995.

Outside Over There by M. Sendak. Harper, 1981.

The Paper Crane by M. Bang. Greenwillow, 1985.

People of Corn: A Mayan Story by M. Gerson. Illustrated by C. Golembe. Little, Brown, 1995.

Perspective by J. Welton. Dorling Kindersly, 1993.

Picture This: Perception and Composition by M. Bang. Bulfinch Press, 1991.

Puppies, Dogs, and Blue Northers by G. Paulsen. Illustrated by R. W. Paulsen. Harcourt, 1996.

Reflections by A. Jonas. Greewillow, 1987.

Return of the Wolf by D. H. Patent. Clarion, 1995.

A River Ran Wild by L. Cherry. Harcourt, 1992.

Round Buildings, Square Buildings, and Buildings That Wiggle Like a Fish by P. M. Isaacson. Knopf, 1988.

Round Trip by A. Jonas. Greenwillow, 1983.

Sacred Places by J. Yolen. Illustrated by D. Shannon. Harcourt, 1996.

Scorpions by W. D. Myers. Harper, 1988.

The Sculptor's Eye: Looking at Contemporary American Art by J. Greenberg & S. Jordan. Delacorte, 1993.

Shimmy Shimmy Shimmy Like My Sister Kate: Looking at the Harlem Renaissance through Poems by N. Giovanni. Holt, 1996.

A Short Walk Around the Pyramids and Through the World of Art by P. M. Isaacson. Knopf, 1993.

Sierra Club Book of Our National Parks by D. Young. Sierra Club, 1990.

The Skyscraper Book by J. C. Giblin. Crowell, 1981.

Slake's Limbo by F. Holman. Macmillan, 1974.

The Sleepers by J. L. Curry. Illustrated by G. Floyd. Harcourt, 1968.

A Song in Stone: City Poems by L. B. Hopkins (Ed.). Photographs by A. H. Audette. Crowell, 1983.

Soulfire by L. Hewett. Dutton, 1996.

The Stinky Cheese Man and Other Fairly Stupid Tales by J. Scieszka. Illustrated by L. Smith. Viking, 1992.

Stories I Ain't Told Nobody Yet by J. Carson. Orchard, 1989.

Story of Johnny Appleseed by Aliki. Prentice-Hall, 1963.

A Street Called Home by A. B. L. Robinson. Harcourt, 1997.

Street Music: City Poems by A. Adoff. Illustrated by K. Barbour. HarperCollins, 1995.

This Land Is My Land by G. Littlechild. Children's Press, 1993.

Three Days on a River in a Red Canoe by V. B. Williams. Mulberry Books, 1981.

Toughboy and Sister by K. Hill. McElderry, 1990.

The True Adventures of Grizzly Adams by R. M. McClung. Morrow, 1985.

The Twenty-One Balloons by W. P. duBois. Viking, 1947.

Two Bad Ants by C. Van Allsburg. Houghton, 1988.

Underground by D. Macaulay. Houghton Mifflin, 1976.

Visiting the Art Museum by L. Brown & M. Brown. Dutton, 1986.

Visual Magic by D. Thomson. Dial, 1991.

Voices from the Streets: Young Former Gang Members Tell Their Stories by S. B. Atkins. Little Brown, 1996.

Where On Earth Am I? by R. Gardner. Watts, 1996.

Where the Lilies Bloom by V. Cleaver & B. Cleaver. Illustrated by J. Spanfeller. Lippincott, 1969.

The Wild, Wild Cookbook by J. C. George. Crowell, 1982.

Winter Camp by K. Hill. McElderry, 1993.

The World of Hidden Forces by J. White. Dodd Mead, 1987.

Yellowstone 1988: Summer of Fire by P. Lauber. Orchard, 1991.

CHAPTER 4

Prototypes for Integrated Language Classrooms

Starting a Thematic Unit

Reflective, Disciplined Inquiry

Reflective, Disciplined Inquiry* is crucial to theme studies.

Reflective, disciplined inquiry is the underlying rationale for a thematic unit. As we mentioned in Chapter 3, the creation or discovery of a problem can lead students to generate questions, create and test hypotheses, explore variations on an initial problem, and study a theme in depth. This process is crucial to the development of a thematic unit because it helps children understand *why* they are engaged in a particular study or topic, *how* they can investigate important questions, and *how* they can "master perplexity" by making sense out of what did not initially make sense.

An initiating event sets the stage for inquiry.

In an integrated language classroom, children do not pursue a topic simply because it has been assigned, but because they are perplexed; their existing schemas have been challenged or they perceive a problem to investigate. This problem or perplexity may be provoked by events in the school or community beyond the school, or it may be initiated by the teacher. In either case, a wide variety of learning experiences develops from the initiating event and provides opportunities for lively conversation and intellectual negotiation, engagement with substantive content from a variety of sources, and classroom thoughtfulness—thinking carefully and thoroughly before responding to questions or attempting to resolve problems. In sum, Reflective, Disciplined Inquiry* supports children's efforts toward informing themselves, directing their own studies, and becoming intellectually independent.

Atwell (1990); McGinley & Madigan (1990)

There are a number of ways to spark this kind of inquiry. Once you have organized possible activities, projects, and resources in your WEB, you have to decide where to begin. The first few moments and activities in a thematic unit set the stage for what is to come and can either generate interest, enthusiasm, and learning or create difficulties that are hard to overcome. The stage must be set with *meaning-full* work if children are to be engaged as *meaning makers*. What follows are some ideas that can be used to begin inquiry-based thematic units.

Begin with Children's Interests

Support inquiry with a variety of genres.

As already noted in Chapter 3, children's interests can be used to inspire a thematic unit. Sometimes a vacation trip can generate interest in a study. One teacher sets up an interest center based on the seashells, sand, and seaweed brought back from a child's trip to the shore. She also arranges a selection of information books, poetry, and fiction in the center. Among these resources, she places several cards with different questions for children to consider. The children then use the resources to choose a line of inquiry that starts them on a LIFE IN AND NEAR THE WATER thematic unit.

In another classroom, children become interested in a rhododendron branch that has been wilting in a corner. When they start asking questions about the dying plant, the teacher uses this interest as the beginning point for a WEB on the effect of water on living things. Students conduct experiments to chart changes caused by dehydration, they study the uses of dried plants, and they measure plant growth.

A butterfly cocoon brought into a second- and third-grade class has similar results, serving as the beginning point for the teacher's WEB. Throughout the thematic unit, children observe the cocoon and use reference books to help make inferences about what may emerge. The culminating activity of the unit includes the excitement of seeing the cocoon hatch and then the ceremony accompanying the butterfly's release into the wild.

In each of these instances, children's ideas and interests provide a theme for further study and elaboration. The teacher's task is to help children focus on substantive issues and the kinds of essential questions relevant to the theme. At the same time, the children's initiative generates interest and motivates in-depth inquiry around these essential questions.

Begin with an Artifact

Another way to begin a thematic unit is to present students with an artifact or use one brought in by a student or community member so that curiosity is aroused and speculation begins. One teacher introduces a unit on Japan by gathering her class about her in a semicircle and pulling a wooden mask out of a bag. As the children pass the mask around the circle and peer through its eyes, the teacher asks students to share their observations. The children then write a few lines—poetry for some, simple Thought Ramblings* for others—about who this character might be. Several of these observations are shared, then all are mounted and displayed with the mask. Next the teacher records the students' questions about the mask on a large piece of paper and tells the children that she is going to share a book with them that comes from the same part of the world as the mask.

The teacher leads the class to discover a topic-of-interest by focusing children's attention on an unusual object and by maintaining its mystery while she draws children into another culture. Any artifact, from a fossil to a painting, can serve as the first step in implementing a thematic unit.

Begin with a Book

Literature is a rich source of ideas and starting points for thematic units. One teacher uses Eve Bunting's *Going Home* to spark interest in a thematic unit on JOURNEYS. In Bunting's book, a family returns to Mexico to visit the relatives left behind when the family emigrated to the United States. After discussing why the family in the book came to the United States and why the parents someday want to return to Mexico, students decided that they would interview immigrants in their own community. They developed a set of questions to ask: Why did you immigrate? What made you decide to come to the United States? What do you miss most about your old home? What were the most difficult parts of moving from one place to another? Did you find new opportunities here? Eventually, they organized their questions into categories and decided that one essential question they were investigating was, "How have the journeys of immigrants changed the world?" This question helped students organize the museum of immigration that concluded their study.

(1996) Bunting

Provide many opportunities for children to share their work with peers.

Begin with Drama

Creative dramatics, role playing, and simulation can lead children to explore a theme by establishing a context for investigation and a need for research. A fifth-grade unit on AMERICANS ON THE MOVE begins when students are assigned the roles of family members on a New England farm in the 1840s who must decide whether to head for land in Kansas. To resolve the family conflict raised in the role playing, students need more information. They list some of the things they need to know: How much can they get for their present land? How much will the trip cost? How can they

Record student questions on chart paper to encourage continued reference.

Clements, Tabachnik, & Fielder (1966)

get to Kansas? What supplies will they need? Who else might be going? What crops can be grown there? Are there Indians already living on the land? How might these native peoples feel about the influx of new settlers?

Minnesota Educational Computer Consortium (1985)

These questions form the backdrop for organizing student inquiry and lead to the use of the computer simulation *The Oregon Trail*, to questions about the politics of pioneering across times and places, and to exploration of the body of literature about pioneers. At different points throughout the unit, dramatic techniques are used to focus on such issues as Native American rights, the power of the railroads and industry, establishment of free and slave states, Spanish and French claims in the West and North, and women's suffrage. Each of these issues raises important questions about how history is studied (Who narrates the story? Whose voice is heard or unheard?), challenges children's thinking, and furthers careful reflection on decisions made in the initial pioneer-oriented simulation.

Empowering Teachers and Children

Each of the teachers described here assumed that one of a teacher's roles is that of motivator and facilitator of learning. Teachers in the classroom know the curriculum and the children, linking both so that children are more likely to develop schemas for understanding the world, not just as it is in their immediate experience but as it was in the past, is now elsewhere, and could be in the future. The intent is to empower children by creating a learning environment in which content, process, and intellectual excitement are connected. By encouraging reflective inquiry, teachers do not separate the processes of learning from the content learned. Instead, they link processes to specific contents or domains of knowledge. As children debate whether to move west, for instance, they use data sources specific to history—primary documents, such as diaries or letters written by actual pioneers, speeches and treaties representing native peoples, census information, period art, and music. To evaluate these sources, they learn such historical processes as cross documentation: Is this information supported by other documentation? Are there documents that give a contrary point of view? Whose perspective is gained? Whose is missing?

Blake (1981); Feshback (1975); Shaftel & Shaftel (1982)

By role playing or participating in a simulation, they also gain skill in perspective-taking, an important element in developing historical as well as global understanding. As in the "black box" experience described in Chapter 3, children practice careful observation, inference, hypothesis making and testing, and scientific speculation. They also focus on significant themes and essential questions that do not have single or simple solutions. In short, they learn research skills by using them as they were intended to be used—to better understand the world.

Finally, the focus on identifying essential questions helps teachers and students concentrate their efforts on worthwhile content related to significant issues. Instructional time is limited, however the possibilities for themes are limitless. There is no time for themes that cannot generate the kinds of essential questions discussed in Chapter 3. As a result, teachers need constantly to ask themselves the "so what" question. *So what* if children learn this material? What importance does this knowledge have? What essential questions does it help them answer? Does it help them more effectively participate in the world around them? In the prototypes that follow you will see how a variety of teachers answered these questions.

Prototypes in Action

The first steps are taken, the unit initiated, and then . . . what? Prototypes—excerpts from integrated language classrooms in action—provide an overview of what happens when teachers and children work together to explore themes and engage in the various activities that make up a school day. Eight prototypes offered in this chapter demonstrate the versatility and flexibility of this approach while spanning grade levels:

Prototype	Grade	Theme
1	K	SPACES
2	1	SOUNDS ALL AROUND
3	2	LET'S EAT!
4	2/3	JOURNEYS
5	4	CHANGES (two versions)
6	4/5	EXPLORATIONS
7	5	EXPLORING OUR ROOTS
8	6	DIGGING UP THE PAST

There are samples taken from self-contained, family-grouped, and departmentalized settings, from thematic units that begin in different ways, and from teachers with very different styles of engaging children.

Each of the eight prototypes contains five parts:

- A WEB demonstrating the range of choices available to the teacher(s) and students
- A schedule demonstrating how time is used in the classroom
- An "Into the Classroom" component that follows children and teacher(s) through one entire day and portions of two other days
- A summary pointing out particular features of the prototype
- A bibliography of the books and resources referred to in the WEB

What to Look for in Prototypes: Tips on How to Read Them

The prototypes are provided in chronological order. There are some advantages in reading all the prototypes in the order presented. It enables you to compare and contrast the various features illustrating different prototypes to better observe and abstract developmental characteristics. However, the prototypes have been written so that you can skip around to read individual prototypes by focusing on a particular grade level, a certain classroom feature (e.g., family grouping or departmentalization), or a specific theme.

It is important to point out four features ahead of time so that you can read the prototypes more easily. First, the information in the component called "Into the Classroom" is presented in tables with four columns. The first column, "Time," indicates how activities are scheduled and the amount of time designated for different parts of the day. The second column, "Children," describes the activities children are engaged in, according to the time allotments depicted in the "Schedule" section of that prototype. The third column, "Teacher," highlights teacher roles, showing what the teacher does during children's activities. The fourth column, "Teacher Research," shows some of the activities related to the teacher's ongoing classroom research on teaching and learning, whereby the idea of reflective inquiry by students is extended to teachers as well. Thus, besides everyday assessment and ongoing evaluation of children's learning, each teacher is focusing on a particular inquiry during the course of the thematic unit. (See also the "Guidelines for Teacher Inquiry" at the end of the book).

Second, various classroom routines, such as Comparison Charts*, Sustained Silent Reading (SSR)*, and Big Books*, which are mentioned in these tables and elsewhere, may be unfamiliar to you. These routines, which are marked with an asterisk, are explained in more detail in Chapter 7, the "how-to" chapter.

Third, each web includes *essential questions*—the big questions around which an inquiry is organized. Some of these questions can be found in the headings for categories on each web. Others are listed on the web as research activities within a larger category. As you read the "Into the Classroom" sections and the webs you can see how these questions are used to organize and focus student work. For instance, in the LET'S EAT prototype, the essential questions range from "Where does food come from?" to "How can we help the hungry?" The CHANGES prototype involves students in exploring questions such as "What changes have created the most problems for your community?" and "How does an artist make you 'see' in a particular way?"

Fourth, certain features of ongoing assessment are explicitly noted throughout the prototypes. Assessment and instruction in these classrooms is a reciprocal process—part of an ongoing interplay of teacher actions and evaluations, student learning, and teachers' everyday decisions as to what and how to teach. These kinds of interactions provide both teachers and students with information that is useful in promoting student learning. Many of these ongoing routines and assessments are described in Chapters 7 and 8. However, certain assessment strategies or terms, such as performance assessment or portfolios, are explained further in Chapter 9.

Prototype 1: Half-Day Kindergarten—SPACES

Schedule

The SPACES thematic unit is geared to half-day kindergarten, a time frame typical of many school districts around the country. Beth Busch's classroom is self-contained and organized into centers. There is a large open area for creative dramatics, dance, music, and whole-class read-aloud reading. There is a library filled with books and comfortable places to read. Many of the books are on shelves, but many more are displayed cover-forward on wooden racks or tables or lined up along the floor for easy access. There is an art corner with a sink, supply cupboards, table, and several easels. A building or construction corner with large wooden blocks, a playhouse made out of plastic pipes, and sand and water tables provide many opportunities for dramatic play and scientific exploration. The classroom looks like a place where exciting things are happening. The children's artwork, writing, projects, and shared and dictated writing are displayed in every available space.

Children learn through play and active participation.

See Bergen (1987), for example.

The thematic unit SPACES began because Beth wanted to develop a unit that would allow her five- and six-year-olds to explore the world around them and their relationships to it, particularly in terms of spatial relationships. She felt that an understanding of different perspectives and the concepts relating to spatial relationships is important in language, mathematics, science, and geography, as well as for social development. The theme SPACES also enabled her to capitalize on children's fascination with outer space and gave many opportunities for dramatic play.

As Beth's planning developed, she also began to think about "inner" spaces, such as hiding places, spooky houses, tunnels, and submarines. As Beth looked through several of the indexes to children's books, she found other titles that helped her further develop categories for the WEB. Many of the print materials, songs, and finger plays were chosen because they included and often repeated words such as *in, into, inside, out, behind, in front of, above, below, under, over, through, high, low, up, down, bottom,* and *top.*

Aliki (1988)

Activities were planned to give children occasions to explore these relationships firsthand, to use the words orally in meaningful ways, and to see these words in print. *Dinosaur Bones* by Aliki, a book featured in a library display, opened up another category of "Inside Spaces"—those inside animals and animal eggs. Eventually the hatching of baby chicks from a classroom incubator provided the children with one of the most rewarding experiences of the entire year because it helped them to take on the perspective of another living thing when they tried to imagine what it is like to live inside an egg.

Beth has woven these activities throughout the unit, planning them in such a way that children move from more familiar experiences to more unfamiliar, difficult concepts, and focusing them on such *essential questions* as: What is the difference between "inside" and "outside" spaces? Between "public" and "private" spaces? How can I move in space? What is "outer space"? How are different kinds of spaces used?

Table 4.1 shows a typical weekly plan for Beth's half-day program. The outdoor time was often used for free play, but during this unit Beth sometimes planned more focused activities: trips to a municipal park and other special community spaces, obstacle courses, and solar system walks. The presence of an aide and frequent parent and other family volunteers allowed Beth to work regularly with individual children or small groups.

Into the Classroom

The unit begins with a favorite song and dance, "The Hokey Pokey." This and other songs that incorporate movement ("The Bear Went Over the Mountain," "Roll Over, Roll Over," and "Put Your Hands Up on Your Head") are an ideal beginning point for active kindergartners and give them concrete experiences for talking about direc-

Table 4.1 *Weekly Schedule, Beth Busch's Half-Day Kindergarten*

Time	Monday	Tuesday	Wednesday	Thursday	Friday
8:00	Arrival				
8:10	Center. Teacher reads books or tells story, leads singing or finger play. Children prepare to go to activities.				
8:30	Activity time. Water or sand table, building, library, art, or writing corner. Teacher works with small groups or individuals.				
9:40	Snack time				
9:50	Outdoor play	Obstacle course	Walk to local park	Solar system race	Outdoor play
10:35	Activity time. Book reading. Big Book*, or shared writing activities with small or large groups. Children work with teacher or in centers.				
11:35	Cleanup and evaluation				
11:55	Dismissal				

tional and spatial terms. In the ensuing weeks, the children will have had a variety of experiences to help them further explore and refine their understanding of spatial relationships—their own space and that of others. These experiences provide them with a range of perspectives for looking at and talking about their worlds.

The children enjoy the building that goes on in the block corner. A spaceship, submarines, and space stations have been planned for and constructed so that they can "live in" these places through their imagination. They are busily engaged in the experiments and activities occurring at the sand and water tables and in the constructive play that these experiences promote. They laugh at the antics of the characters in "crowded" stories—stories in which too many characteristics are gathered in too small a space—and they delight in acting out these situations or writing their own versions. They like finding out about animals and insects that live inside something or underground. Joanne Ryder's stories *The Snail's Spell* and *Chipmunk Song* are particularly good in helping children visualize the world from the perspective of the animal, and Mary Ann Hoberman's delightful poem "A House Is a House for Me" gives children new ways to think about things that contain other things. Children also enjoy the delicious scariness of such stories as *A Dark, Dark Tale* and frequently retell or act these out. They are also intrigued with seeing normally scary skeletons in a new light when local veterinarians and doctors visit to show X-rays of animal and human skeletons.

As you read Table 4.2, you can see how the outer-space activities and books have been planned to occur at the end of the unit so that children can become more familiar with spatial concepts and orientation in their immediate environment before deal-

Ryder (1982, 1987)

Hoberman (1978)

Brown (1983)

Prototype 1: Half-Day Kindergarten—SPACES

Spatial Relations

SHAPE SPACE

Movement, Exploration, Bubble gum bubble, other activities.
Buried body, bottomless bottles, video viewing, the gate game, and other games.

TOPS AND BOTTOMS
OUTSIDE, INSIDE
WHERE'S SPOT?
LOOK OUT, HE'S BEHIND YOU
GUINEA PIGS FAR AND NEAR
INSIDE, OUTSIDE, UPSIDE DOWN
SNAKE IN, SNAKE OUT
BECCA BACKWARD, BECCA FRONTWARD
BIG AND LITTLE
BIG WORLD, SMALL WORLD
FROM WHERE YOU ARE
LOOK UP, LOOK DOWN
ALL ABOUT WHERE

Look at things from different perspectives. Describe them. Label classroom locations.
Plan an obstacle course and map it. Tell directions for getting through it successfully.
Dance the Hokey Pokey.

WHERE DOES IT GO?

What are some other silly places for familiar things? Write your own version of this book.

It's Dark Inside

BUZ
A DARK, DARK TALE
IN A DARK, DARK ROOM

Make pictures for a Big Book*.
Retell the story. Use sound effects.

THE FAT CAT
THE TERRIBLE TIGER
THE GREEDY PYTHON

Play with nesting dolls.
Make a sock puppet. Have the puppet eat all the characters in the story.

WHAT'S HATCHING OUT OF THAT EGG?
HATCH, EGG, HATCH

Make a classroom incubator. Keep a calendar of observations.

Inside Spaces

ALFIE GETS IN FIRST
THE CAT IN THE HAT
I UNPACKED MY GRANDMOTHER'S TRUNK

Play the unpacking game.

WHAT'S INSIDE THE BOX?

Hide something in a box. Have others guess what's inside.

THE INSIDE OUTSIDE BOOK OF NEW YORK CITY
THE INSIDE-OUTSIDE BOOK OF LIBRARIES
THE HOUSE FROM MORNING TO NIGHT

Draw your house inside and out.
Play with a dollhouse.
Make a list of things you find inside and things you find outside.

THE WILD INSIDE
A HOUSE IS A HOUSE FOR ME

Think up other houses for things.

Underneath Spaces

UNDERGROUND
UNDER THE GROUND
CHIPMUNK SONG
HOW TO DIG A HOLE TO THE OTHER SIDE OF THE WORLD
A RUMBLY TUMBLY GLITTERY GRITTY PLACE

Pretend you are in a spaceship or a submarine. Radio back to the surface and tell what you see or how you are feeling.

THERE'S AN ALLIGATOR UNDER MY BED

What hides under *your* bed?

THE THREE BILLY GOATS GRUFF

Build a bridge for the ogre. Tell the story from the ogre's point of view.

SPACES

Over, Under, and Through

Water and sand table; play with pipe constructions; observe water run through and come out.

OVER, UNDER, AND THROUGH
OVER, UNDER, AND ALL AROUND: RELATIONSHIPS IN SPACE
TUNNELS

Make an obstacle course.

THE VERY HUNGRY CATERPILLAR
ACROSS THE STREAM
OVER IN THE MEADOW
"The Bear Went Over the Mountain"
TEN IN A BED
"Roll Over, Roll Over"

Sing the songs. Make up new verses.

ROSIE'S WALK

Play hide and go seek. Tell whether you hid under, over, behind, or inside something.

Outside Spaces

SPOT'S FIRST WALK

Pretend to be Spot. Look behind, go through, and look under things.

THE PARK BOOK
PLAYGROUND
IN MY GARDEN
MY BACKYARD

Visit an outdoor place. Tell what you see. How is it different from indoors?

IN MY TENT

Make a tent. Play inside.

OUTSIDE OVER THERE

Recreate the story in pantomime as the teacher reads aloud.

Your Own Space

A PLACE FOR BEN
EVAN'S CORNER

Write a letter inviting a friend to visit your special place. Measure your place.

SOPHIE'S HIDEAWAY
YOUR OWN BEST SECRET PLACE
SECRET PLACES

Draw a picture of a secret place.
Make a list of things to keep in your secret place.
Write a poem about your secret place.

EVERYTHING HAS A PLACE

Make a plan for where to put things in your room, your classroom.

Animals Inside and Out

SNAIL IN THE WOODS
THE SNAIL'S SPELL
INSIDE TURTLE'S SHELL
TURTLE AND SNAIL
TURTLE WATCH
LOOK OUT FOR TURTLES!

Pretend you are an animal that lives inside something.
   Tell what it is like.
Why do some animals need protective shells?
Make a hermit crab home in a glass aquarium.
Categorize the types of animals in your
   neighborhood.

Outside and Inside Living Things

OUTSIDE AND INSIDE YOU
OUTSIDE AND INSIDE TREES
OUTSTANDING OUTSIDES
SKELETONS! SKELETONS! ALL ABOUT BONES
A BOOK ABOUT YOUR SKELETON
SKELETON
THE SKELETON INSIDE YOU
YOUR INSIDES
THE SKELETON BOOK: AN INSIDE LOOK AT
   ANIMALS
DINOSAUR BONES
A CAT'S BODY

Invite a doctor or a vet to show X rays.
Have a classmate trace your body on large brown
   paper. Draw what you think your X ray would
   look like.

Up-Above Spaces

HIGHER ON THE DOOR
HOW HIGH IS UP?
UP GOES THE SKYSCRAPER
SKYSCRAPER GOING UP
ELEPHANTS ALOFT
A GREAT DAY FOR UP
UP, UP, AND AWAY
ON TOP
THE CROSS-COUNTRY CAT
HIGH WIRE HENRY
MIRETTE ON THE HIGH WIRE
LOOKING DOWN

Pretend you are taking a balloon ride or walking on a
   tightrope. Tell how the world looks from up above.

THE SEA-BREEZE HOTEL
THE EMPEROR AND THE KITE
THE DRAGON KITE

Make a kite and have a kite-flying festival.

THE TURNAROUND WIND

Draw "turnaround" people.

THE CLOUD BOOK

Make a chart of different kinds of clouds.

DREAMS

Imagine what shapes and creatures you see in the clouds.
   Make them in soft sculpture.

SKY SONGS
SPACE SONGS

Read other space poetry.

Outer Space

A SPACE STORY

Interview an astronaut. Design a mission patch for your class.

EARTH, OUR PLANET IN SPACE
THE PLANETS IN OUR SOLAR SYSTEM
THE PLANETS

Make a solar system on your own football field.
   Compare the number of laps it takes to reach each planet.
Learn planet order chant.
Use vegetables and dried beans as models for planets.

WHAT THE MOON IS LIKE
THE MOON
LET'S FIND OUT ABOUT THE MOON

Play "moon buggy."

JOURNEY INTO A BLACK HOLE

Plan a space mission, make props, and blast off. Tell about your trip
   when you return.
Dress up in many layers of clothes. Why do astronauts need so much
   protection? How does it feel to move?

ROCKETS AND SATELLITES

Watch "The Secret City." Build a classroom space lab.

LET'S FIND OUT ABOUT THE SUN
COMETS
LOOK TO THE NIGHT SKY: AN INTRODUCTION TO STAR
   WATCHING
THE SKY IS FULL OF STARS
STAR GAZERS
MY PLACE IN SPACE
COMETS, METEORS, AND ASTEROIDS

Make star viewers. List the steps it took.

THE LEGEND OF THE MILKY WAY
HER SEVEN BROTHERS
WHY THE SUN AND THE MOON LIVE IN THE SKY
COYOTE PLACES THE STARS

Compare stories.

IS THERE LIFE IN OUTER SPACE?
SPACE CASE
LET ME OFF THIS SPACESHIP!

Interview the alien for television. Find out how it feels to be on
   another planet far from home.
Write secret messages from the alien to its spaceship.

Crowded Spaces

THE BIG RED BUS
PIGS APLENTY, PIGS GALORE
KNOCK, KNOCK, TEREMOK!
MR. GUMPY'S MOTOR CAR
MR. GUMPY'S OUTING
MUSHROOM IN THE RAIN
WHO SANK THE BOAT?
THIS BOOK IS TOO SMALL
HOW MANY ARE IN THIS OLD CAR?
   A COUNTING BOOK
IT COULD ALWAYS BE WORSE
SHEEP IN A JEEP
MILLIONS OF CATS
ALWAYS ROOM FOR ONE MORE
"The Old Woman Who Lived in a Shoe"

How many is too many? Count the
   characters in each story. Compare the
   numbers. Show the different sets on a
   graph. Which story had the most
   characters? The fewest?
Make a mural of crowded stories.
Make a clay model.
Act out one of the stories.
Find out which story your classmates
   like best.

I KNOW AN OLD LADY WHO
   SWALLOWED A FLY

Make up new verses to the song.

ing with those on a more distant plane. Note also how responsive Beth is to the needs and interests of the children during these activities.

Finally, Beth has decided that her own inquiry will focus on gender differences in how children learn and use spatial concepts. She is familiar with research that suggests that boys' pretend play involves different uses of motor skills and space. Beth wants to explore possible differences between her students and to see if her emphasis on spatial concepts in a variety of contexts will have a positive effect on girls' use of spatial concepts. She has arranged to videotape some of her class sessions so that she can more carefully analyze student activity. She has also selected four focus children—two girls and two boys—for whom she will keep comparative response records, noting how each child responds to spatial tasks over the course of the unit.

Table 4.2　*Detailed Schedule, Beth Busch's Half-Day Kindergarten*

Day 1

Time	Children	Teacher	Teacher Research
Teacher Arrival 7:30		Teacher Beth and aide Sandy arrive to set up new centers, take care of paperwork.	
Children Arrival 8:00	Children come in; put away coats and lunches. Many move to centers. Some talk to Beth or Sandy.	Beth greets the children, talking informally with several.	
Center 8:10	The children gather in the open areas of the classroom.	Beth leads the children in a favorite dance, "The Hokey Pokey." She encourages children to watch her if they get confused.	Beth has arranged to videotape this activity to give her good baseline data about the children's spatial awareness. She will view the tape later to observe children's sense of direction, knowledge of body parts, and spatial orientation, and to note any children who seem to be having particular difficulties.
	Some children have trouble sorting right from left. All enjoy the active movement. Several children remember "in," "out," and "all about."	After they have sung the song several times, Beth invites them to sit on the rug. She asks them to recall the action of the game: Where did they put their hands, legs, and so on?	
	Children respond with chairs, desks, televisions, people, pets for inside; cars, trees, grass, flowers, birds for outside.	Beth asks them to think of other things that are inside and outside. As they volunteer ideas, she makes a list on a large sheet of chart paper divided into two columns, reading each word as she writes it.	
	One child knows that birds can be found inside and outside because he has a pet parakeet. Others recall their pet dog or cat that goes outside.	She then asks children if there are some things found both inside and outside. She reads back through the list, pointing to each word and reading it. "Could we find birds inside and outside?" When the children respond yes, she marks it with a star.	
	The children are unsure about this concept.	She explains that "inside" and "outside" are names we give to spaces. "What other names do we have for spaces?" she asks. She prompts children by asking about birds: "Where are spaces birds might be?"	
	The child with the pet parakeet replies, "In a cage." Another child says, "Outdoors." "Up in a tree," "In the sky," "On the ground," volunteer others.		
	"All about," says one child. "That's where we shook all about."	"Where outdoors?" Beth asks. Beth responds, "Up in the tree, down on the ground. These are	

(continued)

Table 4.2 *Detailed Schedule, Beth Busch's Half-Day Kindergarten (continued)*

Day 1

Time	Children	Teacher	Teacher Research
		words that tell about places and spaces. We're going to start a unit today that's all about spaces. We'll find out about spaces that are inside and outside, up above and down under, over and through, and all about."	
	The children name the block corner, art corner, and housekeeping corner.	"Who can think of some special spaces right here in our classroom?"	
		Beth explains that for the next several weeks they will find many activities in these centers that will help them explore many different spaces. She suggests that this morning, the block corner may be a good place to build a spaceship to go to outer space. She has set up a special activity at the sand table and a game called the gate game at another center. She points out several books that show insides and outsides and sets them in the reading corner.	
		After children have looked at these, they may want to draw pictures of their houses inside and outside or play with the dollhouse she has brought in.	
		She asks each child what he or she plans to do during activity time. She reminds four children that they are helpers during snack time.	
Activity Time 8:30	Children move to centers. Four children enthusiastically enter the building center and begin to pull out blocks to build a spaceship. They exchange suggestions about its size. One child begins to make blast off noises as he puts bricks together. Other children are in the reading center looking at *the Inside-Outside Book of Libraries*. Two children reading together begin to chant, "Inside, outside," as they turn the pages. Another child is excited by the skeleton views of a large house in *The House from Morning to Night*. She takes it to the children who are playing with the dollhouse to show them the different rooms.		
	Several children play the gate game. They soon realize that, to roll a ball through cardboard gates or arches and to knock over the objects placed there, they have to reposition their bodies in space.	Sandy stands by to reposition objects behind the arches each time they are knocked down. She purposefully moves the objects so that the children have to move their bodies to aim at the objects. She helps the children articulate what they are doing.	Beth has arranged to videotape this activity in order to observe the children's problem-solving responses.

(continued)

Table 4.2   *Detailed Schedule, Beth Busch's Half-Day Kindergarten (continued)*

Day 1

Time	Children	Teacher	Teacher Research
	Some of the children are intrigued by the activity at the sand table and move to play at that center. Several children begin to imitate Beth, and Michelle uncovers a paper drawing.	Beth joins the children at the sand table and tells them she is going to dig down deep.	
	Michelle is not sure at first what is under the sand, and a friend helps her move more sand away. They discover a hand. One child guesses that the bottom of the table is under the sand. Others begin to move sand away from the paper hand. Eventually the children uncover a life-size doll. Several children think the doll is looking at them. Another puts his head down near the doll's and looks up at the ceiling.	Beth asks Michelle what she has found. Beth asks the children what they think is under the sand. Beth talks with the children as they make predictions about what they are doing and uses words like *covered over, under, bottom,* and *top.* She asks the children what the doll might be able to see.	
9:35	Four children move to help prepare snacks. Each child counts out snacks for six children.	Sandy takes out Fig Newtons, peanuts in shells, and olives. She asks the children what is inside each of the snacks.	
Snack Time 9:40	Children enjoy eating snacks and begin to name other foods that have something inside. They then expand to talking about foods with outsides, such as apples with skin or sandwiches with bread.	Beth and Sandy help the children think about insides and outsides of food.	
Outdoor Play 9:50	Children enter into the imaginary bubbles and move carefully to Beth's directions.	Beth takes the first part of outdoor time to do some movement exploration. She asks the children to crouch down on the ground and imagine they are chewing a big piece of bubble gum. They are then to imagine blowing a gigantic bubble and stepping inside it. Once inside, they can gently touch the inside of their bubbles. Then she tells them that they can move slowly to the right but that their bubble cannot touch anyone else's bubble or it will burst. She leads them in various movements inside their bubbles. If anyone bumps, he or she must leave the group.	
Activity Time 10:35	The children enjoy chiming in and predicting where the snake will go next. Some of the children want to play snake.	Beth reads *Snake In, Snake Out.*	
	Children enjoy being leaders and followers.	Beth helps the children to line up and hold each other's waists so that the line is like a snake. She then gives children directions in a "Simon says" manner: "Snake go around the art table. Snake go through the reading center. Snake step over the block bridge." She then invites the children to take turns at giving directions to the snake.	

(continued)

Table 4.2 *DETAILED SCHEDULE, BETH BUSCH'S HALF-DAY KINDERGARTEN (CONTINUED)*

Day 1

Time	Children	Teacher	Teacher Research
	Several children have trouble with some of the positions like "front" and "back." A lively discussion ensues.	When the game is finished, Beth asks the children to help her label positions in the classroom. She writes out tagboard labels with the words *under, over, up, down, front,* and *back* and gives them to children to place around the room.	Beth jots down notes about individual responses on yellow Post-it Notes. She is interested in the children's thinking and hopes that as she looks over her notes and reviews videotapes she will see some patterns emerging in the children's responses. She wants to identify four of the children to study more closely in ensuing weeks. In addition, this will help her plan subsequent activities for the unit.
Cleanup and Evaluation 11:35	Children clean up centers and put away materials.	Beth asks children to think about more inside/outside things and foods for tomorrow. She ends by leading the children in a favorite song, "I Know an Old Lady Who Swallowed a Fly."	

Day 4

Time	Children	Teacher	Teacher Research
Outdoor Play 9:50	Children proceed through the obstacle course one by one. When they have finished, they ask to do it again.	Beth and the P.E. teacher have set up an obstacle course on the playground using old tires and the standard playground equipment. They walk children through the course verbally, telling them to step into the first tire, run around the tire tower, crawl under the cargo net, climb up the ladder, and slide down the slide. She, Sandy, and the P.E. teacher station themselves along the course. All give directions to the children. After the children have completed the race several times, Beth asks different children to serve as leader and give directions.	Beth has asked the P.E. teacher and Sandy each to observe two children, Jason and Michelle, noting their responses to the activities. She will be watching Mark and Kerry and making notes on the ease or difficulty they are having. These four children have been chosen for the case study portion of her inquiry.
Activity Time 10:35	Children work in centers with activities begun earlier in the week. In addition, several children have taken a large cardboard box and decorated it as a car. They are acting out *Mr. Gumpy's Motor Car.* In the reading center, children are playing school with the Big Book* version of *Where's Spot?* The teacher has printed the words and glued flaps over the hidden animals, and the children have created the pictures. The children decide they want the bear to change directions in their version. They suggest that he go	Beth works with a small group to write a version of a song they learned the previous day, "The Bear Went Over the Mountain."	

(continued)

Table 4.2 DETAILED SCHEDULE, BETH BUSCH'S HALF-DAY KINDERGARTEN (CONTINUED)

Day 4

Time	Children	Teacher	Teacher Research
	under a bridge, climb up a tree, and run into a cave.		
		Beth makes the process of composition explicit. She tells the children where she would begin writing and says each word as she writes it on a large sheet of tagboard. She stops to ask the children's opinion about word choices and reminds them of the pattern of the original song. She suggests they add adjectives so that their sentences better fit the rhythm of the song ("the bear ran into a dark cave"). She writes each verse on a separate sheet of tagboard and gives pairs of children verses to illustrate.	
	Several children have difficulty remembering which verse they are to illustrate.		
	Susan remembers the labels they placed around the room. She can match up the label with a word in the written text. She knows the order of the words they composed and can match the words in her head to the words on the page until she comes to the word *under*. "The bear went. . . ." She and Richard look at the labels and find the same word on a label under the table. Richard looks at the word *under*. "There's an *r* there," he points out. "That's in my name."	Beth asks if there are any clues to help them figure out the words.

Beth asks if they had any other clues. | |

Day 15

Time	Children	Teacher	Teacher Research
Activity Time 8:30	The children are working in centers. Several are creating a collage mural of crowded story characters. Others are busy decorating kites. Some are building a space station in the block corner. In an open area, three children are playing with a moon buggy. The buggy has a large seat, a metal frame, and casters that rotate. The children are seated facing outward and have to cooperate to get the buggy to move in any one direction. They have decorated the buggy with tin foil, flags, and "antennas" and are wearing space paraphernalia they have made.	Beth moves from group to group.

Sandy works with the group to help them understand how to move the vehicle. | Beth has set up the videotape recorder and asked her case study children to work on the moon buggy project together so that she can have a record of their interactions as well as individual reactions. |
| Snack Time 9:40 | | Beth has set out a "solar system" salad. A dried pea represents the moon, a fresh pea is Pluto, and walnuts represent the Earth and Venus. Beans stand for Mars and Mercury, | Beth is particularly interested in the responses of her four case study children to this task and jots down their responses in her notebook. |

(continued)

Table 4.2 *Detailed Schedule, Beth Busch's Half-Day Kindergarten (continued)*

Day 15

Time	Children	Teacher	Teacher Research
	The children are intrigued by the sizes of the objects. They seem to have trouble with the representation of large sizes with small objects.	and cabbages for Jupiter and Saturn. An orange stands for Neptune, and a small grapefruit for Uranus. She places them in order on the snack table, then serves children a mixture cut up earlier. Beth suggests they think about the dollhouse and the smaller scale of objects and people. She suggests that the children look at several of the information books in the library, especially *The Planets in Our Solar System.*	
Outdoor Play 9:50	Terrestrial planet children (Mars, Venus, Mercury, and Earth) match their name cards to the signs on the track.	Beth selects children to represent the inner planets. She hangs a name and picture label on each child and gives him or her the appropriate vegetable, fruit, or nut from the snack table. She then leads the children to the school track. Sandy has placed planet signs around the track at intervals that correspond to miles in the solar system. She helps children find their stations.	
	The children enjoy imagining that they are on spaceships as they "walk" the solar system. The children who have been planets want to take the walk, too. They place their fruit at the foot of the planet sign and join Sandy in a walk of their own.	Beth asks other children to imagine they are on a journey from Earth to all the planets in the solar system. She then leads them on a walk around the track where a yard equals 211,265 miles. Imagining that the beginning is the sun, they will have to walk $\frac{2}{5}$ of a lap to reach Mercury, $\frac{3}{4}$ to Venus, 1 to Earth, and $1\frac{1}{2}$ to Mars. The journey to the outer planets would require many more laps: $5\frac{1}{2}$ laps to get to Jupiter, $9\frac{1}{2}$ to Saturn, $19\frac{1}{8}$ to Uranus, 30 to Neptune, and $39\frac{2}{5}$ to Pluto. She suggests that bicycles might be needed to complete the rest of the journey.	Beth divides up her case study students between the planet group and the travelers so that she and Sandy can better observe their reactions during the activity. Later she will ask the four children to draw a "map" of their trip. She is interested to see how they will represent the experience on paper and will note any differences in their talk while they are drawing and in their final products.
	Several children who live near the school volunteer to bring their bikes tomorrow so that they can complete the solar system trip.	Beth agrees to set up signs for the outer planets on the following day and help the children count off laps.	

Summary

Beth's classroom is a place where children have the opportunity to be children and explore their environments and spaces in ways that make sense to them. She believes that kindergarten is a place where children learn best through play and active participation rather than through teacher-directed formal lessons. To this end, Beth is a facilitator. She observes carefully and listens closely, trying to understand how it is that her students are constructing knowledge. This is carried on throughout the day, using informal and formal observation techniques. (See Chapters 8 and 9.) In addition, she has identified the topic of gender differences as an area-of-interest and has carried out a systematic inquiry that seeks to identify patterns in the way the boys and girls in her class deal with spatial concepts. Through these observations and inquiries, she attempts to respond to what the children are trying to do. She demonstrates and collaborates as a fellow, and more experienced, learner.

The language that accompanies children's experiences involves and engages them in many language modes and registers. Beth believes that they are already readers and writers when they enter her classroom, so she gives them many opportunities to use written language in natural, authentic ways. As they share reading and writing with each other and adults, they are thus able to refine and further build on the emergent literacy understandings that had been developed before they came to school.

Children's Literature: SPACES

Across the Stream by M. Ginsburg. Illustrated by N. Tafuri. Greenwillow, 1982.

Alfie Gets in First by S. Hughes. Morrow, 1981.

All About Where by T. Hoban. Greenwillow, 1991.

Always Room for One More by S. N. Leodhas. Illustrated by N. Hogrogian. Holt, 1965.

"The Bear Went Over the Mountain" in *If You're Happy and You Know It: Eighteen Story Songs Set to Pictures* by N. Weiss. Greenwillow, 1987.

Becca Backward, Becca Frontward: A Book of Concept Pairs by B. McMillan. Lothrop, 1986.

Big and Little: A Beginning Concept Book by J. Satchwen. Random House, 1984.

The Big Red Bus by J. Hindley. Illustrated by W. Benedict. Candlewick, 1995.

Big World, Small World by J. Titherington. Greenwillow, 1985.

A Book About Your Skeleton by R. B. Gross. Illustrated by D. Robinson. Hastings House, 1979.

Buz by R. Egileski. HarperCollins, 1996.

The Cat in the Hat by T. Geisel (Dr. Seuss). Random House, 1957.

A Cat's Body by J. Cole. Photographs by J. Wexler. Morrow, 1982.

Chipmunk Song by J. Ryder. Dutton/Lodestar, 1987.

The Cloud Book by T. de Paola. Holiday, 1984.

Comets by F. M. Branley. Illustrated by G. Maestro. Crowell, 1984.

Comets, Meteors, and Asteroids by S. Simon. Morrow, 1994.

Coyote Places the Stars by H. P. Taylor. Bradbury Press, 1993.

The Cross-Country Cat by M. Calhoun. Illustrated by E. Ingaham. Morrow, 1979.

A Dark, Dark Tale by R. Brown. Dial, 1983.

Dinosaur Bones by Aliki. Harper & Row, 1988.

The Dragon Kite by N. Luenn. Illustrated by M. Hague. Harcourt Brace Jovanovich, 1982.

Dreams by P. Spier. Doubleday, 1986.

Earth, Our Planet in Space by S. Simon. Four Winds, 1984.

Elephants Aloft by K. Appelt. Illustrated by K. Baker. Harcourt Brace, 1993.

The Emperor and the Kite by J. Yolen. Illustrated by E. Young. Philomel, 1988.

Evan's Corner by E. S. Hill. Illustrated by S. Speidel. Viking, 1991.

Everything Has a Place by P. Lillie. Illustrated by N. Tafuri. Greenwillow, 1993.

The Fat Cat: A Danish Folktale by J. Kent. Parents, 1971.

From Where You Are by J. Wakefield. Illustrated by T. Dunnington. Children's Press, 1978.

A Great Day for Up by T. Geisel (Dr. Seuss). Random House, 1974.

The Greedy Python by R. Buckley. Illustrated by E. Carle. Picture Book Studio, 1985.

Guinea Pigs Near and Far by K. Duke. Dutton, 1984.

Hatch, Egg, Hatch by S. Roddie. Illustrated by F. Cony. Joy Street, 1991.

Her Seven Brothers by P. Goble. Bradbury, 1988.

High Wire Henry by M. Calhoun. Illustrated by E. Ingraham. Morrow, 1991.

Higher on the Door by J. Stevenson. Greenwillow, 1987.

The House From Morning To Night by D. Bour. Kane Miller, 1985.

House Is a House for Me by M. A. Hobeman. Illustrated by B. Fraser. Viking, 1978.

How High Is Up? by B. Kohn. Illustrated by J. Pyk. Putnam, 1971.

How Many in this Old Car? A Counting Book by C. and J. Hawkins. Putnam, 1988.

How to Dig a Hole to the Other Side of the Earth by F. McNulty. Illustrated by M. Simont. Harper & Row, 1979.

I Know an Old Lady Who Swallowed a Fly adapted by N. Bernard. Joy Street, 1981.

I Unpacked my Grandmother's Trunk by S. R. Hoguet. Dutton, 1983.

In a Dark, Dark Room by A. Schwartz. Illustrated by D. Zimmer. Harper & Row, 1984.

In My Garden by R. Maris. Greenwillow, 1987.

In My Tent by M. Singer. Illustrated by E. A. McCully. Macmillan, 1992.

The Inside-Outside Book of New York City by R. Munro. Dodd, Mead, 1985.

The Inside-Outside Book of Libraries by J. Cummins. Illustrated by R. Munro. Dutton, 1996.

Inside, Outside, Upside Down by S. Berenstain & J. Berenstain. Random House, 1968.

Inside Turtle's Shell by J. Ryder. Illustrated by S. Bonners. Macmillan, 1985.

Is there Life in Outer Space? by F. M. Branley. Illustrated by D. Madden. Crowell, 1984.

It Could Always Be Worse by M. Zemach. Farrar, Straus & Giroux, 1976.

Journey into a Black Hole by F. M. Branley. Illustrated by M. Simont. Crowell, 1986.

Knock, Knock, Teremok! A Traditional Russian Tale by K. Arnold. North-South, 1994.

The Legend of the Milky Way. Retold by J. M. Lee. Holt, Rinehart & Winston, 1982.

Let Me Off this Space Ship by G. Greer & R. Ruddnick. Illustrated by B. L. Sims. HarperCollins, 1991.

Let's Find Out about the Moon by C. Shapp & M. Shapp. Illustrated by S. Later. Franklin Watts/Random House Sound Film Strip.

Let's Find Out about the Sun by M. Shapp & C. Shapp. Illustrated by S. Later. Franklin Watts/Random House Sound Film Strip.

Look Out for Turtles! by M. Berger. Illustrated by M. Lloyd. HarperCollins, 1992.

Look Out, He's Behind You by T. Bradman. Illustrated by M. Chamberlain. Putnam, 1988.

Look to the Night Sky: An Introduction to Star Watching by S. Simon. Viking, 1977.

Look Up, Look Down by T. Hoban. Greenwillow, 1992.

Looking Down by S. Jenkins. Houghton, 1995.

Millions of Cats by W. Gag. Putnam, 1988.

Mirette in the High Wire by E. A. McCully. Putnam, 1992.

The Moon by S. Simon. Macmillan, 1984.

Mr. Gumpy's Motor Car by J. Burningham. Crowell, 1973.

Mr. Gumpy's Outing by J. Burningham. Holt, Rinehart & Winston, 1970.

Mushroom in the Rain by M. Ginsberg. Illustrated by J. Aruego & A. Dewey. Macmillan, 1974.

My Backyard by A. Rockwell & H. Rockwell. Macmillan, 1981.

My Place in Space by R. Hirst & S. Hirst. Illustrated by R. Harvey & J. Levine. Orchard, 1990.

"The Old Woman Who Lived in a Shoe" in *The Mother Goose Book* by A. Provensen & M. Provensen. Random House, 1976.

On Top by M. MacGregor. Morrow, 1988.

Outside, Inside by C. Crimi. Illustrated by L. A. Riley. Simon, 1995.

Outside and Inside Trees by S. Markle. Bradbury, 1993.

Outside and Inside You by S. Markle. Bradbury, 1991.

Outside Over There by M. Sendak. Harper & Row. 1981.

Outstanding Outsides by H. Matchotka. Morrow, 1993.

Over in the Meadow by E. J. Keats. Scholastic, 1971.

Over, Under, and All Around: Relationships in Space by S. Tester. Child's World, 1977.

Over, Under, and Through by T. Hoban. Macmillan, 1973.

Parents in the Pigpen, Pigs in the Tub by A. Ehrlich & S. Kellogg. Dial, 1993.

The Park Book by C. Zolotow. Illustrated by H. A. Rey. Harper, 1972.

Pigs Aplenty, Pigs Galore by D. McPhail. Dutton, 1993.

A Place for Ben by J. Titherington. Greenwillow, 1987.

The Planets by G. Gibbons. Holiday House, 1993.

The Planets in Our Solar System by F. M. Branley. Illustrated by D. Madden. Crowell, 1981.

Playground by G. Gibbons. Holiday, 1985.

Rockets and Satellites by F. M. Branley. Illustrated by G. Maestro. Crowell, 1987.

"Roll Over, Roll Over" in *If You're Happy and You Know It: Eighteen Story Songs Set To Pictures* by N. Weiss. Greenwillow, 1987.

Rosie's Walk by P. Hutchins. Macmillan, 1968.

A Rumbly Tumbly Glittery Gritty Place by M. L. Ray. Illustrated by D. Florian. Harcourt Brace, 1993.

The Sea-Breeze Hotel by M. Vaughan. Illustrated by P. Mullins. HarperCollins, 1992.

Secret Places: Poems by C. Huck. Illustrated by L. B. George. Greenwillow, 1993.

Shape Space by C. Falwell. Clarion, 1992.

Sheep in a Jeep by N. Shaw. Illustrated by M. Apple. Houghton Mifflin, 1986.

Skeleton by S. Parker. Knopf, 1988.

The Skeleton Book: An Inside Look at Animals by M. Livaudis & R. Dunne. Walker and Co., 1972.

The Skeleton Inside You by P. Balestrino. Illustrated by T. Kelley. Crowell, 1989.

Skeletons! Skeletons! All about Bones by K. Hall. Illustrated by P. Billin-Frye. Platt & Munck, 1991.

The Sky Is Full of Stars by F. Branley. Illustrated by F. Bond. Crowell, 1981.

Sky Songs by M. C. Livingston. Illustrated by L. E. Fisher. Holiday House, 1984.

Skyscraper Going Up by V. Cobb. Illustrated by J. Strejan. Crowell, 1987.

Snail in the Woods by J. Ryder & H. S. Feinberg. Illustrated by J. Polseno. Harper & Row, 1979.

The Snail's Spell by J. Ryder. Illustrated by L. Cherry. Frederick Wame, 1982.

Snake In, Snake Out by L. Banchek. Crowell, 1978.

Sophie's Hideaway by R. Kozikowski. Harper & Row, 1983.

Space Case by J. Marshall. Dial, 1980.

Space Songs by M. C. Livingston. Illustrated by L. E. Fisher. Holiday House, 1988.

A Space Story by K. Kuskin. Illustrated by M. Simont. Harper & Row, 1978.

Spot's First Walk by E. Hill. Putnam, 1981.

Star Gazers by G. Gibbons. Holiday House, 1992.

Ten in a Bed by M. Rees. Joy Street, 1988.

The Terrible Tiger by J. Prelutsky. Illustrated by A. Lobel. Macmillan, 1970.

There's an Alligator Under My Bed by M. Mayer. Dial, 1987.

This Book Is Too Small by A. Wouters. Dutton, 1992.

The Three Billy Goats Gruff by P. C. Asbjornsen & J. E. Moe. Illustrated by M. Brown. Harcourt, 1957.

Tops and Bottoms by J. Stevens. Harcourt Brace, 1995.

Tunnels by G. Gibbons. Holiday, 1984.

The Turnaround Wind by A. Lobel. Harper & Row, 1988.

Turtle and Snail by Z. O'Neal. Illustrated by M. Tomes. Lippincott, 1979.

Turtle Watch by G. Ancona. Macmillan, 1987.

Under the Ground by P. de Bourning. Illustrated by D. Bour. Scholastic, 1995.

Underground by D. Macauley. Houghton Mifflin, 1976.

Up Goes the Skyscraper by G. Gibbons. Four Winds, 1986.

Up, Up, and Away by M. Hillert. Follett, 1982.

The Very Hungry Caterpillar by E. Carle. Philomel, 1983.

What the Moon Is Like by F. M. Branley. Illustrated by T. Kelley. Crowell, 1986.

What's Hatching Out of that Egg? by P. Lauber. Crown, 1979.

What's Inside the Box? by E. Kessler & L. Kessler. Dodd, Mead, 1976.

Where Does It Go? by M. Miller. Greenwillow, 1992.

Where's Spot? by E. Hill. Putnam, 1980.

Who Sank the Boat? by P. Allen. Putnam, 1985.

Why the Sun and the Moon Live in the Sky by N. Daly. Lothrop, 1995.

The Wild Inside: Sierra Club's Guide to the Great Outdoors by A. Allison. Sierra Club/Little, Brown, 1988.

Your Insides by J. Cole. Illustrated by P. Meisel. Putnam, 1992.

Your Own Best Secret Place by B. Baylor. Illustrated by P. Parnall. Scribner, 1979.

Prototype 2: First Grade—SOUNDS ALL AROUND

Schedule

The plans for the SOUNDS ALL AROUND WEB are meant for a first grade in an open area school whose students represent many cultures and countries from the large urban area nearby. In the school organization, grades are grouped together in "pods"—areas that are separated from the other grades by walls but open to other classes in the grade level. The teachers work together to organize space, blocking off areas with bookcases and mobile bulletin boards. They have also found that dressmakers' cutting boards and old appliance boxes can be cut into folding display panels to help organize space and allow display of work at the perfect eye level for first graders. The teachers in the first grade pod also work well as a team, and although each takes responsibility for his or her own class they sometimes plan themes together. They also make sure to schedule quiet times when all the teachers read aloud or all children are involved in Sustained Silent Reading (SSR)*. Table 4.3 shows the weekly schedule for Michael Silverman's first-grade classroom.

Michael planned the SOUNDS ALL AROUND unit for autumn, following the theme WHO AM I? meant to introduce children to each other, a new school year, and the school community. This first unit gave Michael an excellent opportunity to observe children as language learners, to get to know their diverse backgrounds, interests, and abilities, and to cover key social studies and science concepts related to identity and growth.

As Michael observed children in a variety of talking, reading, and writing activities during the first weeks of school, he was able to gather data about his students' understanding and awareness of reading and writing conventions—to identify their "literacy set" (See Figure 1.6 in Chapter 1). He found that many of his students readily engaged in pretend book reading and tried a variety of written forms. Still others were beginning to focus on conventional letter-sound relationships as they read and wrote. In Michael's school district, a central emphasis was placed on literacy learning in the primary grades. In addition, as a first-grade teacher he received many questions from parents who were concerned that he was not teaching phonics and spelling in familiar ways. He was knowledgeable about research in emergent reading and writing and the role of phonological awareness—the ability to segment words into sounds—as a part of this process. Michael decided to plan a unit that would give him an opportunity to demonstrate to parents his beliefs about meaningful, contextually based learning. This would also give him a way to provide his children with many opportunities to explore the sounds of spoken language at the same time that he supported their discovery of written codes.

When he found during the WHO AM I? unit that Claire, one of his students, had a sister who was Deaf, he decided to plan a unit on sound that would build on the concepts from the first unit. This would give the children opportunities to explore the idea of different cultural viewpoints, in this case the culture of the Deaf. A unit about Sounds would also give children a natural context for developing concepts about letter-sound relationships, word knowledge, and language play. A SOUNDS ALL AROUND theme would personalize the learning at the same time that it might help children develop empathy and concern for others' ways-of-living, one of the key concepts in the first-grade state social studies program. Such a theme would allow excellent opportunities for teacher research and kid watching as his children engaged in a variety of emergent literacy activities. He therefore planned to keep notes on teacher-pupil conferences and to tape-record children's use of strategies in ongoing activities such as Big Books* sessions. As a way of helping himself identify a range of possible behaviors, he also devised an emergent reading checklist to help him keep track of children's use of specific strategies such as book awareness, cueing systems, and print and word awareness. He hoped such a checklist would be a useful tool for reporting to parents. (See Chapter 9.) The understandings gained through these processes would help him make sense of classroom life and identify and plan for individual needs.

See Goodman, Bird, & Goodman (1992, pp. 110–116) for a discussion of checklists.

As he began to develop the unit, he found that while he was able to cover some requirements of the science and math curriculum with the activities and resources he collected, the theme particularly lent itself to exploring concepts in social studies and music. While he felt comfortable developing projects and activities for the former, he was less knowledgeable about covering some of the musical concepts. He enlisted the help of Jon Petrillo, the school music specialist, who was delighted to be his coteacher. Finally, he involved Claire and her family and Ida Sylvester, a specialist in Deaf education, all of whom helped him to plan activities and projects that focused on the Deaf.

Integrated language teachers are good collaborators.

Table 4.3 *Weekly Schedule, Michael Silverman's First-Grade Class*

Time	Monday	Tuesday	Wednesday	Thursday	Friday
8:00	Teacher preparation time				
8:25	Children arrive, put down chairs, get supplies, and work on assignments or read a book.				
9:00	Group time. Discuss ongoing projects, introduce new assignments, introduce new materials, or share completed work.				
9:20	Integrated work time. Children work on individual or group projects. Teacher meets with small groups or has individual conferences.				
9:45	Recess				
10:00	Book time. Read book or poem to class. Discuss or follow up with an activity.				
10:30	Integrated work time. Continue with projects begun earlier or inspired by Reading Aloud*.				
11:10	Cleanup. Put away materials, supplies, projects, and assignments in storage areas.				
11:15	Sharing. Children share work with class, or teacher shares information relevant to the unit.				
11:30	Lunch and outdoor play				
12:15	Art	Music	Library	Art	Music
1:00	SSR* (Teacher has conferences with individual children.) Twice a week children have Buddy Reading* with second graders.				
1:35	Group time. Teacher reads aloud or focuses on special activity.				
1:55	Recess				
2:10	Integrated work time				
2:45	Cleanup. Pass out papers. Evaluate the day.				
3:00	Dismissal				

Into the Classroom

Michael begins the unit by bringing a large model of the human ear and a poster showing the manual alphabet that the speech pathologist Ida Sylvester has provided. He has arranged these and some other items (a conch shell, several glass bottles, a stethoscope, a drum, and a tuning fork) in a display in a corner of the room. As the children enter the room, many of them are attracted by the display. When the class gathers on the rug for morning meeting, Michael encourages them to hypothesize how they hear, asking if they can remember times when sounds seemed different. He asks the children what happens to sounds when they cover their ears. Several children talk about how sound is different when they are swimming underwater and others recall having a bad cold and getting an ear infection. One child tells how her ears got blocked up when she went for an airplane ride. Michael has planned some simple experiments with sounds for the unit, and at some point he may introduce more formal concepts of sound waves and vibrations, depending on the children's understandings. At this point, however, he asks the children to help him start a Graffiti Wall* listing some of the kinds of sounds that they hear throughout the day. The children decide to categorize the sounds according to the places they hear them and whether the sounds are pleasant or unpleasant.

Prototype 2: First Grade—SOUNDS ALL AROUND

Farmyard Sounds

THE COUNTRY NOISY BOOK

What noises would Muffin hear in your neighborhood? Make up new versions to fit the weather, a time of year, or a place.

OH, WHAT A NOISY FARM?
FIDDLE-I-FEE
A FARMYARD SONG
EARLY MORNING IN THE BARN
IT'S A PERFECT DAY
MY BARN
BARNYARD BANTER
BARNYARD SONG

Are the sounds these animals make the ones you expected? Make a chart of animal sounds. Draw pictures of animals that could make those sounds. Let people match the animal with the sound they think it could make.

WHO SAYS A DOG GOES BOW-WOW?

Interview people from other countries or cultures. Find out the sounds they have for these familiar animals.

COCK-A-DOODLE-MOO
"QUACK!" SAID THE BILLY-GOAT
THE COW THAT WENT OINK
THE PIG IN THE POND
OINK OINK

Act out other versions of these silly stories.

Familiar Farms

"Old Macdonald Had a Farm"
Sing this familiar song and make up new verses.

OLD MACDONALD HAD A FARM (HELLEN)
OLD MACDONALD HAD A FARM (ROUNDS)
OLD MACDONALD HAD A FARM (JONES)
OLD MACDONALD (SOUHAMI)
E-I-E-I-O

Read these versions. Construct a Comparison Chart*.

OLD MACDONALD HAD AN EMU

Make a list of animals you didn't know. Match them to the sounds that they make. Find out more about these Australian animals. Compose a version of the song for other countries or regions.

MS. MACDONALD HAD A CLASS
ONCE UPON MACDONALD'S FARM

Act out or retell the stories with a Puppet Show* or make up a new version.

Noisy Birds

BLACK CROW, BLACK CROW

Write your own counting book for a different bird or animal. Use a similar pattern.

COCK-A-DOODLE-DOO
COCK-A-DOODLE-DOO!
ONE RED ROOSTER
PROUD ROOSTER AND THE FOX
WHEN THE ROOSTER CROWED

Make a mural or Story Map* of the characters and events in these stories.

THE BROODY HEN
QUACK QUACK
QUACKY QUACK-QUACK
THE STORY OF LITTLE QUACK

Plan Choral Reading* or Readers' Theater* of these stories.

Too Much Noise

How much noise is too much for you? Do some sounds make you uncomfortable? Survey classmates and create a graph showing your findings.
Can too much noise hurt you? How can you protect yourself from too much noise?
Are there places in your school or community where there is too much noise? Find out what you can do to solve the problem.

TOO MUCH TALK
IT COULD ALWAYS BE WORSE
IT'S TOO NOISY
TOO MUCH NOISE
POSSUM COME A-KNOCKIN'
THE NOISEMAKERS
THE NOISY BOOK
NOISY NORA
THE NOISY BARN
BABY-O

Create dioramas and use them to retell these stories.

Buggy Sounds

What kinds of insects make noises? List all the insects you can think of. What purposes do sounds serve insects and other animals?

IN THE TALL TALL GRASS
OLD BLACK FLY
BUZZ BUZZ BUZZ
WHY MOSQUITOES BUZZ IN PEOPLE'S EARS
JOYFUL NOISE

Listen to several voices read these poems. How do the sounds of the words mimic the behavior of the insects?

THE VERY BUSY SPIDER
THE VERY QUIET CRICKET

Find out how insects and animals communicate. Is sound the only way to "talk"?

SOUNDS ALL AROUND

Noises at Night

How is noise different at night? Make a day/night comparison of noises in your house or neighborhood. Write words to describe the sounds you hear at each time.

DON'T WAKE THE BABY
I HEAR A NOISE
NIGHT NOISES
NO THUMPIN', NO BUMPIN', NO RUMPUS TONIGHT!
ONCE A LULLABY
THE SPOOKY EERIE NIGHT NOISE
WHOO-OO IS IT?

Tell a story of a noise that scared you at night.

SHADOWS OF THE NIGHT
ZIPPING, ZAPPING, ZOOMING BATS
AMAZING BATS
A FIRST LOOK AT BATS
A PROMISE TO THE SUN

Study bats. How do they hear noise?

The Sound of Music

RAT-A-TAT, PITTER PAT
ROOT-A-TOOT-TOOT
THUMP, THUMP, RAT-A-TAT-TAT TOOT!
PATAKIN: WORLD TALES OF DRUMS AND DRUMMERS

Listen to different types of musical instruments. Classify them as to the types of sound they make.

MUSICAL INSTRUMENTS OF THE WORLD
WHAT INSTRUMENT IS THIS?
MUSIC

Create your own classroom orchestra with simple instruments. Compose music to accompany a favorite story or poem.

Rainy Day Sounds

RAIN TALK
LISTEN TO THE RAIN
FOG
WHAT DOES THE RAIN PLAY?

Keep a weather observation Journal* and keep track of the sounds you hear on different weather days. Write your own weather story.

RUMBLE THUMBLE BOOM
FLASH, CRASH, RUMBLE AND ROLL

Find out what causes thunder.

Machine Sounds

"Bam, Bam, Bam"
CLICK, RUMBLE, ROAR: POEMS ABOUT MACHINES

Do Choral Readings* of some of these poems.

CRASH! BANG! BOOM!
ZIP, WHIZ, ZOOM!

Listen to the noises of machines in your neighborhood. Add some to the list.

Listen to the Story

Listen to storytellers, recordings of radio broadcasters, and audiotapes of poets reading their work.

How can we use our voices in interesting ways?

Tell a story and record it on audiotape. Plan a Storytelling* festival. Invite family members to come and tell stories.

Plan a Choral Reading* of some favorite poems. Use solo voices, small groups of voices, and the whole class. Change loudness and softness, and adjust pitch high and low.

Find out how sound effects are created for radio, television, or film. Create your own sound effects for a story you tell on audiotape or for a cartoon you draw.

Sounds of the Train

COUNTRY CROSSING
"Song of the Train"
"Riding on the Train"
TRAIN SONGS
TRAIN WHISTLES: A LANGUAGE IN CODE

Are there machine codes in your community? What other types of codes communicate messages?

Family Sayings

FIRST THINGS FIRST: AN ILLUSTRATED
  COLLECTION OF SAYINGS
SAY SOMETHING
YO! YES?
HONEY I LOVE AND OTHER POEMS
NATHANIEL TALKING
"Grandma's Bones"

Interview family members or neighbors. What are some sayings that are important to them? Make a Graffiti Wall* of sayings. Are there some from different cultures or countries that are alike?

What are conversation routines in your family? Does everyone talk at the dinner table or is everyone quiet? In your family is it all right for children to interrupt adults or should children always be quiet around adults?

Make a Comparison Chart* of talk etiquette, showing the differences and similarities that you find.

HOW YOU TALK

How are hearing and talking alike?
What were your first words?
What different languages are represented in your class? In the families of your class? Make a chart showing all the different languages spoken by the families in your class.
Find out if there are words in other languages that are similar to each other.

Listen for the Sound

QUIET, PLEASE
IF YOU LISTEN
JUST LISTEN
THE LISTENING WALK
THE OTHER WAY TO LISTEN
WHEN THE WOODS HUM
GOBBLE, GROWL, GRUNT

Take a walk outdoors. Listen for sounds of the natural world or the human-made world. Compile a list of all the sounds you hear that are natural or human-made. Make a picture or mural to show your findings.

Experiment with different kinds of sound. How would you categorize them?

ONE WINDY WEDNESDAY
THE QUIET FARMER
THE QUIET NOISY BOOK
THE QUIET MOTHER AND THE NOISY LITTLE
  BOY
SPEAK UP, BLANCHE!
THE TINIEST SOUND

Think of the quietest sound you know. Make a class book of "small" sounds.

City Sounds

GARAGE SONG
WHO'S THAT BANGING ON THE CEILING?
CITY SOUNDS (EMBERLEY)
CITY SOUNDS (BROWN)
CITY NOISE

How are city sounds different from country sounds?
What are some sound problems for people who live in a city?

How We Hear

EARS ARE FOR HEARING

Study a plaster model of the ear.
Interview an audiologist and learn about audiometers.
Find out what causes ear infections.
Make a survey about how many in your class have had ear infections. How many have had tubes in their ears?
Are there things that can cause you to lose your hearing?

THE MAGIC OF SOUND
THE SCIENCE BOOK OF SOUND
SOUND AND MUSIC

Conduct experiments with sound. Find out about people who work with sound.

Instead of Sound

HANDTALK BIRTHDAY: A NUMBER AND
  STORY BOOK IN SIGN LANGUAGE
HANDTALK
THE HANDMADE ALPHABET

Interview someone who knows sign language. Learn to sign.
Watch Linda Bove from *Sesame Street* sign a favorite story. Learn to do it, too.

AMY: THE STORY OF A DEAF CHILD
A BUTTON IN HER EAR
I HAVE A SISTER, MY SISTER IS DEAF
ANNA'S SILENT WORLD
WHAT IS THE SIGN FOR FRIEND?

How do people with hearing difficulties hear such things as alarms, doorbells, or the telephone?
Investigate inventions and other helps for the deaf. Borrow a closed-captions device from the library. Find out how it works.
Try out a TDD (Telephone Device for the Deaf). How could you help someone who cannot hear?

PUFF. . . FLASH. . .BANG!
  A BOOK ABOUT SIGNALS

Study the many ways to "talk."

Sounds in the Wild

CHICKA CHICKA BOOM BOOM
DO BUNNIES TALK?
17 KINGS AND 42 ELEPHANTS
AWFUL AARDVARK
CROCODILE BEAT
THE HAPPY HIPPOPOTAMI
IN THE TALL, TALL GRASS
IN THE SMALL, SMALL POND
JUNGLE SOUNDS
THE ANIMAL THAT DRANK UP
  SOUND

Create sound effects to go with one of these stories.
Find out how sound effects are created for radio and television.

HOOT, HOWL, HISS
POLAR BEAR, POLAR BEAR,
  WHAT DO YOU HEAR?
ROAR AND MORE
JUNGLE SOUNDS

Make a book of wild animal noises. Write the words so they look like the sound.

Underwater and Underground

WHALE SONG
THE WHALE'S SONG
ALL ABOUT WHALES

Find out how whales, dolphins, and other sea creatures use sound to communicate.
Listen to whale songs and dolphin talk.
Find out about ultrasound pictures. Did you have a sound picture taken of you?
Study bat communication.
Does the earth talk? Find out how seismographs work.

This discussion will allow Michael to introduce children to some of the topics to be explored during the course of the unit and will eventually develop into other central inquiries—the topic of noise pollution in and out of the classroom and a study of personal, family, and cultural linguistic patterns. This initial activity will also set the stage for the topic of "Instead of Sound" and provide children with the opportunities to learn about Claire's sister and other Deaf people and their rich culture. Claire's mother, Mrs. Jensen, has volunteered to work with the children over several days, answering questions and teaching them the manual alphabet and simple signs. Her sister Melanie has been invited to visit later with a sign language interpreter. Michael feels that in addition to learning about alternative forms of communication, learning manual signs will provide a wonderful kinesthetic mode of representing letters for young children learning the alphabet. Mrs. Jensen has also suggested that the class explore technological and other aids, such as pets, that are available to help the hearing-impaired. Michael is hoping that as the children talk about what they have learned from their experiences, they may make suggestions for helping people in the community who have a hearing loss and also understand how they might improve the environment for the Deaf and the hearing.

In addition to these important investigations, Michael has a great sense of fun and, as Table 4.4 shows, he has planned many opportunities for playing with language during the course of the unit. The topics "Familiar Farms," "Farmyard Sounds," and "Noisy Birds" incorporate favorite songs and funny characters, and he expects that many children will want to dramatize, retell, or respond to the stories with art and music of their own. Many of the books and activities offer opportunities for children to explore written codes for sounds and to see how these can be manipulated. For example, while many of the books use traditional animal sounds, such as "bow-wow" for *Brown (1991)* dogs and "cock-a-doodle doo" for roosters, others such as *My Barn* by Craig Brown use "ruff-ruff-ruuuufff" and "er-er-errrr-er-ererer-errr" instead. The patterns of these books offer the children models for making up their own versions and exploring letter-sound relationships and the concept of onomatopoeia.

Many of the books Michael has chosen use print in unusual graphic ways: the print is as much a part of the pictorial text as of the verbal text. In *Quacky Quack-Quack!* by *Whybrow (1991)* Ian Whybrow, the animal sounds are printed in a large decorative type that flows across *Most (1990)* the page, while in Bernard Most's *The Cow That Went Oink*, the sounds are printed in speech balloons. Stories like these draw children's attention to the written language code and also offer opportunities for shared reading, Readers' Theater*, and individual or small group rereading. As Michael has planned to observe the children's emergent reading abilities during this unit, these books provide many opportunities for him to engage in kid watching and systematic data collection, using an emergent reading and writing checklist he has developed.

Table 4.4 *Detailed Schedule, Michael Silverman's First-Grade Class*

Day 5

Time	Children	Teacher	Teacher Research
Teacher Arrival 8:00		Michael arrives to set out special supplies. He takes time to look through children's work folders.	Michael identifies several papers that will be useful beginning writing samples. These will form a basis for comparison over time.
Children Arrival 8:25	Children arrive and begin putting away lunches. Many go to the reading corner. Several assemble at the display table and examine the objects that Michael set up for sound experiments.	Michael greets the children, prepares the lunch count, and take attendance.	
Group Time 9:00	Several children have brought objects that they want the others to "listen" to. These include a dried seed pod, a snake skin, and a bird's nest.	Michael calls on children who want to share their listening objects with the class. He suggests that they might want to write about why they	

(continued)

Table 4.4 *Detailed Schedule, Michael Silverman's First-Grade Class (continued)*

Day 5

Time	Children	Teacher	Teacher Research
	They were inspired by the book *The Other Way to Listen* that Michael read several days before. They suggest that these be added to the sound center.	chose those objects or make a label for the display. He reads a poem by Eloise Greenfield he has found called "Nathaniel Talking." He asks children if there are special sayings or "talk" in their families. He invites them to write them or dictate them for the Graffiti Wall* during the course of the unit.	
Integrated Work Time 9:20	Children move to the work area, stopping to get supplies they need from their dishtubs (stored on shelves). Many are involved in ongoing projects begun in previous days. Four children are working on a Puppet Show* for their version of *Old Macdonald Had an Emu.* Several are working on illustrations for a Big Book* version of *In the Tall, Tall Grass.* Another group is completing a Comparison Chart* of the different illustrated versions of *Old Macdonald.* The children in Mrs. Jensen's group negotiate the new text as she demonstrates the process of composing. A group is conducting a simple experiment in which they bounce sound off different types of materials; another is making instruments out of found objects.	Michael asks for volunteers to participate in a shared writing experience with Mrs. Jensen, Claire's mother, and another group to work with him on a sound experiment. He writes the ongoing activities on the blackboard. As part of a Group-Composed Writing* exercise, Mrs. Jensen works with a group of children in writing a first draft of a new version of *A Farmyard Song.* Michael gets the sound experiment group started with an experiment in which they bounce sound off different hard and soft surfaces. He encourages them to hypothesize or predict results and gives them a simple chart to record their findings.	Later, Michael will return to observe the Group-Composed Writing* session to take notes on the children's contributions and their knowledge of written text.
Recess 9:45	The children who have been working on homemade instruments take them outside to practice.		
Book Time 10:00	Children enjoy hearing the story.	After recess Michael reads *Too Much Noise.* After the children have responded to the book Michael asks children if they think there are places in the school or community where there is too much noise. He invites them to be on the "listen-out" and be prepared to share findings tomorrow.	
Integrated Time 10:30	Children continue projects begun earlier. The children who worked with Mrs. Jensen on their version of *A Farmyard Song* begin work on illustrations for a bulletin board display.	Michael uses the time to visit the different groups and observe children's literacy behaviors. Mrs. Jensen transfers their draft to sheets of construction paper that will accompany their drawings on the bulletin board.	During his observation, Michael uses an emergent literacy observation checklist he has developed.
Sharing 11:15	Children share the work they've been involved in throughout the morning.	Michael asks for volunteers from several of the groups to share their morning experiences.	
Music 12:15	The children respond with a variety of words. Some describe the instruments as having a happy, sad, ringy, high, and low sounds.	The children go to the music room where teacher Jon Petrillo has assembled different instruments to illustrate four major classifications of musical instruments. He breaks the children into groups, gives them time to try the instruments out, and	

(continued)

Table 4.4   *Detailed Schedule, Michael Silverman's First-Grade Class (continued)*

Day 5

Time	Children	Teacher	Teacher Research
		then asks them to listen carefully and try to describe the types of sounds they hear. He makes a list of their findings and then shows them that the instruments can also be classified as wind, string, keyboard, or percussion instruments, demonstrating each one. He asks the children if they can add some of the instruments they have been making in class to these categories. He invites children to plan to incorporate simple instruments and compositions into the projects they will be doing in the coming weeks. The group brainstorms some ways that they might add more music to their activities.	
SSR 1:00	Children engage in Buddy Reading* with members of a second grade class. Each child has brought a book to read aloud to the other child.	Michael holds individual conferences with three children. He listens to them read, takes dictation, or reads their writing with them.	Michael takes notes on the emergent literacy concepts and patterns of phonological awareness he observes during the sessions. Although he doesn't give a Modified Miscue Analysis (see Chapter 8) at this time, he jots down information about miscues and the strategies the children are using.
Group Time 1:35	The children try out some of the signs they are introduced to on the tape.

Several children tell the class that they have met Claire's sister Melanie who is deaf. | Michael shows a videotape of Linda Bove from *Sesame Street* signing the story "Little Red Riding Hood." He asks how signing is another way to speak and he asks them what they know about deafness. Michael reintroduces Mrs. Jensen, Melanie and Claire's mother, who has been working with the class, and tells them she will be coming to class all week. Next week she will bring Melanie to visit the class. Mrs. Jensen does several short book talks on some of the books about sign language and the deaf and hands these out to interested children. | |
| Integrated Work Time 2:10 | Some children return to activities begun earlier. The sound experiment group and the musical instrument group change places. | Michael gets the new groups started and then meets with children who have finished activities for individual conferences. | Michael continues to collect data during these conferences. He uses the checklist he has developed, noting print and word awareness and whether he feels the child is beginning to use particular visual cues. |
| Cleanup/ Evaluation 2:45 | Children put away supplies and join the group. | Michael asks each child what project was worked on during the day and whether it was completed. He notes which children are finished with a project and suggests some choices they might like to consider the following day. He finishes with another poem by Eloise Greenfield called "Grandma's Bones" and reminds them to ask about family sayings to add to the Graffiti Wall*. | |

(continued)

Table 4.4 *Detailed Schedule, Michael Silverman's First-Grade Class (continued)*

Day 6

Time	Children	Teacher	Teacher Research
Group Time 9:00	Some of the children mention that they like to read in quiet places. One of the children tells the class that his older brother likes to do homework with the radio playing and that his mother argues about this with him. Other children say that they don't mind noise when they are writing but sometimes they can't hear when Michael does experiments because of the noise from the other classes in the pod. One of the children says that sometimes the noise during lunch in the cafeteria gives her a headache.	Michael reads *The Quiet Noisy Book* and invites the children to talk about their feelings about noise and quiet. Michael suggests that they make a chart of the things they do that need quiet places and the things they do that need noisy places. He invites children to interview some of their classmates about their noise preferences.	
Integrated Work Time 9:20	Many children are involved with ongoing projects. Other children elect to be involved in the activities previously done by other groups. The interview group decides they want to interview other students in the pod about whether they think they should be allowed to talk during lunch.	Michael works with one group to generate questions for their interviews. Michael suggests that they might want to interview the principal and some teachers about this issue, too.	He encourages the children to write down their questions on separate sheets of paper and takes notes on comments they make as they attempt to spell the words. He encourages them to help each other and is interested in the kind of strategies they have to share.
Book Time 10:00	The class reads through the poem together several times and then decides to make their voices loud and soft and high and low in different places. One of the children suggests that they do physical movements to the poem as well as sound effects.	Michael reads the poem "Bam, Bam, Bam" by Eve Merriam. He has written it out on chart paper and suggests that the class try a Choral Reading* of the poem. He asks for their advice on changing the sound of their voices for different parts of the poem.	
Library 12:15	SSR* with library books. George reads a mystery he has been dying to finish. Several children talk about their books at the end of the time.		
Group Time 1:35	The children have many questions for both Mrs. Jensen and Claire. They want to know how she became deaf and if it can happen to them. Some cover their ears with their hands to try and imagine what it is like to be deaf. Soon all the children are trying this. They have a good time learning the signs. One child says watching Linda Bove and Mrs. Jensen sign is like looking at people dancing.	Mrs. Jensen has returned to talk with the children about the hearing-impaired and how the family has learned to communicate with Melanie. She teaches them the signs for *hello, my,* and *name*. She asks them to think of ways that they might help people who have trouble hearing and promises to return at a later date to hear their ideas.	

Day 10

Time	Children	Teacher	Teacher Research
Group Time 9:00	The children have found that students and teachers feel there are two important noise problems in the school. One is the noise in the open areas. A second is the noise in the	Michael asks the group of children who have been interviewing to share the results of their study.	

(continued)

Table 4.4 *DETAILED SCHEDULE, MICHAEL SILVERMAN'S FIRST-GRADE CLASS (CONTINUED)*

Day 10

Time	Children	Teacher	Teacher Research
	cafeteria during lunchtime. In the discussion, children decide that they could put posters up in the pods to remind people to use "indoor" voices. They wonder if there is an enclosed space that classes could use for times when they might make more noise. They decide that the noisy cafeteria is a big problem and something they want to try and work on as a group.	Michael asks if there might be something they can do to solve the problem. Michael suggests that they all talk the problem over with their families and see if they can suggest some solutions. He promises more time the following day to brainstorm ideas.	
Integrated Work Time 9:20	Children continue on previous projects. One group is planning a Puppet Show* with sound effects. Another group is working with Mrs. Jensen on a sign language version of "The Three Bears."	Michael has conferences with individual children.	
Book Time 10:00	The children volunteer to use the masking device. They look for various features of print, and many can articulate the strategies they use in looking at the printed language. The children enjoy the idea of the marching band and decide that this is a story that they want to use their instruments with.	Michael reads a Big Book* version of *Thump, Thump, Rat-a-Tat-Tat*. He then uses a masking device and asks different children to use it to mask things such as a letter they know, a small word, or a word with a short *a* sound. As children carry out these tasks, he asks them to talk about why or how they made their choices. Their answers provide useful information about strategies and concepts of print.	Children's responses and their explanations of why and how they made choices provide useful information about strategies and concepts of print, as well as of their growing familiarity with phonology. Michael makes notes about individual strategies in a small notebook.

Summary

The SOUNDS ALL AROUND theme provides these first graders the means to explore the world of printed language in a variety of developmentally appropriate ways. The children's growing understanding of emergent reading and writing, concepts that Michael was able to document through his own research, was reassuring to parents and district professionals who had at first been unsure about his integrated language perspective. Just as importantly, the literature that was part of the unit was experienced and enjoyed in natural ways. Michael does not feel that he has to "use" a book or a poem to teach phonics; he knows that planned activities and the experiences the children have chosen to respond to the books naturally support the development of their literacy sets.

The unit also provides Michael's first-graders with many opportunities for focused inquiry around such *essential questions* as: How does sound effect us? How can we control sounds? How can we communicate without sound? How can we use what we have learned to change our environment? As a result of their study of the effects of sound, they campaigned to have a traffic light installed in the cafeteria. When the noise level during lunchtime is acceptable, the light shows green, but when it increases, the light changes to yellow. A red light indicates that talk should stop for a minute. In realizing their ability to make changes in their school surroundings, they are learning how citizens can effect change in the larger society. Through other inquiries they have become involved in their environment in a variety of ways and gained understanding and respect for individual differences within their class and cultural differences between their classmates' families. They have discovered interesting differences in family talk at meal-

Children take action to solve real problems.

times and found several wonderful storytellers among the relatives of several children. These family members were invited to class for a Storytelling* festival that culminated the unit. Finally, because one of their classmates is directly affected by a sister who is deaf, they have a unique opportunity to learn firsthand about the differently abled and to participate in that special world in a personal way. The understandings the children have gained over the course of the unit not only support their growth as competent language learners but also heighten their sensitivity to the diversity in the world around them and their future role as change agents.

Children's Literature: SOUNDS ALL AROUND

All about Whales by D. H. Patent. Holiday House, 1987.

Amazing Bats by F. Greenway. Photographs by J. Young & F. Greenway. Knopf, 1991.

Amy: The Story of a Deaf Child by L. A. Walker. Photographs by M. Abramson. Dutton, 1985.

The Animal that Drank Up Sound by W. Stafford. Illustrated by D. Fraser. HBJ, 1992.

Anna's Silent World by B. Wolf. Lippincott, 1977.

Awful Aardvark by Mwalimu. Illustrated by A. Kennaway. Little Brown, 1989.

Baby-O by N. W. Carlstrom. Illustrated by S. Stevenson. Little, Brown, 1992.

"Bam, Bam, Bam" in *Jamboree Rhymes for Everyone* by E. Merriman. Illustrated by W. Gaffney-Kessell. Dell, 1984.

Barnyard Banter by D. Fleming. Holt, 1994.

Barnyard Song by R. Greene. Illustrated by R. Bender. Simon, 1997.

Black Crow, Black Crow by G. F. Guy. Illustrated by N. W. Parker. Greenwillow, 1991.

The Broody Hen by O. Dunrea. Doubleday, 1992.

A Button in Her Ear by A. B. Litchfield. Illustrated by E. Mill. Whitman, 1976.

Buzz Buzz Buzz by B. Barton. Puffin, 1979.

Chicka Chicka Boom Boom by B. Martin & J. Archambault. Illustrated by L. Ehlert. Simon & Schuster, 1989.

City Noise by K. Kuskin. Illustrated by R. Flowers. HarperCollins, 1994.

City Sounds by C. Brown. Greenwillow, 1992.

City Sounds by R. Emberley. Little, Brown, 1989.

Click Rumble Roar: Poems About Machines. Selected by L. B. Hopkins. Photographs by A. H. Audette. Crowell, 1987.

Cock-A-Doodle-Doo! by J. Runcie. Illustrated by L. Lorenz. Simon & Schuster, 1991.

Cock-A-Doodle-Doo by F. Brandenberg. Illustrated by Aliki. Greenwillow, 1986.

Cock-A-Doodle-Moo by B. Most. Harcourt, 1996.

Country Crossing by J. Aylesworth. Illustrated by T. Rand. Atheneum, 1991.

The Country Noisy Book by M. W. Brown. Illustrated by L. Weisgard. Harper, 1993.

The Cow that Went Oink by B. Most. HBJ, 1990.

Crash! Bang! Boom! by P. Spier. Doubleday, 1972.

Crocodile Beat by G. Jorgensen. Illustrated by P. Mullins. Bradbury, 1988.

Do Bunnies Talk? by D. A. Dodds. Illustrated by A. Dubanevich. HarperCollins, 1992.

Don't Wake the Baby by J. Franklin. Farrar, Straus, & Giroux, 1992.

E-I-E-I-O by G. Clarke. Lothrop, 1992.

Early Morning in the Barn by N. Tafuri. Greenwillow, 1983.

Ears Are for Hearing by P. Showers. Illustrated by H. Keller. Crowell, 1990.

A Farmyard Song by C. Manson. North-South, 1992.

Fiddle-I Fee by D. Stanley. Little, Brown, 1979.

A First Look at Bats by M. Selsam & J. Hunt. Walker, 1991.

First Things First: An Illustrated Collection of Sayings Useful and Familiar for Children by B. Fraser. Harper, 1990.

Flash, Crash, Rumble, and Roll by F. Branley. Illustrated by B. Emberley & E. Emberley. Crowell, 1985.

Fog by S. G. Fowler. Illustrated by J. Fowler. Greenwillow, 1992.

Garage Song by S. Wilson. Illustrated by B. Kaplan. Simon & Schuster, 1991.

Gobble, Growl, Grunt by P. Spier. Doubleday, 1971.

"Grandma's Bones" in *Nathaniel Talking* by E. Greenfield. Illustrated by J. S. Gilchrist. Black Butterfly Children's Books, 1988.

The Handmade Alphabet by L. Rankin. Dial, 1992.

Handtalk Birthday: A Number and Story Book in Sign Language by R. Charlip & M. B. Miller. Photographs by G. Ancona. Four Winds, 1987.

Handtalk: An ABC of Finger Spelling and Sign Language by R. Charlip & M. B. Miller. Photographs by G. Ancona. Macmillan, 1974.

The Happy Hippopotami by B. Martin Jr. Illustrated by B. Everitt. HBJ, 1991.

Honey I Love and Other Poems by E. Greenfield. Illustrated by L. Dillon & D. Dillon. HarperCollins, 1978.

Hoot, Howl, Hiss by M. Koch. Greenwillow, 1991.

How You Talk by P. Showers. Illustrated by M. Lloyd. HarperCollins, 1992.

I Have a Sister, My Sister Is Deaf by J. Peterson. Illustrated by D. Ray. HarperCollins, 1984.

I Hear a Noise by D. Goode. Dutton, 1987.

If You Listen by C. Zolotow. Illustrated by M. Simont. Harper, 1980.

In the Small, Small Pond by D. Fleming. Holt, 1993.

In the Tall, Tall Grass by D. Fleming. Holt, 1991.

It Could Always Be Worse by M. Zemach. Farrar, Straus, & Giroux, 1977.

It's a Perfect Day by A. Pizer. HarperCollins, 1990.

It's Too Noisy by J. Cole. Illustrated by K. Duke. Crowell, 1989.

Joyful Noise: Poems For Two Voices by P. Fleischman. HarperCollins, 1988.

Jungle Sounds by R. Emberly. Little, Brown, 1989.

Just Listen by W. Morris. Illustrated by P. Cullen-Clark. Atheneum, 1990.

Listen to the Rain by B. Martin Jr. & J. Archambault. Illustrated by J. Endicott. Henry Holt, 1988.

The Listening Walk by P. Showers. Illustrated by Aliki. Harper-Collins, 1991.

The Magic of Sound by L. Kettlekamp. Illustrated by A. Kramer. Morrow, 1982.

Ms. Macdonald Had a Class by J. Ormerod. Clarion, 1996.

Music by N. Ardley. Photographs by D. King. Knopf, 1989.

Musical Instruments of the World by UNICEF. Facts on File, 1976.

My Barn by C. Brown. Greenwillow, 1991.

Nathaniel Talking by E. Greenfield. Illustrated by J. S. Gilchrist. Black Butterfly Children's Books, 1988.

Night Noises by M. Fox. Illustrated by T. Denton. Harcourt, 1989.

No Thumpin', No Bumpin', No Rumpus Tonight! by N. Patz. Atheneum, 1990.

The Noisemakers by J. Caseley. Greenwillow, 1992.

The Noisy Barn by H. Zeifert. Illustrated by S. Taback. Harper-Collins, 1991.

The Noisy Book by M. W. Brown. Illustrated by L. Weisgard. HarperCollins, 1993.

Noisy Nora by R. Wells. Dial, 1997.

Oh, What a Noisy Farm! by H. Zeifert. Illustrated by E. Bolam. Tambourine, 1995.

Oink Oink by A. Geisert. Houghton Mifflin, 1993.

Old Black Fly by J. Aylesworth. Illustrated by S. Gammell. Holt, 1992.

Old Macdonald by J. Souhami. Illustrated by P. McAlindon. Orchard, 1996.

Old Macdonald Had a Farm by N. Hellen. Orchard Books, 1990.

Old Macdonald Had a Farm. Illustrated by C. Jones. Houghton Mifflin, 1988.

Old Macdonald Had a Farm. Illustrated by G. Rounds. Holiday House, 1989.

Old Macdonald Had an Emu by D. Niland. Hodder and Stoughton, 1986.

Once a Lullaby by B. P. Nichol. Illustrated by A. Lobel. Greenwillow, 1986.

Once Upon Macdonald's Farm by S. Gammell. Four Winds, 1981.

One Red Rooster by K. S. Carroll. Illustrated by S. Barbier. Houghton Mifflin, 1992.

One Windy Wednesday by P. Root. Illustrated by H. Craig. Candlewick, 1996.

The Other Way to Listen by B. Baylor. Illustrated by P. Parnall. Scribners, 1978.

Patakin: World Tales of Drums and Drummers by N. Jaffe. Illustrated by E. Eagle. Holt, 1994.

The Pig in the Pond by M. Waddell & Jill Barton. Candlewick, 1992.

Polar Bear, Polar Bear, What do You Hear? by B. Martin Jr. Illustrated by E. Carle. Henry Holt, 1991.

Possum Come A-Knockin' by N. Van Laan. Illustrated by G. Booth. Knopf, 1990.

A Promise to the Sun: A Story of Africa by T. Mollel. Illustrated by B. Vidal. Little, Brown, 1992.

Proud Rooster and the Fox by C. Threadgill. Tambourine, 1991.

Puff . . . Flash . . . Bang! A Book About Signals by G. Gibbons. Morrow, 1993.

Quack Quack by P. Casey. Lothrop, 1988.

"Quack!" Said the Billy-Goat by C. Causley. Illustrated by B. Firth. Lippincott, 1986.

Quacky Quack-Quack! by I. Whybrow. Illustrated by R. Ayto. Four Winds, 1991.

The Quiet Farmer by M. Mcgee. Illustrated by L. Dennis. Atheneum, 1991.

The Quiet Mother and the Noisy Little Boy by C. Zolotow. Illustrated by M. Simont. Harper, 1989.

The Quiet Noisy Book by M. W. Brown. Illustrated by L. Weisgard. HarperCollins, 1950.

Quiet, Please by E. Merriam. Illustrated by S. Hamanaka. Simon & Schuster, 1993.

Rain Talk by M. Serfozo. Illustrated by K. Narahshi. McElderry, 1990.

Rat-A-Tat, Pitter Pat by A. Benjamin. Illustrated by M. Miller. Crowell, 1987.

"Riding on the Train" in *Honey I Love and Other Poems* by E. Greenfield. Illustrated by L. Dillon & D. Dillon. Harper-Collins, 1978.

Roar and More by K. Kushkin. Harper, 1990.

Root-A-Toot-Toot by A. Rockwell. Macmillan, 1991.

Rumble Thumble Boom by Hines. A. G. Greenwillow, 1992.

Say Something by M. Stolz. Illustrated by A. Koshkin. Harper-Collins, 1993.

The Science Book of Sound by N. Ardley. HBJ, 1991.

17 Kings and 42 Elephants by M. Mahy. Illustrated by P. MacCarthy. Dial, 1987.

Shadows of the Night: The Hidden World of the Little Brown Bat by B. Bash. Sierra, 1993.

"Song of the Train" in *One at a Time* by D. McCord. Little, Brown, 1986.

Sound and Music by D. Evans & C. Willins. Dorling Kindersley, 1993.

Speak Up, Blanche! by E. A. McCully. HarperCollins, 1991.

The Spooky Eerie Night Noise by M. R. Reeves. Illustrated by P. Yalowitz. Bradbury, 1989.

The Story of Little Quack by B. Gibson. Illustrated by K. M. Denton. Joy Street, 1991.

Thump Thump Rat-A-Tat by G. Baer. Illustrated by L. Ehlert. Harper & Row, 1989.

The Tiniest Sound by M. Evans. Illustrated by N. W. Parker. Greenwillow, 1991.

Too Much Noise by A. McGovern. Illustrated by S. Taback. Houghton Mifflin, 1967.

Too Much Talk by A. S. Meddaris. Illustrated by S. Vitale. Candlewick, 1995.

Toot! by T. Gomi. Morrow, 1979.

Train Songs by D. Siebert. Paintings by M. Wimmer. Crowell, 1990.

Train Whistles: A Language in Code by H. R. Sattler. Illustrated by G. Maestro. Lothrop, 1985.

The Very Busy Spider by E. Carle. Philomel, 1985.

The Very Quiet Cricket by E. Carle. Philomel, 1990.

Whale Song by T. Johnson. Illustrated by E. Young. Putnam, 1987.

The Whale's Song by D. Sheldon. Illustrated by G. Blythe. Dial, 1990.

What Does the Rain Play? by N. W. Carlstrom. Illustrated by H. Sorensen. Macmillan, 1993.

What Instrument Is This? by R. Hausherr. Scholastic, 1992.

What Is the Sign for Friend? by J. E. Greenberg. Photographs by C. Rothschild. Franklin Watts, 1985.

When the Rooster Crowed by P. Lillie. Illustrated by N. W. Parker. Greenwillow, 1991.

When the Woods Hum by J. Ryder. Illustrated by C. Stock. Morrow, 1991.

Who Says a Dog Goes Bow-Wow? by H. De Sutter. Illustrated by S. MacDonald. Doubleday, 1992.

Who's That Banging on the Ceiling? by C. McNaughton. Candlewick, 1992.

Whoo-oo Is It? by M. McDonald. Illustrated by S. D. Schindler. Orchard, 1992.

Why Mosquitoes Buzz in People's Ears by V. Aardema. Illustrated by L. Dillon and D. Dillon. Dial, 1975.

Yo! Yes? by C. Raschka. Orchard Books, 1993.

Zip, Whiz, Zoom! by S. Calmeson. Illustrated by D. Stott. Little, Brown, 1992.

Zipping, Zapping, Zooming Bats by A. Earle. Illustrated by H. Cole. HarperCollins, 1995.

Prototype 3: Second Grade—LET'S EAT!
Schedule

The schedule for Prototype 3 is based on activity in a self-contained, integrated-day second-grade classroom. As the LET'S EAT! WEB indicates, there are activities planned to involve parents and other adults from outside the school. Although this technique is not always necessary, it can be an important way in which to involve other adults in the school and to build interest in and support for school programs.

The theme in this classroom fits with a common primary health and science unit on nutrition and attempts to put the concept of nutrition into cultural context, focusing on different customs and occasions for eating, problems of hunger and malnutrition, and ways in which children can be problem alleviators even in the primary grades. The teacher, Carol Hagihara, introduces the theme with a piece of literature, *The Hungry Thing* by Jan Slepian and Ann Seidler, a humorous story about hunger and communication that is enjoyable for young children and that easily leads into a variety of extension activities. Table 4.5 (see p. 110) shows how Carol blocks class time for the week. Note that Carol's schedule allows for movement from whole group to small group to individual activities throughout the day and allows for quieter times—poetry sharing, for instance—to follow more active periods such as physical education.

Slepian & Seidler (1967)

Carol has also organized the integrated worktime around activity centers. Children rotate through groups over the course of the day or week, but not every child will spend time or the same amount of time in each center. Instead, Carol plans with the children for individual, group, and whole class responsibilities. Carol also uses a parent volunteer in one center. Although this is not necessary, it is certainly a worthwhile involvement of an interested parent, and it allows Carol to use a cooking experience in a small group that might otherwise have been awkward to arrange. Carol's school also has an outdoor education program that culminates in a fifth-grade overnight and a sixth-grade four-day camping trip. As a result, Carol has responsibility for planning outdoor experiences (one block of time on Fridays) to prepare her children for the overnight and camping trips when they are older. On Monday through Thursday, however, her children go to classes in art, music, and physical education, and Carol has a fifty-minute planning period on each of those days.

Carol has also established a Buddy Reading* program in which older students are matched with children in her class for an allotted time to read together. Finally, Carol's teacher research project will study how children apply and learn mathematical concepts. She asks children to keep a special journal where they can keep all their work related to this inquiry. Carol also keeps a triple-entry journal. In one column she records suggestions and activities she develops that relate to mathematics; in the second column, her observations of student responses to these tasks; and in the third column, her evaluation of the task and student response. By collecting student journals and comparing them to her own journal, Carol can begin to see patterns and compare her own observations with those of students.

Prototype 3: Second Grade—LET'S EAT!

Where Does Food Come From?

TRAINS AT WORK
THE TORTILLA FACTORY
HOW A SEED GROWS
KNOW YOUR FRUITS
KNOW YOUR VEGETABLES
HOE, HOE, HOE, WATCH MY GARDEN GROW
MILK
THE AMAZING EGG BOOK
THE AMAZING POTATO

Make a chart of different types of food and where
   they come from.
Make a diagram of the travels one kind of food
   takes to get to your table.
Grow food plants. Chart their growth.
Classify seeds and plants. Label your categories and
   display them in the room.
Try new fruits and vegetables.

Food Changes

GROWING VEGETABLE SOUP
WHAT HAPPENS TO A HAMBURGER?
ICE CREAM SOUP
OF CABBAGES AND CHEMISTRY
FOODWORKS

List all the ways food changes when it is cooked
   and eaten.
Bake bread, and observe the changes. Write the recipe.
Grow mold on food. View under a microscope. Keep a
   log of changes under different conditions, using
   different foods.
Find out what uses can be made of mold.
Find out how food changes in the body. Make a chart
   of how food helps humans.

Food Chains

Make food chains/pyramids to
   hang from ceiling.
Play "Food Chain." (OBIS).
Build a terrarium or aquarium.

FOOD SCIENCE

Arts

Display art with a food theme.
Display ways in which food can be
   used to make art (potato prints and
   the like).
Illustrate stories or poems about food.
Make scenery for a performance.
Make invitations to a luncheon.
Collect examples of artistic ways to
   display or hold foods. Make cross-
   cultural comparisons.

FOOD ART

Advertisements

AN EDIBLE ALPHABET

Write ads for favorite foods.
Collect ads in newspapers and magazines. Analyze
   techniques used.
Make a display of the best ads you can find for foods
   that are necessary for good health. Compare them
   with ads for foods high in sugar.

FUN WITH FOOD

Food in Poems and Stories

CLIVE EATS ALLIGATORS
THE HUNGRY THING
THE FUNNY LITTLE WOMAN
RHINOS FOR LUNCH, ELEPHANTS FOR SUPPER
THIS DELICIOUS DAY: 65 POEMS
CLOUDY WITH A CHANCE OF MEATBALLS
"I'm Hungry" section of RANDOM HOUSE BOOK POETRY
THE LITTLE PIGS' COOKBOOK
BON APPETIT, MR. RABBIT
THE CHOCOLATE TOUCH
"Adelaide"
PASS THE FRITTERS, CRITTERS
BURGOO STEW
SEVEN LOAVES OF BREAD
PEOPLE OF CORN
JALAPENO BAGELS
A SPACEBURGER
MEAN SOUP
THE FINE ROUND CAKE
TOPS AND BOTTOMS

Share food stories. What are the common elements in each of
   these stories? Make a chart of food in literature,
   categorized by real, magic, and so on.
Make a literary feast. Make foods described in stories (pasta,
   rice balls).
Write poems about favorite, least favorite, or funny foods.
What is the most common food in poetry?
Write a script for a performance to be given during the luncheon.
Compose a food symphony.

Food Jokes

GOING BANANAS: JOKES FOR KIDS
MY LITTLE SISTER ATE ONE HARE

Make a Big Book* of food jokes,
   collected by surveying community
   people.
Share food jokes.
Make up your own food jokes.

Field Trips

ROUND TRIP
A FRUIT AND VEGETABLE MAN
SATURDAY SANCOCHO

Try international food in a restaurant.
Inventory types of food, prices, etc.
   in a grocery store.
Pick apples or berries at a farm or
   orchard.
See how peanut butter, cereal, or
   other food is made at a food
   processing plant.
Volunteer to help at a food bank or
   community kitchen.

Cooking Math

Calculate measurements for recipes.
How much is a teaspoon, tablespoon, or other quantity?
Match the spoon with the proper measurement.
List all the food items that come in fractions.
Measure the difference in volume between cooked and uncooked food.
Display all the types of measures used in cooking. Label the display and use it during cooking.

Grocery Math

A GRAIN OF RICE
WHAT COMES IN 2'S, 3'S AND 4'S?
COUNT YOUR WAY THROUGH AFRICA
JELLY BEANS FOR SALE

Calculate the cost of a meal or groceries on a list.
Cut out food ads from the paper, and categorize by cost.
Figure cost of "average" American and Third World meals.
Visit the grocery store and purchase food for class use.
What foods come in 2's, 3's, and 4's?

Helping the Hungry

KIDS ENDING HUNGER: WHAT CAN WE DO?
UNCLE WILLIE AND THE FOOD KITCHEN
FOOD FIGHT
THE RETURN OF THE BUFFALOES

Collect food for a local food bank. Check to see what is needed.
Donate time to help with boxing food, stacking shelves, and other activities at a pantry or food bank.
Write letters to community officials and newspapers about hunger-related issues.
Raise funds to help CARE or a similar organization fight hunger.

Comparing Past and Future

Find out what "average" meals were like when your grandparents were young. What things have changed since then?
Conduct an "eating out" survey.
Make a "prediction" almanac of future meals and food habits.
Survey grocery stores to see what foods sell best, what "new" foods and new packaging are, etc.

Sharing Food

Invite a greengrocer and do a taste test.
Invite guests to the luncheon and perform or share what you have learned.
Invite an international guest to speak about customs. Share some of your own with him.

FOOD MATH

LET'S EAT

WHO EATS?

Who Has the Food?

Make a world distribution simulation.
Distribute a snack on the basis of food distribution in the world. Consider ways to resolve problems.
"Please pass the potatoes" activity.
Find articles on hunger in the world.
What is being done? Is there hunger in your area?
Fill grocery sacks with the food that an average American family consumes in a week and one for a developing nation. Discuss.

Food Geography

OX-CART MAN
BREAD, BREAD, BREAD
POSSUM MAGIC
HOW TO MAKE APPLE PIE AND SEE THE WORLD

Find ways to represent the number of people who do not have enough to eat.
Place markers on a world map to indicate the places of origin for different types of food.
Make a chart showing all the countries that contribute ingredients to a favorite snack (candy bar, ice cream, etc.).
Trace different names for food by region (e.g. sub, hoagie, hero sandwich).
Follow a single food through different cultures or look at variations on a meal (e.g., What's for breakfast?).

Who Eats What?

SLUMPS, GRUNTS AND SNICKERDOODLES
LITTLE HOUSE COOKBOOK

Make a graph of the most popular foods in the class, showing the most often and least often eaten foods.
Survey teachers and people from different cultures.
Interview an agricultural extension agent about food production in your state.
Map production areas on a state map.
Find out who has the healthiest diet in the world.

Eating Customs

HOW MY PARENTS LEARNED TO EAT
I KNOW A PLACE
FROM HAND TO MOUTH
A MEDIEVAL WEDDING
A MEDIEVAL FEAST
GREGORY THE TERRIBLE EATER
SUNSHINE
DUMPLING SOUP
POTLATCH
HALMONI AD THE PICNIC

Study eating customs around the world.
Eat with chopsticks.
Eat English or Middle Eastern style food.
Make a guide to eating in different cultures.
Collect data on eating customs from your class.
What are favorite foods or special celebration foods?

Table 4.5 *Weekly Schedule, Carol Hagihara's Second-Grade Class*

Time	Monday	Tuesday	Wednesday	Thursday	Friday
7:35	Opening exercises. Attendance, lunch count, sign-ups.				
8:05	Sharing time. Projects, writing, solutions to work-related problems, planning, progress reports.				
8:25	Whole group activity. Theme introduction, simulation, guest speaker, Readers' Theater*.				
9:00	Integrated work time. Move between centers. Work in small groups.				
9:45	Recess				
10:00	Art	Music	Physical education	Library	Outdoor education
10:50	Poetry time. Teacher shares poetry. Children share poetry.				
11:00	Integrated work time. Rotate groups.				
11:30	Lunch				
12:10	Integrated work time				
12:30	Sustained Silent Reading* and individual conferences.				
12:55	Literature time	Buddy Reading*	Writing workshop	Buddy Reading*	Author's Chair*
1:30	Integrated work time				
2:15	Evaluation and cleanup				

Into the Classroom

The schedule is simply the bare bones of Carol's planning. In Table 4.6, the entire first day of the thematic unit is outlined, along with portions of the second and fifteenth days of the unit. Notice how much activity is generated on the first day and how Carol concentrates that focus during sharing and whole group times on Day 2. She uses writing—a child-constructed Big Book* on eating customs in the United States and Japan—to move into a discussion of the mechanics of punctuation, and she asks children to attend to this feature of their writing. Carol also uses Day 2's activities to help children focus on the concept of "fairness" relative to problems of food distribution and to consider issues of hunger. However, instead of simply telling children there are problems of hunger, she encourages them to think of ways they can make a difference in the larger community. In addition, Carol teaches the children how to acquire the information they need. She helps them write down questions they need answers to and people who might be able to help them. This provides the impetus for the integrated work time that follows, during which children call a local food bank to find out what supplies are most needed, locate articles on hunger in newspapers and magazines, and discover how much food an average family eats in a week.

Between Days 2 and 15, children will have worked through a number of activities suggested and depicted on the WEB, as well as working with their reading buddies, having Sustained Silent Reading (SSR)* each day, and going to their regularly scheduled art, music, physical education, and library classes. Day 15 is selected for a luncheon and theme-related performance for invited guests. This sharing brings together other strands from the WEB—celebrating food, the communal importance of eating, and the children's literary and artistic endeavors related to the theme. Notice that Carol has rescheduled the day to accommodate this activity and the children involve themselves in decorating the room with examples of their work. A book written and illustrated by the children to represent the various types of experiences they have had is placed near each visitor's seat. There are chapters on where food comes from, favorite foods around the world, and the use of food in literature. A glance at the WEB indicates the projects children might represent in their book. Day 15 also begins with a report on the food pantry that the children have "adopted" as one response to their study of the problems of hunger. There are also quiet times just before and after guests come. This helps Carol and the children cope with the excitement of performance and guests without resorting to harsher disciplinary tactics. Carol has also worked with the children so that they take on the responsibilities of hosts, including appropriate behavior.

As the children move through centers and engage in various activities, Carol works with them on particular center projects. In one case (Day 1), after checking to ensure that everyone understands the morning's work, Carol meets with a small group needing extra assistance in math. During this time she also tries out material she has developed as part of her teacher research. Carol subsequently leaves the math group and moves in and out of small group and individual encounters with other children as they work.

Table 4.6 *DETAILED SCHEDULE, CAROL HAGIHARA'S SECOND-GRADE CLASS*

Day 1

Time	Children	Teacher	Teacher Research
Teacher Preparation 7:25		Carol checks setups for class, writes announcements on board, and checks mail in office.	
Opening Exercises 7:55	Children arrive and fill in attendance and lunch count, dropping the forms in the appropriate box. Several sign up for Sharing Time.	Carol greets children as they enter, makes sure forms are filled in, and makes announcements.	
Sharing Time 8:05	Two groups share projects from the previous unit. Peers ask questions and comment on work done.	Carol invites children to the sharing area. She shares a limerick as an introduction to Sharing Time, and then monitors time and participates in the group discussion.	
Unit Introduction 8:25	Children stay in sharing area, listen to the story, and discuss it. They read along with the Big Book* version of the story.	Carol introduces a new story, *The Hungry Thing,* and leads a discussion of hunger, "What might happen if no one could figure out what you wanted?"	
	Children take different parts to read, and all recite the Hungry Thing's lines.	Carol uses the Big Book* and reads it along with the children. She points out features of the text and of individual words and phrases. As children suggest additional things to feed the Hungry Thing, Carol adds lines to the Big Book* text.	
	Several children suggest activities for a class work chart.	Carol introduces the new unit on eating, solicits children's suggestions, and goes over some possible activities.	
	Children help plan their work for integrated work time. Planning sheets are checked off, and work assignments made.		
Integrated Work Time 9:00	Children move to work areas throughout the room: • *Grocery list.* Children locate advertisements for luncheon foods and figure math problems related to serving a luncheon. A grocery store in the area provides practice in careful shopping, making change, adding money, and checking work with a calculator. Finished work is put in a folder for the teacher to review.	Carol moves between groups, helping children get started on their work.	As Carol works with the "grocery list" and Z"food measures" groups, she explains about keeping the special math Journal*.
	• *Food measures.* This group works with an assortment of measuring devices and dry foods to measure. They work to establish equivalencies and make a chart to use in cooking activities.	Carol works with a small group who have been having difficulty with previous math activities. The children then work in pairs to check their work.	Carol records her observations of student work in her triple-entry journal. She has focused much of the math in this unit on the very practical problem of planning for and feeding guests at a class luncheon. She wants children to see mathematics as a common human activity.

(continued)

Table 4.6 DETAILED SCHEDULE, CAROL HAGIHARA'S SECOND-GRADE CLASS (CONTINUED)

Day 1

Time	Children	Teacher	Teacher Research
	• *Growing food.* Assorted seeds and reference books help children with sorting and matching seeds to full-grown plants. Children set up experiments to observe root growth and chart development of different types of food plants.	Carol leaves the math group and joins the children who are planting seeds. She shares part of *Hoe, Hoe, Hoe, Watch My Garden Grow* and discusses the types of plants children have decided to grow. She asks children for a report on their progress during today's evaluation time.	
	• *Food in fiction.* Children select books from the reading center to read to each other. Each child picks a book to read during individual conferences.		
	• *Eating around the world.* Children listen to the story and try to use chopsticks. They discuss the experience and try to find interesting words to describe it. They locate Japan and the United States on their inflatable globes and on the Peter's Projection world map. In pairs, they create directions for eating in America and in Japan.	A parent volunteer (prepared by Carol) is working in this area today. She has a pot of Japanese noodles bubbling in a corner, and *How My Parents Learned to Eat* in hand. She shares the story and invites children to eat the noodles with chopsticks. In between helping children manage the chopsticks, she records the descriptive words and phrases the children use to describe this experience. These will be added to children's Learning Log* and used in their writing.	
Recess and Special Classes			
Poetry 10:50	Children recite their favorite poems after the teacher shares some poetry. A child suggests illustrating Shel Silverstein's "Adelaide" and several other children decide to put together a book of eating poems and illustrations.	Carol shares several "eating" poems from *The Random House Book of Poetry.* Carol points out other books of poetry in the reading center and suggests asking the librarian for help, too.	
Integrated Work Time 11:00	Children rotate groups or move to writing tables to complete projects begun earlier in the day.	Carol works with a child who is ready for an "editor" for part of "How to Eat in Japan and the United States." She also checks with the poetry group to see that they have themselves organized for work.	
Lunch Followed by a Third Integrated Work Time			
Sustained Silent Reading* 12:30	Children read selections of their choice.	Carol has conferences with individual children or with small groups to hear them read and to discuss their reading.	
Literature 12:55	After discussing food preferences, children decide to survey a grocery store to find out what foods are best sellers. They select a committee to work with the teacher in developing a survey.	Carol shares *Gregory the Terrible Eater* and leads discussion of favorite and least favorite foods.	
	Children retrieve *How My Parents Learned to Eat* to find parts that	Carol asks children to share what was learned about Japanese food and	

(continued)

Table 4.6 *Detailed Schedule, Carol Hagihara's Second-Grade Class (continued)*

Day 1

Time	Children	Teacher	Teacher Research
	refer to American eating customs. They reread some parts.	customs. What part of the story helped them to understand how complicated American style eating was? She invites several children to share parts of the story by reading them aloud.	
Integrated Work Time 1:30	The children complete work for today's projects and plan for next day.	Carol works with the survey committee to get them started, and then moves between groups to help children decide on future directions, or bring closure to a project.	One of the things Carol wants to study is how children learn to communicate mathematically. The survey project will give her a rich source of data as children negotiate how they will collect data and then how they will represent it for others.
Evaluation and Cleanup 2:15	Children put work in notebooks and begin end of day jobs.	Carol asks children to survey food products at home and to see if they can find two foods that did not come from the United States.	

Day 2

Time	Children	Teacher	Teacher Research
Sharing Time 8:05	One group shares their Big Book* of eating customs in the United States and Japan. Children discuss punctuation in the Big Book* as the group explains that they had some difficulty in this area. Several children read sentences as if other punctuation had been used (i.e., question marks rather than an exclamation mark or a period). They begin to construct some helpful hints for punctuation. Several children come to the board to put punctuation marks in sentences and to see if their hints are really helpful.	Carol points out interesting words and ideas, comments on their careful attention to punctuation, and asks the class why they think certain choices were made. Carol writes some sentences on the board and asks children to use their new helpful hints to punctuate them: "Let's see if we can use these hints to make our writing more interesting. Why don't you bring some examples of good use of punctuation to 'group' today?"	
Whole Group Activity 8:25	Children match passports from a previous activity to country names posted in the room and sit in those areas. Children quickly note that the snack is not "fairly" distributed. The children discuss as a class how to solve the problem; they rank order their solutions then pick one and act on it. Children discuss ways to help hungry people. Select several possibilities to work on.	Once children are seated by country, Carol distributes snack based on food distribution in the countries represented. Carol introduces a new book, *Kids Ending Hunger: What Can We Do?* Carol asks them to outline the problem and then offer possible solutions: "How do we decide which solution to pick?" Compare to problems in the world. "Can we think of possible solutions to some of these problems?" Carol divides the class into groups based on the suggestions and student interests.	This book uses statistical information on hunger that can be a source of students' own problem setting. Carol records the problems the children pose, as well as their attempts to solve them.
Integrated Work Time 9:00	Children work in groups to plan for hunger projects (see WEB). The children share plans and make schedule for accomplishing them.	Carol helps make plans workable and serves as recorder.	

(continued)

Table 4.6 *Detailed Schedule, Carol Hagihara's Second-Grade Class (continued)*

Day 15

Time	Children	Teacher	Teacher Research
Sharing Time 8:05	A committee that went to the food pantry reports on the need for cardboard boxes. The class decides to collect boxes and deliver them the following week.	Carol participates in the discussion that is led by the committee of students.	
Dress Rehearsal 8:25	The children run through the play, poems, and other readings planned for guests.	Carol organizes a runthrough of the program, including a play adapted from *The Funny Little Woman*.	
Room Arrangement 9:00	Children put final touches on decorations, and organize food.	She works with children on room decoration.	
Recess and Special Classes 9:45			
Literature 10:50	The children gather quietly for story.	Carol shares *Bon Appetit, Mr. Rabbit*.	
Special Program 11:00	Children greet guests and show them to seats. They introduce the program and put on their performance.	Carol also greets guests. She assists and directs as necessary and makes sure guests receive books made for them.	
	Children serve luncheon (all planned and made by children).		
	Children bid guests goodbye.		
	After all the guests leave, everyone goes out for recess.		
Cleanup 12:15	Everyone helps put the room back into working order.		
Sustained Silent Reading* 12:55	Children read books of their own choosing.	Carol reads book of her own choosing.	

Children learn content and concepts from different subject matter.

Summary

Over the course of this thematic unit, Carol strives to balance individual and small and whole group activities. She provides for vigorous movement, discussion, and quiet reflective time. Each part of the day is planned to incorporate a wide variety of language use. There is reason to practice oral reading and plenty of time for pleasurable, private reading, as well as listening when the teacher shares books. There are opportunities to talk and to listen, to organize thoughts in writing, to express ideas in art, charts, graphs, and action. Children make choices, as when they decide to adopt the food pantry and to collect food and volunteer time there. With Carol's guidance, children are engaged in activities that allow them to participate in the community beyond the school. They learn in graphic ways about a community's responsibility in helping to feed its members. They are also involved in learning the content and concepts of such subject areas as science and social studies when they compare cross-cultural patterns of food use or try raising their own food crops, and of mathematics when they solve problems related to cooking for large groups. Carol's role as facilitator helps children see the connections between these domains more clearly, and helps focus the children on such *essential questions* as: Why do we eat what we do? How have eating and eating customs changed over time? Who has food? How does food get to our table? How can we share food with those who need it? Also, as Carol begins to keep track of student responses to mathematical activities, she notices two things that help her change her instruction. First, as children write about mathematics, their questions about mathematics become more focused and the children seem better able to ask for and understand help from Carol and peers. Second, linking mathematics to real problems (i.e., planning a meal) and literature (i.e., *Count Your Way Through Africa*) seem to help less secure students feel more confident of their ability to do math.

Haskins (1989)

Certainly, Carol's placement in a self-contained setting and her school's interest in integrated-day planning support her move toward an integrated language curriculum. However, other settings—for example, the following second/third-grade family-grouped setting—can also support integrated language programs at this elementary level.

References: LET'S EAT!

Food chain in OBIS. Delta Education.

"Please Pass the Potatoes," in M. Hartoonian (1992). *A Guide to Curriculum Planning in Global Studies,* Milwaukee: Wisconsin Department of Public Instruction.

Children's Literature: LET'S EAT

"Adelaide" in *Where the Sidewalk Ends: Poems and Drawings* by S. Silverstein. Harper & Row, 1974.

The Amazing Egg Book by M. Griffin & D. Seed. Dale Seymour, 1993.

The Amazing Potato: A Story in Which the Incas, Conquistadors, Marie Antoinette, Thomas Jefferson, Wars, Famines, Immigrants, and French Fries All Play a Part by M. Meltzer. Harper & Row, 1992.

Bon Appetit, Mr. Rabbit by C. Boujon. McElderry, 1987.

Bread, Bread, Bread by A. Morris. Mulberry, 1989.

Burgoo Stew by S. Patron. Illustrated by M. Shenon. Orchard, 1991.

The Chocolate Touch by P. S. Catling. Bantam-Skylark, 1981.

Clive Eats Alligators by A. Lester. Houghton Mifflin, 1986.

Cloudy with a Chance of Meatballs by J. Barrett. Macmillan, 1978.

Count Your Way Through Africa by J. Haskins. Carolrhoda, 1989.

The Delicious Day: 65 Poems by P. Janeczko. Orchard, 1987.

Dumpling Soup by J. K. Rattigan. Illustrated by L. Hsu-Flanders. Little, Brown, 1993.

The Fine Round Cake by A. Esterl. Translated by P. Hejl. Illustrated by A. Dugin & O. Dugina. Four Winds, 1991.

Food Fight: Poets Join the Fight Against Hunger with Poems to Favorite Foods by M. J. Rosen, Harcourt, 1996.

An Edible Alphabet by B. Christiansen. Dial, 1994.

Foodworks by Ontario Science Centre. Dale Seymour, 1993.

From Hand to Mouth, or How We Invented Knives, Forks, Spoons and Chopsticks and the Table Manners to Go with Them by J. C. Giblin. Crowell, 1987.

A Fruit and Vegetable Man by R. Schotter. Illustrated by J. Winter. Little, Brown, 1993.

The Funny Little Woman by A. Mosel. Illustrated by B. Lent. Dutton, 1972.

Going Bananas: Jokes for Kids by C. Keller. Treehouse, 1975.

A Grain of Rice by H. Pittman. Hastings, 1986.

Gregory the Terrible Eater by M. Sharmat. Illustrated by J. Aruego & A. Dewey. Four Winds, 1987.

Growing Vegetable Soup by L. Ehlert. Harcourt Brace Jovanovich, 1987.

Halmoni and the Picnic by S. N. Choi. Illustrated by K. M. Dugan. Houghton, 1993.

Hoe, Hoe, Hoe, Watch My Garden Grow by M. Daddona. Addison-Wesley, 1980.

How a Seed Grows by H. J. Jordan. Harper & Row, 1960.

How My Parents Learned to Eat by I. Friedman. Illustrated by A. Say. Houghton Mifflin, 1984.

How to Make Apple Pie and See the World by M. Priceman. Knopf, 1994.

The Hungry Thing by J. Slepian & A. Seidler. Scholastic, 1967.

Ice Cream Soup by F. Modell. Greenwillow, 1988.

I Know a Place by K. Ackerman. Houghton Mifflin, 1992.

"I'm Hungry" section of *The Random House Book of Poetry* by J. Prelutsky (Ed.). Illustrated by A. Lobel. Random House, 1983.

Jalapeno Bagels by N. Wing. Illustrated by R. Casilla. Atheneum, 1996.

Jelly Beans for Sale by B. McMillan. Scholastic, 1996.

Kids Ending Hunger: What Can We Do? by T. A. Howard with S. Howard. Andrews & McNeil, 1992.

Know Your Fruits by S. S. Bose. Jules Books, 1988.

Know Your Vegetables by S. S. Bose. Jules Books, 1988.

Little House Cookbook by B. Walker. Harper & Row, 1979.

The Little Pigs' Cookbook by C. N. Watson. Little, Brown, 1987.

Mean Soup by B. Everitt. Harcourt, 1992.

A Medieval Feast by Aliki. Harper & Row, 1983.

A Medieval Wedding by Aliki. Crowell, 1983.

Milk by D. Carrick. Greenwillow, 1985.

My Little Sister Ate One Hare by B. Grossman. Illustrated by K. Hawkes. Crown, 1996.

Of Cabbages and Chemistry by J. Barber. Dale Seymour, 1993.

Ox-Cart Man by D. Hall. Illustrated by B. Cooney. Viking, 1979.

Pass the Fritters, Critters by C. Chapman. Illustrated by S. L. Roth. Macmillan, 1993.

People of Corn: A Mayan Story by M. Gerson. Illustrated by C. Golembe. Little, 1995.

Possum Magic by M. S. Fox. Illustrated by J. Vivas. Abingdon, 1987.

Potlatch: A Tsimshian Celebration by D. Hoyt-Goldsmith. Photographs by L. Migdale. Holiday, 1997.

The Return of the Buffaloes: A Plains Indian Story About Famine and Renewal of the Earth by P. Goble. National Geographic, 1996.

Rhinos for Lunch, Elephants for Supper by T. Mollel. Houghton Mifflin, 1992.

Round Trip by A. Jonas. Greenwillow, 1983.

Saturday Sancocho by L. Torres. Farrar, Straus, & Giroux, 1995.

Slumps, Grunts and Snickerdoodles by L. Perl. Houghton Mifflin, 1977.

Seven Loaves of Bread by F. Wolff. Illustrated by K. Keller. Tambourine, 1993.

A Spaceburger: A Kevin Spoon and Mason Mintz Story by D. Pinkwater. Macmillan, 1993.

Sunshine by J. Ormond. Lothrop, 1981.

The Tortilla Factory by G. Paulsen. Illustrated by R. W. Paulsen. Harcourt, Brace 1995.

Tops and Bottoms by J. Stevens. Harcourt Brace, 1995.

Trains at Work by R. Ammon. Photographs by D. Peterson & R. Ammon. Atheneum, 1993.

Uncle Willie and the Soup Kitchen by D. DiSalvo-Ryan. Morrow, 1991.

What Comes in 2's, 3's, and 4's by S. Aker. Simon & Schuster, 1990.

What Happens to a Hamburger? by P. Showers. Harper & Row, 1985.

Prototype 4: Second/Third Grade—JOURNEYS

Schedule

Dehea Munioz's family-grouped class includes children who would be identified as second- and third-graders in more traditionally organized schools. Dehea's school houses a "magnet" program that emphasizes cross-cultural and multicultural studies and includes students from all over the city and from various sociocultural and economic backgrounds. The school is also managed by a site-based school council that includes parent, teacher, student, and administrative representatives. The school council decided that family grouping had many pluses, given their situation. Children of various backgrounds and abilities could more easily work together. Older children could benefit from helping younger children and acting as their tutors. The council felt that the older students' familiarity with the classroom organization could help them initiate the younger members into the routine of the thematic unit approach. This type of mentoring supports the school's goal of developing cross- and multicultural understanding by building strong personal relationships between children from disparate backgrounds. Family grouping also accommodates children with a variety of capabilities and gives them plenty of time to develop as learners. In this particular class, the teacher is responsible for teaching all subject areas except art, music, health, and physical education. (See Table 4.7.) The school staff believes in cooperative planning, however, and specialists in these subject areas enjoy extending classroom themes through their areas of expertise.

Teachers draw on their own experience.

The JOURNEYS theme was the culmination of several needs and interests that Dehea saw in her school and classroom. First, the school has a long-term relationship with a "sister school" in France. Children were already exchanging letters, pictures, and videotapes. Second, Dehea was a cross-cultural traveler herself, having lived in several countries before returning to the United States for college and work. She wanted her students to learn to see themselves as world citizens, interested in cross-cultural travel and open to people from different backgrounds. She also wanted to capitalize on the fact that many of her students had already moved a number of times as recent immigrants from Southeast Asia or having lived in several different regions of the United States or their own community. Journeys were already a part of their lives. Finally, Dehea knew from conferences with some of the parents and comments from children that many of her students had experienced hostility because of cultural differences. Dehea was aware that one of the most important opportunities for developing openness to differences is in the early elementary years. The JOURNEYS theme would allow her to begin the process of developing the cross- and multicultural perspective that was a school goal and a real issue in her students' lives.

Dehea also decided to make developing cross- and multicultural understanding the focus of her teacher inquiry during the thematic unit. Her background reading led her to look carefully at several issues. First, she was interested in the impact of

Table 4.7 *WEEKLY SCHEDULE, DEHEA MUNIOZ'S SECOND/THIRD-GRADE FAMILY-GROUPED CLASS*

Time	Monday	Tuesday	Wednesday	Thursday	Friday
7:30	Teacher preparation time.				
8:00	Children arrive, put away coats, prepare lunch count, and take attendance.				
8:10	Group time. Initiating activity: setting the stage for individual and small-group activities for the day. Plans for the day are discussed.				
8:30	Physical education	Art	Health	Music	Library
9:30	Recess				
9:45	Integrated work time. Children work in small groups or individually. Teacher works with small groups or has individual conferences. Time is flexible.				
11:15	Math				
12:00	Lunch and outdoor play.				
1:00	Book sharing. Teacher reads a book aloud. Several children talk about the books they have been reading.				
1:30	Integrated work time. Children continue work time, or teacher works with whole class.				
2:15	Group sharing. Children report on their group work. Teacher may conduct a lesson on relevant topics.				
2:45	Read Aloud* or SSR*. Teacher reads aloud or everyone engages in SSR*.				
3:00	Cleanup and dismissal.				

"culturally conscious" books—literature that speaks from *inside* a culture, not just *about* it. Dehea found several books representing some of the cultures in her class. She decided to study the impact of these texts by analyzing the children's Literature Response Group* journals and classroom discussions. Second, Dehea decided to look at the impact of planned reflection based on multiple exposures to different cultures. Her experience led Dehea to believe that simple exposure was not enough. The children needed to reflect on what they had experienced, and they needed enough experience to begin to appreciate both cultural universals (elements of culture common to all people and nations—food, language, arts, recreation, beliefs, and the like) and cultural differences (the variety of manners, myths, and customs and institutionalized practices that develop around cultural universals). As a result, Dehea planned for regular opportunities for the children to have and reflect on cross- and multicultural experiences. She also decided to focus on five children and carefully monitor their responses in their journals and other written and oral work. The five children selected—three boys and two girls—appeared to be having difficulty with cultural differences. Two were children whose parents had expressed concern to Dehea about intolerance directed at their children in the community. Three were children who seemed to Dehea to resort to stereotyping in many of their cross- and multicultural interactions. She thought their reactions would provide her with some evidence of the impact of the thematic unit's cross- and multicultural component.

Finally, in looking over the school's curriculum guides, Dehea noted that the science curriculum required that she deal with aspects of physical and biological science, and the social studies guide called for a study of neighborhoods and communities of the past and present, with an emphasis on human interaction with the environment. As she developed her plans, she constantly looked for ways to incorporate these topics into her thematic unit, and developed a set of *essential questions* to guide her work, including the following: Why do people move? How is movement influenced by geography? How is the environment changed by people's journeys? What happens when people from different cultural backgrounds live and work in the same place? What kind of personal journeys help people grow and mature? Are there patterns to plant, animal, and geological movement? How do ideas travel?

"Culturally conscious" texts are insider perspectives.

Cultural universals are common to all people.

Prototype 4: Second/Third Grade—JOURNEYS

Immigration to North America

THE LAND I LOST
ELLIS ISLAND
ELLIS ISLAND: LAND OF HOPE
HECTOR LIVES IN THE UNITED STATES NOW
THE LONG WAY TO A NEW LAND
IMMIGRANT GIRL
MY GRANDMOTHER'S JOURNEY
ALL THE LIGHTS IN THE NIGHT
A PEDDLER'S DREAM
WATCH THE STARS COME OUT
MAKING A NEW HOME IN AMERICA
I HATE ENGLISH
TO BE A SLAVE
HOW MANY DAYS TO AMERICA?
A BOOK OF AMERICANS
IMMIGRANT KIDS
WHEN AFRICA WAS HOME
HELLO, MY NAME IS SCRAMBLED EGGS
EMMA'S DRAGON HUNT
GRAB HANDS AND RUN
HOANG ANH: A VIETNAMESE-AMERICAN BOY
FATHER'S RUBBER SHOES
OVER HERE IT'S DIFFERENT: CAROLINA'S STORY
MY NAME IS MARIA ISABEL
IF YOUR NAME WAS CHANGED AT ELLIS ISLAND
THE DREAM JAR
ACROSS THE WIDE DARK SEA
COMING TO AMERICA
GRANDFATHER'S JOURNEY

Survey: Why do people move?
Chart: Places class members have lived or visited.
Use a variety of maps to locate foreign place names
   used in the United States.
Storyteller: Stories with African roots
Interview new immigrants:
   What brought you here?
   What is most strange in new country?
   What is most missed from old country?
Comparison Chart*: Different immigrant groups and
   why they came.
Discuss difference between voluntary and involuntary
   immigration.
Have a multicultural fair: Share what has been learned
   about the people who come to America and the
   native peoples who lived here first. Make and share
   ethnic foods, art, crafts, dance, and music.

Migrations of First Peoples

THE PEOPLE SHALL CONTINUE
THE GIRL WHO LOVED WILD HORSES
THE MUD PONY
BABY RATTLESNAKE
KEEPERS OF THE EARTH
KEEPERS OF THE ANIMALS
SEES BEHIND TREES
WHO CAME DOWN THAT ROAD?

Map movement of native people from your area.
Video: section of Scott Momaday on Onondaga Nation.
Discuss: Why do the people of the Six Nations call themselves a
   separate nation?
Mural comparing life in three different nations.
Compare Native American journey stories with those from other cultures.

Historic Journeys in the United States

ARMINTA'S PAINT BOX
AURORA MEANS DAWN
AUNT HARRIET'S UNDERGROUND RAILROAD IN THE SKY
CASSIE'S JOURNEY
DEATH OF THE IRON HORSE
JOSHUA'S WESTWARD JOURNAL
THE JOSEPHINA QUILT STORY
FOLLOW THE DRINKING GOURD
DAKOTA DUGOUT
SARAH, PLAIN AND TALL
JOURNEY CAKE, HO
GREAT MIGRATION
SWEET CLARA AND THE FREEDOM QUILT
A TRAIN TO SOMEWHERE
ORPHAN TRAIN RIDER: ONE BOY'S STORY

Visit a historic site. Use trip book to collect data on life at that site,
   why people came there.
People moving in the past: Make time line of U.S. migrations.
If you were going west, what would you want to take with you?
If you were Native American, what would you want to say to these new people?
What If . . .? activity:
   What if Native Americans and European Americans had settled
   their differences peacefully?
Classroom museum: Create displays that show historic journeys.
Plan a frontier community: Give students picture map of area. What
   resources can you use? What kind of jobs will you need in your
   town? Make an ad for your town to attract new people.
Make a model of a Native American community (select group from
   your area, or near neighbor). Show how people used the natural resources.

Journeys Toward Growth and Understanding

SITTI'S SECRETS
GRANDPA'S FACE
NATHANIEL TALKING
MARIA TERESA
TURTLE KNOWS YOUR NAME
HOW DOES IT FEEL TO GROW OLD?
UNDER THE SUNDAY TREE
ALL THE COLORS OF THE RACE
AT THE CROSSROADS
NOT SO FAST, SONGOLOLO
YOUNG MARTIN'S PROMISE
VIVA MEXICO
AMAZING GRACE
WORKING COTTON
MIRETTE ON THE HIGH WIRE

K-W-L*: What is a journey?
Interview people of different ages:
   What is the best thing about being your age?
   What can you do now that you couldn't do before?
   What would you like to do that you can't do easily at this age?
Classroom meetings: Plan for the class's progress on theme, deal
   with interpersonal and management issues.
Current events time. Discuss current issues that concern children.
Display news items, pictures, etc. about current issues.
Write letters of concern about issues of importance.
Compare different kinds of work in community and in other parts
   of the world (i.e., Crossroads).
What kinds of work require travel? Begin bulletin board to display
   student findings.
Read biographies and compare types of personal journeys.
Make collage of things important to own journeys.
Make a life line showing important things you have learned to do
   and some challenges you have faced over time.

HUMAN JOURNEYS

Magical and Fantastic Journeys

THE WRETCHED STONE
THE MYSTERIES OF HARRISON BURDOCK
POSSUM MAGIC
MIRANDY AND BROTHER WIND
JUNE 29, 1999
ALADDIN AND THE ENCHANTED LAMP
THE FOOL OF THE WORLD AND THE
   FLYING SHIP
THE MAGIC HORSE
AIRMAIL TO THE MOON
ANNO'S JOURNEY
TRAVELING TO TONDO
SHEEP ON A SHIP
THE TREK
MOLASSES FLOOD
WHERE THE WILD THINGS ARE
ZORAH'S MAGIC CARPET
THE LEGEND OF THE PERSIAN CARPET

Make a list of magical elements in stories.
Make a museum of literary quests.
Compare quests in book with those in popular
   children's films.
Write "What happened next . . ." after reading one of
   the magical journey stories.
Using *Possum Magic* as a model, write a version for
   another culture.
What foods would you eat and where would you go?
Make a collection of time travel books.
Draw a picture of a time you would like to visit. Who
   would you be? What would you like to do? Find out
   as much as you can about the time you have selected
   and share your findings with class.
"When are you?" Identify time clues in pictures.

Getting There

FREIGHT TRAIN
ROUND TRIP
AIRPORT
BICYCLE MAN
LIFE ON A BARGE
THE ERIE CANAL
INCREDIBLE CROSS-SECTIONS
SCHOOL BUS
FLYING
JONATHAN AND HIS MOMMY
FILL IT UP
THE WAY THINGS WORK
THE SECRET LIFE OF HARDWARE
TRUCKER
TRUCK SONG
CARS AND HOW THEY GO
BIKES
CARAVAN
MAPS: GETTING FROM HERE TO THERE
WHERE ARE YOU GOING, MANYONI?

Mechanical connections. Study how simple and
   compound machines used for household
   gadgets and tools work. Chart the national
   origins and organize by continent or region.
How would the history of the world be different
   if air travel (or cars, etc.) did not exist?
Design a new way to travel, using what you know
   about simple and compound machines. Make
   a cross–section of your invention.
Read maps to plot routes around the community.
Take a "Jonathan and Mommy" walk.
Use maps to plan a field trip.
Follow maps to explore the school or
   neighborhood.
Take a trip on a bus, train, or boat.
Design paper airplanes that can glide, do loops, etc.
Do clay boats activity: Design a boat that can
   carry the most cargo.
How much travel do you do in one day?
Categorize and chart types and purposes for travel.
Visit an airport or other transportation centers .
Make a model city. Plan for transportation, as
   well as other services. What would make your
   city a good place to visit?
Make a collage of different ways to travel.
Goods travel, too. Make a list of all places your
   clothes came from (check tags).
The world in a chocolate bar. Where do all the
   ingredients in a candy bar come from?
   Locate on map.

IMAGINARY JOURNEYS

Journeys in Traditional Literature

WHEN SCHLEMIEL WHEN TO WARSAW
EAST OF THE SUN AND WEST OF
   THE MOON
ANANSI THE SPIDER
THREE JOVIAL HUNTSMEN
THE PEOPLE COULD FLY
GREEK MYTHS
SUNDIATA
HER SEVEN BROTHERS
TAM LIN
SUN
FLIGHT
LEGENDS OF JOURNEYS
THE THREE BEARS AND 15 OTHER
   STORIES
PERSEPHONE
THE TALE OF ALADDIN AND THE
   WONDERFUL LAMP
ARTHUR, HIGH KING OF BRITAIN

Locate culture of origin for each story and
   mark on world map.
Make a story map based on one of the literary
   journeys.
Compile a list of travelers and their reasons
   for travel.
Display*: When . . .travels, it is because . . .
   Study illustrations. What do they tell about
   the time and place in the story?
Create a cartoon strip of a journey tale.
Write: If I were a story traveler. . .
Put on the Interact musical version of
   Goldilocks.

Language Travels

TALK ABOUT ENGLISH
BEN'S TRUMPET
TAKE MY WORD FOR IT
MARMS IN THE MARMALADE
WHO SAYS A DOG GOES BOW–WOW?

Collect words from other languages that have become part of English.
On world map, place names on their country of origin.
Collect slang words and regional variations, and make a dictionary of slang or regionalisms. Where did these words come from? Why don't they stay around very long? Make a Graffiti Wall* to collect new words as they are found.
Collect language used for specific activities: athletics, music, etc.
Study the "language" of art and music: How have sounds and images journeyed around the world?
Collect travel words, and put on Graffiti Wall*.

Out-of-this World Journeys

FLYING TO THE MOON AND OTHER
    STRANGE PLACES
FIRST TRAVEL GUIDE TO THE MOON
MY TRIP TO ALPHA 1
THE FORGOTTEN DOOR
THE SNOW QUEEN
THE SEARCH FOR DELICIOUS
PETER PAN
TUESDAY

Create a cross–cultural space colony.
How many miles? Find out how many miles it is to different parts of the solar system. Place these "astronomical" numbers on large strips of paper around the room.
Make a time line of space travel.
Plan for the future. What should NASA tackle next?
Write to NASA to find out what their plans are.
Write stories about future space journeys.
Study alternative worlds in literature. What do they have in common?
Which might you want to visit?
Dramatize scenes from favorite fantasies.
Make a literature guide for fantasy. What are the characteristics of different types of fantasy? How are journeys used in these books?

Journeys in Art, Music, and Movement

I SPY: AN ALPHABET IN ART
I SPY A FREIGHT TRAIN: TRANSPORTATION IN ART
LINNEA IN MONET'S GARDEN
DRAWING FROM NATURE: DRAWING LIFE IN MOTION
THE TURN ABOUT, THINK ABOUT, LOOK ABOUT BOOK
WALK TOGETHER CHILDREN: BLACK AMERICAN SPIRITUALS
A VERY YOUNG DANCER

Use *The Turn About . . .*book, and create own turn about pictures.
Analyze art: How do artists get their work to "move"? Use art in children's books, as well as that of other visual artists. Look at art from all over the world.
Make art that moves. Try making mobiles, using line alone to imply motion.
Listen to journey music (e.g., "Four Seasons," "The Moldau," "Grand Canyon Suite," "Peter and the Wolf"). What makes the music "journey"?
Collect sounds of movement. Use tape recorders and record sounds of movement (footsteps, cars, wind blowing, etc.).
Make a symphony of natural movement sounds.
Make a mural of a journey using techniques studied in other artists' work.
Put "journey" poetry to music, or do Choral Readings*.
Listen to recordings of different types of vocal music. What types of journeys are found in songs?
Turn a journey story or poem into dance.
Learn movement that will make you healthier. Plan a fitness journey.
Make a fitness path on the school grounds or plan an obstacle course in the gym.

Numerical Journeys

ANNO'S COUNTING HOUSE
WORLD OF WONDERS: A TRIP THROUGH
    NUMBERS
MAPS AND GLOBES
SPLASH!
MOVING FROM ONE TO TEN

Work the problems in Anno's Counting House.
Create a different journey with number problems.
Present children with a mathematical quest.
Work on reading astronomical numbers.
Cooking math.
How numbers grow: addition and multiplication.
Are we there yet? Calculating mileage on maps.

Geological Migrations

ROCKS AND MINERALS
VOLCANO
VILLAGE OF ROUND AND SQUARE HOUSES
HOW TO DIG A HOLE TO THE OTHER SIDE OF THE EARTH
FOLLOW THE WATER BROOK TO OCEAN
WATER'S WAY
THE MAGIC SCHOOL BUS AT THE WATERWORKS

Field trip to stream/creek. Find evidence that rocks and soil have moved. Take photos for exhibit.
Use sand table to observe erosion by wind and water.
Make mural of cause and effect: How volcano, earthquake, water change how the earth looks.
Walking trip to collect evidence that earth and rock have moved or been moved.
Class book: *Earth Movers.*
Use globe to look for evidence of continental shifts.
How does the earth's movement change people's lives? Small group report.
Field trip to water treatment plant.

JOURNEYS THROUGH TIME AND SPACE

NATURE'S JOURNEYS

PERSONAL JOURNEYS

Family Journeys

GOLD CADILLAC
I GO WITH MY FAMILY TO
    GRANDMA'S
RELATIVES GAME
BIGMAMA'S
TAR BEACH
ABUELA
FIRST ONE FOOT, NOW
    THE OTHER
THREE DAYS ON A RIVER
    IN A RED CANOE
STRINGBEAN'S TRIP TO
    THE SHINING SEA
NIGHT DRIVING
DIA'S STORY CLOTH
GOING HOME

Learn traveling songs.
Draw or write about a favorite family trip.
Make a travel brochure for a place you want to visit.
Make a "trip book" of journeys taken by class members.

Plant Migrations

PLANT
TREE
THE REASON FOR A FLOWER
PLANTS THAT NEVER EVER BLOOM
SEEDS: POP, STICK, GLIDE
HOW SEEDS TRAVEL
EAT THE FRUIT, PLANT THE SEED

Have students plant seeds from fruit and vegetables they have prepared and eaten.
Collect and categorize plants by how they travel.
Grow plants from different beginnings: seeds, roots, cuttings.
Write the adventures of a seed.
Guest speaker: Plants that travel where you don't want them (kudzu, creeper, poison ivy).
Conduct experiments on how far a seed moves in a breeze.
How many plants come from a package of seeds? Record numbers.

Astronomical Migrations

JOURNEY TO THE PLANETS
JOURNEY INTO A BLACK HOLE
JUPITER
SATURN
SEEING EARTH FROM SPACE
LOOK TO THE NIGHT SKY
THE CONSTELLATIONS
PICTURE ATLAS OF THE UNIVERSE

Field trip to planetarium.
Collect star charts for each month and trace movement.
Guest speaker: Sailing by the stars.
Make a class planetarium; read stories about constellations.
Act out motion of planets around the sun. Make a mural of solar system.
Study different planets. Write the story of a planet as if the planet could tell its own story.

Animal Migrations

BIRD
BUTTERFLY AND MOTH
MONARCH BUTTERFLIES:
    MYSTERIOUS TRAVELERS
HOME IN THE SKY
SHELL
WHERE THE WAVES BREAK
WHERE DO THEY GO? INSECTS
    IN WINTER
TOWNSEND'S WARBLER
THE MOON OF THE
    MONARCH BUTTERFLIES
MONARCH
HOW DO BIRDS FIND
    THEIR WAY?

Map bird and butterfly migrations.
Guest speaker: Why animals migrate.
Observation in school yard: Keep track of living things in area. What movement patterns can be observed?
Set up a living system in classroom and observe and record movement patterns.
Visit the zoo. How did animals get to the zoo?
Compare zoo behavior to behavior in the wild as seen in videos.

Into the Classroom

As you enter Dehea Munioz's classroom and watch the interactions between members, you note that the use of natural resources and people in the larger community sets the stage for a wide variety of activities, including studying other cultures and customs, exploring movement in the arts, and investigating the cross-cultural and multicultural origins of English. You will recall that the concepts of "custom" and "movement" were subthemes in the "LET'S EAT!" WEB (Prototype 3). Sometimes such subthemes develop into full-length thematic units. In other cases, they provide a base of experience for later in-depth study. In Dehea's school, these strands run through the entire curriculum. As children move from one level to another within the school, they encounter these concepts in increasingly diverse and complex forms. These concepts motivate enough interest and offer enough rich possibilities to support multiple encounters.

Collaboration on themes includes working with art, music, and physical education teachers.

Two other features of this prototype are important to note. First is Dehea's excellent support from the specialists in art, music, and physical education, each of whom consults with Dehea and introduces a sequence of activities that encourage children to experience movement physically and aesthetically. As you will see in Day 1 of Table 4.8, these specialists also work together to help Dehea set the stage for the unit. This is an important stage if students are to generate ideas for study. By the time Dehea meets with the children to work on a class WEB, they have been immersed in some aspect of the unit all morning and are ready to think about the theme topic in more depth than if they had been asked to generate ideas "cold." Second is the way in which Dehea integrates assessment into her ongoing instruction to meet her content and process goals. As you read through the days' activities, you will note that she collects samples of children's work at different stages for their portfolios. She has specific ways in which children collect data, from Learning Logs* to double-entry Journals*. She includes assessment on Day 15, when she collects both observational data and the exhibit folders.

Table 4.8 samples the first day of the JOURNEYS theme and provides an overview of how Dehea draws children into planning activities, works with the specialists, shares books with her students, and sets the stage for her own inquiry. Day 4 provides a look at the variety of science activities that have developed since Day 1. Day 15 represents a midpoint opportunity for children to communicate what they have been studying in one aspect of the unit and shows how Dehea refocuses the class to maintain momentum and keep interest in the unit high. She is particularly sensitive to the choreography of this day as she plans for quiet time to follow high-energy activities and precede guest speakers.

Table 4.8   *DETAILED SCHEDULE, DEHEA MUNIOZ'S SECOND/THIRD-GRADE FAMILY-GROUPED CLASS*

Day 1

Time	Children	Teacher	Teacher Research
Teacher Arrival 7:30		Dehea arrives to complete paperwork and get materials ready for the children. She has already arranged an interest center focusing on a terrarium containing a cocoon attached to a leafy branch. Now she sets out literature on butterflies and moths and displays Activity Cards* with the books.	
Children Arrival 8:00	As the children come in, they place their colorful name tags in the attendance envelope. Several children are assigned to record the lunch count and attendance. Others move to the interest center to study the new addition to their classroom.	Dehea takes time to chat with individual children.	

(continued)

Table 4.8 *Detailed Schedule, Dehea Munioz's Second/Third-Grade Family-Grouped Class (continued)*

Day 1

Time	Children	Teacher	Teacher Research
Group Time 8:10	Children have many questions about the cocoon and have already begun looking at the books and Activity Cards* on butterflies and moths. They volunteer many comments on what they have seen.	Dehea calls children to group time, where she has a large pad of chart paper set up on an easel for Observation and Interference*. She asks the children to describe what they have observed in the terrarium and records their comments on the chart paper under the heading "Observations." She stops several times to ask if something is really an observation (something we can test with our senses) or an inference (something we think our observations mean). She adds a new column to the chart, and heads it "Inferences."	
	Students refer to the books in the center to clarify their observations.		
	Most of the children are sure that the cocoon will produce a butterfly.		
		Dehea explains that she found the cocoon while hiking near a stream. The creature who made the cocoon, she explains, has already had a long journey and has a longer one ahead. Perhaps they will learn a bit more about the caterpillar's journey in their next class.	
Physical Education 8:30	Children line up to go to physical education.	Ruth Rabinowitz, the P.E. teacher, has been alerted to the introduction Dehea has planned for the JOURNEYS theme. She is able to combine her time this week with the music teacher, Fred Bechtel, because another class is on a field trip. She and Fred decide on a dramatic beginning for a subtheme on movement.	
	Children enter a slightly darkened gymnasium where images of butterflies flash on the walls.	Ruth and Fred use slides and two projectors to cast butterfly images on the walls. Fred's selection of music ("Rites of Spring" and "Four Seasons") fits the theme and plays softly in the background. Fred shares *The Very Hungry Caterpillar.*	
	Children listen as Fred reads.		
	Children fit their movement to the story and then to the music.	Ruth asks children to act out how they think the caterpillar felt at each stage of the story. Fred has them listen to the music and think about which music best fits each feeling. Ruth asks them to imagine themselves in a cocoon, using as little space as possible to move, struggling out of their cocoons, and then swooping and soaring with large movements, finally settling on a branch or flower.	
	They swoop and soar, wiggle, and inch their way along an imaginary branch.		
		Next, Fred teaches the class the "Inchworm" song, using an autoharp as accompaniment. He invites several of the older students who have some experience with the autoharp to accompany their classmates' singing.	
	Children sing. Several try the autoharp.		
Recess 9:30	Several students decide to be caterpillars and butterflies during recess.	Dehea meets her students to walk out to recess with them.	

(continued)

Table 4.8 *Detailed Schedule, Dehea Munioz's Second/Third-Grade Family-Grouped Class (continued)*

Day 1

Time	Children	Teacher	Teacher Research
Integrated Work Time 9:45	After a morning immersed in butterflies and movement, children are ready to think about the unit as a whole. They have many questions and are excited about what the have done so far. Children have many ideas about studying cocoons and insects. Children volunteer ideas: vacation trips, moving from one home to another, and journeys into outer space. One child recalls the time another classmate was new to the school and did not speak English well. This triggers interest in journeys to foreign places and how interesting it would be to visit their sister school in France.	Dehea asks children to brainstorm the idea of JOURNEYS. She writes their ideas on a class WEB. Dehea asks questions to point them in other directions, too. She asks them about journeys they have taken—journeys that changed them just as a cocoon changes to a butterfly, journeys that were fun, or journeys that moved them from one place to another to live. She asks if they know people who go on many journeys or who might have interesting stories to tell and reminds them that they can continue to add to the WEB as new ideas come up. Dehea explains that the unit will involve activities connected to journeys and should help them to think about journeys in new ways. She summarizes some of the activities they will be involved in during the course of the unit and introduces some books with journeys themes.	Dehea points children toward discussing cross– and multicultural journeys, her research interest during this unit.
10:15	Children volunteer for "Out-of-This-World Journeys," Magical and Fantastic Journeys," "Getting There," and "Journeys Toward Growth and Understanding." Children look through the book selections, and each child chooses a story to read.	Dehea has grouped the books and asks for volunteers for each, explaining the basic theme of each group of stories. Dehea has more than enough books for each group. She allows each child to choose from the ten to twelve stories available for each type of journey story. Next, she asks children to work together in groups of three or four. She explains that when each child has finished his or her story, the group will take turns telling each other about the stories. As each person speaks, children are asked to think about how their stories are similar and different. Then they will decide on categories in order to construct a Comparison Chart*.	The "Journey's Toward Growth and Understanding" books form the foundation of Dehea's research on how to help children deal with cross– and multicultural issues in their own lives.
	Children read silently. As some finish before other members of their group, they jot down details in their Learning Logs*. Several get art paper and draw pictures from their stories. Several groups begin telling each other about their stories.	Dehea monitors SSR*, stopping to listen to several children who want to read to her. She suggests that one member in each group jot down details that seem to be alike in the stories.	Data gathering begins. As groups begin discussion, Dehea moves from group to group taking notes and observing the children at work. She records the selections made by the five focus children.
Math 11:15	One group of children uses a yard wheel (a wheel that clicks off yards as it is rolled along a surface) to measure the distance from the office to the classroom. Several of the children are ready for a more challenging	Dehea wants children to be able to use basic measurements and to see the need for accuracy in reporting distances measured. She sets before each student the task of calculating either the distance they travel from	

(continued)

Table 4.8 DETAILED SCHEDULE, DEHEA MUNIOZ'S SECOND/THIRD-GRADE FAMILY-GROUPED CLASS (CONTINUED)

Day 1

Time	Children	Teacher	Teacher Research
	problem, and they use a map of the city to calculate distances from home to school. Some of them use a ruler to do a simple "as the crow flies" measurement. Others use their calculators to figure actual driving or walking distances. They have some difficulty with interpreting the distances on the map and ask for Dehea's help.	home or bus stop to the school each day, or the distance from the front office to their classroom. She also challenges some of the students to see if they can figure out their travel for the week and month. This allows her to assess understanding of days in a week, weeks in a month, and calculator functions.	
	Distances are recorded on a graph. A few children calculate their travel for the school year and decide to find out if they travel further to school than their parents travel to work.	Dehea encourages children to use their calculators. As she moves from child to child, she monitors progress. She spends more time with the group that asks for special help, and makes notes about the specific problems they seem to be having with map reading or making calculations. She decides that she will add a selection on map reading to the WEB. As this is the first time some of the children have attempted this type of measurement, she reminds them to put their work in learning portfolios so that she and they can monitor progress on this new skill. Dehea works with the whole group on adding multiple-digit numbers. Students check their work with calculators.	
Book Sharing 1:00	Children listen to the reading, sometimes asking for clarification or to see the pictures that head each chapter.	Dehea begins reading *The Land I Lost*. The stories in the book are funny and touching, and Dehea hopes they will help her students understand that new immigrants to America might miss their old homes very much. In particular, Dehea wants the children to learn something about the country that was home to the parents of several of her students. Dehea suggests that someone might want to find out more about the animals in the story.	Dehea selected this book for her teacher inquiry. She thinks it will provoke considerable discussion and provide an opportunity to invite Tran's parents to class to talk about their childhoods in Vietnam. This is a culture with whom the children can have multiple contacts, mediated by discussion and further study.
	They are particularly interested in the chapter "Tank, the Water Buffalo."		
	Children volunteer information about books they are reading. Some exchange books. One child shares part of a book he is writing about his dog, Edison, who got his name after chewing on a lamp cord.	Dehea asks students to share some of their own reading.	
Integrated Work Time 1:30		Dehea explains that many people have journeyed to the United States from other countries. One way of seeing the influence of these people on the United States is to notice how many words we borrow from other languages and other places.	
	One child says that his favorite foreign word is "taco." Most of the children who studied Mexico last year laugh. Others wonder what is so foreign about "taco."		

(continued)

Table 4.8   *Detailed Schedule, Dehea Munioz's Second/Third-Grade Family-Grouped Class (continued)*

Day 1

Time	Children	Teacher	Teacher Research
		Dehea tells them that there are many more foreign words that they use every day—they may even have lived in places named for foreign countries, cities, or people. She divides the children into groups of four or five. Each group gets a map of a different region of the United States. Their task is to see how many place-names they can find that come from other countries. They may use the globes, world maps, and atlases already in the social studies center to check their work. She reminds them that some of them are quite good at the names of different countries and cities because they have been playing *Where in the World Is Carmen Sandiego?*	
	Children work in groups to find place-names from other countries. One group wonders if such unfamiliar words as "Montauk" and "Massapequa" are foreign. The names don't appear in the class atlas, so children decide to put them in a separate category called "Strange Names." Another group finds lots of foreign names, such as Paris and Athens, but they find some that are so funny, such as Monkey's Eyebrow and Rabbit Hash, that they make a new category called "Funny Names." A third group notices two cities named Columbus and starts looking for duplications of place-names.	Dehea helps each group categorize the names they have found by regions of the world. She tells them that some of the names they have found come from native peoples who lived in the Americas long before the first settlers from other parts of the world came here. She helps one group compile a list of names used in several different places, such as Columbus, Lexington, and Middletown.	
Group Sharing 2:15	Children report on their group work and comment on how many names come from Europe. They locate place-name origins on the world map and wonder why they found only one name from all of Asia (China), and one from Africa (Cairo). They want to add that question to the topics on the WEB begun in the morning. Children give their pronunciations for different words. Children add "Language Travels" to the WEB and decide to collect samples of regional variations.	Dehea asks children to identify parts of the world that are often represented in U.S. place-names. Dehea adds their new question to the WEB. She also points out that pronunciations of names change as words journey from one country to another. She points out that Lima, Peru, is pronounced as if the *i* were a long *e*, while Lima, Ohio, is pronounced with a long *i*, just like Lima beans. She writes several other words on the board. Dehea, whose accent differs from her students', tells them how each word is pronounced in the region where she grew up. She asks why language changes so much from location to location.	
Reading Aloud 2:45	Children listen to book. Some write in their Response Journals* or make sketches to go with the story.	Dehea reads *I Hate English,* a book about an immigrant's struggle with the English language.	Dehea is anxious to see what students have to say in their art and Journals*. These responses will give her some idea of how children are thinking about other cultures.
Dismissal 3:00	Weekly class leader reminds children that tomorrow is library day and time to return last week's books.		

(continued)

Table 4.8 *Detailed Schedule, Dehea Munioz's Second/Third-Grade Family-Grouped Class (continued)*

Day 4

Time	Children	Teacher	Teacher Research
Group Time 8:10	Children listen and participate in storytelling with a guest storyteller. They have found Nigeria on the world map and seen slides Jameel shared from his father's trip to West Africa. They have many questions about some of the characters in the stories. The trickster is familiar from other traditional literature they have read, and they note the similarities between the tricksters they know and those in the Nigerian tale Mr. Burton tells.	Dehea has arranged for Jameel's father, Mr. Burton, to visit class today to share stories from Nigeria. He can only stay a short while, but he has brought several small "talking drums" that he collected while traveling in West Africa. After telling one of the trickster tales from Nigeria, he plays a tape recording of African drummers and lets children try to make the drums talk.	Dehea takes careful notes on student responses, especially on the focus children in her teacher inquiry. This is the second culture to include visits from parents. Dehea notes that one focus child has just told another, "Be quiet. I need to know this stuff!"
Music 8:45	Children discover the range of sounds that can be made with different percussion instruments. They use the instruments to accompany several songs that have roots in both Africa and the United States. They especially enjoy some of the spirituals in *Walk Together Children*.	Mr. Bechtel begins class fifteen minutes late today, to accommodate Mr. Burton. Mr. Bechtel has a number of percussion instruments set up for the class. He plays some modern music that uses percussion and asks children to listen for some of the similarities between modern American music and the Africa music Mr. Burton shared with them. Mr. Bechtel makes a note to tell Dehea of student interest in the spirituals.	Mr. Bechtel reports to Dehea that children are interested in the music and in how the spirituals were used to send messages. Two students asked why Africans came to this country when things were so bad.
Integrated Work Time 9:45	Children begin work on trickster stories. They use the books in the reading center to remind them of the story patterns they have previously discussed. Other books help them decide on appropriate settings and figure travel routes. Several of the children place their stories in countries they have been studying. A couple of children are trying to use dialogue in their stories and are uncertain in their use of punctuation.	A display of trickster stories is set up in the reading center and organized by country of origin. All the stories involve a journey of some sort. There is also a display of books with rich illustrations of different parts of the world. Dehea asks children to write their own trickster stories involving a journey of some sort. These can be illustrated and made into a book and a copy sent to thank Mr. Burton for his visit. Dehea moves from child to child, talking with children about their stories and listening as several read what they have written. Dehea makes a note on her own Observation Chart to pull a small group aside tomorrow to edit for punctuation in dialogue. She encourages children to use their personal dictionaries and best-guess spelling so that they can get all of their ideas organized in a first draft. Tomorrow, she tells them, there will be time for peer Editing Conferences*.	These stories are also a source of data for Dehea's research as they provide insight into how children understand the cultural settings for their stories.
10:30 (Note: Dehea extends integrated work time today.)	Children work in small groups or individually on the following: • A survey of trips class members have taken, with graph of results. • A world map showing routes of literary journeys in books read by classmates.	At 10:30 most of the children have a rough draft of a story. Dehea tells them it is a good idea to move on to something else now and come back to the story a little later: "Give the story time to percolate in your thoughts!" Dehea directs students	*(continued)*

Table 4.8   *Detailed Schedule, Dehea Munioz's Second/Third-Grade Family-Grouped Class (continued)*

Day 4

Time	Children	Teacher	Teacher Research
	• Observation of cocoon and note taking in Learning Log*. • Development of a board game based on the journey of a monarch butterfly. • Preparation for a trip to the planetarium, including collecting sky charts from local newspapers and displaying them on the bulletin board with captions based on student research. • Conducting an experiment on propulsion (balloon rockets), based on directions on the *Journey to the Planets* bulletin board.	into individual and group activities. Dehea works with one group on how to display data they have collected. Dehea also checks the bulletin board in the science area where she has set up a display to get children ready for a simulation she is planning for the following week. Each day a new picture, question, or riddle appears on the bulletin board. Books, pamphlets, and manipulatives for experiments are displayed on the shelf below to help students follow the clues that will prepare them for their space journeys.	
Group Meeting 11:45	Children report on group work. The group that made the balloon rockets demonstrates, and most of the other students also want to sign up for that area.	Dehea helps make explicit the connections between student work and the JOURNEYS theme, asking students why jet propulsion would be important in space journeys. She asks if anyone could answer the riddle about an animal that propelled itself much like a rocket. She notes what still needs to be done after lunch and collects student's self-reports.	

Day 15

Time	Children	Teacher	Teacher Research
	Children put finishing touches on the class museum of "Nature's Journeys."	Dehea makes sure children are prepared for guests. She reminds them to use the museum guides they prepared.	
Group Time 8:10	In addition to preparing a piece of the exhibit, each child is responsible for one part of either the museum guidebook or the tour notes used by the guides. In one corner of the room is a planetarium made from a refrigerator carton. Its insides are painted black, and students have made perforated sky charts showing constellations at different seasons of the year. A student guide reads over her notes and makes sure that visitors will be able to see the pictures and stories about the planets that are exhibited on the outside walls of the planetarium. On a table, books, children's writing and artwork, charts of butterfly metamorphosis, and the remains of the cocoon are displayed with student-created labels and photographs of the new butterfly as it stretched its wings and was released into the	Dehea uses this event as a midpoint performance assessment for one of the aspects of the thematic unit. As part of the preparation for the museum opening, Dehea checks the notes and guides against the criteria she and the students developed. During the tours she will move among her students, checking their work with their guests.	

(continued)

Table 4.8 *Detailed Schedule, Dehea Munioz's Second/Third-Grade Family-Grouped Class (continued)*

Day 15

Time	Children	Teacher	Teacher Research
	outdoors. Another student guide arranges the board games his peers completed and makes sure the rules are easy to see.		
	Other displays include projects on bird migration, reports on observations of life on the school yard, movement in the class aquarium, and murals showing the impact of volcanoes and earthquakes on the earth's surface. Further along one wall, students have set up a hands-on science display where different types of plants and plant parts are arranged with instructions for categorizing the way plants move from one place to another.		
	On a table near the door, student-created museum guidebooks contain a map of the exhibits, brief explanations of how the exhibits fit the JOURNEYS theme, pictures and poems, and a suggested reading list.		
Museum Opening 8:30	Children take turns as tour guides, helping younger children read stories and exhibit descriptions, and operating the planetarium. When not acting as guides, they read to one of the groups of children waiting to come to the exhibit. Stories have been selected from those written by classmates so that they fit the theme and are short enough to be completed in just a few minutes of reading.	Dehea turns on the tape recorder to play Holtz's "The Planets," as guests from other classes arrive.	
Book Sharing 9:30	Children are exhausted and pleased with their museum opening. They place their notes in folders and gather in the reading area.	Dehea knows the children need some time to relax and restore energy levels before moving on to other work for the day. She also wants to refocus the group so that the theme does not become stale. She selects a class favorite, *Mirandy and Brother Wind* to read.	
	Children sit comfortably and listen to the story, joining in on favorite parts.		
	They join in singing "Waltzing Matilda," one of the traveling songs Mr. Bechtel taught them.	Dehea leads the class in singing "Waltzing Matilda." She tells them that after lunch they will be meeting someone who knows a great deal about the place where this song comes from and about the unusual words in it.	
	As they line up to go to the library, they are already talking about the funny words in the song.		
Library 9:45	As they enter the library, each child tells Dehea how many steps their journey took.	Dehea has the children count the number of steps it takes to complete their journey to the library.	
	Children participate in the scavenger hunt, using card catalog and book-finding guides.	Mr. Schwartz, the librarian, greets the children and tells them that he is going to help them journey around	

(continued)

Table 4.8 *Detailed Schedule, Dehea Munioz's Second/Third-Grade Family-Grouped Class (continued)*

Day 15

Time	Children	Teacher	Teacher Research
		the world. He has set up a scavenger hunt that will help them find information books about different parts of the world.	
		Dehea returns to her class, where she collects the exhibit folders. The children still have to write self-evaluations, and then Dehea will give each child written feedback on their performance. This information will also be sent to parents, along with samples of student work and suggestions for activities to try at home and books that might be shared.	
		Dehea pulls out a cardboard trunk decorated with pictures from all over the world. Inside are "culture clues"—a plastic beef cow, a stuffed koala, real kiwi fruit, a turtle mask, raw wool, a boomerang, and a variety of pictures representing Australia, New Zealand, and some of the surrounding South Pacific Islands.	
Group Time 10:15	Children speculate on the contents of the trunk. Several recognize the kiwi fruit, but no one knows where it is from or how it got to the United States. They ask for more clues.	Dehea asks children to observe the trunk. What do they think is in it? What clues can they use to help them guess? She reaches in one hand and pulls out a kiwi fruit. She pulls out artifacts and pictures one by one, as the children make guesses.	Dehea is especially pleased by the children's response to the pictures. They note similarities between Nigeria, Vietnam, and the places in the pictures. They are eager to provide their ideas.
	Children begin to try to figure out the problem as each new clue appears. Some of the artifacts make them think this must be a place with farms. Others notice that some of the pictures have beaches, so it must touch the ocean.	Dehea records their suggestions.	
	Someone remembers an ad for Qantas airlines and says, "They go down under!"	She pulls out a tiny stuffed koala bear.	
	Children list the possibilities as Antarctica, Australia, Tasmania, and New Zealand. They aren't sure about South Africa and think Indonesia could be "down under," too.	Dehea calls their attention to the globe, and asks what part of the world might be "down under."	
		Dehea introduces *Possum Magic* to the class and asks them to listen for some of the things they saw in the trunk. This story, she tells them, takes place down under.	
	Children listen as Dehea reads, and all call out, "Australia," when the answer becomes obvious.	Dehea tells them that their special guest this afternoon comes from Australia, and she will let him tell them more about down under. She	While the guest is talking to the children, Dehea plans to take notes on student comments and questions. So far, her study supports

(continued)

Table 4.8 *Detailed Schedule, Dehea Munioz's Second/Third-Grade Family-Grouped Class (continued)*

Day 15

Time	Children	Teacher	Teacher Research
		then tells them that some of the things in the trunk were from Australia, some from New Zealand, and some from other islands in the South Pacific. Perhaps they will be able to figure out which are which.	her hypothesis that sustained study, multiple exposure to another culture, and time to reflect will have a positive impact on children's attitudes to their own and others' cultures. The most effective experience seems to be the opportunity for children to meet people from other cultures. Dehea has noticed that the children treat their "international" classmates with great respect after such a visit and talk about visiting that person's home country some day.
Math 11:15		Dehea shows children six kiwi fruits: "I want you all to taste this fruit from down under, but you will need to help me make sure there is enough for everyone." She then asks the children how to divide up the fruit so that everyone gets a taste.	
	The students work on figuring out how to divide the kiwi fruits evenly. They decide it would be easiest to divide the class into six groups, and then each group could divide one kiwi fruit into the same number of pieces as they had group members.	Dehea cuts the fruit as each group tells her how many pieces it needs. She then works through the problem on the board. Some of the children are ready for division, and they are allowed to work in the math center on problems set up for them there. Most of younger children still need practice with manipulatives, and Dehea distributes materials for them to work with.	
	Children work either in the math center on problems involving division or with the teacher, using manipulatives to show sets and subsets.		

Summary

The opportunity to work with like-minded and cooperative colleagues is certainly a plus for Dehea Munioz. She benefits from a schoolwide commitment to the goals of cross- and multicultural understanding that Dehea feels are fundamental to her teaching. It is also representative of her approach to teaching and learning that her collegial relationships benefit her students. Dehea does not pretend to know everything there is to know about each theme introduced in the course of a year. Instead, she embarks as a learner, albeit a more expert one, with her students. As a fellow learner and researcher with her students, Dehea taps resources and asks for help in constructing new knowledge as her students do. She also uses what she has learned to improve teaching and learning in her classroom. As a result, Dehea made some interesting discoveries. First, she found distinct differences in how children responded to the "culturally conscious" books she selected. The children whose cultures were represented seemed to find a voice in these books. Several children who had rarely spoken up in class began participating in Literature Response Groups*. Initially, some expressed anger about what they experienced in school and in their home neighborhoods. Their journal entries became longer and included more commentary on life in and out of school. Other students expressed surprise and sometimes distress that differences might be more than "just skin color." Dehea noted a change, however, as each international visitor came for several visits and became a classroom friend. In this role the visitor also became a "neutral" reference point for discussions of cultural differences. The children's fascination with other countries and customs also allowed them to look differently at differences closer to home. Through their joint and individual inquiries, Dehea, her students, her peer teachers, and members of the school community were better able to negotiate some of the tensions in their own cross- and multicultural community.

Exploration is a joint student and teacher venture.

Children's Literature: JOURNEYS

Abuela by A. Dorros. Illustrated by E. Kleven. Dutton, 1991.

Across the Wide Dark Sea by J. Van Leeuwen. Illustrated by T. B. Allen. Dial, 1995.

Airmail to the Moon by T. Birdseye. Illustrated by S. Gammell. Holiday House, 1988.

Airport by B. Barton. Harper & Row, 1982.

Aladdin and the Enchanted Lamp by M. Mayer. Illustrated by G. McDermott. Macmillan, 1985.

All the Colors of the Race by A. Adoff. Lee & Shepard, 1982.

All the Lights in the Night by A. Levine. Illustrated by J. E. Ransome. Tambourine Books, 1991.

Amazing Grace by M. Hoffman. Illustrated by C. Burch. Dial, 1991.

Anansi the Spider by G. McDermott. Holt, Rinehart, and Winston, 1972.

Anno's Counting House by M. Anno. Harper & Row, 1986.

Anno's Journey by M. Anno. HarperCollins, 1977.

Araminta's Paint Box by K. Ackerman. Atheneum, 1990.

Arthur, High King of Britain by M. Morpugo. Illustrated by M. Foreman. Harcourt, 1995.

At the Crossroads by R. Isadora. Greenwillow, 1983.

Aunt Harriet's Underground Railroad in the Sky by F. Ringgold. Crown, 1992.

Aurora Means Dawn by S. Sanders. Bradbury, 1989.

Baby Rattlesnake by T. Ata. Children's Book Press, 1989.

Ben's Trumpet by R. Isadora. Greenwillow, 1979.

Bicycle Man by A. Say. Parnassus Press, 1982.

Bigmama's by D. Crews. Greenwillow, 1991.

Bikes by A. Rockwell. Dutton, 1987.

Bird by D. Burne. Knopf, 1988.

A Book of Americans by R. S. Benét & R. Benét. Illustrated by C. Child. Henry Holt, 1984.

Butterfly and Moth by P. Whalley. Knopf, 1988.

Caravan by L. McKay Jr. Illustrated by D. Ligasan. Lee & Low, 1995.

Cars and How They Go by J. Cole. Crowell, 1983.

Cassie's Journey: Going West in the 1860s by B. Harvey. Illustrated by D. K. Ray. Holiday House, 1988.

Coming to America by B. Maestro. Illustrated by S. Ryan. Scholastic, 1996.

The Constellations by R. A. Gallant. Four Winds, 1979.

Dakota Dugout by A. Turner. Macmillan, 1985.

Dia's Story Cloth by D. Cha. Compendium by J. Herold. Illustrated by C. Cha & N. T. Cha. Lee & Low, 1996.

Death of the Iron Horse by P. Goble. Bradbury, 1987.

Drawing from Nature: Drawing Life in Motion by J. Arnosky. Lothrop, 1987.

The Dream Jar by B. Pryor. Illustrated by M. Graham. Greenwillow, 1996.

East of the Sun and West of the Moon by D. J. MacHale. Rabbit Ears Press, 1991.

Eat the Fruit, Plant the Seed by M. Selsam. Morrow, 1980.

Ellis Island by C. Reef. Dillon, 1991.

Ellis Island: Land of Hope by J. L. Nixon. Bantam Books, 1992.

Emma's Dragon Hunt by C. Stock. Lothrop, 1984.

The Erie Canal by P. Spier. Doubleday, 1970.

Father's Rubber Shoes by Y. Heo. Orchard, 1995.

Fill It Up by G. Gibbons. Crowell, 1985.

First One Foot, Now the Other by T. dePaola. Putnam, 1981.

First Travel Guide to the Moon: What to Pack, How to Go, and What to See When You Get There by R. Blumberg. Four Winds, 1980.

Flight by B. Burleigh. Putnam, 1991.

Flying by D. Crews. Greenwillow, 1986.

Flying to the Moon and Other Strange Places by M. Collins. Farrar, Straus, & Giroux, 1976.

Follow the Drinking Gourd by J. Winter. Knopf, 1988.

Follow the Water from Brook to Ocean by A. Dorros. HarperCollins, 1991.

The Fool of the World and the Flying Ship by A. Ransome. Illustrated by U. Shulevitz. Farrar, Straus, & Giroux, 1968.

The Forgotten Door by A. Key. Scholastic, 1965.

Freight Train by D. Crews. Greenwillow, 1978.

The Girl Who Loved Wild Horses by P. Goble. Bradbury, 1978.

Going Home by E. Bunting. Illustrated by D. Diaz. HarperCollins, 1996.

Gold Cadillac by M. Taylor. Bantam, 1987.

Grab Hands and Run by F. Temple. Orchard Books, 1993.

Grandfather's Journey by A. Say. Houghton Mifflin, 1993.

Grandpa's Face by E. Greenfield. Illustrated by F. Cooper. Putnam/Philomel, 1988.

Great Migration by J. Lawrence, HarperCollins, 1993.

Greek Myths by O. Coolidge. Houghton Mifflin, 1949.

Hector Lives in the United States Now: The Story of a Mexican-American Child by J. Hewett. Photographs by R. Hewett. Lippincott, 1990.

Hello, My Name Is Scrambled Eggs by J. Gilson. Lothrop, 1985.

Her Seven Brothers by P. Goble. Bradbury, 1988.

Hoang Anh: A Vietnamese-American Boy by D. Hoyt-Goldsmith. Holiday House, 1992.

Home in the Sky by J. Baker. Greenwillow, 1984.

How Do Birds Find Their Way? by R. Gans. Illustrated by P. Mirocha. HarperCollins, 1996.

How Does It Feel to Grow Old? by N. Farber. Illustrated by T. S. Hyman. Dutton, 1979.

How Many Days to America? by E. Bunting. Clarion, 1988.

How Seeds Travel by C. Overbeck. Lerner, 1982.

How to Dig a Hole to the Other Side of the Earth by F. McNulty. Harper, 1979.

If Your Name Was Changed at Ellis Island by E. Levine. Illustrated by W. Parmenter. Scholastic, 1993.

I Go with My Family to Grandma's by R. Levinson. Dutton, 1986.

I Hate English by E. Levine. Scholastic, 1989.

Immigrant Girl: Becky of Eldridge Street by B. Harvey. Illustrated by D. K. Ray. Holiday House, 1987.

Immigrant Kids by R. Freedman. Dutton, 1980.

Incredible Cross-Sections by R. Platt. Knopf, 1992.

I Spy: An Alphabet in Art by L. Micklethwait. Greenwillow, 1991.

I Spy a Freight Train: Transportation in Art by L. Mickelthwait. Greenwillow, 1996.

Jonathan and His Mommy by I. Smalls-Hector. Little, Brown, 1992.

The Josephina Quilt Story by E. Coerr. Harper & Row, 1986.

Joshua's Westward Journal by J. Anderson. Photographs by G. Ancona. Morrow, 1987.

Journey Cake, Ho by I. McLennan. McMeekin & Messer, 1942.

Journey into a Black Hole by F. M. Branley. Crowell, 1986.

Journey to the Planets by P. Lauber. Crown, 1982.

Jupiter by S. Simon. Morrow, 1985.

Keepers of the Animals by M. J. Caduto & J. Bruchac. Fulcrum, 1988.

Keepers of the Earth by M. J. Caduto & J. Bruchac. Fulcrum, 1988.

The Land I Lost by H. Q. Nhuong. HarperCollins, 1982.

The Legend of the Persian Carpet by T. dePaola. Illustrated by C. Ewart. Putnam, 1993.

Legends of Journeys by O. J. Norris. Cambridge University Press, 1988.

Life on a Barge by H. Scarry. Prentice-Hall, 1982.

Linnea in Monet's Garden by C. Bjork. R & S, 1987.

The Long Way to a New Land by J. Sandin. Harper & Row, 1989.

Look to the Night Sky by S. Simon. Puffin, 1979.

The Magic Horse by S. Scott. Greenwillow, 1985.

The Magic School Bus at the Waterworks by J. Cole. Illustrated by B. Degan. Scholastic, 1986.

Making a New Home in America by M. Rosenberg. Lothrop, 1986.

Maps and Globes by J. Knowleton. Illustrated by H. Barton. Crowell, 1985.

Maps: Getting from Here to There by H. Weiss. Houghton Mifflin, 1991.

Maria Teresa by M. Atkinson. Illustrated by C. E. Eber. Lollipop Power, 1979.

Marms in the Marmalade by D. Morley. Carolrhoda, 1984.

Mirandy and Brother Wind by P. McKissick. Illustrated by J. Pinckney. Knopf, 1988.

Mirette on the High Wire by E. A. McCully. Putnam, 1992.

Molasses Flood by B. Lent. Houghton Mifflin, 1992.

Monarch Butterflies: Mysterious Travelers by B. Lavies. Dutton, 1992.

Monarchs by C. Lasky. Photographs by C. G. Knight. Gulliver Green, 1993.

The Moon of the Monarch Butterflies by J. C. George. Illustrated by K. Mak. HarperCollins, 1993.

Moving from One to Ten by S. Halpern. Macmillan, 1993.

The Mud Pony by C. L. Cohen. Scholastic, 1988.

My Grandmother's Journey by J. Cech. Illustrated by S. McGinley-Nally. Bradbury, 1991.

My Name Is Maria Isabel by A. F. Ada. Atheneum, 1993.

Night Driving by J. Coy. Illustrated by P. McCarty. Holt, 1996.

The Mysteries of Harris Burdock by C. Van Allsburg. Houghton Mifflin, 1984.

My Trip to Alpha I by A. Slote. HarperCollins, 1992.

Nathaniel Talking by E. Greenfield. Illustrated by J. Gilchrist. Black Butterfly, 1989.

Not So Fast, Songololo by N. Daly. Macmillan, 1986.

Orphan Train Rider: One Boy's Story by A. Warren. Houghton Mifflin, 1996.

Over Here It's Different: Carolina's Story by M. L. Dawson. Photographs by G. Ancona. Macmillan, 1993.

A Peddler's Dream by J. Shefelman. Illustrated by T. Shefelman. Houghton Mifflin, 1992.

The People Could Fly by V. Hamilton. Knopf, 1985.

The People Shall Continue by S. Ortiz. Children's Book Press, 1988.

Persephone by W. Hutton. McElderry, 1994.

Peter Pan by J. M. Barrie. Samuel French, 1956.

Picture Atlas of the Universe. Rand-McNally, 1991.

Plant by D. Burne. Knopf, 1989.

Plants That Never Ever Bloom by R. Heller. Grosset & Dunlap, 1984.

Possum Magic by M. Fox. Illustrated by J. Vivas. Abingdon, 1987.

The Reason for a Flower by R. Heller. Grosset & Dunlap, 1983.

Relatives Came by C. Rylant. Bradbury, 1985.

Rocks and Minerals by D. J. Arneson. Kidsbooks, 1990.

Round Trip by A. Jonas. Greenwillow, 1983.

Sarah, Plain and Tall by P. McLachlan. Cranston, 1988.

Saturn by S. Simon. Morrow, 1985.

School Bus by D. Crews. Greenwillow, 1984.

The Search for Delicious by N. Babbitt. Farrar, Straus, & Giroux, 1969.

The Secret Life of Hardware by V. Cobb. Lippincott, 1982.

Seeds: Pop, Stick, Glide by P. Lauber. Crown, 1981.

Seeing Earth from Space by P. Lauber. Orchard Books, 1990.

Sees Behind Trees by M. Dorris. Hyperion, 1996.

Sheep on a Ship by N. Shaw. Houghton Mifflin, 1989.

Shell by A. Arthur. Knopf, 1989.

Sitti's Secrets by S. Nye. Illustrated by N. Carpenter. Four Winds, 1994.

The Snow Queen by H. C. Andersen. Macmillan, 1985.

Splash! by A. Jonas. Greenwillow, 1995.

Stringbean's Trip to the Shining Sea by V. B. Williams & J. Williams. Scholastic, 1988.

Sun by S. Simon. Morrow, 1986.

Sundiata by R. Bertol. Crowell, 1990.

Sweet Clara and the Freedom Quilt by D. Hopkinson. Illustrated by J. Ransome. Knopf, 1993.

Take My Word for It by V. Pizer. Dodd, Mead, 1981.

The Tale of Aladdin and the Wonderful Lamp by E. Kimmel. Illustrated by J. Cheng. Holiday House, 1992.

Talk about English: How Words Travel and Change by J. Klausner. Crowell, 1990.

Tam Lin by S. Cooper. Macmillan, 1991.

Tar Beach by F. Ringold. Crown, 1991.

The Three Bears and 15 Other Stories by A. Rockwell. Crowell, 1975.

Three Days on a River in a Red Canoe by V. B. Williams. Mulberry Books, 1981.

Three Jovial Huntsmen by S. Jeffers. Bradbury, 1973.

To Be a Slave by J. Lester. Dial, 1968.

Townsend's Warbler by P. Fleischman. HarperCollins, 1992.

Train to Somewhere by E. Bunting. Illustrated by R. Himler. Clarion, 1996.

Tree by D. Burne. Knopf, 1988.

The Trek by A. Jonas. Greenwillow, 1985.

Traveling to Tondo by V. Aardema. Knopf, 1991.

Trucker by H. H. Wurmfeld. Macmillan, 1990.

Truck Song by D. Diebert. Illustrated by B. Barton. Crowell, 1984.

Tuesday by D. Wiesner. Clarion, 1991.

The Turn About, Think About, Look About Book by B. Gardner. Lothrop, 1983.

Turtle Knows Your Name by A. Bryan. Macmillan, 1989.

Under the Sunday Tree by E. Greenfield. Harper & Row, 1988.

A Very Young Dancer by J. Krementz. Dell, 1986.

Village of Round and Square Houses by A. Grifalconi. Little, Brown, 1986.

Viva Mexico by A. Palacios. Steck-Vaughn, 1992.

Volcano: The Eruption and Healing of Mount St. Helens by P. Lauber. Bradbury, 1986.

Wagon Wheels by B. Brenner. Illustrated by D. Bolognese. Harper & Row, 1978.

Walk Together Children: Black American Spirituals by A. Bryan. Aladdin, 1981.

Watch the Stars Come Out by R. Levinson. Illustrated by D. Goode. Dutton, 1985.

Water's Way by L. W. Peters. Illustrated by T. Rand. Little, Brown, 1991.

The Way Things Work by D. Macaulay. Houghton Mifflin, 1988.

When Africa Was Home by K. L. Williams. Orchard Books, 1991.

When Schlemiel Went to Warsaw by I. B. Singer. Farrar, Straus, & Giroux, 1986.

Where Are You Going, Manyoni? by C. Stock. Morrow, 1993.

Where Do They Go? Insects in Winter by M. Selsam. Four Winds, 1982.

Where the Waves Break: Life at the Edge of the Sea by A. Malnig. Nature Watch Books, 1985.

Where the Wild Things Are by M. Sendak. Harper & Row, 1963.

Who Came Down That Road? by G. E. Lyon. Illustrated by P. Catalanotto. Orchard, 1992.

Who Says a Dog Goes Bow-Wow? by H. De Zutter. Illustrated by S. MacDonald. Bantam, 1993.

Working Cotton by S. A. Williams. Harcourt Brace Jovanovich, 1992.

World of Wonders: A Trip Through Numbers by S. Ockenga & E. Doolittle. Houghton Mifflin, 1988.

The Wretched Stone by C. Van Allsburg. Houghton Mifflin, 1991.

Young Martin's Promise by W. D. Myers. Steck-Vaughn, 1992.

Zorah's Magic Carpet Ride by S. Czernecki. Hyperion, 1996.

Prototype 5A: Fourth Grade—CHANGES

Changes Prototypes 5A and 5B

The same theme can take very different directions.

There are two CHANGES themes described in this prototype. You will notice some similarities between the two approaches, but each teacher thinks very differently about how to approach this theme. Some of the decisions are based on the resources available in a particular location (i.e., rural versus urban or suburban); others are based on different curricular requirements. Still others grow out of the teacher's plans for future studies or on what has already happened in the course of the school year. As you read, think about the ways in which you might have approached this theme.

Schedule

Prototype 5A takes place in a rural setting.

Ted Jackson's fourth grade is located in a building that used to house classes for children with special needs. Classrooms were designed to accommodate ten children, but Ted has twenty-five fourth graders, two rabbits, science equipment, boxes of math manipulatives, and assorted paraphernalia related to other subject areas. A grant Ted wrote two years ago means that there are also two computers, a printer, and some software. Noise from an ancient heating system accompanies much of the work in the classroom, but large windows on one wall provide sunlight and an uninterrupted view of the mountains behind the school.

Because there are no art or music specialists, Ted and the other fourth-grade teacher, Amber Richardson, arrange their schedules so that Ted teaches music and his colleague teaches art. They schedule planning time during the children's P.E. and library periods. In addition, the two teachers jointly sponsor a monthly school/community newspaper, so they schedule a weekly time for editorial conferences with student reporters. (See Table 4.9.)

Themes can connect community and world.

Both teachers feel strongly that their students need to understand their community and how it is connected to the world. As a result, they try to bring the community into the school and students into the community as often as possible. But at the beginning of the year, children told Ted that social studies was their least favorite subject, declaring it boring and not useful. Because Ted is determined to help children see the relevance of social studies to their lives, he has focused his teacher inquiry on building student interest in this area. Ted is particularly interested in the success that some teachers have had with "Foxfire" types of oral history projects, especially in small communities such as his. As a result, a major part of his teacher inquiry is the effect of a school/community newspaper on students' interest in social studies.

Table 4.9 *Weekly Schedule, Ted Jackson's Fourth-Grade Class*

Time	Monday	Tuesday	Wednesday	Thursday	Friday
7:30	Teacher arrival and setup				
8:00	Children arrival and "jobs" time				
8:10	Whole-class activity		Physical education Library	Newspaper	Whole-class activity
9:15	Integrated work time				
10:00	Recess				
10:15	Integrated work time			Art/Music	Integrated work time
11:30	Literature				
12:00	Lunch				
12:45	Art/Music	Math			
1:30	Individual or group time				Physical education Library
2:00	Cleanup				
2:15	Dismissal				

Into the Classroom

The idea for the theme CHANGES began with the newspaper. Ted and Amber had been working with students on determining what counted as "news." After much discussion, the students began writing a list titled "It's News If . . ." At the top of the list was this sentence: "It's news if it makes things change." This seemed like a perfect opportunity to introduce a concept that was important to much of the fourth-grade curriculum. The science curriculum was supposed to emphasize physical science, while social studies was supposed to be local and state studies, and U.S. regional geography, with attention to global connections.

At first, Ted thought that change might be too enormous a concept to deal with in a single thematic unit. After all, he told Amber jokingly, how many things could she think of that didn't change? As he planned, however, Ted decided to emphasize aspects of change most directly related to the fourth-grade science and social studies curriculum and to the local community. As you read through Table 4.10, you will notice that on the first day, Ted uses a whole-class activity that generates a lot of discussion about various aspects of two kinds of communities—urban and rural. Later, he uses these ideas to help children analyze their own community. Ted also moves the concept of change into the area of science immediately after children have considered it in terms of human communities. On Day 1, students are engaged in changing the shape or state of matter. Ted emphasizes the move to science by changing the room into "Jackson Laboratories." The children love the role playing and easily adapt to the rules for laboratory behavior, including inventing some rules of their own.

Ted also schedules a separate time each day to work on literature and mathematics. These are flexible time periods, and on Day 15 he substitutes a special program for the math time period. Generally, however, Ted tries to provide intensive work in both areas every day.

Prototype 5A: Fourth Grade—CHANGES

Imaginary and Magical Changes

SYLVESTER AND THE MAGIC PEBBLE
THE DONKEY PRINCE
THE FROG PRINCE
THE FROG PRINCESS
DAWN
THE CRANE WIFE
GRAHAM OAKLEY'S MAGICAL CHANGES
CHANGES CHANGES
FISH IS FISH
"YOU LOOK RIDICULOUS," SAID THE
   RHINOCEROS TO THE HIPPOPOTAMUS
THE MIXED-UP CHAMELEON
THE BOGGART
THE FIREBIRD
JOURNEY OF THE NIGHTLY JAGUAR

Experiment with changes in color mixing.
Interview the "changelings" in stories. What are
   their lives like now?
Make a mural showing all the characters before
   and after.
Make a Comparison Chart* of magical changes.
Imagine that you can change your community—
   draw a picture of what you would like it to
   look like in 100 years.
Make a list of folk and fairy tale characters who
   can change shape. Invent a shape changer and
   write your own folk or fairy tale. What will be
   the moral of your story?
Discuss: What do these characters learn from
   their shape changing?

Changes in Countries and Cultures

WHEN I WAS YOUNG IN THE MOUNTAINS
IN COAL COUNTRY
TREE OF CRANES
THESE LANDS ARE OURS
THE DISCOVERY OF THE AMERICAS
THE INVENTION BOOK
THE WAY THINGS WORK
LOTUS SEED
MY PLACE

How do countries or cultures change?
What if. . .? activity. How would life be
   different if some historical events/inventions
   had been different? What if cars were not
   invented? What if Native Americans had
   kept control of the Americas? What if all
   people could read and write? What if
   everyone had enough food to eat?
What events in your community have brought
   about the most change?

Changing Mathematically

ANNO'S MYSTERIOUS MULTIPLYING JAR
WHAT COME IN 2'S, 3'S AND 4'S
THE GREATEST GUESSING GAME: A
   BOOK ABOUT DIVIDING
BUILDING TABLES IN TABLES: A BOOK
   ABOUT MULTIPLICATION
THE DOORBELL RANG
ED EMBERLEY'S PICTURE PIE
"Little Bits"

Create designs using fractional parts of
   geometric shapes.
How many bites does it take to eat a "whole"?
Discuss equivalent names for a "whole"
   (2/2, 24/24).
Do a fraction hunt (Door 1/2 shut;
   a pane =1/8 of a window).
Create a class book out of findings.
Figure the number of seating possibilities at
   a table.
Make a list of common sets of objects
   (days of the week, pairs of socks, etc.).
How many ways do students use fractions
   in their daily lives (half past three, 10% off)?

CHANGES

Changing Feelings

THERE'S A NIGHTMARE IN MY CLOSET
THE WAY I FEEL...SOMETIMES
SHADES OF GRAY
HEARTBREAK: A STORY OF VIETNAM
THE BOOK OF CHANGES

Make "then" and "now" pictures of how feelings have changed.
Practice conflict management techniques.
Set up a class system for peer discussion of interpersonal issues.
Discuss: How do disagreements get settled in a democracy?
   What happens if they can't be settled?

Changing Environments

The Changing Earth

SAVE THE EARTH
THE SALAMANDER ROOM
THE WORLD THAT JACK BUILT
RECYCLE: A HANDBOOK FOR KIDS
WERE YOU A WILD DUCK, WHERE WOULD YOU GO?
THE GREAT KAPOK TREE
JUST A DREAM
WHERE THE FOREST MEETS THE SEA
SOMEWHERE TODAY
GOING GREEN: A KID'S HANDBOOK TO SAVING THE PLANET
LETTING SWIFT RIVER GO
YOU'RE ABOARD SPACESHIP EARTH
IT'S OUR WORLD, TOO!

Create a mural showing natural features in different regions of the United States and how people have
   changed those features.
Identify an environmental problem in your community and work on helping solve the problem.
Invite local people to talk about how the community takes care of garbage and waste.
Visit a recycling center.
Start a recycling project in your school.
Make "trash" puppets out of discarded material.
Create a Puppet Show* on environmental issues.
Test air and water in area for pollutants.
Write to major polluters with suggestions for cleaning up their act.
Study effects of erosion.
Design an environmentally "friendly" invention.
Compare regions of the United States in terms of pollution. Compare with other parts of the world.
Create a "Declaration of Environmental Rights" for the UN that guide countries as they deal with
   environmental issues.
Video: *Rainforest Voices*
Group Composed Writing* based on video.
What could you live without? Make a chart of those appliances/products that do the most damage to
   the environment. Make a plan for limiting usage.
Survey products to see how many use recycled material.

Seasons, Weather, Day, and Night

CLOUDY WITH A CHANCE OF MEATBALLS
YEAR AFTER YEAR
WEATHER WATCH
MY FAVORITE TIME OF THE YEAR
SUN UP, SUN DOWN
ALL IN A DAY
THE MOON SEEMS TO CHANGE
WONDERS OF SEASONS
GRANDFATHER TWILIGHT
EARTHQUAKE!
WEATHER
HURRICANES
THE MAGIC SCHOOLBUS INSIDE A
   HURRICANE

Build a weather station and collect data. Compare with
   data in newspaper. Compute percentage for accuracy.
Interview a meteorologist.
Paint the same place as seen at different times of the day.
Make a calendar showing phases of the moon.
How does weather affect how people live?
After reading *Earthquake*, collect data on weather-related
   problems. Write a "Be Prepared" booklet or a news
   article to help people in your community.
Interview people about their memories of natural disasters
   (drought, fire).

Changes in Ideas, Attitudes, and Perspectives

THE TRUE STORY OF THE THREE LITTLE PIGS
JIM AND THE BEANSTALK
ROUND TRIP
BEAUTY AND THE BEAST
DRAWING ON THE RIGHT SIDE OF THE BRAIN

Do frame of reference activity.
Make a Comparison Chart* of alternative fairy tales.
Write a story from a different point of view.
View optical illusions (M.C. Escher, Anno).
Draw a picture of an optical illusion.
Do some of the activities in *Drawing on the Right Side of the Brain*.
Act out *Jim and the Beanstalk* from Jim's mother's perspective.

W.E.B. DU BOIS
SOJOURNER TRUTH
TO FLY WITH THE SWALLOWS
THEY SHALL BE HEARD
THE MOUNTAIN MAN AND THE PRESIDENT
WALKING FOR FREEDOM
A LONG HARD JOURNEY
"Dreams"

Read and discuss biographies of people who tried to change society.
Make a "Hall of Change." Include people who have changed society for the better. Develop criteria for admission. Submit candidates and debate merits for inclusion. Select people from your own community and have an introduction ceremony.
What ideas and attitudes still need to be changed? Make a plan for change.
Dramatize the lives of people who are change agents.
Invite speaker to class to talk about how they are trying to change people's ideas and attitudes.

I SPY: AN ALPHABET IN ART

Study perspective in art. How does an artist make you "see" in a particular way? Collect examples of different styles of art. Categorize by the artist's perspective or how the viewer responds. Look for art that is also social commentary.
Practice using perspective in own artwork.
Create political cartoons on an issue you feel is important.

Social Changes

Changes in Fashions

FASHIONS OF THE DECADE
COSTUME
FROM TOP HATS TO BASEBALL CAPS, FROM BUSTLES TO BLUE JEANS
AMERICA'S CHILDREN
WHERE WILL THIS SHOE TAKE YOU?

Make a T-shirt.
Put on a historical fashion show.
Create a mural of fashions that show changing attitudes toward men's and women's roles.
Create advertisements for the next fashion trend.
Listen to music from different eras. What major changes do you note?
Collect advertisements that show changing fashion/pop culture.
Make a "Fashions of the Nineties" book.

Changes in Matter: From One State to Another

POPCORN
THE POPCORN BOOK
WHAT HAPPENS TO HAMBURGER
MESSING ABOUT WITH BAKING CHEMISTRY

Experiment with different states of water: Heating, cooling. Try to make a container that can keep an ice cube from melting.
Bubble explorations: How can you change the shape of a bubble? Make it bigger or smaller?
Make bread. Keep track of all the changes the ingredients undergo.
Grow crystals.
Visit a food processing plant.
Record observations of a rusting nail or a tarnishing silver spoon.
Make popcorn, butter, Jell-O. Record the changes observed.
Time evaporation/dehydration rates for various liquids/plants.

Changes in Communities

THE STORY OF A FARM
THE STORY OF AN ENGLISH VILLAGE
THE STORY OF A MAIN STREET
THE CHANGING CITY
THE CHANGING COUNTRYSIDE
WHO CAME DOWN THAT ROAD?
DAYS OF COURAGE
OLD HOME DAY
WHEN THE WHIPPOORWILL CALLS
HOMEPLACE

Find evidence of change in your community.
Discuss: How can we tell what is good and what is bad?
What problems are associated with change?
What changes have created the most problems for your community?
What should your community look like in the year 2000?
Collect oral histories from people who have lived in the community a long time.
Write books and articles based on community study.
Predict what changes you think are most likely to happen next in your community.
Pick different aspects of community and create a time line showing how they have changed over time (i.e., schooling, fire fighting, shopping).
Graph changes in population and develop a written explanation of graph.
Compare maps of community for different time periods.
Put oral histories on a time line.
Plan a community celebration or festival.
Survey different occupations in the community. What were the most common occupations 25 years ago? 50 years ago? 100 years ago? And so on. Display data set.
Study community services. Which have been most helpful to you or your family? What services do you think your community needs? Which would you change?
What's really in your school yard?
Clip pictures, charts, and diagrams from local newspaper for one week. Sort and display. Make Observations and Inferences*. What changes do these data indicate?
Trace language changes in your community. Make a dictionary of current slag. Interview older people to find out what slang they used.

Changes in Families

CECIL'S STORY
MOM'S NEW JOB
DAYS WITH DADDY
SARAH, PLAIN AND TALL
THE WALL
MISSING MAY
THREE NAMES
"Mother Doesn't Want a Dog"
"I Am Cherry Alive"
SUN AND SPOON
WALK TWO MOONS
TROUT SUMMER
UNCLE JED'S BARBERSHOP

Make a family photo album that shows change over time in families.
Make a chart showing some of the ways in which families change.
Pictures of families in other countries/cultures. How does culture influence/change a family? Make a book showing family customs.
Survey the different roles family members have. How/when do these roles change? (Son may become husband, father, grandfather.)
Discuss how "family" changes in *Missing May*.
Make a life history for a toy. Invent a toy for the future.
Collect popular games, songs, etc. from different periods of time.

Table 4.10 *Detailed Schedule, Ted Jackson's Fourth-Grade Class*

Day 1

Time	Children	Teacher	Teacher Research
Teacher Arrival 7:30		Ted checks his mail and organizes materials for the day.	
Children Arrival 8:00	Children enter room and greet teacher and peers. They go immediately to jobs: check on the class animals, take attendance and water plants. Most notice the pictures hung along one wall and gather to look at each panel.	Ted greets children, talks individually with several, and collects permission slips for walking trip.	
Whole-Class Activity 8:10	Students look over the travel guide and begin their observations. Different teams work on the following: • finding evidence of change over time • finding evidence that some things do not change over time. • selecting a point in time when it would be best to live in their location • finding evidence of people's occupations • finding evidence of changes that helped or hurt people. Students are excited about what they have found, and all want to share. One team points out a blind man who appears in each of *The Changing City* pictures. They want to tell his story. Another team suggests having a mock interview with one of the characters in *The Changing Countryside*.	Ted gives pairs of children "time travel guides" and tells them that they will be taking a tour of the pictures they see hanging in the room. The pictures from *The Changing City* and *The Changing Countryside* show change over a long period of time in two locations. Each picture represents a three-year change from the last picture. Ted explains that the travel guides will help focus the students' observations. Ted monitors student work, asking questions when a team seems stuck or observations seem unsupported. Ted gathers students for discussion of their Observations and Inferences*. Ted helps students decide how they could share what they have discovered. He suggests that Friday would be a good day to share these projects and plans with the children to organize their work time.	
Integrated Work Time 9:15	Most children work on ideas generated during whole group time. Two children continue work begun last week on a computer program on Graphing*.	Ted works with small groups. He then meets with the computer team and suggests that they use their new Graphing* skills with their data on occupations in *The Changing City*. Could they compare occupations in the pictures with those in their own community?	
Recess 10:00		Ted sets up for laboratory stations.	
Integrated Work Time 10:15	Children put on their "lab coats"—adult-size shirts that Ted has collected over the years—and go to their laboratory stations. Stations include background reading and experiments to: • Create a container that can keep an ice cube from melting • Study bubble states. (Can you change the size and shape of a bubble?) • Grow crystals • Dissolve substances • Prevent erosion on a slope	As children reenter the room from recess, they are greeted with a large sign that reads "Jackson Laboratories: We study change." Each receives a laboratory station assignment and a "lab coat." Ted reminds students of lab rules. He moves between groups, taking notes on problem areas and topics to be discussed in follow-up. He makes sure that students are recording their experiments in their logs, periodically stopping the class to point	

(continued)

Table 4.10 *Detailed Schedule, Ted Jackson's Fourth-Grade Class (continued)*

Day 1

Time	Children	Teacher	Teacher Research
	Children take careful notes in their Learning Logs*.	out a particularly interesting piece of record-keeping or experimenting.	
	Stations are cleaned and materials put away.	Ted calls for cleanup, reminding children that good scientists are careful of their equipment.	
	Children report on the status of their experiments. Groups working on similar projects compare results and all discuss what could account for differences and the impact of changes observed.	Ted explains how important careful notes are in doing experiments. He asks children to confirm their reports by referring back to their logs. He asked whether people can benefit from the changes they observed.	
Literature 11:30	Children discuss transformation stories. They decide that transformations are sometimes used to teach a person a lesson (i.e., *Beauty and the Beast*). Children listen to two versions of frog-to-human transformations. Some are familiar with *The Frog Prince* and comment on how awful it would be to kiss a frog: "You'll get warts on your lips!"	Ted talks about the ancient belief in alchemy and about how many stories involve change. He introduces the term "transformation:" Why would someone want to transform? How are transformations used in the literature they are familiar with? Ted introduces *The Frog Prince*. Ted explains that neither frogs nor toads cause warts, but he doesn't suppose that would make kissing one much better. He then introduces *The Frog Princess*.	
Math 12:45	Children create designs using fractional parts of geometric shapes. For homework, they are to see how many geometric shapes and fractions of shapes are in one room.	Ted reads *Ed Emberley's Picture Pie* and introduces geometric shapes and how changing them can create interesting designs. He collects children's work and displays it.	
Individual or Group Time 1:30	Children work on projects begun earlier in the day or meet with Ted to discuss books they have been reading.	Ted meets with Literature Response Groups*: • *Shades of Gray*. He asks students to talk about how each of the major characters changed during the course of the story. • *Heartbreak: A Story of Vietnam*. He listens as the students discuss what this war must have been like and suggests that this might be an important topic to add to their new unit.	
Cleanup 2:00	Children put all work away and gather at the front of the room.	Ted leads a discussion of the day's work and how it relates to the CHANGES theme. He asks students to think about other aspects of changes, as they will be planning for the new unit tomorrow.	
Dismissal 2:15			

Day 4

Time	Children	Teacher	Teacher Research
Whole Class Activity	Children gather supplies for walking trip, meet their assigned team of reporters, and confirm jobs. Some students have already made a map to guide the walking tour of the	Ted reminds children of their job: to find evidence of change in their own community, using some of the categories they used with the pic-	Ted keeps a small notebook for recording his observations of students as they work in the community. He

(continued)

Table 4.10 DETAILED SCHEDULE, TED JACKSON'S FOURTH-GRADE CLASS (CONTINUED)

Day 4

Time	Children	Teacher	Teacher Research
	small town where the school is located. Children gather data about change in their own community as they walk. They note the presence of window air conditioners, of fresh paint on one store front, and a "For Lease" sign on another. As they walk toward the hillside that borders one side of the town, they note evidence of erosion and illegal garbage disposal. They also note signs of a change in seasons—woolly worms inching across the street, and orange and red in the leaves on the hillside. One group gathers natural material and found objects to be used for an art project. Another group takes texture rubbings from manhole covers, a cornerstone on the courthouse, even an out-of-state license plate. The mechanic at the gas station stops to chat and ends up giving an interview. Their excitement is contagious and they stay on task and are not ready to return to class when the trip is over.	tures on Day 1. Ted makes sure that the parent volunteers all have the right group of five children and the right maps and assignments.	also has a folder where he is keeping files of student work on their newspaper/community activity. Ted moves from group to group, noting questions and discoveries in his notebook. The walking trip provides him with plenty of data about student enthusiasm for their own community.
8:10 Integrated Work Time	Children work in groups on projects begun during the morning walk. Some of their ideas include the following: • Describe the physical features of the community. This group decides that, as they only saw the top of the physical features, they should make a cross section of the community. This could make an interesting article in the newspaper, too—a story called "What's Under Our Town?" • Graph changes in employment in the community. Based on their conversation with the mechanic, this group decides to do further research on the relationship between jobs and population. • Study maps of the community for different time periods. • Who lives here? This group decides to work with the jobs people and compile information by interviewing representative members of the community.	Ted works with children, helping them make decisions about how to organize their work. There are so many ideas that he tells the children they will concentrate on some of their ideas now and work on others later in the unit. He also reminds them that they will be able to put articles in the paper all year long, so some projects can extend throughout the year. As they work, they will have to make decisions about what projects need to be extended.	Ted asks students to use their Learning Logs* to tell him why they think the projects they are suggesting are important. This will provide data on how the children are making sense of the work at this point.
10:15 Literature	Children listen to the book. They discuss how the town in the story compares with their community. Pairs of children analyze individual pictures, looking for clues to time. Each group lists useful clues.	Ted reads *The Story of a Main Street*. He shows them a set of pictures that show their town at different times in history and asks if they can figure out what order the pictures go in. He tells them they will work on this project after lunch.	

(continued)

Table 4.10 *Detailed Schedule, Ted Jackson's Fourth-Grade Class (continued)*

Day 15

Time	Children	Teacher	Teacher Research
11:30 Newspaper	Depending on how far along their articles are, children meet with peer editors, with one of the two fourth grade teachers, or with the layout editor. Work is intense as stories are scrutinized and decisions made about what articles should go in which issue of the newspaper. By-lines and length are negotiated, with reporters wanting more space and editors trying to cut to fit in more articles.	Ted and his colleague, Amber, check final drafts, show students how to use the spell check on the computer, and help negotiate disputes. Ted discusses how people should not be quoted in an article and why it is important to be accurate. Amber works with the layout editor. The two of them are learning a new computer program for this project.	There is no time now to take notes, but Ted tape records his thoughts on the drive home. He is amazed at how careful the children are to accurately represent the people they interviewed so that they will be pleased with what is written about them. Ted now has documents in which children developed editorial rules for checking facts, confirming interviews, and establishing ethical behavior of reporters. Some of the people they are interviewing are, after all, their parents, and they all want to "get it right."
8:10 Integrated Work Time 9:15	Children watch video.	Because newspaper time is so intense, Ted plans a quiet introduction to integrated work time on Fridays. Today he shares a video on Appalachian stereotypes from Appalshop. The topic of regional stereotypes has come up several times, and this seems a good way to move the children toward looking at how environment and culture are linked.	
	Children make a list of stereotypes they have heard for different regions and parts of the world. Different groups form to find out what several of these places are really like. Their task is to prove that stereotypes stop us from seeing what is really there.	Ted asks where they think these ideas came from. He then conducts a frame-of-reference activity with the children in which they "see" what they expect to see. Ted views this activity as a good introduction to the concept of region that is part of the social studies curriculum.	
Integrated Work Time 10:15	Groups and individuals work on projects begun earlier: • Mural of how their community should look in 100 years. • Chart of changes due to dehydration. • A "Be Prepared" booklet based on an interview with a forest ranger. • Time line of trends in fashion as they relate to changing social roles for men and women. They have also been able to use interview data. • Changes in family roles. • Biography of people who change ideas and attitudes.	Ted works with the time line group in organizing their data. He suggests that they try the computer program "Timeliner." Ted also spends time with the biography group as they debate whether peaceful protest is the best way to get people to change. He asks them to list all the ways they can think of that would get people to change their ideas, and then to prioritize them: Which would be most effective? Could any be used in their own class?	Ted takes notes on the suggestions students make for dealing with conflict over public issues. He particularly notes evidence on students' use of the "democratic principles" they developed earlier in the year. Besides being interested in social studies, he also wants his students to draw on their knowledge to solve problems.
Literature 11:30	Children practice interpretive readings based on *Sojourner Truth, W. E. B. Du Bois, Walking for Freedom,* and *They Shall be Heard.* Children have selected passages that they thought	Ted listens to different groups and makes suggestions for more effective or dramatic readings. He asks two groups to share their readings with the rest of the class.	Children have written about these readings in their Journals*, and Ted has been interested in how often they

(continued)

Table 4.10 *Detailed Schedule, Ted Jackson's Fourth-Grade Class (continued)*

Day 15

Time	Children	Teacher	Teacher Research
	best capture the spirit of particular events or characters. They plan to incorporate these readings into the Hall of Change induction ceremony to be held after lunch.		have said that the books "tell them the truth" about historical events. "We didn't know people did these things," they say. This is a pattern he has observed throughout the unit, as children tell him orally and in writing that they "need to know" about the things they are now studying.
Special Program 12:45	Children enter the auditorium to begin the induction ceremony into the Hall of Change. They have invited people from the community and other classes. Several students act as reporters. This event will be on the front page of the next issue of their newspaper. Students conduct the program, including a brief slide show of Hall of Change inductees selected from historic figures. Each group presents their choral reading as a slide depicts the face of the person or persons honored. The student emcee then reads the criteria for admission. Other children present each of the honorees from the community and explain why he or she was selected. A final student speaker invites everyone in the audience to become a change agent—someone who makes the community a better place. She also invites everyone to send suggestions for improving the community to the class newspaper, where these ideas will be published and discussed. The program closes with a poem titled "Keep on Changing," written by one of the children and performed by several children.	Ted greets the honorees and shows them to their seats on the stage. The principal welcomes guests and turns the program over to the fourth grade. Ted keeps a program in hand to prompt students as necessary, but everyone is prepared and anxious to start. Each honoree comes forward and receives a certificate designed by the students and a giant golden key to the school, also made by the students. Each key is inscribed with some of the qualifications or activities of the recipient.	

Summary

The community becomes a laboratory.

Like many of the other teachers described in these prototypes, Ted provides a variety of opportunities for students to share their work. Two major ways presented in Table 4.10 are the newspaper project and the Hall of Change. The newspaper project provides a regular outlet for student inquiry and receives a great deal of attention in the community. This is a small town and the school is an important community center. Adults stop children on the street to comment on their articles, suggest other stories, or simply to tell the students that their work is enjoyed. Parents and relatives hang articles on refrigerator doors and send them to out-of-town relatives. Community members also enjoy being interviewed for stories so much that they dig old items out of attics and call students to come see unusual crafts and artifacts or hear stories. There is an enormous sense of pride as the children see their work getting this kind of attention, and older community members are pleased to have their past respected and made part of the children's present. This has been particularly useful for children from the more rural parts of the community. Some had been shy about the more traditional ways of some of their family, but the oral history and newspaper projects have made their relatives celebrities. A grandfather who couldn't read taught students how to make Whimmydiddles—old-fashioned wooden toys. An aunt who used to seem old-fashioned now teaches children how to identify edible and medicinal plants. Equally importantly, the regional dialects and local idioms gain respect by being studied. As children try to render speech accurately, they also pay careful attention to the differences between written and oral language as well as between different English variants.

The Hall of Change grew out of children's interviews with community members. They had met people who worked to get improved safety conditions in area mines or set up crafts cooperatives to market traditional crafts. One woman was the first woman mayor in the county. Another man worked to get part of the mountain behind the school set aside as protected land. The children wanted them honored and got the principal's permission to set aside one hallway to display pictures and articles about these people. They also included historical figures who brought about important changes. Both the hall display and the induction ceremony provide further audiences for children's work.

Obviously not every school is set in an Appalachian town where the modern and traditional meet in such distinctive ways. Nonetheless, schools in other locales have equally interesting communities around them that can provide similar laboratory experiences. It is important to note, however, that Ted moves the children beyond the local. He helps children see the connections between local events and those in the rest of the world. When children study local environmental issues, they look for other parts of the world where similar problems exist. They continually ask: Has this happened anywhere else? How did people there react? Ted subscribes to the "think globally, act locally" doctrine. His teacher research not only supports his notion that local problems will engage children's interest and lead them to better understand larger social issues but also demonstrates the power of real audiences for student work. His work has raised questions about what counts as "truth" in relation to social studies and how teachers might help children understand the importance of multiple perspectives without losing their desire to take action. Some of the *essential questions* that guide student work include: How can we tell what is good change and what is bad? How do ideas and attitudes change? What ideas and attitudes still need to change? How can we be change agents? How does change in the environment change us? How can we study change?

Children's Literature: CHANGES (A)

All in a Day by M. Anno. Philomel, 1986.

America's Children: Real-Life Stories and Poems about Children by L. Etkin & B. Willoughby (Eds.). Golden, 1992.

Anno's Mysterious Multiplying Jar by M. Anno. Philomel, 1983.

Beauty and the Beast by M. Mayer & M. Mayer. Four Winds, 1978.

The Boggart by S. Cooper. McElderry, 1993.

The Book of Changes by T. Wynne-Jones. Orchard, 1995

Building Tables in Tables: A Book about Multiplication by J. Trivett. Crowell, 1975.

Cecil's Story by G. E. Lyon. Orchard Books, 1991.

Changes Changes by P. Hutchins. Macmillan, 1971.

The Changing City by J. Muller. Macmillan, 1977.

The Changing Countryside by J. Muller. Macmillan, 1979.

Cloudy with a Chance of Meatballs by J. Barrett. Macmillan, 1978.

Costume by L. Rowland-Warne. Knopf, 1992.

The Crane Wife by S. Yagawa. Translated by K. Paterson. Illustrated by S. Akaba. Morrow, 1981.

Dawn by M. Bang. Mulberry, 1983.

Days of Courage by R. Kelso. Streck-Vaughn. 1993.

Days with Daddy by P. Waston. Prentice-Hall, 1977.

The Discovery of the Americas by B. Maestro & G. Maestro. Mulberry, 1991.

The Donkey Prince by J. M. Craig. Illustrated by B. Cooney. Doubleday, 1977.

The Doorbell Rang by P. Hutchins. Greenwillow, 1986.

Drawing on the Right Side of the Brain by B. Edwards. St. Martins, 1988.

"Dreams" by L. Hughes. In *The Random House Book of Poetry for Children* by J. Prelutsky (Ed.). Random House, 1983.

Earthquake! by K. Wilson. Steck-Vaughn, 1993.

Ed Emberley's Picture Pie by E. Emberley. Little, Brown, 1984.

Fashions of the Decade (Vols. 1–8) by V. Cumming and E. Feldman (Eds.). Facts on File, 1991.

The Firebird by Demi. Holt, 1994.

Fish Is Fish by L. Leoni. Pantheon, 1970.

The Frog Prince by W. Gag. Coward, McCann, 1936.

The Frog Princess by E. Isele. Illustrated by M. Hague. Crowell, 1984.

From Top Hats to Baseball Caps, From Bustles to Blue Jeans by L. Perl. Clarion, 1990.

Going Green: A Kid's Handbook to Saving the Planet by J. Elkington, J. Hailes, D. Hill, & J. Makower. Puffin, 1990.

Graham Oakley's Magical Changes by G. Oakley. Atheneum, 1979.

Grandfather Twilight by B. Berger. Philomel, 1984.

The Greatest Guessing Game: A Book About Dividing by R. Froman. Crowell, 1978.

The Great Kapok Tree by L. Cherry. Harcourt Brace Jovanovich, 1990.

Heartbreak: A Story of Vietnam by W. D. Myers. Steck-Vaughn, 1993.

Homeplace by S. A. Halperin. Illustrated by W. Anderson. Orchard, 1995.

Hurricanes: Earth's Mightiest Storms by P. Lauber. Scholastic, 1996.

"I Am Cherry Alive" by D. Schwartz. In the *Random House Book of Poetry for Children* by J. Prelutsky (Ed.). Random House, 1983.

In Coal Country by J. Hendershott. Knopf, 1987.

The Invention Book by S. Caney. Workman, 1985.

I Spy: An Alphabet in Art by L. Micklethwait. Greenwillow, 1991.

It's Our World, Too! Stories of Young People Who Are Making a Difference by P. Hoose. Little, Brown, 1993.

Jim and the Beanstalk by R. Briggs. Putnam, 1989.

Journey of the Nightly Jaguar: Inspired by an Ancient Mayan Myth by B. Albert. Illustrated by R. Roth. Atheneum, 1996.

Just a Dream by C. VanAllsburg. Houghton Mifflin, 1990.

Letting Swift River Go by J. Yolen. Illustrated by B. Cooney. Little, Brown, 1992.

"Little Bits" by J. Ciardi. In *You Read to Me, I'll Read to You.* Lippincott, 1962.

A Long Hard Journey: The Story of the Pullman Porter by P. McKissack & F. McKissack. Walker, 1989.

Lotus Seed by S. Garland. Illustrated by T. Kiuchi. Harcourt, 1993.

The Magic School Bus Inside a Hurricane by J. Cole. Illustrated by B. Degen. Scholastic, 1995.

Messing about with Baking Chemistry by B. Zubrowski. Illustrated by S. Hanson. Little, Brown, 1981.

Missing May by C. Rylant. Orchard Books, 1992.

The Mixed-up Chameleon by E. Carle. Crowell, 1984.

Mom's New Job by P. Sawyer. Raintree, 1978.

The Moon of the Monarch Butterflies by J. C. George. Illustrated by K. Mak. HarperCollins, 1993.

The Moon Seems to Change by F. M. Branley. Illustrated by B. Emberley & E. Emberley. Crowell, 1987.

"Mother Doesn't Want a Dog" by J. Viorst. In *The Random House Book of Poetry for Children* by J. Prelutsky (Ed.). Random House, 1983.

The Mountain Man and the President by D. Weitzman. Steck-Vaughn, 1993.

My Favorite Time of the Year by S. Pearson. Harper, 1988.

My Place by N. Wheatley. Illustrated by D. Rawlins. Kane Miller, 1992.

Old Home Day by D. Hall. Illustrated by E. A. McCully. Browndeer, 1996.

Popcorn by M. Selsam. Photographs by J. Wexler. Morrow, 1976.

The Popcorn Book by T. dePaola. Holiday House, 1978.

Recycle: A Handbook for Kids by G. Gibbons. Little, Brown, 1992.

Round Trip by A. Jonas. Greenwillow, 1983.

Sarah, Plain and Tall by P. MacLachlan. HarperCollins, 1986.

The Salamander Room by A. Mazer. Knopf, 1991.

Save the Earth by B. Miles. Knopf, 1991.

Shades of Gray by C. Reeder. Avon, 1989.

Sojourner Truth by P. McKissack. Franklin Watts, 1992.

Somewhere Today by B. Kitchen. Candlewick Press, 1992.

The Story of a Farm by J. S. Goodall. Macmillan, 1989.

The Story of a Main Street by J. S. Goodall. Macmillan, 1987.

The Story of an English Village by J. S. Goodall. Macmillan, 1978.

Sun and Spoon by K. Henkes. Greenwillow, 1997.

Sun Up, Sun Down by G. Gibbons. Harcourt Brace Jovanovich, 1983.

Sylvester and the Magic Pebble by W. Steig. Simon & Schuster, 1969.

There's a Nightmare in My Closet by M. Mayer. Weekly Reader Books, 1968.

These Lands Are Ours: Tecumseh's Fight for the Old Northwest by K. Connell. Steck-Vaughn, 1993.

They Shall Be Heard: Susan B. Anthony and Elizabeth Cady Stanton by K. Connell. Steck-Vaughn, 1993.

Three Names by P. MacLachlan. HarperCollins, 1991.

To Fly with the Swallows by D. C. de Ruiz. Steck-Vaughn, 1993.

Tree of Cranes by A. Say. Houghton Mifflin, 1991.

Trout Summer by L. J. Conly. Holt, 1995.

The True Story of the Three Little Pigs by J. Schieszka. Scholastic, 1989.

Uncle Jed's Barbershop by M. K. Mitchell. Illustrated by J. S. Ransome. Simon, 1993.

Walking for Freedom: The Montgomery Bus Boycott by R. Kelso. Steck-Vaughn, 1993.

Walk Two Moons by S. Creech. HarperCollins, 1994.

The Wall by E. Bunting. Illustrated by R. Himler. Clarion, 1990.

The Way I Feel. . .Sometimes by B. De Regniers. Houghton Mifflin, 1988.

The Way Things Work by D. Macaulay. Houghton Mifflin, 1988.

Weather by S. Simon. Morrow, 1993.

Weather Watch by V. Wyatt. Addison Wesley, 1990.

W. E. B. DuBois by P. McKissack. Franklin Watts, 1990.

Were You a Wild Duck, Where Would You Go? by G. Mendoza. Stewart, Tabori, & Chang, 1990.

What Comes in 2's, 3's and 4's? by S. Aker. Simon & Schuster, 1990.

What Happens to a Hamburger? by P. Showers. Crowell, 1985.

When I Was Young in the Mountains by C. Rylant. Dutton, 1982.

When the Whippoorwill Calls by C. Ransom. Illustrated by K. Root. Tambourine, 1995.

Where the Forest Meets the Sea by J. Baker. Greenwillow, 1988.

Where Will This Shoe Take You? A Walk Through the History of Footwear by L. Lawlor. Walker, 1996.

Who Came Down That Road? by G. E. Lyon. Orchard Books, 1992.

Wonders of Seasons by K. Brandt. Illustrated by J. Watling. Troll, 1982.

The World that Jack Built by R. Brown. Dutton, 1991.

Year After Year by B. Binzen. Coward, McCann, & Geohegan, 1976.

"You Look Ridiculous," Said the Rhinoceros to the Hippopotamus by B. Waber. Houghton Mifflin, 1966.

You're Aboard Spaceship Earth by P. Lauber. HarperCollins, 1996.

Other Resources

Rainforest Voices (1990). Nature Science Network.

Prototype 5B: Fourth Grade—CHANGES
Schedule

Lisa Bridges is a second-year teacher in a fourth-grade classroom. The school, a relatively new one, serves a growing suburban population, with some children bused in from outlying rural areas. When she interviewed for the position, Lisa was heartened to find that many of the ideas and beliefs she had learned about in her teacher education program were being implemented in many classrooms in the district. She was hired late in August, however, and this did not give her much preparation time. She decided to move into integrated units slowly as she became accustomed to her daily responsibilities and got to know the culture of the classroom, the school, and the community. She knew from the beginning that she would read aloud several times each day. In addition, she wanted to include reading and writing workshops and to provide children with lots of reading materials in addition to the textbooks.

During her first year she decided to schedule her day in a fairly traditional manner, with reading and writing time planned for the morning and the afternoons set aside for content areas: math, science, and social studies. She planned some short themes that connected to one or more of these content areas, several genre studies, and an author study. Early in the year she found the willing and enthusiastic help of Connie Peterson, the school librarian, who suggested several of the genre studies, helped her pull together text sets of books, and gave her a list of paperback books that were available in multiple copies. Lisa appreciated Connie's interest in her students' responses to books and found her suggestions invaluable. When toward the end of that first year she decided to plan a fully-integrated unit for the following year, it seemed natural to enlist Connie's help in the planning.

As she looked ahead to her second year of teaching, Lisa consulted the state curriculum guides, where she found the word *changes* over and over again, particularly in the social studies and science guides. In social studies these concepts or content understandings included the ideas that families and places in the community, such as schools, change over time, while in science living things are affected by and affect the environment. Lisa felt that the exploring questions relating to change seemed particularly important for the children in this community, as it had been culturally homogeneous for a long time but was undergoing tremendous change—the population was spreading into the area as a result of both economic growth and flight from nearby urban areas. She realized that she could also incorporate the mathematics concepts of equivalence (by including the subtopic "No Change") and conversion (metric to feet and inches) or systems (Arabic and Roman numerals) that represented the same amount. She did some preliminary brainstorming, which included plans for possible Reflective Inquiries* into these changes, and then enlisted Connie's help.

As the two looked over Lisa's preliminary WEB, Connie made additional suggestions. The two enlisted the help of the art teacher whose suggestions helped them identify book titles that would extend the theme of change in art. Connie showed Lisa several books that she thought might be particularly relevant to the children's

Prototype 5B takes place in a suburban setting.

Prototype 5B: Fourth Grade—CHANGES

Changing Viewpoints

THE TRUE STORY OF THE THREE LITTLE PIGS

Retell other stories from different viewpoints.

MORNING GIRL
DISCOVERING CHRISTOPHER COLUMBUS

Interview people following a dramatized event. Did everyone see what happened in the same way?
Compare different versions of an event as covered on television or in newspapers.

GEORGE WASHINGTON'S BREAKFAST
IMMIGRANT KIDS
WATCH THE STARS COME OUT
THE EXPLORERS AND SETTLERS: A SOURCEBOOK OF COLONIAL AMERICA

Consult Primary Sources* about historical events. Do these give you information different from a recently published book on the topic?
Study a conflict or encounter from history. Consult as many sources as possible about the event. Dramatize the event and include the points of view of all participants.

Changing Your Mind

THE GIVER
THE LAMPFISH OF TWILL
RANDALL'S WALL
DOG FRIDAY
THE GREAT GILLY HOPKINS
A GIRL CALLED BOY
SHADES OF GREY
ARTHUR FOR THE VERY FIRST TIME
THANK YOU DR. MARTIN LUTHER KING, JR.
PLAYING BEATIE BOW

How do the characters in these books change their thinking? Have you ever had a change of mind (or heart)?

MISSISSIPPI BRIDGE
THE FRIENDSHIP
THE WELL
UNCLE JED'S BARBERSHOP
MAYFIELD CROSSING

How have events changed since the time these stories took place?
How can you get others to change their minds? Find out more about groups who have worked for human rights or to improve the human condition.
Study techniques of advertising, political campaigning, political action committees, or lobbyists.

Generational Changes

HOW DOES IT FEEL TO BE OLD?
EDDIE'S LUCK
HUMBUG
GROWING OLDER
GRANDPA'S MOUNTAIN
GRANNY THE PAG
GRANDADDY AND JANETTA
FAMILY PICTURES
HIGHER ON THE DOOR
GO FISH
THE HOUSE OF WINGS
THE UPS AND DOWNS OF CARL DAVIS III

What happens as we grow and age? Has your family been affected by aging relatives?
Are there older people in your community who could use your help or who could help you? Invite members of the older generation to become part of your classroom community. Adopt a retirement home and make regular visits. What can you learn from these people?

Changing Communities

THE BEST TOWN IN THE WORLD
MY PLACE
ISLAND BOY
EVERYTHING FROM A NAIL TO A COFFIN
MY BACKYARD HISTORY BOOK
NEW PROVIDENCE: A CHANGING CITYSCAPE
OLD HOME DAY
HOMEPLACE
SAN RAFAEL: A CENTRAL AMERICAN CITY THROUGH THE AGES
LEBEK: A CITY OF NORTHERN EUROPE THROUGH THE AGES

Study the changes in your community over time. Interview older residents; consult Primary Sources*.

CHANGES

Unnatural Changes

FARMING AND THE ENVIRONMENT
WHO REALLY KILLED COCK ROBIN?
THE MISSING 'GATOR OF GUMBO GROVE

What happens when humans interfere with nature?

GRANDPA'S MOUNTAIN
SHAKER LANE
WHEN THE WHIPPOORWILL CALLS
LETTING SWIFT RIVER GO

How are humans affected by efforts to change the environment?

Changing Language

TALK ABOUT ENGLISH: HOW WORDS TRAVEL AND CHANGE
ILLUMINATIONS
ALEF-BET: A HEBREW ALPHABET
ALPHABET ART: THIRTEEN ABC'S FROM AROUND THE WORLD
AHYOKA AND THE TALKING LEAVES
VOICES OF THE HEART
WORDS: A BOOK ABOUT THE ORIGINS OF EVERYDAY WORDS AND PHRASES

Study changing forms of symbols in different languages. Make up your own alphabet. Teach it to someone else and use it to write notes with.

WHO SAYS A DOG GOES BOW WOW?

Interview family members or community members. Make a dictionary of different words or phrases for the same thing (pop, soda, tonic, bubbly, coke).

JACK AND THE WONDER BEANS
JACK AND THE BEAN TREE
YO, HUNGRY WOLF: A NURSERY RAP

Retell a familiar story in different styles.
Find out how new words come into the language. Make a list of words from products or modern technology.

I HATE ENGLISH

Dramatize the encounter of two people who speak different languages. Find ways to make yourself understood.
Interview someone who has had to learn a new language.

Natural Changes

CHANGES
THE BIG TREE
FROM FLOWER TO FRUIT
FROM SEED TO PLANT
THE SKY TREE
APPLE VALLEY YEAR
HOW DO APPLES GROW?
THE LIFE AND TIMES OF THE APPLE
HOW THE FOREST GREW
FROM THE BEGINNING: THE STORY OF EVOLUTION
EVOLUTION

How do plants and animals grow, change, and adapt?
What changes are a natural part of the life cycle?
How do plants and animals change the environment?

SUMMER OF FIRE: YELLOWSTONE, 1998
VOLCANO: THE ERUPTION AND HEALING OF MT. ST. HELENS
ANTARCTICA: THE LAST UNSPOILED CONTINENT

How does the environment change plants and animals?

People Who Made Changes

CESAR CHÁVEZ
FANNIE LOU HAMER: FROM SHARECROPPING
   TO POLITICS
MOTHER JONES AND THE MARCH OF THE
   MILL CHILDREN
THE GREAT LITTLE MADISON
HARRIET TUBMAN: THE ROAD TO FREEDOM
MARION ANDERSON
MARTIN LUTHER KING, JR.
NATIVE AMERICAN DOCTOR: THE STORY OF
   SUSAN LAFLESCHE PICOTTE
RACHEL CARSON: VOICE FOR THE EARTH
STATESWOMAN TO THE WORLD: A STORY OF
   ELEANOR ROOSEVELT

Study the life story of a person who helped change
   the world. What were the steps they had to take
   to make these changes? What were the
   difficulties they faced?
Make a time line showing the major events in
   their lives.

Numerical Change

Compare Roman numerals to
   Arabic numerals.
Compare negative and
   positive numbers.
Learn about bases.
Compare metric to English
   measures.

Magical Changes

THE SEAL MOTHER
THE SELKIE GIRL
GREYLING
THE BOY WHO LIVED WITH THE SEALS
THE SEA KING'S DAUGHTER
THE SEAL PRINCE
THE CHILDREN OF LIR
THE FISH SKIN
THE GIRL, THE FISH, AND THE CROWN:
   A SPANISH FOLKTALE
A WHITE WAVE: A CHINESE STORY
MERMAID STORIES FROM AROUND THE WORLD
THE CRANE WIFE
THE HEDGEHOG BOY
THE DONKEY PRINCE
THE FROG PRINCE
THE FROG PRINCESS
TAM LIN

Make a Comparison Chart* of these folktales about
   transformation or shape changing. How are they
   alike and different?

THE ADVENTURES OF KING MIDAS
PONDLARKER
THE FROG PRINCE CONTINUED
A FROG PRINCE

Write a reversal or a sequel to a familiar story.

Sea Changes

SHADOWS IN THE WATER
BENEATH THE WAVES
WORLD WATER WATER
CITY UNDER THE SEA
WHEN THE RIVERS GO HOME
OCEANS: ECOLOGY WATCH
THE GREAT ASTROLABE REEF
SWIMMING WITH SEA LIONS
   AND OTHER ADVENTURES
   IN THE GALAPAGOS ISLANDS

Study marine ecology. How are water
   environments changed by pollution?

Changing Shapes

A STRANGER CAME ASHORE
SEAL CHILD
THE SEA CHILD
THE CHANGELING SEA
DAUGHTER OF THE SEA
THE MOORCHILD
SHAPE–CHANGER

Read these and other books with a
   transformation theme. What motifs
   from folklore do you find?

FINN'S ISLAND

Study the ecology of the Shetland
   Islands. How has the oil spill
   affected the sea and land habitats?

No Change

TWELVE WAYS TO GET TO ELEVEN

Study equivalence. How many ways can
   you find to represent the same
   number?
Compare equivalencies in music, money,
   cooking, and distance.

Family Changes

MAMA'S GOING TO BUY YOU A MOCKING BIRD
DEAR MR. HENSHAW
RAMONA AND HER FATHER
LOVE YOU SOLDIER
MAMA, LET'S DANCE
MY BROTHER STEVIE
BELLE PRATER'S BOY
SUN AND SPOON

How is the family affected by death, divorce, and
   unemployment? What happens when new siblings
   arrive or when someone changes jobs?

Making Changes

COME BACK, SALMON
A RIVER RAN WILD
MISS RUMPHIUS
SEEDFOLKS
JACKSON JONES AND THE PUDDLE OF THORNS
GREENING THE CITY STREETS
CARTONS, CANS, AND ORANGE PEELS: WHERE
   DOES YOUR GARBAGE GO?
THE GARDEN IN THE CITY
LIVING TREASURE: SAVING THE EARTH'S
   BIODIVERSITY
OUR VANISHING FARM ANIMALS: SAVING
   AMERICA'S RARE BREEDS
PLACES OF REFUGE: OUR NATIONAL WILDLIFE
   REFUGE SYSTEM
RECYCLING: MEETING THE CHALLENGE OF
   THE TRASH CRISIS
THE KID'S EARTH HANDBOOK
THE SIERRA CLUB KID'S GUIDE TO PLANET
   CARE AND REPAIR
IT'S OUR WORLD, TOO!

Study ways in which you can improve your local
   environment.

Changing Government, Changing Schools

GOVERNING AND TEACHING: A SOURCEBOOK
   ON COLONIAL AMERICA
THE PRESIDENT'S CABINET AND HOW IT GREW

Study changes in government over time. Visit your local
   town council and watch a town meeting. Report on the
   proceedings.

FRONT PORCH STORIES AT THE ONE ROOM
   SCHOOL
HANNAH
MILLIE COOPER, 3B
MY GREAT AUNT ARIZONA
THE ONE-ROOM SCHOOL AT SQUABBLE HOLLOW

Study educational change. How have schools in your
   community changed over time? What changes do you
   foresee in the future?

Difficult Changes

TREE OF CRANES
LITTLE BROTHER
THE LAND I LOST
LUPITA MAÑANA
MY NAME IS MARIA ISABEL
MY NAME IS SAN HO
HOLD FAST TO DREAMS

How does it feel to leave a
   familiar place? How have you
   coped with similar changes?

THE AGONY OF ALICE
LAST SUMMER WITH
   MAIZON
RABBLE STARKEY
THE CUCKOO'S CHILD
WALK TWO MOONS
MISSING MAY

How do these characters cope
   with change?

Cone (1992)

Reeder (1991)

Ransom (1995); Yolen (1992); Provensen (1987)

Dorris (1992); Yolen (1992); Pelta (1991)

Hunter (1975); Doherty (1997)

experience. One, an information book called *Come Back, Salmon,* told of a fifth-grade class that cleaned up a local river so that salmon returned to spawn. Another was *Grandpa's Mountain,* a novel set during the depression, which told of a family's fight to keep their home when the Shenandoah National Park was created. She found picture books with similar themes, *When the Whippoorwill Calls, Letting Swift River Go,* and *Shaker Lane* and suggested that these and other titles would provide an important background for helping children understand how change can be effected and the consequences of change on people and communities. This idea led to the decision to include biographies of famous change makers. As they looked over the curriculum guides, Connie noted that the social studies guide called for children to learn that history is subject to individual interpretation. She knew of many books that would fit the theme CHANGES and that would give children an opportunity to explore the idea that there are multiple perspectives of historical events. Among these were books about the prelude to and aftermath of Columbus's voyages to America, *Morning Girl,* a novel by Michael Dorris, a picture book by Jane Yolen called *Encounter,* and an information book by Kathy Pelta titled *Discovering Christopher Columbus: How History Is Invented.* Because Lisa planned to implement the unit in the fall prior to the Columbus Day holiday, the "Changing Viewpoints" subtopic seemed a particularly appropriate way to introduce the theme.

As Lisa and Connie pored over library holdings and consulted such indexes as *Adventuring with Books* and *Kaleidoscope* (see Chapter 3), they identified other titles related to the topic and goals of the unit. As they considered opportunities for inquiry that were beginning to emerge, they looked for titles that would support these possible studies. Connie's suggestion that studying the connections between transformation motifs in traditional folk literature would provide a literary aspect to the unit opened up even more titles, including the changing viewpoints and time periods that were part of a whole collection of frog prince variations. Picture books from a variety of cultures could lead into a study of more complex modern-day fantasies about transformation and shape shifting, such as Mollie Hunter's *A Stranger Came Ashore* and Berlie Doherty's *Daughter of the Sea.* As they accumulated titles, Connie was able to identify those that were already part of the library holdings, those that might be borrowed from the town library (which had a generous teacher loan policy), and those they felt were crucial to the unit and so could be ordered as part of the library budget for the following year.

Thanks to Connie, when the year began the following September, Lisa had a collection of over one hundred titles and additional resources. She also had found a partner for classroom collaboration and research. As the two women had discussed resources and shaped the WEB one of the questions that emerged was whether they were choosing titles and experiences appropriate for nine- and ten-year-olds. It had been Connie's experience that children were sometimes rushed into reading well-known books, particularly novels, that were not connected to their developmental understandings, and so she was careful to suggest titles she felt were appropriate to the interests and understandings of fourth graders. Lisa, too, felt she had chosen subtopics that were right for her children, but she wondered whether some of the topics she had chosen for inquiry might be beyond the real understanding of fourth graders and so might be covered in only superficial ways. These included not only the understanding of racial prejudice and changes effected by the civil rights movement, which were part of the subtopic "Changing Your Mind," but also that of the ability to take on a viewpoint that was very different from one's own, which would be explored as part of the subtopic "Changing Viewpoints." They decided to collaborate on researching children's responses to the topics and the literature in this thematic unit with the aim of identifying developmental patterns that might emerge in these fourth graders as well as on recording the range of variations they expected to find among children. Lisa, who would have more contact time with the children, decided to tape-record Reading Aloud* sessions and to use the children's Literature Response Group* journals and projects as sources of information. Connie volunteered to transcribe the tape recordings and to monitor library circulation to see how the theme study might influence children's book selections. (See Table 4.11.)

Table 4.11 *WEEKLY SCHEDULE, LISA BRIDGES'S FOURTH-GRADE CLASS*

Time	Monday	Tuesday	Wednesday	Thursday	Friday
8:00	Teacher preparation time				
8:45	Children arrive, put away coats, take attendance, and prepare lunch count.				
9:00	Group time. Teacher reads poetry, novel, or information book. Plans for the day are discussed.				
9:30	Integrated work time. Children work on individual or group projects. Teacher meets with small groups or has individual conferences.				
10:50	Cleanup. Put away materials, supplies, projects, and assignments in storage areas.				
11:00	Recess				
11:15	Art	Music	Library	Art	Music
12:00	Author's Chair*. Children share work with class. Teacher checks on Status of the Class*.				
12:20	Lunch and outdoor play				
1:00	SSR*. Teacher conferences with individual children.				
1:20	Book Talk*. Several children share books they have been reading.				
1:30	Focus Lesson* on Math				
2:00	Integrated work time. Children continue working on projects.				
2:50	Cleanup				
3:00	Reading Aloud*. Teacher reads aloud or asks children to share their work.				
3:30	Pass out papers. Evaluate the day. Dismissal.				

Into the Classroom

Lisa, with Connie's help, organized the unit to lead children through experiences that would build the necessary firsthand experience with ideas and contexts that they might need for the more difficult concepts to follow. A new version of a familiar folktale introduced them to the idea of different viewpoints and led into a critical study of Columbus's journeys to coincide with the Columbus Day holiday. This study, because it provided family, cultural, and historical viewpoints of Columbus's time, opened up investigations into change in their families and community. They went on to study "Magical Changes" and the familiar genre of folktales, connecting the water settings in fantasy to the study of watery ecosystems in their immediate environment. As Lisa and Connie examined the children's projects during these weeks and carefully reviewed their field notes and transcripts, they felt that the children's interest and the quality of their work warranted additional time for inquiry. After consulting the children, Lisa decided to continue the study at least until Christmas.

As you enter the classroom on Day 45 of the unit, these preliminary studies have been completed and the class is now involved in the final leg of their inquiries. (See Table 4.12.) Remember that in the previous weeks, in addition to studying science, social studies, and mathematical concepts related to change, Lisa also prepared children to think about the often very difficult issues involved in environmental, political, and social change that they are now covering. By studying differences in viewpoints between themselves, their families, and their communities, she prepared them to find that there are not always clear-cut answers or easy solutions to problems and that some people may suffer in the name of progress. Lisa hopes that by considering differing viewpoints through the eyes of characters in the books they have read and the important ideas they have researched, the children will approach their class project with energy and an understanding of the time and hard work it may require to see it through to conclusion.

Table 4.12 *Detailed Schedule, Lisa Bridges's Fourth-Grade Class*

Day 45

Time	Children	Teacher	Teacher Research
Teacher Arrival 8:00		Lisa arrives to set out special supplies.	She takes time to look through some of the children's Literature Response Group* journals and make notes in her own field notebook regarding their responses.
Children Arrival 8:45	Children arrive and begin putting away lunches. Assigned children take attendance and lunch count.	Lisa greets the children.	
Group Time 9:00	Children discuss their feelings about the fact that someone's home could be taken away by the government. Many side with Grandpa and agree that they would not allow it to happen. Others argue that sometimes this is best for most of the people or to save the environment. They mention the studies of changes in their own community they recently completed. They agree that some changes were good and some were unpleasant.	Lisa has been reading from *Grandpa's Mountain*. Lisa asks how they feel about Grandpa and Grandma's different reactions to losing their home: Do they think Grandma was wrong to let the government appraiser come? Would they have shown him around if they had been Carrie? She suggests that some of them might like to write a letter to Carrie, Grandpa, or Grandma, telling them what to do.	
Integrated Work Time 9:30	Children read materials relating to the topics of "Changing Your Mind" and "Making Changes." Some are novels, others biographies. One group is reading information books and periodicals about making ecological changes.	Lisa asks the children to read for at least thirty minutes and to respond to their journals when they reach a good stopping place. Lisa conferences with individual children.	Lisa monitors groups and sits in one of the discussions, taking notes on student response in her field notebook.
	Following their reading, the children write in their Literature Response Group* journals and work on ongoing writing projects in response to their books. Several elect to write to the Grandpa character in *Grandpa's Mountain*. One child wants to do a picture of the mountain and asks to borrow the book from Lisa. Then they meet in Literature Response Groups* to share their book responses and the writing they have been working on. One member of each group fills out a group discussion response form, and the group decides who and what they will share with the whole class after recess and art.		She will collect the writing and artwork they are doing in response to *Grandpa's Mountain* as part of the data for her study.
Cleanup 10:50	Children put away materials used that morning and prepare work to share after recess and art.	Lisa collects group response forms.	These forms give Lisa an overview of what the children have talked about in groups she didn't visit. She will use them to follow up with individual children later.
11:00	Recess	Lisa reads through the group and takes note of pertinent questions, connections, or problems.	
Art 11:15	The children are enthusiastic about the idea of decorating their own initial. They enjoy practicing different letters with the pens.	The art teacher, Joe Scott, has tied into the unit through Lisa's subtopic "Changing Language" and developed a study of art and the alphabet to tie into a traveling exhibit that is currently at the local art museum. He has introduced	

(continued)

Table 4.12 *Detailed Schedule, Lisa Bridges's Fourth-Grade Class (continued)*

Day 45

Time	Children	Teacher	Teacher Research
	One child suggests that they make a class alphabet book like *Illuminations*.	children to changing alphabets and letter forms over time. He shows them the book *Illuminations* and suggests that they design an illuminated letter for their name. Then he teaches a lesson on calligraphy, using chisel-tipped marking pens. Joe thinks this is a great idea and suggests that they also make a study of alphabet books prior to visiting the art museum.	
Author's Chair* 12:00	One child from each group becomes reporter for the morning's work. In several groups a child is ready to share a piece of writing that has been completed. Other children have questions for the authors and the group about their topics.	Lisa returns the group response sheets to the children to refresh their memory about what they discussed and worked on.	She has taken notes about what topics the children discussed and jotted down some questions that might probe for deeper responses.
SSR* 1:00	Children read silently, selecting from books, newspaper articles, or magazines relating to the CHANGES theme.	Lisa is reading Walter Dean Myers' *Now Is Your Time!* about the history of African-Americans and the civil rights movement.	
Book Talk* 1:20	Four children share their reading. One mentions that he has read a newspaper article about a fourth grade class on Long Island that was trying to prevent a developer from building on wetlands. The other children wanted to know what happened, but the article only tells that they planned to write to the legislature and the governor. Several children point out that this is what Grandpa is doing in *Grandpa's Mountain*.	Lisa shares her own interest in Myers' book and tells some of the things she hadn't known about. Lisa suggests that they start taking note of and making a list of the steps people can take to make changes. In addition to the books they are reading, she suggests they use family members and others as possible sources of information.	She tries to demonstrate her own thinking process as she responds to books. She has begun to watch for similar responses in the children's Literature Response Group* journals.
Math Focus Lesson* 1:30	Children work in pairs, giving each other Roman numerals to change into Arabic numerals.	Lisa teaches a lesson on Arabic and Roman numerals.	
Integrated Work Time 2:00	Children return to books and activities begun that morning. After reading they return to groups to brainstorm the types of things the people they are reading about did to make changes.	Lisa suggests that they continue reading for about twenty minutes, this time with an eye toward the list they have just discussed. Lisa meets with children for individual conferences.	
Cleanup 2:50	Children put away supplies and join the group.		
Reading Aloud* 3:00	Many children feel the people in this book aren't as upset about losing their homes as Grandpa. They draw parallels between these characters and some of those in the novel who are glad about the changes.	Lisa reads *Shaker Lane,* a picture book about a community relocated for a dam. She asks children to compare the feelings of the narrator of this book to Carrie's feelings in *Grandpa's Mountain.* Lisa collects some of the Book Response Journals* to take to a meeting with Connie Peterson.	
Dismissal 3:30			She and Connie will meet for about half an hour to go over the latest transcribed book discussion and follow up on patterns of response they have identified.

(continued)

Table 4.12   *Detailed Schedule, Lisa Bridges's Fourth-Grade Class (continued)*

Day 47

Time	Children	Teacher	Teacher Research
Group Time 9:00	Many children are disappointed that Grandpa couldn't save his home. They debate whether they would be like Grandma or Grandpa if the same thing happened to them. Others don't feel Grandpa did enough. They feel he should have gone right to the President to protest. Children contribute ideas such as letter writing, personal visits, boycotts, and newspaper and TV reports.	Lisa finishes *Grandpa's Mountain* and asks the children how they felt about the ending: Was it what they predicted? Were they satisfied? Lisa suggests that they make a chart of the types of recourse for change that they have been researching. As they list these on the board, she asks if they can group these actions into categories or make a sequential map of where to go first, next, and so on.	She is recording their reactions for future analysis. She is particularly interested in how they react to the less-than-happy ending.
Integrated Work Time 9:30	Children begin with reading time. When they come to their Literature Response Groups*, they talk about some of their ideas for projects. One group decides to do a Comparison Chart* summarizing their information books about ecological changes. Another group decides to do a TV interview of characters from their biographies. Other children choose individual responses.	Lisa suggests that as the children near the end of their reading they choose a way to respond to the books or topics as a whole and report back to the rest of the class. She asks each group to brainstorm activities as part of their meeting time.	
Library 11:15	Children share the inquiries and books they have been reading. The children love the book and mention that, except for the newspaper article they found about kids on Long Island, it is the first book in their studies that shows kids making changes in their community. They are enthusiastic about trying a project like this in their own community.	Connie asks the children to report on the work they have done on their study the past week. Then she begins a book called *Come Back, Salmon* about a fifth grade class in Washington that adopted a polluted stream and began a campaign to bring it back to life so that the salmon would return there to spawn. Connie checks the book out to one of the children who promises to share it with Lisa.	
Author's Chair* 12:00	The children want to share their reactions to *Come Back, Salmon* and beg Lisa to finish the book. They work back through the book, listing the events that took place over the two-year period.	Lisa knows the book and is happy to finish it with them. She suggests that they make a map of the steps the class in the book took toward accomplishing their goal. She suggests that they begin thinking about a similar project they could tackle in their own community.	

Day 50

Time	Children	Teacher	Teacher Research
Group Time 9:00	The children are fascinated with the borders of the book, which show natural and human-made artifacts found in the area at the times depicted. One child suggests that they are like the Primary Sources* they studied when they worked on their community history projects. The children have been interviewing schoolmates and families to find out what kind of community change	Lisa reads *A River Ran Wild,* a story of a group that cleans up the Nashua River in New Hampshire. She asks the children how long the cleanup project took. Lisa takes extra time this morning to lead discussion from the book to the possibilities for their own class project. They have previously listed possible sources of changes they could make in the community.	

(continued)

Table 4.12 *Detailed Schedule, Lisa Bridges's Fourth-Grade Class (continued)*

Day 50

Time	Children	Teacher	Teacher Research
	they think is needed. Many are in favor of cleaning up a pond behind the school that they studied earlier for their pond ecosystem project. Others want to improve the school playground.	Lisa asks them to think about possible problems in each of these projects. She suggests that during work time their groups make a list of steps they would need to take and any help they might require. They will come back together in the afternoon to discuss findings and see if they can reach a consensus.	
Integrated Work Time 10:00	Children read or finish projects from the previous week. When they assemble in groups, they discuss the pros and cons of the two projects suggested and then make a list of things to do, people to contact for permission, help they will need, and an estimate of how much it might cost.	Lisa meets with individual children. She monitors groups, taking notes on their discussions.	
Art 11:15	Children work on their illuminated initials.	Connie has helped Joe gather a selection of the libraries' alphabet books and other books that have unusual fonts or graphics. Joe shares some of these with the children and they talk about how the letter-forms change.	
Author's Chair* 12:00	The group that has biographies presents their dramatized interview of characters using a Phil Donahue format. The other children play the role of audience members and ask questions following the interview.	Lisa plays the part of a telephone caller and asks her own questions.	

Summary

The careful planning that went into the CHANGES unit gave children new and different perspectives on the concepts they were studying on a recurring basis, helping to deepen their understanding of important ideas as they focused on such *essential questions* as: Who and what creates change? How do different people interpret change? Why are there differences in how people interpret change? Why are some changes so difficult? When is change necessary?

Their teacher research project, Lisa and Connie felt, provided the evidence of this and increased their own knowledge of learning processes of fourth graders. Their documentation allowed them to present these positive outcomes to parents and other professionals. The CHANGES unit represented a collaboration between a beginning teacher and an experienced library professional. Not only did Connie help Lisa find books and other printed resources, but she provided valuable knowledge of and interest in children's responses to books. In return, Lisa expanded Connie's awareness of curriculum development and the processes involved in Reflective, Disciplined Inquiry* so that her own professional understandings were enhanced. They were excited about the possibilities for a continuing relationship.

Children's Literature: CHANGES (B)

The Adventures of King Midas by L. R. Banks. Morrow, 1992.
The Agony of Alice by P. R. Naylor. Atheneum, 1985.
Ahyoka and the Talking Leaves by P. Roop & C. Roop. Illustrated by Y. Miyake. Lothrop, 1992.

Air Alert: Rescuing the Earth's Atmosphere by G. Christina & A. Berry. Atheneum, 1996.
Alef-Bet: A Hebrew Alphabet by M. Edwards. Lothrop, 1992.

Alphabet Art: Thirteen ABC's from around the World by L. E. Fisher. Four Winds, 1978.

Antarctica: The Last Unspoiled Continent by L. Pringle. Simon & Schuster, 1992.

Apple Valley Year by A. Turner & S. W. Resnick. Macmillan, 1993.

Arthur for the Very First Time by P. MacLachlan. HarperCollins, 1980.

Belle Prater's Boy by R. White. Farrar, Straus, & Giroux, 1996.

Beneath the Waves: Exploring the Hidden World of the Kelp Forest by N. Wu. Chronicle, 1992.

The Best Town in the World by B. Baylor. Illustrated by R. Himler. Macmillan, 1982.

The Big Tree by B. Hiscock. Atheneum, 1991.

The Boy Who Lived with the Seals by R. Martin. Illustrated by D. Shannon. Putnam, 1993.

Cartons, Cans, and Orange Peels: Where Does Your Garbage Go? by J. Foster. Clarion, 1991.

Cesar Chavez by R. Franchere. Crowell, 1970.

The Changeling Sea by P. A. McKillip. Atheneum, 1988.

Changes by M.N. Allen & S. Rotner. Macmillan, 1991.

The Children of Lir by S. MacGill-Callahan. Illustrated by G. Spirin. Dial, 1993.

Children Save the Rain Forest by D. H. Patent. Illustrated by D. L. Perlman. Cobblehill, 1996.

City under the Sea: Life in a Coral Reef by N. Wu. Atheneum, 1996.

Come Back, Salmon by M. Cone. Illustrated by S. Wheelwright. Little, Brown, 1992.

The Crane Wife by S. Yagawa. Translated by K. Paterson. Illustrated by S. Akaba. Morrow, 1981.

The Cuckoo's Child by S. Freeman. Greenwillow, 1996.

Daughter of the Sea by B. Doherty. DK, 1997.

Dear Mr. Henshaw by B. Cleary. Morrow, 1983.

Discovering Christopher Columbus: How History Is Invented by K. Pelta. Lerner, 1991.

Dog Friday by H. McKay. McElderry, 1995.

The Donkey Prince by M.J. Craig. Illustrated by B. Cooney. Doubleday, 1977.

Earth Keepers by J. Anderson. Photographs by G. Ancona. Gulliver Green, 1993.

Eddie's Luck by K. Stevens. Atheneum, 1992.

Everything from a Nail to a Coffin by I. Van Rynbach. Orchard, 1991.

Evolution by J. Cole. Illustrated by Aliki. Crowell, 1987.

The Explorers and Settlers: A Sourcebook on Colonial America edited by C. Smith. Millbrook, 1991.

Family Pictures/Cuardos de Familia by C. L. Garza. Children's Book Press, 1990.

Fannie Lou Hamer and the Fight for the Vote by P. Colman. Millbrook, 1993.

Farming and the Environment by M. Lambert. Steck-Vaughn, 1991.

Finn's Island by E. Dunlop. Holiday House, 1992.

The Fish Skin by J. Oliviero & B. Morrisseau. Hyperion, 1993.

The Friendship by M. Taylor. Dial, 1987.

A Frog Prince by A. Berenzy. Holt, 1989.

The Frog Prince by W. Gag (Translator). Illustrated by W. Gag. Coward McCann, 1936.

The Frog Prince Continued by J. Scieszka. Illustrated by S. Johnson. Viking, 1991.

The Frog Princess by J. P. Lewis. Illustrated by G. Spirin. Dial, 1994.

From Flower to Fruit by A. O. Dowden. Crowell, 1984.

From Seed to Plant by G. Gibbons. Holiday House, 1991.

From the Beginning: The Story of Evolution by D. Peters. Morrow, 1991.

Front Porch Stories at the One Room School by E. E. Tate. Bantam, 1992.

The Garden in the City by G. Muller. Dutton, 1992.

George Washington's Breakfast by J. Fritz. Illustrated by P. Galdone. Coward McCann, 1969.

A Girl Called BOY by B. Hurmence. Clarion, 1982.

The Girl, the Fish, and the Crown: A Spanish Folktale by M. Heyer. Viking, 1995.

The Giver by L. Lowry. Houghton Mifflin, 1993.

Go Fish by M. Stolz. Illustrated by P. Cummings. HarperCollins, 1991.

Governing and Teaching: A Sourcebook on Colonial America edited by C. Smith. Millbrook, 1991.

Grandaddy and Janetta by H. V. Griffith. Illustrated by J. Stevenson. Greenwillow, 1993.

Grandpa's Mountain by C. Reeder. Macmillan, 1991.

Granny the Pag by N. Bawden. Clarion, 1996.

The Great Astrolabe Reef by A. Siy. Dillon, 1992.

The Great Gilly Hopkins by K. Paterson. Crowell, 1978.

The Great Little Madison by J. Fritz. Putnam, 1989.

Greening the City Streets: The Story of Community Gardens by B. Huff. Photographs by P. Ziebel. Clarion, 1990.

Greyling by J. Yolen. Illustrated by D. Ray. Putnam, 1991.

Growing Older by G. Ancona. Dutton, 1978.

Hannah by G. Whelan. Illustrated by L. Bowman. Knopf, 1991.

Harriet Tubman: The Road to Freedom by L. Johnson. Troll, 1982.

The Hedgehog Boy by J. Langton. Illustrated by I. Plume. HarperCollins, 1985.

Higher on the Door by J. Stevenson. Greenwillow, 1987.

Hold Fast to Dreams by A. D. Pinkney. Morrow, 1995.

Homeplace by S. A. Halperin. Illustrated by W. Anderson. Orchard, 1995.

The House of Wings by B. Byars. Viking, 1972.

How Do Apples Grow? by B. Maestro. Illustrated by G. Maestro. HarperCollins, 1992.

How Does It Feel to Be Old? by N. Farber. Illustrated by T. S. Hyman. Dutton, 1979.

How the Forest Grew by W. Jaspersohn. Illustrated by C. Eckart. Greenwillow, 1980.

Humbug by N. Bawden. Clarion, 1992.

I Hate English by E. Levine. Illustrated by S. Bjorkman. Scholastic, 1989.

Illuminations by J. Hunt. Bradbury, 1989.

Immigrant Kids by R. Freedman. Dutton, 1980.

Island Boy by B. Cooney. Viking, 1988.

It's Our World, Too! Stories of Young People Who Are Making a Difference by P. Hoose. Little, Brown, 1993.

Jack and the Bean Tree by G. E. Haley. Crown, 1986.

Jack and the Wonder Beans by J. Still. Illustrated by M. Tomes. Putnam, 1977.

Jackson Jones and the Puddle of Thorns by M. Quattlebaum. Delacorte, 1994.

Kids' Earth Handbook by S. Markle. Atheneum, 1991.

The Lampfish of Twill by J. T. Lisle. Orchard, 1991.

The Land I Lost by Q. N. Huynh. HarperCollins, 1982.

Last Summer with Maizon by J. Woodson. Delacorte, 1990.

Lebek: A City of Northern Europe through the Ages by X. Hernandez & J. Ballonga. Translated by K. Leverich. Illustrated by F. Corni. Houghton Mifflin, 1991.

Letting Swift River Go by J. Yolen. Illustrated by B. Cooney. Little, Brown, 1992.

The Life and Times of the Apple by C. Micucci. Orchard, 1992.

Little Brother by A. Baillie. Viking, 1992.

Living Treasure: Saving the Earth's Biodiversity by L. Pringle. Morrow, 1991.

Love You Soldier by A. Hest. Four Winds, 1991.

Lupita Manana by P. Beatty. Beech Tree, 1992.

Mama's Going to Buy You a Mockingbird by J. Little. Viking, 1984.

Mama, Let's Dance by P. Hermes. Little, 1991.

Marion Anderson by T. Tobias. Illustrated by S. Shimin. Crowell, 1972.

Martin Luther King, Jr. by D. Patrick. Watts, 1990.

Mayfield Crossing by V. M. Nelson. Putnam, 1993.

Mermaid Stories from around the World by M. P. Osborne. Scholastic, 1993.

Millie Cooper, 3B by C. Herman. Dutton, 1985.

The Missing 'Gator of Gunbo Grove: An Ecological Mystery by J. C. George. HarperCollins, 1992.

Missing May by C. Rylant. Orchard, 1992.

Mississippi Bridge by M. D. Taylor. Dial, 1990.

Miss Rumphuis by B. Cooney. Viking Penguin, 1982.

Morning Girl by M. Dorris. Hyperion, 1992.

The Moorchild by E. McGraw, McElderry, 1996.

Mother Jones and the March of the Mill Children by P. Colman. Millbrook, 1993.

My Backyard History Book by D. Weitzman. Little, Brown, 1975.

My Brother Stevie by E. Clymer. Holt, 1967.

My Great Aunt Arizona by G. Houston. HarperCollins, 1992.

My Name Is Maria Isabel by A. F. Ada. Illustrated by K. D. Thompson. Atheneum, 1993.

My Name Is San Ho by J. Pettit. Scholastic, 1992.

My Place by N. Wheatley. Illustrated by D. Rawlins. Kane Miller, 1992.

Native American Doctor: The Story of Susan Laflesche Picotte by J. Ferris. Carolrhoda, 1991.

New Providence: A Changing Cityscape by R. von Tscharner & R. L. Fleming. Illustrated by D. Orloff. Gulliver/HBJ, 1987.

Now Is Your Time! by W. D. Myers. HarperCollins, 1991.

Oceans Ecology Watch by R. Aldis. Dillon, 1991.

Old Home Day by D. Hall. Illustrated by E. A. McCully. Browndeer, 1996.

The One-Room School at Squabble Hollow by R. Hausherr. Four Winds, 1988.

Our Vanishing Farm Animals: Saving America's Rare Breeds by C. Paladino. Joy Street, 1991.

Places of Refuge: Our National Wildlife Refuge System by D. H. Patent. Photographs by W. Munoz. Clarion, 1992.

Playing Beatie Bow by R. Park. Atheneum, 1982.

Pondlarker by F. Gwynne. Simon & Schuster, 1990.

The President's Cabinet and How It Grew by N. W. Parker. HarperCollins, 1991.

Rabble Starkey by L. Lowry. Houghton, 1987.

Rachel Carson: Voice for the Earth by G. Wadsworth. Lerner, 1992.

Ramona and Her Father by B. Cleary. Morrow, 1977.

Randall's Wall by C. Fenner. McElderry, 1991.

Recycling: Meeting the Challenge of the Trash Crisis by A. Silverstein, V. Silverstein, & R. Silverstein. Putnam, 1992.

A River Ran Wild by L. Cherry. Gulliver/HBJ, 1992.

San Rafael, A Central American City Through the Ages by X. Hernandez. Translated by K. Leverich. Illustrated by J. Ballonga & J. Escofet. Houghton Mifflin, 1992.

The Sea Child by C. Sloane. Holiday House, 1987.

The Sea King's Daughter by A. Shepard. Illustrated by G. Spirin. Atheneum, 1997.

Seal Child by S. Peck. Morrow, 1989.

The Seal Mother by M. Gerstein. Dial, 1986.

The Seal Prince by S. MacGill-Callahan. Illustrated by K. Waldherr. Dial, 1995.

Seedfolks by P. Fleischman. HarperCollins, 1997.

The Selkie Girl by S. Cooper. Illustrated by W. Hutton. McElderry, 1986.

Shades of Grey by C. Reeder. Macmillan, 1989.

Shadows in the Water by K. Lasky. HBJ, 1992.

Shaker Lane by A. Provensen & M. Provensen. Viking, 1987.

Shape-Changer by B. Brittain. HarperCollins, 1994.

The Sierra Club Kid's Guide to Planet Care and Repair by V. McVey. Illustrated by M. Weston. Little, Brown, 1993.

The Sky Tree by T. Locker & C. Christiansen. HarperCollins, 1995.

Stateswoman to the World: A Story of Eleanor Roosevelt by M. N. Weidt. Carolrhoda, 1991.

A Stranger Came Ashore by M. Hunter. HarperCollins, 1975.

Summer of Fire Yellowstone, 1988 by P. Lauber. Orchard, 1991.

Sun and Spoon by K. Henkes. Greenwillow, 1997.

Swimming with Sea Lions and Other Adventures in the Galapagos Islands by A. McGovern. Scholastic, 1992.

Taking Care of the Earth: Kids in Action by L. Pringle. Illustrated by B. Moore. Boyds, 1996.

Talk About English: How Words Travel and Change by J. Klausner. Crowell, 1990.

Tam Lin by J. Yolen. Illustrated by C. Micolaycak. HBJ, 1990.

Thank You, Dr. Martin Luther King, Jr.! by E. Tate. Watts, 1990.

Tree of Cranes by A. Say. Houghton Mifflin, 1991.

The True Story of the Three Little Pigs by J. Scieszka. Illustrated by L. Smith. Viking, 1989.

Twelve Ways to Get to Eleven by E. Merriam. Illustrated by B. Karlin. Simon & Schuster, 1993.

Uncle Jed's Barbershop by M. K. Mitchell. Illustrated by J. Ransome. Simon, 1993.

The Ups and Downs of Carl Davis III by R. Guy. Delacorte, 1989.

Voices of the Heart by E. Young. Scholastic, 1996.

Volcano: The Eruption and Healing of Mt. St. Helens by P. Lauber. Bradbury, 1986.

Walk Two Moons by S. Creech. HarperCollins, 1994.

Watch the Stars Come Out by R. Levinson. Illustrated by D. Goode. Dutton, 1985.

The Well by M. Taylor. Dial, 1995.

When the Rivers Go Home by T. Lewin. Macmillan, 1992.

When the Whippoorwill Calls by C. Ransom. Illustrated by K. Root. Tambourine, 1995.

White Wave: A Chinese Story by D. Wolkstein. Illustrated by E. Young. Gulliver, 1996.

Who Really Killed Cock Robin?, An Ecological Mystery by J. C. George. HarperCollins, 1991.

Who Says a Dog Goes Bow Wow? by H. De Zutter. Illustrated by S. MacDonald. Doubleday, 1992.

Wings along the Waterway by M. B. Brown. Orchard, 1992.

Words: A Book about the Origins of Everyday Words and Phrases by J. Sarnoff. Illustrated by R. Ruffins. Macmillan, 1981.

World Water Watch by M. Koch. Greenwillow, 1993.

Yo, Hungry Wolf: A Nursery Rap by D. Vozar. Illustrated by B. Lewin. Doubleday, 1993.

Prototype 6: Fourth/Fifth Grade—EXPLORATIONS

Schedule

These plans are based on activity in a departmentalized fourth- and fifth-grade family-grouped situation. This arrangement is becoming fairly common in intermediate classrooms, especially when middle school settings include fifth and sixth grades. Integrating the curriculum in such a condition necessitates joint planning by the entire grade-level faculty, along with faculty from across-grade classes such as art, music, and physical education.

The topic EXPLORATIONS is an adaptation of the required curriculum at both fourth- and fifth-grade levels in many states—regional studies in fourth grade and national history in fifth—and can be adjusted accordingly to meet local requirements. It is also an example of a broad thematic approach that encourages children to study explorations at different periods and across disciplines. This theme helps children link past, present, and future, and it broadens the scope of history to include past developments in the sciences, math, and language. Children study past explorations in comparison to those in modern times (e.g., the European exploration of the Americas compared to the exploration of space by the United States and the former Soviet Union), and then they speculate about and make plans for the future—their future. You will note that the JOURNEYS theme in the second- and third-grade family-grouped classroom includes topics that could be considered subthemes in this EXPLORATIONS unit. At this level, however, the concept of JOURNEYS is dealt with in a way more appropriate to older children (i.e., literature about inner journeys or the study of forced journeys, such as the Trail of Tears or Japanese internment).

The WEB for this unit was initially planned around topics rather than curricular areas. In a departmentalized situation, teachers may then allocate parts of themes to the separate disciplines for which they are responsible. Planning emphasizes the connectedness of the various disciplines, however, and an effort is made to help children see that many of the disciplinary categories artificially divide what is rarely separated in the real world.

The schedule shown in Table 4.13 shows four groups of children and four teachers working together. Each teacher is responsible for a homeroom of twenty-five children, has lead-teacher responsibility for one content area, and is a team teacher for at least one other area. Team planning is scheduled during the blocks of time when students are in art, music, P.E., and library classes. Because this arrangement excludes cross-grade teachers from the planning time, the team leader meets separately with these teachers to get their input and share team plans. Group sizes in classes vary, and schedules are frequently adjusted to accommodate special programming, single or multiple teacher involvement, or small group needs.

Into the Classroom

To show how this thematic unit would operate in a departmentalized setting, Table 4.14 (see p. 158) depicts the fairly typical pattern that a child might follow through several days of the unit. Other children might take these classes in a different order or with a different team teacher, but the activities would be basically the same. Thus, the table is different

Table 4.13 *Weekly Schedule, Departmentalized Fourth/Fifth-Grade Family-Grouped Class*

Time	Monday	Tuesday	Wednesday	Thursday	Friday
8:00	Homeroom, opening exercises, attendance, lunch count				
8:10	Language arts or Math			Art or Physical education (8:10–9:00)	
9:50	Social studies or Science		Music/Library	Social studies or Science	
10:50	Recess				
11:05	Social studies or Science		Art/Physical education	Social studies or Science	
12:05	Lunch and recess				
12:40	Language arts or Math				Music or Library (1:30–2:30)
2:30	Homeroom and dismissal				

from those found in the other prototypes in that it describes the activities of different groups of children and teachers within the same team settings. As a result, under the column headed "Teacher," activities are those of the teacher in charge of that period.

The team teachers arranged this unit to begin with a broad overview of some of the myriad ways in which exploration occurs. Day 1 shows some of the ways in which this is done. Excerpts from Days 14 and 20 then outline students' movement into more focused and intensive study—their use of Primary Source* materials, role playing, and Reflective, Disciplined Inquiry*. Children are expected to share this work with their peers and to participate in other activities depicted on the WEB or developed on the basis of student interests.

A life-story strand runs throughout most of the classes on Day 1 and continues on Day 14. This strand involves children in exploring other lives through reading poetry, biography, autobiography, and historical fiction, and through writing a "fictionalized" biography and role playing. It invites children to address such *essential questions* as: How can we understand our own and others' lives through different written and oral genres? How can we distinguish between inference and observation? Why is careful observation crucial in all forms of exploration? A second strand centers around exploration as problem solving and is carried out by activities in math, art, and science by role playing, student writing, and experiments in magnification. These activities are intended to draw student attention to a second set of *essential questions:* What kinds of problems are explored in different fields of study? What procedures and resources can be used to investigate and, perhaps, solve these problems? Day 20 moves students into contemplating possible futures.

You will notice that some classes are shortened when art, music, physical education, and library are scheduled. This adjustment is distributed across the classes so that no part of the curriculum is regularly shortchanged. State requirements in reading and language arts are met not by cutting out science or social studies, as is so often the case in elementary schools, but by making language activities integral to the curriculum. Literature is used across the curriculum, and social studies and science offer content for communication (e.g., European Americans' expansion and conflict with native peoples provide data for the creation of fictionalized biographies).

The team teachers also incorporate a joint teacher research strand focusing on how students' writing changes across and between disciplines: Are students able to use different genres appropriately? Are they able to manipulate these genres in interesting and creative ways? Does their work show the influence of the different genres being used during the thematic unit? You can follow some of their work in the "Teacher Research" column in Table 4.14.

Prototype 6: Fourth/Fifth Grade—EXPLORATIONS

Exploring Dialects/Accents/Regionalisms

JACK AND THE WONDER BEANS
A REGULAR ROLLING NOAH
THE PEOPLE COULD FLY
THE DARK–THIRTY

Make a list of regional expressions.
Collect regional ways of naming or pronouncing words.
Tell a story from your region. How would someone from another region tell it?
Compare regional versions of common stories ("Jack and the Beanstalk," "The Night Before Christmas").
Invite a storyteller to class who can use dialect effectively.
Make a Comparison Chart* of similarities and differences in regional story versions.
Locate language/dialect regions on a U.S. map. Where does "standard English" come from?
Survey television or radio for use of dialects/accents/regionalisms.

Exploring Word Origins and Uses

WORDS FROM THE MYTHS
WORDS OF STONE
AHYOKA AND THE TALKING LEAVES
WHEN BLUE MEANT YELLOW

Make a dictionary of word origins for new terms in science and social studies. Illustrate your dictionary.
List all the suffixes and prefixes you can discover and categorize by use and meaning.
Make a chart of confusing "word additives" (such as nonflammable/inflammable).
Make a current slang dictionary–use the *Dictionary of American Slang* for ideas.

Figurative Language

WHITE SNOW, BRIGHT SNOW
REFLECTIONS ON A GIFT OF WATERMELON PICKLE
THE PIRATE'S MIXED–UP VOYAGE
QUIET, PLEASE

Go on an adverb and adjective hunt. Collect descriptive words for environmental phenomena.
Collect beautiful ways of saying things from poems or other literature.
Create metaphors and similes to describe a favorite place or event.
Make an anthology of favorite poems that use interesting language.

Codes and Special Languages

OVER SEA, UNDER STONE
HANDTALK

Review sign language. Work with hearing-impaired children in school as a learning buddy.
Tell a story in sign language.
Read a story in several different languages.

EXPLORING WITH LANGUAGE

EXPLORATIONS

Inventions That Changed Music

Make a display showing the earliest known instruments.
Make a time line showing the history of musical instruments.
Listen to recordings of ancient instruments.
Listen to different styles of music over time.
What inventions changed musical styles?
    Prepare a demonstration of electronic music.
    Compose and play your own music.

EXPLORING THE ARTS

PERSONAL EXPLORATION

New Dance Forms

A VERY YOUNG DANCER
I HAVE ANOTHER LANGUAGE

What is the language of dance? Make a dictionary of dance.
Create a photo essay to illustrate your dictionary.
Find out how dance is used in other cultures. Learn a dance from another culture. Compare ways you use dance.
Create a dance to represent the EXPLORATION theme.

Wishes and Dreams

WHERE THE WILD THINGS ARE
THERE'S A NIGHTMARE IN MY CLOSET
POLAR EXPRESS
THE MOON AND THE FACE
THE BLUE SWORD
TOM'S MIDNIGHT GARDEN
THE DREAM KEEPER AND OTHER POEMS

Where do dreams come from?
Gather information on dreams and share with the class.
Survey the ways in which dreams are used in literature.

Artistic Breakthroughs

ON THE FRONTIER WITH MR. AUDUBON
DOROTHEA LANGE: LIFE THROUGH THE CAMERA PERSPECTIVE
PICTURE THIS
PERSPECTIVE
SELF-PORTRAIT: TRINA SCHART HYMEN
A STRANGE AND DISTANT SHORE

Create a museum of different art styles. Make a guide to the museum and invite others to visit.
Write to a variety of artists and survey them on questions of interest.
Visit a print shop to see how art is reproduced.
Make a survey of the uses made of art in the community. Create a guide to community art.
Raise money to buy a piece of art for the school.
Explore different artistic mediums. Use art to share findings from other investigations.

Inner Journeys

ON MY HONOR
A FINE WHITE DUST
IOU'S
THE ELEPHANT IN THE DARK
THE HIDEOUT
THE CUCKOO'S CHILD
SLAM!

Make a time line of important events in your life. What makes an event good or bad?
What makes a good person?
Make a list of the characteristics of a good person. Make a Comparison Chart* of literary and real characters using your list.
Discuss what each character in *A Fine White Dust* and *IOU's* is exploring.
Write a tentative plan for things you want to accomplish this year, in 3 years, and so on.

Exploring Life Stories: Fiction and Nonfiction

HARRIET AND THE RUNAWAY BOOK

"Mother to Son"
"Nikki Rosa"

PETER THE GREAT
GRACE
LETTERS FROM A SLAVE GIRL
AJEEMAH AND HIS SON
THE CAPTIVE
TO BE A SLAVE

Add these lives to class time line.
Write a biography.
Study biography as a genre.

Exploring the Future

THE GREEN FUTURES OF
    TYCHO
THE WHITE MOUNTAINS
THE GIVER
SHADE'S CHILDREN

What might lead to the futures
    depicted in these books? Make
    a future wish list of things we
    need to do to ensure a better
    future. Write to find out what
    is being done to make a good
    future.
Make a predictions chart, listing
    things you think are likely to
    happen.

20,000 LEAGUES UNDER
    THE SEA

What things did Jules Verne
    predict accurately?
Write a history of your time
    as if you were living 100 years
    from now.

Understanding Time

ALL IN A DAY

Make a Display* of all the ways
    time can be measured.
Make a sundial and compare it
    with digital clock time.
How are time zones calculated?
What happens at the
    International Time Line?
All of China is on one time. List
    problems and advantages of this
    system.

A WRINKLE IN TIME

Compare the time travel in
    L'Engle's book with other time
    fantasy. Is there a scientific
    basis for wrinkles in time?
Make a model showing how a
    clock works.

Time Travels

TOM'S MIDNIGHT GARDEN
THE FORGOTTEN DOOR
THE TIME MACHINE
THE ROOT CELLAR
A CONNECTICUT YANKEE IN
    KING ARTHUR'S COURT
PLAYING BEATIE BOW
BOTH SIDES OF TIME

Make a Display* that illustrates the ways
    in which characters travel in time.
Show *Back to the Future:* Discuss the use
    of time travel in the movie. Compare to
    literature.
Write: "Rules for Time Travelers."
Write: "If I could visit the year _____."

Exploring Under the Sea

CORAL REEF
OCEANS
A CITY UNDER THE SEA
WINDOW ON THE DEEP

Make a time line of underwater
    exploration.
Sink or float experiments.
Experiment with the cartesian diver.
Make a Display* of the benefits of
    undersea exploration.
Debate: Should the Titanic be left
    alone or artifacts removed?
Locate the deepest trenches and
    tallest undersea mountains.
Create a bibliography of sea-related
    stories and legends.

EXPLORING TIME

SCIENTIFIC EXPLORATIONS

HISTORIC EXPLORATIONS

Exploring the Earth's Surface

HIMALAYAS
HEARTLAND
SIERRA

Compare surface and undersea features.
Research: How does environment
    influence how people meet basic needs?

LETTING SWIFT RIVER GO
AN INDIAN WINTER
CHILDREN OF THE DUST BOWL
POWWOW
OUR PATCHWORK PLANET
COMMON GROUND

Find evidence of human interaction with
    the environment.

Ages of Exploration

MORNING GIRL
FOLLOW THE DREAM
MARCO POLO
LIFE THROUGH THE AGES
THE DOUBLE LIFE OF POCAHONTAS
CONSTANCE: A STORY OF EARLY PLYMOUTH
SING DOWN THE MOON
LET THE CIRCLE BE UNBROKEN
BEYOND THE DIVIDE
SAVE QUEEN OF SHEBA
A LANTERN IN HER HAND
THE TAINOS
LINCOLN
DISCOVERING CHRISTOPHER COLUMBUS
AROUND THE WORLD IN A HUNDRED YEARS

Make a time line all around the room and place
    noteworthy explorations on it.
On a large world map (floor map) trace
    explorations of Magellan, Henry the Navigator,
    Eric the Red, etc.
Make a Comparison Chart* showing positive and
    negative effects of explorations.
Collect maps showing how different people have
    viewed the world over time.
Compile a list of explorers: Categorize by
    fact/fiction, century, age, goals, and so on.
Role-play "natives" deciding how to treat
    explorers. Reverse roles.
Explore the history of forced journeys.

ONLY THE NAMES REMAIN
VALLEY OF THE SHADOW
JOURNEY TO TOPAZ

Turn one of these tales into an epic poem or
    ballad.
Write a newspaper report or editorial about one of
    the forced journeys.

Political Explorations

NORTH TO FREEDOM
THE NIGHT JOURNEY
JOURNEY OF THE SHADOW BAIRNS
IMMIGRANT KIDS
HOW MANY DAYS TO AMERICA?
THE ROAD FROM HOME
BULL RUN
THE WIDOW'S BROOM
GRAB HANDS AND RUN
WESTMARK
ZOAR BLUE
THE GIFT OF SARAH BARKER
THE INGENIOUS MR. PEALE
WHO WERE THE FOUNDING FATHERS?
JOURNEY HOME

What forms of government did explorers bring to the
    Americas? What types already existed here?
Invent a "good government." What rights and
    responsibilities would people have? Compare your
    system with the constitutions of several countries.
    What did you leave out? Add?
Who should be President?
Research other people's ideas of ideal societies—utopias.
Collect news articles about issues of human rights; a just
    society.
Set up a classroom government.
Debate: Should the United States intervene in
    international disputes (i.e., Bosnia, Somalia)?

Exploring Air and Space

NEBULAE
SATURN
JUPITER
FLIGHT
WHY THE SKY IS FAR AWAY
COMETS, METEORS, AND
    ASTEROIDS
GALILEO AND THE UNIVERSE

Research the history of flight. Create a
    gallery of famous pilots and astronauts.
    Write a brief caption for each.
Make an aerospace museum. Visit flight-
    related agencies; interview workers.
    Explain how a place works.
Demonstrate jet propulsion with a
    balloon, string, and straw.
Set up a jet-propelled race and a paper
    airplane race.
Analyze effective designs for carrying
    cargo, smooth landings, etc.
Find out how recent unmanned
    explorations of distant planets have
    changed what we know about the
    universe.
Invite an astronomer to class to discuss
    recent discoveries related to planets,
    nebulae, etc.
Construct a mural of the known
    universe and incorporate recent
    discoveries.
Write a story of travel to Saturn or
    Jupiter.

Table 4.14 *Detailed Schedule, Departmentalized Fourth/Fifth-Grade Family-Grouped Class*

Day 1

Time	Children	Teacher	Teacher Research
Homeroom 8:00	Children fill in attendance and lunch count, engage in quiet conversation with friends, prepare for first two classes, and change classes.	Homeroom teacher greets children as they enter, checks lunch and attendance count, and makes announcements.	
Language Arts 8:10	On large sheets of paper, children draw life lines and mark important events in their lives (that they are willing to share).	Teacher displays biography and autobiography in the library area. Bulletin board with questions and quotes is arranged to spark curiosity. Teacher introduces idea of life line.	Teacher observes which books seem to capture student attention. Is there any pattern to selection by discipline?
	Children discuss what makes an event positive or negative. Students tally positive and negative items on class lists and discuss what they have in common (classification). What things on the lists are unique?		
	Children write memorable event and then work on their stories. Several students share their drafts.	Teacher asks children to take five minutes to write a brief description of a memorable event in their lives, and then to use that description as the basis for a story.	These will be kept in student portfolios after being displayed. They will serve as a beginning point for the study of how children use different genres in their own writing.
		Finished stories are collected to display with life lines, and the teacher introduces genres of biography and autobiography, shares the beginning of *Harriet and the Runaway Book*, notes copy of *Uncle Tom's Cabin* in reading area. Teacher conducts individual reading conferences.	
	Children select books to read after teacher has read. Most read for fifteen minutes; several work with teacher in individual conferences.		
	Children try different ways to read "Mother to Son" and "Nikki Rosa" by changing pacing, emphasis, or intensity. With teacher's help they arrange the poems as a Readers' Theater* piece.	Teacher ends SSR* by sharing Langston Hughes's "life-story" poem, "Mother to Son," and Nikki Giovanni's poem "Nikki Rosa" and passes out copies of each poem. Teacher helps orchestrate the poetry reading. Agrees that these would be good poems to share with other classes.	Teacher has deliberately started with poetry to see if that will have any influence on how children perceive biography and autobiography. Each poem also has a distinct "voice" that she wants children to hear and discuss in relation to their own writing.
	Children make note of homework assignment.	Teacher gives homework, selects a biography or autobiography, and read the introductory chapter, note, how the author begins the story and how the reader is drawn into the tale, and make notes for class discussion tomorrow.	
Social Studies 9:50	Children discuss trips in small groups and write names of places they have visited on flags. They try to locate the places they have visited on the map given to their group.	A variety of maps are displayed around the room, including traditional Mercator projections, a Peter's projection, a fifteenth-century world map, a U.S. map, and state and local maps. Each desk has a supply of flags and a smaller world map. The teacher begins by asking children to work in small groups to describe the most memorable or interesting trips they have ever taken.	
	Children discuss changes in countries and accuracy of maps. Are there places left to explore? How might one explore them?	Each group has been assigned a different type of map and the teacher anticipates that they will have some difficulty locating their trip destinations. "What has happened to	

(continued)

Table 4.14 *Detailed Schedule, Departmentalized Fourth/Fifth-Grade Family-Grouped Class (continued)*

Day 1

Time	Children	Teacher	Teacher Research
		change the world from one map to another?" Teacher writes "exploration" on the board and leads discussion of what that term means.	
	Students list types of explorations and then decide which might be interesting to pursue. Groups are responsible for submitting a work plan by the second class period.	Teacher divides class into exploration teams and passes out exploration guides as a research aid for each group. Teacher moves between teams, makes suggestions on resources and strategies, helps negotiate work loads, and allocates time. A portion of class time for the next two weeks will be devoted to team explorations of such subthemes as "Exploring Time," "Ancient Explorations," "Finding New Worlds," etc.	This is the first step in helping students organize data that can be drawn on for writing.
Science 11:05	As children enter and receive their observation guide, they follow directions to the pictures around the room and attempt to identify what they see. Students participate in guided observation and discuss the difference between observation and inference.	Pictures of undersea and beach life are hung all around the room. The teacher greets students at the door and distributes an observation guide and directions. The teacher assembles the class for discussion of their observations and calls attention to *Coral Reef* and *Oceans.* Lights are dimmed and a video begins a second guided observation.	These two books provide models of interesting scientific reading. The teacher is interested in seeing if students use the model in their own writing.
	Students set up their laboratory books for work in each station. Stations involve students in learning to do careful observations of natural phenomena: tree rings, fish in plastic-bag aquaria, seashells, rocks, and coral.	Teacher assigns students to stations around the room and then moves between stations, keeping a check sheet of problem areas for later discussion or activity. Students are drawn back into the central area to discuss the impact of microscopic observation.	
	Students share observations and explain what can be inferred from patterns and variations in patterns in natural objects. Several students select books to use for their language arts assignments.	Teacher suggests reading about scientific explorers and calls attention to books displayed for student use.	Biographies and autobiographies provide another model for writing about science. Teacher keeps track of what books are checked out.
Art 12:40	Student monitors pass out materials. Class moves outside to work on watercolors of natural objects in the environment.	Biographies and autobiographies of artists are on display, with the caption "Exploring the Arts." The teacher begins by sharing samples of the art of Winslow Horner and a small section of *The Island,* in which a boy experiments with watercolors.	
Math 1:40	For the first ten minutes of class, students work on challenge problems involving calculations of the length of voyages of exploration. Children discuss possible solutions to the challenge problems and explain how they arrived at their answers.	Teacher puts challenge problems on the board for immediate attention. For the next ten minutes, teacher works with a small group who had difficulty with homework. Teacher records possible solutions and asks for proof. Participates in resulting discussion.	

(continued)

Table 4.14 *Detailed Schedule, Departmentalized Fourth/Fifth-Grade Family-Grouped Class (continued)*

Day 1

Time	Children	Teacher	Teacher Research
Home-room 2:40	Children make up three problems that use the operations practiced in homework and exchange problems, working in small groups to solve the problems.	Teacher asks students to construct three problems and then distributes the problem for solutions or adjustments.	
	Children clean up, collect supplies needed for homework, listen to end-of-day announcements, and perform class jobs.		

Day 14

Time	Children	Teacher	Teacher Research
Library (as part of Language Arts class) 8:10		Librarian has displayed historical fiction set in the United States and emphasizing themes of exploration. The listening center has a tape and filmstrip interview with children's author Jean Fritz discussing her works of biography and historical fiction.	
	Browsing time. Children return books and pick new ones. A few children work in listening center.		
	Children gather in story area to share favorite parts of books read since last week. They listen while librarian gives a Book Talk* on *The Double Life of Pocahontas*.	Librarian gives a Book Talk* on Fritz's biography of Pocahontas, then draws children's attention to *Lincoln: A Photobiography* by Freedman, reading several quotes from the end of that book. Librarian asks children to find quotable quotes in the biographies they are reading.	
	Children take home strips of tagboard to write quotes on. The children decide to make this a guessing-game bulletin board titled "Who said that?"		
Language Arts 9:10	Children participate in discussion, adding information gathered from library class. They help make a tentative set of criteria for writing historical fiction. Children work in small groups with Primary Source* material related to a person from the U.S. westward movement. Over the next five days, this information will form the basis for student writing.	A large wall chart shows the student-generated list of criteria for biography and autobiography. Teacher reviews these with students and asks if any will work for historical fiction. They discuss historical fiction and what an author might need in writing it. As children make suggestions, teacher serves as recorder. She then introduces the Primary Source* material and divides the class into small groups.	This is important data for the study. Teachers will use this to see if students use these criteria in their own work.
	Children begin developing a primary source vocabulary.	Teacher leads discussion of problems with source material: What information can a document give us? What can't it tell us? How do you suppose an author uses this material?	This is another step in the teacher research. The teacher is interested in helping children think about the author behind the words.
Social Studies 9:50	Children enter and seat themselves in a semicircle in front of a table and five chairs. A wall poster behind the table announces land for sale in Kansas.	Teacher refers to character introduced in language arts. Where is this person going? How would students feel if suddenly faced with such a move? Calls attention to poster.	
	Children read poster and list salient points of information (e.g., date, location of land, conditions of sale).	Teacher asks children to read poster carefully and list all the information given on the poster that could help a person decide whether to buy this land.	

(continued)

Table 4.14 *Detailed Schedule, Departmentalized Fourth/Fifth-Grade Family-Grouped Class (continued)*

Day 14

Time	Children	Teacher	Teacher Research
	As children participate in the role playing, they discover that they need more information to make decisions. Questions are listed, and committees formed to find answers. They break into groups to get necessary information. (This information will be used in writing their biographies in language arts as well as for the role playing.)	Teacher passes out role cards involving a New England family's decision to buy land in Kansas and move west. Teacher suggests reconvening the role play as a town meeting where information can be shared and discussed. She points out reference works located in the room and helps students divide into committees based on the questions raised during the role play.	Role play also sets the scene for later writing by the students and for consideration of the differences between fictional and non-ficitional historical accounts.
Science 11:05	Children report latest observations of living systems. Children watch video on ocean exploration.	Teacher begins with groups reporting on aquaria and filling in class observation charts. Teacher introduces video and suggests specific things to look for related to the just-completed group reports.	
Math 12:40	Children work on challenge problems related to time and as a follow-up to work on the discovery of time. Students then work with math partners on calculating time differences between different points on the globe.	Teacher works with individual student who is working with metric problems. As students move into math partner work, teacher refers them to charts on writing mathematical "sentences," and then moves between groups checking to see how students are formulating their problems, and guiding their work.	

Day 20

Time	Children	Teacher	Teacher Research
Language Arts 8:10	Author's Chair*. Students share their completed biographies. Discussion centers on how sources were used and whether authors slipped into "presentism" or included anachronisms in their writing. Students discuss historical fantasies they have read. Sustained Silent Reading (SSR)* Children work in small groups or individually on several projects related to their reading, including Plot Profiles* and Character Sociograms*. Several children go to a primary classroom as Reading Buddies* for children there. They check their plans with the teacher before they leave.	Teacher asks if historical fantasy is a literary genre. Introduces *Playing Beatie Bow*. Teacher meets with individuals and small groups for reading conferences.	The biographies allow the teacher to assess children's facility with this genre, and to see how they incorporated content into their writing. The fantasies introduce a new genre.
Social Studies 9:50	Children have participated in the simulation "Powderhorn" on the previous day. As a three-tiered society was created, the students in the bottom "class" planned a rebellion, and today they create a document of protest. The other two groups prepare responses.	The simulation begun the previous day has reached the point of rebellion. The teacher posts the documents and responses and then passes out several documents that outline a just society (Declaration of Independence, Bill of Rights, and Declaration of Human Rights).	

(continued)

Table 4.14 *Detailed Schedule, Departmentalized Fourth/Fifth-Grade Family-Grouped Class (continued)*

Day 20

Time	Children	Teacher	Teacher Research
	Students decide to interview parents and other adults about their ideas of a just society. Two students volunteer to write to the governor and local congressional representatives to ask for their ideas.	Each "class" is asked to analyze how each answers the concerns of their "class." What is left out? What does the document include that was not in the documents prepared by the students?	
Science 11:05		Teacher suggests inviting the mayor to class to talk about her view of a good and just society.	
	Students work on individual and small group projects including: • Developing a book of experiments on altering the flight of paper airplanes. • Creating a board game based on efforts to clean water supplies. • Designing clay boats that will carry different arrangements of cargo, followed by a writing up of the results. • Creating a display of undersea geography. • Preparing a presentation on women in science.	Teacher works with individuals and groups as needed. Most of these projects are well under way and need only some help in organizing for presentation.	

Summary

Team meetings facilitate planning thematic units and build community.

Clearly, this type of teaming requires considerable cooperation on the part of all team members. It also requires a theme that is broad enough to cross disciplinary lines. Sometimes, however, a theme may be selected that more actively involves, say, social studies but not mathematics. In this case, team members make the necessary adjustments and adapt to a more domain- or discipline-specific type of instruction for this period.

However, regular team meetings generally allow teachers to build on activities in other classes or to introduce a topic from one perspective that another teacher will deal with from a different disciplinary perspective. Thus, when students began work on writing biographies, they use primary resources in language arts, but they also gain background material from their research for the role-playing situation in social studies. It is expected that they will cross disciplines in using their sources and work cooperatively in acquiring information. Learning in this team setting is seen as a collaborative venture for teachers and students. Teachers model collaboration as they plan and work together. Students then take responsibility, along with the teachers, for constructing meaning out of the diverse sources of information. A sense of community emerges that supports speculation, problem solving, and intellectual risk taking.

Teaming also facilitates collaborative research.

One advantage of this team arrangement is the potential for teachers to develop areas of content expertise that are sometimes more difficult for a single teacher to manage. The lead teacher for a curricular area can be the team expert and focus his or her energies on generating essential questions that are subject specific as well as theme related, collecting resources and keeping up with developments in a field. Another advantage is the potential for collaborative research. At the conclusion of this thematic unit, each of the teachers had data to contribute to the joint research project and brought a unique disciplinary perspective to bear on analyzing the data. The social studies teacher found that students seemed quite adept at turning Primary Source* data into historical fiction and were able to make good use of the techniques of biography and autobiography, often experimenting with styles found in the literature read as part of their language arts program, but the science teacher found that children were having much more trouble turning scientific data—observations and experiments—into interesting nonfictional reports. The team decided to incorporate more nonnarrative literature into the next unit and to continue their documentation of student writing.

Children's Literature: *EXPLORATIONS*

Ahyoka and the Talking Leaves by P. Roop & C. Roop. Lothrop, 1992.

Ajeemah and His Son by J. Berry. Harper, 1992.

All in a Day by Fern Hollow. Outlet, 1985.

Around the World in a Hundred Years: From Henry the Navigator to Magellan by J. Fritz. Illustrated by A. B. Vanti Putnam, 1994.

Beyond the Divide by K. Lasky. Macmillan, 1983.

The Blue Sword by R. McKinley. Greenwillow, 1982.

Both Sides of Time by C. B. Cooney. Delacorte, 1995.

Bull Run by P. Fleischman. HarperCollins, 1993.

The Captive by J. Hansen. Scholastic, 1994.

Children of the Dust Bowl: The True Story of the School at Weed Patch Camp by J. Stanley. Crown, 1992.

A City under the Sea: Life in a Coral Reef by N. Wu. Atheneum, 1996.

Comets, Meteors, and Asteroids by S. Simon. Morrow, 1994.

Common Ground: This Water, Earth, and Air We Share by M. Bang. Scholastic, 1997.

A Connecticut Yankee in King Arthur's Court by M. Twain. Illustrated by T. S. Hyman. Morrow, 1988.

Constance: A Story of Early Plymouth by P. Clapp. Penguin, 1986.

Coral Reef by B. Taylor. Houghton Mifflin, 1992.

The Cuckoo's Child by S. Freeman. Greenwillow, 1996.

Discovering Christopher Columbus: How History Is Invented by K. Pelta. Lerner, 1991.

The Dark-Thirty: Southern Tales of the Supernatural by P. McKissack. Franklin Watts, 1992.

Dorothea Lange: Life through the Camera by M. Meltzer. Viking, 1985.

The Double Life of Pocahontas by J. Fritz. Illustrated by E. Young. Putnam, 1983.

The Dream Keeper and Other Poems by L. Hughes. Illustrated by B. Pinkney Knopf, 1994.

The Elephant in the Dark by C. Carrick. Illustrated by D. Carrick. Tichnor & Fields, 1988.

A Fine White Dust by C. Rylant. Bradbury, 1986.

Flight by R. Burleigh. Illustrated by M. Wimmer. Trumpet, 1991.

Follow the Dream by P. Sis. Knopf, 1991.

The Forgotten Door by A. Key. Scholastic, 1986.

Galileo and the Universe by S. Parker. HarperCollins, 1992.

The Gift of Sarah Barker by J. Yolen. Viking, 1981.

The Giver by L. Lowry. Houghton Mifflin, 1993.

Grab Hands and Run by F. Temple. Orchard Books, 1993.

Grace by J. P. Walsh. Farrar, Straus, & Giroux, 1992.

The Green Futures of Tycho by W. Sleator. Dutton, 1981.

Handtalk: An ABC of Finger Spelling and Sign Language by R. Charlip & M. Miller. Macmillan, 1980.

Harriet and the Runaway Book by J. Johnston. Harper, 1977.

Heartland by D. Siebert. Illustrated by W. Minor. Crowell, 1989.

The Hideout by E. Bunting. Harcourt Brace Jovanovich, 1981.

Himalayas: Vanishing Cultures by J. Reynolds. Harcourt Brace Jovanovich, 1991.

How Many Days to America? A Thanksgiving Story by E. Bunting. Illustrated by B. Peck. Tichnor & Fields, 1988.

I Have Another Language: The Language Is Dance by E. Schick. Macmillan, 1992.

Immigrant Kids by R. Freedman. Dutton, 1980.

The Ingenious Mr. Peale: Painter, Patriot, Man of Science by J. Wilson. Atheneum, 1996.

An Indian Winter by R. Freedman. Holiday House, 1992.

IOU's by O. Sebastyen. Dell, 1986.

Jack and the Wonder Beans by J. Still. Putnam, 1977.

Journey Home by Y. Uchida. Atheneum, 1978.

Journey of the Shadow Bairns by M. J. Anderson. Knopf, 1980.

Journey to Topaz by Y. Uchida. Atheneum, 1976.

Jupiter by S. Simon. Morrow, 1988.

A Lantern in Her Hand by B. Aldrich. Appleton, 1932.

Letters from a Slave Girl: The Story of Harriet Jacobs by M. E. Lyons. Scribner's, 1992.

Let the Circle Be Unbroken by M. Taylor. Dial, 1981.

Letting Swift River Go by J. Yolen. Little, Brown, 1992.

Life through the Ages by G. Caselli. Grosset & Dunlop, 1987.

Lincoln: A Photobiography by R. Freedman. Clarion, 1987.

Marco Polo by R. Stefoff. Chelsea House, 1992.

The Moon and the Face by P. A. McKillip. Berkley, 1986.

Morning Girl by M. Dorris. Hyperion, 1992.

"Mother to Son" by L. Hughes. In *The Dream Keeper and Other Poems*. Illustrated by B. Pinkney. Knopf, 1992.

My Side of the Mountain by J. George. Dutton, 1988.

Nebulae by N. Apfels. Lothrop, 1988.

The Night Journey by K. Lasky. Macmillan, 1982.

"Nikki Rose" by N. Giovanni. In *Ego-Tripping*. Illustrated by G. Ford. Lawrence Hill, 1993.

North to Freedom by A. Holm. Peter Smith, 1984.

Oceans by S. Simon. Morrow, 1990.

Only the Names Remain: The Cherokees and the Trail of Tears by A. Bealer. Illustrated by W. S. Bock. Little, Brown, 1972.

On My Honor by M. Bauer. Tichnor & Fields, 1986.

On the Frontier with Mr. Audubon by B. Brenner. Putnam, 1977.

Our Patchwork Planet: The Story of Plate Tectonics by H. R. Sattler. Illustrated by G. Maestro. Lothrop, 1995.

Over Sea, Under Stone by S. Cooper. Harcourt Brace Jovanovich, 1966.

The People Could Fly by V. Hamilton. Knopf, 1985.

Perspective by A. Cole. Dorling Kindersley, 1993.

Peter the Great by D. Stanley. Four Winds, 1986.

Picture This: Perception and Composition by M. Bang. Bulfinch, 1992.

The Pirates' Mixed-up Voyage: Dark Doings in the Thousand Islands by M. Mahy. Dial, 1993.

Playing Beatie Bow by R. Park. Atheneum, 1982.

Polar Express by C. VanAllsburg. Houghton Mifflin, 1985.

Powwow by G. Ancona. Harcourt Brace Jovanovich, 1993.

Quiet, Please by E. Merriam. Simon, 1993.

Reflections on a Gift of Watermelon Pickle by S. Dunning (Comp.). Scott Foresman, 1966.

A Regular Rolling Noah by G. E. Lyon. Bradbury, 1986.

The Road from Home: The Story of an Armenian Childhood by D. Kherdian. Greenwillow, 1979.

The Root Cellar by J. Lunn. Macmillan, 1983.

Saturn by S. Simon. Morrow, 1988.

Save Queen of Sheba by L. Moeri. Dutton, 1981.

Self-Portrait: Trina Schart Hyman by T. S. Hyman. Addison-Wesley, 1981.

Shade's Children by G. Nix. HarperCollins, 1997.

Sierra by D. Siebert. HarperCollins, 1991.

Sing Down the Moon by S. O'Dell. Houghton Mifflin, 1990.

Slam! by W. D. Myers. HarperCollins, 1996.

A Strange and Distant Shore: Indians of the Great Plains in Exile by B. Ashabranner. Cobblehill, 1996.

The Tainos: The People Who Welcomed Columbus by F. Jacobs. Putnam, 1992.

There's a Nightmare in My Closet by M. Mayer. Dial, 1976.

The Time Machine by H. G. Wells. Raintree, 1983.

To Be a Slave by J. Lester. Dial, 1968.

Tom's Midnight Garden by P. Pearce. Harper & Row, 1984.

20,000 Leagues Under the Sea by J. Verne. Airmont, 1964.

Uncle Tom's Cabin by H. B. Stowe. Modern Library, 1985.

Valley of the Shadow by J. Hickman. Macmillan, 1974.

A Very Young Dancer by J. Krementz. Dell, 1986.

Westmark by L. Alexander. Dutton, 1981.

When Blue Meant Yellow: How Colors Got Their Names by J. Heifetz. Holt, 1994.

Where the Wild Things Are by M. Sendak. Harper & Row, 1963.

The White Mountains by J. Christopher. Macmillan, 1967.

White Snow, Bright Snow by A. Tresselt. Illustrated by R. Duvoisin. Morrow, 1947.

Who Were the Founding Fathers? Two Hundred Years of Reinventing American History by S. H. Jaffe. Holt, 1997.

Why the Sky Is Far Away by M. Gerson. Joy Street, 1992.

Window on the Deep: The Adventures of Underwater Explorer Sylvia Earle by A. Conley. Franklin Watts, 1992.

The Widow's Broom by C. VanAllsburg. Houghton Mifflin, 1992.

Words from the Myths by I. Asimov. Dutton, 1969.

Words of Stone by K. Henks. Greenwillow, 1992.

A Wrinkle in Time by M. L'Engle. Farrar, Straus, & Giroux, 1962.

Zoar Blue by J. Hickman. Macmillan, 1976.

Prototype 7: Fifth Grade—EXPLORING OUR ROOTS
Schedule

"Identity" can be complex for ESL students.

Karen Beeman teaches fifth grade in a bilingual program in a predominantly Mexican/Mexican-American urban Midwestern school. All the students speak Spanish at home, but their level of English proficiency varies. Identity is one of the most important issues Karen's students must deal with in her classroom and in the larger community. Being a Latino in an urban area is very complex, with success or failure dependent on such variables as socioeconomic status, the family's motivation for migrating, place of origin, length of time in the United States, and treatment by mainstream Americans. Some of Karen's students identify themselves as "American" because they have witnessed the discrimination, embarrassments, and difficulties their parents have endured for being "Mexican." They try not to identify with many aspects of Mexican culture. Often they lose touch with their home language and culture and as adolescents have difficulties dealing with identity issues. Karen wanted to incorporate a positive stance toward Latin America in the classroom, identifying and studying what is not often publicly spoken about (language differences, culture shock, identity crisis, and discrimination) so that students would be more energized to learn and would grow both personally and academically. She had also noted that her students learned a great deal more when content was linked to their personal issues and concerns.

Karen weighed many variables in designing her thematic unit, most important of which were the students' cultural identity and language. The theme EXPLORING OUR ROOTS was first conceived as a way of incorporating all these issues into the classroom and linking students' personal experiences to academic subject areas. The unit covers some of the fifth-grade curriculum objectives in Karen's district but goes further by merging aspects of Mexican and American cultures. Karen feels particularly strongly about this issue. She was born to American parents in Mexico and attended bilingual schools through high school, so she had struggled with some of the same issues her students faced. Because of her concerns about identity issues, Karen's teacher research focused on students' reactions to studying identity issues. She plans to observe any changes in students' attitudes, particularly on the student-created segregation between "brazers" (a word coined in the community, based on the Spanish braceros and connoting something akin to "wetback"), more Americanized Mexican-Americans, and the "mainstream" English-speaking fifth graders who also attend the school. To see if the quantity and quality of reading and writing increased as a result of studying identity issues, Karen plans to keep a journal of observations to focus on activities where students naturally tend to group themselves heterogeneously, mixing recent immigrants with those who had been in the United States longer. She also plans to document the relationship between classroom activities and discussion and students' efforts to work on community issues. Finally, Karen hopes to share her observations with parents and colleagues in hopes that her work would be the beginning of a schoolwide plan. (See Table 4.15.)

Into the Classroom

Because the theme EXPLORING OUR ROOTS deals with issues of conquest, encounter, and the blending of cultures, Karen has begun it right after Columbus Day. The unit begins with a glimpse into the roots of Mexican culture. Though there are many areas of Mexican culture that could begin the theme, Karen concentrates on the Aztecs, who survived by creating a novel irrigation and anti-erosion form of agriculture by making islands (or chinampas) in the Lag Texcoco with mud from the lake bottom. This symbol of creating roots in the chinampas appealed to Karen and so the theme begins with a simulation of the chinampas. Students then delve into various aspects of culture, family, art, history, and agriculture. The primary focus is on family roots and elements that form culture throughout time. Social studies and reading/writing are integrated easily in the activities about family, cuisine, and identity. Math and science are also integrated through activities that enable students to analyze the Mayan place value system and then study their own community to highlight its strengths and improve its weaknesses. Parents and the community are essential participants in this thematic unit. Students rely on them for data and help in planning for the future. Many activities bring in parents and community members to share their expertise and visions.

The unit is planned for three months of study. Throughout the unit, most morning integrated work time begins with a structured activity or discussion planned by Karen. Frequently, the activity is a Focus-Lesson*. The Focus-Lessons* include such things as examining writing or comparing trade book and textbook versions of the same events. Other times Karen uses class meetings to review information or highlight exciting things that happen in the classroom. Class meetings also provide a forum for student-led demonstrations of work in progress or for hearing a guest speaker. A variety of group work takes place. Some projects are student-initiated and lead to small group work; other projects involve small groups in contributing a part of a larger project (i.e., writing the bilingual cookbook). Throughout the day, students work in integrated activities. Mornings, however, usually focus on reading, writing, and social studies and afternoons on science and math. Students also analyze their surroundings and plan activities that move them into the community as active participants in its betterment. Finally, the unit culminates in a celebration of both

Class meetings can be important forums for sharing.

Table 4.15 *WEEKLY SCHEDULE, KAREN BEEMAN'S FIFTH-GRADE BILINGUAL CLASS*

Time	Monday	Tuesday	Wednesday	Thursday	Friday
9:00	Student/teacher duties (attendance, lunch tickets)				
9:10	Integrated work time. Reading, writing, and social studies.				
10:35	Art	Music	Gym	Integrated work time	Library
11:30	Crafts/Art reflective of EXPLORING OUR ROOTS				
12:00	Reading Aloud*				
12:20	Lunch				
12:50	SSR*				
1:25	Integrated work time. Math, science, and art.				
2:30	Dismissal				

Prototype 7: Fifth Grade—EXPLORING OUR ROOTS

Identity Roots

CHILDREN AND THE YUCATAN
MY MEXICO/MÉXICO MÍO
PASSPORT TO MEXICO
THE STORIES JULIAN TELLS
BLESS ME, ÚLTIMA
TALES OF FAR NORTH
THE HOUSE ON MANGO STREET
HENRY CISNEROS, ALCÁLDE MEXICO-AMERICANO
… AND NOW MIGUEL
HELLO, AMIGOS!
MEXICAN PROFILES: BILINGUAL BIOGRAPHIES FOR TODAY
CESAR CHÁVEZ
BARRIO GHOSTS

Write your autobiography.
Interview a person you respect and write a short biography.
Write about your experiences. How are they alike or different from
    those of children in Mexico or other parts of the United States?
Invite a person you admire from the community to speak to the class.
Write about what you would like to be doing in 10 years.

Me and My Family

THE HUNDRED PENNY BOX
GATHERING THE SUN
IN MY FAMILY/EN MI FAMILIA
MAMA'S BIRTHDAY SURPRISE
LOCAL NEWS
THE WALLS OF PEDRO GARCIA
A FAMILY IN MEXICO
YOUR NAME–ALL ABOUT IT
BLUE WILLOW
COME SPRING
IMMIGRANT KIDS
EL LIRÓN SIN NOMBRE
FAMILY PICTURES
TAKE A TRIP TO MEXICO
LA HISTORIA DE ERNESTO
ONLY JODY
AL OTRO LADO DE LA PUERTA
RAMONA AND HER FATHER
ANNIE AND THE OLD ONE

Trace your family's migration to the United
    States and/or around the United States on a
    map. Chart their migration on a time line.
Interview relations about life in Mexico
    compared with that in the United States.
Write about your home town using maps and
    historical references.

Literary Roots

WHERE THE SIDEWALK ENDS
CANTO FAMILIAR
NEIGHBORHOOD ODES
VERSITLAN
THE DAY IT SNOWED TORTILLAS
ANTONIO MACHADO Y LOS NIÑOS
JUAN RAMÓN JIMÉNEZ Y LOS NIÑOS
CUENTOS JUVENILES DE AMÉRICA
HANSEL AND GRETEL
CINDERELLA
RED RIDING HOOD
TALES OF THE FAR NORTH
THREE LITTLE PIGS
RUMPELSTILTSKIN
LA VOZ DE COATL
LA MONTAÑA DEL ALIMENTO
FOLK TALES: FOUR PLAYS FOR THE CLASSROOM
TORTILLAS PARA MAMÁ AND OTHER NURSERY RHYMES
I AM PHOENIX: POEMS FOR TWO VOICES
EL LIBRO DE LAS ADIVINANZAS
THE WOMAN WHO OUTSHONE THE SUN/LA MUJER
    QUE BRILLABA AUN MÁS QUE EL SOL
THE WITCH'S FACE
THE HUMMINGBIRD'S GIFT
THIS TREE IS OLDER THAN YOU ARE

Make a play of a favorite tale and present it.
Compare and contrast origins of folktales—use maps and
    historical references.
Write a poem or tale reflective of your culture.
Identify the main components or a folktale and write a
    retelling or present an oral Storytelling* version.

EXPLORING OUR ROOTS

Establishing Roots for the Future

GREENING THE CITY STREETS
THIS HOME WE HAVE MADE/ESTA CASA QUE HEMOS HECHO

Create a plan to actively work on issues in the community that are
    important to you. Negotiate how to implement your plan. Enlist
    school, community, and parental support.
Suggestions:
    Conduct a survey of fourth-sixth graders about their community
        concerns. Write up results for the class paper.
    Conduct a survey of classroom parents and see what their major
        concerns are. Are they similar to yours? How can you work together?
    Invite area leaders to speak about your concerns. Try to enlist their help.
    Begin a letter-writing campaign to city officials to urge them to act on
        your concerns.

Celebration Roots

ARROZ CON LECHE
¡FIESTA! CINCO DE MAYO
A PUMPKIN IN A PEAR TREE
TOO MANY TAMALES
THE SPIRIT OF TIO FERNANDO
PIÑATA MAKER
FIESTA USA
LA BODA
PABLO REMEMBERS

Research Mexican *posadas* (celebrations); write
    an explanation and present one to the school.
Make a year-long calendar, marking celebrations
    in both Mexico and the United States. How
    does each reflect the culture of its country of
    origin?
Prepare a show reflecting games and oral
    traditions of both cultures.

Culinary Roots

THE STINGY BAKER
TORTILLA FOR EMILIA
NEW JUNIOR COOKBOOK
210 RECETAS DE COCINA INTERNACIONAL
VOY A COCINAR
COCINA NAVIDEÑA MEXICANA
COOKING THE MEXICAN WAY
THE TORTILLA BOOK
EVERYBODY COOKS RICE
ESPECIALIDADES DE LA COCINA MEXICANA
THE TORTILLA FACTORY

Write a (bilingual) class cookbook to sell.
Mark a day to celebrate cooking traditions. Invite
   special people.
Analyze why and how the cuisines of the United
   States and Mexico are different.

Indigenous Roots

CORN IS MAIZE
HEIRS OF THE ANCIENT MAYA
THE FLAME OF PEACE: A TALE OF THE AZTECS
AZTEC INDIANS
LA MÚSICA DE LA CHIRÍMIA
BUFFALO DANCE: A BLACKFOOT LEGEND
POPOL VUH
DE TIGRES Y TLACUACHES: LEYENDAS ANIMALES
LA CIVILIZACIÓN MAYA
EL MAÍZ TIENE COLOR DE ORO
THE MONKEY'S HAIRCUT, AND OTHER STORIES TOLD BY THE MAYA
MITOS Y LEYENDAS
MONTEZUMA AND THE AZTECS
LEYENDAS MEXICANAS
MAYA
THE ANCIENT MAYA
THE WITCH'S FACE
PEOPLE OF CORN

Build a model of an indigenous living area.
Study the calendars of the Mayans and Aztecs and analyze them
   mathematically.
Make a time line of events affecting indigenous people. Begin with pre-
   Columbian time. Chart changes on tables and graphs.
Write and illustrate your own version of the Aztec tale of settlement in the
   valley of Mexico.
Compare Mexican indigenous myths and legends and Native American
   myths and legends. Use a Graphic Organizer*.
Invite a Native American and/or indigenous Mexican to class to discuss his
   or her heritage.

My Family Roots

GOING HOME
ME AND MY FAMILY TREE
ANCESTOR HUNTING
THE GREAT ANCESTOR HUNT
WHERE DID YOU GET THOSE EYES? A GUIDE TO
   DISCOVERING YOUR FAMILY HISTORY
GROWING OLDER
EL ABUELO TOMÁS

Make a family tree and photo gallery across as many
   generations as possible, either for yourself or for
   someone in your community.
Document the oral history of an older person in your
   family or community.

Life Support Roots

PRIETTA AND THE GHOST WOMAN
JOURNEY OF THE NIGHTLY JAGUAR
QUETZAL: SACRED BIRD OF THE CLOUD FOREST
POPPY SEEDS
BEING A PLANT
PLANT EXPERIMENTS
WATER PLANTS
PLANTS
ROOTS ARE FOOD FINDERS
A FIRST LOOK AT THE WORLD OF PLANTS
SKY SONGS
COLOR DE TIERRA
COME SPRING
EXPERIMENTOS ATMOSFÉRICOS
AIR
NATURE'S WEATHER FORECASTERS
OBSERVANDO EL CLIMA
STORMS
THE TRIP OF A DRIP
WATER (WEBB)
WATER (BUNSTON)
WATER FOR THE WORLD
WHAT MAKES IT RAIN?
WEATHER EXPERIMENTS
FLASH, CRASH, RUMBLE AND ROLL
IT'S RAINING CATS AND DOGS: ALL KINDS OF WEATHER
   AND WHY WE HAVE IT
LAS CHINAMPAS: UNA TÉCNICA AGRICOLA MUY
   PRODUCTIVA

Write a booklet describing the chinampas for class visitors.
Investigate why certain herbs and plants are grown in Mexico
   and not the United States.
Classify plants. Develop a plant key for identification purposes.
Conduct experiments on different rooting systems of plants.

Artistic Roots

DIEGO
FRIDA KAHLO
JOSEPHINA
MAYA ART DESIGN COLORING BOOK
FOLK TOYS AROUND THE WORLD AND HOW TO MAKE THEM
SLAB, COIL, AND PINCH
LATIN AMERICAN CRAFTS AND THEIR CULTURAL BACKGROUNDS
MEXICAN CRAFTS AND CRAFTS PEOPLE
WHEN CLAY SINGS
THE POTTERY PLACE
THE FLAME OF PEACE: A TALE OF THE AZTECS

Make a craft reflecting either U.S. or Mexican culture.
Compile a collection of favorite Mexican and U.S. crafts. Write a manual
   explaining how to make them and how they reflect their culture.
Study traditional and modern artists in the United States and Mexico.
   Experiment with their styles in your own art.

American and Mexican cultures. Food from the cookbook is shared, a play presented, and other projects exhibited.

Karen must carefully choreograph the use of language in this unit. The bilingual program in which she works is a transitional, late-exit program. Students are heterogeneously mixed according to their English proficiency. Some are about to be moved into programs where all instruction is in English. Others have just arrived from Mexico with no English. They receive instruction in Spanish in major content areas; their more English-fluent peers also benefit from ongoing instruction in Spanish. As a result, major explanations and discussions are conducted by Karen in Spanish, especially at the beginning of the year. Reading in both languages is done daily, both aloud by the teacher and individually or in small groups. Because Karen feels that it is unreasonable to expect students to speak one language specified by the teacher when all people in the classroom are bilingual, an explanation may be given in Spanish but students may respond in either language. Many group activities are also carried out utilizing both languages. However, Karen must also monitor students' English language proficiency, so she carefully orchestrates some activities so that they are carried out in each language. For example, when working on writing with the students, Karen finds that two variables influence the choice of language for writing: (1.) the language of the materials used as references, and (2.) the language preference of the audience. If writing on family issues, such as the interviews in this unit, the writing tends to be in Spanish; when the audience is the English-speaking classroom to whom students present their projects, students write in English regardless of their English proficiency. (See Table 4.16.)

Table 4.16 *DETAILED SCHEDULE, KAREN BEEMAN'S FIFTH-GRADE BILINGUAL CLASS*

Day 1

Time	Children	Teacher	Teacher Research
Student/ Teacher Duties 9:00	Children take care of assigned duties. Attendance, lunch count taken, library books returned, and homework collected.	Prior to students' arrival, Karen posted an "EXPLORING OUR ROOTS" WEB on the wall. The WEB presented a compilation of suggestions children had made, along with some of Karen's ideas.	
	Children add activities to the WEB and negotiate ideas with peers. Ricky adds "Research recycling centers and set one up in the classroom," and Catherine suggests writing and illustrating an Aztec legend.	As children enter the room, Karen supervises assignments and responds to students who have written to her on the Message Board*.	
Integrated Work Time 9:10		Karen gathers the children around her. She places a large plastic sweater box, potting soil, rock, and stones the students have brought in, pitted chiles and epazote (an herb from Mexico), and beans.	
	Children share what they learned in interviewing their parents about the chinampas in Mexico City. They jot down notes of the creation of the chinampas.	She begins by asking the children what they learned in interviewing their parents. Karen records questions for small group discussion and investigation.	Karen makes mental notes of students' comments and plans to use some of what they say in the sections of the theme on family and cultural knowledge.
	The volunteers work with Karen to create several model chinampas, using class discussion to guide their work.	The sharing and discussion is led in Spanish by Karen, though some students interject English, too. Karen and student volunteers begin to create a model of the chinampas.	
	Students move into small groups, select roles, decide on resources and begin working on the following:	Karen organizes cooperative learning groups, models with a group the roles students will use, and	Karen keeps notes on which students have decided to work together, and moves between groups, listening to

(continued)

Table 4.16 DETAILED SCHEDULE, KAREN BEEMAN'S FIFTH-GRADE BILINGUAL CLASS (CONTINUED)

Day 1

Time	Children	Teacher	Teacher Research
	• Why the chinampas were important to the Aztecs. • Where the idea for the chinampas came from. • The destruction of the chinampas. • Why it might be important to study ancient people such as the Aztecs. • What the Spaniards thought of the chinampas and the Aztecs. Any group that finishes early goes to their EXPLORING OUR ROOTS Learning Log* and writes reactions to the morning activities. Each group reports to the whole class on their investigation and discussion.	introduces the questions students will investigate. Questions are introduced in Spanish, but students may speak in the language most comfortable to them as long as everyone understands, including those with the least English.	discussions and focusing on students' perceptions of and possible identification with the Aztecs.
Music 10:35	Students watch a video (in Spanish) on the Aztecs that explains Aztec culture: family, agriculture, religion, food, art, music, and dance. Students discuss the video: *Ernesto:* "Teacher, the movie says the Indians were smart, but I thought they were dumb. Why do people think they're dumb?" *Maribel:* "Mi mamá me contó que los indios vivian muy saludablemente y sabian curar todo. No tenian tanta violencia y enfermedad como nosotros." (My mother told me the Indians lived very healthy lives and knew how to heal many things. They didn't have as much illness and violence.)	Karen and the music teacher have planned this time to connect the music with the EXPLORING OUR ROOTS unit. Karen leads a brief discussion in Spanish after the video. She focuses on the relevance of the Aztecs to the lives of the students and tries to bring out their background knowledge on indigenous peoples of Mexico and Latin America. Karen suggests that they add a time line of events affecting indigenous people to their WEB. The music teacher says that the Aztecs also had a rich artistic tradition, including music and dance, then she introduces students to instruments that may have been used by Aztecs and versions that are still used today.	Later, Karen reflects on the following questions: • How much cultural knowledge do students have? • How important is that knowledge to them? • How do students' different perceptions about their cultural identity come out in the discussions?
Crafts/Art 11:30	Students move to groups, following Karen's instructions. They discuss the possible uses of different artifacts and the meaning of the symbols. Some recognize forms from the video on the Aztecs.	As children return to class, Karen places a set of pictures and artifacts on the center of each group of tables. She asks students to study the material in each group and then decide what each item might be used for and figure out what the decorations on each item represent.	
Reading Aloud* 12:00	Students offer predictions, comments, and reactions to the book.	Karen reads *La Música de la Chirimía* to the class.	
SSR* 12:50	Students take ten minutes to look at the new books in the room and select one to read during SSR*. They then read and write to the teacher about their reading in their Learning Logs*.	Karen explains that she would like the students to be reading about topics related to the EXPLORING OUR ROOTS theme during SSR* and has brought a number of books they might want to try.	Karen logs books being read by students and later reviews and responds to literature logs, keeping track of student comments related to her teacher research interests.
Integrated Work Time 1:25	Students join groups. In front of each group is a large piece of chart paper and pens. They participate in the discussion led by Karen and then	Karen asks students to group themselves. She then facilitates whole-group discussion on the neighboring community. She asks what they	*(continued)*

Table 4.16 *Detailed Schedule, Karen Beeman's Fifth-Grade Bilingual Class (continued)*

Day 1

Time	Children	Teacher	Teacher Research
	work in smaller groups to discuss the following: • Five major strengths of the community. • Five major weaknesses of the community. • What the community should be like. • Five ways we could improve the community.	think the strengths and weaknesses of the community are.	
	The resulting discussion is lively and generates many possibilities for community projects, including working with the priests to sit down with the gang members and stop the shooting, and cleaning up the garbage by the aqueduct.	Karen records suggestions, nothing that no decision will be made today. This is a brainstorming session. Later, they can pick a project they really want to work on.	
Dismissal 2:30			

Day 5

Time	Children	Teacher	Teacher Research
Student/ Teacher Duties 9:00	Children carry out morning duties.	Karen had previously noted that her students were not accustomed to reading and writing recipes. Though their parents had a wealth of culinary expertise, most did not use recipes. Karen decided to tap into the parent's knowledge and introduce the students to a new written genre. She has asked students to write a recipe that reflects a special meal from their family.	
Integrated Work Time 9:10	Children bring their recipes to the whole-group portion of integrated work time. As they gather around Karen, they find sets of measuring cups, measuring spoons, utensils, and mixing bowls. Students help Karen remember directions for the recipes. One of the students tells Karen that her mother learned to cook from her father's mother. The only time she uses a recipe is if the food is not Mexican and is all new to her.	Karen demonstrates a cooking recipe, highlighting the directions and quantities of measurement. She explains orally what she is doing, with no written recipe. She then asks students to talk her through the same recipe.	
	Students select one of the recipes from each group and use water to practice measuring out quantities. They try to write clear instructions for others to follow. They also estimate equivalencies, and measure to confirm their estimates.	Karen reviews measurements with students, including some equivalences (e.g., 2 cups = 1 pint). Karen asks students if they would like to make a bilingual cookbook and asks them to think about what might be involved in doing so (i.e., editing, illustrating, publishing, and distributing).	
	Each group rewrites their recipes in English and Spanish.		

(continued)

Table 4.16 *Detailed Schedule, Karen Beeman's Fifth-Grade Bilingual Class (continued)*

Day 25

Time	Children	Teacher	Teacher Research
Integrated Work Time 9:10	Small group reports on community issues are presented today on the results of the following: • Survey of other students in the school on community concerns. • Parent survey. • Interview with two area leaders • Interview with leader of community center in area Students decide that they want to combine two projects, both their celebration of EXPLORING OUR ROOTS planned for the end of the unit and a thank you for those who have helped in their community project.	Karen monitors group reports, making sure that everyone who wants to gets a chance to participate. Karen leads a discussion of the results of the group studies, asking where the students want to go from here. Karen agrees to student suggestion, and planning begins for this new venture.	Karen is very excited about this part of the theme. Parents have been interested, as have community leaders. A local priest has told students he will ask for support from the parish if students decide to pursue their plan for a community cleanup. The city council member for the area has volunteered equipment to help, too. Part of Karen's research interest was in whether this study would connect outside the school setting and this is exciting evidence that it has.

Summary

While Karen Beeman's classroom is officially bilingual, the issues she faces are not unfamiliar to many teachers in areas where more and more students acquire English as a second language. As with Dehea Munioz (Prototype 4), she is concerned about the cultural identities of her students and with the impact that entering a different culture has on their success in and out of school. Like Dehea, Karen also has cross-cultural experience and recognizes the points of dissonance for students. As the unit progressed, Karen found that focusing her *essential questions* on issues such as identity, migration, bilingualism, conquest, and subjugation—What are our major concerns about our community? How can we work together to make our community better?— seemed to make school relevant and appealing to her students. She used some of the same techniques Ted Jackson used in his Appalachian community (Prototype 5A) to make positive connections between school and community. Children went out into the neighborhood; the neighborhood was invited into the school. Multiple audiences for children's written, oral, and artistic productions helped to break down some of the barriers between groups of children. Karen's documentation of her and the students' experience allowed her to argue for more schoolwide attention to issues of cultural identity. The students' public performances provided concrete evidence to parents and school personnel that students were both interested in and capable of handling these issues. Finally, Karen noted that her students became more adept at register switching (using the language appropriate to the situation), more comfortable in using both Spanish and English in their studies, and more likely to see bilingualism as a positive attribute.

Children's Literature: EXPLORING OUR ROOTS

Air by A. Webb. Franklin Watts, 1986.

Al Otro Lado De La Puerta by M. Medero. Editorial Novaro, 1982.

Ancestor Hunting by L. Henriod. Messner, 1979.

The Ancient Maya by I. F. Glum. Benchmark, 1996.

...and Now Miguel by J. Krumgold. Harper & Row, 1953.

Annie and the Old One by M. Miles. Illustrated by P. Parnell. Little, Brown, 1971.

Antonio Machado Y Los Niños by J. M. Garrido Lopera. Everest, 1983.

Arroz Con Leche: Popular Songs and Rhymes From Latin America by L. Delacre. Scholastic, 1989.

Aztec Indians by P. McKissack. Children's Press, 1985.

Barrio Ghosts by E. Cervantes & A. Cervantes. New Readers Press, 1988.

Being a Plant by L. Pringle. Crowell, 1983.

Bless Me, Ultima by R. A. Anaya. Tonatiuh International, 1972.

Blue Willow by D. Gates. Viking, 1948.

La Boda: A Mexican Wedding Celebration by N. Van Lann. Illustrated by A. Arroyo. Little, Brown, 1996.

Buffalo Dance: A Blackfoot Legend by N. Van Loan. Little, Brown, 1993.

Canto Familiar by G. Soto. Illustrated by A. Nelson. Harcourt, 1995.

Cesar Chavez by R. Franchere. Illustrated by E. Thollander. Crowell, 1970.

Children of the Yucatán by F. Staub. Carolrhoda, 1996.

Las Chinampas: Una Técnica Agrícola Muy Productiva by J. Aguilar. Arbol Editorial, S.A. de C.V., 1982.

Cinderella, Or the Little Glass Slipper by C. Perrault. Illustrated by E. LeCain. Bradbury, 1973.

La Civilizacion Maya by S. Gerson & S. Goldsmith. Trillas, 1988.

Cocina Navideña Mexicana by E.O. de Sanz. Editorial Continental, 1987.

Color De Tierra by I. Suarez de la Prida. Editorial Amaquemecan, S.A. de C.V., 1987.

Come Spring by K. O. Galbraith. Atheneum, 1979.

Cooking the Mexican Way by R. Coronado. Lerner, 1982.

Corn Is Maize: The Gift of the Indians by Aliki. Crowell, 1976.

Cuentos Juveniles De América by M. Vich Adell (Ed.). Gente Nueva, 1974.

The Day It Snowed Tortillas by J. Hayes. Mariposa, 1986.

De Tigres Y Tlacuaches: Leyendas Animales by M. Kurtycz. Editorial Novaro, 1981.

210 Recetas De Cocina Internacional by V. Ramos Espinoza. Editorial Diana, 1979.

Diego by J. Winter. Translated by A. Price. Illustrated by J. Winter. Knopf, 1994.

El Abuelo Tomás by S. Zavrel. Ediciones S.M., 1987.

El Libro de las Adivinanzas by C. Bravo-Villasante. Editorial Minon, 1984.

El Lirón Sin Nombre by J. Moran. Illustrated by C. Buskuets. Susaeta Ediciones, S.A., 1983.

El Maíz Tiene Color de Oro by S. Martinez-Ostos. Editorial Novaro, 1981.

Especialidades de la Cocina Mexicana by A. de la Rosa. Editores Mexicanos Unidos, 1981.

Everybody Cooks Rice by N. Dooley. Illustrated by P. I. Thornton. Carolrhoda, 1991.

Experimentos Atmosféricos by V. Webster. Children's Press, 1986.

A Family in Mexico by P. Jacobsen & P. Kristensen. Bookwright, 1984.

Family Pictures/Cuadros de Familia by C. L. Garza. Children's Book Press, 1990.

¡Fiesta! Cinco de Mayo by J. Behrens. Children's Press, 1986.

Fiesta U.S.A. by G. Ancona. Lodestar, 1995.

A First Look at the World of Plants by M. E. Selsam. Walker, 1978.

The Flame of Peace: A Tale of the Aztecs by D. Lattimore. Harper and Row, 1987.

Flash, Crash, Rumble and Roll by R. M. Branley. Crowell, 1964.

Folk Tales: Four Plays for the Classroom by L. Swinburne & S. Bank. Walker, 1989.

Folk Toys Around the World and How to Make Them by V. Fowler. Prentice-Hall, 1984.

Frida Kahlo by R. M. Turner. Little, Brown, 1993.

Gathering the Sun: An Alphabet in Spanish and English by A. F. Ada. Illustrated by Simon Silva. Lothrop, 1997.

Going Home by E. Bunting. Illustrated by D. Diaz. HarperCollins, 1996.

The Great Ancestor Hunt: The Fun of Finding Out Who You Are by L. Perl. Clarion, 1989.

Greening the City Streets: The Story of the Community Gardens by B. A. Huff, Photographs by P. Ziebel. Clarion, 1990.

Growing Older by G. Ancona. Dutton, 1978.

Hansel and Gretel by J. Grimm & W. Grimm. Illustrated by A. Lobel. Delacorte, 1971.

Heirs of the Ancient Maya: A Portrait of the Lacondon Indians by C. Price. Scribner's, 1972.

Hello, Amigos! by T. Brown. Henry Holt, 1986.

Henry Cisneros, Alcálde Mexico-Americano by N. Roberts. Children's Press, 1988.

La Historia de Ernesto by M. Company. Ediciones S.M., 1986.

The House on Mango Street by S. Cisneros. Vintage Contemporaries, 1989.

The Hummingbird's Gift by S. Czernecki. Illustrated by T. Rhodes. Hyperion, 1994.

The Hundred Penny Box by S. B. Mathis. Puffin, 1986.

I Am Phoenix: Poems for Two Voices by P. Fleischman. Harper & Row, 1985.

Immigrant Kids by R. Freedman. Dutton, 1980.

In My Family/En Mi Familia by C. L. Garza. Children's Press, 1996.

It's Raining Cats and Dogs: All Kinds of Weather and Why We Have It by F. M. Bradley. Houghton Mifflin, 1987.

Josephina by J. Winter. Harcourt Brace, 1996.

Journey of the Nightly Jaguar: Inspired by an Ancient Mayan Myth by B. Albert. Illustrated by R. Roth. Atheneum, 1996.

Juan Ramón Jimenez y los Niños by J. R. Ramirez. Everest, 1980.

Latin American Crafts and Their Cultural Backgrounds by J. Comins. Lothrop, Lee and Sheppard, 1974.

Leyendas Mexicanas by R. Morales. Aguila, S.A. de Ediciones, 1968.

Local News by G. Soto. Harcourt Brace, 1993.

Mama's Birthday Surprise by E. Spurr. Illustrated by F. Davalos. Hyperion, 1996.

Maya Art Design Coloring Book. Editorial San Fernando, 1988.

Maya by P. McKissack. Children's Press, 1985.

Me and My Family Tree by P. Showers. Crowell, 1978.

Mexican Crafts and Craftspeople by M. Harvey. Art Alliance Press, 1987.

Mexican Profiles: Bilingual Biographies for Today by J. Nava & M. Hall. Aardvard Media, 1974.

Mitos y Leyendas translated and adapted by J. Oleza. Ediciones Gaisa, 1968.

The Monkey's Haircut, and Other Stories Told by the Maya by J. Bierhorst. Morrow, 1986.

La Montaña del Alimento adapted by H. Rohmer. Illustrated by G. Carrillo. Children's Book Press, 1988.

Montezuma and the Aztecs by N. Harris. Bookwright, 1986.

La Música de la Chirimia by J. A. Volkmer. Carolrhoda, 1991.

My Mexico/México Mío by T. Johnston. Illustrated by F. J. Sierra. Putnam, 1996.

Nature's Weather Forecasters by H. R. Sattler. Nelson, 1978.

Neighborhood Odes by G. Soto. Illustrated by D. Diaz. Harcourt Brace, 1992.

New Junior Cookbook by *Better Homes and Gardens*. Meredith, 1989.

Observando El Clima by A. Ford. Everest, 1982.

Only Jody by J. Delton. Houghton Mifflin, 1982.

Pablo Remembers: The Fiesta of the Day of the Dead by G. Ancona. Lothrop, 1993.

Passport to Mexico by C. Irizarry. Franklin Watts, 1987.

People of Corn: A Mayan Story by M. Gerson. Illustrated by C. Golembe. Little, Brown, 1995.

The Piñata Maker by G. Ancona. Harcourt Brace, 1994.

Plant Experiments by V. Webster. Children's Press, 1982.

Plants by L. Bender. Gloucester Press, 1988.

Popol Vuh translated by A. Recinos. Fondo de Cultura Económica, 1982.

Poppy Seeds by C. R. Bulla. Crowell, 1955.

The Potter Place by G. Gibbons. Harcourt Brace, 1987.

Prietita and the Ghost Woman/Prietita y la Llorona by G. Anzaldúa. Illustrated by C. Gonzalez. Children's Press, 1996.

A Pumpkin in a Pear Tree by A. Cole. Little, Brown, 1974.

Quetzal: Sacred Bird of the Cloud Forest by D. H. Patent. Illustrated by N. Waldman. Morrow, 1996.

Ramona and Her Father by B. Cleary. Illustrated by A. Tiegreen. Morrow, 1977.

Red Riding Hood by J. Marshall. Dial, 1987.

Roots Are Food Finders by F. M. Branley. Crowell, 1975.

Rumpelstiltskin by E. Hunter. Viking, 1981.

Sky Songs by M. C. Livingston. Holiday House, 1984.

Slab, Coil, and Pinch: A Beginner's Pottery Book by A. T. Gilbreath. Morrow, 1977.

The Spirit of Tio Fernando/El Espiritin de Tio Ferando: A Day of the Dead Story/Una Historia del Dia de los Muertos by J. Levy. Translated by T. Mlawer. Illustrated by M. Fuenmayor. Whitman, 1995.

The Stingy Baker by J. Greeson. Carolrhoda, 1990.

The Stories Julian Tells by A. Cameron. Pantheon Books, 1981.

Storms by R. Broekel. Children's Press, 1982.

Take a Trip to Mexico by K. Lye. Franklin Watts, 1983.

Tales of the Far North by E. Martin. Dial, 1984.

This Home We Have Made/Esta Casa Que Hemos Hecho by A. Hammond and J. Matunis. Crown, 1993.

This Tree Is Older Than You Are: A Bilingual Gathering of Poems and Stories with Paintings by Mexican Artists by N. S. Nye. Simon, 1995.

Three Little Pigs by P. Galdone. Seabury, 1970.

Too Many Tamales by G. Soto. Illustrated by E. Martinez. Putnam, 1993.

The Tortilla Book by D. Kennedy. Harper & Row, 1975.

The Tortilla Factory by G. Paulsen. Illustrated by R. W. Paulsen. Harcourt Brace, 1995.

Tortilla for Emilia by M. Angeles. Sundance, 1992.

Tortillas para Mamá and Other Nursery Rhymes by D. Griego. Holt, Rinehart & Winston, 1981.

The Trip of a Drip by V. Cobb. Little, Brown, 1986.

Versitlan by R. López Moreno. Presencia Latinoamericana, S.A., 1983.

Voy a Cocinar by M. Lasa. Sitesa, 1988.

La Voz de Coatl by L. Ramos. Editorial Novaro, 1983.

The Walls of Pedro Garcia by K. McColley. Delacorte, 1993.

Water by A. Webb. Franklin Watts, 1986.

Water by B. Bunston. Silver Burdett, 1982.

Water for the World by F. M. Branley. Crowell, 1982.

Water Plants by L. Pringle. Crowell, 1975.

Weather Experiments by V. Webster. Children's Press, 1982.

What Makes It Rain? The Story of a Raindrop by K. Brandt. Troll, 1982.

When Clay Sings by B. Baylor. Macmillan, 1972.

Where Did You Get Those Eyes? A Guide to Discovering Your Family History by K. Cooper. Walker, 1988.

Where the Sidewalk Ends: The Poems and Drawings of Shel Silverstein by S. Silverstein. Harper & Row, 1974.

The Witch's Face: A Mexican Tale by E. A. Kimmel. Illustrated by F. V. Broeck. Holiday House, 1993.

The Woman Who Outshone the Sun/La Mujer Que Brillaba Aun Mas Que el Sol by R. Zubizarreta, H. Rohmer, & D. Scheter. Illustrated by F. Olivera. Children's Book Press, 1991.

Your Name—All about It by M. Prie Lee. Westminster, 1980.

Prototype 8: Sixth Grade—DIGGING UP THE PAST
Schedule

DIGGING UP THE PAST begins with a simulated experience—two archaeological digs—and uses the "unearthing" of artifacts to draw children into an exploration of the processes used to define and resolve problems in various domains. The unit is designed to incorporate the world studies curriculum typical of many sixth-grade programs into a larger unit on the interpretation of human, plant, and animal remains. The major *essential question* in this theme is "How do we know what happened in the past?" It builds on the foundation of independent reading and research begun in earlier years, with the intent of helping children further develop their understanding that knowledge is a human construction subject to change and interpretation, and that students and teachers alike participate in making and interpreting knowledge.

The unit also makes use of a commercial simulation, *Dig* (a unit developed by Interact), and *Bones*, an Elementary Science Study (ESS) science program. Although commercial materials are not necessary to the theme, they do provide resources that are otherwise unavailable or difficult to obtain. Two "digs" initiate the unit. The first is a wastebasket excavation that introduces children to the process of excavation and interpretation of data. The second is the simulation *Dig* that involves students in the

Interact (1974); ESS (1974)

Prototype 8: Sixth Grade—DIGGING UP THE PAST

Building a Prehistory Museum

HOMINIDS: A LOOK BACK AT OUR ANCESTORS
WHERE THE FOREST MEETS THE SEA
TYRANNOSAURUS REX AND ITS KIN
FROM MAP TO MUSEUM
TRACES OF LIFE

Include Displays* of the development of plants and animals.
Make a geological clock.
Display size comparisons of plants and animals over time.

Animals

THE BONE WARS
THE PUZZLE OF THE DINOSAUR-BIRD
DINOSAURS AND THEIR YOUNG
DIGGING UP DINOSAURS
TYRANNOSAURUS WAS A BEAST
DINOSAURS DOWN UNDER AND
   OTHER FOSSILS FROM AUSTRALIA
TRAPPED IN TAR

Do *Bones* unit in ESS   .
Make a time line of an animal species.

Plants

MOONSEED TO MISTLETOE

Make plaster fossils.
Collect plant fossils and label them for
   a Display*.
Make a plant history of the world.
   What are the oldest plants on earth?
   The newest?

Music and Dance

Learn music and dance
   from other cultures.
Invite guests to help
   identify patterns in
   music by region.
Investigate how music
   and dance are used
   in the cultures studied.

FOSSIL REMAINS

THE ARTS

SCIENCE

Arts and Crafts

Try crafts from cultures
   studied.
Make a Display* of crafts
   indigenous to the cultures
   you study.
List all the ways you can find
   that art is used in your own
   culture.
Use found objects and recycle
   them into art.
Set up a class museum of world
   art.

DIGGING UP THE PAST

METHODOLOGY

Architecture as a Time Line

UNBUILDING
CATHEDRAL
CITY
MILL
PYRAMID
PROVINCETOWN
GREAT MOMENTS IN ARCHITECTURE
LEBEK: A HANSEATIC CITY OF
   NORTHERN EUROPE THROUGH
   THE AGES

See if you can unravel the mysteries behind the
   building of the pyramids, Stonehenge, or the
   ancient Mayan buildings. Think of an interesting
   way to share your discoveries.
Make a Display* of distinctive architectural
   features from different times and cultures.
   Look for evidence of these features in
   American culture.

THE CHANGING CITY
THE CHANGING COUNTRYSIDE

Use either of Muller's books, and trace the history of
   one feature of the changing landscape.
Write a story about a person living in any of the places
   you've read about in these books. Do as a
   performance assessment.
Theory building: How is architecture related to:
• the natural environment
• people's religious beliefs and other values
• technological development

In the Social Sciences

"History Lesson"
MOTEL OF THE MYSTERIES
DIGGING TO THE PAST
THE BOYS' WAR
LETTERS OF A WOMAN HOMESTEADER
THE BONE DETECTIVES
FROZEN MAN
FINDING THE LOST CITIES
SHIP
BURIED IN ICE

Do a wastebasket excavation.
Do simulation DIG.
Collect articles on "garbageology"—the study
   of landfills.
Interview different social scientists about their
   work (anthropologist, archaeologist,
   sociologist, etc.).
Conduct an observation of human interaction.
Study the different types of information that
   can be gathered from Primary Sources*.
Create a Jackdaw*.

In the Sciences

WHITE BEAR, ICE BEAR
TRACKING WILD CHIMPANZEES
BEAVER AT LONG POND
THE COMPLETE FROG
PLACES OF REFUGE
WATCH OUT FOR SHARKS!
BORN FREE
MUMMIES, DINOSAURS, AND
   MOON ROCKS
INTO THE SEA

View films/videos of scientific studies
   (Goodall in Africa, Cousteau on the
   Calypso, and other field researchers).
How do scientists study plants and
   animals?
Interview scientists about their work.
Plan and conduct a study of a
   classroom pet or pets. Keep field notes,
   and make a final report. Take photos
   for support data.

Information Books

MUMMIES MADE IN EGYPT
EARLY HUMANS
LIFE THROUGH THE AGES
THE BLACK DEATH
CALLIOPE: WORLD HISTORY
  FOR YOUNG PEOPLE

Write a history of your island culture.
Compare burial and other practices
  and beliefs between cultures.
Make a "life through the ages" book
  for your culture. Illustrate.
Study influence of ancient Africa and
  Asia on western cultures.
Look for common patterns in ancient
  and modern cultures.

Traditional Literature

IN THE BEGINNING
WORDS FROM THE MYTHS
SHAMROCKS, HARPS, AND SHILLELAGHS
SWEET AND SOUR: TALKS FROM CHINA
ORACLE BONES, STARS, AND WHEELBARROWS:
  ANCIENT CHINESE SCIENCE AND TECHNOLOGY
DAUGHTER OF EARTH

Compare folktales, myths, and legends from other cultures.
Hypothesize a type of folktale for a culture (e.g., an island
  culture might have water sprites).
Write a catalog of common themes, characters, and so on
  in traditional literature.
Write a tale that would fit your island culture.
Collect folklore from your own area/region; compare with
  those from other places.
Analyze: What do these tales tell us about values of different
  cultures?

Historical Fiction

I, TUT
HIS MAJESTY, QUEEN HATSEPSHUT
THE EYE IN THE FOREST
SETH OF THE LION PEOPLE
DAWN WIND
THE STRONGHOLD
THE SAMURAI'S TALE
THE AMETHYST RING
MALU'S WOLF

How have different authors visualized the
  past? What evidence do they use? What
  is their point of view? Are there instances
  of presentism or anachronisms?
Write a piece of historical fiction that could
  come from your island culture.
Discuss: Slides of "developed" and
  "developing" cultures. Is "development"
  always "progress?"

LITERATURE

Problem Solving

INCREDIBLE CROSS-SECTIONS

Express size comparisons as fractions,
  decimals, and ratios.
Calculate proportions for museum
  Displays★.
Figure the cost benefit of recycling
  in the school.
Weigh recycled goods; calculate resale.

MATH

Field Math

Find out how math is used in archaeological
  and anthropological work.
Set up problems from your island culture and
  share them via computer with your
  classmates.
Invent a base system for your culture.
Make size comparisons of plants and animals.

SOCIAL STUDIES

Inventing Culture

BAAA
BARMI: A MEDITERRANEAN CITY
  THROUGH THE AGES
CRANBERRIES
THE IGLOO
THE PUEBLO

Construct an island culture. How will
  you meet your basic needs? Use the
  resources in environment?
Prepare geographic and historic reports,
  decide on government, and so on.
Write documents, laws, create art,
  literature, music.
Communicate and trade with others.
Provide evidence that your creations
  are possible by finding parallels in
  past or present.

Burying the Present

CARTONS, CANS, AND ORANGE PEELS:
  WHERE DOES OUR GARBAGE GO?
RECYCLOPEDIA

Investigate ways your community deals with waste.
Investigate cross-cultural issues of
  pollution/waste disposal.
Create a school plan for recycling.
Debate: Should a local industry be able to dump
  waste into a lake that is a major tourist attraction?
Visit a recycling center and/or a water treatment plant.

Interpreting Cultures

SHAKA, KING OF THE ZULUS
DAWN WIND
THE STRONGHOLD
LOST AND FOUND
THE LAND I LOST
FAMILIES
MUMMIES, TOMBS, AND TREASURE
STEPPING ON THE CRACKS

Make a catalog of ways in which cultures take
  care of necessities.
What values do these choices represent?
Write a set of "Laws for Cross-Cultural
  Travelers."
Create a traveler's guide to a culture or country.
  Be sure to let the traveler know about customs
  that could cause misunderstandings.
Make a comparative time line for cultures and
  countries from different regions of the world.
Do parallel culture studies: Begin with island
  culture and real-world parallels.
Trace evidence of cultural diffusion in your own
  community.
Study families in a cross-cultural perspective.
Conduct an in-depth study of several cultures
  over time.

replication of an archaeological excavation. These activities take approximately one week, with about forty-five minutes to an hour per day devoted to the digs.

Although it has become common to departmentalize at sixth grade, the teacher in this class, Caitlin Cooper, works in a self-contained sixth grade in a school noted for its integrated language curriculum. Her schedule is given in Table 4.17.

Caitlin has been developing this unit over the past several years. Over time and as a direct result of her teacher inquiries, her plans have changed. Caitlin now puts more emphasis on methodology as a category that cuts across both science and social studies. She finds that this better supports a Reflective, Disciplined Inquiry* approach and makes more explicit the kind of attention she wants to pay to how knowledge is acquired in specific domains. She now helps students report on how they acquired information, not just on the product of their research. She also makes more explicit the connections between the work her students do this year and their prior studies of American history in fifth grade. She found that her students were not making these connections on their own and were confused as to when events in American history happened in relation to world history. Finally, she has added a section called "Burying the Present" not only to capitalize on student interest in burial practices in ancient civilizations but also to move her students beyond a fascination with the techniques of mummification or buried treasures to current practices and issues, including waste management and land use. This year, Caitlin intends to continue her research into how students become more reflective inquirers. To better understand how children are approaching problems in the different disciplines, Caitlin requires that her students keep a specific type of Learning Log* in which they record problems they are investigating, the approaches and sources that are working best, and the problems they are encountering in their work. These logs, based on the I-Search* approach to inquiry, provide data on common research techniques and problems that are applied across disciplines or that appear to fit one discipline better than another.

Into the Classroom

Caitlin's use of integrated work time is similar to that in Carol Hagihara's second grade (Prototype 3). Students move among work centers distributed throughout the room and a central grouping of tables and chairs arranged for projects using reading and writing. We begin on Day 6, after children have worked with the excavations. (See Table 4.18.) Caitlin uses most of the morning on this day to establish the idea of interpretation of artifacts and to set the stage for the later introduction of the *Bones* unit and

Table 4.17 *WEEKLY SCHEDULE, CAITLIN COOPER'S SELF-CONTAINED SIXTH-GRADE CLASS*

Time	Monday	Tuesday	Wednesday	Thursday	Friday
8:00	Opening exercises				
8:10	Forum. Children gather to share work, group plan, and learn about activity choices for the day.				
8:30	Integrated work time. Children sign up to work in various areas, participate in special projects (i.e., digs). Opportunity for problem solving, creative thinking, self-expression, communication, and content engagement.				
9:50	Special classes: art, music, physical education, library				
10:30	Recess				
10:45	Integrated work time				
12:00	Lunch				
12:45	SSR*				
1:00	Forum. Whole group experiences that include introducing new material, guest speakers, writing/editing workshops, math reviews, and the like.				
2:00	Integrated work time				
2:30	Cleanup, announcements, and dismissal				

a study of fossils and geological interpretation. She has done some background reading on the use of fossilized bones in studying early humans and on the controversies surrounding the interpretation of human remains. Caitlin's plans also call for inviting an anthropologist to class. The traditional task of the guest expert is to deliver a speech (with short discussion afterward) and then leave. In this case, however, Caitlin has asked the guest to talk about the concept of culture and serve as consultant to the children as they develop their own island cultures. Caitlin may be the only teacher assigned to this classroom, but she regularly invites guests to provide other points of view, different types of expertise, and a range of audiences for children's work. During this unit guests include, in addition to the anthropologist, an architect, a storyteller, several parents who have traveled to the areas being studied, a dancer, and international students from a nearby university.

Invite guests to serve as consultants for student work.

Another project that involves students in interpreting data and communicating their results is the development of a museum of prehistory and the creation of artifacts and documents related to a student-developed culture. (Compare this to the "Nature's Journeys" museum in Prototype 4.) In each case, children simulate the activity of experts in a domain. They have recourse to some of the same data that an expert might have, and they can consult experts as they develop their ideas. They make approximations in their interpretations in the same ways that they use approximations in other forms of communication. Caitlin is anxious to see if this activity will show up in the student I-Search* reports. She also encourages this type of intellectual risk taking by sharing literature such as Ray Bradbury's short story "History Lesson," in which the tentative nature of historical interpretation and the possibility of error are humorously pointed out.

Bradbury (1974)

Between Days 6 and 10, students use a teacher-developed simulation to construct an island culture and begin reconstructing plant and animal histories. Portions of the schedule of Day 20 highlight the continued development of the theme as children prepare to share their findings.

Table 4.18 *Detailed Schedule, Caitlin Cooper's Self-Contained Sixth-Grade Class*

Day 6

Time	Children	Teacher	Teacher Research
Forum 8:10	Children make a chart of what can be known or inferred from artifacts, using digs and slides of Viking dig as data.	Caitlin shares parts of *Digging to the Past* and asks students what other digs they know of. She shows slides of the Viking excavation, Yorvik, at York, England.	Caitlin's teacher inquiry begins here, as she presents the idea of archaeology as a form of data collection and points out the methods explained in *Digging to the Past*.
Integrated Work Time 8:30	Children select a settlement location on Mystery Island and list factors influencing their decisions. Breaking into groups based on location, they discuss what it would take to survive in their group's area. Each group takes a clan name and begins to plan for the kind of civilization that they will be able to develop in that area.	Caitlin distributes a map of an uninhabited island and asks children to select a location where they could survive. Each group is then given a list of supplies they will have to work with.

After students have worked in groups, Caitlin leads a discussion of problems encountered and ideas tried. She calls on a student to record some of the considerations each clan must deal with. This is posted in the room for student reference throughout this activity. | |
| Literature 9:50 | Children listen to a story and discuss connections to interpreting artifacts. | Caitlin shares the "History Lesson" and participates in discussion. | |
| Integrated Work Time 10:15 | Children try to identify artifacts from their state's prehistory and infer their use. | A specialist from the local museum brings artifacts to class and leads a discussion of how the museum staff | *(continued)* |

Table 4.18 *DETAILED SCHEDULE, CAITLIN COOPER'S SELF-CONTAINED SIXTH-GRADE CLASS (CONTINUED)*

Day 6

Time	Children	Teacher	Teacher Research
		reconstructs the past and builds displays based on fragments from the past.	
Whole Group Activity 11:00	Children observe slides and discuss the observations that led to the archaeologist's misinterpretations of the artifacts in the slides.	Caitlin follows up the guest talk with a slide show based on *Motel of the Mysteries*, a spoof on artifact interpretation.	
Integrated Work Time 11:20	Children return to their clans and work on developing their culture, using some of the ideas gathered during the earlier part of the morning.	Caitlin moves among groups, asking questions and listening to students' discussions.	
Forum 1:00	Children work in pairs to identify groups of bones. They measure bones and calculate the possible size of the creature.	During this period, Caitlin introduces a new type of artifact—bones—using the ESS unit *Bones*.	
Integrated Work Time 2:00	Children work in pairs or individually on the following: • comparing traditional literature from ancient cultures • investigating arts and crafts common to ancient cultures • using *Tyrannosaurus Was a Beast* as a model for writing poems about the creatures reconstructed during forum • making size Comparison Charts* of features of Mystery Island	Caitlin works with small groups for part of this period and conducts several Reading Conferences* for the rest of the time.	Caitlin's emphasis here is on how to use different sources. She asks students to keep track of the sources they use and to remember to record both their sources and why they chose particular sources in their Learning Logs*.

Day 10

Time	Children	Teacher	Teacher Research
Forum 8:10	Children listen to a story.	Caitlin reads portion of *The Bone Wars*.	
Integrated Work Time 8:30	Children are conducting inquiries into a variety of topics. They have engaged in source sharing discussions, developed specific questions, and used a variety of data sources.		As students have engaged in inquiries throughout the unit, Caitlin has systematically introduced them to different research techniques. Now Caitlin wants them to focus more carefully on the process of researching as well as the final product. She reminds them that good researchers want to know about the process because it helps them evaluate the product. She reminds them to use their double-entry Journals* to take notes.
	Children listen and talk with the guest. They take notes as she talks, leaving enough room for their own questions and comments. They then move into centers, including: • *Mystery Island*. Present part of their culture to the anthropologist and use expert help in solving problems. • *Plants*. Organize a plant history that connects plants and agriculture with human culture.	Guest anthropologist speaks about what a "culture" is and responds to student questions. The anthropologist works with small groups as they rotate into the Mystery Island center. Caitlin works with the plant history group as they organize data.	Caitlin is particularly interested in observing how students handle this stage of their inquiry. *(continued)*

Table 4.18 *DETAILED SCHEDULE, CAITLIN COOPER'S SELF-CONTAINED SIXTH-GRADE CLASS (CONTINUED)*

Day 10

Time	Children	Teacher	Teacher Research
	• *Literature*. Create a Comparison Chart* of "origin" stories from different cultures. Note how plants and animals are explained in these stories.	Caitlin brings a pomegranate and a copy of *Daughter of Earth* to share with this group. After everyone tastes the seeds and discusses whether they were worth the months in Hades, Caitlin calls students' attention to several other "origin" myths and to Hamilton's *In the Beginning*, a collection of creation stories from around the world.	
	• *Animal observations*. View video on Jane Goodall's work and begin to read *Born Free*.	Caitlin enters this area as the video ends and talks with the students about careful observation of live animals, then introduces *Born Free*.	Later, Caitlin will collect samples of student observation reports as part of her inquiry.
Art 9:50	Children construct mosaics similar to those in illustrations of ancient Greece and Rome, except that they use symbols representing different aspects of their island cultures.	An art specialist works with the class and plans some of her activities to coincide with units Caitlin has developed.	
Recess 10:30	Children rotate between groups.	Caitlin continues as during the first integrated work time.	
Integrated Work Time 10:45 Forum 1:00	Students working with a base 5 number system present their work to the class, giving some base 5 problems. Three students share their most recent writing.	Caitlin helps as students do base 5 problems, congratulating those who figure it out: "Looks as if you're ready to try another base system!" She also joins in the discussion of the writing presented, using an overhead to answer questions about quotations and paragraphing in dialogue.	
Integrated Work Time 2:00	Students work in centers.	Caitlin works with small groups and then holds a Reading Conference* on *The Stronghold* and *Dawn Wind*.	

Day 20

Time	Children	Teacher	Teacher Research
Forum 8:10	A small group reports on their ten-day study of Ethel, the classroom guinea pig. They have made charts of growth and a video of Ethel's behavior. The class discusses the study and compares it to the video on Goodall and to *Born Free*. They decide that several comparison studies would be useful and begin to plan how to conduct them.	Caitlin encourages other animal studies. When two children suggest a study of sixth graders, she tells them to think about what their questions might be to guide the study, how they would collect data, and how they would protect their "subjects" privacy. She suggests they submit a plan to the class for discussion and approval.	Caitlin takes notes on student work. She is especially interested in how the children deal with ethical issues at this point. She makes a note to remind herself to show them guidelines for human subjects research.
Integrated Work Time 8:30	Several new groups have grown from previous work, including: • *Museum group*. Construction is under way on a diorama-type museum of the prehistoric world. Students have designed exhibits to compare interpretations of		Many of these activities serve as both performance assessment and data in Caitlin's study. As she has gathered data throughout the unit, several issues seem particularly salient. First, she wants to see how (or if) chil-

(continued)

Table 4.18 *Detailed Schedule, Caitlin Cooper's Self-Contained Sixth-Grade Class (continued)*

Day 20

Time	Children	Teacher	Teacher Research
	what the prehistoric world was like. They have found conflicting accounts in reports about the work of paleoarchaeologists Don Johannsen and Richard Leakey. • *Architecture.* After working with the art teacher, students are preparing a report "The Bones of Buildings," using *Unbuilding* and *Incredible Cross-Sections* as models for planning their report. • *Human culture.* Three groups have each looked at a different culture and are now collaborating on a way to share the results of their studies. • *Leaders.* After questions of leadership arose in the Mystery Island activity, a group of students decided to study the influence of different types of leaders in history and are preparing a news conference with Shaka Khan, Mao Zedong, Saladin, Henry VIII, and Franklin D. Roosevelt.	Caitlin works carefully with this group in planning how to share their findings. This will be used as a performance assessment. Children have conducted several studies throughout the unit, and received regular feedback from peers and from Caitlin. Caitlin uses these group tasks to assess children's progress toward two of the major goals for the unit—learning to use and understand the processes for solving problems in various domains and using content appropriately and accurately.	dren represent or account for differing interpretations in their final reports. Second, she wants to see how children handle the different genres they will use in reporting their studies. Third, she wants to see whether they report both process and results. Performance assessment also provides Caitlin with rich data for her own inquiry.
Forum 1:00	Author's Chair*. Students share some of their writing with peers.	Caitlin participates in listening to and discussing each author's work.	Caitlin takes notes on peer evaluations related to appropriateness of genre.

Summary

Departmentalized teaching requires careful team planning and coordination of efforts by an entire team of teachers, but a teacher in a self-contained classroom such as Caitlin must also use her planning periods wisely. She must be constantly alert to student interests and possible extensions. She makes extensive use of the services of the school librarian and the surrounding community for human and material resources, and works with the art, music, and P.E. teachers to enrich her themes. Caitlin also spends time carefully organizing her room and thinking about her students' needs. She uses a variety of methods and media, especially videotapes. Sometimes children watch prepackaged programs and often they make their own. In this way, Caitlin capitalizes on early adolescents' fascination with the video medium to promote careful observation and support their inferences, as well as to help them recognize and appreciate the perspective of the filmmaker.

The advantage of this type of self-contained, integrated approach to study is the ease with which Caitlin and her students can cross and relate disciplinary categories. Time is as flexible as the class's inclinations and the requirements of their studies. In addition, Caitlin can pursue long-term research goals in which she revises her teaching strategies, documents student response, and adjusts thematic units accordingly. As a result of her teacher research during this thematic unit, Caitlin finds that the students' I-Search* reports are especially useful for student self-evaluation. For instance, she discovers that, while students can *report* other interpretations, they become confused in *evaluating* the merits of different interpretations. She notes that students seem to confuse interpretation and opinion, and are reluctant to evaluate something that "is his opinion, but I don't agree with it."

Children's Literature: *DIGGING UP THE PAST*

The Amethyst Ring by S. O'Dell. Houghton Mifflin, 1983.

Baaa by D. Macaulay. Houghton Mifflin, 1989.

Barmi: A Mediterranean City through the Ages by X. Hernandez & P. Comes. Houghton Mifflin, 1992.

Beaver at Long Pond by W. T. George and L. B. George. Illustrated by L. B. George. Greenwillow, 1988.

The Black Death by J. Day. Franklin Watts, 1989.

The Bone Detectives: How Forensic Anthropologists Solve Crimes and Uncover Mysteries by D. Jackson & C. Felllenbaum. Little, Brown, 1996.

The Bone Wars by K. Lasky. Morrow, 1988.

Born Free by J. Adamson. Random House, 1974.

The Boys' War: Confederate and Union Soldiers Talk about the Civil War by J. Murphy. Houghton Mifflin, 1990.

Buried in Ice by O. Beattie & J. Geiger. Illustrated by J. Wilson. Scholastic, 1992.

Calliope: World History for Young People by R. Baker & C. Baker, III (Eds.). Cobblestone. (Periodical)

Cartons, Cans, and Orange Peels: Where Does Our Garbage Go? by J. Foster. Houghton Mifflin, 1991.

Cathedral by D. Macaulay. Houghton Mifflin, 1977.

The Changing City by J. Muller. Atheneum, 1977.

The Changing Countryside by J. Muller. Atheneum, 1977.

City by D. Macaulay. Houghton Mifflin, 1974.

The Complete Frog: A Guide for the Very Young Naturalist by E. A. Lacey. Illustrated by C. Santoro. Lothrop, 1988.

Cranberries by W. Jaspersohn. Houghton Mifflin, 1991.

Daughter of Earth by G. McDermott. Delacorte, 1984.

Dawn Wind by R. Sutcliffe. Walck, 1962.

Digging To the Past: Excavations in Ancient Lands by W. J. Hackwell. Scribner's, 1986.

Digging Up Dinosaurs by Aliki. Crowell, 1981.

Dinosaurs and Their Young by R. Freedman. Illustrated by L. Morill. Holiday House, 1983.

Dinosaurs Down Under and Other Fossils from Australia by C. Arnold, Photographs by R. Hewett. Clarion, 1990.

Early Humans by N. Merriman. Knopf, 1989.

The Eye in the Forest by W. & M. Steele. Dutton, 1975.

Families: A Celebration of Diversity, Commitment and Love by A. Jenness. Houghton Mifflin, 1990.

Finding the Lost Cities by R. Stefoff. Oxford, 1997.

From Map to Museum: Uncovering Mysteries of the Past by J. Anderson. Photographs by G. Ancona. Morrow, 1988.

Frozen Man by D. Getz. Illustrated by P. H. McCarty. Holt, 1994.

Great Moments in Architecture by D. Macaulay. Houghton Mifflin, 1978.

His Majesty, Queen Hatshepshut by D. S. Carter. Lippincott, 1987.

"History Lesson" by R. Bradbury. In *Transformations 2: Understanding American History through Science Fiction*. Fawcett Crest, 1974.

Hominids: A Look Back at Our Ancestors by R. Sattler. Illustrated by C. Santoro. Lothrop, 1988.

The Igloo by C. Yue and D. Yue. Illustrated by D. Yue. Houghton Mifflin, 1993.

Incredible Cross-Sections by S. Biesty. Knopf, 1992.

In the Beginning by V. Hamilton. Illustrated by B. Moser. Harcourt Brace Jovanovich, 1988.

Into the Sea by B. Z. Guiberson. Illustrated by A. Berenzy. Holt, 1996.

I, Tut: The Boy Who Became Pharaoh by M. Schlein. Four Winds, 1979.

The Land I Lost by H. Q. Nhuong. HarperCollins, 1982.

Lebek: A Hanseatic City of Northern Europe through the Ages by X. Hernandez & J. Ballonga. Illustrated by R. Corni. Houghton Mifflin, 1991.

Letters of a Woman Homesteader by E. P. Stewart. Houghton Mifflin, 1982.

Life through the Ages by G. Caselli. Putnam, 1987.

Lost and Found by J. P. Walsh. Andre Deutsch, 1985.

Malu's Wolf by R. Craig. Orchard, 1995.

Mill by D. Macaulay. Houghton Mifflin, 1983.

Moonseed to Mistletoe: A Book of Poisonous Wild Plants by C. Lemer. Morrow, 1988.

Motel of the Mysteries by D. Macaulay. Houghton Mifflin, 1980.

Mummies, Dinosaurs, and Moon Rocks: How We Know How Old Things Are by J. Jesperson & J. Fitz-Randolph. Illustrated by B. Hiscock. Atheneum, 1996.

Mummies Made in Egypt by Aliki. Crowell, 1979.

Mummies, Tombs, and Treasure by L. Perl. Houghton Mifflin, 1990.

Oracle Bones, Stars, and Wheelbarrows: Ancient Chinese Science and Technology by F. Ross, Jr. Illustrated by M. Goodman. Houghton Mifflin, 1982.

Places of Refuge by D. Patent. Clarion, 1992.

Provincetown by M. Oliver. Edited by J. Wheatcroft. Press Alley, 1987.

The Pueblo by C. Yue & D. Yue. Illustrated by D. Yue. Houghton Mifflin, 1990.

Pyramid by D. Macaulay. Houghton Mifflin, 1975.

The Puzzle of the Dinosaur-Bird by M. Schlein. Illustrated by M. Hallett. Dial, 1996.

Recylopedia by R. Simons. Houghton Mifflin, 1993.

The Samurai's Tale by E. C. Haugaard. Houghton Mifflin, 1990.

Seth of the Lion People by B. Pryor. Morrow, 1988.

Shaka, King of the Zulus by D. Stanley & P. Vennema. Illustrated by D. Stanley. Morrow, 1988.

Shamrocks, Harps, and Shillelaghs by E. Barth. Illustrated by U. Arndt. Houghton Mifflin, 1982.

Ship by D. Macaulay. Houghton Mifflin, 1993.

Stepping on the Cracks by M. Hahn. Houghton Mifflin, 1992.

The Stronghold by M. Hunter. Harper & Row, 1974.

Sweet and Sour: Tales from China by C. Kendall & Y. Li. Illustrated by S. Felts. Clarion, 1979.

Traces of Life by K. Lasky. Illustrated by W. Powell. Morrow, 1989.

Tracking Wild Chimpanzees by J. Powzyk. Lothrop, 1988.

Trapped in Tar: Fossils from the Ice Age by C. Arnold. Photographs by R. Hewett. Clarion, 1987.

Tyrannosaurus Rex and Its Kin by H. K. Sattler. Illustrated by J. Powzyk. Lothrop, 1988.

Tyrannosaurus Was a Beast by J. Prelutsky. Illustrated by A. Lobel. Greenwillow, 1988.

Unbuilding by D. Macaulay. Houghton Mifflin, 1983.

Watch Out for Sharks! by C. Arnold. Photographs by R. Hewett. Clarion, 1991.

Where the Forest Meets the Sea by J. Baker. Greenwillow, 1988.

White Bear, Ice Bear by J. Ryder. Illustrated by M. Rothman. Morrow, 1988.

Words from the Myths by I. Asimov. Dutton, 1969.

Other Resources

Elementary Science Study (ESS). (1974). *Bones*. New York: McGraw-Hill.

Interact. *Dig*. Learning Through Involvement. Lakeside, CA:

Conclusions

Each of the teachers visited in the eight prototypes in this chapter is a unique individual in strength, interests, and enthusiasm. Some are more likely to think initially in disciplinary or curricular categories when planning; others prefer to follow a theme across categories first and attend to disciplinary or curricular requirements later. Some work well in teams or in open classrooms; others enjoy the flexibility of self-contained or family-grouped settings. Despite these and other differences, there are also commonalities among them that identify their classrooms as integrated language environments. First, these classes are distinguished by the joint participation of adults and children in meaning making. Dehea Munioz, for instance, regularly involves children in planning at the outset of a thematic unit so that they see themselves as active participants not just in learning about something or someone but in selecting what to learn about. As a result, her plans evolve over the course of the unit as student investigations trigger new questions for inquiry. Dehea is also a researcher in her own right. As the thematic unit progresses, she introduces specific experiences or information, collects data on student responses, analyzes those responses, and develops theories supported by her research, thereby better learning how to support student learning.

Distinguishing features of integrated language classrooms.

A related feature of these integrated language classrooms is a different view of error. Children hypothesize, make approximations, develop theories, and test them against new data. Their hypotheses and theories may not be supported by these new data, and their approximations may be refined as they learn more, but that is the nature of learning. Hypothesis-making requires risk, and these classes provide a context within which intellectual risk taking is encouraged, supported, and expected. Caitlin Cooper depicts this perspective as her students first develop the tools of archaeological observation and inference and then use those tools to construct their own civilization. Carol Hagihara also encourages hypothesizing in the "How do we decide which solution to pick?" activity that points children toward assuming responsibilities in the larger community.

Teachers and children in these classes develop a different view of "error" and intellectual risk taking.

Teachers in integrated language classrooms see themselves as child developmentalists rather than teacher technicians. They are professionals responsible for developing a child-centered curriculum that has solid intellectual content. Child developmentalists know that content and context are inseparable. They strive to arrange the kind of context that fosters student engagement in their process of building theories about the world. These classrooms are full of participants, not recipients. Children are the active makers of meaning.

Teachers become child developmentalists rather than technicians.

These classroom contexts are filled with a range of materials, but they are not expensive resources. Rather, they are gathered from many sources, including materials donated by or borrowed from families, friends, acquaintances, and other members of the community. Books and print resources are easily obtained from libraries. As pointed out in Chapter 3, experienced integrated language teachers frequently use approximately 400 to 500 books during a thematic unit. Space does not allow us to list that many books on the WEBs. Consequently, the WEBs in this chapter include only a portion of the books available on these themes.

Integrated language classrooms are content rich and community oriented.

Related to this feature of resources is the way the community serves as a resource. An important characteristic of the integrated language classrooms you have seen here is how frequently the boundaries between the community and the classroom are crossed. Time after time, the community is brought into the classroom to provide expertise or help. Parents and friends and children from other classes join class participants to celebrate and support children's efforts. Children go on field trips into the community to gain important information and data for their projects. In turn, the larger community provides a real audience for student work. Through this two-way process, the classroom culture is enlarged and expanded, and bridges are constructed to span the gulf between the school and the world at large.

Finally, the various classroom and teaching arrangements depicted here are not specific to a particular grade or age. A teacher working on a seventh- or eighth-grade team in a middle school setting, for instance, would be more likely to use patterns such as those suggested in the fourth- and fifth-grade departmentalized setting than those in the sixth-grade self-contained model. Obviously, ideas from one prototype can be used in others, and activities set up for younger children can often be adapted for use with older students, and vice versa. Classrooms, as with any human community, change over time. What is crucial is that each of these teachers constantly seeks to enrich children's lives by making them more interested and able learners.

REFERENCES

Atwell, N. (Ed.). (1990). *Coming to know: Writing to learn in the intermediate grades.* Portsmouth, N.H.: Heinemann.

Barr, R., Barth, J., & Shermis, S. S. (1977). *Defining the social studies (Bulletin No. 51).* Washington, DC: National Council for the Social Studies.

Bergen, D. (Ed.). (1987). *Play as a medium for learning and development: A handbook of theory and practice.* Portsmouth, NH: Heinemann.

Blake, D. W. (1981). Observing children learning history. *The History Teacher, 14,* 533–549.

Clements, M., Tabachnik, R., & Fielder, W. (1966). *Social study.* New York: Bobbs-Merrill.

Feshback, N. D. (1975). Empathy in children: Some theoretical and empirical considerations. *Counseling Psychologist, 4,* 25–30.

Goodman, K., Bird, L., & Goodman, Y. (1992). *The whole language catalog: Supplement on authentic assessment.* Santa Rosa, CA: American School Publishers.

Hartoonian, M. (1992). *A guide to curriculum planning on global studies.* Milwaukee: Wisconsin Department of Public Instruction.

McGinley, W., & Madigan, D. (1990). The research "story": A forum for integrating reading, writing, and learning. *Language Arts, 67,* 474–483.

Perry, T., & Fraser, J. (1993). *Freedom's plow.* London: Routledge.

Ryan, F., & Ellis, A. (1974). *Instructional implications of inquiry.* Englewood Cliffs, NJ: Prentice-Hall.

Shaftel, F. R., & Shaftel, G. (1982). *Role playing in the curriculum (2nd ed.).* Englewood Cliffs, NJ: Prentice-Hall.

Sims, R. (1982). *Shadow and substance: Afro-American experience in contemporary children's fiction.* Urbana, IL: National Council of Teachers of English.

Spears-Bunton, L. A. (1990). Welcome to my house: African-American and European-American students' responses to Virginia Hamilton's "House of Dies Drear." *Journal of Negro Education, 59,* 566–576.

Stone, L. C. (1986). International and multicultural education. In V. Atwood (Ed.), *Elementary social studies: Research as a guide to practice (Bulletin No. 79, pp. 34–54).* Washington, DC: National Council for the Social Studies.

More Ideas to Integrate the Curriculum

Two major characteristics of the integrated language perspective are the use of oral and written language across the curriculum and the integration of the various curricular areas. Chapters 3 and 4 explained how this integration is accomplished through thematic units. This chapter provides more specific details and ideas to help teachers integrate language and content in five curricular areas: social studies, science, mathematics, art, and music. In each curricular area, there are two emphases: (1) a brief overview of current views, principles, and concepts, and (2) more ideas for ways to integrate language within and across the curriculum.

Social Studies

What Is Social Studies?

Gamberg, Kwak, Hutchings, & Altheim (1988); McGinnis (n.d.); NCSS (1994)

Social studies connects children to the world.

Levstik & Barton (1997)

We see social studies as the integration of the processes of learning about people as they arrange to live together in groups, and the content of history and the social sciences as they relate to these human activities. How children learn and what they learn are both fundamental parts of social studies. In the social studies, children learn to recognize and evaluate social data, build causal theories, draw conclusions, and make and challenge generalizations about human behavior. These are important behaviors in a culturally diverse society in an interdependent world. Students need to make *informed* and *reasoned* decisions, not just to enhance their individual lives—although this is certainly important—but to enable them to better work for the public good. Thus, the basic subject matter and constant focus of the social studies is people *in community*. Social studies connects children to the world, whether engaging them in studying family history, looking at the influences of the Nile River on Egyptian society and how Egyptians have attempted to control those influences, or in examining the economic, social, and political impact of urbanization in a developing nation. In our perspective, social studies is often the core of the integrated curriculum, for it provides powerful themes for study and opportunities for children to engage in important conversations about race, class, gender, ideology, and the distribution of power in human societies. Because these issues divide societies, they are among the most controversial—and potentially interesting—parts of the curriculum. As a result, social studies is one of the most powerful contexts within which children use all the forms of language discussed in previous chapters. Sometimes however, this feature of social studies makes teachers, as well as some students and parents, uncomfortable. This explains, at least in part, why social studies is too often reduced to its least interesting and least controversial aspects. In too many classrooms, social studies is little more than perfunctory studies of such topics such as community helpers or transportation, without any real attention to the human consequences of social studies content. But if we are to prepare students to live in community with others, to make informed and reasoned decisions, and to participate fully in a democratic society, we cannot ignore controversies. Instead, we can use the social studies to help children develop the knowledge, skills, and attitudes necessary to un-

184

derstand and cope with controversy. In the context of an integrated curriculum, then, social studies gains an importance that it often lacks in the traditional classroom.

Like science, social studies is not a single discipline but an integration of content, concepts, and generalizations from a number of disciplines. Social studies generally draws on history, geography, anthropology, sociology, political science, economics, psychology, and the arts. Combining these disciplines encourages children to see the way in which these forces together influence human activity. Figure 5.1 shows the way content from several disciplines can pose different questions to be used in exploring a single theme. The integrated nature of social studies, however, makes it more complicated to define than science, due in part to the multiple perspectives or purposes that can be attributed to this curricular area. As a result, teachers need to think carefully about building a classroom context that supports social studies.

Social studies is an integration of content, concepts, and generalizations from several disciplines.

Barr, Barth, & Shermis (1977); Maxim (1987); Stodolsky (1988)

See also Barr, Barth, & Shermis (1977) and Barth (1996) for a discussion of the implications of differing definitions of social studies.

Building the Social Studies Context

Linking Process and Content

As we have already mentioned, social studies involves integrating the processes of learning about history, the social sciences, and the arts with content drawn from each domain. This is a crucial idea in understanding the place of social studies in an integrated curriculum. Good teaching focuses on helping students learn important organizing ideas. Because each of the component fields within social studies focus on different, though related, organizing ideas, students need plenty of opportunity to study the content of each field; they also need to learn *how* each field acquires and organizes knowledge. The way knowledge is constructed in history, for instance, is quite different from the way in which scientists understand chemistry. A scientist can observe the way in which hydrogen combines with oxygen to produce water and can generate laws based on this observation. A historian can never observe the phenomena under investigation. Instead, history is constructed from the partial residue of the past. The historian constructs a plausible explanation of how that residue fits into the past but cannot construct laws to explain this phenomenon. History is particularistic and resists our attempts to construct a full account of the past.

Downey & Levstik (1991); Levstik & Pappas (1987); Wilson & Wineberg (1988)

"Knowing" in a domain is more than remembering discrete "facts."

History is interpretation based on the residue of the past.

These are very different ways of thinking about evidence, hypotheses, and proofs. For children to develop understanding in social studies, they need to understand these differences. They need experience in using and interpreting various kinds of social data

Figure 5.1

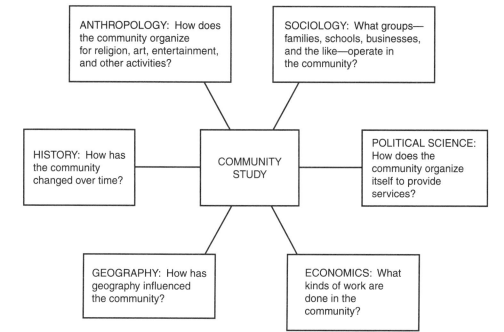

Gamber, Kwak, Hutchings, & Altheim (1988)

from history, the social sciences, and the arts. Yet process alone is not social studies. No matter what processes are used, there is always a subject of study—the question or content under investigation. In addition, not all subjects are equally worthy of study. Given the limited amount of time and the almost infinite variety of topics that can be studied in any school year, part of the teacher's obligation is making sure that the topics studied are worthwhile. Thus the teacher might ask, with regard to content, if selected topics help children:

NCSS (1994); NCSS Focus Group (1992)

> View a period or culture from the perspective of those who live or lived in that time and place.
> Recognize the impact of interactions between humans and the environment.
> Develop deeper understanding of themselves and others as individuals and members of groups.
> Act as knowledgeable, critically-minded citizens
> Resist prejudice and avoid stereotyping.
> Critically evaluate social data and interpretations of social data.

From this perspective, time spent investigating apples or bears may not seem worthwhile, despite some possibilities for helping children learn to use the processes of gathering and analyzing data or communicating findings. On the other hand, consider the possibilities from both process and content perspectives when third-grade children study a problem in their community.

No More Litter

Harlan (KY) Elementary School (1986)

Children in a mountainous rural district were engaged in a thematic unit centered on their community and containing the areas outlined in Figure 5.1. After touring the community, they discussed a real problem in their area: the illegal dumping of trash and garbage. They thought that something ought to be done about the garbage that littered their hillsides, but they were not sure what that could be or if children could make any difference. Their teacher suggested that they investigate and collect data to help them decide. She then arranged a series of field trips to garbage collection sites: illegal dumps, the county landfill, and a recycling center. The children planned and collectively wrote interview questions, recorded their observations and interviews, and then set about analyzing their data. Their teacher encouraged them to express their findings in a variety of ways. Soon the classroom was full of captioned artwork detailing what had been found. Some children made a mural showing how the plants and animals might feel about all the garbage. The trees, birds, and even the sun commented on how awful the litter was. Only germs, maggots, and rats had good things to say. The children had been researching in information books, and they shared their findings about the relationship of germs, maggots, and rats to garbage.

Children study an authentic problem and record their observations.

Next, the class began a recycling campaign. Their trip to the recycling center had convinced them that this would have several benefits. Not only would it clean up the environment, but they could also earn money to pay for the videotapes they were using. The second grade sponsored a can-collecting contest in the school, and they soon were recycling huge amounts of aluminum cans. They also began writing a play about a community where it was illegal not to litter. They made up songs and dialogue and constructed props as a way to convince the rest of their school to participate in an antilitter campaign.

Children participate in alleviating a problem.

The next step was to visit their local government representatives to find out what was being done about the litter problems. They discovered that their county had begun an adopt-a-spot campaign to encourage a sense of responsibility and ownership about the environment. The class adopted their school yard to educate others in the community about their responsibility. Before long, the children had edited their tapes, selected artwork and writing as well as musical background, and produced a videotape called *No More Litter*. The tape was used at parent-teacher meetings to encourage adults to join the adopt-a-spot program.

Accomplishing the goals of social studies

Consider what these children accomplished in terms of the goals of social studies:

1. The topic had power and reality for them. It helped them understand the diverse factors that shape societies (geography, history, sociology, and economics).
2. The unit allowed the children to critically examine a public issue in their community and act as knowledgeable, critically-minded citizens by helping to alleviate that problem (citizenship and political science).
3. They learned something about the community services available to help people take care of such basic problems as garbage disposal and recycling (economics, political science, and sociology).
4. They discovered that elected officials shared their concerns and were willing to work with the community to solve problems (political science).
5. They learned what resources could be used to investigate a problem, how to critically evaluate those resources, and how to effectively communicate their findings to other people (reflective inquiry).
6. They learned to see the problem from the perspective of different community members and interest groups (history, economics, sociology, and psychology).

At the end of this unit, the children had a sense of efficacy rather than defeat. They had discovered a powerful motivation for using their writing and reading skills, and as a result, they improved the very skills that had caused them problems in their previous schooling. Finally, this thematic unit broke down the walls between school and the surrounding world.

Little would have happened if the children had not had time to study in depth and reflect on what they had learned, ask new questions, and select ways to respond to their findings.

Depth

For children (and adults) to understand a particular cognitive domain, they need enough time to study in such depth that they begin to build theories about how knowledge in that domain is used. They need to see how particular information fits in the larger context of a domain. In geography, for instance, how does one piece of information (the location of a mountain range) relate to another (a slow density of population)? What can one find out about people by knowing and developing understanding? Providing context means providing an opportunity to study something in depth as the second grade children studied the problem of litter in their community. To have depth, a topic must have *extensiveness*; that is, it must be rich enough to generate subtopics, activities, and interest. Study is equally important in that it encourages the kind of thinking that relates to theory building in a domain. As a result, social studies is not just the accumulation of information but a way of asking questions about a subject and a way of answering and understanding the answers. Some incongruity or anomaly must therefore strike children as they encounter the social studies. Read the following account of a classroom and think about how the teacher uses incongruity to involve children in thinking about interpretation in the social studies.

Carey (1985a, 1985b); Keil (1984); Newmann, et al. (1985); Whitin & Whitin (1993)

Context can facilitate depth.

Hyde & Bizar (1989)

Social studies is a way of asking and answering questions.

Immigrant Children

As part of a thematic unit titled MIGRATIONS, a teacher brought a selection of books on U.S. immigration into his fifth-grade classroom. He hoped to generate interest in a recurrent theme in American history and a current topic of debate in the surrounding community. He brought one of his favorite books, *Immigrant Kids* by Russell Freedman, to share orally. As he read to the class, he pointed out the photographs that illustrated the text. One picture of a child bathing in a metal sink generated a good deal of discussion; children noted how difficult it would be to keep clean and how little privacy families would have had in the tenement pictured. Some days later, as the teacher shared *Watch the Stars Come Out* by Rikki Levinson, one of the children called attention to Diane Goode's illustration of a child bathing in a metal sink in a New York ten-

Using incongruity

Freedman (1980)

Levinson (1997)

Looking at history as interpretation

Meltzer (1964); Hurmence (1982)

Teachers gather resources.
Riis (1971)

Children share findings and chart results.

Children create their own texts.

Albert & Groth (1997); Levstik & Barton (1996)

ement—clearly based on the photograph they had seen earlier. The children were amazed at the difference between Goode's soft pastel treatment of the same scene that the photographer had captured in all its squalor. At this point, the teacher saw an opportunity to help children look at the interpretive nature of historical reporting. He gathered other examples of authors and illustrators who treated issues of voluntary and involuntary immigration. He brought to the classroom Meltzer's *In Their Own Words*, a compilation of the memories of enslaved African Americans, and Hurmence's *A Girl Called Boy*, a historical fiction based on slave narratives. He also located copies of the slave narratives preserved at his State Historical Society so that a group of students could study these books' source material. He found collections of pictures of the ethnic and tenement neighborhoods of Manhattan that were taken by Jacob Riis at the turn of the century and published in *How the Other Half Lives*, a photo essay on illegal immigration by Ashabranner, and photographs from the collection.

Students also located reference material in the school and public library and in their textbooks and set to work analyzing the varying interpretations in the sources. One group developed charts to show the following:

The sources for information used by authors and illustrators
The ways in which illustrations were used to help interpret information
The types of interpretations authors used
Specific information selected for inclusion or omission
Evidence of point of view (ideological perspective, bias, distortion)

Soon these fifth graders were developing criteria for evaluating information books and historical fiction. (See Figure 5.2.) The children went on to create their own information books and historical fiction based on their studies and the criteria they had developed. One of their texts was titled *How to Read History*. As a result of their study, these children had learned a great deal about the interpretive nature of history:

1. They were engaged in comparing and contrasting interpretations that would not only help them understand the history of immigration but also serve them well when they studied other history and read historical literature.
2. They learned to look for certain types of errors, bias, and misinterpretation—an important part of understanding history and the social studies.
3. They learned some of the ways in which historical information can be "mythologized" and misunderstood.

Visualizing the Social World

Part of the impact of the MIGRATIONS theme came through visual images—photographs, paintings, and drawings—that gave immigration not only a human face, but a material world. The visual arts provide information about clothing, work and leisure activities, gender roles, religious practices, household goods, and children's play. A student can study the faces of immigrant children as they pick over rags, work in sweatshops, or walk among the vendors on Hester Street in New York. In the same way,

Figure 5.2

Criteria	Biography	History	Historical Fiction
Conversation	Not invented.	Must have evidence.	Invent only for fictional characters.
Order of events	Can't change if it's true.	Definitely can't change.	Only for made-up events.
Invented actions	Not for real people.	Never. Infer with support.	Yes, as long as it doesn't change history.
Invented people	No. Maybe disguise the identity of real people.	No. Must be based on evidence.	Yes. Put invented people in real situations.

pictures of the bleak, windswept Gila River Relocation Center in Arizona make vivid the indignities of Japanese internment. One photograph of a long line of people waiting in the blowing dust to use the latrines in the camp speaks volumes to students. Similarly, Wendall Minor's paintings in *Mojave* and *Heartland* provide students with powerful images of American landscapes.

Seibert (1988); Seibert (1990)

Visual images provide different vantage points, or perspectives, from which to view the world and make explicit some of the powerful emotions that often defy words to fully express. They are also accessible to even very young children. This does not mean that visual images are always simple to comprehend. Think about how challenging it can be to "read" the imagery in, say, a painting by Chagall, or Magritte. Even relatively "realistic" paintings can be interpreted at many different levels and in many different ways. Beyond their aesthetic purposes the arts are also social and ideological data. Gheeraert's painting of Queen Elizabeth I standing astride a map of the world is not just a picture of a historical figure, anymore than Steen's *The World Upside Down* is only a picture of a social gathering. Each provides social and political commentary—a perspective on the social world—that is neither wholly aesthetic nor the whole picture of a particular time, place, or person. One teacher finds *The Kids' Art Pack* a helpful resource here. He began with a picture—Ford Madox Brown's "The Last of England"—and set of questions from the book. In the picture, a somber couple sit in the foreground, clasping hands and gazing back towards England from the deck of a ship. The questions require students to look closely, speculating on how the two main figures might be feeling, what the woman is holding in her left hand (a baby's hand), the significance of the name of the ship (El Dorado), the weather, and other details in the painting. Students then construct an interpretation of the "story" told in the painting. Finally, their teacher shares the event that inspired the painting—emigration to Australia in 1855—and engages the class in a discussion of how the artist captured that event and some of its accompanying emotions.

Mitchell (1994)

Visual images can be interpreted in many ways.

Van der Meer & Whitford (1997)

The visual arts also shape popular opinion and behaviors by boosting consumerism, discouraging particular personal or social habits, memorializing people and events, and encouraging participation in various activities. Depictions of individuals, groups, or events have enormous influence on the ways in which students think about the social world. Think about the impact of pictures of waif-like models on young girls' body image, the stereotyping of Arabs as bomb-throwing terrorists in different media, or of World War II propaganda posters presenting the Japanese as a "yellow peril." Perhaps most powerfully, consider the ways in which images from television and film influence students. After looking at pictures representing five hundred years of American history, children from kindergarten through sixth grade identified a picture of a 1950s drive-in restaurant as the "Happy Days" picture. They also recognized other aspects of material culture from television shows or in popular movies that depicted historical events. Sometimes this helps children in sequencing events in time; sometimes visual images perpetuate stereotypes, myths, and oversimplifications of the social world.

The visual arts shape popular opinion and behaviors.

Barton & Levstik (1996); Kammen (1996)

Because social studies in the integrated curriculum should make people next door as well as those in other times, places, and circumstances real to children, it is important to find visual images that present people as complex beings who share the students' humanity. When carefully selected, such images provide important social data to children. They help children answer such questions as: What is it like to live in this time or place? What is it like to be this person? To feel this way? And, perhaps most significantly, images help children visualize what it means to be fully human in a diverse and interdependent world.

Images should show the complexity and diversity of human life.

Besides their use as social data, however, the arts are also an important form of problem solving. In one class, students studying American history were asked to see if they could come up with a multicultural timeline of ten events they considered to be significant in American history. After considerable debate about what constituted a "multicultural" timeline as well as what constituted "significance," students set about building their timelines. Their teacher asked that they use illustrations and captions rather than long explanations for each point on the timeline. First, the students col-

The arts are a form of problem solving.

lected a set of events that they all thought were significant. Next, they began sorting these events into time periods. They debated about whether an event or individual was significant multiculturally, or only for one group. Once they had settled on ten events or individuals, they set about deciding how to illustrate the significance of each. This turned out to be an important discussion; in order to depict the *significance* of an event, they had to understand it well enough to *symbolize* it. One group, for instance, drew a slave breaking out of manacles to represent the Emancipation Proclamation. Another group drew the face of a Native American and placed arrows next to the face. At the top of the downward-pointing arrow, the students printed the population of Native Peoples in the Americas at the time of Columbus' arrival; at the bottom of that arrow, they listed the population one hundred years later. The other arrow, pointing up, began with the population of Europeans after Columbus' arrival, and then one hundred years later. Once the timelines were complete, the class discussed each group's choices. By this time they could provide solid support for their choices, explain their significance, and discuss the challenges inherent in telling a multicultural story while accurately depicting the impact of each individual and event. The timelines provided a lively forum through which student expressed their moral judgments as well as their historical analyses.

The arts transform information into visual representation.

In another classroom, students working on a DIGGING UP THE PAST theme also sought to transform linguistic information into visual representation. After collecting evidence of cultural diffusion in their small, largely rural community, they decided to develop a map that traced certain practices from other countries and other parts of the United States to their community. First, they used digital cameras to take photographs of cultural artifacts and practices in their community. Their pictures included a restaurant and two grocery store signs, photographs of international cookbooks in the local library, names from storefronts, pictures of themselves, of their homes, and public art. They grouped these images into categories—What We Eat, How We Dress, Celebrations, Language, and Built Environment—and used the computer to create collages for each category. They designed their explanatory text as a series of letters and postcards that could be attached to the large map. They also designed symbols to indicate how each practice or artifact made its way to their community. A couple of students experimented with digitally enhancing their photographs to dress local people in clothing representing some of their countries of origin. In the end, they created a visually exciting map that kept their peers and families interested for some time. The students came away from the experience with a better understanding of the sources of their own cultural practices and a growing awareness of how cultural diffusion operates, even in relatively homogeneous communities.

Technology helps students manipulate visual images.

Avoiding Social Studies Mythologies

Freeman & Levstik (1988)

Helping children see the ways in which history and the social sciences use social data and the kinds of problems that can arise in these domains is an important way to help children recognize mythologized information. Unfortunately, the tendency to simplify complex subject matter for children has often resulted in a social studies curriculum that is little more than an accumulation of myths and misunderstandings. Children learn about such a complex figure as Abraham Lincoln only that he freed the slaves, split rails as a boy, and grew to be a very tall man in a stovepipe hat. Lincoln as a person is lost. As we mentioned earlier, one of the purposes of social studies in an integrated curriculum is recapturing the humanity of such people not by presenting children with historical "dirty linen" but by connecting them with real people so that they can better understand the nature of their nation's and the world's past, present, and possible future. Few people are entirely heroic or completely unassailed by doubts, whether they are children or famous adults. Social studies can provide a context in which to look at the decisions both good and bad that people have made and to see how they responded to the challenges life offered them.

Oversimplification leads to misunderstanding.

Egan (1979); Zarnowski (1997)

Connect children with real people and provide a context for studying human decision making.

One of the most popular units in one teacher's third-grade class is MEETING CHALLENGES. She and her third graders interview people in the community selected by the students as people who meet challenges in a variety of ways, not only firefighters and police officers but also news reporters, who talk about the challenges of accurately reporting the news, and people who have met physical challenges. In addition, the teacher sets up a "history roundtable" in which children learn about figures from the past, with an emphasis on the challenges they met (e.g., Should Rosa Parks have moved to the back of the bus? Should Washington have been king? Why did Lindbergh think he should/could fly across the Atlantic?). Children come to the roundtable in character, prepared to talk to each other and to classmates about how they might respond to these historical challenges. They use a variety of literature as background material and often end by asking very interesting questions. One boy, for instance, found George Washington most admirable. But, he wondered, why had Washington continued to own slaves? The class discussed the possibility of a person's being heroic in some ways but not in others. Could such a person still be a hero? they debated, concluding that most people probably were not heroic all the time.

Encourage children to see history as the story of people meeting challenges.

These children chose their heroes and heroines not because they were presented with myths but because they were beginning to understand the strengths and weaknesses of the people they admired. Aside from this being a more accurate view of history as well as of human nature, children can also better imagine themselves meeting challenges and overcoming weaknesses.

Encourage children to see themselves as able to meet challenges.

Attending to the Language of Social Studies

All the foregoing examples describe language use in the content areas that constitute the social studies. A teacher in an integrated language classroom seeks ways to use language across the curriculum, but that means attending to the uses of language peculiar to many knowledge domains. What is the language of geography, for instance? How are symbol systems used on maps and globes to transmit geographic information and a sense of place? What do placenames tell us about human geography?

Hyde & Bizar (1989)

A short activity using one symbol system—maps—may point out the way language shows the interconnectedness of our world. You need only a map of your state. Lay the map out and begin to look for names borrowed from other places. In one small section of central Kentucky, for example, you can locate Paris and Versailles. Ohio has Lima, Cadiz, and Schoenbrun. Where in the world did the placenames in your state come from? What parts of the world predominate? Are there also names borrowed from Native Americans? You may want to try this with a map of Australia. What could account for this geographic phenomenon?

Part of the teacher's job is to help children learn to use the vocabulary of history and the social sciences intelligently. There should be opportunities for children to express what they are learning in charts, graphs, and maps and in informational genres. They should have experience taking surveys and talking about the limitations of survey methods. (Did the survey really ask the right questions? Who answered the survey? Are they representative?) When children use the data sources common to each of these fields, they can use these sources as models for communicating the results of their studies. Children studying immigration produce maps of migration patterns and bar graphs comparing immigration from and to different parts of the world. They may collect historic photographs from their own community along with oral history interviews and create a history of local immigration that includes a table of contents and bibliography. In other words, they use the language of historians and social scientists to talk about these domains of knowledge.

In addition, students may decide to represent what they have learned in genres less commonly associated with a particular domain. These could include such things as letter writing between real or imagined historical personages (e.g., an East German and a West German discussing the problems of reunification) or to individuals outside the classroom (e.g., pen pals or relatives) describing what students are learning. They could include scripts for radio and TV plays to be tape-recorded or videotaped; speeches, plays, and skits to be performed; or filmstrips to be produced. Or they could include annotated catalogs of artifacts (e.g., the dress of men and women of pioneer America or eating utensils from different cultures) or calendars, each page containing a drawing and text related to a topic (e.g., a calendar of archeology or technological change). And finally, as we mentioned earlier, not all representations need be written. Paintings, murals, mobiles, dioramas, musical compositions, and drama can be powerful forms through which children share learning.

Beaty (1997)

Perspectival Social Studies

Any time students represent what they have learned—and any time they pick up a source to help them learn—they must deal with *perspective*. At the beginning of this book, we outlined our perspective—our point of view and basic assumptions—about language and learning. However, whether authors explicitly explain their perspective or not, *all texts represent some world view*. There is no such thing as *just the facts*. Someone sorts through the available data, perceives some facts as more relevant than others, organizes those facts, and presents his or her interpretation in a written narrative, a museum exhibit, a piece of art, or in the classroom. A series of nineteenth-century photographs of sod houses and homesteaders on the Kansas "frontier," for instance, represents a very different perspective or interpretive stance than would an exhibit that focused on the life of Kickapoo Indians in Kansas during the same period, or one that interspersed images of homesteaders with images of the Kickapoo people.

All texts represent some world view.

Appleby, Hunt, & Jacoby (1994); Kammen (1996); Levstik (1997)

As perspectives change, so too do interpretations. Consider, for instance, the lack of attention given in the past to women in history and much of the social sciences. While many of the facts about women's lives were there all along, it was not until people began asking different questions about the social world that they began assigning new significance to those facts. Gradually, scholarship not only included but sometimes focused on women's activities. As a result, the old assumptions, as well as the interpretations that accompanied them, altered. You can see similar patterns in the treatment of other previously underrepresented groups. If we did not regularly revise the questions we ask and the data we use in making sense out of the world, we would be trapped in old ideologies, less able to think about changes in the present or future because we have incomplete or erroneous information. Social studies *must* be subject to revision—to hearing new voices, rethinking old assumptions, and searching for more complete evidence. There can be no "last word"—instead, revision and reinterpretation are basic to social studies.

Social studies must be subject to revision.

In order to help children recognize how perspective shapes interpretation teachers have to carefully consider how to select the books and other resources used in instruction. One primary teacher carefully orchestrates a FAMILY theme so that children can see that a variety of family structures and relationships are normal. She and her students discuss different types of family members—uncles, aunts, cousins, stepparents, mothers, fathers and siblings—as well as different types of family arrangements and family activities. In order to help students understand some of these differences, she uses a variety of literature. She introduces the topic of family travel with two books, *Night Driving*, a gentle story about a father and son as they take a nighttime road trip, and *Nine for California*, a humorous nineteenth-century stagecoach journey in which a resourceful mother averts a series of potential disasters. Later, when discussing how families care for each other, she shares *When We Married Gary*, a warm story about two little girls and their new stepfather, *Mountain Wedding*, about another blended family whose transition to unity is a little rockier, and quite humorous, and *More Stories Huey Tells*, a little boy's stories about his engaging family. Through these and other stories, the teacher tries to establish a sense of positive family relationships and mutual responsibilities. Students then create lists of things families can do to work well together, and suggestions for strategies to use when things are not going well. The class talks about how different family members might view the same events differently, and how that can sometimes cause problems. They listen to *The Year of the Ranch*, about a family's move to Arizona and the different ideas each member of the family has about their year on the ranch. Finally, the teacher invites parents or other interested adults to participate in a special project with students in the class. This is a *participatory research* pro-

Coy (1997); Levitan (1977)

Hines (1997); Gibbons (1997)

Cameron (1997)

McLerran (1997)

Participatory research links children, parents, teachers and the community.

ject in which children and adults work together on a project of their choice. In this case, some of the participants wrote books about a time when the child and adult had worked together on something important. Others wrote and illustrated posters of favorite memories from childhood. One parent and child wrote a poem together about a trip they had made to the mother's childhood home in Venezuela, and then each made an illustration of the poem. Their pictures provoked considerable conversation in the class about how differently each had remembered some parts of the trip. This project was very popular with the children, whether they worked with their own parents or some other adult, but it was also an eye-opener for the teacher. As a result of this classroom interaction, she found adults in the community much more supportive of her work, more willing to talk to her about children's work, and more willing to volunteer in the school. As each year passes, more and more adults show up. Interestingly, some parents continue with the program even after their own children have moved on in school. These volunteers ensure that every child in the class has an adult with whom to work. As a result, social studies instruction includes the perspectives of many community members as well as the teacher and children in the class.

Teacher As Learner

With seven areas—history, geography, anthropology, sociology, political science, economics, and psychology—and multiple perspectives on each one to consider, the elementary teacher may not have a great deal of background in any single field related to social studies. Although this is often seen as a disincentive for teaching social studies, it is also an opportunity to try a role other than that of dispenser of information. Traditionally, many elementary teachers rely on the textbook to delineate the curriculum and to form the boundaries of knowledge. The teacher's role in that case is to help children acquire the information that is within those boundaries. The teacher and the children share the same source of information, and the teacher has the "answers" at least insofar as the text and teacher's guide provide them. However, an integrated approach to the curriculum proposes a different way of looking at the teacher's role. There is no way a teacher can know everything there is to know about the topics that can come up in the course of a thematic unit. As a result, the teacher studies the topics with the children as a fellow learner. The teacher is a more sophisticated learner and probably has more background knowledge to bring to bear in trying to understand a new area, but the task is a joint endeavor by students and teacher. This dramatically alters the teacher's stance. Think about a teacher as one who engages in the following four activities.

Teachers are both decision makers and fellow learners.

Arranging Opportunities for Children to Think Critically About the Content of Social Studies

Observe how this fourth-grade teacher leads children to clarify their understanding of the geographic concept of desert through a Sketch to Stretch* exercise.

The children begin by drawing what they imagine a desert to look like. Most of the children include sand (yellow), snakes, lizards, and cacti. One child draws a tent strung between two saguaro cactus plants and surrounded by people in turbans and long robes. After the class discusses what features they think most deserts have in common and lists some of the areas of uncertainty, the teacher records the results on chart paper as a Semantic Map* (See Figure 5.3.) She also asks that they save their pictures until the end of the investigation.

During the next class session, a guest from Yemen shares slides of the desert and other features of Yemen. The children are surprised by pictures of corrugated tin houses surrounded by a brown, stony, and arid landscape. They have many questions to ask, and later they add to and amend their semantic map considerably. (See Figure 5.4.)

The teacher shows a short filmstrip of the high tableland in the desert sections of Arizona and Nevada. The children express surprise at the difference between the black hills of Nevada and the red landscape of parts of Arizona. As they add more information to their semantic map, they become involved in a debate about whether saguaro

Teachers learn to elicit student questions.

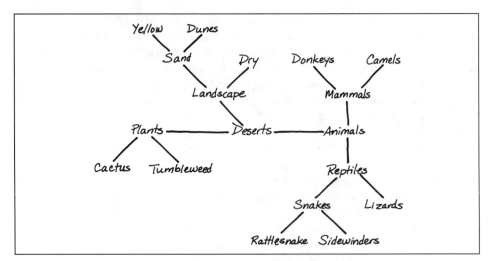

Figure 5.3

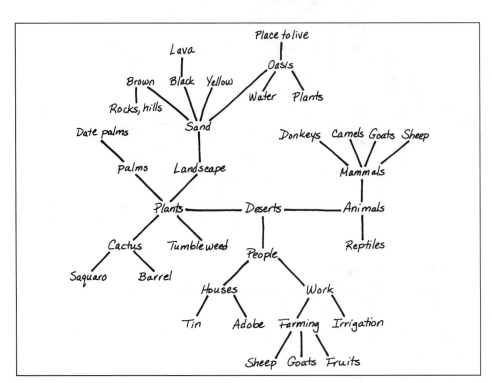

Figure 5.4

cactus grows in all deserts. The teacher asks them to work in groups to construct questions that still need to be asked about deserts. She suggests that they think about the pictures they drew on the first day of their discussion. What questions would help them to make their pictures more accurate?

After the small groups have developed their questions, the teacher leads a debriefing session, during which the children share their work and begin to organize their questions and to consider the sources they can use to find answers.

Providing Challenges to Assumptions

Most of us prefer to let our assumptions go unchallenged, and we work hard to fit new information into old schemas. For children to enrich their schemas relative to social studies, some entrenched ideas must be challenged and other possibilities presented. The teacher must find out what children know about a topic and what assumptions, or schema, they already have in place. The teacher in the foregoing example did this by asking children to draw their ideas of a desert. The teacher's next task is to deal with the anomalies or incongruities—the discrepant events—that do not fit with the children's existing schema.

A fifth-grade teacher found that his students were sure that the work of men on the frontier was much more strenuous and difficult than that done by women. The teacher did not tell students that their information was inadequate. Instead, he brought in diary excerpts describing a day's work done by a young mother on the Oregon frontier. He also brought in several artifacts: kitchen implements necessary for meal preparation and reproductions of period clothing borrowed from a costume shop. These artifacts caused children to question their assumptions because it became clear that household work on the frontier was considerably more taxing than they had assumed.

Teachers learn to arrange for incongruities.

Helping Children Formulate Questions and Generate Opinions

As children confront discrepant events and begin to think about problems and issues to explore, the teacher helps them formulate their questions so that when it is time to communicate findings and draw meaning from their study, children will be able to make supported claims and understand the claims made by others. One simple activity that helps older children distinguish between observing data and drawing inferences based on those data involves the concepts of developed and less-developed countries. The teacher introduces the terms and asks for student response in listing the characteristics or properties of each classification (thus establishing the existing schema). Next, a series of eight to ten slides showing scenes in countries generally considered developed (e.g., United States, England, Germany, and Russia) and developing (e.g., Rwanda, Indonesia, Philippines, and Yemen) are shown, but the slides contradict the stereotypes. A U.S. slide shows a poor rural area without electricity or indoor plumbing, and an Indonesian slide pictures a large, modern city. Children are asked to quickly classify the scene in each picture as either developed or developing. After they have done so, the slides are shown again and discussed so that the problems with these common terms are demonstrated and students are forced to think differently about how parts of the world are categorized.

Children learn to distinguish between observation and inference and between supported and unsupported claims.

Organizing Resources for Student Inquiry

As topics are chosen for investigation, the teacher must also be prepared to search out multiple sources at a variety of levels for student use. This is not as daunting a task as it may at first seem. A number of organizations are anxious to help teachers provide good materials for social studies. The National Geographic Society has launched an extensive program to improve the instruction of geography, including their National Geographic Kids Network Project from Technical Education Research Centers, Inc., while State Councils on Economic Education and the American Bar Association provide materials, activities, and support for teachers who want to include more economic and law content. Historical agencies provide suggested activities and materials for use in classrooms. Some colleges and universities have programs that link international students with area classrooms so that students can meet and talk with people from other cultures. In addition, private and public funds support centers for the dissemination of information in many areas of the social studies, from history and civics to global studies. The resources are there; teachers are the vital link between resources and students.

Links with colleges and universities can match classrooms with international students studying in the United States.

Kraus International (1992)

Obviously, no single book can suggest everything there is to do in a field as diverse as social studies. The activities suggested here will get you started in thinking about how to use social studies as the context for integrating the curriculum.

References: Social Studies

Appleby, J., Hunt, L., & Jacob, M. (1994). *Telling the truth about history*. New York: Norton.

Albert, M., & Groth, J. (1997). Arts alive in the development of historical thinking. *Social Education, 61*, 42-44.

Arnheim, R. (1981). *Visual thinking*. Berkeley: University of California Press.

Bardige, B. (1988). Things so finely human: Moral sensibilities at risk in adolescence. In C. Gilligan, J. Ward, & J. M. Taylor (Eds.), *Mapping the moral domain: A contribution of women's thinking to psychology and education* (pp 87-110). Cambridge, MA: Harvard University Press.

Barr, R., Barth, J., & Shermis, S. S. (1977). *Defining the social studies.* (Bulletin No. 51). Washington, DC: National Council for the Social Studies.

Barth, J. (1996). NCSS and the nature of social studies. In O.L. Davis (Ed.). *NCSS in retrospect.* (pp 9-19) Washington, DC: National Council for the Social Studies.

Barton, K. C., & Levstik, L. S. (1996). "Back when God was around and everything": The development of elementary children's understanding of historical time. *American Educational Research Journal, 33,* 419-454.

Beaty, J. J. (1997). *Building bridges with muticultural picture books.* Portsmouth, NH: Heinemann.

Brophy, J., VanSledright, B. A., & Bredin, N. (1992). Fifth-graders ideas about history expressed before and after their introduction to the subject. *Theory and Research in Social Education, 20,* 440–489.

Carey, S. (1985a). *Conceptual change in childhood.* Cambridge: MIT Press.

Carey, S. (1985b). Are children fundamentally different kinds of thinkers and learners than adults? In S. B. Chipman, J. W. Segal, & R. Glaser (Eds.), *Thinking and learning skills: Research and open questions* (Vol. 2, pp. 485–517). Hillsdale, NJ: Erlbaum.

Downey, M., & Levstik, L. S. (1988). Teaching and learning history: The research base. *Social Education, 52,* 336–342.

Egan, K. (1979). What children know best. *Social Education, 43,* 130–139.

Ellis, A. (1986). *Teaching and learning elementary social studies.* Boston: Allyn-Bacon.

Freeman, E., & Levstik, L. (1988). Recreating the past: Historical fiction in the social studies curriculum. *Elementary School Journal, 88,* 329–337.

Gamberg, R., Kwak, W., Hutchings, M., & Altheim, J. (1988). *Learning and loving it: Theme studies in the classroom.* Portsmouth, NH: Heinemann.

Hardy, B. (1978). Narrative as a primary act of mind. In M. Meek, A. Warlow, & G. Barton (Eds.), *The cool web: The patterns of children's reading.* New York: Atheneum.

Harlan (KY) Elementary School (1986). *No more litter* [Videotape made by third grade class]. Harlan, KY: Author.

Hyde, A. A., & Bizar, M. (1989). *Thinking in context: Teaching cognitive processes across the elementary school curriculum.* White Plains, NY: Longman.

Kammen, M. (1996). Some patterns and meanings of memory distortion in American history. In D. L. Schacter (Ed.), *Memory distortion: How minds, brains, and societies reconstruct the past* (pp. 331–345). Cambridge: Harvard University Press.

Keil, F. C. (1984). Mechanisms of cognitive development and the structure of knowledge. In R. J. Stemberg (Ed.), *Mechanisms of cognitive development.* New York: Freeman.

Kraus International. (1992). *Social studies: Curriculum resource handbook.* Millwood, NY: Author.

Levstik, L. S. (1986). The relationship between historical response and narrative in a sixth-grade classroom. *Theory and Research in Social Education, 14,* 1–15.

Levstik, L. S. (1989). Historical narrative and the young reader. *Theory Into Practice, 28,* 114–119.

Levstik, L. S., & Barton, K. C. (1997). *Doing history: Investigating with children in elementary and middle schools.* Mahwah, NJ: Lawrence Erlbaum.

Levstik, L. S., & Pappas, C. C. (1987). Exploring the development of historical understanding. *Journal of Research and Development in Education, 21,* 1–15.

Levstik, L. S., & Pappas, C. C. (1992). New directions for studying historical understanding. *Theory and Research in Social Education, 21,* 369–385.

McCaleb, S. P. (1997). *Building communities of learners: A collaboration among teachers, students, families, and community.* Mahwah, N.J.: Lawrence Erlbaum.

McGinnis, K. (n.d.). *Educating for a just society.* St. Louis, MO: The Institute for Peace and Justice.

Maxim, G. W. (1987). *Social studies and the elementary school child* (3rd ed.). Columbus, OH: Merrill.

Mitchell, W. J. T. (1994). *Picture theory.* Chicago: University of Chicago Press.

NCSS Focus Group. (1992). *Initial response to national history standards.* Unpublished document, Washington, DC: National Council for the Social Studies.

Newmann, R., Secada, W., & Whlage, G. (1995). *A guide to authentic instruction and assessment: Vision, standards and scoring.* Madison, WI: Wisconsin Center for Educational Research.

Riis, J. (1971). *How the other half lives.* New York: Dover.

Stodolsky, S. S. (1988). *The subject matters.* Chicago: University of Chicago Press.

Wilson, S. M., & Wineberg, S. S. (1988). Peering at history through different lenses: The role of disciplinary perspectives in teaching history. *Teachers College Record, 89,* 525–539.

Wineberg, S. S., & Wilson, S. M. (in press). Subject matter knowledge in the teaching of history. In J. E. Brophy (Ed.), *Advances in research on teaching.* Greenwich, CT: JAI.

Winner, E. (1982). *Invented worlds: The psychology of the arts.* Cambridge, MA: Harvard University Press.

Zarnowski, M. (1997). It's more than dates and places: How nonfiction contributes to understanding social studies. In R.A. Bamford & J. V. Kristo (Eds.), *Making facts come alive: Choosing quality nonfiction literature K-8.* Norwood, MA: Christopher-Gordon.

Children's Literature: Social Studies

A Girl Called BOY by B. Hurmence. Clarion, 1982.

Immigrant Kids by R. Freedman. Dutton, 1980.

In Their Own Words by M. Meltzer. Crowell, 1964.

The Kids' Art Pack by R. Van der Meer & R. Whitford. DK Publishing, Inc., 1997.

Mojave by D. Seibert. Illustrated by W. Minor. Crowell, 1988.

More Stories Huey Tells by A. Cameron. Farrar, 1997.

Mountain Wedding by F. Gibbons. Morrow, 1997.

Night Driving by J. Coy. Holt, 1997.

Nine for California by S. Levitan. Orchard, 1997.

Sierra by D. Seibert. Illustrated by W. Minor. Crowell, 1990.

Watch the Stars Come Out by R. Levinson. Illustrated by D. Goode. Dutton, 1987.

When We Married Gary by A. G. Hines. Greenwillow, 1997.

The Year of the Ranch by A. McLerran. Viking, 1997

Science

What Is Science?

Carl Sagan once suggested that human beings are predisposed by intellect, emotional makeup, and evolution to be interested in those things we label science. Science is a categorical label used to encompass such domains as biology, chemistry, physics, and geology. Most significantly, science is a way of knowing. In fact, some people prefer to talk about "sciencing" rather than "science." Advocates of sciencing emphasize that science is more than a collection of facts and formulas; science is a way of dealing with and ordering experience, usually by rigorous investigation of physical and biological phenomena. Because experience rarely arranges itself tidily into discrete disciplines, much of modern science crosses disciplinary boundaries. You are probably familiar with biochemistry as a cross-disciplinary category, but you may be less used to thinking about the science of social science—the search for the patterns and processes that influence the way in which people think and behave. Much of our discussion of how children think and learn is drawn from scientific studies of such cross-disciplinary phenomena, as recognized by some of the science programs designed for elementary schools. One of these, the Biological Sciences Curriculum Study (BSCS), explains its stance this way:

> Children should learn about science, technology, and health as they need to understand and use them in their daily life and as future citizens. Education in the elementary years should sustain the natural curiosity of children, allow exploration of their environments, improve explanations of phenomena in their world, develop understanding and use of technology, and contribute to informed choices in their personal and social lives.

Blocks to Learning Science

If science is intrinsically interesting as a forum for children's exploration of the natural world, why do many students, especially young women, leave school thinking of science as dull and hard? Data from the National Assessment of Educational Progress indicates that at age nine, boys and girls perform about equally in all sciences except physical science, and by age thirteen there is a significant gender gap across the sciences. In the physical sciences the gap at age nine grows extremely large by age seventeen. Interestingly, the NAEP data showed that further schooling increasingly widened the gender gap.

Several factors account for the problems some students have with science. First, there is growing evidence of differential treatment and opportunities in science teaching. Teachers often have different levels of expectation for boys and girls and for children from some racial, ethnic, or socioeconomic groups. Sometimes this shows up in the roles assigned to students during science instruction. Boys tend to be assigned— or take—more active roles, girls more passive ones. In addition, parents, peers, the media, and some curriculum materials may reinforce these roles for females and minority students.

Another problem is that science is too often taught as vocabulary, not problem solving. It is taught in the abstract, with an emphasis on "getting it right" rather than on posing questions, taking intellectual risks, or learning from mistakes. As a result, too many children come to fear science and avoid it whenever possible.

An integrated language perspective approaches science quite differently. Science is seen as more than information accumulation. In this perspective, doing science has values in common with doing social studies, encouraging wonderment, curiosity, openness to new ideas, and skepticism. As with social studies, the prime motive behind doing science is to provide children with a variety of ways of finding out about the world and themselves.

Science As a Way of Knowing

Perhaps it will help to think about teaching and learning science as having five major elements.

Sagan (1978)

Science encompasses many domains.

"Sciencing" implies active participation in investigations.

Carin & Sund (1985); Kyle, Bonnstetter, Gadsden, & Shymansky (1988); Labinowicz (1980)

Bybee, Ellis, Muscsella, & Robertson (1988)

Learning science includes making informed choices about health and technology.

Malcolm (1986); Mullis et al. (1988); Oakes (1985)

Teachers often have different levels of expectation for boys and girls as well as children of color.

Saul et al. (1993); Whitin & Whitin (1997)

Science is more than information accumulation; learning science involves maintaining a sense of wonder.

Components of sciencing

Science Is a Way of Thinking

Scott (1992); Whitin & Whitin (1997)

Science offers a unique way of looking at the world and of asking questions, gathering and interpreting data, and explaining findings. Scientific thinking involves particular attitudes that include making judgments based on adequate data, striving to be rational and analytical, and maintaining a sense of wonder at the complexity and beauty of the universe. You have probably learned to call this process the scientific method. What you may not have considered is that science is also a process of false starts and fortunate accidents. Sometimes, presentations of the "scientific method" make it seem that inquiry in science is a neat, linear pathway to knowledge, rather than the exhilarating though riskier and more halting exploration of pathways that sometimes turn into blind alleys, and accidents that sometimes turn into insights.

Science Is a Way of Problem Solving

Doris (1991); Saul et al. (1993)

Science draws on and constructs the body of facts, principles, laws, and theories that attempt to explain physical, biological, and behavioral phenomena. This body of knowledge is both the framework for scientific understanding and thinking and the "product" of the sciencing process. It is the outcome of inquiry—a way of solving problems related to the natural world. When science is presented as a finished product, or as a set of simple steps, we misrepresent the power of this discipline. Authentic learning in science involves children in confronting anomalies, formulating questions, dealing with unanticipated results, and offering possible explanations.

Science is a Living Tension Between Theory and Observation

Brown & Shavelson (1996); Whitin & Whitin (1997)

As scientists work, they create theories based on observation and alter those theories as new observations reveal new information. There is always a productive tension between theory and observation. This tension encourages a willingness to revise and abandon theories in the face of new information, and is an important component of sciencing in the classroom.

Science Includes a Technological Component

Technology uses knowledge from science to accomplish tasks and solve problems. Sometimes too, technology creates new problems, and people are faced with moral and ethical dilemmas. Children as well as adults must learn to examine the benefits and risks of this aspect of sciencing and to understand the relationship between science, technology, health, and society. In addition, technology is a problem solving tool in science. Children engage tools for measuring or drawing, for looking closely, and for imagining alternatives. These tools help children look more closely at their world, but also require attention to their appropriate uses and possible limitations.

Science Involves a Behavioral Component

Science can help us understand certain phenomena, but knowing is not always doing. We can know that certain foods are bad health risks yet eat them anyway. Science education links knowing and behaving so that children learn to adopt and maintain health behaviors.

Science Involves a Social Component

Carter (1991); Heath (1992); Merryfield (1991)

Science and technology have complex global social ramifications. Current social, political, technological, and ecological choices affect the possible futures available to the world's people. The nuclear accident at Chernobyl, for instance, affected food crops and animals from Norway to Italy. Increased population in California affects water resources as far away as Colorado. Science education helps children envision the social impact of scientific and technological knowledge. A unit on CHANGES, for instance, would include not only how something changed but also the social impact of that change: not simply *can* we build a dam to stop flooding but *should* we do so? Not can we use fiber optics to increase telecommunications but what will be the social impact of this technological change?

You may have noticed some similarities between this definition of science and the previous definition of social studies. Both fields stress the integration of process and content, of a way of thinking about the world and of observing and building theories about what we observe. Both emphasize the recognition of problems and the central role of perspective in social and scientific inquiry. Thus, there is "science" in the social sciences, and there are social issues in the sciences. There are also differences that make it useful to consider separately these two ways of knowing.

Science is essentially a search for explanatory laws and principles—a search rarely possible in history and not always possible in the other social sciences. Gravity operates according to laws that do not respond to changing social conditions, political upheavals, or economic trends. Little in social studies can be said to be subject to physical laws. Science attempts to control social factors so that results can be generalized beyond a specific event; history and the social sciences often seek to understand and explain specific events. There are places where these two parts of the curriculum intersect—in ecology, for instance—but each also offers a particular way of knowing that can challenge children to think in increasingly mature ways. Think about the difference in approach taken in the No More Litter example, which used a social studies theme, and the following example that approaches an environmental issue from a more science-like perspective.

Hyde & Bizar (1989)

Science looks for generalizations; history studies the particular

Water Cleanup

A sixth-grade class in Iowa became concerned about pollution in their community's water supply. Their reading had led them to conclude that suds and phosphates were a contributing factor. In class discussions, the children hypothesized that laundry detergents must be putting the suds into the streams and rivers. Several had seen evidence of suds at the water treatment plant, and others had observed overflowing washers and rinse water full of suds going into drains. They wanted to find out if there were some detergents that did not make as many suds.

McShane (1988)

Building hypotheses

The enterprising teacher arranged for the donation of a washing machine, and a parent set up a suds collector. The class then made arrangements with the school janitor to use white cotton cleaning cloths of equal size. Students decided that they would need to test the cleaning power of detergents as well as the suds production, especially if they were to convince others to use lower sudsing detergents. With this in mind, they decided to test a variety of stains: catsup, mustard, motor oil, salad dressing, lipstick, marker and ballpoint pen inks, tea, coffee, chocolate, soil, and blood.

Testing hypotheses

The next steps involved setting up procedures for testing and recording results. The students were most concerned about the importance of using scientific methods and procedures. They tried to keep their work accurate by maintaining the same brands for making stains and ensuring that the same amount of the staining substance was used in each trial. They set up a data sheet for recording each trial that included information about the water temperature, brand of detergent, type of stain, amount of suds in the wash and rinse cycles, and results of a litmus test.

Controlling variables

Interviews with a representative from the local sewage treatment plant helped students understand some of the social and environmental problems that resulted from excessive sudsing and phosphates. Interviews with parents helped them understand the consumer's dilemma when there is a choice between better cleaning power in a detergent and fewer pollutants in the public's water. Finally, the children shared their results with the community, letting others know how each detergent in their study had fared and how clean the low-sudsing detergents got laundry.

Studying community impact

Meeting the goals of sciencing

Consider what these children accomplished in terms of the goals of sciencing:

1. Like the litter study for the younger children, this topic dealt with how people managed their environment, especially in making decisions about the uses of technology versus protecting the environment (technology, ecology, and society).
2. The methods used in designing the study—establishing hypotheses, gathering and analyzing data, and reporting results—engaged children in learning and using the scientific method essential to sciencing.
3. As part of their study, children drew on content from various sciences. They investigated the impact of suds and phosphates on water environments and on the humans who used the water (biology). The children studied the action of detergents as they interacted with water, stains, and cloth (chemistry). They also learned something about the machinery used to conduct the experiments (physics).
4. They learned that problems in science do not always have simple, clear-cut solutions. This is a point of intersection with social studies, where human interests conflict and problems are not easily resolved.
5. They learned that the process of solving one problem in science frequently raises other questions, so that sciencing is a continuous feature of living.

Seeing science as an aspect of living

Using the Language of Science

Communicate ideas and share information with accuracy and clarity.

Rutherford & Ahlgren (1990); Scott (1992); Saul et al. (1993)

One of the hallmarks of the language of science is the ability to communicate ideas and share information with accuracy and clarity. Throughout this study, students had opportunities to do just that. They wrote letters, set up their experiments, wrote descriptions of observations, and wrote reports of their data. They referred to other sources: library references, technical material from manufacturers, and expert testimony. They cooperated with people in the community: the companies that donated goods and services, the parent who helped set up the suds-gauging machine, and their peers. For eight weeks, these children conducted a rigorous, controlled study into a real problem in their community. Because it was a real problem, and because the results would be shared publicly and could have significant social impact, accuracy and clarity were crucial. In addition, they had to read other scientific writing as well as other forms of public writing: government reports and newspaper articles. Thus, there were many models for student reporting.

Making cross-curricular connections

This scientific investigation could also have been integrated into a larger study of the community or of ecology, or it could have spurred a series of investigations into water purity historically, culturally, and scientifically. Certainly, the students had to be aware of the social and economic issues related to their study, especially as they engaged in debate and discussion about cleanliness versus decreased pollutants.

Depth

Doris (1991); Hyde & Bizar (1989); Wassermann & Ivany (1988)

As you have probably gathered by now, understanding in a cognitive domain requires depth. Their teacher knew that an eight-week study would require enough time to really think about the investigation, plan carefully, and conduct accurate tests. At the end of eight weeks, the children knew a great deal more than which low-sudsing detergent was the most effective cleaning agent. It might have been possible to give them that information based on EPA tests. What they had learned, however, was how to "know" in science. They were building the scaffolding that would support future learning in science and help them to evaluate other scientific claims. Imagine, for instance, that these children were watching a commercial for a detergent that got clothes "whiter than white." What problems might they have with such claims? What questions might they have about supporting evidence? How might they understand such issues of water quality as the salt content in rivers and streams? They are likely now to think very differently about these issues because they have had an opportunity to think in depth about related issues and to build a framework for understanding new information. Depth also allows children to understand the connections between "pure" science and the applications of science that we term technology.

Science and Technology

We all take much of science for granted, especially as it relates to technology. One primary teacher, inspired by Macaulay's *The Way Things Work*, decided to try a thematic unit built around MACHINES. She remembered wondering as a child how a pencil sharpener worked and what made the toaster pop. She was sure from watching her young students that they shared her interest in the way things work. To begin the unit, the teacher gathered a number of machines that were easily dismantled and safe for small children to experiment with. She arranged a machine center in the room and laid out a manual meat grinder, pencil sharpener, coffee grinder, eggbeater, flour sifter, and pepper mill. She then gathered the children around her in a circle on the floor and introduced the concept of the wheel. While children experimented with moving objects of various shapes across the floor, the teacher asked: "Why is it easier to move the toilet paper roll and the ball than the cracker box and the block? How could you use the roll or ball to move the box?" As children made suggestions, the teacher put several wheeled vehicles in the circle. "Were there any shapes like the paper roll on these vehicles?" Children quickly identified the wheels and proceeded to load the wagons and trucks with boxes and blocks.

At this point, the teacher shared the section of Macaulay's book about wheels. Over the next several days, children kept track of all the ways in which they observed wheels being used. They also used construction toys (e.g., Erector sets and LEGO blocks) to build wheeled vehicles. They drew pictures of new uses for wheels and collected pictures from magazines to make wheel collages.

Their teacher pointed out that many of the things they had worked with were machines. She asked the children to separate some of the things that used wheels into two categories: one to include wheels used as machines and the other to include wheels that were not machines (e.g., a single disc attached to nothing). There was much discussion as children tried to decide what constituted a machine. With help from the teacher and *The Way Things Work*, they wrote this definition: "A machine does work. Some parts of machines move."

With this definition written on chart paper, the students set to work listing all the machines they could find in their classroom. For homework, they listed all the machines they could find in one room at home. Before long, children began bringing in samples of machines to add to the collection in the machine center. As this unit progressed, students tried using a variety of machines. They took machines apart and tried to figure out how they worked. They used information books to help them understand machines, built machines to do various simple tasks, and drew machines for doing work in the future. They wrote about, talked about, and experimented with machines. Their teacher left messages for them in the center, asking them to think about such questions as: How is an eggbeater like a meat grinder? or Can you find a machine that uses a ratchet?

Teachers' Roles in Sciencing

If children are engaged in the kind of sciencing described, it soon becomes clear that they are, as Carl Sagan suggests, disposed to be curious about the area we label science. It is also clear that we are talking about a particular kind of activity that requires teachers to present activities across the sciences (physics and chemistry as well as biology and geology), structured to engage all children in identifying, posing, and attempting to solve problems. The teacher described above did this by arranging the machine center and making sure that everyone participated. Another teacher began a unit on MOVEMENT by hanging a large animal mobile labeled "How Do I Move?" In each case, materials are organized so that children not only are bound to ask questions but also know how to set about answering those questions. There are materials, time, and a place to work, and the teacher interjects carefully considered questions. When one

Connecting "pure" science to its applications

Macaulay (1988)

Establish an interest center, encourage initial exploration and experimentation, and use questions to move explorations in new directions.

Use information books as a resource.

Bamford & Kristo (1997)

Provide practice with examples and nonexamples.

Help children construct definitions.

Maintain excitement and enthusiasm.

See also Lind & Milburn (1987) for another good example of a primary unit on MACHINES, Chaillè & Britian (1991) for a unit on HOW DOES IT MOVE, and Shaw & Dybdahl (1996) for a unit on WHEELS.

Doris (1991); Rutherford & Ahlgren (1990)

Science should engage all children.

Chaillè & Britian (1991)

Children need materials, time, and a place to work.

Hoban (1995); Greenway (1992); Ehlert (1993)

Watts & Parsons (1993)

Consciously give girls active roles in sciencing.

Mullis et al. (1988)

Chaillè & Britain (1991)

Providing organizational help

Pearce (1993)

Saul et al. (1993); Shaw & Dybdahl (1996); Whitin & Whitin (1997)

Saul et al. (1993); Shaw & Dybdahl (1996); Whitin & Whitin (1997)

group of children struggles to decide how to organize their observations of animal movement, the teacher provides three possible models: Hoban's *A Children's Zoo*, a book that matches a picture of an animal with descriptive words, Greenway's *Animals Q & A: How Do I Move?* a book with a question and answer format, and Ehlert's *Nuts to You!* a combination of collage and poetry depicting the behavior of a squirrel. In another group, the teacher helps children make model sycamore (or maple) seeds that spin like helicopters. When it appears that two boys are taking over the task, she intervenes, asking the girls to demonstrate the task for new group members. She then sets up an activity that involves finding plants whose seeds "work like a parachute" or "stick to fur or cloth" and carefully balances the working groups to make it less likely that one group or one person will dominate. She also uses literature, films, and guest speakers to introduce her students to a variety of male and female scientists from various racial and ethnic backgrounds. Perhaps most importantly, the teacher listens to her students' questions, monitoring herself to make sure that she does not allow one child or group of children to dominate the discourse in her classroom.

Children's scientific investigations do not develop in a vacuum. Instead, they are nurtured through carefully planned experiences, including some teacher presentation to individuals, small and whole class groups modeling from literature as well as from peer observation, judiciously chosen teacher questions, and regular opportunities for individual and group reflection. Students thus acquire scientific knowledge and thinking processes as they repeatedly engage in science in many different contexts. In addition, teachers provide organizational help—the kind of scaffolding that allows students to be both independent and accountable for their work.

Question Board

A primary teacher finds that a "question board" is a useful tool. She found that many questions came up in class that would be worth later investigation, but were too often lost in the press of ongoing work. Now she uses a large erasable board on an easel. When a question is raised but there isn't time to investigate immediately, the question goes on the board. Later, these questions are categorized as those they can test themselves, those they can look up, and those that cannot yet be answered. Students can select individual or small group investigations, if they choose, or the whole class may decide to pursue one or more of these questions as part of a new theme.

Class Journals

An intermediate teacher uses a "Wonder Journal." This is a class journal that functions much as the question board does. As children pursue an investigation, they share their "wonders"—unanswered questions about observations they have made. These wonderings often inspire other children to respond, adding their own observations and inferences to the journal. Much like the Wonder Journal, a "Body of Knowledge" booklet is also an opportunity for students to share, but in this case, they share their discoveries rather than their questions. Students record the date, their discovery, how it was discovered, and by whom. Other students provide feedback, add observations, and the like.

Log Sheets

When children are engaged in a variety of projects it is helpful for teacher and student to keep a record of work. Log sheets are simple forms that students complete as they work, in the same way that adult scientists might keep a log of their work. However, because one of the focuses for children is learning to spend their time productively, some of the entries are a bit different than might be the case for an adult scientist. One fifth-grade teacher developed different types of log sheets. One includes sections where students describe their activity for the inquiry period, including how they spent their time and what they found particularly interesting. Finally, they write a section to "convince someone else that your activity was a worthwhile use of time." A second log sheet includes large spaces for sketches of different attempts to solve a scientific problem, along with places where students describe each attempt and how it worked. These pictures help students to observe in more detail, as well as to talk through their work.

Scientists' Meetings

One of the ways that new information is refined and disseminated is through meetings. Just as Ted in the CHANGES theme had his students change into lab coats to mark the seriousness of their investigations, so do some teachers find scientists' meetings a useful way to share and refine children's investigations. Usually one or two children share their work at a time. One teacher suggests that children keep their initial comments brief, reporting an observation, a wonder, or something they did in a sentence or two. Other students listen, ask questions, and talk about what they hear. They may jot down questions in their own notebooks next to the name of the person reporting. Meanwhile, the teacher records each report on a large chart that includes a column headed "Plans." Next, students indicate what their next plans are, and the names of people with whom they might collaborate. Sometimes students decide to replicate an investigation done by another child; sometimes they decided to try another tack related to a problem raised during the meeting.

Doris (1991); Scott (1992); Saul (1993); Whitin & Whitin (1997)

Science Surveys

At other times, students need help in thinking about the skills they are developing as novice scientists. Science surveys, like the reading and writing surveys common to integrated language classrooms, establish the parameters of good sciencing and provide a starting point for conferences with students and caregivers. Together with their students, teachers list the behaviors that mark good sciencing. Students can self-assess by using checking their own behavior against this list. This survey can be kept in their science notebooks to show growth over time, as well as areas that need work.

Blackwood (1993)

Reading and Writing About Science

Like adult scientists, children read and write about science. Reading or hearing read different genres of science writing helps students imagine different ways of writing about their own work. A third-grade class used elements of the "Magic Schoolbus" series to create a shadow play about the rainforest, while another group of sixth graders were inspired by Jennifer Dewey's *Rattlesnake Dance* to create their own book combining mythology, stories, and science about the mice they were observing in their own classroom. In addition to books about science, children need to hear about different kinds of scientists. For example, a group of students studying the environment near their own school particularly enjoyed Wadsworth's *John Burroughs: The Sage of Slabsides*.

Scott (1992); Fredericks (1997)

Dewey (1997)

Wadsworth (1997)

Science As a Way of Doing

As you can see from the preceding discussion, science is learned in the doing. As children act on objects, they begin to build theories based on their actions and observations. We are not describing a simple "hands-on" approach to science. Manipulating objects is necessary but not sufficient in and of itself. Certainly children learn most readily about things that are directly accessible to their senses, but there is evidence that simply performing tasks using concrete objects does not necessarily mean that children understand the scientific content or the relationship of that content to any other situation or context. Children's experiences need to be linked to particular contexts—the themes and questions we have already discussed—but they also need opportunities to express their experiences in a variety of ways, to apply what they have learned to novel situations, to receive appropriate feedback from teachers and peers, to reflect on that feedback, and then to make adjustments and try again. In sum, children need time to build theories, test them, revise them, and represent them.

In shifting from a science curriculum that emphasizes information accumulation to one that concentrates on the quality of children's understanding, starting simply is

Science is learned in the doing.

Link experiences to context.

Provide opportunities to apply learning in novel situations and time to build, test, revise, and represent theories.

Start simply.

Chaillè & Britain (1991); Heath (1992)

Connect explorations to themes and other parts of the curriculum.

Merryfield (1991)

Anticipate the unexpected.

a key idea. Begin with questions and topics that are interesting and familiar to children. In the LET'S EAT! prototype, children work with an assortment of measuring devices and dry foods (rice, beans, and pasta). Variations and complexity are built into the activity as children compare different ways to measure dry and wet ingredients, establish equivalences, and compare cooked and uncooked food measurements. They represent their work in a variety of ways, from making displays of different types of measures used in cooking, to matching measuring devices to directions in a recipe, to giving demonstrations for peers.

This exploration of measurement connects to other theme-related science activities, including preparing food, observing and measuring the changes as foods cook, dehydrate, grow mold, or are digested. (See the "LET'S EAT!" WEB in Chapter 4 for more ideas.) There are also connections with other parts of the curriculum, from exploring eating customs to studying the use of food in literature. Questions from one activity often generate questions that cut across the curriculum. The teacher anticipates many of these possibilities in developing a planning WEB yet is prepared to move in unanticipated directions, led by careful observation of students and the recognition that children's own questions may generate powerful activities and good science. This kind of activity is motivating and challenging, and it provides an excellent context for integrating science across the curriculum. It is also an approach that appears more likely to improve the participation of females and others underrepresented in science.

References: Science

Bamford, R. & Kristo, J. (Eds.) (1997). *Making facts come alive: Choosing quality nonfiction literature, K-8.* Norwood, MA: Christopher-Gordon.

Blackwood, D. (1993). Connecting language and science assessment. In W. Saul, et al. *Science workshop: A whole language approach* (pp 95-118). Portsmouth, NH: Heinemann.

Brown, J. H., & Shavelson, R.J. (1996). *Assessing hands-on science: A teacher's guide to performance assessment.* Thousand Oaks, CA: Corwin Press.

Bybee, R., Ellis, J. D., Muscella, D., & Robertson, W. C. (1988). *New designs for elementary school science: A study conducted by the Biological Sciences Curriculum Study (BSCS).* Colorado Springs: Colorado College.

Carin, A. A., & Sund, R. B. (1985). *Teaching modern science.* Columbus, OH: Merrill.

Carter, C. (1991). Science-technology-society and access to scientific knowledge. *Theory Into Practice, 30,* 273–279.

Chaillé, C., & Britain, L. (1991). *The young child as scientist: A constructivist approach to early childhood science education.* New York: Harper & Row.

Doris, E. (1991). *Doing what scientists do: Children learn to investigate their world.* Portmouth, NH: Heinemann.

Fredericks, A. D. (1997). Evaluating and using nonfiction literature in the science curriculum. In R. Bamford & J. Kristo (Eds.), *Making facts come alive: Choosing quality nonfiction literature, K-8.* Norwood, MA: Christopher-Gordon.

Heath, P. (1992). Organizing for STS teaching and learning: The doing of STS. *Theory Into Practice, 31,* 52–58.

Hyde, A. A., & Bizar, M. (1989). *Thinking in context: Teaching cognitive processes across the elementary school curriculum.* White Plains, NY: Longman.

Kyle, W. C., Bonnstetter, R. J., Gadsden, T., & Shymansky, J. (1988). What research says about hands-on science. *Science and Children, 25 (7),* 39–40, 52.

Labinowicz, E. (1980). *The Piaget primer: Thinking, learning, teaching.* Reading, MA: Addison-Wesley.

Lemke, J. L. (1990). *Talking Science: Language, learning, and values.* Norwood, NJ: Ablex.

Lind, K. K., & Milburn, M. J. (1987). Mechanized childhood. *Science and Children, 25 (5),* 322–333.

Martin, J. (1990). Literacy in science: Learning to handle text as technology. In F. Cristie (Ed.) *Literacy for a changing world* (pp. 79–117). Victoria: Australia Council of Education Research.

McShane, J. B. (1988). The mean machine. *Science and Children, 26 (3),* 19–21.

Merryfield, M. M. (1991). Science-technology-society and global perspectives. *Theory Into Practice, 30,* 288–293.

Mullis, I., Jenkins, B., Berry, R., Champagne, A., Penick, J., Raizen, S., Weiss, I., & Welch, W. (1988). *The science report card: Elements of risk and recovery.* Princeton, NJ: Educational Testing Service.

Oakes, J. (1985). *Keeping track: How schools structure inequality.* New Haven, CT: Yale University Press.

Pearce, C. (1993). What if? . . . In W. Saul, et al. *Science workshop: A whole language approach* (pp 53-77). Portsmouth, NH: Heinemann.

Rutherford, F. J. & Ahlgren, A. (1990). *Science for all Americans.* New York: Oxford University Press.

Sagan, C. (1978). *Address given at the 26th annual national convention of the National Science Teachers Association,* Washington, DC.

Saul, W., Reardon, J., Schmidt, A., Pearce, C., Blackwood, D., & Bird, M. D. (1993). *Science workshop: A whole language approach.* Portsmouth, NH: Heinemann.

Scott, J. (1992). *Science & language links: Classroom implications.* Portmouth, NH: Heinemann.

Shaw, D. G., & Dybdahl, C. S. (1996). *Integrating science and language arts: A sourcebook for K-6 teachers.* Needham Heights, MA: Allyn-Bacon.

Stodolsky, S. S. (1988). *The subject matters.* Chicago: University of Chicago Press.

Wassermann, S., & Ivany, J. W. G. (1988). *Teaching elementary science. Who's afraid of spiders?* New York: Harper & Row.

Whitin, P., & Whitin, D. (1997). *Inquiry at the window: Pursuing the wonders of learners.* Portsmouth, NH: Heinemann.

Children's Literature: Science

Animals Q & A: How Do I Move? by S. Greenway. Ideals Children's Books, 1992.

A Children's Zoo by T. Hoban. Mulberry Books, 1985.

Get It in Gear: The Science of Movement by B. Taylor. Random House, 1991.

John Burroughs: The Sage of Slabsides by G. Wadsworth. Clarion, 1997.

Nuts to You! by L. Ehlert. Harcourt Brace Jovanovich, 1993.

Rattlesnake Dance: True Tales, Mysteries, and Rattlesnake Ceremonies by J. O. Dewey. Boyds, 1997.

Plants: A Creative Hands-on Approach to Science by C. Watts & A. Parsons. Macmillan, 1993.

The Way Things Work by D. Macaulay. Houghton Mifflin, 1988.

World Water Watch by M. Koch. Greenwillow, 1993.

Mathematics

Recent research in mathematics gives validity to the integrated language perspective in helping children learn math. Having opportunities to use math as a tool, an aid to tackle a problem or the means to accomplish a project within a thematic unit of study, is consistent with what we know about how children learn mathematical understandings during the preschool years and form mathematical knowledge in out-of-school activities in general.

Besides being emergent readers and writers, it is clear now that young children during the preschool years are also emergent mathematicians. Preschoolers engage in a variety of everyday activities that involve numbers: playing store-bought games or those invented by parents and children (e.g., counting stairs), watching educational TV shows (e.g., *Sesame Street*), helping parents on shopping trips, discussing how long it is till supper or till they get to Grandma's house, and noting how many floors yet to go in an elevator to the doctor's office. Moreover, numbers depicting the cost of products, mileage and speed limits, and the like are frequently incorporated into the public print of the signs and labels of our culture. As a result of this exposure, even two- and three-year-olds have considerable competence in counting objects. By the age of four, most children extend their early counting knowledge to comparing and reproducing number sets and to addressing simple arithmetic problems with small sets. When kindergartners begin school, they have already constructed important mathematical understandings; they have considerable arithmetic prowess on which to build and extend.

> **Emergent mathematicians**
>
> *Gelman & Gallistel (1978); Hughes (1986); Saxe (1988a); Saxe, Guberman, & Gearhart (1987)*

In this new view of the emergent mathematician, language plays an important role. In fact, the origin of numbers can be traced to one of the earliest uses of language by the child. There is ample evidence to show that babies' early utterances of "up," "more," "all gone," and so on represent functional expressions that also serve as precursors of numbers in children's subsequent language. Relying on the number words (and numerals) found everywhere in their world and used repeatedly in interactions with themselves and others, children try to make sense of what they see and hear by employing their versions of "counting" to answer their own questions of how many or how much. That is, the development of mathematical understandings is also learning through language. Thus, the view that children learn mathematics principally through math lessons in school—and then only when they enter what Piaget has described as the concrete operational stage of development—has been questioned by cognitive developmentalists, mathematicians, and mathematics educators alike.

> *Language is integrally related to early understanding of math.*
>
> *Nesher (1988)*
>
> *Piaget (1952, 1953)*

A critical aspect of the recent views on the development of mathematical understandings is the importance of sociocultural influences on the process. That parents and others engage young children in everyday activities and games involving mathematical concepts and that these interactions support the children's efforts in learning math suggest that similar collaborative experiences are needed in the classroom to strengthen and extend these understandings. Another important related issue is the movement from the performance of techniques to a more reflective way of knowing. Rather than emphasize a curriculum in which children practice or perform techniques to get "right" answers, the current view envisions a curriculum in which chil-

> *Donaldson (1978); Gelman & Gallistel (1978); Lave, Murtaugh, & de la Rocha (1984)*
>
> *Social-cultural factors affect mathematical development.*
>
> *There is a shift from performance techniques to reasoning and thinking about math.*

Burns (1992); Hyde & Hyde (1991); Mokros, Russell, & Economopoulos (1995); Rutherford & Ahlgren (1990); Van de Walle (1994)

Bishop (1988); Borasi (1992); Cobb, Yackel, & Wood (1991); Hiebert (1984); Siegel & Fonzi (1995); Zaslavsky (1996)

National Council of Teachers of Mathematics (1989)

Math is a system of relationships.

Rutherford & Ahlgren (1990); Van de Walle (1994)

A problem-solving atmosphere in math requires a different role for the teacher.

The teacher dominated initiate–respond–evaluate (IRE) discourse has to be replaced with more collaborative talk. (See Chapter 2.)

Brillian-Mills (1994); Corwin, Storeygard, & Price (1996); McCallum & Whitlow (1994); Pimm (1987); Whitlin & Wilde (1995)

Problems need to be selected so that children's current math understandings can be assessed and extended.

Hyde & Hyde (1991); Lampert (1991); Mokros, Russell, & Economopoulos (1995); Moon & Schulman (1995)

dren develop an understanding and critical awareness of how and when to use mathematical techniques as well as why they work and how they are developed. Such a curriculum requires personal interpretation and invention, with opportunities to read, talk, and write about others' views and opinions on mathematical problems and issues. Thus, controversy, ambiguity, doubt, and risk taking all play important roles in the development of children's understandings and their attitudes towards mathematics. Moreover, these experiences contribute to their appreciation of the value of mathematics as a discipline and a certain way of knowing.

This new view can be seen in the key goals that the National Council of Teachers of Mathematics (NCTM) has recently set for students of mathematics in the 1990s:

1. To learn to value mathematics
2. To become confident in their ability to do mathematics
3. To become mathematical problem solvers
4. To learn to communicate mathematically
5. To learn to reason mathematically

These goals are radically different from those found in traditional classrooms but consistent with those fostered in integrated language classrooms. The following section underscores the importance of a problem-solving atmosphere in mathematics teaching and learning. The last two sections cover more ideas for integrating mathematics in thematic units and other ways in which mathematics can be incorporated in language and literacy activities.

Promoting a Problem-Solving Atmosphere in Mathematics

Mathematics is essentially the science of patterns and relationships. This *relational understanding* is the major objective in the teaching and learning of mathematics. It consists of helping children develop (1) mathematical ideas or concepts—*conceptual knowledge*; (2) a facility with the symbolism, rules, and methods of performing mathematics processes—*procedural knowledge*; and (3) connections between the methods/symbols and the corresponding concepts—*connections between conceptual and procedural knowledge*. Thus, fostering relational understanding in children requires that they know both the what and the why of mathematics. Traditionally school mathematics instruction has implied that there is a right way to do mathematics, and too frequently the symbolic method to produce mathematical results has been separated from the meaning. Facility with computation does not ensure that children have the ability to know when to use those skills when they encounter a particular problem. When children are seduced solely into the symbolism of math, they cannot create and recreate math relationships in their minds. Knowing mathematics means being able to use it in purposeful ways.

Thus, in integrated language classrooms, problem solving—the spirit of inquiry—is promoted. The challenge is to provide motivating problems that spark children's natural curiosity in a safe and supportive environment so that they can develop and use the mathematical skills and strategies they will need to solve real-life problems.

Such a problem-solving curriculum has a different role for the teacher. The teacher cannot control instruction by being the key person to provide information, explain concepts or skills, or give examples. The teacher cannot direct all classroom interactions in an IRE-like discourse fashion—asking all of the questions, leading all of the discussions, and prompting student responses to the "right" answers. Instead, the teacher shares power with children by providing opportunities for them to grapple with problems on their own, search for strategies and solutions that make sense to them, and learn how to evaluate their results. Thus, choosing and using "good problems" is a critical feature of the integrated approach. Good problems are ones that have multiple routes to resolution, thereby encouraging children to express their thinking and approximations about the mathematical concepts underlying computational procedures while leading them to encounter new and unfamiliar mathematical territory that is an important curricular agenda or goal of the teacher. That is, solving good problems leads children to relational understanding because it is accomplished through collaborative talk where teachers are able to assess children's sense of these problems and then provide contingent, responsive feedback.

Learning is never an all-or-nothing enterprise. In a good problem-solving activity, children develop a tentative understanding of the concept(s) involved. As they engage in additional activities, more sophisticated and elaborate thinking evolves as they see and appreciate more connections. They also begin to view mathematical knowledge not as a stable body of facts but as a dynamic process of inquiry constructed by human, social activity—where uncertainty and conflict lead to a search for a more refined understanding of the world.

Children learn math best when the math they encounter is embedded in meaningful activities, where their problems involve real purposes for using and exploring math. In thematic units, children can analyze complex problems, arrive at reasonable solutions, and justify and evaluate the effectiveness of their solutions. In these contexts children care about the results and outcomes of their math activity.

Problem solving and math inquiry encourage children to view mathematics as a humanistic discipline shaped by cultural and personal values.

Borasi(1992); Zaslavsky(1996)

Baker & Baker (1990); Cobb (1991); Corwin, Storeygard, & Price (1996); Mokros, Russell, & Economopoulos (1995)

Using Mathematics in Projects in Thematic Units

Like any symbolic system, mathematics involves both pure and applied aspects. The pure aspects are the abstractions of the symbolic language of mathematics (its concepts, principles, and theories); the applied aspects are the variety of ways mathematics explains the physical world and helps us in various everyday social interactions. These aspects are not separate. In fact, in the history of mathematics, new abstract formulations of mathematics have almost always been developed because specific situations or problems had to be addressed. These new notions have subsequently found applications to many other situations or problems. Before coming to school, children's knowledge of pure mathematics has been acquired in a dynamic, interactive way and anchored in applied circumstances. Unlike traditional classrooms, where frequently only pure or abstract math is emphasized, integrated language classrooms incorporate both aspects of math. In various thematic units, children continue to learn the abstract aspects of math *within* meaningful problem-solving contexts that facilitate their understanding of, and thinking about, mathematical concepts.

Hyde & Bizar (1989); Saxe (1988a, 1998b)

See Zasluvsky (1996) for useful ideas for incorporating math ideas along various across–the–curriculum multicultural thematic units.

See also Cordeiro (1988) for an example of a sixth grade unit on infinity.

Math consists of many concepts and topics: number sense, numeration, and number systems; fractions and decimals; measurement, geometry, and spatial sense; estimation; statistics and probability; and algebra. Though only a hint of the possibilities can be provided here, mathematizing—using mathematics as reasoning and as active problem solving—is an integral feature of all the suggestions presented.

Graphing*

Graphing* can be used in practically any and every thematic unit and by children at any level in the elementary school. In developing graphs, children compare, count, add, and subtract. Other mathematical operations such as multiplying and dividing are also possible in organizing data in a systematic way to discover patterns. Graphs can be the result of surveys children have conducted on a range of topics or issues. Graphs may come about when children have opportunities to observe data accumulation in the course of a thematic unit, for example, in gathering specific information in particular scientific experiments or conducting interviews or surveys related to a social studies issue.

See Baratta-Lorton (1995) for a useful discussion of graphing.

Graphing* activities can easily be incorporated in any of the prototypes in Chapter 4. In the SPACES unit, graphs can show how children get from one space to another—how many children in the class go to school by walking, by car, or by bus. Older elementary children in a SPACES unit could collect this information for the whole school and expand the number of space categories beyond school to spaces such as stores or entertainment places. In JOURNEYS, children plant various kinds of seeds, roots, and cuttings, and chart daily growth. Graphs showing and comparing growth patterns of propagation could be constructed. Information on types of and purposes for travel could also be organized and displayed through a graph in the JOURNEYS unit.

Older children can develop more complex graphs that incorporate percentages, averages, and other complex mathematical operations rather than those that may rely mostly on adding and subtracting. For example, in a fourth grade version of the LET'S EAT! thematic unit, children could keep journals of their food consumption for a week and plot their average number of calories for each day of the week and contrast the average number of calories consumed through nutritious food versus junk food. They might also explore various types of graphs to display their data in bar graphs, line graphs, circle graphs, and especially computer-generated graphs. In the departmentalized fourth/fifth-grade EXPLORATIONS unit, children collect slang expressions for a dictionary as part of their study of word origins in the subtheme "Exploring with Language." Besides this dictionary, they could document the percentage of use of certain slang expressions in the different grades. Or in the subtheme "Exploring Careers," graphs reflecting percentages could emerge as the result of children's taking inventory of the necessary skills required at the various work sites they visit.

In sum, graphs can be incorporated in many ways in any thematic unit. Teachers can consider Graphing* activities as part of planning a WEB. Although you could review the prototype WEBs in Chapter 4 and brainstorm a range of other possibilities, some of the most valuable graphs are those that evolve spontaneously. Recognizing the natural opportunities in the classroom allows for an integration of math with every curricular area. A growth graph can be developed when children notice some pollywogs with developed feet and others with less-developed feet. Contrasting the books that have been read on various topics within a unit, charting miles traveled by various explorers, and depicting types of foods eaten by people in various regions or countries all incorporate various Graphing* activities that require meaningful mathematical experiences for children across the curriculum. As children learn to use graphs to answer purposeful questions about their world and to make sense of the data they collect, they extend their knowledge of the communication potential of graphs—they learn graphs, learn about graphs, and learn through graphs.

Measurement

Only a few ideas of the limitless possibilities for measurement can be presented here. Various cooking activities, which can be incorporated in most units, readily incorporate measurement of ingredients: liquids such as milk, water, and oil, solids such as butter or shortening, particles of "matter" such as flour and sugar. As children follow various recipes, they begin to understand fractions and comparable amounts. The doubling or tripling of recipes requires estimating and confirming equivalences of particular ingredients.

In the SPACES prototype (in the "Over, Under, and Through" subtheme), many water activities are incorporated that could have children measuring liquids. Various containers that have both cup and milliliter markings could be available for measuring water. Comparing English and metric liquid and dry measurements could be included in the LET'S EAT! unit. Children could bring in weight information for various packaged and canned goods from the grocery store and then try to represent these weights (in terms of pounds and grams) by using scales and a range of objects in the classroom.

As you may have already noted, measurement is usually an initial step of Graphing*, especially when linear measurement is involved. Measuring the growth of plants from seeds, for example, is a prerequisite to graphing plant differences in the JOURNEYS and CHANGES units. It is important that children have opportunities to use both the English and metric systems in linear measurements. In a SPACES unit, for example, children could measure their favorite spaces at home (the length and width of their room, their bed, etc.) in inches, feet, and yards *and* in centimeters and meters. Older children could consider the notion of perimeter by figuring out the perimeters of objects in the various spaces in the classroom.

Graphing opportunities should be planned for, but many can also emerge spontaneously.

See Chapter 7 for more information on graphing.

Whitlin, Mills, & O'Keefe (1990); Mills, O'Keefe, & Whitlin (1996)

Food measurement

Contrasting English and metric systems

"Body Spaces" could also be explored in both the SPACES and EXPLORATIONS thematic units (as well as other units such as TAKING CARE, where taking care of the environment, others, and your body, etc., were explored). Children's heights, as well as lengths and widths of various body parts, could be measured. For older children, the concept of circumference could be explored by measuring the circumferences of children's waists, heads, wrists, or thighs. Having children estimate the sizes of their body parts and then compute how far off their "real" measurements are adds even more to these problem-solving activities.

Add estimation to measurement activities.

Measurement of time can frequently be incorporated in a range of thematic units. In a FLIGHT unit, children, using a stopwatch, can chart the time it takes their miniature parachutes, which are attached to objects of various weights, to land from the top of the playground equipment. A study of some of the timed events from the *Guinness Book of World Records* can lead children to track their everyday events to identify their own records. In a thematic unit on TIME, encouraging children to determine the time elapsed by noting both the hands on an analog clock and the digits on a digital clock helps them to begin a study of the ways people have described time.

Time measurement

Many scientific experiments involve the measurement of time. In a unit on DISAPPEARING ACTS, older elementary students studied a range of topics: various magic tricks and magicians such as the famous Houdini, certain aspects of pollution (many materials are not easily biodegradable and are therefore not good disappearing acts), and famous missing persons such as Amelia Earhart. They also timed the evaporation rates of various liquids (water, oil, alcohol, and soapy water). Another possible scientific activity is an exploration of the disappearing acts (the "demise" of soapy bubbles) and an examination of why certain bubbles last longer than others. Measuring various transformations is frequently an integral aspect of the careful observation required also in the process of sciencing. In sum, measurement can be easily incorporated in various ways in thematic units. Just as in Graphing*, possible measurement ideas should be considered ahead of time in planning WEBs, but more natural opportunities emerge frequently if the teacher is alert enough to spot and support them.

Fostering Geometric and Spatial Sense

In traditional elementary classrooms, geometry is usually limited to children learning the labels of various geometric shapes, and in the older grades, sometimes memorizing formulas to compute the area of various shapes. However, when engaged in activities and experiences in various thematic units, children can be encouraged to think about and analyze the shapes in more meaningful ways. The formula for calculating the area of a rectangle is much more understandable when children are asked to determine the area of a construction paper "rug" to cover the bottom of a diorama constructed as an extension of a book they have read. Other such constructions—making Strega Nona's house (found in dePaola's *Strega Nona, Big Anthony and the Magic Ring,* and *Strega Nona's Magic Lessons*) or the houses of the *Three Little Pigs*—require that children visualize the three-dimensional nature of geometric figures. As part of a fourth-, fifth-, or sixth-grade SPACES unit, children's attempts to construct accurate scaled-down versions of their favorite spaces at home can foster a concentrated effort to understand geometric and spatial sense. This project also means that children employ a range of measurements, deal with ratios, and apply certain algebraic expressions. Children gain similar understandings when, after having architects and city planning personnel come to visit the classroom in a HOUSES thematic unit, they decide to design and construct a model of a town depicted in a story.

Burns (1992); Mokros, Russell & Economopoulos (1995); Pappas & Bush (1989); Van de Walle (1994)

de Paola (1975, 1979, 1982)

In a thematic unit such as DESIGNS AND PATTERNS, children are able to explore geometric figures in depth. Besides studying the symmetrical patterns of plant and animal organisms and various crystal formations, children examine all kinds of patterns and geometric designs. Children construct many patterns and designs by using a range of material (pennies, buttons, seeds, small sticks, attribute blocks, LEGO blocks, etc.) and then describe them through writing or illustrations so that others can

See Larke (1988), Mokros, Russell & Economopoulos (1995), and Van de Walle & Holbrook (1987) for good classroom examples on geometric and pattern units.

try to replicate them. Musical patterns are examined, patterns of three in stories are compared, and quilts are designed using various geometric shapes. Children use rubber bands to construct shapes on student-made or commercially-made geoboards and compasses to make circles. They construct various triangular designs as well as pentomino or hexomino puzzles. They use dot or centimeter paper to make hexagons or equilateral triangles to create tessellating patterns. Geometry circuit boards are set up to show various geometric shapes, arranged so that when a match is made, a bell rings.

Burns (1992); Van de Walle (1994)

Geometric understandings can be fostered not only in thematic units in which geometric sense is a major focus. The development of a range of geometric concepts (e.g., shape, size, symmetry, congruence, and similarity in two- and three-dimensional space) along with the appropriate geometry vocabulary can also be fostered in many other units when teachers are aware of the possibilities. These understandings and experiences in geometric thinking provide an important foundation for learning the more formal generalizations in geometric relationships in the upper-elementary, middle-, and high-school grades.

Other Miscellaneous Ideas for Integrating Math

Give children responsibilities for everyday "housekeeping" activities that involve math.

There are many everyday routines in which children can use math in the classroom. Giving children responsibility for various routine tasks such as taking roll, keeping track of lunch or milk money or book orders, or distributing materials fosters mathematical understandings. Understanding of decimals is developed when real money is computed and handled for real purposes. There are many opportunities for dealing with money in thematic units as well. Money can be exchanged in grocery stores or restaurants set up in the classroom in units such as LET'S EAT! Children can trade and sell stocks in hypothetical accounts as part of a DISAPPEARING ACTS unit. Store-bought and student-made games also provide many opportunities for developing the concept of number and other mathematical principles. (Games are discussed in the next section as well.)

See Kamii (1985) for examples of using games in a first grade classroom.

Having many manipulatives available for children to use encourages many kinds of mathematical understandings. We know of a kindergarten teacher who fosters the idea of number sets by having children tell how many sets (of ten, three, four, etc.) of blocks are counted out when they work in the construction area. The teacher observes the strategies the children employ and intervenes to support their efforts or to point out how peers' sets are different or equivalent. By the end of the year, most of these children know that two sets of ten blocks are equivalent to four sets of five blocks.

Borasi (1992); Hyde & Hyde (1991); Van de Walle (1994); Zaslavsky (1996)

Math anxiety and avoidance are greatly reduced for all children when there are many meaningful math experiences.

What is important in these mathematical activities and experiences is that children recognize the socially constructed nature of mathematical knowledge—that alternative interpretations and debate are integral elements of the discipline. Moreover, underlying these authentic problem-solving approaches is the expectation that *all* children—boys *and girls* from diverse ethnolinguistic backgrounds—will not only be attracted to such mathematical sense making but will also be confident in developing mathematical understandings.

Many ways to use math are possible in the classroom no matter what the thematic unit is. Ideas that more directly integrate language and literacy are suggested in the following pages.

Language, Literacy, and Mathematics

Fostering Talk about Math

Discussion of math problems fosters math understandings.

Speaking and listening are naturally integrated in children's discussions of mathematical concepts. Comparing information obtained or accumulated as part of projects fosters mathematics as a way of knowing. In small groups or as whole class, they debate how, when, and why certain mathematical operations are appropriate for the issues being investigated. Addition, subtraction, multiplication, division, fractions, and decimals are not pursued as separate subjects of math. In real-life situations, problems frequently require solutions that integrate several techniques. Consequently, children have

Corwin, Storeygard, & Price (1996); McCallum & Whitlow (1994); Whitlin & Wilde (1995)

to talk about and consider others' views when they decide which mathematical operations are necessary.

To further math talk, many teachers regularly gather a range of text sets of children's literature having math concepts in them and have children read and discuss them in Literature Response Groups*. In these small group discussions, students talk about what they don't understand or what seems puzzling to them, explain math ideas in their own words, use open questions ("What did you notice?" What did the story remind you of?"), and ask their own questions that they then attempt to answer. In these experiences, students understand that math is an integrated part of living; they make personal connections with math. They realize that that math can be intrinsically rewarding topic that they can learn and think about. (See also below for ideas for using literature books for teaching math.)

Integrating Reading and Writing about and around Math

Many opportunities for reading and writing about math are also possible in an integrated language classroom. Reading and writing occur when children jot down survey data or organize their various calculations in Learning Logs* and then share these notes with others. The construction of graphs also incorporates reading and writing. Reading and writing reports of scientific experiments or other investigations include opportunities to express and comprehend mathematical data. Constructing and playing games as extensions of books read and studied in class can also provide meaningful occasions to apply and use math. Board games may depict important significant events of a story or a biography, or stages of transformation in an experiment on animal and plant growth. As children decide on and write their directions so that others can play, particular mathematical operations are considered and clarified. Players then develop these mathematical understandings as they try to comprehend and follow the directions.

Many teachers include specific math Journals* where children are encouraged to write about the difficulties they might have with math problems, to record new learnings, and to compare and contrast various procedures or strategies to solve problems. These journals serve as personal records of the experience of doing mathematics. Beginning a school year by having children write their own mathematics autobiography provides teachers, as well as the students themselves, many insights into children's views and attitudes toward math. Asking students to tell about their accomplishments or disasters, and what they like or do not like about math, reveals ideas about their thinking on the nature of mathematics, as well as their abilities to learn and understand it. It also uncovers their perceptions of how they have been taught math in school and how math has functioned in their out-of-school, everyday life. Using these ideas, teachers have a better sense about individual students' beliefs, needs, interests, and feelings regarding math and are therefore able to develop appropriate instruction.

Another possible way for children to do both reading and writing of math is through Student-Initiated Inquiries* on math topics of choice. "Math search" papers can cover a range of topics, such as African mathematics, ancient math, paper folding, paradoxes, tessellations, gambling, numerology, and the work of M. C. Escher, that both teachers and students can develop together. Besides generating initial questions to guide and frame their inquiries and papers, children can also address other questions on the process of their inquiry: what they knew and didn't know before the inquiry, what they did to find out about their topic of inquiry, and what they learned and did not learn from their study. (See Organizing/Monitoring Student-Initiated Inquiry* in Chapter 7 for more ideas on implementing math inquiry projects.) The purposeful reading and writing involved in studying these math topics encourages in-depth relational thinking.

Using "Mathematical" Books

As already noted, many wonderful books that have mathematical concepts in them can be included in thematic units. Below we suggest only some of the possibilities.

See Thiessen & Matthias (1992) and Whitlin & Wilde (1992, 1995) for lists of mathematical books to use in these small-group discussions.

Whitlin & Wilde (1995)

Burns (1995); Fulwiler (1980, 1982)

Countryman (1992); Short & Harste (1995)

Math autobiographies

See Burns (1995) and Mills, O'Keefe, and Whitlin for other authoring ideas in math.

Student-Initiated Inquiry can occur around math topics, too.*

Borasi (1992); Countryman (1992); Macrorie (1988)

Freeman & Person (1998)

Murphy (1996a, 1996b; 1996c)

Scieszka (1995)

Clement (1991)

See Whitlin & Wilde (1995) for children's writing based on ideas in *Counting on Frank*.

Math literature books show children how math is embedded in real life.

Birch (1988)

See also A *Grain of Rice* by Pittman (1986) for another book that illustrates a similar mathematical progression.

Nozaki & Anno (1985)

Anno & Anno (1983)

Murphy has written several books about everyday events for primary grade children that help demystify math. *A Pair of Socks* is a concept book that has a striped sock looking for its missing mate. *Give Me Half! Understanding Halves* explains fractions by having a brother and sister figure out how to divide a pizza or cookies into half so they can share equally. *Get Up and Go!* concretely introduces timelines by depicting the minutes a young girl uses to get ready for school.

In a similar way, older elementary children enjoy *Math Curse*, which presents how a girl begins to see how almost everything in her life can be seen as math inquiry, even choosing what she will that day. Also, *Counting on Frank* could be used for many ages. It is a humorous book in which a boy is always measuring, figuring out, and musing about mathematics and things around the house. He calculates how many Franks (his dog) could fit in his room or how long of a line an average ballpoint pen can make before running out of ink. He estimates that if he "accidentally" knocked down fifteen peas off his plate for the last eight years, the peas they would now be at the level of the table top. Because all of these books have to do with familiar, everyday events, children can extend the books by writing and illustrating their own stories that involve a mathematical point of view.

Another book, *The King's Chessboard* by David Birch, is a story that takes place in ancient India. The King of Deccan is so pleased with his wise man's services that he wishes to give him a reward. The wise man does not think he needs a reward, but the king is insistent. The wise man reflects, and then noting the king's chessboard, asks the king for the number of grains of rice that would be required if one grain were placed on the first square, two on the second square, four on the third square, and so on for all 64 squares on the chessboard. Because the king isn't sure how much rice would be necessary, and because he is too proud to let on to anyone that he doesn't know, he grants the wise man's request as his reward. With only half the squares accounted for, however, the royal granaries are nearly bare from meeting the requirements of the reward.

As children discover how the king finds a way to save face over being outwitted by the wise man, they begin to reflect on the mathematical power of a simple request. Extensions of this book could involve children in posing other "simple" requests that require different kinds of mathematical patterns—adding 10 or some other number for each chessboard square, for example. These could be incorporated in stories or expressed by short descriptions of various patterns (e.g., on day 1 there are ten pennies; on day 2, twenty; day 3, fifteen; day 4, twenty-five; then thirty-five, thirty, and so on) for other classmates to figure out. Possible mathematical abstractions can be considered by children because the abstractions are begun in a meaningful way and are initiated and controlled by the children.

Mitsumasa Anno has several books incorporating various mathematical concepts. In *Anno's Hat Tricks*, Anno and Nozaki introduce children to the deductive reasoning that is the basis of binary logic. As the hatter encourages Shadowchild (the reader) to play tricks about red and white hats, the power of "if" is explained as it is used by computer programmers, mathematicians, and other scientists. Children enjoy making their own hats to dramatize the book or writing plays to illustrate other examples of the process of elimination and binary logic.

In Anno's *Mysterious Multiplying Jar*, Anno and his son, Masaichiro, illustrate the concept of factorials in a manner that children with a basic understanding of multiplication can grasp. Like a cumulative folktale, the authors present an island in a sea; and on that island, two countries; and in each country, three mountains; and so on up to ten jars. How many jars altogether? Well, there were 10! jars. As children discover a new function of the exclamation point, they begin to realize how it signals a special kind of numerical relationship. The !, called a *factorial*, means that the number it follows stands for the product of that number multiplied by the next smaller number, multiplied by the next smaller number, and so forth all the way down to 1. Extensions can involve children in trying to figure out other real-life scenarios that depict factorials (e.g., the possible arrangements of the desks of four students). In addition, because the Anno book is like a cumulative tale, a study of some of these folktales leads children to discover how the part-whole relationship in these tales compare with the relationships of the mathematical factorial idea. Sometimes this investigation can result in children's writing a new genre—"cumulative factorial" tales.

In Konigsburg's *From the Mixed-up Files of Mrs. Basil E. Frankweiler*, Claudia, aged eleven, decides to run away to the Metropolitan Museum of Art in New York City. She's given up hot fudge sundaes for three weeks, but she still has saved only $4.18, so she invites her younger brother Jamie to go along because he can help bankroll the expedition. This book is filled with story problems for children to figure out, and more can be constructed as extensions. For example, children can compare the amount of Claudia's allowance with theirs, and they can figure out how much money Claudia and Jamie have left for meals after paying train fare. Children can also determine the rate of inflation by comparing how much things cost in 1969 (the year the book was published) with how much things cost now. This book can also encourage children to write their own books filled with real-life mathematical problems.

Konigsburg (1967)

Indeed, the topic of money is a good one to incorporate in many thematic units, and many books, both fiction and nonfiction, are available to support children's inquiries in this domain. Because children become aware of money at an early age, and because the economy is so much in the news, books can help them begin to learn about fiscal responsibility. Vera Williams has three books—*A Chair for My Mother*, *Something Special for Me*, and *Music, Music for Everyone*—in which Rosa, her mother, and her grandmother save in a jar her mother's tips from her job as a waitress at the Blue Tile Diner, and other extra family money, to buy various items. Ellen Conford also has several chapter books about Jenny Archer, who tries to raise money in some interesting but not always popular ways: *A Job for Jenny Archer*; *What's Cooking, Jenny Archer?*; and *Can Do, Jenny Archer*. Other books of fiction cover money topics that children can relate to. In Viorst's *Alexander, Who Used to be Rich Last Sunday*, Alexander squanders his money in foolish ways; in *Martin and the Tooth Fairy* by Chardiet and Maccarone, buying children's teeth to make a profit from the tooth fairy is foiled; and in *Alice* by Whoopi Goldberg, Alice's dream-come-true sweepstakes ends up a scam.

See Stan (1993) for a good bibliography of money books.

Williams (1982, 1983, 1984)

Conford (1988, 1989, 1991)

Viorst (1978); Chardiet & Maccarone (1991); Goldberg (1992)

A range of nonfictional titles about money also appeal to children. Maestro's *The Story of Money* traces the history of money and shows how the medium of money has changed from salt to electronic cards. *The Money Book* by Wyatt and Hinden is a paperback that covers a range of topics—even some unusual ones, such as collectibles, betting, and charity. Several books—*Jobs for Kids*; *Making Cents: Every Kid's Guide to Money*; and *Better Than a Lemonade Stand*—cover innumerable ways children can earn money or begin a business for profit.

Maestro (1993)

Wyatt & Hinden (1991)

Barkin & James (1990); Wilkinson (1989); Bernstein (1992)

Another informative book that children love is *The I Hate Mathematics! Book* by Marilyn Burns. A range of activities convinces children that math can be fun and that there is more to math than arithmetic. Topology (the study of surfaces) is examined in "A Topological Garden," exponential growth is introduced in "Doing Dishes," and a palindrome is discovered in "The Perfect Palindrome." Children can reenact in the classroom many of the tricks and games described in the book. Trying them out on the unsuspecting in other classes or at home can lead to shared writings about reactions. Because the activities are frequently illustrated by cartoons, children are sometimes spurred to use this medium to express other math tricks they have discovered.

Burns (1975)

See *Math for Smarty Pants* by Burns (1982) for even more games and activities in various mathematical areas.

As already noted, mathematical literature books are written in a range of genres. There are poetry book, such as *One, Two, Three, and Four—No More?*. Here, Catherine Gray's verses and Marissa Moss's illustrations depict various animals in combinations of the first four numbers, thereby providing a delightful introduction of simple numeration, addition, and subtraction for young mathematicians. Besides reading these verses over and over, children can extend the book in many ways. They can make stick or other animal puppets and dramatize these arithmetical operations. They can also write their own verses, using other animals and mathematical operations that involve numbers over four. Older elementary children can try writing similar verses (or verses that use other kinds of poetic structures or that focus on objects or people rather

Mathematical literature books come in all genres.

Gray (1988)

than animals), using other operations, such as multiplication and division. Writing verses that incorporate mathematical notions can be part of children's Learning Logs* as they engage in various projects in thematic units throughout the year.

There are "fuzzy" books as well, where the language of various genres are incorporated or intermingled (see more about "fuzzy" books in Chapter 6). In *Emeka's Gift: An African Counting Story*, Ifeoma Onyefulu has Emeka setting off to visit his grandmother in the next village. The book is storylike in that he is engaged in various events and has conversation with people on his journey. He meets, for example, three women on their way to the market who stop to say hello. Then as he passes through the market and sees many things that Granny would like, he worries whether she will understand that he has no money to buy anything for her. Stunning photographs of Emeka's village in southern Nigeria are included (rather than illustrations) and various topics about the village related to the storyline, such as markets, are further explained in informational "boxes" (e.g., "Markets are important meeting places...").

Writing Story Problems

One of the best ways children can make mathematics meaningful is to write their own story problems. These can be constructed and collected in every thematic unit throughout the year, perhaps in a special journal designated for this purpose. Ideas are generated as the children read a range of genres and investigate problems across the curriculum. For example, they can incorporate their mathematical data by spinning a yarn using the characters and episodes in a story they are enjoying. Problems can be expressed by describing the behaviors of animals or by relating historic events. As writers, children begin with a solution and then work backward to construct an interesting problem. As readers of their peers' problems, they do the opposite: They begin with trying to figure out the problem and work toward the solution. These reading and writing experiences and the spirited discussions surrounding them are invaluable mathematical problem-solving activities.

Writing their own mathematics book for children in other classes or for children next year provides opportunities to display and reflect on what they know about math. Math becomes meaningful, even for kindergartners, as they try to explain and illustrate the mathematical concepts and procedures they know so that other children can understand them. By sketching classroom and real-world scenarios, children come up with interesting and novel ways to express these mathematical understandings.

Summary

In an integrated classroom, problem-solving is emphasized across the curriculum. Both pure and applied aspects of mathematics are integrated so that relational understanding is developed. Math is concrete and meaningful because it has to do with real-world problems and scenarios. Because math activities and experiences make sense to children, the mathematical concepts they acquire by being engaged in these activities serve as launch pads for expanding these concepts to greater levels of abstraction in meaningful ways. As children discuss the process of mathematical operations or techniques, they examine their appropriateness; risk taking is fostered when they consider and evaluate alternative methods. They also learn the diverse ways that mathematical meanings are expressed through the "language" or "texts" of mathematics and its genre-specific forms and structures: graphs, proofs, definitions, algorithms, and equations.

Teachers need to demonstrate mathematical operations, strategies, models, or approaches to problems in Focus-Lessons* (see Chapter 7) and/or have regular sessions in which math is the focus. Rather than spend a lot of rote practice on many problems, children tackle a smaller number of problems in depth. In so doing, they develop an appreciation of the coherence of a problem and the process involved in attempting to solve it. Children see math as a powerful way of knowing and themselves as confident mathematicians.

References: Mathematics

Andersen, A. (1993). Making math connections. *The Five Owls, 7,* 109–110.

Baker, A., & Baker, J. (1990). *Mathematics in process.* Portsmouth, NH: Heinemann.

Baratta-Lorton, M. (1995). *Mathematics their way.* Menlo Park, CA: Addison-Wesley.

Bishop, A. (1988). *Mathematical enculturation.* Dordrecht, The Netherlands: Kluwer Academic Publishers.

Borasi, R. (1992). *Learning mathematics through inquiry.* Portsmouth, NH: Heinemann.

Brilliant-Mills, H. (1994). Becoming a mathematician: Building a situated definition of mathematics. *Linguistics and Education, 5,* 301–334.

Burns, M. (1992). *About teaching mathematics: A K–8 resource.* White Plains, NY: Cuisenaire Co. of America.

Burns, M. (1995). *Writing in math class: Resource for grades 2-8.* White Plains, NY: Math Solutions.

Cobb, P. (1991). Reconstructing elementary school mathematics. *Focus on Learning Problems in Mathematics, 13,* 3-32.

Cobb, P., Yackel, E., & Wood, T. (1991). Curriculum and teacher development: Psychological and anthropological perspectives. In E. Fennema, T. P. Carpenter, and S. J. Lamon (Eds.), *Integrating research on teaching and learning mathematics* (pp. 83–119). Albany: State University of New York Press.

Cordeiro, P. (1988). Playing with infinity in the sixth grade. *Language Arts, 65,* 557–566.

Corwin, R. B., Storeygard, D., & Price, S. L. (Eds.) (1996). *Talking mathematics: Supporting children's voices.* Portsmouth, NH: Heinemann.

Countryman, J. (1992). *Writing to learn mathematics: Strategies that work, K–12.* Portsmouth, NH: Heinemann.

Donaldson, M. (1978). *Children's minds.* Glasgow: William Collins Sons.

Freedman, E. B., & Person, D. G. (1998). *Connecting informational children's books with content area learning.* Boston: Allyn & Bacon.

Fulwiler, T. (1980). Journals across the disciplines. *English Journal, 69,* 14–22.

Fulwiler, T. (1982). Writing: An act of cognition. In C. W. Griffin (Ed.), *New directions for teaching and learning: No. 12. Teaching writing in all disciplines* (pp. 15–26). San Francisco: Jossey-Bass.

Gelman, R., & Gallistel, C. R. (1978). *The child's understanding of number.* Cambridge, MA: Harvard University Press.

Hiebert, J. (1984). Children's mathematics learning: The struggle to link form and understanding. *Elementary School Journal, 84,* 497–513.

Hughes, M. (1986). *Children and number: Difficulties in learning mathematics.* New York: Basil Blackwell.

Hyde, A. A., & Bizar, M. (1989). *Thinking in context: Teaching cognitive processes across the elementary curriculum.* Oxford: Longman.

Hyde, A. A., & Hyde, P. R. (1991). *Mathwise: Teaching mathematical thinking and problem solving.* Portsmouth, NH: Heinemann.

Kamii, C. K. (1985). *Young children reinvent arithmetic: Implications of Piaget's theory.* New York: Teachers College Press.

Lampert, M. (1991). Connecting mathematical teaching and learning. In E. Fennema, T. P. Carpenter, & S. J. Lamon (Eds.), *Integrating research on teaching and learning mathematics* (pp. 121–152). Albany: State University of New York Press.

Larke, P. J. (1988). Geometric extravaganza: Spicing up geometry. *Arithmetic Teacher, 36,* 12–16.

Lave, J., Murtaugh, M., & de la Rocha, O. (1984). The dialectic of arithmetic in grocery shopping. In B. Rogoff & J. Lave (Eds.), *Everyday cognition: Its development in social context* (pp. 67–94). Cambridge, MA: Harvard University Press.

Macrorie, K. (1988). *The I-search paper.* Portsmouth, NH: Boynton/Cook.

McCallum, R., & Whitlow, R. (1994). *Linking mathematics and language: Practical classroom activities.* Markham, Ontario, Canada: Pippin.

Moon, J., & Schulman, L. (1995). *Finding the connections: Linking, assessment, instruction, and curriculum in elementary mathematics.* Portsmouth, NH: Heinemann.

Mokros, J., Russell, S. J., & Economopoulos, E. (1995). *Beyond arithmetic: Changing mathematics in the elementary classroom.* Palo Alto, CA: Dale Seymour Pulications.

Mills, H., O'Keefe, T., & Whitlin, D. (1996). *Mathematics in the making: Authoring ideas in primary classrooms.* Portsmouth, NH: Heinmann.

Mousley, J., & Marks, G. (1991). *Discourse in mathematics.* Victoria, Australia: Deakin University Press.

National Council of Teachers of Mathematics (1989). *Curriculum and evaluation standards for school mathematics.* Reston, VA: Author.

Nesher, P. (1988). Precursors of number in children: A linguistic perspective. In S. Strauss (Ed.), *Ontogeny, phylogeny, and historical development: Human development* (vol. 2, pp. 106–124). Norwood, NJ: Ablex.

Pappas, C. C., & Bush, S. (1989). Facilitating understandings of geometry. *Arithmetic Teacher, 36,* 17–20.

Piaget, J. (1952). *The child's conception of number.* London: Routledge & Kegan Paul.

Piaget, J. (1953). How children form mathematics concepts. *Scientific American, 189,* 74–79.

Pimm, D. (1987). *Speaking mathematically: Communication in mathematics classrooms.* London: Routledge & Kegan Paul.

Rutherford, F. J., & Ahlgren, A. (1990). *Science for all Americans.* New York: Oxford University Press.

Saxe, G. B. (1988a). Candy selling and math learning. *Educational Researcher, 17,* 14–21.

Saxe, G. B. (Ed.) (1988b). *New directions for child development: No. 41. Children's mathematics* (pp. 55–70). San Francisco: Jossey-Bass.

Saxe, G. B. Guberman, S. R., & Gearhart, M. (1987). *Social processes in early number development* (Monograph No. 52, Serial No. 216). Society for Research in Child Development.

Siegel, M. & Fonzi, J. M. (1995). The practice of reading in an inquiry-oriented mathematics class. *Reading Research Quarterly, 30,* 632-673.

Stan, S. (1993). Children and money. *The Five Owls, 7,* 101–108.

Thiessen, D., & Matthias, M. (1992). *The wonderful world of mathematics: A critically annotated list of children's books in mathematics.* Reston, VA: National Council or Teachers of Mathematics.

Van den Brink, J. (1987). Children as arithmetic book authors. *For the Learning of Mathematics, 7,* 44–47.

Van de Walle, J. A. (1994). *Elementary school mathematics: Teaching developmentally.* New York: Longman.

Van de Walle, J. A., & Holbrook, H. (1987). Patterns, thinking, and problem solving. *Arithmetic Teacher, 34,* 6–12.

Whitlin, D. J., Mills, H., & O'Keefe, T. (1990). *Living and learning mathematics: Stories and strategies for supporting mathematical literacy.* Portsmouth, NH: Heinemann.

Whitlin, D. J., & Wilde, S. (1992). *Read any good math lately? Children's books for mathematical learning, K–6.* Portsmouth, NH: Heinemann.

Whitlin, D. J., & Wilde, S. (1995). *It's the story that counts: More children's books for mathematical learners, K-6.* Portsmouth, NH: Heinemann.

Zaslavsky, C. (1996). *The multicultural math classroom: Bringing in the world.* Portsmouth, NH: Heinemann.

Children's Literature: Mathematics

Alexander, Who Used to Be Rich Last Sunday by J. Viorst. Illustrated by R. Cruz. Atheneum, 1978.

Alice by W. Goldberg, Illustrated by J. Rocco. Bantam, 1992.

Anno's Hat Tricks by A. Nozaki & M. Anno. Philomel, 1985.

Anno's Mysterious Multiplying Jar by M. Anno & M. Anno, Illustrated by M. Anno. Philomel, 1983.

Better Than a Lemonade Stand by D. Bernstein, Illustrated by R. Husberg. Beyond Words, 1992.

Big Anthony and the Magic Ring by T. dePaola. Harcourt Brace Jovanovich, 1979.

Can Do, Jenny Archer by E. Conford. Illustrated by D. Palmisciano. Little Brown, 1991.

A Chair for My Mother by V. Williams. Greenwillow, 1982.

Counting on Frank by R. Clement. Gareth Stevens, 1991.

Emeka's Gift: An African Counting Story by I. Onyefulu. Dutton, 1995.

Get Up and Go! by S. J. Murphy, Illustrated by D. Greenseid. HarperCollins, 1996.

Give Me Half! Understanding Halves by S. J. Murphy. Illustrated by B. Karras. HarperCollins, 1996.

From the Mixed-up Files of Mrs. Basil E. Frankweiler by E. I. Konigsburg. Atheneum, 1967.

A Grain of Rice by H. C. Pittman. Hastings House, 1986.

The I Hate Mathematics! Book by M. Burns. Illustrated by M. Hairston. Little, Brown, 1975.

A Job for Jenny Archer by E. Conford. Illustrated by D. Palmisciano. Little, Brown, 1988.

Jobs for Kids by C. Barkin & E. James. Illustrated by R. Doty. Lothrop, 1990.

The King's Chessboard by D. Birch. Illustrated by D. Grebu. Dial, 1988.

Making Cents: Every Kid's Guide to Money by E. Wilkinson. Illustrated by M. Weston. Little, Brown, 1989.

Martin and the Tooth Fairy by B. Chardiet & G. Maccarone. Illustrated by G. B. Karas. Scholastic, 1991.

Math Curse by J. Scieszka. Illustrated by L. Smith. Viking, 1995.

Math for Smarty Pants by M. Burns. Illustrated by M. Weston. Little, Brown, 1982.

The Money Book by E. Wyatt & S. Hinden. Illustrated by A. Levin. Tambourine, 1991.

Music, Music for Everyone by V. Williams. Greenwillow, 1984.

One, Two, Three, and Four—No More? by C. Gray, Illustrated by M. Moss. Houghton Mifflin, 1988.

A Pair of Socks by S. J. Murphy. Illustrated by L. Ehlert. HarperCollins, 1996.

Something Special for Me by V. Williams. Greenwillow, 1983.

The Story of Money by B. Maestro. Illustrated by G. Maestro. Clarion, 1993.

Strega Nona by T. dePaola. Prentice-Hall, 1975.

Strega Nona's Magic Lessons by T. dePaola. Harcourt Brace Jovanovich, 1982.

What's Cooking, Jenny Archer? by E. Conford. Illustrated by D. Palmisciano. Little, Brown, 1989.

Art and Music

Langer (1978)

Gardner (1982)

Language and the arts are our humanistic vehicles for constructing and conveying meaning. Langer has argued that, whereas language is linear and the arts nonlinear, both are branches of the same root. Language is a way of naming and the arts a way of knowing. Gardner suggests that through language and the arts the human mind creates, revises, transforms, and "recreates wholly fresh products, systems and even worlds of meaning".

Arnheim (1974)

Caldwell & Moore (1991)

Dyson (1986)

Olshansky (1994)

In Western mainstream cultures, the attention of educators has been on the acquisition of verbal language and the teaching of "literacy." We cannot afford, however, to ignore the potential of the arts for constructing and representing ourselves and our particular culture. Arnheim has called this potential the neglected "gift of comprehending through our senses" (p. 1). The arts seem to be integrally intertwined with children's need to make sense of themselves and their world through symbols. Very young children quickly pick up the intonation or musical patterns of various registers of language. They sing little rhymes to themselves, savoring the sounds and patterns of words. They create metaphors and tell stories as they explore their world. They exhibit an astonishing creative artistry in the manipulation of the elements and principles of the visual arts. We also know that artistic expression seems to enable children in the creation of oral and written texts.

Thus, there is good reason to include the arts as natural vehicles for exploring the topics in thematic units. We need, argues Gardner, "to acknowledge forms and intensities of thought other than" those traditionally valued by our school systems (p. 214). Yet too often arts education has been considered a frill. If not the first to be eliminated in the face of budget cuts, it is limited to the production of art and music (i.e., students engaged in making art or music) only once a week for twenty minutes to an hour in a room apart from the day-to-day business of the classroom.

Gardner (1982)

Donmoyer (1995)

In recent years, however, a broadening and redefining of arts education curricula have occurred. Arts educators have increasingly made efforts to put the arts at the center of the school restructuralization movement. This revitalization of the arts has taken several directions. In the visual arts, an approach called discipline-based art education (DBAE) has grown out of a collaboration between Elliott Eisner and the Getty Center for Education in the Arts. DBAE programs call for experiences in four major areas: art making, art history, art criticism, and aesthetics. According to Eisner, there are four things people do with art: "They make it, they understand it, they make judgments about it and they appreciate it" (p. 7). He suggests that when children make pots out of clay coils, for example, they should have the opportunity to think about proportion and technique, to consider the feelings conveyed when pots are delicate or heavy, and to make connections to the uses and forms of pots in other times and cultures.

Arts curricula have been re-examined.

Aesthetics raises the question: What is art and what is my response to it?

Brandt (1988a).

Many art educators have been critical of DBAE for several reasons. London, for example, argues that DBAE is "shallow in its appreciation of what art is, how art and artists serve society, and what is entailed in the creative process in art, art education and education in general" (p. 3). He and other arts educators have called for art training based in "spontaneous emotional activities, attunements, discernments, appraisals, and imaginary experiments of the child" (p. 20). Such an approach has developed out of the work of Howard Gardner and his colleagues at Harvard Project Zero, a group that has had major influence on arts research and education. This approach focuses on the arts as alternative ways of knowing, and it emphasizes artistic production as a central focus of the curriculum interwoven with strands of perception (discrimination) and reflection (introspection and critical analysis about productive and perceptual endeavors). The heart of arts education, he argues, should be "the capacity to handle, to use, to transform different artistic symbol systems—to think with and in the materials" (p. 163).

London (1988)

Ewens (1988)

See Gardner (1988) for an overview of Project Zero research and its school-based initiatives.

Gardner's work has been especially helpful in clarifying how teachers can respond to the child's artistic development in ways that are similar to their response to the child's development of language systems. He suggests, for example, that across cultures the years from two to about seven are spent "coming to grips with the world of 'symbols.'" During this time "the child's capacity to use, manipulate, transform and comprehend various symbol systems matures at a ferocious pace" (pp. 211–212). These young children should be given every opportunity to explore media and forms of expression in a way that allows natural processes to unfold. Older children, however, become increasingly aware of the culture in which they live and become occupied with the rules and standards of those around them. Thus, the type of experimentation with art forms and the lack of conformity children exhibit before formal schooling begins give way to a period of wanting to know how to make a drawing look "real" or a song sound "right." At this point, a teacher can step in with experiences that help children gain mastery of various techniques and media at the same time they introduce them to questions and concepts regarding standards and criticism. In addition, by introducing children to many different cultural traditions teachers can broaden the range of possibilities children see for their own art making.

Gardner (1988)

Gardner (1980, 1982)

Gardner (1982)

Giving the preteenager a knowledge of techniques and a familiarity with various media should make it less likely that during the critical years of adolescence, when teens begin to recognize the range of the finest art and performance that exist, they give up because they cannot measure up. If instead they see their work within the context of broad cultural and historical traditions, it is more likely that they will remain willing participants in the arts throughout their lives.

The arts are resources and vehicles for learning.

See Levstik & Barton (1997)

We have already explored the arts as resources in thematic units in Chapter 3, specifically in SPACES AND PLACES, which included the study of many aspects of two- and three-dimensional space in art and explored movement in space as it relates to art, music, and dance. Such themes also allow children to study paintings, sculptures, and musical compositions and to consider how artists, choreographers, and composers have explored and represented space in their creations throughout history and across cultures. Furthermore, because the arts exist in historical, cultural, and political contexts they become important sources for Reflective, Disciplined Inquiry*. In Chapter 4, many of the prototypes represent collaboration between art, music, and physical education specialists and the classroom teacher.

Because of the limitations of space in this book, we cannot deal with the wide range of genres that exist within the scope of the disciplines called the arts. In Chapter 7, we look at the language-related arts of drama and literature. In the remainder of this section we look more closely at two of the arts—visual art and music—as vehicles for exploring and responding to the content in thematic units and as domains of knowledge in their own right. However, we encourage teachers to explore other art forms such as movement and dance through web sites and other resources.

See Bang (1991), Barrett, McCoy, & Veblen (1997), McFee and Degge (1980), and Upitis (1990) for help in understanding and applying concepts about art and music.

Because the arts often require special skills or talents as well as specialized knowledge, you may feel a bit intimidated by developing experiences that involve children with techniques used in art and music production or in discussing their critical, historical, or aesthetic dimensions. There are many excellent resources that will boost your confidence and suggest practical methods for developing art and music activities. Some of these resources are included in the bibliography of Books for Exploring the Arts below, along with books that engage children in various ways of thinking and experiencing these art forms.

Books for Exploring the Arts (Including Dance and Movement)

The Visual Arts

Agee, J. (1988). *The Incredible Painting Of Felix Clousseau*. New York: Farrar, Straus, & Giroux.

Ashabranner, B. (1996). *A Strange and Distant Shore: Indians of the Great Plains in Exile*. New York: Cobblehill.

Berry J. (1996). *Rough Sketch: Beginning*. Illustrated by R. Florczak. San Diego: Harcourt Brace.

Bonafoux, P. (1992). *A Weekend With Rembrandt*. New York: Rizzoli International.

Carle, E. (1992). *Draw Me A Star*. New York: Philomel.

Cummings, P. (1995). *Talking with Artists: Volume Two*. New York: Simon & Schuster.

de Trevino, E. B. (1965). *I, Juan de Pareja*. New York: Farrar, Straus, & Giroux.

dePaola, T. (1991). *Bonjour, Mr. Satie*. New York: Putnam.

Dewey, J. O. (1996). *Stories on Stone: Rock Art: Images from the Ancient Ones*. Boston: Little, Brown.

Dionetti, M. (1996). *Painting the Wind*. Illustrated by K. Hawkes. Boston: Little, Brown.

Dunrea, O. (1995). *The Painter Who Loved Chickens*. New York: Farrar, Straus, & Giroux.

Everett, G. (1992). *Li'l Sis and Uncle Willie: A Story Based on the Life and Paintings of William H. Johnson*. Illustrated by W. H. Johnson. New York: Rizzoli International.

Geisert, A. (1997). *The Etcher's Studio*. Boston: Houghton Mifflin,

Greenburg, J., & Jordan, S. (1995). *The American Eye: Eleven Artists of the Twentieth Century*. New York: Delacorte.

Isaacson, P. (1993). *A Short Walk around the Pyramids and through the World of Art.* New York: Knopf.

Konigsburg, E. L. (1967). *From the Mixed-up Files of Mrs. Basil E. Frankweiler.* New York: Atheneum.

Konigsburg, E. L. (1967). *The Second Mrs. Giaconda.* New York: Atheneum.

Krull, K. (1995). *Lives of the Artists: Masterpieces, Messes (And What the Neighbors Thought).* Illustrated by K. Hewitt. San Diego: Harcourt Brace.

Lattimore, P. N. (1991). *The Sailor Who Captured the Sea: The Story of the Book of Kells.* New York: HarperCollins.

Lionni, L. (1991*). Matthew's Dream.* New York: Knopf.

Llorente, P. M. (1993). *The Apprentice.* Illustrated by J. R. Alonso. New York: Farrar, Straus, & Giroux.

Lyons, M. E. (1996). *Painting Dreams: Minnie Evans Visionary Artist.* Boston: Houghton Mifflin.

McClintock, B. (1996). *The Fantastic Drawings of Danielle.* Boston: Houghton Mifflin.

Micklethwait, L. (1991). *I Spy: An Alphabet Book in Art.* New York: Greenwillow.

Niemark, A. E. (1992). *Diego Rivera: Artist of the People.* New York: HarperCollins.

Paterson, K. (1979). *Bridge to Terabithia.* New York: HarperCollins.

Peppin, A. (1991). *Places in Art.* Brookfield CT: Millbrook.

Presilla, M. E. (1996). *Mola: Cuna Life Stories and Art.* New York: Holt.

Ringgold, F. (1993). *Dinner at Aunt Connie's House.* New York: Hyperion.

Rylant, C. (1993). *The Dreamer.* Illustrated by B. Moser. New York: Blue Sky.

Say, A. (1996). *Emma's Rug.* Boston: Houghton Mifflin.

Shaw, M., & Gal, L. (1996). *Tiktala.* New York: Holiday House.

Sills, L. (1993). *Visions: Stories about Women Artists.* Niles, IL: Whitman.

Stanley, D. (1996). *Leonardo Da Vinci.* New York: Morrow, 1996.

Sullivan, C. (1992). *Children of Promise: African American Literature and Art for Young People.* New York: Abrams.

Sullivan, C. (1994). *Here Is My Kingdom: Hispanic-American Literature and Art for Young People.* New York: Abrams.

Turner, R. M. (1993). *Frida Kahlo.* Boston: Little, Brown.

Wilson, E. (1994). *Bibles and Bestiaries: A Guide to Illuminated Manuscripts.* New York: Farrar.

Wright-Frierson, V. (1996) *A Desert Scrapbook: Dawn to Dusk in the Sonoran Desert.* New York: Simon & Schuster.

Music

Adoff, A. (1995). *Street Music: City Poems.* Illustrated by K. Barbour. New York: HarperCollins.

Ardley, N. (1995). *A Young Person's Guide to Music.* New York: DK.

Awmiller, C. (1996). *This House on Fire: The Story of the Blues.* New York: Watts.

Axelrod, A. (1991). *Songs Of The Wild West.* New York: Simon & Schuster.

Brett, J. (1991). *Berlioz the Bear.* New York: Putnam.

Eversole, R. (1995). *The Flute Player/La Flautista.* Illustrated by G. B.Karas. New York: Orchard.

Fenner, C. (1995). *Yolanda's Genius.* New York: McElderry.

Fleischman, P. (1988). *Rondo in C.* Illustrated by J. Wentworth. New York: Harper & Row.

Haskins, J. (1996). *The Harlem Renaissance.* Brookfield CT: Millbrook.

Hopkins, L. (1997). *Song and Dance.* Illustrated by C. M. Taylor. New York: Simon & Schuster.

Jaffe, N. (1994). *Patakin: World Tales of Drums and Drummers.* Illustrated by E. Eagle. New York: Holt.

Krull, K. (1993*) Live of the Musicians: Good Time, Bad Times (and What the Neighbors Thought)*. Illustrated by K. Hewitt. San Diego: Harcourt Brace.

Lasker, D. (1979). *The Boy Who Loved Music*. Illustrated by J. Lasker. New York: Viking.

MacLachlan, P. (1988). *The Facts and Fictions of Minna Pratt*. New York: HarperCollins.

Martin B. Jr. (1994). *The Maestro Plays*. Illustrated by V. Radunsky. New York: Holt.

Melmed, L. K. (1993). *The First Song Ever Sung*. Illustrated by E. Young. New York: Lothrop.

Monceaux, M. (1994). *Jazz, My Music, My People*. New York: Knopf.

Moss, L. (1995). *Zin! Zin! Zin! A Violin*. Illustrated by M. Priceman. New York: Simon & Schuster.

Namioka, L. (1992*) Yang the Youngest and His Terrible Ear*. Illustrated by K. de Kiefte. Boston: Little, Brown.

Paterson, K. (1985). *Come Sing, Jimmy Jo*. New York: Dutton.

Philip, N. (1995*) Singing America: Poems that Define a Nation*. Illustrated by M. McCurdy. New York: Viking,

Pinkney, B. (1994). *Max Found Two Sticks*. New York: Simon & Schuster.

Raschka, C. (1992). *Charlie Parker Plays Be Bop*. New York: Orchard.

Raschka, C. (1997). *Mysterious Thelonious*. New York: Orchard.

Schroeder, A. (1996). *Satchmo's Blues*. Illustrated by F. Cooper. New York: Doubleday.

Silverman, J. (1996). *Just Listen to This Song I'm Singing: African American History through Song*. Brookfield CT: Millbrook.

Steig, W. (1994). *Zeke Pippin*. New York: HarperCollins.

Strickland, M. (1993). *Poems That Sing to You*. Illustrated by A. Leiner. Honesdale, PA: Wordsong.

Voigt, C. (1983). *Dicey's Song*. New York: Atheneum.

Williams, V. B. (1984). *Music, Music for Everyone*. New York: Greenwillow.

Wilson, C. (1996). *The Kingfisher Young People's Book of Music*. New York: Kingfisher.

Wolfe, V. E. (1991). *The Mozart Season*. New York: Henry Holt.

Dance and Movement: Informational Books

Gherman, B. (1994). *Agnes DeMille: Dancing of the Earth*. New York: Macmillan.

Haskins, J. (1992). *Black Dance in America*. New York: HarperCollins.

King, S. (1993). *Shannon: An Ojibway Dancer*. Illustrated by C. Whipple. Minneapolis, MN: Lerner.

Kuklin, S. (1989). *Going to My Ballet Class*. New York: Bradbury.

Pinkney, A. D. (1993). *Alvin Ailey*. Illustrated by B. Pinkney. New York: Hyperion.

Dance and Movement: Fiction and Poetry

Carlstrom, N. W. (1993). *How Does the Wind Walk?* Illustrated by D. K. Ray. New York: Macmillan.

Cauley, L. B. (1992). *Clap Your Hands*. New York: Putnam.

Esbensen, B. (1995). *Dance With Me*. Illustrated by M. Lloyd. New York: HarperCollins.

Gauch, P. L. (1994). *Tanya and Emily in a Dance for Two*. Illustrated by S. Ichikawa. New York: Philomel.

Giovanni, N. (1996). *The Genie in the Jar*. Illustrated by C. Raschka. New York: Holt.

Gray, L. M. (1995). *My Mama Had a Dancing Heart*. Illustrated by R. Colon. New York: Orchard.

Hughes, L. (1995/1954). *The Book of Rhythms*. Illustrated by M. Wawiorka. New York: Oxford.

Isadora, R. (1993). *Lili At Ballet*. New York: Putnam.

Lowery, L. (1995). *Twist with a Burger Jitter with a Bug*. Illustrated by P. Dypold. Boston: Houghton Mifflin.

Martin, B., & Archambault, J. (1986). *Barn Dance*. Illustrated by T. Rand. New York: Holt.

Noll, S. (1987). *Jiggle Wiggle Prance*. New York: Greenwillow.

Rodanas, K. (1994). *Dance of the Sacred Circle: A Native American Tale*. Boston: Little, Brown.

Ryder, J. (1996). *Earthdance*. Illustrated by N. Gorbaty. New York: Holt.

Schaefer, C. L. (1996). *The Squiggle*. Illustrated by P. Morgan. New York: Crown.

Schick, E. (1992). *I Have Another Language, the Language Is Dance*. New York: Macmillan.

Tadjo, V. (1988). *Lord of the Dance: An African Retelling*. New York: Lippincott.

Tamar, E. (1996). *Alphabet City Ballet*. New York: HarperCollins.

Van Laan, N. (1993). *Buffalo Dance: A Blackfoot Legend*. Illustrated by B. Vidal. Boston: Little, Brown.

Walsh, E. S. (1993). *Hop Jump*. San Diego: Harcourt Brace.

Consider also the artists within your own community as resources. With support from corporate sponsors, many museums and arts groups are developing outreach programs for local schools. School districts often have artist-in-residence programs that can provide children with a valuable firsthand look at the creative process inherent in the production of a work of art. In the light of our new understanding about children's conceptions of the arts and the call for developing their critical and aesthetic awareness, it seems especially important that children see these artworks evolve over time rather than simply examine or listen to the finished product.

Don't hesitate to enlist the support of your school or district's art and music specialists. They have expertise in developing critical, aesthetic, and historical perspectives for children in their respective fields, and you should enlist them as team members and resource persons for all thematic units. They can suggest composers, musicians, and musical compositions or art and artists from many historical periods that can be incorporated into the units. They may also have libraries of recordings or art reproductions, or know of other sources that they would be willing to share with the children. They themselves may be practicing artists or know of artists who can share their work and processes with the children. At other times, a theme may suggest some important critical or aesthetic factors to the specialists on which they can expand during their time with the children. Such would be the case in a CHANGES unit when an art teacher introduces children to op art, or when a music teacher concentrates on critical factors such as dynamics and crescendo.

In a PATTERNS unit an art teacher introduced children to American quilt-making traditions that began in Africa and are realized today in the work of artists like Faith Ringgold. Themes can also provide specialists with the opportunity for developing experiences with special techniques. A theme of SPACES for older children can provide the opportunity for teaching different techniques in two- or three-point perspective so that they could represent views of a scene or an object from below or above.

Art or music can often serve as the focus in a thematic unit (a subtopic on the books of a particular illustrator or on exploring art or music through books) or as a springboard to a unit. The art teacher who worked with Lisa Bridges on the CHANGES unit coordinated the study of "changing languages" with an exhibit of alphabet books from many countries that was on view at the art museum. (See Chapter 4.) A middle-school music teacher helped classroom teachers develop a unit for studying American history through American music.

Thus, keep in mind the important role played by artists in the community and by the art and music specialists in your school. The following classroom activities can serve

Specialists are resources and team members.

as foundations, easily laid by teachers, that will allow the specialists to build further expertise and understanding in the realms of art and music.

Art and Music Makers

Children learn through the languages of art and music.

See Barrett, McCoy, & Veblen (1997); Upitis (1990); and Walther (1981) for other ideas.

Art and music are not simply tools for teaching concepts in other content areas but ways of knowing these concepts. They allow children to explore a theme, act on it, and transform it. The integrated language classroom thus provides many opportunities to create art and music and many materials and avenues of expression. Try to make available as full a range of materials and instruments as the school budget will allow and encourage children to consider their use as they choose ways to explore a given theme. These would include simple musical instruments and basic art supplies as well as donated items and found objects. For your wish list consider the use of computers or synthesizers that would allow children to compose, play, read, and listen to music as well as to learn notation and orchestration, and to experiment with the sounds of various instruments. Or consider how the Internet and CD-ROM would allow children to have immediate access to the art of the world's great museums.

Made readily available, the simplest materials and instruments can give children the means for creating a variety of art and music in response to themes being studied. As part of the subtheme "Exploring Nature" in an EXPLORATIONS unit, for example, first graders may want to translate sounds and rhythms they noted on a nature walk into a symphony of sounds using child-made instruments or some of the simple percussion instruments. Some children may choose to make block prints, gluing natural objects such as leaves and grasses to cardboard, inking them with a brayer (a roller used in printing), and then pressing a sheet of construction paper onto the inked surface. Others may want to create a natural hanging by suspending found objects from a stick with yarn and weaving twigs, grasses, and other elements into this warp.

Brandt (1988b)

As part of a TIME theme, children may take a simple and familiar tune such as "Twinkle, Twinkle, Little Star," and play it on recorders, then change it into a morning or afternoon song, or a summer or winter song, varying tempo, pitch, and dynamics. They can then listen to Ferde Grofe's "Grand Canyon Suite," which depicts different times of day, or listen to the variations that Mozart wrote for "Twinkle, Twinkle, Little Star."

Children involved in a theme of CHANGES, having decided to do a painting of a local scene, could discuss what colors or media to choose to express changes at different times of the day, or seasonal or weather changes. By thinking about the ways that colors can affect feelings or the way that qualities of media such as acrylic or watercolor paints can convey meaning, children can also be led to appreciate the choices made by artists such as Claude Monet or Winslow Homer, who spent much of their careers depicting the changing light in landscapes and cityscapes.

Books often weave into a story a musical or artistic theme that suggests a musical or artistic response. Reading about "Sea Journeys" (as a subtheme of JOURNEYS) may lead children to listen to the many musical interpretations of the sea, then create their own sea symphony with voice and instrument. As part of a study of "Personal Journeys," children can read Gary Paulsen's *Dogsong*, in which a young Inuit boy, Russel, braves the arctic wilderness in search of himself and his cultural heritage. They may then seek to interpret the story through a melody and instrument that represent Russel's song or through a monochromatic painting, using shades and tints of blue not only to represent the frigid arctic landscape but also to convey the mood of the character's isolation.

Paulsen (1985)

Students involved in the theme DIGGING UP THE PAST may want to make sketches of animal symbols found on fragments of Native American pottery, noting the abstraction of form and pattern. They may then choose to create their own artifacts by building clay coil pots and decorating them with their own personal symbols. A group of children could create a ceramic tile mural or a mosaic of key events and understandings gleaned from their study. Others may read John Bierhorst's *A Cry from the Earth: Music of North American Indians*, a book that suggests and presents Native

Bierhorst (1979)

American instruments, songs, dances, and masks that were part of music making. It could serve as a springboard for some remarkable art and music activities. These last suggestions, many of which incorporate music making, dance, and art, could serve to summarize a unit such as DIGGING UP THE PAST in ways that are every bit as effective as writing a research report. However art and music making are incorporated into the integrated classroom, they provide children with a richness of expression and an added depth of understanding. Although there is not space enough here to include detailed instructions for art and music projects, we have summarized some of the activities that would be possible as part of a thematic unit.

The arts can be used to summarize a unit.

Music and Art As Ways of Knowing

Music

Listen to or sing theme-related music.

Do finger plays and movement exploration.

Compose music to interpret stories or poems.

Choose theme music for a story or novel.

Orchestrate poems for Choral Reading*.

Make instruments.

Listen to sounds in nature or sounds in the city; represent pitches and rhythms on a musical scale.

Collect old song lyrics. What do these say about the time in which they were written?

Compare musical forms in your own culture.

Compare musical taste and music makers in other cultures.

Art

Weave natural objects into wall hangings.

Create a class theme quilt out of embroidered panels.

Draw a map for a work of fiction.

Make a sculpture out of cardboard and plastic pipe.

Create character portraits out of clay.

Make a diorama or shoe box scene in miniature.

Create a collage to represent a book or concept.

Paint a mural of a theme's important ideas.

Sculpt papier-mâché masks.

Illustrate with watercolor or other media.

Sketch with charcoal or pastel chalk.

Make linoleum or meat-tray prints.

Make batik or crayon-resist wall hangings.

Compare art forms in your own culture.

Compare art tastes and artists in other cultures.

Compare illustrators' media and styles.

Talking about Art and Music

When children are involved in the production of various forms of art and music, they gain control over such media as clay, watercolor, and pastels or such simple instruments as the human voice, recorder, percussion, and string instruments. In addition, they may begin to think about the expressive properties inherent in these art forms. Having time to explore a given instrument or medium in-depth gives children opportunities to think about themselves as choice makers as they seek to express meaning through an art form. They may come to understand that they may choose an element of art or music for its literal property (a piece of music has tempo, while a painting has shapes), but that element also has expressive or metaphorical properties (a fast tempo can convey tension or the hectic pace of life, while a rectangular shape can convey weight or repose).

Encourage children to reflect on and talk about their experiences with the arts. It is through talk that questions essential to aesthetic understandings can be raised: Does art have to be beautiful? Do we have to know what a piece of music is "about" to enjoy it? Can truth be found in fiction? Talk also provides children with the experience necessary for developing critical awareness: What makes this picture more effective than that? What criteria do I apply when I listen to a new piece of music?

Talk provides a focus for developing aesthetic and critical awareness or for reflecting on art forms.

Gardner & Winner (1982)

Being able to talk with children about the arts does not require expert knowledge in any of these disciplines. Teachers can ask some simple but powerful questions that will help children to think about the emotive power of art and music, which is another key to developing aesthetic awareness: Why did you choose watercolor instead of tempera paint for your painting? Did you choose these colors for a particular reason? What were you thinking about as you looked at (listened to) that picture (song)? How did that painting (composition) make you feel? Why would you say that? Young children will probably respond with idiosyncratic reasons: I chose red because I like red. However, older children begin to understand the stylistic choices available to them and other artists: I chose red because I was feeling angry. In addition, teachers may want to use some of the critical vocabulary associated with the forms of each particular discipline in the same way they use words such as word, sentence, character, setting, story, or report in discussing the elements and forms of language. Such words or terminology help children begin to think about how artists or musicians convey meaning through a given art form, which in turn can provide fertile ground for developing aesthetic and critical awareness.

To illustrate how this might be done, let us take an art form that is already a familiar part of integrated language classrooms and show how talking about picture books can develop an aesthetic awareness in children. It may seem surprising to think that such a familiar object as a picture book could be considered an art form, but today's picture books are part of an artistic tradition dating at least as far back as 1300 B. C. to the Egyptian Book of the Dead. During the Middle Ages, the book illustrator or painter was held in equal esteem with the painter and sculptor, and well into the nineteenth-century religious or cultural stories were often the subject matter of paintings and sculpture. With today's sophisticated printing techniques, book illustration is attracting many talented artists who are working in a variety of original media (e.g., watercolor, pen and ink, stitchery, or collage) that is then reproduced by means of printing techniques.

Marantz (1983)

As an art form the picture book is a combination of image and idea in a sequence of turned pages. When words are present, they support the pictures just as the pictures extend and enhance the meaning of the words. When we have closed the best picture books, we experience something that is much more than the sum of the parts.

Studying the art of the picture book has advantages over studying reproductions of paintings or listening to recordings of a symphony. A reproduction of a painting may not be faithful to the color of the original, and the texture of the painting's surface cannot be accurately reproduced. More important, the size of the original may have a great impact on the viewer's response, yet reproductions are seldom faithful to a painting's original size. The picture book, on the other hand, keeps its integrity as an art object. It does not matter if we cannot see the original artwork, because these originals were created so that they could be photographically reproduced and bound together within the covers of the book.

Kiefer (1995)

When you are talking with children about the art of the picture book, it may be helpful to connect children's experiences in making choices in their own art to the choices made by the artist seeking to convey some visual meaning. Just as writers use words and sentences to create character, setting, theme, and mood in a story, illustrators use line, shape, color, value, and texture to convey these same properties. As previously mentioned, the elements of art have their objective, or exemplified, qualities (lines can be jagged or curving, while shapes can be sharp-edged or biomorphic) and their expressive qualities (jagged lines convey a feeling of excitement or danger, while curved lines seem restful or rhythmic). These elements are chosen and composed according to the principles of design: balance, rhythm, repetition, variety, unity, and eye movement. In a painting, of course, these elements and principles are present only on a single pictorial plane. In a picture book the artist can use elements and principles to unify the entire book and bring added power to the final art object.

See Kiefer (1995) for a more detailed discussion of elements of art in picture books.

An illustrator is also concerned with the technical aspects of book production. The artist's choice of original media, typeface, endpapers, pictorial content, or viewpoint can add meaning and depth to the book. Likewise, illustrators may also rely on historical or cultural conventions—aspects of art that have come to be identified with a particular period or culture. When adapted by an illustrator, these conventions can add to our understanding of a tale set in the past or a distant place. Paul Zelinsky in his illustrations for Susan Isaacs' American tall tale, *Swamp Angel*, used aspects of early American portraiture and landscape painting borrowed from itinerant painters called limners. He chose very different conventions for *Rapunzel*. This tale, with its roots in Northern Europe, is visualized by Zelinsky through the forms, textures, and lighting of Renaissance painting. Ed Young uses devices and perspectives reminiscent of Chinese silk screen paintings in books like *Lon Po Po*. Not only do these adaptations of historical and cultural conventions help make children more sensitive to the many choices available to an artist, but they also provide possibilities for connecting art in the classroom to art in the museum.

Isaacs (1994)

Zelinsky (1997)

Young (1989)

Understandings of style in picture books will help teachers bring the best picture books into their classrooms and add depth to discussions about them. These ideas are also applicable to music and the other arts. Notice, for example, how concepts of form and composition such as movement, balance, mood, harmony, repetition, pattern, and motif are present when we talk about either music, literature, or art. In all these areas the composer, the writer, and the artist must make choices in order to convey meaning, just as children make choices in constructing their world.

It is not always necessary or profitable to teach these elements to children or to expect them to apply abstract stylistic labels. Instead, aesthetic understandings grow in the broader context of the integrated language classroom. In the act of creating art, music, or writing, children may come to see how various elements convey and enhance meaning. In discussing these art forms, they acquire the words for talking about their elements and mechanics. In observing and talking with artists, musicians, and other professionals, they become more insightful about their own processes of creation. We hope that they will use these understandings to broaden the scope of the art forms that provide enjoyment, and we also hope that they will become increasingly sophisticated in their search for quality.

Children discover style by being choice makers.

Art and Music in the Wider World

The suggestions for using art and music in the integrated classroom are highly compatible with recent trends in arts education. The knowledge represented by art and music extends beyond the range of a single genre such as painting or choral performance to encompass broader domains. Take the case of children engaged in making clay pots. In addition to producing, perceiving, and reflecting on the art of ceramics and considering the aesthetic, historical, and critical ramifications of pottery, children can come to understand how the decoration on a piece of pottery represents accurate Primary Source* material and gives us access to the culture and social structure of other times, sometimes in the absence of any written history: What legend is retold on the surface of the Greek vase? What symbols were important to Native Americans of the Southwest? Moreover, as they create their own pottery, children must think about the object's use as a container: Will it hold liquids or solids? Will it be used for cooking or storage? They will gain experience with concepts of volume, mass, and density. They will have a chance to consider the object's weight in relation to its structure and form: Will it stand up if the bottom is narrow and the top wide? They will be able to consider the physical makeup of soils, to note changes in matter, and to think about chemical changes that may occur during the firing process: Is a pot more likely to hold liquids after it is fired? Why might it explode in the kiln? What happens to the colors in glazes during the firing? They must consider an object's placement in space and contrast two- and three-dimensional space: When does an object have not only a bottom and a top but also a front and a back? Such powerful understandings are possible through other arts experiences as well and form the basis for the suggestions we have made in this chapter. These understandings show how children learn art and music as domains of knowledge. Their experience with certain media, such as clay or watercolor,

See Grallert (1991).

Children develop understandings beyond the range of a single work or single art discipline.

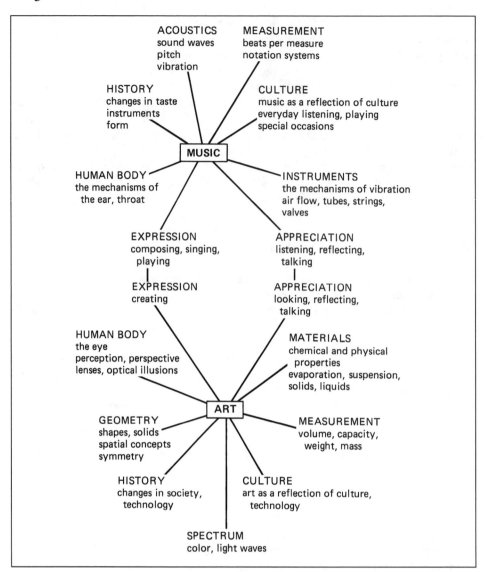

Figure 5.5

INTERRELATIONS BETWEEN
DOMAINS OF KNOWLEDGE IN
MUSIC AND ART

or percussion instruments or voice, help them to explore more specific domains in different ways. Figure 5.5 is a visual summary of the ways in which art and music encompass and connect to many domains of knowledge.

Part of helping children to develop an aesthetic awareness involves helping them to become sensitive to the sights and sounds in the world around them and to look and listen with a practiced eye and ear. In an integrated language classroom, children's experiences with art and music can develop their sensitivities in a variety of subtle ways. Sketching objects or scenes as a prelude to writing, for example, may make children more aware of small nuances of detail, pattern, or texture that they can describe with words. Discovering the details or visual subplots that many illustrators include in pictures, children may look more carefully at the world around them, noting, for example, the subtle changes taking place in the tadpole aquarium or in the textures and colors of an early spring day.

As children gain experience as makers of music, they may become more sensitive to the qualities of the human voice that they can use in Reading Aloud* or creative dramatics. As they listen to music, they may become aware of the subtle effects of such qualities as pitch and volume on their understandings and feelings when they listen to a sales pitch or the evening news. This attention to detail and the aesthetic qualities of the world can lead to a heightened concern with the environment (both in and out of

The arts make children more sensitive to sensory aspects of the world around them.

the classroom) and with their own work. A sensitivity to musical sound, for example, can lead to greater understanding of noise in the outside world and its positive and negative effects on the emotions. Involvement with the visual arts can help sensitize children to pollution and urban clutter.

However you and your students get involved and whatever the outcomes, art and music need to happen frequently for children of all ages. Limiting children's involvement with the arts deprives them of a powerful means of expression and understanding and the fullest opportunity for knowing themselves and their world.

References: Art and Music

Arnheim, R. (1974). *Art and visual perception: A psychology of the creative eye.* Berkeley: University of California Press.

Bang, M. (1991). *Picture this: Perception and composition.* Boston: Bullfinch Press/Little, Brown.

Barrett, J. R., McCoy, C., & Veblen, K. K. (1997). *Sound ways of knowing.* New York: Schirmer Books.

Brandt, R. (1988a). On discipline-based art education: A conversation with Elliott Eisner. *Educational Leadership, 45 (4),* 6–9.

Brandt, R. (1988b). On assessment in the arts: A conversation with Howard Gardner. *Educational Leadership, 45 (4),* 30–34.

Caldwell, H. & Moore, B. H. (1991). The art of writing: Drawing as preparation for narrative writing in the primary grades. *Studies in Art Education, 32,* 207–219.

Donmoyer, R. (1995). The Arts as modes and methods of teaching: A (borrowed and adapted) case for integrating the arts across the curriculum. *Arts Education Policy Review, 96(5),* 14–20.

Dyson, A. H. (1986). Transitions and tensions: Interrelationships between the drawing, talking, and dictating of young children. *Research in the Teaching of English, 20,* 379–409.

Ewens, T. (1988). Flawed understandings: On Getty, Eisner and DBAE. In J. Burton, A. Lederman, & P. London (Eds.), *Beyond DBAE: The case for multiple visions of art education* (pp. 6–22). North Dartmouth, MA: University Council on Art Education.

Gardner, H. (1980). *Artful scribbles: The significance of children's drawings.* New York: Basic Books.

Gardner, H. (1982). *Art, mind, and brain: A cognitive approach to creativity.* New York: Basic Books.

Gardner, H. (1988). Towards more effective arts education. *Journal of Aesthetic Education, 22,* 157–167.

Gardner, H., & Winner, E. (1982). Children's conceptions (and misconceptions) of the arts. In H. Gardner (Ed.), *Art, mind, and brain: A cognitive approach to creativity* (pp. 103–209). New York: Basic Books.

Grallert, M. W. (1991). Working from the inside out: A practical approach to expression. In M. R. Goldberg & A. Phillips (Eds.), *Arts as education* (pp. 79–90). Cambridge, MA: Harvard Educational Review.

Kiefer, B. (1995). *The potential of picturebooks: From visual literacy to aesthetic understanding.* Columbus, OH; Merrill/Prentice Hall.

Langer, S. (1978). *Philosophy in a new key.* Cambridge, MA: Harvard University Press. (Originally published in 1942)

Levstik, L. S., & Barton, K. C. (1997). *Doing history: Investigating with children in elementary and middle schools.* Mahwah, NJ: Lawrence Erlbaum.

London, P. (1988). Introduction. In J. Burton, A. Lederman, & P. London (Eds.), *Beyond DBAE: The case for multiple visions of art education.* (pp. 1–40). North Dartmouth, MA: University Council on Art Education.

McFee, J. K., & Degge, R. M. (1980*). Art, culture and environment: A catalyst for teaching.* Dubuque, IA: Kendall Hunt.

Olshansky, B. (1994). Making writing a work of art: Image making within the writing process. *Language Arts, 71(5),* 350–357.

Upitis, R. (1990). *This too is music.* Portsmouth, NH: Heinemann.

Children's Literature: Art and Music

A Cry from the Earth: Music of North American Indians by J. Bierhorst. Four Winds, 1979.

Dogsong by G. Paulsen. Bradbury, 1985.

Make Mine Music by T. Walther. Little, Brown, 1981.

Swamp Angel by S. Isaacs. Illustrated by P. Zelinsky. Dutton, 1995.

Lon Po Po by E. Young. Philomel, 1989.

Rapunzel by P. Zelinsky. Dutton, 1997.

CHAPTER 6

Learning about Written Language

Chapter 1 provided a preliminary review of the theoretical foundation of the integrated language perspective. The following three major interrelated principles were emphasized:

Children (all humans) are active, constructive learners.

Language is organized in different ways and in different patterns or registers because it is used for different purposes in different social contexts.

Knowledge is organized and constructed by individual learners through social interaction.

This chapter builds on and extends the second principle—the variation of language—by focusing more on the nature of written language and the processes—reading and writing—of using it. Although this chapter concentrates on the second principle, the other two are involved in our discussion as well, because all three are interrelated and cannot be separated.

Registers of Written Language

What Is a Genre?

In the previous chapters we have argued that it is important for children to have many opportunities to use a range of written genres in the classroom. We have argued that a major advantage of the use of a thematic unit is that such an approach provides a means to accomplish this. However, what is really meant by the term *genre*? You probably have met this term in English literature courses during which you have read and studied various written genres such as short stories, odes, sonnets, novels, novellas, and plays. We will use genre much more broadly, not only to include these literary genres but also to incorporate the potentially limitless number of written texts available in our culture.

Although we focus mostly on written texts in this chapter, our meaning of genre also includes a similar limitless range of spoken texts. Our culture consists of a variety of structured activities occurring in a range of contexts of situation. When the particulars in these situations are similar, the spoken texts constructed by participants end up being similar and having a similar form or organization. When the factors in these situations are different, the spoken texts related to these contexts result in different forms and organizations. Think of the kinds of texts and the types of discourse patterns that are used when people participate in service encounters, such as shopping in stores or markets, buying stamps or sending packages at post offices, or buying tickets at travel agencies. Contrast these texts with the kind of spoken language employed when people visit a doctor, consult with a lawyer, or perhaps seek advice from a university academic advisor. Now consider the language patterns that are likely to occur in very different activities: when people attend a party, have lunch with friends at a restaurant, participate in a religious service, or conduct a public meeting.

The range of written genres is limitless.

There are many spoken genres, too.

Bakhtin (1986); Christie (1987, 1990); Collerson (1988); Cope & Kalantzis (1993); Halliday & Hasan (1985); Hasan (1995); Himley (1986); Martin (1992); Martin, Christie, & Rothery (1987); Swales (1990)

228

Can you "visualize" the variations of spoken language—the different registers of language—in these examples? Can you "sense" similarities or commonalities and differences in these examples? Certain texts appear to be similar or go together into certain sets or categories because they seem to be part of certain socially ordered activities serving similar purposes. For example, the texts in the service encounters might resemble each other even though different "goods"—groceries, stamps, or plane tickets—might be bought and sold. Moreover, this set of texts would be somewhat different from the discourse patterns in which we seek a service from a professional such as a physician or lawyer. And both of these sets would be very different from the text registers of a party or lunch at a restaurant with friends. We can call these various categories of texts—these similar sets, ways, or registers of using language—*genres*.

A genre is a conventional way of using language.

Just as there are numerous kinds of spoken genres, there are numerous types of written genres. Besides the literary ones already mentioned, there are mysteries, westerns, fantasies, science fiction, historical fiction, romances, biographies, poems, how-to manuals, editorials, advertisements, information books, commentaries, business letters, newsletters, recipes, and reviews of books, films, and movies, and so forth.

Thus, prior knowledge, in terms of both our direct experiences and activities of life and our verbal (oral and written) experiences and encounters, contributes to the development of genres. Thus, the recurring situations in which people interact and enact social activities give rise to regularities in texts. Schemas of content and form converge because genres have to do with *what* is "sayable" along with *when* and *how* it is said or written. That is, genres are types or classes of communicative events or texts.

Both nonverbal and verbal experiences contribute to the development of genres.

Hasan (1995); Kress (1993); Swales (1990)

Genres—spoken or written—have two characteristics that at first glance appear to be contradictory. First, genres are *stable*. They have fixed elements or patterns: A story is organized in a different way from an essay, which in turn is different from a recipe. Genres are stable because they do certain jobs in our culture, allowing us to choose from a range of genres to communicate various intentions.

Genres are stable patterns of language use.

Although they are stable, genres always involve *change* because we put together various available options from different genres in a different way or borrow elements or features from different genres in new, novel ways; we create new subgenres. Because we frequently have new language goals or purposes to be accomplished in everyday life, aspects of the patterns of genres are altered. Genres are *evolved* and *evolving systems*.

Genres reflect change in patterns of language use.

The generic characteristics of stability and change lead to predictable and creative texts. A particular text is always a new, creative instance of some genre, but at the same time it is always predictable, being in some sense "old hat" for its users. Thus, genres are inherited social forms, but they are also historical entities that change and merge.

Stability in generic patterns leads to predictability in texts; change in generic patterns leads to creativity in texts.

Bakhtin (1986); Pappas & Pettegrew (1998); Slevin (1992); Wertsch (1991)

The Organization of Written Genres

The predictability and creativity, or novelty, of written texts in particular genres is owed to their linguistic organization. Authors do not simply sequence words, sentences, and paragraphs in a random, helter-skelter fashion. Instead, they structure their texts in particular ways that are influenced by the purposes they want the language to accomplish. In doing so, they draw on their language of the linguistic conventions of various genres.

Genres consist of organized linguistic schemes.

The organization of genres is related to how language is used for social processes.

The Textural Patterns of Written Texts

Let's consider again the storybook *The Owl and the Woodpecker* and the information book *Squirrels* that were discussed in Chapter 1. Each of these texts represents a typical example of its respective genre, that is, everyone would agree that *The Owl and the Woodpecker* is a storybook and that *Squirrels* is an information book. We have already observed (in Chapter 1) that each possesses different linguistic patterns, *textural* differences. That is, the storybook has linguistic patterns (identity chains) to refer to the *same* characters or objects (woodpecker, owl, or woodpecker's tree, for example) in the text, whereas the information book includes patterns (coclassification chains) in which the same classes of objects or animals (in our case, squirrels) are referred to in   the

Wildsmith (1971, 1974)

Hasan (1985a)

Texture involves meaning relations.

text. Other aspects of texture were mentioned—the use of the past tense in the story versus the present tense in *Squirrels*, and the fact that this information book contains many more descriptive constructions than does the story.

If we looked at these two texts from these two genres, and at other texts that are typical examples of the genres, we would probably notice even more linguistic differences. You were surely aware of these linguistic differences in storybook and information books even before you read this textbook, but you probably have never examined them in any explicit way. This chapter points out other linguistic patterns of a range of written genres—patterns that you already know about in a tacit or subconscious way—to render them more explicit and make you more aware of the nature of written genres. This awareness enables teachers to know how to select books of various genres for children to read in the classroom and to know how to respond to children as they attempt to read and write in various genres.

The Global Structure of Written Texts

Besides textural differences, texts of written genres are structured in a more global way; they are organized into big "chunks," which vary for different genres. Each genre has a shape, or global structure, of its own. For example, stories are typically formed into elements according to what many researchers call a *story grammar*. Although researchers have described and labeled the components of these global frameworks in different ways, the schemes are very similar. We use the framework (and terminology) developed by the linguist Ruqaiya Hasan, who has studied the language of bedtime stories in depth.

According to Hasan's scheme, there are chunks or elements that every story must have to be considered a story, and there are optional elements that a particular story may or may not include. The elements she calls the Initiating Event, Sequent Event, and Final Event are the necessary (or obligatory) elements in this framework, and the Placement, Finale, and Moral are optional. Remember, these elements are not just one sentence or event but big chunks of text that may include many events or sentences. These elements are described and illustrated by the storybook *The Owl and the Woodpecker* (Table 6.1). See if you can recognize them in other storybooks that you know.

Storybooks have to do with interpersonal understandings, how characters' goals interrelate and how their plans to achieve these goals mesh or clash. This genre shapes its message so that inferences about human beliefs, purposes, or motives can be expressed. In contrast, the information book genre does not involve specific characters and their goals, personal motives for action, and the like. As a result, just as a different texture exists, the information book genre has a different global structure or a different "grammar." We use Pappas's scheme to describe this genre which, like Hasan's story framework, has both necessary global chunks, or elements, that every information book has to include and optional elements that particular information books may or may not express. *Squirrels* is used to illustrate the global elements in this genre. (See Table 6.2. Refer also to Figure 1.5 in Chapter 1.)

These two generic schemes, for both storybooks and information books, are provided to illustrate how two genres are organized and how they differ with respect to their global patterns. These schemes also have other organizational features. For example, each generic text structure has rules for how the global elements are ordered, specifically whether elements have a fixed or flexible order. For example, the Moral story element, if included, must always follow the Final Event of the story. However, if the story also includes the Finale global element, the Moral element can come either before or after the Finale. The Placement (if included), the Initiating Event, the Sequent Event, and the Final Event have a fixed order, following one another as listed in Table 6.1.

The generic scheme for information books also has fixed and variable aspects of order. The Topic Presentation is always the first element, but the order of the next three elements shown in Table 6.2—Description of Attributes, Characteristic Events,

Genres are also organized in global ways.

Pappas (1991)

Hasan (1984, 1985b, 1996)

Storybook genre

Hasan (1984, 1996)

Bruce (1980, 1984)

Information book genre

Pappas (1986, 1987, 1988, in press)

Part of a genre's organization is the order of its elements.

The order of elements can be fixed or variable.

Table 6.1 GLOBAL ELEMENTS IN THE OWL AND THE WOODPECKER

Description of the Global Elements	Examples from *The Owl and the Woodpecker*
Placement—an author may introduce or "place" characters on "stage" in the story, provide time or locale information, relate what characters habitually do, talk about certain attributes of characters, and so on (optional).	"Once upon a time" information, as well as something about the locale ("in a forest, far away") and about the habitual behavior of the woodpecker character ("lived in a tree in which he slept all night and worked all day") are included.
Initiating Event—the conflict or problem of the story emerges.	The owl, who has sleeping and working habits that are the opposite of those of the woodpecker, moves into a nearby tree. The woodpecker's daily tapping keeps the owl awake and he becomes so bad tempered that something has to be done.
Sequent Event—a recount of characters' attempts to resolve the problem or conflict. *Final Event*—resolution of the problem or conflict.	Other animals in the forest have a meeting and decide that the owl has to leave, because the woodpecker was there first. One night, they try to push down his tree while the owl is out hunting, with no success.
Finale—a restoration of the habitual or normal state of affairs (optional).	The tree is blown down by a terrible storm. Fortunately, however, the owl, who had been sound asleep and was not aware that he was in danger, is saved by the woodpecker's tapping, and the owl and the woodpecker remain "good friends all the rest of their lives."
Moral—a moral statement or claim is made (optional).	Not realized in this book. Can you think of a story in which it is included?

Table 6.2 GLOBAL ELEMENTS IN SQUIRRELS

Description of the Global Elements	Examples from *Squirrels*
Topic Presentation—the topic of the text is presented or introduced.	The topic of squirrels is presented.
Description of Attributes—a description of the attributes of the class or topic the book is about.	That squirrels are furry, have long bushy tails, strong back legs, two big front teeth, and so on are described.
Characteristic Events—characteristic or habitual or typical process/events are expressed.	How squirrels live and build homes, use their tails, have babies, what they eat, and so on are explained.
Category Comparison—compares or discusses different members of the class or topic that a book is about. (common, but optional)	Not realized in this book. See *The Squirrel* by Lane (1981) for a book on squirrels in which it is realized—where red and gray squirrels are compared.
Final Summary—summary statements are made about the information covered in a book.	Summarizes that if you walk in the woods, you might see squirrels jumping and frolicking on trees or hiding a store of nuts.
Afterword—extra information about the topic is included. (optional)	Not realized in this book. See *Tunnels* by Gibbons (1984) for an example of this element—where extra specific details about tunnels are provided.

and Category Comparison—can vary. The Final Summary always follows all of these, and the Afterword (if included) always ends the book.

Another characteristic of generic schemes is whether certain elements can be discrete, separate chunks or interspersed in other elements. Both of the generic schemes we have discussed have such features. The story scheme allows for the possibility that in certain stories Placement information can be interspersed in the Initiating Event. The

Certain elements of a generic scheme can be discrete or interspersed.

information book generic scheme permits even more interspersion. The Topic Presentation can be interspersed in any one of the three elements—Description of Attributes, Characteristic Events, or Category Comparison—and any of these three can be interspersed in each other.

You already know about this structure of storybooks and information books, although the organization of these two written genres and many others may seem complicated when it is described in this explicit way. Nevertheless, these generic text structures provide a sense of stability. Knowledge of these schemes makes texts more predictable and comprehensible to readers. Reading a range of written genres to children and providing many opportunities for children themselves to read texts of various genres helps them internalize knowledge of the shape, rhythm, and flow of the various registers, or genres, of written language. Moreover, experiences with various genres provide children with a wide range of models to draw on in their own writing. Thus, children are now able to extend their communicative competence and expertise as semioticians to include meaning making in written language.

Although generic schemes have structure, order, and specificity, they also allow for the creation of new texts that show variation and novelty. We have noted how creativity in particular texts can occur through the inclusion of certain optional elements, changes in their order, or interspersion of some elements in others. The potential for creativity in written texts is even greater, however. Creativity in written texts can be best understood and appreciated by examining texts from other written genres and by developing a general model of genres.

A General Model of Written Genres

We have already mentioned that the storybook *The Owl and the Woodpecker* and the information book *Squirrels* are typical texts from their respective genres. In reading or reviewing them, no one would disagree that the former is a storybook and the latter an information book. However, many texts are not so clear-cut or typical. There are many "fuzzy," or atypical, texts. Let's consider two texts—*Mouse* by Sara Bonnett Stein and *Panda* by Susan Bonners—to illustrate the notion of "fuzziness." Figure 6.1 shows the first part of each text.

Learning about various generic schemes helps readers and writers.

Calkins (1991, 1994); Fletcher (1993); Smith (1988, 1997)

Newkirk (1989); Pappas (1993a, 1993b, in press)

**The Owl and the Woodpecker *and*
Squirrels *are typical examples of their genres.**

Some texts are "fuzzy" examples of genres.

Stein (1985); Bonners (1978)

Figure 6.1

Mouse	
P? TP?	A mouse lives in a dark closet where the family never sees her.
CE?	She makes her nest of soft things she finds in the closet–white stuffing, blue wool, red cloth.
	The outside of the nest is round, with a hole just big enough for a mouse to get through.
	The inside of the nest is hollow, just the right size for the mouse and her babies.
	When the nest is finished, the mouse is ready to have her babies. Her belly tightens.
IE?	She pushes out a wet, pink baby in a thin wrapper.

Panda	
P?TP?	In a mountain forest of southwestern China, a giant panda sits in a birch tree.
DA/CE?	Snowflakes fall on her black and white fur, but she does not look for shelter.
	She has lived in snow most of her life.
IE?	Early one autumn, she found a den in a rocky mountainside. There she made a nest out of broken bamboo stalks. While frosty winds blew through the forest, she gave birth to her cub.

KEY
From the Storybook Genre:
Global Elements P—Placement
                 IE—Initiating Event
From the Information Book Genre:
Global Elements TP—Topic Presentation
                 DA—Description of Attributes
                 CE—Characteristic Events

As you review the texts in Figure 6.1, consider whether these texts are information books or storybooks. To the left of the two excerpts are the abbreviations of possible global elements from the two genres. (See the key at the bottom of Figure 6.1.) The dotted lines indicate pages in the books. First, approach each as an example of the storybook genre. The first four pages of *Mouse* seem like a Placement. A mouse is introduced, and the actions of the mouse—where she lives and how she makes her nest—could be considered habitual behavior. The last page of the excerpt could be seen as the beginning of the Initiating Event in which a baby is born. A similar case can be made for *Panda*. A sort of Placement can be established for the first three pages of the excerpt, in which a panda is introduced and habitual information is included. The Initiating Event also begins with the birth of an offspring. Moreover, in each text, identity chains for the mouse and panda can be established, which is a textural feature of the storybook genre.

Now consider each text as an example of the information book genre. The first page of each book seems to be a Topic Presentation, each presenting the topic, mouse and panda, respectively. The second page begins the second global element. In *Mouse* this is the Characteristic Event, whereas in *Panda* it could be either Description of Attributes with information from the Characteristic Event in it or the other way around. Although it seems that identity chains are involved in each, neither book has the theme of "human" conflict that characterizes stories. However, *Mouse* is in the present tense, a textural feature of the information book genre, and *Panda* begins with the present tense but switches to the past tense.

Thus, these are "fuzzy" or atypical texts because they do not fit clearly in either genre. They seem to have some features of each genre; thus, they lie where the boundaries of these genres overlap. To help you visualize this overlap, Figure 6.2 uses genre "curves" or "mountains" to both depict the typical texts of each genre (*The Owl and the Woodpecker* and *Squirrels*) and the more atypical or fuzzy texts (*Mouse* and *Panda*).

Mouse and **Panda** *include features from the storybook and information book genres.*

The fact that a text is atypical does not mean that it is necessarily less coherent or comprehensible or of low quality. It is because authors have knowledge of the structure and features of various genres that they are able to select and write a text that is creative, novel, and interesting. Thus, we need a model of genres that can deal with such creativity.

An atypical text can be coherent, comprehensible, and of high quality.

Genres do not have absolute boundaries, as Figure 6.2 shows. Real texts are not the result of all-or-nothing formulas. Instead, some texts are typical of particular genres; they lie in the shaded part of the genre mountains—at the "peaks"—and are very distinctively different from typical texts of other genres. Other texts reflect degrees of atypicality and are less distinctive; they lie on the nonshaded "slopes" or "valleys" of the genre mountains, or where the genre mountains overlap and intersect.

Typical texts are found in the "peaks" of genre mountains.

Consequently, our model of genres has to depict these characteristics of texts that are a matter of degree. We cannot go into every type of text in this chapter, but let's try to extend Figure 6.2 to consider other genres. First, how should we treat the genres of poetry and how-to manuals? We add these genres to the storybook and information book genres by placing them in multidimensional space. Figure 6.3 depicts this by adding two new genre mountains.

Atypical texts are found in the "slopes" or "valleys" of genre mountains.

Figure 6.2

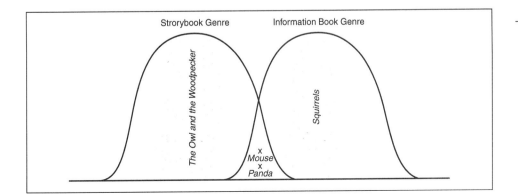

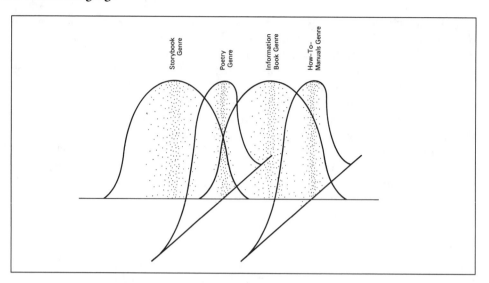

Siebert (1988)

Figure 6.3

Now, let's consider two atypical texts that show overlap between genres. The first is the book *Mojave* by Diane Siebert (1988). The first two pages of this book about the Mojave Desert—an area that covers thousands of square miles of southern California, southern Nevada, and small portions of Utah and Arizona—are reprinted here.

Mojave

> *I am the desert.*
> *I am free.*
> *Come walk the sweeping face of me.*
>
> *Through canyon eyes of sandstone red*
> *I see the hawk, his wings outspread;*
> *He sunward soars to block the light*
> *And casts the shadow of his flight*
> *Upon my vast and ancient face,*
> *Whose deep arroyos boldly trace*
> *The paths where sudden waters run—*
> *Long streams of tears dried by the sun.*
>
> *I feel the windstorm's violent thrust;*
> *I feel the sting of sand and dust*
> *As bit by bit, and year by year,*
> *New features on my face appear.*

Mojave includes features from the information book, poetry, and personal narrative genres.

The book goes on by talking about mountain ranges (that "crease my face"), lakes, the animal jacks, dust "devils" (winds or storms), and so forth. Can you see how this text is atypical? In what ways is it fuzzy? Is it like an information book because it provides information about the Mojave Desert, the creatures that live there, the vegetation, the sand and sun, and how the desert changes with the seasons. However, this information is expressed by lyrical prose and a poetic register. Thus, there is an overlap of information book and poetry features. We could even make the case that *Mojave* also has some features of yet another genre, that of the personal narrative (a genre not included in Figure 6.3). That is, the message seems also to be communicated through the experiences of an "I"—in this case, the "I" being the desert.

Haldane (1984)

Another book, *The See-Through Zoo: How Glass Animals Are Made* by Suzanne Haldane, also shows fuzziness. Unlike excerpts from the other books, the excerpts that follow start with page eight, then skip to other parts of the book.

The See-Through Zoo: How Glass Animals are Made

Glass is made from materials that could be found in any backyard: sand, soda, ash, and lime. Yet from these familiar ingredients, objects both ordinary and unique have been fashioned for many thousands of years. (p. 8)

In a large open area, several paces from where the craftsmen work, the furnace is fired up to the melting temperature of 2600°F—more than ten times the heat needed to boil water.

At night, while the glassmakers are home sleeping, the batch is cooked. During the ten to twelve hours it takes to fuse—melt and blend—the ingredients, the intense heat must be kept constant, or the furnace will be damaged and the glass ruined....

Too hot ever to touch, the molten glass, now referred to as "metal," is ready to be worked.

Two people are needed to turn metal into animals. One is the teacher, the other the pupil.

The master craftsman is called the gaffer, from an old English word meaning grandfather.

He has had years of experience and familiarity with glass. Guided only by his imagination, he pulls and pushes the glass into the shapes of more than fifty different animals, using a variety of tools.

His helper, called a gatherer because he collects or gathers the glass, assists and learns from the master. (p. 15)

The two artisans must work fast. They are always racing against time, because glass cools rapidly, and below a certain temperature it can no longer be shaped.

Tiny animals may be pulled and pinched into shape in a matter of seconds. But larger animals, especially those composed of several pieces of metal, must be reheated before the addition of each piece, because hot glass will only stick to hot glass.... (p. 18)

An animal starts as a ball of molten glass. The gaffer begins most animals at either the head or tail. Cats, horses, and unicorns begin at the head; dolphins, sharks, and seals at the tail.

When making an elephant, however, the gaffer begins with the body.... (p. 19)

These excerpts illustrate that the book is like an information book in that it provides an account of what glass is made of, how it is made, and so forth. It also includes features of a how-to manual in that it describes the step-by-step work of a master glassmaker (the gaffer) and his assistant (the gatherer) in fashioning glass animals in general and a glass elephant specifically. Thus, this text seems also to overlap genres.

The See-Through Zoo includes features from the information book and how-to manual genres.

Authors create typical texts of particular genres, as well as atypical texts that reflect overlapping genres. Our model must therefore have a multidimensional perspective to explain both the typicality *and* the overlap, or atypicality, of texts in a range of genres.

Discussions of genres are frequently simplified by depicting them as two large all-or-nothing categories, such as fiction and nonfiction or narrative and expository. Unfortunately, many texts do not fit easily into these categories. Although most fiction is narrative, a personal narrative is not fiction. What about biography? Or letters? Or newspaper stories? They are narrative, but they are nonfiction. Two major categories or general types of genres cannot account for the complexity and the range of the genres present in our culture.

Classifying all texts into two large genres is too simplistic.

When we consider the subgenres, it is clear that no two-category model will work. Are mysteries, fantasies, westerns, science fiction, or historical fiction part of the storybook genre or genres on their own? What is the distinction between biographies and historical fiction? How do they overlap? How do recipes and reports of science experiments overlap with information books and how-to manuals? How do epics, sonnets, and odes relate? Where should letters—personal and business letters, thank-you notes, and invitations—fit? Figure 6.4 tries to depict such a model of genres. (Activity 1 at the end of the chapter can help you explore more about the multidimensional, overlapping aspects of written genres.)

See Activity 1

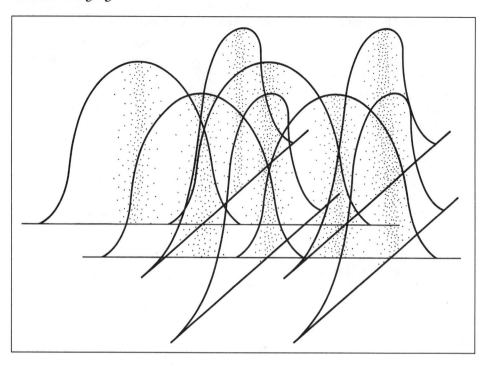

Figure 6.4

The Ideology of Texts/Genres: Examining The "Element" of Description in Different Genres

In Chapter 1 (and the Introduction), we talked how ideologies—our values, biases, and perspectives—are embedded in the texts that we read and write. Sometimes ideology is very apparent and easy to spot; sometimes it is very subtle and hard to detect. And it isn't necessary to consider ideology in an explicit way in every texts that students read or write. Nevertheless, we want to give you some more examples of how ideology is expressed so that you can be alert to consider it when it might be relevant to do so.

We extend this discussion by examining how the "element" of description is realized in different kinds of genres. This exploration also gives us another way to show both the conventionality and the complexity of linguistic patterns in written language. (This section also provides background to Teaching Grammar in Context* in Chapter 7.)

We also introduce a new term—*lexicogrammar*—which emphasizes several ideas. First, when we talk about *grammar* we are talking about patterns or constructions at the text (and genre) level. Too frequently, "formal grammar" has meant solely focusing on parts of speech or types of sentences, isolated from the context of reading and writing texts. Second, grammatical constructions are not concerned with form alone; they consist of certain vocabulary, or "*lexis.*" Certain kinds of vocabulary or content words are related to different kinds of texts or genres. Thus, the use of "lexicogrammar" better explains how texts do what they do in the world. Finally, it is our attention on these lexicogrammatical patterns expressed in texts and genres that enables us to understand how ideology or perspective might manifest itself.

Description is found in many genres. It is especially found in factual genres, which we will examine first, because the major purpose of this broad class is to explore the world around us, focusing on what things are like or how things are done. Then we will see how it occurs in fiction.

Description in Factual Genres

Certain types of lexicogrammatical patterns are prevalent in factual texts. For example, refer again to Figure 1.5 in Chapter 1 that shows the beginning of the typical infor-

All texts express ideology—values, biases, points of view, and power in relation to others.

Eggins (1994); Fairclough (1989, 1992); Lemke (1995); Luke (1988); Nodelman (1996); Stephens (1992)

'Lexicogrammar' is a term that incorporates the content or vocabulary expressed by linguistic patterns of texts/genres.

mation book *Squirrels*. You will note that there is a density of constructions that include relational processes, or verbs. These are attributive processes ("he *looks* happy and mischievous"); identifying processes ("he *is* a furry small animal . . ."); and possessive processes ("he *seems to have* little socks on his feet"). We have mentioned other kinds of lexicogrammatical patterns in *Squirrels*: the fact that these processes are expressed as "timeless" verbs in simple present tense; and the idea that a class of an animal, namely, squirrels, is included (as opposed a particular woodpecker or owl, which we saw in *The Owl and the Woodpecker*). Other typical information books include similar features. For example, some of the early sentences of *The Ladybug* are "The ladybug *is* an insect./Lady bugs *are* often red with black spots./Like all insects, the ladybug *has* six legs." And, the first sentence of *Tunnels* is: "Most tunnels *are* long holes dug underground." Thus, these three features of lexicogrammatical structure (constructions that include relational processes, present-tense verbs, and class or generic nouns) are characteristic in the description in the information book genre.

So far we have illustrated descriptive constructions that include relational processes and depicted *what things are like*. However, description can also expressed by action verbs or processes. For example, in the book *Squirrels*, the last sentence in Figure 1.5 (in Chapter 1)—"Squirrels live in trees."—begins the beginning of the global element Characteristic Events (see Table 6.2). Other characteristic actions or behavior—they *build* homes, *scamper* up and down trees, *leap* through the air, *gather* nuts and acorns, and so forth—all describe *how things are done*. In *How Do Bees Make Honey?* similar constructions are found: "Honeybees *live* together in big groups called colonies.", "[Some honeybees] *build* honeycomb nests out of wax." When the things being described are nonliving things, such as in *Tunnels*, the processes or verbs in the lexicogrammatical constructions functions as actions of use (e.g., "People *dig* tunnels . . .").

Thus, these are some of the major lexicogrammatical structures that are realize description in the information book genre. They are also predominant in description found in many adult factual reports and scientific genres.

The factual genre of advertisements also realizes description to a great extent. In an advertisement of a necklace, for example, a company first names the product—THE CLASSIC HEART—and then provides many lexiogrammatical constructions of description: "Timeless symbol of love.", "Tender and eternal.", "Original yet enduring.", "Definitely romantic." Note that many of these sentences "break" the common "rule" where a sentence *must* have a subject and verb. Yet all of them work as description. Most of the sentences in the advertisement represent relational processes, despite the fact that these key verbs are absent and they and other language must be understood. For example, in the first sentence above, an identifying process is involved ([the classic heart *is* the] "timeless symbol of love") and the next one "has" an attributive process ([the classic heart *is*] "tender and eternal").

Thus, the lexicogrammatical structures here are both similar to and different from the ones in the informational book texts. We have already discussed in Chapter 1 about the possible ideological implications of some of the wordings in *Squirrels*, namely, the use of "happy and mischievous" and having "little socks on his feet," as well as the predominance of singular masculine pronouns for refer to squirrel (instead of *it* or *its*). Ideological issues are much more blatant in the advertisement. The elliptical structures serve to emphasize the emotionally laden vocabulary, thereby enticing readers of the ad to become customers of the product.

What if someone had bought such a heart and then had it stolen? How different the descriptive words would be if a description of it was needed for an insurance or police report (two other factual genres). Here the owner would have used relational constructions, but he or she would have used alternative wordings to describe the physical features of the heart—shape, size, color, and so forth. Thus, the owner would not have used "tender and eternal," "original yet enduring," and "definitely romantic"!

Thus, when descriptions are realized in various factual genres, they are similar but different. See also how the description was accomplished in the fuzzy or atypical texts in this chapter (e.g., how the Mojave Desert or the construction of glass animals was

Relational processes or verbs are: *attributive processes; identifying processes; and possessive processes.*

Eggins (1994); Halliday (1985); Pappas & Pettegrew (1998)

First Discovery Books (1991)

Many descriptive constructions depict what things are like.

Many descriptive constructions depict how things are done.

Claybourne (1994)

Gibbons (1984)

Halliday & Martin (1993)

Description in advertisements is frequently expressed through short sentences that "assume" relational processes.

described). Moreover, note how very different ideology or values may be present in the language used in these texts and other examples provided in this section.

Description in Fictional Genres

Description occurs in fictional texts as well, but because the major aim of these genres is to entertain or amuse readers, the lexicogrammatical patterns are realized differently. Characters and their motivations and feelings or reactions influence action and drive the plot. In fiction, description depicts the places that characters go, the objects they come across, or the other characters they meet. These descriptions are woven in the text along with lexicogrammatical constructions that include a different type of verbs called *mental* processes. There are three classes of mental-process verbs: *cognition* (verbs of thinking, knowing, understanding), *affection* (verbs of liking, fearing, hating), and *perception* (verbs of seeing, hearing). For example, there is a mental process in sentence 3 in Figure 1.4 in Chapter 1—"Owl . . . *liked* to work all night and sleep all day." That is, the description of how things were done (note the past tense) is connected to the character's verb of affection towards this characteristic behavior.

In the beginning of storybook, *Amelia's Road*, it is stated that Amelia hated roads. They are described via an attributive relational process, then Amelia's mental reactions to them are included: "*Los caminos*, the roads, were long and cheerless. They never went where you *wanted* them to go."

In the fictional novel *Child of the Owl*, the character Casey is sent to Chinatown to live with her grandmother, Paw-Paw. Although her parents had been raised in Chinatown, this was Casey's first time. Note again how Casey's mental responses are interwoven with the description of Chinatown.

> I didn't know what to make of the buildings . . . They were mostly three- or four-story stone buildings but some had fancy balconies, and others had decorations on them like curved tile roofs . . . —one building had bright yellow balconies decorated with shiny, glazed purple dolphins—and there was a jumble of neon signs, dark now in the daytime, jammed together. Most of the buildings, though, had some color to them— bright reds and rich golds with some green thrown in.
>
> But it was the people there that got me. I don't think I'd ever seen so many Chinese in my life before this.

The first sentence includes two mental processes of cognition ("didn't know" and "make of" [think]). Then the description is realized by past-tense constructions having several relational processes (e.g., "they *were*. . .three- or four-story stone buildings"; "one building *had* bright yellow balconies"). In the last two sentences of the excerpt, Casey's reactions to the Chinese people in Chinatown is expressed through all three types of mental processes—affection ("*got* me"); cognition ("don't *think*"); and perception ("I'd *seen*").

Thus, the lexicogrammatical patterns in each of the fictional examples of fictional description are unlike those found in factual genres. Description in fictional genres generally uses the past tense (except in dialogue); it deals with particular people, places, and objects. Description is steeped in human mental reactions. As a result, the human values are also more apparent. For example, we know how Amelia and Casey feel about the places they find themselves.

Summary

Written genres are *products* of our culture, but these products are the result of various social *processes* that have certain purposes or goals. Genres are organized to provide both *stability* (they have certain fairly predictable elements and an accepted sequence, and so forth) and *change* (although they are somewhat "fixed," they reflect new versions of structure and sequence elements in novel and creative ways). *Typical texts* of a particular genre reflect that genre as a whole; they are exemplars for which consensus can be found. However, many *atypical* texts exist as well; they

---

Sidenotes:

Mental *processes are verbs of cognition, affection, and perception.*

Eggins (1994); Halliday (1985); Pappas & Pettegrew (1998)

Altman (1993)

Yep (1977)

Description in fictional texts/genres is frequently interwoven with human mental reactions and responses.

Genres are products of social processes.

are borderline cases or instances of subgenres that contain features of one or more other genres.

Because of the complexity of written genres, their lexicogrammatical structures cannot be taught in direct, formal ways; otherwise, children will be misled and given only part of the story. They will miss out and never understand the creativity, limitless options, or potential of language. However, if teachers have an awareness of the various conventions of a range of written genres, they can support and foster children's processes of reading and writing them. They can provide many examples of both typical and atypical texts, point out and compare their elements and features, and facilitate children's comprehension and composition of texts of a variety of genres. They can help children learn to look how values are being expressed in books they read and write. (See Teaching Grammar in Context* in Chapter 7 for some of the possibilities; see also Activity 2 for ways to examine ideology of texts.)

The Reading and Writing Processes

In Chapter 1 we discussed the involvement of the reader-writer contract in processing or using written texts. It was emphasized that both reading and writing are meaning-making process—that is, both readers and writers bring meaning (based on their schemas) to texts. In this chapter, we extend and expand on these important ideas by looking further into each side of the reader-writer contract, and then we reconsider the connections between them.

The Reading Process

Reading is a constructive, problem-solving process. Readers pose problems or ask questions about the text. Inherent in this process is *prediction*, a set of reader expectations. Readers predict what print means—reading consists of informed guesses. They confirm their predictions or they resolve or answer the problems they pose, or they disconfirm their initial predictions and have to set new hypotheses or consider new questions or problems about the meaning of the text. In this process, readers understand or partially comprehend the text.

Goodman (1967, 1997); Hiebert (1991); Smith (1988, 1997)

Using a variety of strategies, readers use the linguistic clues or "cues" provided by the author. The type of genre the author has chosen is a particular source of these clues. Readers employ these clues to build or construct their own useful, personal world of the text. They structure their own knowledge or schema regarding that text. Thus, from the reader's point of view meaning is not in the text itself but arises during the interaction—or what many researchers call the *transaction*—between the written words of the text and the reader. Let's try to get an idea of this transaction by considering the following passage about Rocky and then examining some important issues regarding it.

Goodman & Burke (1985)

Cazden (1992); de Beaugrande (1980); Nystrand (1986, 1987); Nystrand & Wiemelt (1991); Pappas & Pettegrew (1998)

Transaction

Lytle & Botel (1988); Rosenblatt (1978, 1989); Karolides (1992, 1997); Pappas & Barry (1997); Weaver (1988)

Anderson, Reynolds, Shallert, & Goetz (1977)

> Rocky slowly got up from the mat, planning his escape. He hesitated a moment and thought. Things were not going well. What bothered him most was being held, especially since the charge against him had been weak. He considered his present situation. The lock that held him was strong but he thought he could break it. He knew, however, that his timing would have to be perfect. Rocky was aware that it was because of his early roughness that he had been penalized so severely—much too severely from his point of view. The situation was becoming frustrating; the pressure had been grinding on him for too long. He was being ridden unmercifully. Rocky was getting angry now. He felt he was ready to make his move. He knew that his success or failure would depend on what he did in the next few seconds.

Well, who is Rocky? Most readers answer "a wrestler" or "a prisoner" (or "a convict"). How did you respond? This passage has been used in research studies in which some subjects were asked, before reading, to take the perspective that Rocky is a wrestler, and some, that Rocky is a prisoner. After the reading, they were asked to answer questions about the passage. The subjects answered the same questions differently,

Carey, Harste, & Smith (1981)

Different readers have different interpretations of "Rocky."

Cazden (1992); Hiebert (1991); Spiro (1980); Willinsky (1990)

Readers use prior knowledge to understand texts.

Smith (1982a, 1997); Weaver (1988)

The comprehension of texts is a relative phenomenon.

Rosenblatt (1978, 1989)

The characteristics of a text affect readers' interpretations of that text.

Personal and immediate situational factors affect readers' interpretations of texts.

depending on the perspective. In another study, in which the subjects were not asked to take a particular perspective, the researchers got similar findings. Subjects again responded differently to the same questions. In this study the subjects were college students majoring in either physical education or sociology. What is interesting about these findings is that the subjects' answers corresponded to their major. Without being asked to do so, most of the physical education majors took the perspective that Rocky was a wrestler, whereas the sociology students most frequently viewed Rocky as a prisoner.

How can we account for these different reader responses? These readers read the same text—the same words—so the meaning cannot be said to reside totally in the text. Instead, individual readers had different transactions with the text. Some readers with whom we have shared this passage have also reported that Rocky was a horse or a dog. We have even gotten the answer "a kindergartner" from a teacher in a recent workshop with early elementary teachers. In this setting, we were discussing and evaluating how much the bits of language—letters, sounds, words, etc.—were emphasized in the reading lessons in the basal readers used in their schools. Take a kindergartner's point of view and read the passage again.

This Rocky passage was constructed by researchers for a particular experiment. If it were found in any other context, we would probably not consider it complete. It seems to be the beginning of a story in which an author may possibly include many flashbacks to fill in important circumstances or pertinent events in Rocky's life. If it is a story, the subgenre is unclear from the passage as it stands; maybe it's a mystery.

Nevertheless, by using this passage, several important points can be made about the reading process. First, readers use prior knowledge or experience about the world and language to construct meaning. In other words, they construct meaning by bringing meaning *to* the text. Notice that individual words from the passage—*mat, escape, charge, lock,* and so forth—have different meanings depending on whether the perspective of a wrestler or prisoner (or horse, dog, or kindergartner) is taken. The same is the case for the individual sentences. That is, different readers were concerned with different predictions and different questions and answers before, during, and after reading the Rocky passage. This means that, although people might *think* that reading proceeds in a bottom-up or part-to-whole (from letters to words to sentences, etc.) process, the opposite is the case. Because reading is more of a top-down, whole-to-part process, comprehension is a relative—not an absolute, all-or-nothing—phenomenon. In other words, more than one interpretation is possible in transactions with texts.

Second, although varied responses are possible for a particular text, it is not the case that everything goes. No one reading the Rocky passage would say that Rocky is a beautician or a florist. The language and organization of the text are more like a "blueprint." The text offers openness, but it also provides control or constraints. We know, for example, that the Rocky passage is not the beginning of a text that belongs to the poetry, information book, or how-to manual genres.

Third, readers' transactions and interpretations are influenced by factors of social context, including both the background of the reader—cultural, economic, gender, personal, etc.—and the actual situation in which the reading occurs. Remember that the researchers asked the subjects in the study to take on different roles for Rocky. Remember that the sociology and the physical education majors responded to the task without having been asked to take a specific perspective. What personal and situational factors were affecting the teacher's response to the Rocky passage?

These three characteristics, or influences on readers' responses, are summarized in Figure 6.5. A reader's transactions with text are the result of (1) the characteristics of the reader (knowledge, attitudes, skills, values, etc.), (2) characteristics of the text (the genre, text structure, the content or topic, etc.), and (3) the characteristics of the social context (the immediate situational context—perhaps a certain context in a certain classroom—*and* the broader sociocultural contexts such as school, home, neighborhood, town/city, state, region, nation, and culture).

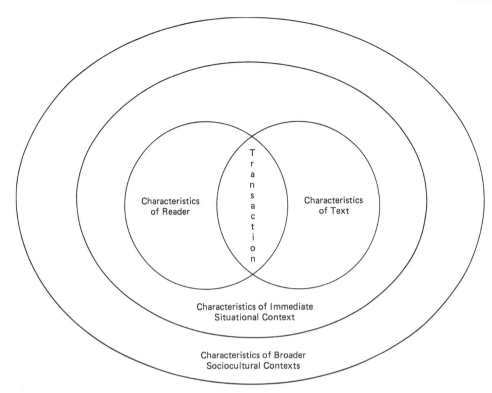

Figure 6.5

*READING AS A SOCIAL READER-
TEXT TRANSACTION*

The term *transaction* thus emphasizes the active meaning-making flavor of the reading process, or how readers experience or "evoke" the text. When children learn to read or use written texts across the curriculum, they acquire the conventions or genres of particular disciplines, the different "ways of knowing," and the various domain-specific rules of evidence for history, science, math, art, and so forth. At the same time, they develop some general approaches to reading across the curriculum. This range of transactions with text is outlined in Table 6.3.

These transactions reflect the ways in which children engage with and respond to texts before, during, and after reading. One type of transaction is the *emotional, experiential, and autobiographical* responses of readers—what stands out (or is salient) for them when they read particular texts. *Connective* transactions have to do with readers' linking prior knowledge of experiences and texts with ideas in texts and fitting these new ideas within their present schemas of various topics or experiences. *Descriptive and analytic* transactions are those in which features of texts are noted and authors' actual structures or wordings—their specific linguistic choices—are examined. *Interpretive and elaborative* transactions deal with the sense-making, problem-solving strategies readers employ to predict, consider, infer, explain, ponder, and question ideas to decide what texts mean for them. *Evaluative* transactions are considerations of appropriateness regarding texts, whereby readers assess authors' ideas and arguments and their effectiveness in relating or expressing their messages to decide whether particular texts are "good" or not or whether certain ideologies or values are presented. Finally, *self-reflective* transactions involve readers' noting and monitoring their own processes of reading.

Thus, in reviewing Table 6.3, you will note that these types of transactions involve a range of reader experiences and questions. These questions, which can be at an awareness level that is tacit or subconscious or more explicit, depend on readers' purposes for reading—whether they are reading for pleasure during Sustained Silent Reading* (see Chapter 7), skimming quickly to decide if a particular book will provide useful information for a project they are doing, or reading to get answers to specific questions for a report or to participate in a discussion with peers. Thus, there is no hierarchy or order in

Reading involves social reader-text transactions.

Geertz (1983); Cope & Kalantzis (1990); Martin (1990); Mousley & Marks (1991)

A range of transactions is possible in reading.

These transaction categories have been taken from Lytle and Botel (1988).

Emotional, experiential, and autobiographical transactions

Connective transactions

Descriptive and analytic transactions

Interpretive and elaborative transactions

Evaluative transactions

Self-reflective transactions

Reader questions about a text can be tacit or explicit.

Table 6.3 *Types of Transactions with Text*

Types	Definitions	Sample Questions
Emotional, experiential, and autobiographical	Initial response, showing involvement with the text; identifying and/or empathizing. Experiencing the text by using mental/sensory imagery.	What stands out for me? How do I feel about this?
Connective	Linking text with prior experiences, with attitudes and ideas and similar texts, and other ideas within the text; making analogies.	What does this text make me think of? remind me of? How does this text fit with what I already know about this subject?
Descriptive and analytic	Noticing features of the text, e.g., choice or function of particular words, syntax, or length of sentences; functions of sentences or paragraphs in the text; characters and events; tone; type of discourse; style; use of metaphor or other figures of speech; author's arguments.	How does this text work? What's going on here? What does it say?
Interpretive and elaborative	Using reasoning or problem-solving strategies to construct meaning, resolve doubts, and make sense of text; hypothesizing; making predictions, asking questions; using evidence to confirm or disconfirm a hypothesis or prediction or to answer own questions. Explaining, exploring, making inferences; questioning and defining intentions, problems, themes, and symbols. Creating, revising, and adding to text. Pondering implications of ideas, including incongruities, discrepancies, ambiguities, and omissions.	What does this text mean? What might be added here? omitted? changed? Where can I apply these ideas? How valid/reliable is this argument?
Evaluative	Evaluating the text according to criteria related to appropriateness, effectiveness, difficulty, relevance, importance of content, or form.	Does this make sense? How [good] is this? What do I agree/disagree with?
Self-reflective	Noticing one's own processes of reading; monitoring or keeping track of current understandings of words, sentences, or discourse level meanings; noticing conflicts between text and own knowledge and beliefs.	What am I doing as I read? What questions do I have? What do I understand? not understand?

Source: Lytle & Botel, 1988.

Many transactions can occur at the same time.
Transactions are influenced by the genre involved.

these transactions. Many occur simultaneously, overlapping and affecting each other. Some predominate in reading particular genres—in reading a storybook versus a biography versus a how-to manual. Some happen because of specific contextual factors.

Summary

Reading is an active, constructive, social meaning-making process that consists of a range of transactions with texts during which readers ask questions, monitor understanding or partial understanding of particular texts, and take control of their reading processes.

Transactions such as these foster abilities to question the authority of texts and to read critically and creatively. Moreover, when children are monitoring and evaluating their reading, they reflect about their thinking. Metacognitive awareness is enhanced.

The Writing Process

The writing process is also an active, constructive, social, meaning-making enterprise. Drawing on their own schemas (which include their knowledge of the language system and the conventions of a range of written genres) writers create texts for readers to use. Because they have to decide what to include in their texts and how to express their messages, the writing process itself engenders in writers new ideas and insights, new meanings, and a deeper thinking.

There are just as many misconceptions about the writing or composing process as there are about the reading process. As a result, instruction in writing has persisted in emphasizing the mechanics of the *product* and the language *parts*—the formation of letters, spelling of words, grammatical relationships between words, etc.—rather than the *whole* of the writing *process* (that is, writers' efforts at meaning making in the creation of texts). To become writers, children need many opportunities from the beginning to write a range of meaningful, authentic texts, rather than to be kept busy with the isolated assigned exercises to "practice writing" that are found in many traditional classrooms.

Current research in writing has changed to emphasize the process of writing and to describe how real writers go about constructing texts. This does not mean that the product and parts of language are ignored. Instead the product, including the ideologies and values expressed in it, is considered *within* the process.

The writing process has been described (but sometimes in different terms) as consisting of prewriting, drafting, revising, editing, and publishing. These five activities are not to be seen as linear, discrete steps or stages of a single composing process. Instead, just as reading involves interacting, simultaneously occurring transactions or experiences, the activities or experiences of writing are also dynamic, and frequently they simultaneously affect and interact with one another. Thus, to counteract the idea that composing is a single, neat, lock-step sequence, act, or process, we consider these five activities different dimensions, aspects, or *experiences of writing* for constructing or creating texts.

Experiences of Writing

Prewriting Experiences

The prewriting experience, sometimes called the rehearsal experience, is more than just what precedes or motivates writing. Instead, prewriting includes almost anything and everything. In some sense, writers' schemas—all their experiences—can be seen as prewriting. Prewriting is generating and exploring, recalling and rehearsing, and relating and probing ideas, as well as planning, thinking, and deciding. Prewriting experiences occur when we talk and listen during discussions, presentations, written passages read aloud, brainstorming sessions, etc. They happen while we read, skim, research, observe experiments or demonstrations, and see films and videotapes. Drawing and sketching constitute prewriting experiences, especially for young children. Moreover, prewriting experiences consist of writing itself: jotting down notes or questions, sketching out patterns or connections between ideas, constructing Semantic Maps* on a topic, charting or outlining commonalities and differences in observations, and transcribing others' talk. Thus, prewriting is an ongoing experience, not some distinct period of writing. It can occur and interact simultaneously with the other writing experiences yet to be described.

Drafting Experiences

Drafting involves attempts to create or construct a whole text. Unlike the language fragments jotted down during brainstorming, discussion, or observation, drafting

Margin notes:

Cazden (1992); Lytle & Botel (1988); Willinsky (1990)

Calkins (1986, 1991, 1994); Graves (1983); Lensmire (1994); Smith (1982b, 1997); Willinsky (1990)

Current views of writing emphasize the process of writing.

Writing activities or experiences are dynamic and interactive.

Prewriting experiences (sometimes called rehearsal experiences)

Drafting experiences
The word drafting implies tentativeness.

consists of spontaneous experiences in producing connected discourse. *Drafting* is a better term than *writing* because it reflects the tentative nature of the text so constructed. It is a matter of trying to get the ideas down, frequently quickly because the mind is always faster than the pen (or the keys of the typewriter or computer). Leaving blanks when the "right" word doesn't pop immediately to mind or periodically suspending concerns about audience sometimes enables a writer to deal with this time factor. Also, during drafting, the writer tries not to worry too much about spelling and punctuation, knowing that the text produced will be reconsidered, crossed out, changed, arranged, and elaborated on. Drafting can be interrupted by prewriting experiences; it can also occur concurrently with revising experiences.

Revising Experiences

Revising experiences

Revising consists of the "re-visioning" of a writer's meanings.

Revising experiences have to do with attempts of "re-visioning." They are occasions to re-think, re-view, re-see, re-make, re-construct, and re-create the text. Revising is also an ongoing activity that can happen during prewriting (as ideas are being simultaneously generated and revised or reexamined) and during drafting (as ideas are being reconsidered so that certain wordings are chosen or selected over others).

Chapters 7 and 8 cover conferences in more detail.

Revising experiences also frequently occur subsequently to or interspersed with drafting experiences; that is, revising exists after or in between the production of sections of text. Revision is an effort to stand back to interact with the text. The writer becomes a reader when the text is reread and its meaning reconsidered to decide whether the writer's intentions or message has been expressed clearly. This is also when other readers (the teacher and peers) may interact—or transact—with the text and provide specific information and feedback about its effect on them. Readers' expectations and questions about the text may lead to more drafting as well as more prewriting experiences.

Editing Experiences

Editing experiences

Editing experiences are those that are intended to "clean up" the draft of a text so that its message is stated in the most comprehensible way, using the most appropriate language possible. Editing involves shaping the message, perhaps changing sentences, or condensing, deleting, or combining them. It can involve replacing one word with another to make it "fit" better or be more vivid. In addition, the tone or style of the text as well as spelling, punctuation, and grammar are checked during editing. Teachers and children may set up different rules or systems for editing experiences. Peer groups and self-editing procedures are frequently established. The important point about editing is that it is done in the context of children's own writing, not as a separate, isolated exercise.

Chapters 7 and 8 cover editing in more detail.

Editing concerns are addressed within the context of the child's writing.

Publishing Experiences

Publishing experiences

Publishing consists of sharing. The publishing of final drafts takes various forms in the classroom, and differs from classroom to classroom. It is different in the nature of the final product and how it is shared. With respect to the product itself, some publishing experiences require only that the children rewrite their texts in their best handwriting. Other publishing entails the teacher, a parent volunteer, or the student typing the final draft. The final draft may have a special cover, or it may be placed in a special format for display. Sometimes the publishing of final drafts ends up in classroom, school, community, or even national newspapers and magazines.

Publishing is sharing.

Because publishing has to do with sharing in general, publishing experiences are not limited to the publishing of final drafts. Thus, any of the children's writing experiences can be "published." Prewriting experiences—plans for projects, questions to be investigated, Semantic maps* on a topic from small-group brainstorming sessions—can be shared; drafts and edited copies can be responded to by peers, teacher, or the whole class. Moreover, as for final drafts, publishing experiences can occur with a range of audiences within the classroom or beyond—with other classes of the school or others in the community.

Summary

Like reading, writing is an active, constructive, social meaning-making process. It consists of a range of writing experiences in the construction of texts from a variety of genres. Writing entails ownership. Writers are given opportunities to take control of the composing process; they decide on their own topics and determine for what purposes their writings are to accomplish, through which genres their texts are to be formed, and for which audiences their messages are to be expressed. In the writing experiences described, the text as a product is a concern but the process of the construction of that text as well as thinking about that process is also emphasized.

Ownership is an important feature of the writing process.

The Reader-Writer Contract Reconsidered

Now that we have looked at reading and writing separately, it is important to consider again the relationships or connections between the two processes. In Chapter 1, we emphasized that *both* readers and writers construct texts and that in doing so they are aware of one another in the reader-writer contract. We learn to read by reading and to write by writing, but we also learn to read by writing and to write by reading. There are similarities in the reading and writing processes, *and* the processes assist each other.

See Dyson (1989); Mason (1989); Shanahan (1990); and Tierney & Shanahan (1991) for more discussions on reading-writing connections.

First, look at some of the commonalities of the two processes. Both readers and writers use their schemas—what they know about the world and language—to *compose* (i.e., *transact*, from the reader's point of view, and *construct*, from the writer's point of view) the text. Tables 6.4 to 6.6 cover the kinds of activities that readers and writers have in common before, during, and after reading and writing.

Similarities exist in the reading and writing processes.
Hammond (1990); Hyde & Bizar (1989); Nystrand (1986, 1987); Rosenblatt (1989); Smith (1982b); Tierney & Pearson (1984)

These are adapted from Butler and Turbill (1984).

As Table 6.5 shows, *before* reading and writing, readers' and writers' expectations and prior knowledge of the topic or content and how it is expressed through the language of the text affect the way they approach their tasks. Thus, prewriting experiences affect both processes. What and how transactions are realized in reading and what and how constructions are expressed in writing are determined by the readers' and writers' questions or hypotheses. Purpose is inherent in both processes.

Similarities *before* reading and writing

There are similarities in reading and writing *during* their respective acts as well, as shown in Table 6.5. As you can see in Table 6.5, during reading and writing, both readers and writers must draft, revise, and edit. In drafting, they deal directly with the text at hand. Revising occurs in rereading and rewriting, when initial purposes,

Similarities *during* reading and writing

Table 6.4 *PREWRITING*

What Readers Do *Before* Reading	What Writers Do *Before* Writing
The proficient reader brings and uses knowledge:	The proficient writer brings and uses knowledge:
• about the topic (semantic knowledge)	• about the topic (semantic knowledge)
• about the language used (syntactic knowledge)	• about the language to be used (syntactic knowledge)
• about the sound-symbol system (grapho-phonic knowledge)	• about the sound-symbol system (grapho-phonic knowledge)
The proficient reader brings certain expectations to the reading cued by:	The proficient writer brings certain expectations based on:
• previous reading experiences	• previous writing experiences
• presentation of the text	• previous reading experiences
• the purpose for the reading	• the purpose of the writing
• the audience for the reading	• the audience for the writing

Adapted from Butler & Turbill (1984).

Table 6.5 *Drafting, Revising, Editing*

What Readers Do *During* Reading	What Writer's Do *During* Writing
The proficient reader is engaged in:	The proficient writer is engaged in:

• draft reading
  –skimming and scanning
  –searching for sense
  –predicting outcomes
  –redefining and composing meaning
	• draft writing
	  –writing notes and ideas
	  –searching for a way in, or a "lead"
	  –selecting outcomes
	  –rereading
	  –revising and composing meaning

• rereading
  –rereading parts as purpose is defined, clarified, or changed
  –taking into account, where appropriate, an audience
  –discussing text and making notes
  –reading aloud to "hear" message
	• rewriting
	  –rewriting text as purpose changes or becomes defined or clearer
	  –considering readers and the intended message
	  –discussing and revising text
	  –rereading to "hear" the message

• using writer's cues
  –using punctuation to assist meaning
  –using spelling conventions to assis meaning
	• preparing for readers
	  –reading to place correct punctuation
	  –proofreading for conventional spelling
	  –deciding on appropriate presentation

Adapted from Butler & Turbill (1984).

Similarities *after* reading and writing

questions, and hypotheses are reexamined, reevaluated, changed, and clarified. Finally, editing is accomplished in reading and writing when medium-related aspects of print—spelling, punctuation, and so on are examined and corrected if necessary.

Table 6.6 depicts what readers and writers do *after* reading and writing. These events are like "publishing" experiences. Responses to and reflections about the meanings expressed in the text are made by the reader or writer. Moreover, attitudes and motivations are developed in both, which leads to more and more successful reading and writing.

This is adapted from Butler and Turbill (1984).

Besides these commonalities, reading and writing influence and aid each other. Table 6.7 outlines the kinds of things the reader and writer learn about the processes while engaged in them.

The reading and writing processes assist each other.

As Table 6.7 indicates, to read like a writer and write like a reader involves learning about three major aspects of texts. Learning the physical presentation or layout—with certain layout features frequently corresponding to specific genres—is the first aspect listed. Contracts, jokes, advertisements, menus, and recipes all look different. Where and how words are physically placed and presented has to do with a text's purpose, which a reader learns through writing and a writer through reading.

Physical presentation/layout features

Register/genre features

The second category of Table 6.7 has to do with how meaning is realized in texts and linguistic messages are organized or patterned. These are the global and textural features of various registers or genres discussed earlier.

The third category has to do with the medium aspects of print—how we learn to use spelling and punctuation to make sense of or express the wordings that constitute the text—as well as the other surface conventions of the print medium.

Surface/medium features

Table 6.6 *Publishing*

What Readers Do *After* Reading	What Writers Do *After* Writing
The proficient reader:	The proficient writer:
• responds in many ways (e.g., talking, doing, writing)	• gets the response from readers
• reflects on reading	• gives to readers
• feels success	• feels success
• wants to read again	• wants to write again

Adapted from Butler & Turbill (1984).

Table 6.7 *INFLUENCE OF READING AND WRITING ON EACH OTHER*

What We Learn *About Writing* While Involved in the Reading Process	What We Learn *About Reading* While Involved in the Writing Process
Physical Presentation/Layout	
The reader learns:	The writer learns:
• the way it is done in different sorts of print matter, in which purpose can be determined by layout, e.g., advertisements, poems, recipes, etc. • that symbols and other patterns of stress or emphasis are used to add impact and meaning to writing.	• to expect different purposes as indicated by presentation layout • to use all the other information on the page, e.g., symbols, pictures, size or boldness of print, etc.
Register/Genre	
The reader learns:	The writer learns:
• that text should follow a logical sequence so it makes sense • that different registers/genres follow different sets of conventions • that there needs to be sufficient information to allow readers to follow what is happening and make predictions about what might be coming • that there are different registers and generic forms for different purposes and different audiences • that there are beginnings, endings, sequencing of ideas, events, etc., appropriate to different registers/genres • that writers use "cohesive ties" (e.g., pronouns, to refer to specific and general persons, objects, places, etc.; conjunctions; repetitions and synonyms of lexical items; etc.) to knit text together (in different genres) so readers can follow it	• to expect text to follow a predictable sequence in order to make sense • to appreciate and notice conventions authors use in registers/genres • to predict likely outcomes based on information given in the text • to expect particular registers and generic forms appropriate to purpose and audience • to expect certain beginnings, endings, sequencing of ideas, events, etc., according to different registers/genres • to expect the range of "cohesive ties" used to knit text together in different genres
Surface/Medium Features	
The reader learns:	The writer learns:
• directional principles of print • the function of punctuation in text • spelling conventions, i.e., how words *look* in print • other print medium conventions, e.g., spacing, use of hyphens, abbreviations, paragraphs, etc.	• to expect a certain direction of lines of print • to expect punctuation to guide us in our reading • letter-sound relationships, i.e., how spoken words can be presented in print • to expect other print medium conventions to guide us in our reading

Adapted from Butler & Turbill (1984).

Summary

This chapter began by examining the nature of written genres. All genres—spoken and written—emerge in a culture as conventional responses to particular and recurrent situations because texts accomplish social action. We have emphasized written genres in this chapter, and we have discovered that genres are organized in various ways because they serve different jobs in our culture. To understand both the stability and the change inherent in genres, a general model of genres that included both typical and atypical texts was presented. Then, by examining how the element of description is realized in various factual and fictional genres, the complexity of lexicogrammatical patterns of different texts were considered, along with how these structures express various ideological stances or perspectives.

Then, the processes of using written texts were examined. First reading, and then writing, was addressed. Reader interactions with texts—transactions—were examined, and the writing experiences constituting the writing process were covered. It was emphasized that both reading and writing are constructive, meaning-making, social processes.

Finally, although writing and authors were alluded to in the section on the reading process, and reading and readers were acknowledged to be part of the writing process, the last section more explicitly examined the reader-writer contract that exists between the two processes. Both commonalities of the two processes and the ways the processes assist each other were covered. Because of this reader-writer contract, Figure 6.5 has to be expanded and modified because it showed only the reader-text transaction. Figure 6.6 adds the other side of the process of the contract, the writer-text composition.

The interaction of the reader and the writer—the reader-writer contract—happens by way of the text. There are similarities in the ways by which both readers and writers activate the semantic potential of the text. In addition, readers always learn about writing when they read as writers learn about reading when they write. When children understand that writers write on the premise of having readers and readers read on the premise of having writers, coherent communication is developed. This bridge between the reader and writer and the connections between the reading and writing processes are shown in Figure 6.6 by the arrows around the top and bottom of the text circle.

In our discussion of the reading and writing processes, speaking and listening were apparent and significant. Sharing readers' responses to a range of texts with others in whole class or small group discussions, brainstorming a particular topic with peers (as a prewriting experience), and listening to authors' published final drafts read aloud illustrate that speaking and listening are integral to the reading-writing processes in the classroom. This integration of speaking and listening (depicted in Figure 6.6 by a shaded area surrounding the reader-writer contract) with reading and writing is the essence of what is meant by an *integrated* language perspective. You may want to review how that

Speaking and listing are integrated with the reading and writing processes.

Figure 6.6

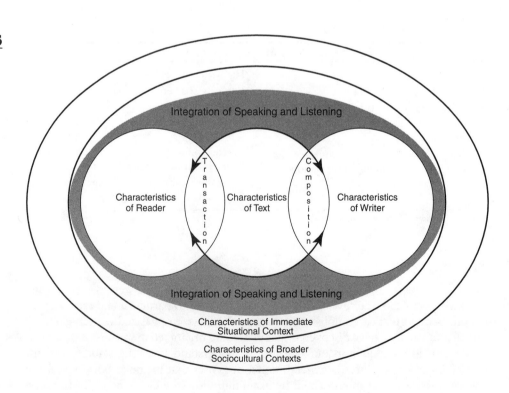

integration was realized in the classroom prototypes in Chapter 4. (Activity 3 at the end of this chapter can help you become more aware of this integration in the prototypes.)

In subsequent chapters, more examples and specific suggestions to facilitate connections between reading and writing and the integration of the language processes in the classroom are provided.

SUGGESTED ACTIVITIES

1. To help you explore more about the multidimensional, overlapping nature of written genres, collect a range of written genres with the help of classmates. Choose texts from many sources —books, magazines, and newspapers, for example—and put them in two piles, one having typical texts, the other having atypical or fuzzy texts. (This activity is similar to Activity 4 in Chapter 1, where you collected storybooks and information books. However, here you are not limiting your examination of texts to two genres.)

   See if you can identify typical texts that everyone would agree belong to a particular genre. Discuss why you think they are typical. Try to look at the language patterns—both the global chunks and the textural organizations—that seem to be involved. Now consider your atypical or fuzzy texts. How are they atypical? What is the nature of the overlap? That is, what genres seem to be involved in the language patterns?

2. To get experience in spotting possible ideologies or values in texts, examine the texts you have collected with this in mind. How are people, places, objects, or events represented? In which texts or genres is ideology easy to recognize? In which texts/genres is it difficult to find? Why? Do you and your classmates have different interpretations regarding the ideology so identified (or not)?

3. To help you make more explicit the integration of speaking, listening, reading, and writing processes in classroom contexts, review the prototypes in Chapter 4. Try to identify instances in which integration occurred. See if you can classify these experiences.

REFERENCES

Anderson, R. C., Reynolds, R. E., Schallert, D. L., & Goetz, T. E. (1977). Frameworks for comprehending discourse. *American Educational Research Journal, 14,* 367–381.

Bakhtin, M. M. (1986). *Speech genres and other late essays* (V. W. McGee, Trans.). Austin: University of Texas Press.

Bruce, B. C. (1980). Plans and social actions. In R. J. Spiro, B. C. Bruce, & W. T. Brewer (Eds.), *Theoretical issues in reading comprehension: Perspectives from cognitive psychology, linguistics, artificial intelligence, and education* (pp. 367–384). Hillsdale, NJ: Lawrence Erlbaum.

Bruce, B. C. (1984). A new point of view on children's stories. In R. C. Anderson, J. Osborn, & R. J. Tierney (Eds.), *Learning to read in American schools: Basal readers and content texts* (pp. 153–174). Hillsdale, NJ: Lawrence Erlbaum.

Butler, A., & Burbill, T. (1984). *Towards a reading-writing classroom.* Rozelle, Australia: Primary English Teaching Association.

Calkins, L. M. (1986). *The art of teaching writing.* Portsmouth, NH: Heinemann.

Calkins, L. M., with Harwayne, S. (1991). *Living between the lines.* Portsmouth, NH: Heinemann.

Calkins, L. M. (1994). *The art of teaching writing.* Portsmouth, NH: Heinemann.

Carey, R., Harste, J., & Smith, S. (1981). Contextual constraints and discourse processes: A replication study. *Reading Research Quarterly, 16,* 201–212.

Cazden, C. B. (1992). *Whole language plus: Essays on literacy in the United States and New Zealand.* New York: Teachers College Press.

Christie, F. (1987). Learning to mean in writing. In N. Stewart-Dore (Ed.), *Writing and reading to learn* (pp. 21–34). Rozelle, Australia: Primary English Teaching Association.

Christie, F. (Ed.). (1990). *Literacy for a changing world.* Victoria: Australian Council for Educational Research.

Collerson, J. (1988). What are these genres, anyway? In J. Collerson (Ed.), *Writing for life* (pp. 12–22). Rozelle, Australia: Primary English Teaching Association.

Cope, B., & Kalantzis, M. (1990). Literacy in the social sciences. In F. Christie (Ed.), *Literacy for a changing world* (pp. 118–142). Victoria: Australian Council for Educational Research.

Cope, B., & Kalantzis, M. (Eds.). (1993). *The powers of literacy: A genre approach to teaching writing.* Pittsburgh, PA: University of Pittsburgh Press.

de Beaugrande, R. (1980). *Text, discourse, and process: Toward a multidisciplinary science of texts.* Norwood, NJ: Ablex.

Dyson, A. H. (Ed.). (1989). *Collaboration through writing and reading: Exploring possibilities.* Urbana, IL: National Council of Teachers of English.

Eggins, S. (1994). *An introduction to systemic functional linguistics.* London: Pinter.

Fairclough, N. (1989). *Language and power.* London: Longman.

Fairclough, N. (1992). *Discourse and social change.* Cambridge: Polity Press.

Fletcher, R. (1993). *What a writer needs.* Portsmouth, NH: Heinemann.

Geertz, C. (1983). *Local knowledge: Further essays in interpretive anthropology.* New York: Basic Books.

Goodman, K. S. (1967). Reading: A psycholinguistic guessing game. *Journal of the Reading Specialist, 6,* 126–135.

Goodman, K. S. (1997). Putting theory and research in the context of history. *Language Arts, 74,* 595–599.

Goodman, Y. M., and Burke, C. (1985). *Reading strategies: Focus on comprehension.* New York: Richard C. Owen.

Graves, D. (1983). *Writing: Teachers and children at work.* Portsmouth, NH: Heinemann.

Halliday, M. A. K. (1985). *An introduction to functional grammar.* London: Edward Arnold.

Halliday, M. A. K., & Hasan, R. (1985). *Language, context, and text: Aspects of language in a social-semiotic perspective.* Victoria, Australia: Deakin University Press.

Halliday, M. A. K., & Martin, J. R. (1993). *Writing science: Literacy and discursive power.* Pittsburgh, PA: University of Pittsburgh Press.

Hammond, J. (1990). Is learning to read and write the same as learning to speak? In F. Christie (Ed.), *Literacy for a changing world* (pp. 26–53). Victoria: Australian Council for Educational Research.

Hasan, R. (1984). The nursery tale as a genre. *Linguistic Circular, 13,* 71–102.

Hasan, R. (1985a). The texture of a text. In M. A. K. Halliday and R. Hasan, *Language, context, and text: Aspects of language in a social-semiotic perspective* (pp. 70–96). Victoria, Australia: Deakin University Press.

Hasan, R. (1985b). The structure of a text. In M. A. K. Halliday & R. Hasan, *Language, context, and text: Aspects of language in a social-semiotic perspective* (pp. 52–69). Victoria, Australia: Deakin University Press.

Hasan, R. (1995). The conception of context in text. In P. H. Fries & M. Gregory (Eds.), *Discourse in society: Functional perspectives.* (pp. 183–283). Norwood, NJ: Ablex.

Hiebert, E. H. (1991). Introduction. In E. H. Hiebert (Ed.), *Literacy for a diverse society: Perspectives, practices, and policies* (pp. 1–6). New York: Teachers College Press.

Hinley, M. (1986). Genre as generative: One perspective on one child's early writing growth. In M. Nystrand (Ed.), *The structure of written communication: Studies in reciprocity between writers and readers* (pp. 137–157). Orlando, FL: Academic Press.

Hyde, A. A., & Bizar, M. (1989). *Thinking in context: Teaching cognitive process across the elementary school curriculum.* White Plains, NY: Longman.

Karolides, N. (Ed.). (1992). *Reader response in the classroom: Evoking and interpreting meaning in literature.* White Plains, NY: Longman.

Karolides, N. (Ed.). (1997). *Reader response in elementary classrooms: Quest and discovery.* Mahwah, NJ: Lawrence Erlbaum.

Kress, G. (1993). Genre as social process. In B. Cope & M. Kalantzis (Eds.), *The powers of literacy: A genre approach to teaching writing* (pp. 22–37). Pittsburgh, PA: University of Pittsburgh Press.

Lemke, J. L. (1995). *Textual politics: Discourse and social dynamics.* London: Taylor & Francis.

Lensmire, T. J. (1994). *When children write: Critical revisions of the writing workshop.* New York: Teachers College Press.

Luke, A. (1988). *Literacy, textbooks, and ideology.* London: Falmer Press.

Lytle, S. L., & Botel, M. (1988). *PCRP II: Reading, writing and talking across the curriculum.* Harrisburg: Pennsylvania Department of Education.

Martin, J. R. (1990). Literacy in science: Learning to handle text as technology. In F. Christie (Ed.), *Literacy for a changing world* (pp. 79–117). Victoria: Australian Council for Educational Research.

Martin, J. R. (1992). *English text: System and structure.* Philadelphia, PA: John Benjamins.

Martin, J. R., Christie, F., & Rothery, J. (1987). Social processes in education: A reply to Sawyer and Watson (and others). In I. Reid (Ed.), *The place of genre in learning: Current debates* (pp. 58–82). Victoria, Australia: Deakin University Press.

Mason, J. M. (Ed.). (1989). *Reading and writing connections.* Boston: Allyn & Bacon.

Mousley, J., & Marks, G. (1991). *Discourses in mathematics.* Victoria, Australia: Deakin University Press.

Newkirk, T. (1989). *More than stories: The range of children's writings.* Portsmouth, NH: Heinemann.

Nodelman, P. (1996). *The pleasures of children's literature.* White Plains, NY: Longman.

Nystrand, M. (Ed.). (1986). *The structure of written communication: Studies in reciprocity between writers and readers.* Orlando, FL: Academic Press.

Nystrand, M. (1987). The role of context in written communication. In R. Horowitz & S. J. Samuels (Eds.), *Comprehending oral and written language* (pp. 197–214). San Diego: Academic Press.

Nystrand, M., and Wiemelt, J. (1991). When is a text explicit? Formalist and dialogical conceptions. *Text, 11,* 25–41.

Pappas, C. C. (1986). *Exploring the global structure of "information books."* ERIC Document No. ED 278 952.

Pappas, C. C. (1987). *Exploring the generic shape of "information books": Applying "typicality" notions to the process.* ERIC Document No. 299 834.

Pappas, C. C. (1988, January). *Exploring the textual properties of information books: A sociopsycholinguistic perspective.* Paper presented at the Ohio State University Children's Literature Conference, Columbus, OH.

Pappas, C. C. (1991). Fostering full access to literacy including information books. *Language Arts, 68,* 449–462.

Pappas, C. C. (1993a). Is narrative "primary"? Some insights from kindergarteners' pretend readings of stories and information books. *Journal of Reading Behavior, 25,* 97–129.

Pappas, C. C. (1993b). Questioning our ideologies about narrative and learning: Response to Egan. *Linguistics and Education, 5,* 157–164.

Pappas, C. C. (in press). *Learning written language: Genre from a social-semiotic perspective.* Cresskill, NJ: Hampton Press.

Pappas, C. C., & Barry, A. (1997). Scaffolding urban students' initiations: Transactions in reading information books in the

Read-Aloud curriculum genre. In N. Karolides (Ed.), *Reader response in elementary classrooms: Quest and discovery* (pp. 215-236). Mahwah, NJ: Lawrence Erlbaum.

Pappas, C. C., & Pettegrew, B. S. (1998). The role of genre in the psycholinguistic guessing game of reading. *Language Arts, 75,* 36-44.

Rosenblatt, L. M. (1978). *The reader, the text, the poem.* Carbondale: Southern Illinois University Press.

Rosenblatt, L. M. (1989). Writing and reading: The transactional theory. In J. Mason (Ed.), *Reading and writing connections* (pp. 153–176). Boston: Allyn & Bacon.

Shanahan, T. (Ed.). (1990). *Reading and writing together: New perspectives for the classroom.* Norwood, MA: Christopher-Gordon.

Slevin, J. F. (1992). Genre as a social institution. In J. Trimmer and T. Warnock (Eds.), *Understanding others: Cultural and cross-cultural studies and the teaching of literature* (pp. 16–34). Urbana, IL: National Council of Teachers of English.

Smith, F. (1982a). *Understanding reading.* New York: Holt, Rinehart & Winston.

Smith, F. (1982b). *Writing and the writer.* New York: Holt, Rinehart & Winston.

Smith, F. (1988). *Understanding reading* (4th ed.). Hillsdale, NJ: Lawrence Erlbaum.

Smith, F. (1997). *Reading without nonsense.* New York: Teachers College Press.

Spiro, R. J. (1980). Constructive process in prose comprehension and recall. In R. J. Spiro, B. C. Bruce, & W. F. Brewer (Eds.), *Theoretical issues in reading comprehension: Perspectives from cognitive psychology, linguistics, artificial intelligence, and education* (pp. 245–278). Hillsdale, NJ: Lawrence Erlbaum.

Stephens, J. (1992). *Language and ideology in children's fiction.* London: Longman.

Swales, J. M. (1990). *Genre analysis: English in academic and research settings.* Cambridge: Cambridge University Press.

Tierney, R. J., & Pearson, P. D. (1984). Toward a composing model of reading. In J. M. Jensen (Ed.), *Composing and comprehending* (pp. 33–45). Urbana, IL: ERIC Clearinghouse on Reading and Communication Skills.

Tierney, R. J., & Shanahan, T. (1991). Research on the reading-writing relationship: Interactions, transactions, and outcomes. In R. Barr, M. L. Kamil, P. Mosenthal, & P. D. Pearson (Eds.), *Handbook of reading research* (vol. 2, pp. 246–280). White Plains, NY: Longman.

Weaver, C. (1988). *Reading process and practice: From socio-psycholinguistics to whole language.* Portsmouth, NH: Heinemann.

Wertsch, J. V. (1991). *Voices of the mind: A sociocultural approach to mediated action.* Cambridge: Harvard University Press.

Willinsky, J. (1990). *The New Literacy: Redefining reading and writing in the schools.* New York: Routledge.

CHILDREN'S LITERATURE

Amelia's Road by L. J. Altman. Illustrated by E. O. Sanchez. Lee & Low Books, 1993.

Child of the Owl by L. Yep. HarperTrophy, 1977.

How Do Bees Make Honey by A. Claybourne. Illustrated by S. Allington & A. Spenceley. Usborne Publishing, 1994.

The Ladybug and Other Insects by First Discovery Books. Translated from French by C. Cramer. (American edition by L. Goldsen). Scholastic, 1991.

Mojave by D. Siebert. Illustrated by W. Minor. Crowell, 1988.

Mouse by S. B. Stein. Illustrated by M. Garcia. Harcourt Brace Jovanovich, 1985.

The Owl and the Woodpecker by B. Wildsmith. Oxford University Press, 1971.

Panda by S. Bonners. Delacorte, 1978.

The See-Through Zoo: How Glass Animals Are Made by S. Haldane. Pantheon Books, 1984.

Squirrels by B. Wildsmith. Oxford University Press, 1974.

Tunnels by G. Gibbons. Holiday House, 1984.

More How-To: Action Approaches in Integrated Language Classrooms

CHAPTER 7

Many traditional school practices separate process from content.

This chapter provides more how-to details of some of the routines, activities, and experiences through which inquiry in integrated language classrooms is realized. Traditional schooling often separates the process of learning from the content to be learned, having generally depended on a model of information accumulation. Children are expected to learn and remember information about particular subjects without necessarily understanding the nature of the information learned, how it came to be accepted as a part of a particular domain, or how to evaluate it relative to other information. You probably remember classes like these. In science, perhaps, you memorized definitions for terms or formulas intended to explain work and force. Too frequently, though, you did not conduct experiments with machines that could do work, or with levers and pulleys that could lessen the force exerted to do a particular type of work. You may have been able to pass the exam, but you didn't really understand the underlying concepts related to the terminology. Much of what you learned probably became dated before you ever had a chance to fit it into some schema to help you explain the forces that operate in the natural world. Not so very long ago, children dutifully memorized that "an atom is the smallest indivisible piece of matter"—not very useful in light of fission and fusion and atomic weapons of frightening power.

The traditional information accumulation model is outmoded.

Lave & Wenger (1991); Rogoff (1990), Vygotsky (1978)

Hyde & Bizar (1989)

Recent research on human cognition suggests that this old model of acquiring information is an inadequate way to teach and learn. Instead, there is mounting evidence that process and content are inextricably bound. The schemas that provide intellectual "scaffolding" for new learning are *situated*—built through experience with a particular body of knowledge in a particular context. Further experience—education—builds our repertoire of knowledge and contexts and allows us to think more abstractly and maturely.

Children need collaborative reflection.

Caine & Caine (1994); Brooks & Brooks (1993); Pierce & Gilles (1993)

As a result, it is not enough to go through the motions of problem-solving in a sort of cookbook approach. Instead, teachers must make time for discussion and reflection. Rather than assign children a problem for homework, collect the results the next day, and move on, teachers need to guide children's research and help select appropriate resources for study. Children need to work collaboratively and to have opportunities to think out loud with a responsive teacher and peer audience; they need to revise, rethink, and test ideas to learn from and with their peers. They need to communicate with one another to consider what things mean. What difference does it make, for instance, if children clean up their school playground as part of an antilitter campaign? What difference does it make if children learn to recognize bias in a newspaper report? What use are these skills in their lives?

Children are adaptive experts.

Hatano (1988); Levstik & Smith (1997); Saul, et. al (1993)

This is not just a "good citizen" view of education and learning. Reflection puts research and learning into the larger context of the world beyond the schoolroom walls. It is also both a communal and a personal endeavor. Children build their own meanings, try them on teacher and peers, and in the process, revise these meanings or find ways to defend them. They are adaptive experts: They learn what it takes to argue for a position and what constitutes adequate evidence. They participate in the give and take

252

and excitement of a community of learners where thinking is respected and good ideas are shared. The activities described in this chapter, many of which have already been mentioned, suggest ways to foster the development of a community of learners. Many of the techniques employed in these activities use kid-watching procedures, which are discussed in even more detail in Chapter 8. The learning portfolios and other methods of evaluation and accountability are discussed in Chapter 9.

Three caveats, however, need to be pointed out. First, the activities or experiences presented do not constitute an exhaustive list. We have been selective, trying to include critical activities that show the range of implementation across the curriculum. Integrated language teachers (and children) are constantly discovering new ways and new activities to implement their own teaching and learning goals. Consequently, what is provided here should be considered only as examples of the possibilities. Second, the activities are only suggestions of how to manage a classroom. It is assumed that these ideas will be modified and reshaped by particular teachers and children to meet particular purposes and circumstances. Finally, we are forced to describe these activities separately and linearly, but it is important not to conceive of them as such. In reality, most of the time these activities are incorporated into other activities, which is one of the reasons that the perspective is called "integrated." In sum, the spirit of this chapter is to describe activities so you have enough information to put into action in the classroom some of the principles of the integrated language perspective.

Activities herein are selective.

Activities herein are suggestions.

Activities herein are interrelated and integrated.

Some of the activities are grouped together under a broad category. For example, Graphic Organizers* is a general category consisting of four types of activities: Graffiti Walls*, Semantic Maps*, K-W-L*, and Comparison Charts*. Two large categories include reading and writing activities and experiences, respectively. Certain experiences (e.g., Reflective, Disciplined Inquiry*, Student-Initiated Inquiry*, Collaborative/Cooperative Groups*, Primary Sources*, Observation and Inference*, and Graphic Organizers*) are explained first because they represent more basic or universal processes and strategies that underlie or incorporate many of the other activities. Status of the Class*, Message Board*, and Focus-Lessons* are covered last because their use is more widespread in the classroom. Figure 7.1 depicts this organization and will help you locate a particular activity or experience within the chapter.

Figure 7.1 depicts the organization of the activities in the chapter.

Reflective, Disciplined Inquiry*

As we discussed in Chapter 3, Reflective, Disciplined Inquiry* is the lifeblood of a thematic unit. It links process and content in the kind of in-depth study characteristic of thematic learning. Note that this approach has three major parts. First, an *inquiry* sets up an investigation into a question or set of questions that have power for a particular group of children. You can see some of the ways in which this is done by reading the prototypes in Chapter 4. We call these "essential" questions because they are crucial to the success of an inquiry. They do not have single or simple solutions, and many lead children into a variety of other explorations along the way to resolving the original concern. Equally importantly, they are linked to the kinds of questions characteristic of the disciplines or domains within which children are inquiring.

Levstik & Barton (1997); Newmann et al. (1995)

Fried (1995); Young (1994)

Once a problem or question is raised, children gather relevant data and use such processes as observation, inference, classification, measurement, ordering, and hypothesizing to analyze the data and propose possible solutions or answers. The processes are similar to those generally referred to as the scientific method.

Ellis provides this description of an inquiry conducted by a second-grade class:

Ellis (1986)

> One morning, members of a second-grade class were excitedly telling their teacher and each other about a near accident that had occurred at a pedestrian crossing next to the school. A primary-age child was nearly struck by a car as she was crossing the street. The students exclaimed that the intersection was dangerous, especially during the winter months when ice and snow were present. The teacher asked the students if they would like to conduct an investigation of the intersection to see how dangerous it really was and to see if they could suggest ways to make it safer. The class agreed that

FOSTERING INQUIRY

Reflective, Disciplined Inquiry*
Organizing/Monitoring Student-Initiated Inquiry* Projects
I-Search Papers*
Collaborative/Cooperative Groups*
Primary Sources*
Jackdaws*
Observation and Inference*
Graphic Organizers*
    Graffiti Walls*
    Semantic Maps*
    K-W-L*
    Comparison Charts*

LITERACY ACTIVITIES AND EXPERIENCES

Reading Activities and Experiences	Writing Activities and Experiences
Reading aloud*	Journals*
Storytelling*	Dialogue Journals*
Sustained Silent Reading (SSR)*	Thought Ramblings*
Buddy Reading*	Learning Logs*
Book Talks*	Group-Composed Writing*
Literature Response Groups*	Teacher-Led Group Composed Writing*
Reading Conferences*	Peer-Led Group Composed Writing*
Big Books*	Author's Folders*
CLOZE*	Writing Conferences*
Say Something*	Content Conferences*
	Editing Conferences*
	Publishing Experiences*
	Displays*
	Bookmaking*
	Author's Chair*

DEVELOPING A REPERTOIRE OF LITERACY STRATEGIES

Teaching Phonics/Spelling in Context*
Teaching Grammar in Context*

EXTENDING LITERACY STRATEGIES

Sketch to Stretch*
Activity Cards*
Graphing*

Book Extensions*   Drama Experiences*
    Story Maps*   Improvisation*
    Plot Profiles*   Television News Broadcasts and
    Character Sociograms*   Talk Shows*
    Puppet Shows*
    Choral Reading*
    Reader's Theater*
    Story Theater*

Status of the Class*
Message Board*
Focus Lessons*

Figure 7.1

ORGANIZATIONAL CHART FOR CHAPTER 7 ACTIVITIES AND EXPERIENCES

this would be a worthwhile project. The class wrote a *statement of the problem* as follows: How can our school crossing be made safer? With the teacher's help, the class decided to use the following data sources in their research: a model of the intersection; the intersection itself; other students in the school; school staff members, including teachers, custodians, the principal, and the secretary; local residents; photographs of the intersection; and drivers who use the intersection. Working all together as well as in teams over the course of several weeks, the class *gathered data* through interviews, observation of traffic flow, timing the speed of cars near the intersection, and taking pictures of pedestrian, bicycle, and automobile traffic at peak crossing times before and after school. The students *processed their data* with a photo essay of the intersection, summaries of interviews, drawings of the intersection depicting the various problems they had discovered, and charts showing the volume of foot, bicycle, and auto traffic at peak hours.

They *made the following inferences:*

1. The crossing is dangerous, especially for younger children, and a safety awareness campaign is needed.
2. Four safety patrol students should be placed on duty rather than two, the present number.
3. Larger, more visible warning signs should be posted along the streets leading to the intersection.
4. The crosswalk lines should be repainted.

Their report was given to the school principal and to the police department. The students were pleased to see that all four of their recommendations were enacted. (pp. 197–199)

As children engage in this study, they create a number of documents, including surveys, graphs, and charts. Some children may have more trouble than others with these forms. Although the teacher may not notice some of these problems by simple observation, the children discuss their projects in their Learning Logs*, and the teacher can respond with suggestions and specific help—perhaps a Focus Lesson*—if a problem is shared by several students. In addition, children may include some of the work from this project in a learning portfolio that is shared with the teacher as part of an evaluation of their work conducted during the study.

A second important feature of inquiry in an integrated setting is that it is *disciplined*. In other words, children learn to recognize how different intellectual communities decide what counts as knowledge, how knowledge is acquired, and what purposes it serves within scholarly communities and in the larger world. Knowledge about freshwater ecosystems, for instance, may be gained and used rather differently by a child setting up an aquarium, a city planning commission debating development along a stream, or a research scientist studying mayflies. In order to better help children build their intellectual schema, it is not enough to acquire information; rather, children need to understand the goals, standards, and procedures of study characteristic of the field or fields within which they are investigating. As they do so, they ask better questions, make better sense out of the information they do acquire, and better understand the uses to which information is put in the larger community.

Levstik & Barton (1997); Newmann et al. (1995)

A final and crucial part of this approach is *reflection*. Some people call this time to think and discuss *debriefing*. We use both terms. In the intersection example, for instance, the teacher may debrief for ten minutes after the investigation is concluded by asking children to consider the processes used, their applicability to other problems, and the uses to which they can put their conclusions. In addition to this final debriefing, reflection occurs throughout a study. Some teachers take five or ten minutes at the end of a work period to reflect with students about problems and successes encountered during that time. Sometimes a spokesperson for each group working on a project will briefly report to the rest of the class; sometimes groups or individuals are encouraged to share information they have found that would be relevant to another person or group. Teachers facilitate this sharing by knowing what the children are working on and by encouraging them to consult other students and resources in the room.

Hyde & Bizar (1989); Wassermann & Ivany (1988)

In one sixth-grade class the teacher encourages the development of peer "experts." As the children read a variety of historical literature in preparation for selecting History Day projects, the teacher keeps track of areas where one child's study will help someone else. A child reading about medicine, for instance, came across information on Elizabeth Blackwell, a pioneer in women's entry into medicine, which was useful to another student reading about women in nontraditional occupations. The teacher organized a Literature Response Group* to include both these students so that they had an opportunity to share their information and expertise. At other times, when children asked the teacher questions, she referred them to a student "expert" who had been reading in that area and could be a knowledgeable resource. The teacher also en-

Levstik (1986)

couraged children to develop particular expertise by asking them to read up on a subject that no one else seemed to know much about: "I'd like you to read this book on David Ben-Gurion. No one else seems to have discovered him, and we will need that background if we are going to discuss what's happening in the Middle East. Could you be our Ben-Gurion expert?" Soon children looked for peer expertise without teacher suggestion and sought opportunities to develop expertise themselves.

Ellis (1986)

Reflection can also be encouraged by involving children in tackling ambiguous problems that may not be a part of a larger thematic unit, such as inventing a new language and a form for writing it, proving that the earth is moving, designing a better human being, and drawing a picture of democracy. These types of activities are exercises in divergent thinking. Children are challenged to think about multiple ways of solving problems rather than converge on a single solution. Each problem is grist for the mill of reflection and an opportunity to use a variety of symbol systems to communicate complex ideas.

Organizing/Monitoring Student-Initiated Inquiry* Projects

We have argued that an essential feature of the integrated language perspective is how much reflective, disciplined inquiry is fostered and promoted throughout the curriculum. However, organizing and keeping track of various Student-Initiated Inquiry* projects, where students pose and pursue their own questions or topics in which they do in-depth studies within a particular thematic unit, are necessary for successful collaborative teaching and learning to occur. Figure 7.2 developed by Wells & Chang-Wells, depicts the major components of a model of an inquiry-centered curriculum.

Well & Chang-Wells (1992)

Topics Identified and Questions Generated

The first step in Student-Initiated Inquiry*, of course, is for students to identify and choose the topics they want to study. In developing the thematic unit, the teacher has already offered many invitations. However, more brainstorming sessions with students are usually done to consider additional possibilities. K-W-L* techniques are useful here to identify what children already know and what they want to find out about. Giving students a few days to browse through books and review a copy of a particular WEB also helps in the process of selecting topics that students will find challenging and engaging, and in beginning the process of question generation.

Generate questions rather than topics for inquiry.

Levstik & Smith (1997); Whitin & Whitin (1997)

One problem that many teachers have when they first try Reflective, Disciplined Inquiry* is that they work with children to generate topics rather than questions. As one child explained, "Like, you get *India*. That's pretty big . . . I like it when we narrow it down. You do research on one thing, so that you can see it in your mind and it would take like ten days to do it . . . just the way I like it."

Of course India *is* too big. It is also not a question. What *about* India is worth investigation? If there is no question that children want to investigate, their work is likely to result in one more report neatly outlining the geographical, political, and economic features of India, without any connection to children's interests or intellectual needs. On the other hand, there are interesting and manageable questions for an inquiry into India. One group of sixth graders wanted to know if British colonialism in India was similar to British colonialism in North America. Were the issues that led to the American Revolution similar to those that led to Indian independence? They decided that these were their essential questions—ones that dealt with some of the most important issues related to an emerging theme of CONQUEST AND RESISTANCE—and would provide the focus for their study of India. Their teacher suggested that they make a comparative time line of Indian and American colonial periods to provide a chronological framework for further question generation. When the time line was completed, the class discussed several questions, including whose points of view had been represented, and whose might have been omitted. This discussion led to the development of a number of interesting subquestions under each of the essential questions.

Essential questions deal with the most important ideas and issues related to a theme.

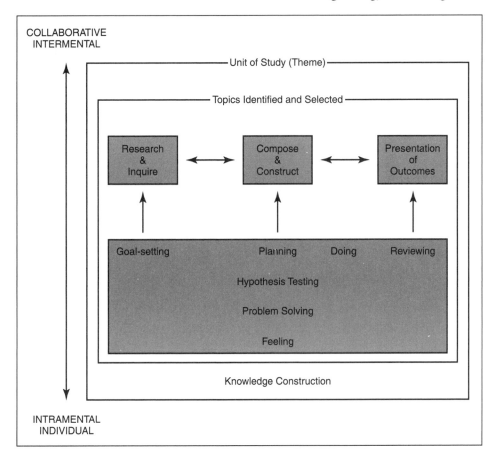

COLLABORATIVE
INTERMENTAL

Unit of Study (Theme)

Topics Identified and Selected

Research & Inquire ⟷ Compose & Construct ⟷ Presentation of Outcomes

Goal-setting   Planning   Doing   Reviewing

Hypothesis Testing

Problem Solving

Feeling

Knowledge Construction

INTRAMENTAL
INDIVIDUAL

Figure 7.2

Source: Wells & Chang-Wells, (1992)

It is important to note that without sufficient time for question generation, students may generate questions that are not worth investigating. In one primary class, children began a study of their community by asking how many bricks were in their city. This dominoed, not surprisingly, and children produced a series of "how many" type questions. If the teacher had simply accepted this array of questions, the inquiry would have been very frustrating for the children and produced little understanding either of the community or of the processes of inquiry. If, on the other hand, she had rejected their initial questions, students might legitimately conclude that their questions were worthless. Instead, she took the time to help children generate richer and more interesting questions. She sent them home to interview people. "See what questions your friends and neighbors have about the city," she suggested. She helped them to categorize their questions and gave them time to see how many they could answer simply by using resources in the room. Finally, the children discussed which questions would be most interesting to investigate and most essential in helping them learn about their community. Their final list included a set of questions manageable for young children, for which there were sufficient and appropriate data sources, and which would generate data from different points of view. This teacher's approach also illustrates *culturally relevant teaching*, which empowers children intellectually, socially, emotionally, and politically by using the knowledge, views, and attitudes from the members of children's cultural communities. Incorporating these kinds of essential questions—and the resulting inquiries—means examining the cultural referents or ideologies of various cultural groups. Thus, such a curriculum helps students who come from diverse ethnolinguistic backgrounds bridge or explain the dominant culture.

Not until this list had been generated were children ready to identify essential questions and select subsets of those questions for small group or individual inquiry. At this point, teachers frequently ask students to prioritize several questions they would want to investigate on an index card or sign-up sheet that shows the various possibilities the

Question generation takes time.

Levstik & Barton (1997)

Ladson-Billings (1994).

Culturally relevant** teaching **takes seriously children's culture in creating curriculum; it attempts to critically understand and evaluate the values or ideologies of student culture, community culture,** and **the dominant culture.

class has come up with. The teacher then goes over student lists and assigns the topics, trying to accommodate children's top choices. Obviously, some negotiation will be necessary because the teacher will want students to investigate as many of the subthemes of the unit as possible, and to incorporate different perspectives on the topic. This last is very important. If children do not select topics representative of different perspectives, their work may reinforce myths and stereotypes. Moreover, if there isn't any use of student culture that culture may not be sustained, and it cannot be employed to resist or transcend the negative effects of the dominant culture. Also, the availability of books and resources is a consideration. If many children choose the same topic, there will not be enough materials to go around to support their inquiries.

Multiple perspectives help children avoid stereotypes and myths.

Many teachers have students choose at least two inquiry projects during a particular thematic unit, one individual and one small group. This is another opportunity to incorporate different perspectives. (See "Collaborative/Cooperative Groups*" in this chapter for further information on managing small groups.) Again, children need help in selecting inquiry projects that are manageable in the time set aside for research.

Conducting the Inquiry Projects

Once questions have been chosen and assigned, many teachers then ask students to develop a proposal regarding their inquiry projects. Figure 9.3 in Chapter 9 shows the kind of information that is usually asked of students. Teachers have found that having students complete such a proposal helps both students and teachers in many ways. First of all, by having students put down questions they have or things they want to find out about, they tend to take their inquiry projects seriously. It assists students in deciding if the topic they have chosen is going to be as interesting and challenging for them as they had initially thought. In completing the form, students sometimes realize that something else might be better for them to study. Consequently, there is plenty of time for them to revise their project topic before putting too much effort into it. As teachers look at the books and other resources listed on the proposals, they can also determine whether other books are needed, whether students are likely to encounter multiple, supportable interpretations, or whether some system might have to be devised to share other types of books. Moreover, the proposals give teachers important information in the beginning about problems students might have so that they can resolve problems before getting bogged down in difficult dilemmas that are hard to overcome. Also, by having students consider the nature of sharing their findings, teachers can see how well students are thinking ahead about their projects. Sometimes there may be a requirement set forth about this aspect of a project, for example, that some of the findings have to be in writing, or that the findings need to be written in a certain genre that a teacher may want to focus on during the thematic unit (biographies or informative reports, etc.). Thus, the proposal enables teachers to remind students early on about such requirements as well as help them find the best, most interesting, or novel ways to "publish" the findings of their inquiry. It is also important at this point to consider what sorts of genres children may be thinking about using. Sometimes children find it difficult to switch from the informational genres used to collect data to the genres they decide they want to use in sharing their findings. Turning data into an interesting presentation may require Focus Lessons* to help children think about the requirements of different genres. Making this information explicit helps children be strategic, selecting genres that are more likely to maintain rather than subvert their focus on the essential questions.

If inquiry projects are to be conducted by small groups rather than by individuals, then the teacher can easily modify the proposal form to ask what individual group members have decided to take responsibility for. Consensus on this issue and on the other areas included on the form helps clear up many initial difficulties members might have so that groups indeed become cooperative and collaborative.

As students work on their inquiry projects—as they research and inquire, compose and construct, and then present outcomes—ongoing documentation and self-evaluation are asked of them. Teachers have several ways to do this. At the beginning of each

Inquiry requires ongoing documentation and self-evaluation.

day or before an integrated work time set aside for inquiry projects, the teacher may use Status of the Class* checks or review individual status reports, including Learning Logs* and planning journals. At the end of the day or work time, students record actual accomplishments and future plans. Or, some teachers have students complete a special inquiry evaluation form each day (see Figure 7.3). This is kept in a special folder with the rest of the work being done on the inquiry project. Whatever system is set up, periodic evaluation of where students are in their projects—what problems they might have and need help on, what they have accomplished already, or what they might need to do next—helps teachers collaborate and provide important responsive feedback. It also enables teachers to know when they might need to have conferences with students or conduct Focus Lessons*.

Final Evaluation of Inquiry Projects

A final evaluation of the inquiry project is an integral feature of Student-Initiated Inquiry* projects, and an important opportunity for children to reflect on their work. Frequently, this evaluation includes ways for both teachers and students to assess a student's work. Criteria categories—usually created collaboratively—are developed to assess the knowledge, understandings, or content of what students have learned, various skills or strategies students might have acquired in the process of conducting their inquiry projects, and students' attitudes toward their learning and work on the inquiry topic or other aspects of the project. Assessment can be given in the more traditional way by giving an A, B, C, and so on for each criterion and then a final grade. Or other rating systems are more frequently used—Excellent, Satisfactory, and Needs Work; or Outstanding, Satisfactory, and Improving (or Working On)—capture positively children's beginning understandings, skills, or strategies. Beside each rating, students are asked to provide a "comment." This important self-evaluation feature helps both

Dalton (1985)

Hill & Hill (1990)

Inquiry projects need to be evaluated for content, process, and student attitude.

Figure 7.3

INQUIRY LOG	
Activity:	Names:
What question(s) did you try to answer today?	
Explain what you did to answer your question(s).	What sources did you use today?
What did you discover today?	What new questions are you curious about?
Are you pleased with your results today?	How would your group rate this activity? Great 10 9 8 7 6 5 4 3 2 1 0 terrible

teachers and students better understand a student's own rationale and perspective on his or her learning.

Many teachers have conferences with students over these final evaluations, especially if the students' and the teacher's assessments are very different, although teachers usually report that most students are quite honest about their assessment, so discrepant ratings are rarely seen. For small-group inquiry projects, student evaluations of their own and their group members' contributions regarding the content of their inquiry as well as how each evaluated the group social processes in doing the project would also be included. (See "Collaborative/Cooperative Groups*" for more details.)

Collaborative Nature of Inquiry Projects

Moll (1992); Wells & Chang-Wells (1992); Wertsch (1985, 1991)

Student-Initiated Inquiry* projects are the best ways for students to engage in reflective thinking, for they have ownership by constructing their own knowledge on topics they find important and interesting. Even when children are involved in individual projects, thematic units still provide many opportunities for them to collaborate with other peers who are working on similar or overlapping projects or on topics they find important and interesting. Moreover, inquiry projects afford ample opportunities for teachers to give collaborative, contingent, responsive feedback. Thus, as indicated on the left side of Figure 7.2, the construction of knowledge in these inquiry projects involves a range of interaction, from collaborative talk with peers and the teacher to communing with self. In Reflective, Disciplined Inquiry* the resources of the culture are encountered in *inter*mental social activity and then acquired and transformed into a personal *intra*mental resource.

I-Search* Papers

Presenting the outcomes of Reflective, Disciplined Inquiry* can take many forms, as can be seen in many of the prototypes in Chapter 4, the experiences mentioned in Chapters 3 and 5, and the activities presented throughout this chapter. The I-Search* paper is one of those forms that is particularly useful in helping children focus on the process of inquiry rather than just on the final product. It is a natural extension of the day-to-day planning and organization involved in any inquiry project.

Macrorie (1988)

Developed by Macrorie, the I-Search* paper is meant to open up the search for knowledge in a very personal way. The I-Search* paper is really the story of "finding out." According to Macrorie, writers conduct a search to find out something they need to know for their own life and write the story of their own adventure. In the process, each writer can begin at the beginning, considering the puzzle or need that led to the question they wanted to answer, identifying the question, narrowing down the topic, searching for information, encountering dead ends and byways along the way, and arriving at the outcome of the search—what was found or not found and where the writer might go next.

I-Searches help children reflect on the process of inquiry.*

One of the advantages of the I-Search* lies in the many sources of information and modes of discovery that children might use. In addition to encyclopedias and traditional reference materials, the personal journey undertaken in an I-Search* paper can lead children to Primary Source* materials, museums, archives, and other community resources, and to telephone and personal interviews with experts, family members, or friends.

See Macrorie (1988) for other examples.

Macrorie suggests that writers follow four simple steps in composing the final paper: "What I Knew," "Why I'm Writing This Paper," "The Search," and "What I Learned (or Didn't Learn)." Another way to approach the paper is to tell the story of the search for information in narrative form, beginning with how the topic or question was identified and where the search for answers led. The actual findings or outcome of the search could then be presented in some other genre, such as the information book or report genre that the child feels is suitable. Thus, the I-Search* provides a focus for talking with children about conventions of written genres as well as processes of inquiry.

One fifth-grade teacher whose class was studying CHANGES found a wide range of interests among her children when she asked them to try an I-Search*. Several wrote about the changes in civil rights laws, while another wrote about changes in fashion from the 1960s to the 1990s. One of them, Karen, began her report on Lyndon Johnson in this way:

> The 1992 election was very interesting and it was the first time I was really aware of the campaign and election. Well, the whole thing got me interested in presidents, and when in reading group I started the book, *Circle of Gold*, taking place in the 1960's, I started wondering who the president was then and what he did in office. So I looked in the encyclopedia, found Lyndon Johnson's name and began research.

Boyd (1984)

While Karen was able to find enough information from secondary sources to satisfy her curiosity, she focused throughout the project on the process of finding out as well as the information gained.

What may be most difficult for many children is finding out where to go when materials in the library don't hold all or even any of the answers to their questions. Many teachers have found that Jean Fritz's book *George Washington's Breakfast* helps children anticipate the problems as well as the rewards of I-Searches*. In the story, a young boy, George Washington Allen, wants to find out what his namesake ate for breakfast. Although he finds four books on President Washington at the library, none of them mention Washington's diet. Young George and his family take a field trip to Washington, D.C., and visit Mount Vernon, where he looks for more information and even interviews the guard in the Mount Vernon kitchen, still to no avail. Eventually, however, George finds a primary source, a type of almanac written at the time Washington lived that gives him the information he wanted: President George Washington ate three small Indian hoecakes every morning. However, young George is not satisfied until he actually eats the same breakfast, which he does after consulting two more sources—a dictionary (to find out what Indian hoecakes are) and his grandmother (who cooks up a batch based on the definition).

Fritz (1969)

In writing about his experience, George could have begun by explaining how he was named and why he was curious about what the first president ate for breakfast. He might have detailed his visit to the library, his trip to Washington, D.C., and his interview with the personnel at Mount Vernon. However, even if he had never found the answer to his question, the I-Search* format would have given him a story to tell and a process to reflect upon.

George's experience can reassure other young searchers who face frustrations when they set out to answer a question. In addition, as McGinley and Madigan point out, the struggles and strategies involved in this kind of research often go unnoticed, yet they provide an important basis for reflection and learning in the classroom. The I-Search* is not only one of many ways of recording and reporting the results of inquiry but also one that may be particularly useful in helping children enjoy the journey to learning as well as the arrival at knowledge.

McGinley & Madigan (1990)

Collaborative/Cooperative Groups*

Much of the work done in integrated language classrooms is done through Collaborative/Cooperative Groups*. Two essential features mark cooperative activity: It has goal similarity and it reflects positive interdependence in that a particular cooperative group is successful because its members work together.

There are two major types of Collaborative/Cooperative Groups*. The first type is short-term and more informal in nature, and the second type is characteristically more formal and long-term. Informal, short-term groups are used when small groups of students may do short activities involving brainstorming ideas, such as K-W-L* or Semantic Map* activities, or work on approaches to solving, say, certain math problems. The group efforts are then shared with the whole class. Short-term collaborative groups also occur frequently during shared or Buddy Reading*, Say Something* activities, or peer conferencing around student writing. In other words, this first type of

Dalton (1985); Hill & Hill (1990)

Collaborative/Cooperative Groups* may be seen to be ongoing in the classroom where membership of the group is frequently changing and of short duration. Thus, membership in this type of cooperative group is usually created spontaneously by students or simply determined by who may be sitting next to each other when a particular activity is initiated.

The second type of Collaborative/Cooperative Group* is more formally constituted and long-term—if not for the whole duration of a thematic unit, then for a large portion of it—because these groups engage students in major projects or work. The following remarks concern mostly this second type of Collaborative/Cooperative Group*, although the ideas presented are good to keep in mind when thinking about the informal, short-term groups, too.

Establishing or Forming Collaborative/Cooperative Groups*

There are several guidelines that are helpful in grouping students for collaborative work. First, the usual number for a group is between two and six members, although most teachers think that a group of four to five students is ideal.

The most successful groups are usually those that are formed around a common interest: the desire to read and talk about the same book in Literature Response Groups* or to pursue the same questions or topics in a Student-Initiated Inquiry* project. Topics are identified and selected and students are assigned to groups as for Student-Initiated Inquiry* projects (described earlier). Although the groups are determined mostly through common interests, an important factor that influences the teacher's grouping decision is diversity in membership. Diversity is considered enriching in integrated language classrooms, so teachers try to make sure that students in particular groups are different—in gender; in ethnic, racial, and cultural background; and in academic *and* social abilities.

Diversity is an important factor in forming groups.

Delpit (1995)

Many children want to work with their friends and may be initially disappointed by not being placed with them. Several strategies are useful. First, talk about the classroom as community all the time (and especially on the first day of school), stressing how important it is for everyone to get to know each other, so that students will expect to be working with lots of different groups during the school year. Second, point out that there will be many opportunities to work not only with old friends in the first type of collaborative group mentioned above—that is, in a peer Writing Conference* or in shared or Buddy Reading*—but also with new friends in other groups. Finally, many teachers also consider this friend issue more directly by asking students to indicate three or four people they would like to work with. This is usually done at the same time that students list their preferred topics for their inquiry projects so that teachers can consider this information when they look at students' interests—as well as at the diversity concerns. In this way, teachers can have each student in a group with at least one person that the student wanted to work with and avoid the problem of having any student being isolated or not chosen.

Having students work on topics that they have chosen usually overcomes a lot of other problems that might occur due to the membership of the groups. That is why grouping around common interests is so successful. However, groups can be formed in other ways. In the beginning of the year, when students do not know each other very well, teachers might establish groups by going around the room or down the class list and counting one, two, three, four, and so forth or by having students pick out a piece of colored paper from a hat, each color indicating a particular group. Or, especially later in the school year, teachers might actually use the criterion of working with someone new as a major means of establishing group membership. In these latter cases, common interests would nevertheless still be a focus.

In sum, in any system of forming Collaborative/Cooperative Groups*, interest and diversity are the important issues to keep in mind. Negotiation with students is very likely, so keeping track of various group membership over the course of a thematic unit and school year is extremely crucial to this end.

Group Process

Group process should be an integral part of real, worthwhile content and authentic purpose. That is, children should *never* be involved in contrived activities set up solely for the sake of "doing cooperative groups." However, if students are not used to working in Collaborative/Cooperative Groups*, there may be a need to scaffold students as they learn how to talk and act in groups. Of course, teacher demonstration and modeling will be an important way to get this done. Through various teacher-student conferences or through periodic teacher interactions in small inquiry groups, teachers are able to ask questions or respond to students in the ways they want students to behave and interact. Another way to help students learn how to work responsibly is for the teacher to work with a small group on group procedures in what one teacher called a "fishbowl technique." Here, the teacher and the small group sit in the middle of the room with the rest of the class circled all around them so that all students can see and hear. Then, the small group models and demonstrates the way the group process should be enacted. Discussion following the demonstration clears up further questions or concerns students might have.

Explicit directions or instruction via Focus Lessons* is yet still another way students can learn the process and procedures of groups. After the teacher's lesson, groups would try out these routines, followed by debriefing and evaluation. Some teachers find that videotaping group work helps during the debriefing. One teacher, for instance, noticed that boys often dominated small-group decision making. When she mentioned this observation in a debriefing session the boys were sure that girls had talked as much as they. The class agreed that they needed to videotape their group work so they could have more data about how boys and girls tended to work in groups. Over the next several days a student teacher in the classroom videotaped several types of interactions: small groups of mixed gender, as well as single gender groups, and whole-class discussions. The children reviewed the tapes and concluded that there were indeed some problems. Not only did some boys dominate in small groups, they found that their teacher tended to call most often on these same boys during whole-class discussion. They also noticed several other things that seemed to be problems in group work. Finally, the class worked to establish new routines to ensure more equitable participation during group work and class discussions. In addition to assigning various roles to group members, they made "turn tickets" to help their teacher call on boys and girls more evenly.

Asking children to notice such specific behaviors in the group and to take turns in having various roles and process are frequently helpful, especially for students who may be unfamiliar with groups. Consider asking children to serve in one of the following roles:

See Hill & Hill (1990) for other ideas for roles group members can take.

Summarizer: Retells or recounts main ideas members made
Recorder: Writes down the group ideas, frequently asking, "Is this what you said?" or "How should I write that idea down?"
Encourager: Encourages by pointing out good points, making sure that everyone has a turn
Organizer: Tries to keep group members on task, reminds members as to problems to be solved or to specific ideas to be considered, and indicates when members agree on points or when there are different views that the group has to resolve

Children can also indicate specifically when they know someone has finished talking, encouraged someone, given specific information to back up points, or used quiet voices or constructive feedback. Making these positive social skills explicit for them in the beginning helps students begin to learn how to work effectively by letting them know what is expected of them and what their responsibilities are as members in a group.

Teachers need to realize that students will internalize these social skills gradually. Students may have to be periodically reminded until these skills become internalized, but if teachers refer to these roles or the specific behaviors, children slowly and surely learn to act responsibly in groups.

Evaluating Group Work and Process

Some of the foregoing ideas involve students in evaluating group process. Many teachers, as part of their general assessment and evaluation program, have students evaluate the work and participation in long-term Collaborative/Cooperative Groups*. (See "Organizing/Monitoring Student-Initiated Inquiry* Projects" in this chapter and Chapter 9 for more details.) At the end of the day or group work, teachers set aside five to ten minutes for students to complete an evaluation sheet that covers both the content of the participants' work and the social skills or group process strategies they displayed. The following kinds of information are elicited:

The group's accomplishment, listing some of the important ideas and contributions that were made by individual members.
Problems that came up and how the group handled or resolved them.
New plans that the group has made, with individual responsibilities, if appropriate.
The ways in which each member helped the others in the group.
The group skills that the members have to work on next time.

Thus, these explicit ongoing group evaluations also foster students' development of the kinds of social skills necessary for meaningful Collaborative/Cooperative Groups*.

Summary

See Bayer (1990), Dalton (1985), and Hill & Hill (1990) for other resources on cooperative groups.

Collaborative/Cooperative Groups* are not a panacea. Problems and mishaps will still occur, but it is through working through these misunderstandings that the classroom becomes a community. Students learn how to deal with the problems, and in doing so, they learn much more. Collaborative groups promote problem-solving and social skills as well as foster the kind of learning that cannot be done alone but that can be accomplished with support. Moreover, well-functioning collaborative groups help students learn about and understand others' perspectives, which undergirds important goals of multicultural education. See Chapter 10 for more information on organizing cooperative learning.

Primary Sources*

History is constructed from the residue of the past. Historians interpret and reinterpret history on the basis of the primary sources that are available to them and on the historiographic or interpretive framework in which the historian operates. The historian uses primary sources—public documents, private papers, newspapers, and artifacts produced during the period under study—and constructs a story to explain the causes and effects of past events. The historian's story, or interpretation of the past, is a secondary source.

Forbes (1943); Collier & Collier (1974)

We see the past filtered through the perspective of the historian, and so our history changes as we change. Even the way history is presented to children changes. Thus, a historical novel such as *Johnny Tremain*, written before the Vietnam War, provides a very different perspective on the American Revolution from that of *My Brother Sam Is Dead*, a novel about the same era but written as America was just coming out of a war in Southeast Asia and reinterpreting its past in light of that traumatic event. Such interpretations are important because they are one way in which we explain ourselves as a culture and as human beings. They provide us with a historical memory and a record of how we have developed over time.

Unfortunately, however, this may be the only history many of us ever encounter. We too easily assume that a secondary historical account is "the way it really was." We forget that history is interpretative and that interpretation is tentative, pending new information. Because of this, it is important for children to understand the sources used by historians in constructing history.

A variety of Primary Sources* are available and appropriate for use with children, especially in grades 4 and up. Local historical societies, archives, and many libraries preserve primary sources in the form of old newspapers, letters, diaries, military papers, census records, period magazines, catalogs, and so forth. Photocopying such documents is relatively inexpensive and can provide children with the raw material for doing their own historical interpretation. It is also possible to buy packaged primary source material at historical sites and museums and from commercial producers.

One of the skills children learn in working with Primary Sources* is careful consideration of the strengths and weaknesses of various sources, possible biases, and inaccuracies. Children should be encouraged to confirm information gathered in one source by reference to other primary and secondary sources and to recognize the difference between a primary source that comes from the time studied and a secondary source that is an interpretation of the past based on an analysis of primary sources.

One way to help older children recognize the differences between primary and secondary sources is to begin with a Primary Source* such as Figure 7.4, a "slave narrative" or transcript of an interview with a person formally enslaved. (Such interviews were conducted during the 1930s as part of President Roosevelt's Works Progress Administration and are a major source of firsthand accounts of slavery.) Put the slave narrative on an overhead transparency and read it with the class, then analyze it in terms of reliability. Can this source be trusted? What things about this source might concern you if you were a historian writing about slavery? Some of the things children may notice include: the age of the person interviewed (slavery ended after the Civil War; interviews were conducted in the 1930s; many of the ex-slaves were in their eighties and nineties and would have been quite young during slavery); concern with whether this person's experience was typical; and who conducted the interview (if the interviewer was white—a likely possibility—would an African-American person who had lived through slavery be likely to trust the interviewer?).

Next, provide students with secondary historical reports of slavery. Milton Meltzer's *In Their Own Words* is a compilation of slave narratives edited and interpreted by the author. How has he used the primary sources? Which parts of Meltzer's work are primary and which interpretative? Then give the children a nonfiction narrative based on slave narratives—perhaps Julius Lester's *To Be a Slave*. How have the primary sources been interpreted here? What purpose may the author have had in writing this narrative? *Meltzer (1964)*

Lester (1968)

Finally, have students read Belinda Hurmence's *A Girl Called BOY*, a novel that also uses slave narratives as background for a story of slavery, or the McKissacks' *Christmas in the Big House, Christmas in the Quarters*, an informational storybook based on primary sources about antebellum plantation life. The children discuss the ways in which the authors seem to have used the primary sources and their purposes in doing so. Can they recognize the primary parts of the novel? How, for instance, has Hurmence woven historical information into the fictional tale of a girl who is taken back in time and mistaken for an escaped slave? How do the McKissacks use historical information to highlight the contrast between life for European Americans and life for enslaved African Americans? *Hurmence (1982)*

McKissack & McKissack (1994)

A similar procedure can be used for other types of primary sources such as photographs. After viewing the picture of a sorghum mill (see Figure 7.5), children are asked to list five observations (observations can be tested by the senses). Be clear that these are observations and *not* inferences—conclusions based on observation—at this point. Working in small groups, the students try to construct three inferences that can be supported by their observations. After a debriefing in which these inferences are shared with the class, each group resumes work and makes a list of additional information needed to confirm or disconfirm their hypotheses (inferences). At this point,

Reporter—Betty Lugabill   Allen County
Editor—Harold Pugh   District 10
Supervisor—R. S. Drum   Ex-slaves

Kisey McKimm Ex-Slave 83 Years

I was born in Bourbon County, sometime in 1853, in the state of Kaintucky where they raise fine horses and beautiful women. Me'n my Mammy, Liza'n Joe, all belonged to Marse Jacob Sandusky the richest man in the county. Pappy, he belonged to the Henry Youngs who owned the plantation next to us.

Marse Jacob was good to his slaves, but his son, Clay was mean. I remember once when he took my Mammy out and whipped her 'cuz she forgot to put cake in his basket, when he went huntin'. But that was the last time, 'cuz the master heerd of it and cussed him like God had come down from heaven.

Besides doin' all the cookin' she was the best in the county, my Mammy had to help do the chores and milk fifteen cows. The shacks of all the slaves was set at the edge of a wood, an' Lawse, honey, us chillun used to have to go out 'n gatha all the twigs 'n brush 'n sweep it jes' like a floor.

Then the Massa used to go to the court house in Paris 'n buy sheep an' hogs. Then we used to help drive them home. In the evenings our Mammy took the old clothes of Mistress Mary 'n made clothes for us to wear. Pappy, he come ovah to see us every Sunday, through the summer, but in the winter, we would only see him maybe once a month.

The great day on the plantation was Christmas when we all got a little present from the Master. The men slaves would cut a whole pile of wood for the fire place 'n pile in on the porch. As long as the whole pile of wood lasted we didn't have to work but when it was gone, our Christmas was over. Sometimes on Sunday afternoons, we would go to the Master's honey room 'n he would give us sticks of candied honey, an' Lawd chile was them good. I ate so much once, I got sick 'nough to die.

Our Master was what white folks call a miser. I remember one time, he hid $3,000, between the floor an' the ceilin', but when he went for it, the rats done chewed it all up into bits. He used to go to the stock auction every Monday, 'n he didn't wear no stockings. He had a high silk hat, but it was tore so bad, that he held the top 'n bottom together with a silk neckerchief. One time when I went with him to drive the sheep home, I heard some of the men with kid gloves call him a "hill-billy" 'n make fun of his clothes. But he said, "don't look at the clothes, but look at the man."

One time, they sent me down the road to fetch somethin' 'n I heard a bunch of horses comin'. I jumped over the fence 'n hid behind the elderberry bushes, until they passed, then I ran home 'n told them what I done seen. Pretty soon they come to the house, 125 Union solders an' asked for something to eat. We all jumped round and fixed them dinner, when they finished, they looked for Master, but he was hid. They was gentlemen 'n didn't bother or take nothin'. When the war was over the Master gave Mammy a house an' 160 acre farm, but when he died, his son Clay told us to get out of the place or he'd burn the house an' us up in it, so we left an' moved to Paris. After I was married 'n had two children, me an' my man moved north an' I've been here ever since.

Figure 7.4

Source: Courtesy of the Ohio Historical Society, Columbus, Ohio

the teacher can introduce further evidence or allow the children to search for it, or explain that the picture shows part of a sorghum-making operation. Not every activity needs to extend for long periods. In this case, the purpose may be to provide practice in analyzing primary source material, not in initiating a study of farm technology. Children can also use Primary Sources* to compare with descriptions in their textbooks. A text passage on the "surprise" attack on Pearl Harbor, for instance, can be compared to earlier news reports that the Japanese were preparing for just such an attack. Various map projections of the world can be used to initiate a discussion of what maps tell us about how people viewed the world at different times. A single coin can be analyzed as a primary source as well. If you were a person who knew nothing of American society, what could you learn by carefully analyzing a penny, a copy of *My Weekly Reader*, or a Barbie doll, for that matter? Jackdaws* provide one way to organize these and other activities using Primary Sources*.

Figure 7.5

A 1930S SORGHUM MILL WORKED BY MULE

Source: Photograph courtesy of the Kentucky Department for Libraries and Archives, Frankfort, Kentucky

Jackdaws*

Jackdaws* are collections of primary and secondary source material, background information, and teaching suggestions for historical and contemporary topics. Commercial Jackdaws* are of this type and are generally geared for high-school students. Commercial Jackdaws* can be easily adapted for use in the intermediate grades and are relatively inexpensive. However, a teacher or the children can also construct Jackdawlike packets.

Jackdaw(TM) *is the commercial name for a series of Primary Source* and activity packets covering a wide range of topics in world and U.S. history.*

Teacher-Made Jackdaws

A teacher can create a Primary Source* packet modeled on the Jackdaws* and geared to specific classroom needs. Because Jackdaws* concentrate on one topic or perspective in a fair degree of detail, they are important ways to provide students with multiple perspectives on larger topics.

Primary Grades Source Packet

A Jackdaw* for younger children might begin with a book such as Peter Spier's *Tin Lizzie* and contain advertisements for cars from Model T's to present models, along with road maps from different eras, pictures of gas stations and roadside merchandising such as drive-throughs, and "before and after" pictures of small towns bypassed by freeways, or connected to other places by roads and cars. Some secondary sources on the history of automobiles (e.g., "coffee table" books with well-done illustrations and clear captions) and suggested activities for children can help students study the history of automotive transportation, and talk about the impact of the car on people's lives.

Spier (1978)

Intermediate Grades Source Packet

Unlike the primary source packet that includes several perspectives in one Jackdaw*, this intermediate packet concentrates on a single historical perspective. Many manuscript collections contain the papers of private individuals of historic interest. In the EXPLORATIONS thematic unit the teacher gathered the letters and journal of a young woman embarking on a trip west into a packet that included other primary sources related to American expansion in the nineteenth century: descriptions of the area the young woman was leaving, copies of newspaper descriptions of western lands and eastern problems, and prints from *Harper's* and *Leslie's* magazines of covered wagons and Native American communities in the west. The teacher also included such sources as information about political conditions, lists of supplies recommended for travelers, a price list for some of these goods, and illustrations of fashions for men, women, and children. A few guide questions were attached to each source so that children had some help in reading a document or picture. These sources were then used by the students as the raw material for constructing a biographical novel of the young woman's journey and settlement in the west. Children also had access to historical novels about the period and to fine secondary sources such as *Pioneer Women: Voices from the Kansas Frontier* and *Women's Diaries of the Westward Journey*, among others.

Harper's and Leslie's were popular illustrated magazines of the Civil War era.

Stratton (1981); Schlissel (1982)

Student-Made Jackdaws*

See also Weber (1989) for many other Jackdaw ideas.*

The second type of Jackdaw* is constructed by students as a way of representing what they have learned in studying a particular topic or in response to a piece of literature. After children have studied the history of automobiles, they may want to put together Jackdaw* histories of their own—of cooking stoves, for instance, to go with the DIGGING UP THE PAST theme. Generally, students need some guidance in this activity. One teacher explains that children can pack a "trunk" (a cardboard box) with items to represent a particular story they have read. In a sense, these children reconstruct Primary Sources.* A child who read *The Cabin Faced West* by Jean Fritz makes a box that looks like an old traveling trunk and fills it with homemade dolls based on those in the story, along with a diary that might have been written by the main character and parts of a letter from "back home." Another turns a shoe box into a replica of an old lunch box similar to those carried by the women in *Rosie the Riveter* by Penny Colman. She fills the lunch box with "artifacts" of women's work during World War II: postcards showing old recruitment posters for war work, a kerchief similar to that worn by Rosie, miniature tools and airplanes, and copies of old articles about war work, along with classified ads. Two older children fascinated by Walter Dean Myers' *Harlem*, borrow a worn instrument case from the band director and fill it with Langston Hughes' poetry, a tape of blues singers, "then and now" pictures of Harlem, and a taped interview with a local jazz musician.

Fritz (1958)

Colman (1995)

Myers (1997)

Such student-created Jackdaws* allow children to represent in interesting and informative ways what they have learned while accommodating children of varying strengths and interests. The Jackdaws* also give the teacher feedback on the kinds of observations children are making and the accuracy of their inferences. One young boy's reconstruction of an 1867 journal, for instance, included reference to stopping off at a saloon to watch the football game on television. His teacher saw this as evidence of a lack of information on technology and made a note to introduce a unit on TECHNOLOGY that would include timelines of inventions.

Observation and Inference*

Although most process skills seem fairly self-evident, children as well as adults have some difficulty distinguishing between observation and inference. Much of the time this is not a problem. We don't really need to distinguish between the observations and inferences that lead us to leap out of the way of a car barreling down the road in our direction. At other times, however, the distinction between what we actually *observe*— what we can discover with our senses and what we *infer*— the meaning we give to what we observe—is crucial, particularly in social studies and science.

Observation and Inference* in Social Studies

We may observe a person of another race or ethnic group as we go about our daily business. Our observation may include seeing skin color, facial features, or clothing. We may notice the aroma of perfume or aftershave or hear the sound of a different language or dialect. But we often infer a number of things that have little to do with our actual observation. Instead, our prejudices and stereotypes interfere with observation, and we may make negative inferences that are unsupported by careful observation.

Young children are as prone to leap to inferences without careful observation as any of us. As teachers, however, we have an opportunity to help hone their observation skills and insist on supported inferences. You will have noted that there are a number of activities in the prototypes in Chapter 4 that provide children with opportunities to observe and build supported inferences, and you have seen from the discussion of Reflective, Disciplined Inquiry* how crucial this distinction can be.

Byrnes (1988); Sonnenschein (1988); Stone (1986); Wilson (1987)

We have evidence that as early as fourth grade, children have developed specific attitudes and ideas about other races, genders, and ethnic groups. These attitudes are often the result of limited observation and experience. In the early years, however, teachers have a wonderful opportunity to build a body of observation and experience that can lead to more open-mindedness as children come in contact with a wider variety of people. Some teachers try to introduce young children to representatives from other cultures, or they do some lessons on African Americans in February (Black History Month) and women in March (Women's History Month). These short-term experiences are interesting but probably do little to change stereotypes. Instead, what seems to work best is consistent, long-term experience. For instance, instead of inviting guests from six different countries for six different visits, try arranging for a person from one culture to come to class for several visits. Talk with the children about their observations after each visit. You will probably notice a change over the course of their acquaintance with their guest. In initial visits, children tend to concentrate on the most unusual features of the visitor. However, over time, they have opportunities to observe other things—that the person enjoys soccer, has a pesky younger sibling, or loves chocolate—that are the common denominators of human contact.

Takaki (1993)

In the same way, do not limit content about people of color, ethnic groups, or experiences with gender roles to a specific month or week. Instead, provide many opportunities for children to see all sorts of people in a variety of roles and situations. The point is to help children search for commonalities, as well as for the deeper differences that not only add interest and variety to human experience, but can cause misunderstandings between people. With young children you might start with Peter Spier's *People*, focusing on the myriad ways in which people develop such cultural universals as clothing, shelter, recreation, and food. Ask children to think about things they do that might seem strange to someone from another country, from another part of their own country, or from their own class. When older children study a topic such as the settlement of California, ask them to imagine how Native Americans might write the history of this era. Or, look at the American Revolution through the eyes of an African American—either free or enslaved—in the colonies. How might a European-American or African-American woman explain the women's rights movement of the nineteenth century? How might a Haitian describe current U.S. immigration policy?

Spier (1980)

Of equal importance, help children to see beyond color, ethnicity, and gender to the unique individual. It is easy enough for children to recognize that all members of the same class do not have the same taste in music or clothes, do not share the same religion or belief system, or exhibit the same interests or abilities. They are less likely, however, to recognize individual differences in other groups. This is part of the reason it is so important, not only to invite people from a variety of different groups into the classroom, but to maintain a rich collection of literature, visual images, and artifacts that represent variety *within* as well as *between* groups.

Delpit (1995); Hollins (1996); Ladson-Billings (1994)

An idea from anthropology is useful here. Anthropologists working in foreign cultures attempt to make the strange familiar. We ask you to help children make the familiar strange: to look with new eyes at phenomena they encounter every day so that they can observe more carefully, infer more justifiably, and learn more richly.

Obviously, Observation and Inference* are not limited to multicultural, cross-cultural, or gender-related interactions. Careful observation is crucial to any social study.

Think, for instance, about the careful observation conducted by the children studying the dangerous intersection or by those studying the problem of litter in their community. In each case, children's careful, accurate observations led to better-supported inferences and, thereafter, to better-conceived responses to the problems under investigation. As you read the next section on Observation and Inference* in science, you will find other examples of these processes in practice.

Observation and Inference* in Science

Saul et al (1993); Whitin & Whitin (1997)

Careful observation is, of course, essential to good science. It was careful observation that led Newton to infer the laws of gravity, Archimedes to deduce the laws of displacement of liquids, and Galileo to conclude that the earth circles the sun. Before Galileo humans had believed—inferred—that the earth was the center of a solar orbit. Such inferences are common to children, too. Perhaps you remember thinking that the moon followed you as you drove along the highway on a clear night, or recall wondering why people on the "bottom" of the world did not fall off.

Alberti, Davitt, Ferguson, & Repass (1974)

When Elementary Science Study (ESS) developers tested some of their procedures while they were preparing their classroom materials and teachers' guides, they discovered that "seeing" isn't always "observing." In one third-grade class, students tried to chill water with crushed ice. Their observations were intended to lead them to conclude that "there is a minimum temperature below which an ice-water mixture will not go, regardless of the quantity of ice and snow added to it" (p. 27). Despite several opportunities to observe that this was the case, the children persisted in thinking that the temperature would drop as more snow or ice was added. It took multiple experiences before children began to accept the evidence gathered from their experiments and to interpret that evidence so as to change their original inferences.

The open-mindedness crucial to science obviously takes practice. In another ESS activity, children observed what happened when they put various objects on ice. Ice cubes and small objects such as pennies, chalk, paper clips, washers, and wooden cubes were distributed, and children were asked to observe what happened when these objects were placed on an ice cube. The teacher helped the children organize their observations as follows:

Didn't Sink In	Sank in a Little	Sank in a Lot
pieces of candle	wood	money
eraser (rubber)	stone	paper clips
pieces of chalk		thumbtack
		washer

In their Learning Logs*, the children speculated about the reasons for these differences—they made inferences—and then planned further experiments to see if their inferences were supported.

Other simple Observation and Inference* activities in science include having the teacher or a student perform an activity while the other students observe carefully. For instance, the demonstrator holds up two white envelopes of equal size. The first envelope is placed against the cabinet and falls to the floor. The second envelope is placed against the cabinet and stays put. Once the observation period ends, children write down and discuss three or four observations. Part of the discussion is separating statements of inference such as "There is glue on one envelope" from statements of observation such as "One envelope is still on the cabinet." Once the class establishes a set of observations, they begin to construct hypotheses or inferences that could explain the observations. Depending on the time available, the teacher can either ask children to create envelopes that will behave as the ones in the demonstration or allow them to suggest further tests of inferences. They may want to see if the "sticking" envelope will also adhere to a wooden cabinet, or they may want to compare the weights of each envelope. None of the student tests should permit opening or destroying the envelopes.

Any number of similar activities can be constructed to help children develop their ability to make the kind of careful observations and supported inferences basic to understanding scientific phenomena. Sometimes teachers introduce these activities in Focus-Lessons* in preparation for a task students want to accomplish or to initiate a new theme. In one fourth-grade classroom the teacher hung several birdfeeders outside the classroom window. She also made a journal labeled "Bird Observation Journal," and hung it by the window. As children wrote in the journal and talked in class meetings, they learned different ways of "looking closely," and observation/inference activities became an important part of the ongoing theme. For instance, children decided that their observations might be more accurate if two people watched the same event, if the observer talked into a tape recorder or used a video camera. In addition, they created a site map to help locate observations, and created a set of abbreviations to use when recording observations. In these ways, observation and inference become techniques that allow children to accomplish their own inquiry goals.

Graphic Organizers*

Graphic Organizers* are visual displays that enable children to organize and represent meanings, ideas, and concepts on a topic, especially while they are engaged in Reflective, Disciplined Inquiry*. They can be used for many purposes: to activate prior knowledge on a topic to be studied or read about and then to show new concepts, connections, or vocabulary that developed as a result of an investigation on that topic; to depict (as a prewriting experience) the meanings or ideas to be included in a piece of writing; to share ideas on a topic or domain in small group or whole class discussions to gain feedback; or to present (or "publish") the findings of a systematic study or analysis done in an inquiry. Just as they reflect different purposes, Graphic Organizers* can also take on different forms. We cover four types: Graffiti Walls*, Semantic Maps*, K-W-L*, and Comparison Charts*.

See Tierney, Readence, & Disher (1995) for another discussion of Graphic Organizers*.

Although Graphic Organizers* can be realized by various forms and may fulfill various purposes, all activities involving Graphic Organizers* have similar features: They all elicit children's own ideas, wordings, and meanings so that children are put into the center of their own learning. They frequently also provide a means for children to share and build on each other's ideas. Hearing others' ideas fosters divergent thinking, and children's own schemas on a topic are likely to be modified or altered. Thus, Graphic Organizers* demonstrate ways to depict knowledge already acquired and to show directions to new learning.

*Graffiti Walls**

The same urge that seems to drive people to leave some permanent record of themselves in public places can be harnessed in a positive way in the classroom through Graffiti Walls*. Graffiti Walls* are free-form spaces for brainstorming or communicating key words, phrases, or ideas on a topic or the thematic unit itself. At the onset of a TIME unit, the teacher may ask children to brainstorm all the words they know about time on a large sheet of butcher paper, chart paper, or newsprint. Contributions are written down in a free-form, loosely organized fashion, using Magic Markers or crayons so that the ideas can be easily seen. The teacher writes children's responses (sometimes first having children work individually or in small groups), or children may add words on their own. Initially, children are likely to think of words such as *minute, hour, second, birthday, morning, evening,* and so on. As the unit unfolds, children are encouraged to add new words or phrases pertaining to time or to illustrate interesting idioms and aphorisms such as "Time flies" or "A stitch in time saves nine." At specific times during the unit, the Graffiti Wall* can take a special focus when children are invited to write words and phrases that describe times of day (e.g., a sunset that was rose-golden) or books and poems that have time in the title (e.g., *Time of Wonder*).

Graffiti Walls focus attention on words and phrases.*

McClosky (1957)

In addition to making children active searchers for new or intriguing words, the Graffiti Wall* can serve as a class thesaurus/dictionary as children become used to consulting it to find words that enrich their writing. The teacher also returns to the Graffiti Wall* during the course of the unit to call attention to particular features of language being used or simply to enjoy the way the display has grown.

Smaller versions of Graffiti Walls* can be used by small groups—perhaps displaying the words, phrases, and so on that reflect initial understandings of a subtopic of a unit and then adding ones that members are coming across in their individual reading. Or, a graffiti notebook could be kept if wall space is at a premium. Once the idea of a Graffiti Wall* is demonstrated, children can use them in many ways: to show possible topics to investigate or write about, to display ideas to pursue in the course of a unit, or to keep track of new words or vocabulary that they have learned to spell.

Semantic Maps*

Heimlich & Pittelman (1986)

Semantic Maps* focus on relationships between ideas and concepts.

Semantic Maps* are similar to Graffiti Walls* in that they encourage children to think about what they already know and then try to build on and extend that knowledge. However, Semantic Maps* are different from Graffiti Walls* in that they are more organized ways to call attention to the relationship between ideas of particular topics by categorizing and connecting wordings or concepts. Semantic Maps* were used in Chapter 1 to illustrate schemas—our mental models of our knowledge—and to depict how Sara developed a schema of the domain of spiders. The WEBs depicted in Chapter 4 are also types of Semantic Maps*.

See also Revel-Wood (1988) for a good classroom example of Semantic Maps*.

To illustrate how Semantic Maps* can be demonstrated in the classroom, let's recall Sara's increasingly complex understanding of the domain for "spider" (in Chapter 1) and the way her teacher built on that understanding by planning a thematic unit on BUGS (in Chapter 3). During the unit, Sara's teacher asked the children to brainstorm about what they know about spiders. As they jotted down ideas, the teacher encouraged them to try to list those words that seem to go together. (Or before their brainstorming, the teacher could have suggested some general categories—what spiders look like, what they do, and where they are found.) Then, on the board or a large sheet of chart paper, the teacher began listing the children's ideas about spiders.

Discussion about words and their categories is one of the most valuable aspects of developing a Semantic Map* while children verbalize, and perhaps argue about, their understanding of already existing schemas. Once the children's categories have been

Figure 7.6
A SEMANTIC MAP* ON SPIDERS

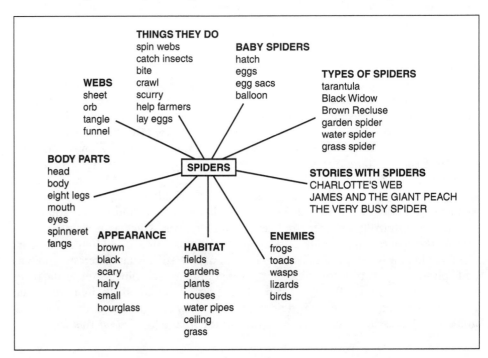

listed on the Semantic Map*, the teacher can help them find labels for the categories. Figure 7.6 illustrates the type of Semantic Map* that can result. Notice that many of the terms may have been contributed by children who have been doing a lot of reading and writing about spiders.

Semantic Maps* can be developed before children start a study, perhaps when they begin some initial observations of some spiders that have been brought into the classroom or seen at a local zoo. Following the discussion of the first map, children engage in some individual research and reading with the goal of enlarging and extending the original map. They then construct a second map and compare the new information they have been able to add. Or instead of writing ideas directly on the board or paper, the children can place them on brainstorming cards or strips and then organize them on a bulletin board with thumbtacks or on a portion of the board with masking tape "loops." As children study the topic, they write down another idea and decide where it should be placed on the map. The advantage of the strips is that children can physically place an idea in one category and then move it if they decide that it is best listed under a different, or new, category. Through the process, the teacher helps children find or change labels for existing categories and to distinguish subtle differences in categories and classes. Thus, the use of strips enables children to construct an ongoing Semantic Map* in a dynamic way.

Semantic Maps* can be constructed in terms of questions or key themes to be considered in an inquiry. A small group studying volcanoes as part of a unit on CHANGES, for example, may initially consider three major questions: Where are volcanoes located? Why do they erupt? What happens during an eruption? Figure 7.7 shows the type of Semantic Map* the teacher developed for the group.

Children are asked to tell, or write individually, what they think they already know regarding each question. Making sure that there is plenty of space left for adding new information later, the teacher then encourages the children to read independently a range of books on the topic (e.g., Branley's *Volcanoes*) to see what else they can find out about volcanoes. The teacher also urges them to be on the lookout for new questions to consider. The children know that following their reading they will come back to the Semantic Map* to confirm or refine their original ideas and to add new information that they have found. During their reading, they may jot down key facts or ideas in their Learning Logs* or perhaps on a smaller photocopied version of the larger Semantic Map*.

When the group comes together following their reading, they reexamine each question. First, they discuss their original ideas and determine if these were confirmed or contradicted by their reading. If confirmed, a star or asterisk is placed by that line. Using a marker of a different color helps children recognize the difference between prior knowledge and new information. If an original idea was a misconception, it is

The finished map represents a summary of prior and new information.

Branley (1985)

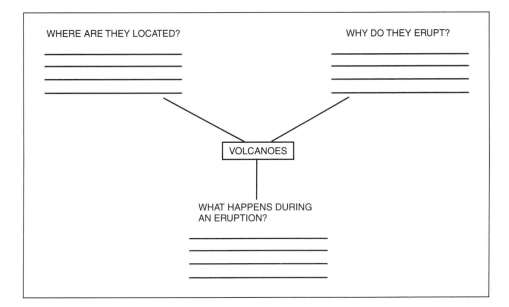

Figure 7.7

An Initial Semantic Map of Questions for the "Volcanoes" Inquiry

crossed out. Then new information gained from the reading is added under each question. Other questions (e.g., What are the consequences of eruptions?) are also considered. The discussion surrounding Semantic Map* activity is important. Children may have to go back to the books or text they have read to support their points of view. They must verbalize and clarify important understandings in the process of negotiating and constructing the map.

Semantic Maps* can be used for a range of purposes. For example, they can be used to document and organize children's observations of snails or to note the transformations involved in a scientific experiment. They can be used as a prewriting experience or as a publication of a small group's (or an individual's) study of a topic. A Semantic Map* can be constructed for one book rather than for a general topic on which information is acquired through reading many books or through other sources such as careful observation and interviews with experts. Semantic Maps* can also be completed for fictional stories or books in which characters, motives, actions, and outcomes are depicted.

See Heimlich & Pittelman (1986) for examples of various kinds of Semantic Maps*.

K-W-L*

Ogle (1986)

Developed by Ogle to help teachers focus on the experiences readers bring to text, K-W-L* began as a framework for actively engaging readers with informational texts. Prior to reading about a particular topic, the blackboard or a sheet of paper is divided into three columns headed "What We Know," "What We Want to Find Out," and "What We Learned and Still Need to Learn." As children brainstorm all the things they know about the topic, teachers might ask, "Where did you learn that?" or "How could you prove that?"

Once children have listed what they know about a topic, they will want to consider what type of information they think they will find as they read. As they list their ideas, the teacher can help them categorize the information in broad subtopics similar to the approach described for Semantic Maps*.

Because this first part of K-W-L* should result in rich discussion and argument, it is likely that individual interests and questions about the topic will arise for each child. Thus, the second step, "What We Want to Find Out," should help each child identify those questions and interests that will be brought to their individual reading and record their questions on individual K-W-L* sheets. The questions help guide each child's reading and then provide a focus for filling in the third column, "What We Learned and Still Need to Know."

Ogle (1986)

Highlights of a transcript reported by Ogle show how the technique works with a group that is preparing to read an article on Black Widow spiders. They have been discussing what they know about the spiders and are getting ready to categorize their ideas.

Teacher: Does anyone else recall anything more about the way they look? [She waits] Look at what we've already said about these spiders. Can you think of any other information we should add?

John: I think they kill their babies or men spiders. I'm not sure which.

Teacher: Do you remember where you learned that?

John: I think I read an article once.

Teacher: Okay, let's add that to our list. Remember, everything on the list we aren't sure of we can double check when we read.

Teacher: . . . OK, before we read this article let's think awhile about the kinds or categories of information that are likely to be included. Look at the list of things we already know or have questions about. Which of the categories of information have we already mentioned?

Peter: We mentioned how they look.

Teacher: Yes, we said they're big and have six legs. And someone said they think

Black Widows have a colored mark on them. Good description is one of the main categories of information we want to learn about when we read about animals or insects. What other categories of information have we mentioned that should be included?

Anna: Where they live; but we aren't sure. (pp. 567–569).

The children went on to name other categories, such as what spiders eat and how they protect themselves. Then, with the teacher's help they listed other things that they wanted to find out about, such as why the spiders are called Black Widows. The teacher encouraged the children to write other questions on their worksheets and to jot down the answers as well as other important information as they read. Following their reading she called them back together and asked:

Teacher: How did you like this article? What did you learn?

Raul: The Black Widow eats her husband and sometimes her babies. Yuck! I don't think I like that kind of spider!

Steph: They can live here—it says they live in all parts of the United States.

Andy: They can be recognized by an hourglass that is red or yellow on the abdomen.

Teacher: What is another word for abdomen? Sara, please look up the word abdomen. Let's find out where the hourglass shape is located. While Sara is looking the word up let's check what we learned against the questions we wanted answered. Are there some questions that didn't get answered? What more do we want to know? (p. 569)

Although the children in this example all read the same article, K-W-L* is equally effective when they are reading from different information books and other resources. The technique is thus well suited for use by small groups or an entire class and allows children to explore a variety of reading materials on a particular topic. In some classes, too, teachers use K-W-L* charts a bit differently. For science workshop, for instance, one class substitutes *Wonder* for *Want to Know*, because *wonder* better conveys the attitude toward scientific inquiry the teacher encourages. In this class, too, children keep individual K-W-L* charts. When they work on individual or small group projects they first list five things they already know about a topic, and five things they wonder about the topic. After reading, listening to a presentation, or conducting an experiment they fill in the Learn column and keep this record in their Learning Logs.*

Saul et al. (1993); Whitin & Whitin (1997)

Comparison Charts*

Comparison Charts* also involve examinations of likenesses and differences among ideas, events, characteristics, and so forth. Comparison Charts* may take a number of forms. Sometimes they may be used to focus characters, events, motifs, and themes within a single story or novel, or the characteristics, features, and attributes in informational materials. At other times, they can be useful in comparing books, events, or properties within a given theme. Comparison Charts* give children opportunities to work individually with texts and then to pool and share details of their reading with their peers in a small group or with the whole class. Comparison Charts* can also give teachers a focus for looking at theme, story structure, character development, or other important features or concepts in a given work.

Comparison Charts allow children to compare and contrast ideas and information.*

Figure 7.8 is an example of a Comparison Chart* that was filled in by five primary children. They first heard their teacher read *Pearl Moscowitz's Last Stand*, a story about taking political action in an urban neighborhood. The class had thoroughly enjoyed Pearl and the way new neighbors and different cultures merged on her block. They particularly liked the ways in which Pearl dealt with the electrician who came to cut down her tree. They talked about what makes people neighbors, and some of the

Levine (1993)

	Problem	Solution	Right	Responsibility
UNCLE JED'S BARBERSHOP	Uncle Jed wants a barbershop. Sarah Jean needs an operation. Uncle Jed lost all his money.	He saves and saves. He gives her his money. He saves and saves, and finally gets his barbershop. His dream came true.	Right to work. Right to be cared for when you are sick. Right to have your money safe in a bank.	Work hard and save. Take care of people when you can. Help people who *really* need it.
PEARL MOSCOWITZ'S LAST STAND	The city wants to cut down the last ginko tree on Pearl's block.	She tries to stop him from cutting down the tree. She chains herself to the tree until the mayor listens and she keeps the tree, and gets more trees.	Right to have a say in what happens where you live. Right to have a mayor listen to you.	To take care of your neighborhood. To have good reasons.
BLOOMERS!	Women's clothes were very uncomfortable. They made it hard for women to do their work. Some women wanted to wear different clothes.	Women made a new kind of clothes, with pants. Some worked for other changes for women; voting and traveling.	Right to wear what you want. Right to vote and be equal.	You should vote.

Figure 7.8
A Comparison Chart* for three books

Mitchell (1993)

Blumberg (1996)

Children become more critical readers when they develop their own categories.

ways that neighbors can work together to protect their neighborhood. Because she wanted them to see other ways of being neighborly, and other challenges that neighbors sometimes face, their teacher also read them *Uncle Jed's Barbershop*. Uncle Jed and his neighbors—mostly Black sharecroppers—lived in the segregated South in the 1920s. There was much need, and Uncle Jed was always willing to help. The children were shocked by the local doctor's refusal to treat Uncle Jed's niece, Sarah Jean, and had many questions about the "whites only" policy in the hospital. When their teacher told them the same had been the case even when she was a little girl they wanted to know how old she had been when things changed. The teacher wrote *rights* on the board and talked about some of the rights people were supposed to share. This conversation carried over into their library period. As a result, the librarian shared *Bloomers!* with the class. Now they had another kind of *right* to think about. Their teacher suggested that it might help to organize some of their ideas if someone would work on a comparison chart. The teacher drew the chart on a large sheet of construction paper and discussed the categories with one group of children. These categories provided them with a focus for problem solving and discussion that centered on the three books. They talked about the three stories and noted details that were alike and different and spent some time talking about the illustrations. They noted stylistic matters; for example, that in two of the books the illustrators drew cartoonlike or stylistic figures, while in *Uncle Jed's Barbershop*, the illustrations were more realistic. They also talked about the kinds of rules that caused problems in each book. The chart thus served as a springboard for a rich and lengthy discussion about characteristics of the books. When it came time to fill in the chart, they were able to draw on each text for specific words as well as ideas about the rights and responsibilities of neighbors.

Children are also quite capable of discovering their own categories. Again, this activity provides a focus for discussion of the many elements in books or other resources. As with the other three types of Graphic Organizers*, the finished chart is only a representation of some of the findings of children's study and analysis; it provides a means and a stepping-stone to writing and talking about findings with others. Therefore, charts frequently serve as a summary of a range of reading transactions children may have had in reading books. The charts are also important prewriting experiences because many of their categories are incorporated into the stories or reports that individual children write. In a third/fourth-grade classroom, for example, a group of children read four "inchling" stories—folktales that center on the tiny size of the main character. Following their reading, each child shared his or her particular story with the group. There was much discussion of themes, events, and other details as the children attempted to choose categories that would capture the features of all or most of their books and then to decide on labels for these categories. Eventually they decided on thirteen: book title, country (of the folktale's origin), magic object, wishes, sacrifices, where they (the parents) worked and what they worked for, where they went and why, size (of the tiny character), what they took (on their journey), Japanese words, whom they met on their journey, how they got the child, and characters. Once the categories were named, the children wrote the details from each book on pieces of paper and glued them on an appropriately labeled piece of chart paper. (See Figure 7.9.)

Following the completion of a Comparison Chart*, many children choose to write their own stories or to illustrate certain events in the books studied. After a study of informational texts, children may write a report on a specific animal or phenomenon that has been included on a Comparison Chart*. A third-grade class read many books on dinosaurs as part of a DISAPPEARING ACTS thematic unit. Comparison Charts* were constructed by small groups to compare dinosaur characteristics such as habitual behavior or physical features. Included in the chart was a category listing other animals that lived at the same time. Several children became interested in one of these animals, the mammoth, and did more research on it. One child wrote a report on her findings, one wrote a cartoonlike saga featuring Wild Willy Mammoth (influenced by Aliki's *Wild and Woolly Mammoths*), and another child (using ideas from Joanna Cole's *Evolution*) constructed his own plaster fossil of a mammoth. In a first-grade unit on FLIGHT, children in a small group completed a Comparison Chart* on various ducks, using the following simple categories: type of duck, looks, home, food, and habits. After they finished the chart, each child illustrated one of the ducks and wrote a brief description of it.

Children can also write about their experience of constructing a Comparison Chart* to enlighten other classmates who may not be so familiar with the process, to explain the activity for a parents' night, or to include in their learning portfolio.

Charts provide a focus or structure for further writing.

Aliki (1977); Cole (1987)

Figure 7.9

A COMPARISON CHART* FOR "INCHLING" STORIES

My Comparison Chart Writing

I did a comparison chart with Terri. The books we compared were The Greatful Crane, The Crane Maiden and The Crane Wife.

First we looked through the books for things we could compare for example how many times the crane changed, the characters and the ending.

Then we wrote everything down on small pieces of paper in a thin black marker. We glued them down on big pieces of blue paper. We made pictures to go with it.

Some neat things I noticed was that in The Crane Wife the crane sings Tankara Tankara and in The Crane Maiden she sings riakola kinkoja.

In The Crane Maiden it doesn't look like it but the illustrator used water color and in The Greatful Crane the illustrator used a well kind of a wooden doll house and collages.

Figure 7.10

Bartoli (1977); Matsutani (1968); Yagawa (1981)

Figure 7.10 is an example of a ten-year-old's report of a comparison of three Japanese tales (*The Story of the Grateful Crane: A Japanese Folktale*, *The Crane Maiden*, and *The Crane Wife*). She and a partner had both read all three tales and then decided on the categories for comparison.

Literacy Activities and Experiences

Reading Activities and Experiences

This section describes various activities or experiences related to reading. It is important to recall that although reading is the focus here, in an integrated language classroom it is integrated with writing, speaking, and listening and it occurs for many purposes across the curriculum.

Reading Aloud*

Cohen (1968); Tunnell & Jacobs (1989); Wells (1986)

Hepler & Hickman (1982); Hickman (1981)

Reading Aloud* to children is a necessary component in integrated language classrooms. Most teachers have times when they read to the whole class; they may also read aloud to small groups during the day. Books should be selected according to children's interests and developmental background and also to stretch their imagination, extend and spark new interests, foster an awareness of various genres, and develop an appreciation of fine writing and illustration. Teachers who want help in selecting quality literature can turn to their librarian for advice or to award lists such as the Newbery and Caldecott winners and honor books. *Booklist* and *The Horn Book* (see Chapter 3) only review books that they recommend for children and star those they judge to be outstanding. Three other professional journals—*Language Arts*, *Social Education*, and *Science Teacher*—publish a yearly list of books that are named as outstanding in the fields of language arts, social studies, and science.

Enthusiasm for the selected book, story, poem, and so on is the first ingredient of good Reading Aloud*. Teachers should always read the text ahead of time so that they are aware of its content and so that their reading is smooth and fluent. A teacher's reading delivery depends on the text being read and that teacher's own style. For example, some teachers are good at doing character voices, sound effects, and physical gestures but children can also be enthralled by the quiet warmth of a gentler voice.

Reading Aloud* seems to work best when children are gathered on a rug or special place close to the teacher. Reading picture books with the book at shoulder level, pages facing the children at their eye level, gives them plenty of time to look at the illustrations and enables them to enter the visual as well as the verbal world of the book.

Books or other texts can be introduced in various ways: by a brief discussion about the author or illustrator; by asking children to predict what the story or text is about by examining the cover and interpreting the title; by linking the topic, theme, author, or illustrator to other books children may know; and so forth. With chapter books, teachers can have children discuss the progress of the book so far and consider what is likely to occur next.

See also Huck, Hepler, Hickman, & Kiefer (1997)

Butler & Turbill (1984); Calkins (1986); Reardon (1988)

Teachers may also plan for places in the text to stop during reading (using small Post-it Notes as reminders) to encourage children's comments or questions about what has been read or to foster predictions about what is yet to be read. It is not a good idea to ask too many questions, and the kinds of questions used should be those that help children make their own discoveries. (See the discourse excerpts in Chapter 2.) Questions to make children aware of the craft of writing—to foster the reader-writer contract—should also be considered. Questions can be posed to get children to recognize the power of particular words or phrases used by the author—how they sound, how they help paint a picture, and how they ask and answer certain questions about the author. We want children to appreciate authors' choices so that they become reflective of their own choices in their writing. Many children like to sketch or write in their journals during the read-aloud time and should feel comfortable about initiating discussion.

Beaver (1982); Morrow (1988)

After they have finished reading, children may want to discuss the book by relating ideas in the text to their own experiences or to other texts. Sometimes, depending on the book, it is useful to give children time to think and ponder about ideas in the text and then to go back and reread particular passages either at the end of a Reading Aloud* session or later in the day. It is important to note, however, that not all texts have to be discussed to be enjoyed, understood, or appreciated. It is also a good idea to frequently read whole texts aloud more than once; often it is during the second or third reading of a book that the most sensitive responses are brought to the surface. This practice also encourages favorites, making certain books "friends" for life.

Holdaway (1979)

Storytelling*

Storytelling* is an important alternative to Reading Aloud*. An art form that needs to be valued and perpetuated, Storytelling* provides opportunities for more intimate rapport with children because no book separates the teacher and the audience. It isn't necessary to memorize stories to be a good storyteller, but careful planning is essential. The teacher needs to be familiar with the plot, the characters, and the "flavor" of the book's language. If certain chants or refrains are repeated in the text, those should be memorized. Stories such as *Goldilocks and the Three Bears* and *The Teeny Tiny Woman* are good for younger children. The use of simple props or visual aids (e.g., a flannel board or puppets) can help teachers recall the story's key elements, and it encourages children to want to retell and reenact their own versions of the story. Bryan's West Indian story *The Cat's Purr* is a favorite of middle elementary children (seven-to nine-year-olds). Fifth and sixth graders also enjoy hearing a story told. Teachers' storytelling may serve as demonstrations for their own efforts to tell stories to younger children in the school, perhaps as an important part of a Buddy Reading* program. Besides the teacher, others who may be happy to tell stories to children in the classroom include librarians, local storytellers, and parents.

Bauer (1977)

Sevens (1986); Galdone (1984)

Bryan (1985)

Sustained Silent Reading (SSR)*

Sustained Silent Reading (SSR)*, sometimes also called USSR (Uninterrupted Sustained Silent Reading) or DEAR (Drop Everything And Read), is simply periods of quiet time set aside during the day when children read books of their own choosing. Usually, an SSR* period is initially ten minutes or so and then gradually lengthened. In many upper-elementary classes, forty-five-minute or longer periods may occur. In some schools, everyone (adults and visitors included) picks up a book and reads. The rationale for SSR* is to demonstrate to children that adults who are important to them also enjoy reading. Thus, SSR* fosters fluency by giving children opportunities to practice reading while it also encourages the joy of reading.

Manning & Manning (1984)

SSR* fosters the enjoyment of reading.

SSR* for younger elementary children may involve looking at the pages and softly telling (or "pretend reading") their own versions of books or quietly reading aloud as they read to themselves. The emphasis should always be on the enjoyment of reading. A wide variety of reading materials of varied reading levels and interests is essential. In the beginning, especially for children who are unfamiliar with SSR* time, teachers may have to guide children to books of interest or remind them to think ahead about what they will be reading during SSR* so that they don't spend a lot of time just finding something to read. A timer of some sort can also be used in the beginning to mark the end of the SSR* period to congratulate children on their capability to sustain a certain number of minutes of reading.

Buddy Reading*

See Mossip (1985) for an example of Buddy Reading* by children of different ages.

Samway, Whang, & Pippitt (1995)

Many teachers implement Buddy Reading* as an alternative to SSR*. Buddy Reading* acknowledges the social nature of reading by having children pair up, each with a book of their own choosing, to read to their partner. Children take turns reading different books or pages of the same book. Buddies do not have to be at the same reading level because they are selecting their own material. Buddy Reading* can occur within one classroom or children from different grade levels can read together. When older elementary children, who might be reluctant or less able readers, are paired with younger children, they have good reasons to practice the books they are to share. Self-confidence as readers is fostered. Older children also frequently enjoy experiences of Storytelling*. Making and sharing Big Books* with younger children is another feature that can be incorporated in a Buddy Reading* program.

Book Talks*

Bauer (1983, 1993)

Book Talks* are great ways to publicize good books. Frequently teachers schedule Book Talk* time right after SSR*. It is important, however, for teachers to model or demonstrate this activity for children, perhaps as they highlight books that will be part of a thematic unit. The first few pages can be read, or an amusing or exciting part recounted. Assuming the role of one of the characters is another Book Talk* technique. Excerpts from several novels or dust jacket summaries can be offered. Special objects that are important elements of stories (a pebble in *Sylvester and the Magic Pebble*, an old key in *The Secret Garden*, or a peach pit in *James and the Giant Peach*) can serve as foci for Book Talks*.

Steig (1979); Burnett (1962); Dahl (1961)

Book Talks* can be about books from a wide range of genres.

Aliki (1981)

Cole (1986)

Freedman (1987)

Hepler (1991)

Book Talks* should not be limited to fiction. Mentioning all the experts involved in finding and digging up dinosaurs—paleontologists, geologists, draftsmen, workers, photographers, and specialists—and what they do may be a selling point for Aliki's *Digging up Dinosaurs*. Or showing the page where the magic school bus rises into the clouds in Cole's *The Magic School Bus at the Waterworks* may draw children to read and find out about water facts. Sharing some of the photographs in Freedman's *Lincoln: A Photobiography* or relating some of the things about Lincoln in the book that were interesting to the teacher may be ways this book might be "sold." Children quickly pick up on these techniques and develop their own ways of "selling" books. It is hard to resist when a friend says, "This is the best book I ever read!" or "This was so interesting, I couldn't put it down!"

Literature Response Groups *

Literature Response Groups*, Literature Circles, and Book Clubs bring children together to talk about books.

See Hepler & Hickman (1982); Hill, et al. (1995); Raphael & McMahon (1994); Samway & Whang (1996); and Short & Pierce (1990) for descriptions of book discussion groups.

Literature Response Groups,* (often called Literature Circles or Book Clubs) are opportunities for a small group to discuss books in depth with one another. At times teachers will ask children to self-select into discussion groups based on books to be read as an exploration of a theme. Frequently, however, these groups are organized and run by the children themselves because they have all read the same book and want to talk about it. Or they may be reading books on a common topic or from a common genre or tackling similar problems in projects in a thematic unit. They may post an announcement on the Message Board* asking for interested participants. Many teachers set some time aside in integrated work time on certain days for such group inter-actions so that they themselves can periodically sit in on the discussions. When a teacher joins in as a member of a Literature Response Group*, the teacher works hard at being a participant, not as someone who asks all the questions or directs and con-trols the discussion.

The way the teacher handles discussion at Reading Aloud* sessions provides a framework that children can adopt in their own Literature Response Groups*. In the beginning of the year, teachers can sit in on the Literature Response Groups* more fre-quently and model ways to phrase questions or comments about texts so that children get ideas about the kinds of transactions possible.

Teachers can demonstrate ways in which readers talk about books during read aloud time.

Children should be encouraged to develop their own questions for Literature Re-sponse Groups.* Most teachers ask children to come to Literature Response Groups* prepared, with their Journals* or Learning Logs* in hand. They have used their Re-sponse Journals* to muse about personal reactions, to wonder about events, themes, and ideas in a book or to note favorite passages and descriptions. Chambers suggests that in discussions, responses to books often fall into three categories: readers share en-thusiasms, share puzzles or difficulties, and share connections or patterns. These "three sharings" could be used as a framework for journal writing and for beginning discus-sions. Many teachers encourage children to mark important places in their books with stick-on notes as they read. These flags mark passages that they want to return to later to think about more carefully. This may have been a place in the book that was par-ticularly moving or exciting or a place where they got confused. These flags might also mark places where they noticed something special about the author's writing or where they had about the author's perspective or point of view.

Book Response Journals are a source for discussion questions.*

Chambers, A. (1996)

See Atwell (1987) for a good example of Book Response Journals in action in the classroom.*

Teachers can conduct Focus-Lessons* on what that preparation for response groups might consist of. They can suggest that children first ask themselves personal, experiential questions about the book at hand: What stands out for me? What do I feel about the ideas in this book? What are my reactions? What's my favorite part? Other questions children might also want to consider are those that connect ideas in the text under discussion with prior experiences or similar ideas in other texts: What did this book make me think of? Other questions or responses—descriptive and analytic, in-terpretive and elaborative, evaluative and self-evaluative—can be illustrated by having children brainstorm ways they could relate to individual texts. (See Chapter 6 for a re-view of reader transactions.)

Focus Lessons can help prepare chil-dren to conduct their own discussions.*

In these responses, comments, or explanations, the author's craft and ideologies should be specifically addressed. Suggestions for questions to consider can be provided: What questions would you ask if the author were here? What sections of the text are effective in relating the setting of the story or in explaining a particular concept or process in an information book? What underlying values does the author seem to have about what he or she is writing? Were the characters believable? What did you like about the author's style? What questions is the author answering in this book on snakes, tunnels, Lincoln, velocity, immigrants, or whatever? Are there questions that the author didn't answer or points of view that the author did not consider?

Questions in Literature Response Groups often center on the craft of writing fiction or information books.*

Calkins (1994); Butler & Turbill (1984); Short & Harste (1996); Reardon (1988)

Literature Response Groups* can also begin by having children do dramatization or writing. The teacher can ask members of the group to take the role of the towns-people in Gauch's *Thunder at Gettysburg*, maybe as they met at a public meeting, at the beginning of the book, or after the Rebel soldiers came to town but before the Union troops arrived. Then children can be asked to have another public meeting af-ter the battle, with discussion revolving around people's changing views about the "vic-tories" of war, and the author's view of war, and how it is communicated in the text. Children's writing responses—perhaps regarding what Tillie, the main protagonist in *Thunder at Gettysburg*, could have written in a letter to her cousin about her experi-ences during the battle and what she saw of death and destruction—can also be a fo-cus of discussion in a Literature Response Group*.

Fostering the reading-writing contract

Gauch (1975)

Discussion in some Literature Response Groups* may result in constructing a Comparison Chart* or some other kind of Graphic Organizer*. These visuals give children a focus for sharing their understandings and responses with other class members. Ideas from the discussion may also spark a range of writing, as well as lead children to read or reread other books on the same topic, by the same author, or in the same genre.

Reading Conferences*

Because children in integrated language classrooms for the most part choose their own reading materials, reading is truly individualized. Consequently, many teachers have individual conferences with children to talk about reading. (Other teachers have many shorter, less formal conferences when they see children reading in the classroom, followed by more general conferences where reading is addressed along with other learning.)

The two primary purposes of Reading Conferences* are to assess and to guide: to assess children's strategies in reading; to understand their range of reading transactions and purposes; to ascertain their abilities to read critically; to determine children's reading needs and interests and their attitudes of reading in general; and to suggest other books, genres, or topics to consider.

Reading Conferences* are usually organized into four parts: sharing, questioning, oral reading, and encouraging and guiding. Most teachers keep a particular notebook or journal in which to make notes and record pertinent information gained in the conferences. They prepare for a conference by going over this and any other information they have observed about the children's reading, so that they know what questions to ask.

Sharing

First, the children share responses about past or present reading materials. They may begin by summarizing briefly what they have written in their Book Response Journals* or Learning Logs*, and then focus more on one or two texts. How and why the texts are being read can be pursued, and any information about a related Book Extension*, activity, or project in which the book is involved can be discussed.

Questioning

The teacher asks one or two searching questions about one of the books or texts the children have read. These questions can concern the theme of the book or the author's style in describing a character or setting, or they may help to explain a concept or process. Teachers may not have read all the books their children are reading, so some teachers take turns addressing a text they know about in one conference and then asking about an unfamiliar text in the next conference. This enables teachers to acquire useful information about the children's awareness of audience.

Oral Reading

The teacher listens to children's reading of a short section of the text that has been chosen for sharing. Teachers usually allow children to select the part they will read aloud, but sometimes teachers may ask them to read a part discussed during sharing or questioning. The teacher notes the child's miscues (see Chapter 8)—how the child is integrating cueing systems, self-correcting, and expressing the language of the text. (Some teachers tape this part of the conference as well as record their impressions of children's reading strategies.)

Encouraging and Guiding

The teacher discusses future plans in reading. Suggestions about the selection of other books written by the same author and with the same theme or topic are made. If children are limiting their reading to one or two genres, teachers may "nudge" them to try books in other genres. Possible ideas for Book Extensions* may also be offered.

Reading Conferences have four parts.*

See also Butler & Turbill (1984), Hepler (1991), and Hornsby & Sukarma (1988) for other ideas for Reading Conferences*.

Teachers can have a Reading Conference* with children once a week or one once every two weeks. As a result of the data acquired in Reading Conferences*, teachers may organize a follow-up conference with a small number of children to foster some specific reading strategies. For example, if children seem to overly rely on graphophonemic cues in their own oral reading, the teacher may develop CLOZE* or other activities to get them to use syntactic and semantic cues as well. Or, if after the set of conferences with children, teachers realize that many children demonstrate such an overreliance (perhaps as the result of instruction in the previous year), they may set up a series of Focus-Lessons* to encourage children to use more meaning-driven reading strategies.

Reading Conferences* can be conducted with students in any elementary grade, even kindergartners and young first graders who may not as yet be reading from print. In these cases, children can be asked to reenact a book by approximating the text ("pretend reading") or retelling it, or by having them "read" a message they have dictated (see Chapter 8). Children show amazing progress in a very short period when they are treated as independent readers, and Reading Conferences* are important ways to demonstrate and emphasize this independence to them.

Big Books*

Big Books* are simply over-sized books containing texts written (and illustrated) on large pieces of paper or cardboard with print big enough for a group of children to see. Big Books* were developed by Holdaway so that children in the classroom could interact with meaningful texts much in the same way that preschoolers interacted with them in book-sharing experiences at home with their parents and other important literate adults. The teacher points, frequently using the handle of a wooden spoon or a ruler, to the words when reading the text in the Big Book*. Then, in rereading the text, children are encouraged to join in. Later, the Big Book* is placed somewhere in the classroom so that children can role-play reading the book. The original, small version of the text is available for children to practice on. Through these book-sharing and other literacy experiences, children learn to read—from many approximations to more competent, accurate renderings—in a self-monitoring, self-correcting manner.

Holdaway (1979)

Holdaway (1979); McKenzie (1977); Pappas & Brown (1989)

Children learn a lot when they are involved in illustrating Big Books*.

Commercially made Big Books* are available, but these are usually very expensive and sometimes not good quality literature but just large versions of basal passages. For these reasons, and because teachers want to use books having to do with a particular thematic unit, teachers usually make (with the help of their children) their own Big Books*. Sometimes the books are made ahead of time by the teacher, a colleague, or parent. Teachers can make simplified drawings or trace pictures enlarged by an overhead projector. Teachers frequently discover that they have many friends or parents who are "closet" artists and enjoy illustrating Big Books*.

Many teachers put in the text only and have children illustrate the books. For example, they share the text with the whole class first, and then a small group of children of varying abilities do the illustrations. The book can be constructed with small metal binders or shower hooks so that individual pages can be worked on separately. Valuable discussion and rereading occur as children decide who will illustrate each page and how. Children can explore many types of media in these illustrations. The teacher usually needs to remind kindergartners and many first-graders to draw "big." Children should also be encouraged to avoid drawing pencil drafts first, for rarely do their resulting illustrations retain the detail of the drafts. After the illustration is completed, children in the group practice the book and read it to the whole class or to children in another class. Large pieces of Plexiglas of several sizes to match varying sizes of books and with holes on the side for the binder rings make excellent book covers that stand up without an easel and are easy for young children to handle. Children's paper covers naturally adhere to the Plexiglas covers due to static electricity, so the expense of supplying sturdier paper book covers is avoided. (Large tablets from art supply stores can also be used to make Big Books*.)

Plexiglas makes great Big Book covers.*

Some teachers go through the whole process of making Big Books* in the presence of a small group of children. Using paper or cardboard strips, the teacher writes

Making Big Books* with children

the words of the text, having children refer to one or more copies of the book to check that mistakes are not made. As the teacher writes the words, he or she talks about the sequence of the message, mentions the characters and other aspects of the book, and refers to spellings and the use of some feature of punctuation (e.g., how quotation marks indicate the words people say). When the whole text is written, both teacher and children read the strips, which are placed on the floor or taped on the board with masking tape. Children pick pages to illustrate, then the group assembles the book by matching strips with illustrations and gluing them on larger pieces of paper.

Clay (1979)

Holdaway (1979)

Besides following words with a pointer—which facilitates children's understanding of one-to-one word correspondences and of the directionality of print—other aspects of written language can be facilitated through the use of Big Books*. Cardboard masks (cardboard frames with holes the width of a line of print and a movable sliding strip) can be made to focus on certain properties of certain phrases or words, thus making children aware of repetitive refrains, or to examine various spelling patterns or graphophonemic relationships. With the use of Post-it Notes, CLOZE* applications can also be made by covering particular words or parts of words to facilitate children's use of surrounding co-text to figure out or predict individual words.

See Fisher (1991) for ideas for using masks with Big Books*.

Patterned books (books that contain rhyme, rhythm, or repetition of certain language patterns) make good Big Books*, but other fictional books and books of informational genres should be considered. For example, children also enjoy Big Book* versions of information books such as *Tunnels, Big City Port*, and *Squirrels*. Teachers can also make their own Big Book* collections of rhymes, poems, recipes, or songs. Big Books* foster children's beginning sight vocabulary quickly, but when children are exposed to a range of genres through Big Books*, a lot more about the registers of written language is fostered. Children, with the help of their teachers and usually in a small group, can write their own Big Books*, perhaps to publish the findings of a project or an in-depth study on some topic in the thematic unit.

Gibbons (1984); Maestro & Del Vecchio (1983); Wildsmith (1974)

Teachers typically use Big Books* of existing literature through the second grade. However, older children may want to make them for use in lower-grade classrooms, or to use with younger children in a Buddy Reading* program.

Cloze*

In Cloze Passages* words are systematically deleted to encourage problem solving.

A CLOZE* passage is a short excerpt—usually several paragraphs—of text in which certain words are deleted. This passage is shared with children in a problem-solving, guided reading lesson. The deletions in an otherwise complete flow of language can be provided in different ways. Usually, one word out of fifteen is deleted, but gaps can occur more frequently if the text still seems meaningful in that way. All the blanks in a CLOZE* can be uniform, or the blanks can resemble the length of the actual word. Some of the letters for the deleted words can be provided, or certain kinds of words can be deleted (e.g., pronouns, adverbs, and adjectives).

Children apply a variety of strategies in a meaningful context.

The CLOZE* passage can be put on a large piece of paper and taped on the board or on a transparency so the group can brainstorm while they try to fill in the blanks. Children can also work on their own copy individually, with a partner, or within a small group. If the beginning of a text is not chosen as the CLOZE* passage, it is important to read the text up to that excerpt. In filling in the blanks, children are encouraged to predict what makes sense. An important aspect of the procedure is for children to justify or tell why their response fits and is meaningful; teachers should accept any reasonable response. In this way, children become sensitive to the linguistic constraints operating on the context—they develop word-attack skills and inferential reasoning. Confirming and self-correcting strategies are induced when children debate as to what the most appropriate response is for a gap. Such strategies can be especially critical for children who believe that reading is merely accurately decoding each word of the text.

Fisher (1991); Goodman & Burke (1985); Holdaway (1979); Routman (1988)

It is also useful to have children engage in CLOZE* activities with passages from different genres so that they can become aware of the different vocabulary and language patterns realized in them.

Say Something*

Harste & Short (1988)

Say Something* activities have been designed by Harste and his colleagues to help children develop a more functional and social view of reading. Partners read the same selection, either aloud or silently. Both read the first several paragraphs, then stop to "say something" to their partner about what they have read. Then the second person says something about what was read. The Say Something* can consist of a range of transactions: responding to something that was just read, predicting what might happen next, or sharing experiences related to the ideas of the text at hand (see Chapter 6 for the types of transactions possible). Then the partners repeat the process: they read the next several paragraphs and take turns "saying something" to each other.

When most partners have finished reading, the teacher sets up a group discussion, perhaps by constructing a Semantic Map*. A central topic is placed in the middle of a large piece of paper or transparency, and children are asked to offer ideas that the author expressed. These ideas are webbed off the central topic. As children contribute, they are asked to explain and justify how and why their responses are relevant concepts and ideas and how and why these ideas relate and interrelate.

Writing Activities and Experiences

The activities and experiences we now discuss have to do with writing, but it is important to emphasize again that writing (like reading) is rarely a separate activity in integrated language classrooms. As discussed earlier, substantial contributions have been made about how to implement in the classroom a process-conference approach to writing, as researchers and educators have termed current views of writing. However, this approach frequently includes a "writing workshop," a certain period set aside each day, during which children write. In an integrated language classroom, writing experiences—prewriting, drafting, revising, editing, and publishing—happen all day across the curriculum. Children take notes during a scientific observation, jot down their responses to a book they may be reading, write questions or comments during their study of some primary materials to prepare for a small group discussion, compose an invitation asking parents or another class to come to a play they have written, or write a thank-you note to a guest speaker who visited their class. The "formal" writing workshops suggested by Graves, Calkins, and Atwell, among others, are therefore not usually implemented as such, but certain important features of these workshops are incorporated by teachers in the writing experiences for children.

Atwell (1987); Calkins (1994); Calkins & Harwayne (1991); Graves (1983)

Instead of a special time, teachers frequently designate a special place—a table or corner of the room—for drafting or peer conferencing, where children share their rough drafts to get feedback. Teachers may then drop in for informal conferences with children, while also checking in with children working elsewhere at other projects. Many teachers routinely set aside some time, perhaps a portion of the integrated work time, to have more formal individual Content Conferences*. Another separate place for Editing Conferences*, where children can receive editing help from peers or teacher, may also be established. Within such a framework, specific properties of writing workshops and other writing activities and experiences of the process-conference writing approach are discussed below in more detail.

Journals*

Fulwiler (1980, 1982)

Journals* can be used in the classroom in many ways. Varying kinds of journals serve varying purposes. We have already discussed Book Response Journals under Literature Response Groups*, in which children write their responses, comments, and questions about the texts they are reading. Other kinds of journals have also been mentioned in this book (e.g., the math story problem Journals* described in Chapter 5). The specific type of journal depends on the needs of the class.

"Notebooks" are Journals that foster "wide-awakeness" in a writer's life— see Calkins (1994)*

Some teachers have children use private, diarylike journals, in which children record their personal feelings, with the agreement that their responses are confidential and therefore are not read or responded to by the teacher or peers. However, most of the time, despite their personal nature, Journals* are communications that can be shared. Three types are covered here: Dialogue Journals*, Thought Ramblings*, and Learning Logs*. Differences between three kinds of Journals* exist, but they are all similar in that they provide for informal writing experiences that allow for personal growth and reflection. (Sometimes teachers use only Learning Logs* in which they incorporate the functions of the other Journals*.)

Journals promote personal expression and reflection.*

Dialogue Journals*

See also Tierney, Readence, & Dishner (1995) for a discussion of Dialogue Journals*.

The rationale for Dialogue Journals* is that they provide a means for children to share with the teacher, privately and without any worry about evaluation, by writing their reactions, questions, and concerns about any aspect of their experiences in and out of school. In this way, the teacher gets to know more about what each child is doing and thinking. Teachers also use Dialogue Journals* to demonstrate the communicative function of writing to children. This is especially important for those who, because of previous instruction, link writing only with evaluation. Dialogue Journals* encourage spontaneity in writing, which in turn fosters self-confidence and writing fluency.

Guidelines for using Dialogue Journals*

Keep the following in mind when implementing Dialogue Journals* in the classroom:

1. Use a separate tablet or spiral notebook for each child. Many teachers make journals simply by stapling some paper together, perhaps using a construction paper cover that children decorate themselves. Have children date each entry. Have a special place in the classroom where the journals are stored so that children know where to get and return their journals for response.

2. Set up a schedule for the children to write in their journals. Many teachers have children write every day; others follow a Monday, Wednesday, or Friday routine. Some teachers also discuss with children the times in the daily schedule that may be good for writing in their journals (e.g., on arrival, after lunch, or after physical education).

3. Encourage children to write about anything they want. Many teachers have a whole-class session in the beginning of the year to brainstorm possible topics for journals. It is important to assure those children who aren't sure that they have anything to write on some particular days that they can write exactly that: "I can't think of anything to write." Sooner or later children (even the most reluctant ones) write in their journals because they see their peers writing and getting responses from the teacher.

4. Assure children that they can use invented spelling and that their entries can be as long or short as they want. If teachers make a big deal about quantity, children are frequently reluctant to write until they have "enough" to say. In the early grades, children should be told that they can make pictures if they don't have anything to write. It may be necessary to get kindergarten and first-grade children (who may be prephonemic, early phonemic, or letter-name spellers—see Chapter 8) to read their entries to the teacher and then have the teacher write down their responses (while saying the message aloud) in front of the child.

5. Respond to children's entries frequently; otherwise, children are likely to see writing in their journal as a drudgery rather than a dialogue.

6. Respond to the content of the message the child has communicated. What is wanted are two-way communications, so teachers should try not to contrive their responses to present conventional forms or grammatical structures.

Evaluations or judgmental responses should also be avoided. For those children who frequently state that they have nothing to write, the teacher can respond, "I'm sorry you can't think of something right now, but I'm sure you will think of something soon." Including a message about something they have observed about the child, followed by a specific question, sometimes breaks the ice. If children then write in their journals, don't congratulate them; simply respond to what they have communicated. If young children have drawn a picture, respond by commenting on the content of the illustration. (Young children also may need help in reading the teacher's responses.) Sometimes adding a question regarding their drawings leads children to try to write back.

In sum, Dialogue Journals* can have many good effects. Teachers get to understand their children better and children's writing fluency is fostered. Teachers' responses provide meaningful resources of the conventions of written language and even help many children in reading, especially in the early grades. Most important, children see themselves as writers, and they begin to feel that they can write for other purposes in the classroom.

See Unia (1985) for a good classroom example of Dialogue Journals.*

Thought Ramblings*

A Thought Rambling* is a way to use writing as a tool for thinking, reflecting, and understanding. It is written for an audience of self, and it helps children to learn more about themselves and their surroundings without regard to correct form or other people's evaluation.

Thought rambling is a way of brainstorming.

Thought Rambling* is brainstorming or putting a stream of consciousness on paper. Children are given five or ten minutes to put their ideas on paper. At the end of that time, they may find they have a page filled with phrases of feelings and sensory data. They may discover a thread of meaning or an insight. They may also find elements or themes that they might want to develop into a more formal piece of writing. Thought Ramblings* can serve as prewriting experiences and seem to work particularly well outside the usual context of the classroom when children have a chance to tune in to the sights, sounds, and other sensory aspects of their environment. Figure 7.11 is a Thought Rambling* done by a second-grader after returning from a walk to a local university campus one spring day. Thought Ramblings* can also occur in other contexts: after seeing a film or demonstration of some sort, after hearing a poem read aloud, or after a field trip.

Also sometimes called "Quickwrites," Thought Ramblings are occasions to ramble on paper to develop ideas and connections among them.*

Moore, et al. (1998); Tompkins (1998)

Learning Logs*

The primary reason for having children use Learning Logs* is to encourage them to be in control of their own learning and think through writing. A Learning Log* is a kind of journal that enables them to write across the curriculum as they plan, map, record, recall, consider, organize, assign, remember, question, predict, and decide in a range of projects and activities. Thinking with pen or pencil on paper gives children awareness and control of their thoughts; it helps them to be constructive, reflective, and adaptive learners.

Fulwiler (1980, 1982); Moore, et al. (1998); Tompkins (1998)

Learning Logs facilitate thinking and writing across the curriculum.*

According to Calkins, Learning Logs* provide a forum for learning within three kinds of interrelated activities: asking questions, making guesses (or stating hypotheses), and organizing information. The three may occur in any subject or domain. (We have mentioned Learning Logs* throughout this book, so you have already come across many examples of these activities.)

Calkins (1986)

Learning Logs allow children to keep track of new material they have learned, and they serve as an important source of self-evaluation.*

Figure 7.11

*A SECOND GRADER'S THOUGHT RAMBLING**

A spray of water shoots swish swish birds tweet sweetly hello
hello rocks rattle down
every 15 minutes chimes ring out loud and clear
distant to where I am sitting I see a lamp post through the bushes
the trance of spring fever spreads
students walk on the long stone path
yellow dandylions are turning white and fluffy and leaves are turning green
big sprouting trees reach over me branches filled with big green leaves
bushes that are big and green
trees that fill the sky.

Asking Questions. In most traditional schools, children don't ask questions but answer others' questions. In an integrated language classroom, we encourage children to initiate and ask their own questions on the basis of their own schemas and for their own purposes. Learning Logs* can help create conditions or contexts for asking questions. Children can record their questions before, during, and after reading and writing, or the questions they pose for Student-Initiated Inquiry* Projects. They can ask what about the subtle ideologies or values that they think various authors are expressing, or what points of view they themselves might be providing in their writing. Questions can be a preparation for a small-group discussion; documentation of what children want to find out about a particular topic or theme; reminders as children plan an experiment or presentation; or follow-up responses of children's own activities or those of their peers and the teacher.

Making Guesses. If it is critical that children have opportunities to ask their own questions, then it is just as important for them to be encouraged to form their own hypotheses as answers for their own and others' questions. Rather than emphasize "correct" answers, Learning Logs* can help children make educated guesses. They look for clues and connections as they read, hear their peers' ideas, see a film, or engage in an experiment; they revise and reconsider as they examine others' feedback, read another book on the same topic, or see a teacher demonstration; and they predict, propose, and confirm in their own reading, in a class discussion or presentation, or in deciding what and how to write.

Organizing Information. If learning is reconstructing knowledge, then encouraging children to be involved in searching for patterns and connections in what they know, and don't know, is crucial. Learning Logs* can help them activate the process of organizing information. Categorizing their questions and guesses can facilitate their reading, writing, and inquiries. Mapping a topic ahead of time helps interactions in small group or whole class discussions and provides a framework for drafting, revising, or Publishing Experiences*.

In summary, Learning Logs* promote child-centered learning. They document both content and process. They provide a way for teachers to observe children's understandings and experiences, and they are a vehicle for children's self-reflection on their learning.

Most teachers use spiral notebooks or three-ring binders for Learning Logs* so that children can work on certain pages at different places in the room or out of school. A separate Learning Log* might be used for each thematic unit, or perhaps for a large project within a unit. All entries in the log are dated. Many teachers respond to children's responses by commenting on content, asking for clarification, and providing questions for the children to consider. If children are not familiar with Learning Logs*, teachers may do a Focus-Lesson* on the ways they can be used, perhaps using as a framework the three categories of asking questions, making guesses, and organizing information. Teacher suggestions or reminders as they interact with children in the first few days of school are usually enough for children to get the idea of Learning Logs*. Learning Logs* are stored in a designated place in the room for easy access by the teacher, who can review them at day's end or at other regular intervals, and the children, who can get them at the beginning of the school day.

Group-Composed Writing*

McKenzie (1985); Short & Harste (1996)

Group-Composed Writing* is a means for children to share the process of writing and to negotiate the form of various types of writing. Group-Composed Writing* can be done in two ways: (1.) Teacher-Led Group-Composed Writing*, in which the teacher does the transcribing and leads the composition process; and (2.) Peer-Collaborated Group-Composed Writing*, in which children contribute portions or sections of a larger piece and do the transcribing themselves. In both versions, children are supported in the writing process because they share the process and learn from one another about their composing strategies.

Teacher-Led Group-Composed Writing*

Teacher-Led Group-Composed Writing* works well with younger children because the teacher takes over some of the mechanical aspects so that children can concentrate on the content. The idea applies to children of any age because it enables the teacher to demonstrate the thinking process involved in getting ideas into print and to make explicit the kinds of choices writers face—choices of voice, purpose, and form, as well as the medium aspects involved in creating a finished piece of writing.

Group writing can be initiated by the teacher or children. Once children have collaborated in a Group-Composed Writing* activity, they are quick to suggest their own ideas. Perhaps the teacher has just finished a particularly delightful story and has seen several children reworking or reenacting versions of the story in their art or play. Using a large sheet of chart paper or an overhead transparency, the teacher may ask for volunteers to help write a group version of the story: How should we begin our story? Children are encouraged to draw on the ideas depicted in their drawings or play routines and to use their own experiences with stories in general to write a new version. As the teacher writes their suggestions, he or she talks about what is happening in the transcribing process, mentioning the need for spaces between words, the use of capitalization and punctuation, and spelling. As the story evolves, parts are reread every so often and questions are posed: How does that sound so far? Is there anything we can change to make it better (clearer, exciting, interesting)? As children make suggestions for changes, parts can be crossed out or written in, even cut and pasted in if necessary to demonstrate that first-draft writing is often messy but dynamic.

After children have agreed on a final version, it can be published—by simply rewriting it on a new piece of paper or by turning it into a Big Book* that children illustrate. In the following excerpt, kindergartners used the pattern in Martin's *Brown Bear, Brown Bear, What Do You See?* to write their own version using characters from *Goldilocks and the Three Bears* and other books they had been reading. (For example: Papa Bear, Papa Bear, what do you see?/I see Mama Bear looking at me./Mama Bear, Mama Bear, what do you see?/I see Paddington looking at me./And so forth . . .) Each child then illustrated one of the bear characters, and their paintings were hung next to the appropriate verse on a large bulletin board display.

Group-Composed Writing* is useful with children at any age. With older children, a group-writing session may center on more advanced understandings of style and form. For example, several children may have decided to create a class newspaper, but their first front-page news seems like a fictional story. By sharing the task of writing one of the newspaper accounts with the children, the teacher can help them use a reporter's voice and present information in a more newslike format. They could also be shown how reading helps writing by looking at some real newspaper samples to get a sense of this style of writing and the ways it differs from other genres (in terms of form and ideology).

Peer-Collaborated Group-Composed Writing*

In Peer-Collaborated Group-Composed Writing*, children do their own transcribing. It is especially useful for less proficient writers who may be overwhelmed by writing a whole book or piece on their own. Children can contribute a "chapter" in an "All About" book (on, e.g., rocks, tunnels, dinosaurs, or bears), collaborate on a fairy tale in which each writer composes an episode that tells how a particular character uses up one wish, or write a biography of a famous person in which each member concentrates on a certain period of the person's life. In Peer-Collaborated Group-Composed Writing*, the teacher's role is one of helping in the coordination of the project and supporting the decision making of the group.

Teachers demonstrate the writing process.

Medium aspects of written language can also be referred to in Teacher-Led Group-Composed Writing.*

Revising strategies are illustrated.

Martin (1983); Stevens (1986)

Harste & Short (1988); Short & Harste (1996)

Authors' Folders*

See also Atwell (1987), Calkins (1986, 1994), Graves (1983), Short & Harste (1996), and Temple, Nathan, Temple, & Burris (1993) for other ideas on Authors' Folders*.

Authors' Folders* are those in which children keep their ongoing current writing. Frequently, the folders are kept in the back of Learning Logs*, of which they are a part. Two other folders for each child are usually kept: one in which children keep copies of final drafts that they have revised, edited, and published (children don't revise, edit, and publish everything they write); and one in which they collect other miscellaneous writings (abandoned partial drafts, prewriting notes, etc.). Many teachers staple or tape blank paper or forms on each of the four sides of the folder.

The organization of an Author's Folder*

Outside Front

The Topics Sheet is where children can jot down ideas or topics for future pieces that emerge as they read, engage in various projects, or interact with other children in the classroom.

Inside Front

The Writing Log is where children provide some information to indicate the status of their pieces. They enter the date in the "Date" column, and in the large column titled "Status" (for younger children, it may be called "What I Did Today"), they note the draft they are working on, the piece they are revising, any prewriting activity they have done, and the piece they have had a peer conference on (and with whom). By reviewing this log, teachers can quickly monitor what's happening in writing for individual children. They can see if a child may be bogged down on a piece and needs help. They can note when children will be ready for more formal Writing Conferences*.

Inside Back

See Chapters 6 and 8 for more information on the Message/Medium aspects of language.

The Evaluation Form includes a "date" column and two other columns, titled "Message Ideas" and "Medium Ideas." (For younger children, these columns can be called "Meaning Ideas" and "Editing Ideas.") Some teachers call the latter column "Spelling/Punctuation/Etc." Observations about what children have learned are written either by the children or the teacher under the appropriate column heading. Comments about children's new strategies for forming the content or meanings in their writing are noted under "Message Ideas," and new growth regarding their use of medium aspects of written language are recorded under "Medium Ideas." This information is gathered by the teacher in everyday informal observations and interactions with children (these informal observations can be jotted down on Post-it Notes or self-adhesive mailing strips and placed on the evaluation form) and in more formal Writing Conferences*. This evaluation sheet provides both a means for monitoring children's writing and a self-evaluation tool in that children are expected to review it when they revise and edit a piece.

Outside Back

Authors' Folders provide sources of evaluation and accountability.*

The Published Writing Form is where children list their published pieces. Children frequently refer to the Published Writing Form when they write an "About the Author" section for a book they are to publish.

Like Learning Logs*, Authors' Folders* are stored in a special place for easy access by both teacher and children. Most teachers go over approximately six folders each night so that they review a child's work at least once a week. Obviously, they can review more folders of younger children who usually write shorter pieces. The folders are important, for they are a means of documenting growth over time and provide an important measure of accountability.

Writing Conferences*

See also Atwell (1987), Calkins (1986, 1994), Graves (1983), Short & Harste (1996), and Temple, Nathan, Temple, & Burris (1993) for other ideas on Writing Conferences*.

Like reading, children's writing is individualized in an integrated language classroom. Children have had different prior writing experiences, know different things about the registers of written language, and choose to write on different topics and genres. Therefore, as for reading, many teachers have separate individual conferences with children about their writing. And, just like reading, other teachers have many more short, less-formal conferences with children as they see them writing in the classroom. They then have more general conferences with children when writing is addressed along with all their other learning.

Two major types of Writing Conferences* are covered here: Content Conferences* and Editing Conferences*. Teachers usually address content or the message aspects of children's writing separately from the medium aspects (spelling, punctuation, etc.). Peer conferencing is an important part of the process-conference approach, so this topic is included in the discussion that follows.

Message aspects of language are addressed in Content Conferences, medium aspects of language in Editing Conferences*.*

Content Conferences*

Teacher-Student Conferences. The major purposes of conferences are to assess and guide. Teachers have roving Content Conferences* all the time when they interact with children who are engaged in the process of writing, either at the designated writing table or elsewhere in the classroom. They may have jotted down information during these interactions, perhaps on Post-it Notes or self-adhesive mailing strips. (These might have been put on the Evaluation Form in the child's Author's Folder* or on sheets in his or her learning portfolio—see Chapter 9.) In the more formal Content Conferences*, teachers will have read the child's text, usually scheduled on the basis of a sign-up sheet on which children indicate their readiness for a Content Conference*. Children will be expected to have already read their text "to the wall" so they can catch omitted words or awkward wordings themselves. They also may have had a peer conference with another classmate, and revised their piece on the basis of that feedback. They will also be expected to have revised their text according to any relevant comments on the Evaluation Form in their Author's Folder*.

Roving Content Conferences*

More formal Content Conferences*

Children prepare before having a conference with the teacher.

In the Content Conference*, the teacher focuses on the content of the text, or the way a child has organized the meanings or message of the text. (See Chapter 6, especially the "Register/Genre" section in Table 6.7, and Chapter 8, particularly the message analyses in the section on kid-watching writing.) First, it is best to comment on something positive about the writing—what the child knows and has done well. A teacher may say how much information about turtles there is in the child's text or remark on some writing strategy: "I felt I was right there because of the way you described that place in the beginning of your story" or "That was an interesting way to conclude your text." Then the teacher asks one or two questions in a way that allows the children to retain ownership of their writing and begin to solve their own problems. Teachers try to assist children with genre or form problems and address difficulties regarding missing (or excessive) information, sequencing, cohesiveness, and so on. They try to respond to children's text as an inquisitive reader: "Tell me more about X" or "I'm not sure that I understand Y." Teachers' final comments or questions concentrate on what the writer plans to do with the text as the result of the conference; they help the writer in the process of revision by asking, "What do you think you'll do next?"

Steps in conducting a Content Conference*

A review of the message aspects of texts discussed in Chapter 6 and of the message questions illustrated in Chapter 8 is important for conducting successful Content Conferences.*

At the end of the Content Conference*, teachers and children go over what should be written under the "Status" section of the Writing Log and under the "Message Ideas" section of the Evaluation Form in the Author's Folder*; usually what was discussed regarding the message aspects of the text or what the child has decided to work on in revising text.

Teachers have Content Conferences* with young elementary children (kindergartners and first-graders) as well, but they are very careful not to dampen the children's spirits by insisting on too much revision too soon. Teachers must show young children delight and excitement with their early writing efforts so that the children see themselves as writers and continue to be motivated to write. However, many young children enjoy Content Conferences* because they like the special attention their writing gets. They also like completing the forms in the Author's Folder*.

Peer Content Conferences.   Children share their writing informally all the time in an integrated-language classroom, but peer-content conferences are occasions to obtain more focused feedback on a finished (or partial) draft from one or two classmates. Many teachers designate certain places in the classroom for peer-content conferences: a corner, a supply closet, or the hall outside the classroom.

Children respond to one another's messages during conferences.

Children internalize ways of acting in peer conferences through their participation in individual conferences with the teacher. Teachers also go over guidelines about how peer conferences are to be conducted. A peer conference usually consists of three parts. First the writer reads the text aloud; older children can read silently. Then the listener/reader makes some positive comment about it (e.g., a part that was particularly exciting, interesting, or clear). Finally, the conference partner points out the place or places that could be improved. All comments to the writer must include a reason; a remark such as "It's good" is not sufficient. After the peer conference, writers have to decide what feedback, if any, to consider in revision. Children are asked to summarize these remarks on their "Status" section of the Writing Log in their Authors' Folders*. Some teachers also develop a special Peer-Conference Sheet with places to jot down both kinds of feedback—positive and "needs-help on"—as well as what the writer was looking for in the conference and what next steps he or she is planning regarding the text. Teachers can then monitor whether children are routinely dismissing useful feedback and can address this problem in their conferences with them.

Procedures for peer conferences

Editing Conferences*

Teacher-Led Editing Conferences.   After children have decided on the content of their draft and done all the revision they want to do, they focus on the medium aspects of their text by editing. Teachers deal with editing in varying ways. Most teachers expect children to address editing matters themselves before a teacher-led conference. Some set up a special place—an editing table or corner supplied with a dictionary and thesaurus, colored pens or pencils, and perhaps specially developed checklists—where children do their editing. Children use a pen or pencil in a different color from that of the text and go over their text, concentrating especially on the issues in the "Medium Ideas" section of the Evaluation Form in their Author's Folder*. They correct spelling and punctuation, delete words or phrases, and insert others for better transitions or clarity.

Teacher-led editing conferences

When the writers have finished editing, they sign up for a conference with the teacher or indicate some other way that their text is to be ready for teacher review. The teacher goes over the text with a pen of a third color, changing only the medium aspects, not the content. Some teachers do this editing alone and then set up an Editing Conference* with the child; some do it with the children, explaining their changes. In either case, usually only one issue is emphasized. At the end of the conference, the children record that issue under "Medium Ideas" on the Evaluation Form in the Author's Folder*.

As in Content Conferences*, teachers must be very careful in dealing with editing matters with emergent writers. Many teachers wait until the end of kindergarten or the beginning of first grade to talk with children about medium aspects. Because the children lack knowledge of many of the conventions of writing, teachers want to encourage them to write using approximations. Of course, teachers do edit the children's work when some of their texts are published (e.g., typed texts that children illustrate and make into books). Children's attempts to read these corrected texts as they illustrate them is one of the best ways to foster reading development.

Peer-Led Editing Conferences.   Many teachers do not edit everything children publish but establish peer teams to play certain editing roles. Peer editing is especially useful in dealing with work that will be published through Displays*, charts, and so on in the classroom, and editorial boards can review classroom newspapers or literary magazines. The teacher and children together can decide what editing procedures will be followed in special class projects.

Peer-led editing conferences

Publishing Experiences*

In Chapter 6, we emphasized that publishing has to do with sharing. For this reason, publishing can include much more than the publishing of final drafts; any of the writing experiences discussed in Chapter 6 can be published. In this chapter, however, three aspects of publishing are covered in more detail: Displays*, Bookmaking*, and the Author's Chair*.

Publishing is a way of sharing.

Displays*

Careful display or presentation of projects helps children develop a sense of accomplishment and pride in a job well done as well as a sensitivity to the effects of their work on others. Displays* can include anything and everything: posters, charts, maps, puppets, games, dioramas, and the like.

Displays should be aesthetically pleasing.*

Children are encouraged to mat finished artwork and writing, thinking about spacing and visual qualities in mounting their work. Mats or borders can be made by gluing the finished work to a larger sheet of construction paper. The mats can vary to include freeform shapes and multicolored backgrounds. A combination of these ideas can be used in mounting several works, thereby adding visual interest or unity to the finished product, as shown in Figure 7.12.

Teachers have several roles in displaying. They provide the materials, demonstrate and suggest some of the possibilities, and support and coordinate children's decision making. Many teachers in traditional schools spend a lot of time and money buying commercially-made pumpkins, valentines, bunnies, etc. to decorate their bulletin boards and classrooms. But do these materials reflect the children's interest or understandings? In integrated language classrooms, they do—the Displays* of children's products depict the work of a community of learners.

Bookmaking*

Publishing in book form lends writing a sense of permanence and value. Many forms of Bookmaking* by children can be used regularly throughout the year, including shape books (made with covers and blank paper cut out in a special shape to tie in with a thematic unit); books with ring binding or binders; books with the edges stapled together with construction paper or wallpaper sample covers; and books made with cloth covers (glued together with white glue or dry mount tissue).

See Chambers (1986); Fennimore (1992); and Johnson (1992, 1993) for good resources on making books.

Cloth-covered books take the most time and effort, but most teachers try to provide the opportunity for children to publish this type of book several times a year. Figure 7.13 outlines instructions for such Bookmaking*.

Children also enjoy experimenting with techniques for papermaking and creating decorative endpapers or cover papers. Waste paper and a kitchen blender can give a finished product that is similar to fine handmade paper. (See Figure 7.14, p. 296.) Block or potato printing or other decorative techniques add special effects to endpapers or covers. (See Figure 7.15, p. 296.)

In Bookmaking*, children are encouraged to include all aspects of a book, such as dedication and title page. The inclusion of an "About the Author" page lets children tell some personal information about themselves as authors: their family, pets, hobbies, interests, and other books they have written. Children search for and read dust covers of real books for the kinds of ideas to include. Having opportunities to write such blurbs about themselves frequently motivates some reluctant writers.

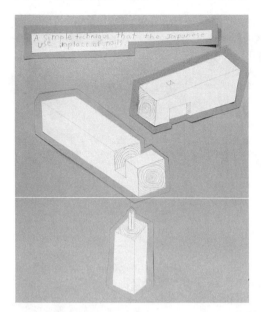

Figure 7.12
*EXAMPLES OF MATTED FINISHED
ARTWORK*

Bookmaking is an art that extends back through the centuries and warrants special attention at some point in the elementary-school years. The study of bookmaking can include a visit to a local printing plant or a small independent press where type is set by hand and pictures are printed from metal etchings or wood blocks. These small print shops sometimes make their own paper, using old rags and handmade molds. Local artisans familiar with oriental techniques of papermaking that use rice paper and such natural items as pressed flowers, or craftspersons familiar with making marbleized paper for endpapers and covers, may be available and willing to visit the classroom.

Author's Chair*

Calkins (1986, 1994); Graves (1994); Graves & Hansen (1983); Thompkins (1998)

The term author's chair has both specific and general meanings in publishing. In a specific sense, the author's chair is an actual chair in a classroom on which writers sit when they present their own writing to peers. In a general sense, however, the Author's

Materials:

Construction paper
Cardboard (Cereal boxes or old file folders are
    best; cardboard boxes are not good.)
Rubber cement or dry mount tissue (available
    from photographic supply stores)
Cloth, wrapping paper, or wall paper

Directions:

1. Measure and cut sheets of construction paper
   for pages. For endpapers, choose 2 sheets of
   contrasting colored construction paper (the
   same size) (Figure A).

2. Fold pages and end pages in half. Keep endpapers on the bottom (Figure B).

3. Sew along fold line with embroidery needles
   (Figure C).

4. Cut cardboard 1/4" to 1/2" larger than the
   pages for the cover.

5. Cut wrapping paper, cloth, or wallpaper 1" to
   2" larger than cover.

6. Cut cover cardboard in half, then trim 1/4" off
   each half.

7. Lay cover paper flat, place 2 cover boards on
   top leaving 1/2" between the top sheets to
   allow book to open and shut (Figure D).

8. a. Glue cover sheets to cover paper with rub-
      ber cement, or
   b. Place 2 sheets of dry mount tissue (cut to
      the same size as the cover board) between
      cover board and cover paper and press
      with dry iron set on wool.

9. Fold corners in to form triangles. Glue to cover board (Figure E).

10. Fold edges over. Glue to cover board.

11. Place pages of book on cover, endpapers on
    bottom. Center pages on cover (Figure F).

12. Glue bottom endpaper to cover.

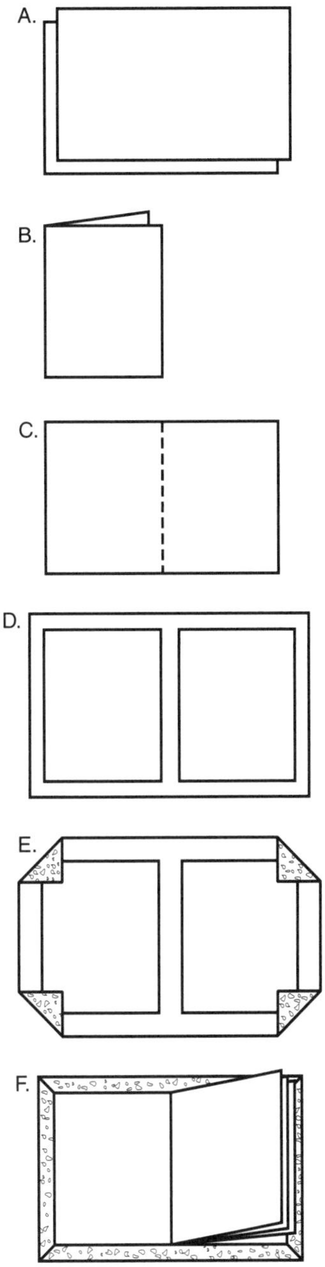

Figure 7.13
MAKING BOOKS

Chair* represents the broad range of sharing possibilities in the classroom. It also establishes linkages between writers and readers (and writing and reading) because it provides opportunities for peers to ask questions about what authors did or were trying to do. It helps authors to understand that readers may have different interpretations and values of their work and facilitates an awareness that both readers and writers have options or choices in the process of reading and writing.

This general sense also means that publishing is more than the act of authors reading final drafts to the class. It includes the sharing of partial drafts that need feedback and suggestions, the presenting of plans or Semantic Maps* to be explored by a small group, giving a play or Puppet Show*, demonstrating a game, the showing of artifacts such as dioramas, topographical maps, or papier-mâché tunnels or animals.

Tierney, Readence, & Dishner (1995)

Many forms of sharing or publishing are possible.

HANDMADE PAPER

Materials:

Large container
Scrap paper (old newspaper, computer paper)
1/4 cup bleach
Toweling
Wooden frame covered with nylon or wire screen (small mesh)
Kitchen blender
2 pieces of wooden board masonite
Weights

Directions:

1. Tear paper into tiny pieces and add to container full of water.
   (Bleach will make paper whiter.)
2. Soak overnight.
3. Add a little water to the blender. Set blender to liquefy. Drop in soaked paper
   a little at a time. (Short pulses on the blender may be more effective.)
4. Pour mixture over screen, distributing it evenly. Let water drain off.
5. Roll pulp onto towel and press with another towel or sponge to remove water.
6. Place pulp between two boards and put weights on top.
7. Let dry.

Figure 7.14

DECORATIVE PAPERS

Chalk Dust Endpapers

Materials:

Oblong pan of water
Construction paper (The paper should have a somewhat absorbent rough texture.)
Pastel chalk (Large single sticks, available in art supply stores, provide the richest color and
   the greatest amount of chalk dust.)

Directions:

1. Using a kitchen knife, scrape the chalk over the pan of water in random spots. A second
   or third color can be added.
2. Place a sheet of paper gently on the surface of the water, tapping it lightly to remove any
   air bubbles.
3. Remove the paper carefully and let it dry. When dry, the chalk dust will be bound to the
   paper in a delicate attractive design.
4. Repeat the processon the reverse side for the sheet of endpaper that is not glued to the
   cover board.

Figure 7.15

It is important to modify Author Chair* if students see it as the "hot seat."

Krogness (1995)

Sometimes children may see Author's Chair as being on the "hot seat." This usually occurs when they have had few experiences in the writing-process approach or when they have poor attitudes about themselves as writers. A modification can be instituted where the sharing is not done by a sole author, but is more of a communal affair. A small group of children may meet with the teacher to celebrate drafts. They can also share good starts in drafts and places in their texts where their writing is going well; in addition, they can talk about the difficulties or struggles they are having in their writing and get suggestions that might help. Thus, in all versions of the Author's Chair*, the context should be a supportive one, and one in which all students are eager to participate.

Developing a Repertoire of Literacy Strategies

See Fisher (1991); Holdaway (1979); and Routman (1988) for similar lists of strategies.

It is important to remember that authentic experiences with reading and writing such as those suggested above provide the best means for the development of literacy and learning. Within this context teachers should use techniques to help children develop strategies that concentrate on meaning at the same time they develop children's understanding of the underlying structures of written language. These techniques should include teacher modeling, direct explanations and demonstrations of the ways that readers seek out meaning. For example, the teacher might make use of the overhead projector to demonstrate how to make inferences about the character of the stranger in a passage from *Tuck Everlasting*. Or he or she might use a selection from an information book like *Rosie the Riveter* to show how she skims material to find out about women's employment opportunities just prior to World War II.

Allington (1994)

Babbitt (1975)
Colman (1995)

Rather than overemphasize word accuracy (especially at the early stages), teachers' guidance should foster good methods for predicting that will get children to make an educated guess using all available information—from the print (physical layout and medium aspects, etc.), the message or register and genre of the text, or their experiences. When readers get "stuck," the following teacher prompts or suggestions help children develop their own strategies:

Rerun. Remind the child to start the sentence again when he or she stops mid-sentence. ("Try it again.") Starting again enables children to gain a refreshed feeling of how the message is structured.

Consider sense and structure. Ask the child if what has just been read made sense. ("Does that make sense? Does that sound right?")

Read on. Tell the child to skip the word by substituting "blank," and read on to the end of the sentence ("Now, what do you think that word is?")

Predict. Encourage the child to make a good guess. ("What do you think it could be?")

Substitute. Tell the child to put in another word that fits or that means the same. ("Can you use something that means the same here?")

Picture. Ask the child to imagine what's going on. ("Can you picture what's happening?")

Use a placeholder. Ask the child to put in a "stand-in" for the same word recurring in text. This is especially useful for proper names of persons and places. ("Can you decide on the same 'stand-in' for this word?")

Identify. Ask the child to find that word on a previous page or paragraph. ("Where else did you see that word?")

Compare. Ask the child if it looks like a more familiar word. ("Does this word look like some word that you know?")

Inspect. Ask the child to take a careful look at the word, keeping the meaning of the text in mind. ("Could it be . . . ? What would you expect to see at the beginning of . . . ? What would you expect to see at the end of . . . ?")

No matter what prompt or suggestion teachers use in supporting children's reading, it is important that they give children time to self-monitor and self-correct. If teachers swoop in with their prompts too soon, children will not have opportunities to apply their own strategies or to self-correct, and the self-regulating behavior that characterizes fluent, effective reading will not be developed. It is also important for teachers to help children be aware of their strategies. When teachers ask questions such as "How did you know?" or "Why did you think it was . . . ?" children become more conscious of the metalinguistic and metacognitive strategies they are using. They are more likely to use them on their own and to gain independence in reading.

Metalinguistic and metacognitive awarenesses are fostered.

Understandings about the underlying structures and conventions of written language will emerge as children engage with meaningful texts. Then, as teachers take time to observe children reading and writing they can begin to make decisions about providing Focus Lessons* on strategies and conventions when (and if) children need more explicit instruction. In the following sections we provide some background and make suggestions for experiences that further support children's growing facility and fluency in reading and writing.

Teaching Phonics and Spelling in Context*

See Adams (1990), Strickland & Cullinan (1990), and Wilde (1992, 1997) for several views on phonics instruction.

English is an alphabetic writing system in which written symbols (graphemes) represent spoken sounds (phonemes). The English spelling system has many irregularities because of the number of cultures that have contributed to the language. (Spanish, in contrast, is much more consistent in its sound/symbol relationships.) While there seems to be a correlation between ability to read and a knowledge of letter/sound relationships, there is no research to tell us whether the knowledge of letter/sound relationships is necessary to learn to read or whether letter/sound relationships *follow* from children's interactions and experiments with written language. Children instructed in intensive phonics and spelling programs may initially show reading gains, but in most studies the advantage of phonics is gone by the sixth grade. More importantly, these intensive, de-contextualized programs take time away from real reading and writing. For children who receive intensive phonics instruction apart from meaningful reading and writing experiences, reading comprehension often suffers in the later grades—they become word callers. Similarly, when teachers concentrate lessons on spelling and grammatical rules at the expense of meaningful composition, children fail to improve in their ability to make meaning through written language.

Hillocks (1986); Weaver (1996)

Cunningham & Cunningham (1992); Yopp (1992)

Research does indicate that in order to benefit from formal phonics instruction, children must be phonemically aware, that is they must be aware that spoken language consists of a series of sounds. Furthermore, research also shows that those children who *are* phonemically aware (have experience in word play, nursery rhymes, nursery songs etc.) don't need much formal instruction in phonics.

Children learn develop concepts about sound-symbol relationships as they listen to stories and play with language and poetry.

Research findings strongly suggest that giving children experience with books and encouraging them to experiment with invented spelling supports their ability to distinguish letter/sound relationships and to segment words into sounds. Thus we can reassure teachers that by creating rich and meaningful learning and literacy activities centered around real books they are providing children with the experiences they will need to become strategic lifelong readers. This includes children who come to school speaking any of the many variations of English or who have acquired English as a second language.

Goodman (1993); Wilde (1992, 1997)

Sendak (1962)

Within this context, teachers become careful observers of children and can determine which children may need more direct instruction in phonics and when they are ready for it. For example, in a first-grade classroom children and the teacher were reading Maurice Sendak's *Alligators All Around: An Alphabet.* On each page, children chimed in with their own words that began with that letter. "P—PUSHING PEOPLE" read the teacher, and children chimed in with "Peter Pan, Pinocchio, peanut butter, Popeye, penguin." When one child volunteered the word "bat," the teacher replied "Pat, bat. Bat is a B word." Later she asked that child to do a word sort with all the words he could find that began with the letters P and B. This is a much sounder approach than giving all children the same instruction at the same time whether they need it, and whether they will benefit from it. Below, we suggest activities on which this focused instruction could center.

Pappas (in press)

Routman (1996)

1. Encourage children's natural inclination to play with language. Collect and share favorite nursery rhymes and playground jingles from around the world and display them around the classroom. Counting out rhymes such as "Hacker packer soda cracker, Hacker packer too. Hacker packer soda cracker, Out goes you." invite further manipulation of sounds when children make up their own verses. Word games also focus attention on sounds in words. Teachers might pronounce the individual sounds of a word and ask children to guess the word, for example, "I'm thinking of fruits we eat, a - pp - le." Or they can help children draw out the sounds of words that they want to spell. The first grader who writes, "A kobra coda cil you. It is a kida saka that is vary poans."(A cobra could kill you. It is a kind of snake that is very poisonous.) is very much aware of the segments of sound in spoken language.

See Yopp (1992) for suggestions for language games.

2. Read books that focus attention on language. Stories and poems with repetitious language draw children's attention to features of words, especially when they are involved in Reader's Theater* or Choral Reading*. Alphabet books

and books like *Roar and More* or *Small Green Snake*, in which printed words are a prominent feature of the visual art, also encourage children's exploration of letter/sound relationships.

Kuskin (1990); Gray (1994)

3. Keep Focus Lessons* simple within the context of meaningful text. Teaching all the letter sound correspondences in English would involve learning some 211 rules. Many of these *do not* have a high degree of consistency. The advice is to keep phonics simple and to teach consistent patterns when children seem ready for them. By simple we mean teaching initial and final consonants, consonant clusters, consonant digraphs, short vowels in a CVC pattern, long vowels with markers (silent partners), "-ed" spelling of past tense, and consonant doubling when adding an ending to a CVC word. These patterns are best learned within the context of real reading and writing. When they read their own writing or use Big Books* such as *The Little Red Hen* or *Mrs. Wishy Washy*, for example, children have many opportunities to find, identify, and use consonant and vowel patterns or word endings.

Barton (1993); Cowley (1981)

4. Teach high frequency word patterns. The teaching of rhyming phonograms (families of words), or the manipulating of onsets (initial consonant sounds) and rimes (e.g., -ack, -eat, -ill, -ock, -ing) is recommended. For example, if a teacher notices that several children are having trouble with the word *fill* she might ask them to list all the words they can think of that end in *-ill*. Their chart could be hung on the wall and added to as they find more words that fit the pattern. Children would then be expected to use these words correctly in their writing. Books such as Charlotte Pomerantz' *If I Had a Paka* and *Here Comes Henny* or favorite poems such as David McCord's "The Pickety Fence," could be transferred to large chart paper with blanks left for onsets or rimes: "The p_ _ _ety fence, the p_ _ _ety fence. Give it a l_ _ _ it's the p_ _ _ety fence . . . " Children who are familiar with the refrains could then write in the proper letters on the charts.

Adams (1990); Routman (1996)

Pomerantz (1993); Pomerantz (1994); McCord (1986)

5. Encourage children to study words. Graffiti Walls* or word walls can become a center for word studies relating to thematic units. Children of all ages can be encouraged to categorize words according to various phonetic and meaning based patterns. Young children might sort pictures or word cards into categories of long and short "e." Older children might group words that are derived from a common base word. (e.g., *lumen, luminous, luminescent, luminescence, luminiferous, luminosity, illuminate*).

See Bear et al. (1996) and Waggstaff (1997–1998) for additional ideas for word study.

*Teaching Grammar in Context**

Traditionally, teaching grammar has usually meant identifying parts of speech (nouns, verbs, adjectives, adverbs, etc.) and their function in sentences, types of sentences (questions, commands, declarative statements), and so forth. Teacher-led lessons on grammar "rules" (e.g., "a sentence must have a subject and predicate [a noun and a verb]" or "never start a sentence with 'and'") are covered, followed by students completing workbook pages on the grammatical concepts. Rarely do these lessons have any relevance to students' current understandings or difficulties in crafting their own sentences in writing texts. As a result, students often find this "formal" study of grammar very boring. Moreover, because its attention is solely at the sentence level instead of the text and genre level, it frequently leads to even more misunderstandings than help. Research has demonstrated over and over that teaching formal grammar systematically and in isolation does not lead to improvement in students' writing, that is, teaching grammar this way just doesn't transfer.

See Weaver (1996) for a recent review of this research.

Grammar, or what we call "lexicogrammar" (which focuses on both vocabulary and linguistic constructions—see Chapter 6), is so complex. We best teach it not by emphasizing "rules" but by helping children see the typical—and atypical—linguistic patterns that are found in various genres. We best teach it in context, that is, by using literature and children's own writing examples in Focus Lessons* and in writing conferences. Chapter 6 illustrates how linguistic patterns are expressed in various typical

The term "lexicogrammar" emphasizes that the wordings chosen in linguistic structures are important in identifying genres.

Krashen (1993); Weaver (1996)

and "fuzzy" texts (ones that include linguistic features from more than one genre) and Chapter 8 shows how an analysis of students' writing could enable a teacher to address grammatical issues in conference. Below we suggest other possibilities.

Show How a Particular Text Feature Is Realized in Different Genres

Explore the same text feature in different genres.

The "element" of description

Wildsmith (1974); First Discovery Books (1991)

Wildsmith (1971)

Yep (1977)

Wright-Frierson (1996)

Siebert (1988)

Children can become language detectives, rather than be bored by formal, rote grammar lessons.

Use several books that can show how different text features work in different genres—how actions work or how time is expressed differently, or how texts begin and end in various genres.

As was illustrated in Chapter 6, the element of description could be examined by showing excerpts from books of different genres. You can point out the many relational processes or verbs in *Squirrels* and *The Ladybug* (e.g., "[A squirrel] *is* a furry, small animal . . ."; "The ladybug *has* two pairs of wings.") that are used in description in most informational books.

Then these could be contrasted with mental verbs (verbs of cognition, affection, and perception) that express the human intentions, reactions, and motivations that are typically found in fiction. Thus, "Owl . . . *liked* to work all night and sleep all day" in *The Owl and the Woodpecker* shows how this verb of affection is intermingled with the description of that character's habitual action in the beginning of the story. Similarly, in the novel, *Child of the Owl*, when Casey goes to live with her grandmother, Paw-Paw, in Chinatown, the description of that place is interspersed with her reactions to it. "But it was the people there that got me. I don't think I'd ever seen so many Chinese in my life before this." All mental processes are used: affection ("got"), cognition ("think"), and perception ("seen"). Another feature you could highlight is how the informational texts use verbs that are in the present tense, whereas in the fictional ones, verbs are in the past tense (except for dialogue or in asides given by the narrator). In *A Desert Scrapbook*, a fuzzy book, Virginia Wright-Frierson includes her personal observations and feelings ("I try to remember some of the patterns I have seen in the desert.", "I love to come outside right after a rain has freshened the air . . .") along with the typical descriptions of the Sonoran desert. And, although her illustrations are in watercolor, they are scientifically accurate, unlike the more "abstract" illustrations in *Squirrels* by Wildsmith, even though his language is typically informational. Another contrast could be how the description of another desert is achieved through poetic language in *Mojave*. Finally, you can point to the short, emotionally-laden descriptions realized through short phrases that are usually found in advertisements and catalogues because the "authors" of these texts hope to entice readers to become consumers of products. (See Chapter 6 for more details on the element of description in various genres.)

Thus, by using different texts, teachers can encourage students to become detectives of how authors/illustrators use language and pictures to express their ideas and their values. Teachers can help students to better understand what people do with language through written texts and how that language is structured for use in different genres.

Have Whole-Class Genre Studies

Classroom genre study

Calkins (1994); Calkins & Harwayne (1991); Lensmire (1994)

For each thematic unit, pick one genre that everyone writes. In the unit WHO IS A HERO? it might be biography; in IT'S NOT FAIR it might be persuasive essays; in a CHANGES unit it might be historical fiction; and in DISAPPEARING ACTS it might be informational reports on animals on the endangered species list. Students would immerse themselves in reading good examples of the genre. Teachers would conduct various Focus Lessons* on the common generic patterns, as well as on students' writing efforts. In this way, children can make more explicit to themselves some of the complexity of the lexicogrammatical structures that characterize particular genres.

Compare and Contrast the Textual Features and Format of a Single Genre or Topic

Text sets on same genre/topic

This is similar to whole-class genre study, but here the inquiry may not lead to writing texts (at least immediately) but carefully studying examples of several books of a particular genre created by different authors and illustrators. They also may include fuzzy examples in the corpus of study. Usually the inquiry is a small-group Student-Initiated Inquiry* project where findings might be depicted in a Comparison Chart*.

One such inquiry might studying biographies, using Adler's *A Picture Book of Frederick Douglass,* Stanley's *The Last Princess: The Story of Princess Ka'iulani of Hawai'i,* and Matthaei and Grutman's *The Ledgerbook of Thomas Blue Eagle.* Besides creating categories that would capture similarities and differences of the lives of the persons involved, specific features of the language, the illustrations, and the format of the books can be examined. For example, the book on Thomas Blue Eagle is actually a fictional, autobiographical account of the life events of a Sioux boy and his imaginary drawings (by the illustrator Cvijanovic) while attending a school in the East to learn about the world of the white man. This book is written in the first person, whereas the other two books are written in the third person. Each book has distinctive format features. The book on Frederick Douglass includes an extra page at the end that lists important dates and extra information about Douglass in an "Author's Note." The book on the Last Princess shows a map of Hawaiian Islands in the beginning of the book with information about the Hawaiian language and a bibliography at the end. The book on Thomas Blue Eagle is published as a ledgerbook with red and blue lines, and it must be turned around to be read; from the top pages then to the bottom ones, instead of reading the typical left- then to righthand pages. No authors or illustrators are listed on the title page. However, information on them is found at the end of the book, along with a glossary and information about pictographs and the actual Carlisle Indian School the fictitious Thomas Blue Eagle attended.

Adler (1993); Stanley (1994); Mattaei & Grutman (1994)

See Duthie (1996) for similar explorations of nonfiction books in the primary classroom.

A similar inquiry might be conducted on a particular topic. Students examine the content *and* how differently authors and illustrators may format that content. For example, books about the honeybee can be used. More typical informational books can be analyzed—*The Honey Makers* by Gibbons; *The Bee* by Crewe; *How Do Bees Make Honey?* by Claybourne; *Questions and Answers about Bees* by Reigot (which uses a question-and-answer format as the title suggests); and *The Life and Times of the Honeybee* by Micucci (which has various sections that include discussions about the different colors and flavors of honey, a depiction of a hive throughout the 12 months of the year, other products using honey, and so forth). The content, language, and the format of these books can also be contrasted with the fuzzy book, *The Magic School Bus: Inside a Beehive,* by author Cole and illustrator Degan. Children may also look at the poem "Honeybees," which can be found in Fleischman's *Joyful Noise: Poems for Two Voices.* In this poem a worker bee and the queen banter back and forth. Children may also want to try to find stories having honeybees to add to their analysis.

Gibbons (1977); Crew (1997); Clayborne (1994); Reigot (1995); Micucci (1995)

Cole (1996)

Fleischman (1988)

Write Two Genres from the Same Student-Initiated Inquiry* Project Data

As students are involved in various individual Student-Initiated Inquiry* Projects in a subtheme or topic of a particular thematic unit, they can report on their findings in two genres. For example, in the DISAPPEARING ACTS theme, they could write a typical informational text on a particular endangered animal. They could then use the same data, the same Semantic Map* they created to organize their questions and answers about that animal in their research, to also write a story or a poem.

Writing two genres from the same data on a topic

Calkins (1994)

Younger children might be given two different inquiry Journals*. In the first they note down the interesting "facts" they have learned about a particular animal—bears or cats or pigs—from reading and hearing informational texts read to them. In the second they jot down the crazy, funny, sad, or happy actions or conflicts that specific animal characters may have experienced in the fictional books the students read in their inquiry. Drawing from each Journal*, they would write an informational book and a story.

Explore the Distinctive Dialects in Books

In a multicultural curriculum, specific dialects should be examined explicitly to help students gain an appreciation of various ethnic and community dialects. The African-

Examine and appreciate dialect differences

Williams (1992)

Haley (1986)
Altman (1993)
Soto (1995)

Examining students' own and others' language patterns enables them to examine attitudes toward dialects and be more comfortable using the "Language of Wider Communication"—the various genres that traditionally have indicated greater status in society.

Conference on College Composition and Communication (1998); Gee (1996); Weaver (1996)

Common grammatical concepts

Waddell (1992)

Cushman (1994)

Base (1986)

Carlson (1997)

Heller (1989)

Teaching grammar usually involves focusing on punctuation.

Raschka (1993)
Lobel (1981)

Fox (1989)

American vernacular dialect is illustrated in William's *Working Cotton* where a day in the field of young girl and her migrant family is described ("We gets us to the fields early, before it's even light. Sometimes I still be sleep. It be cold, cold, cold."). The Appalachian dialect in storytelling ("Poppyseed's a-telling stories tonight . . .") is depicted in Haley's version of *Jack and the Bean Tree*. Another migrant story is told in Altman's *Amelia's Road*, where Spanish words are included in the English ones ("Los caminos, the roads, were long and cheerless."). The street talk of the barrio can be found in Soto's *Chato's Kitchen* ("`No problema, homeboy,' Chato said to himself . . ."). Discussions about the features found in the books and how they contribute to the meanings and feelings expressed in them helps students realize why the language is appropriate in these fictional genres. Thus, they may begin to re-examine their own dialects with new eyes and ears, and write a story or poems incorporating them. They will also begin to understand that these personal, community, and ethnic dialects are not likely to be expressed in their informational reports or other genres.

Use Children's Literature to Teach Common Grammatical Concepts

The concept of a sentence can be taught by providing examples from texts written by a range of authors in various genres and talking with children how and why they think these sentences are constructed. Ask students to create a tentative definition of a sentence and have them examine their own texts of different genres to see how well the definition applies. Make problematic the common rule that sentences must have a subject and a predicate (noun and verb) by using books that have counterexamples. For example, such sentences can be found in Waddell's award-winning picture book, *Owl Babies* ("A big branch for Sarah, a small branch for Percy, and an old piece of ivy for Bill."). Similarly, many occur as entries in Cushman's Newbery Honor novel *Catherine, Called Birdy*, because this book is written as the fictional diary of a young English woman in the year 1290 (e.g., "14TH DAY OF SEPTEMBER "Tangled my spinning again. Corpus bones, what a torture.").

Parts of speech can be taught through books. For example, an alphabet book, *Animalia*, by Graeme Base contains sentences like "An armored armadillo avoiding an angry alligator" for the letter A and "Diabolical dragons daintily devouring delicious delicacies" for D. Here there are opportunities to identify nouns, adjectives, and adverbs and what appear to be verbs (*avoiding* and *devouring*) in a delightful way. In these structures, the adjectives precede the nouns, but in *ABC I Like Me*! by Nancy Carlson they are found in a different kind of construction (e.g., "I am Awesome, Brave, and Cheerful."). The adjectives follow the relational verb "am," similar to the ones we see so frequently in informational texts. Ruth Heller's *Many Luscious Lollipops: A Book about Adjectives* and other books in this series (on adverbs, nouns, and verbs) can also be used to teach these concepts.

Frequently, teaching grammar requires giving attention to punctuation. Reading Raschka's *Yo! Yes?*, which consists of a dialogue between two boys, helps make the use of punctuation become more explicit. How to use commas to punctuate a series of terms can be illustrated in Lobel's *On Market Street*. Here the terms are the one-word items bought on a market street ("I bought . . . apples, books . . . yarns, zippers.") In Mem Fox's *Shoes from Grandpa*, the terms are much longer, as each family member offers to buy some kind of clothes or accessory to go with the new shoes that Jessie has gotten for her birthday from her Grandpa. In a cumulative manner, each idea is repeated throughout the book, and commas are used to mark the series (e.g., "And her mom said, 'I'll buy you a skirt that won't show the dirt, to go with the socks from the local shops, to go with the shoes from Grandpa.'"). Quotation marks could be illustrated with this book as well.

Thus, the idea is not to place that much emphasis on the grammatical terminology or definitions per se, but to help children develop an understanding of the function of punctuation and common grammatical concepts. Teachers might make mention of them again in an incidental way during their conversations with children—"See, how you might use more adjectives to modify these nouns you are using."—as these concepts seem to be relevant in their writing.

Base Focus Lessons* and Individual Editing Conferences* on the Analysis of Students' Writing

Base your instruction on your own observations of what your students are doing in their writing. Figure out—with the child—what genre he or she is attempting, and have your suggestions and feedback address both the message and medium aspects of his or her texts (see Chapter 8 for examples). In Focus Lessons* use texts written by students, with their permission, or your own that reflect particular lexicogrammatical issues or any problems that might have arisen.

Avoid the very popular, commercially produced Daily Oral Language (DOL) Program for teaching punctuation, capitalization, usage, etc. In this program, a teacher writes two sentences that need "correcting" on the board each day, and then invites students to orally provide the necessary corrections. Or students may copy them, correct them, and then discuss them orally as a group. These sentences are isolated sentences, not text- or genre-based. Moreover, too often the errors that the program sentences may be illustrating are not ones your students are making most frequently. Thus, although it seems that only a small amount of time might be used daily on the program, it is usually wasted time if the areas of errors are not related to students' actual difficulties.

Summary

Teach grammar in context. Help students see the typical patterns of various genres and appreciate the complexity of language and how it is used for various social purposes. Most linguistic knowledge is learned incidentally and informally through actual use. You can help children of diverse ethnolinguistic background learn about their own grammatical structures as well those of others by making sure that your thematic units are filled with multicultural books from a range of genres. They can also see the connected nature of reading and writing—the fact that the life of a writer is the life of a reader. However, some of these understandings can be made explicit through Focus Lessons* and conferences with students. With your help, students can see themselves as language detectives and approach grammar as an interesting and exciting area of inquiry.

Extending Literacy Strategies
*Sketch to Stretch**

Sketch to Stretch* activities help children understand that meanings can be communicated through a system other than language. Through drawing, children can transform or extend meanings expressed through language, construct new meanings, or discover insights that language alone cannot afford. Because Sketch to Stretch* activities encourage individual responses, they also help children to understand and value variations in interpretations.

Many teachers suggest Sketch to Stretch* activities as possible responses or extensions to books that children have read or heard. For example, children can sketch what the book (or selection or text) meant to them and then share them with class members. Students can make sketches on what are called "one-pagers" to prepare for discussion in Literature Response Groups*. A one-pager consists of (1.) a drawing of a visual representation of ideas that each reader thinks are significant in a text; (2.) one or two quotes from the text; and, (3.) an interpretative statement or comment (or short paragraph) that explains connections and questions that the reader has developed from the reading. Sketches or one-pagers can be used when reading the same text. Or they might be created for sets of texts that might be on the same topic or theme and thus may serve as a useful first step in creating Comparison Charts*. Or they might be used as part of the writing feedback that students receive in peer Content Conferences*.

Children may also be given a large piece of paper folded into four or more sections and asked to draw a picture of what happened in the beginning of the story in the first section, then what happened at the end of the story in the last section, and then what happened in the middle of the story in the other sections. Children may also include short

Children's own writing as the context for instruction

Create your own Focus Lessons based on your observation of students' current understandings of grammar.*

Make the teaching and learning of grammar exciting!

Short & Harste (1996)

Livdahl et al. (1995)

Cochrane, Cochrane, Scalena, & Buckanan (1984)

sentences or captions in each section to correspond to their drawings. These can then be shared, used for Storytelling*, or as storyboards to support various Drama Experiences*.

Sketch to Stretch activities are possible across the curriculum.*

Sketch to Stretch* activities can be used across the curriculum. With nonfictional information books or topics, children may draw a picture of, say, a squirrel (perhaps also labeling its known characteristics) or a picture of what squirrels do (again including short descriptions of what they think squirrels' habits are). They may then read or

Wildsmith (1974); Lane (1981)

listen to *Squirrels* by Wildsmith and *The Squirrel* by Lane, then create new squirrel sketches, adding, elaborating, and changing their initial drawings to reflect new information gained from these books. Such sketching activities can be used by the class as a whole to begin a new thematic unit or by a small group to depict the initial understandings of a particular topic. Children may try to sketch what they think could happen in a process in a particular science experiment, and then check their ideas by actually doing the experiment. They may illustrate the process as a way of publishing their observations of the experiment. Also recall the example of fourth-graders who were investigating the geographic concept of desert in Chapter 5. They began by drawing what they imagined a desert to look like. Remember how children made their own math books, using illustrations to depict their own understandings of mathematical concepts and procedures. In sum, Sketch to Stretch* activities can complement, extend, and deepen ideas, meanings, and concepts across the curriculum.

Activity Cards*

Activity Cards are invitations or suggestions for learning.*

Activity Cards* encourage children to become active, independent learners by inviting them to engage in learning. The cards are not assignments that children must follow to the letter but open-ended questions or suggestions for possible inquiries that can be interpreted differently by different children.

See Kwak & Newman (1985) for a good classroom example of the use of Activity Cards*.

Many teachers use Activity Cards* to start a thematic unit. When they plan their thematic units, they come up with possible meaningful activities that children can choose from. (See the activities illustrated in Chapter 3 and in the prototype WEBS in Chapter 4.) They then write the activities on different sizes of index cards. Figure 7.16 illustrates Activity Cards* that focus on science topics. Notice how these cards encourage talk and collaboration with others and the integration of literacy. They emphasize thinking and decision making by the children. Activity Cards* do not convey a specific set of expectations or level of competence; children can tackle them at their own level. Sometimes Activity Cards* are designed for more specific support by providing, for example, step-by-step instructions for setting up and conducting a scientific experiment or guidelines for using such materials as Jackdaws* or Primary Sources*.

These science activity card ideas came from Wassermann & Ivany (1998).

Activity Cards can be modified or they can spark altogether new ideas.*

Because Activity Cards* are open-ended suggestions, children are free to modify the ideas on the cards. The cards may even spark altogether different problems or lines of inquiry. Thus, the cards leave room for initiation and negotiation by the children regarding activities. Teachers can specifically encourage this creativity in the beginning of a unit by reading through some of the cards and then having children brainstorm modification or elaborations of the activities or try to construct new activities with the same materials at hand. Thus, teachers have a major role in the use of Activity Cards*. They plan for choices and suggestions in the beginning, then support children's inquiries by raising questions, making comments that lead children to make their own decisions, and pointing out further resources and reading materials.

Reading Activity Cards* and writing modifications or new cards provide meaningful literacy experiences and promote other uses of reading and writing. Reviewing the Activity Cards* at the end of a thematic unit can also help children be more aware of what the classroom community of learners has tackled and accomplished by providing a way of documenting the kinds of learning that have been achieved.

Graphing*

Real graphs

In Chapter 5, Graphing* was suggested as a major way by which children could incorporate mathematical understandings in thematic units. There are three major kinds of graphs: real, picture, and symbolic. Real graphs are especially important at

ACTIVITY CARD #1

* Use the material in this center and make some
  observations about things that sink and things that float.
* Try as many investigations as you can think of.
* Talk with each other about your ideas.
* Then make a record of what you observed.

There may be other ways to use the material in this center. Try some of
your own investigation and see what happens.

MATERIALS: One or two large plastic basins of water. A variety of
materials: Sponges, chalk, ping–pong balls, modeling clay, aluminnm foil,
containers with removable lids, bits of wood, clothespins, stones, shells,
styrofoam chips, plastic dishes and cups, nails, paper cups, glass jars.

ACTIVITY CARD #2

* Use the materials in this center to make some investigations
  with seeds.
* Make some observations and decide how these seeds might be
  classified. Set up some categories and place the seeds
  into the category where each belongs. Then record your
  classification.
* Examine two kinds of seeds and compare them. How are they
  alike? How are they different? Find as many similarities
  and differences as you can, and record your findings.

You may have some other ideas for conducting investigations with these
seeds. Try your ideas and see what discoveries you can make.

MATERIALS: A variety of seeds: fast-growing seeds are preferable—for
example, lettuce, lima bean, mung bean, corn, alfalfa, watercress, radish.
Paper towels or blotting paper, waxed paper or plastic wrap, saucers,
water, sand, potting soil, small pots or other containers (e.g., milk
containers) for planting, large spoons for digging.

ACTIVITY CARD #3

* Study the earthworms for a long time.
* Then, one by one, using the materials in the center,
  change the surfaces on which you place the earthworms.
* What observations can be made about the effect of changing
  the environment on the earthworm's behavior?
* Talk with each other about your observations.
* Then write about what you found.

MATERIALS: Earthworms (found in the school yard or a park, or, if
necessary, purchased from a biological supply house). A variety of items
with flat surfaces, such as pieces of cloth with different textures, wood,
aluminum foil, plastic wrap. Some sand, water, sandpaper. Several
magnifying lenses.

Figure 7.16
*ACTIVITY CARDS**

the lower grades because they enable children to compare groups of real objects and
provide the foundation of all other Graphing* activities. For example, a kindergarten teacher and his students created a real graph to compare and classify their
shoes by considering a variety of attributes—laces or Velcro closings, right or left
shoes, tennis shoes or other kinds, and colors. Once categories had been decided on,
the teacher created a large grid on the floor with masking tape on which children
placed the shoes according to category. Many real graphs are possible using manip-
ulative objects in the classroom: seeds, coins, and buttons; snack items (cookies,
crackers, pieces of vegetables, etc.); or blocks. Grids can be made on the floor or a
table. Smaller grids can be made out of varying sizes of paper or cardboard, or with
any number of rows or categories.

Picture graphs

Picture graphs are also appropriate at the lower elementary grades. A picture graph uses pictures or models to stand for real things. Once the kindergartners had classified their shoes on the real graph, their teacher helped them create a picture graph. The children counted and labeled each category on the real graph, then made smaller picture graphs using cutout construction paper shoes to stand for the shoes on the real graph. The possibilities for picture graphs are unlimited.

Symbolic graphs

Symbolic graphs, which are the most abstract level of graphs, use symbols to represent real things. The kindergartners could have constructed a symbolic graph by using an X instead of the cutout paper shoe. Symbolic graphs can be extended to represent increasingly more complex patterns and relationships and incorporate increasingly more mathematical operations. Bar graphs can be created as a result of a survey of the type of fruit children prefer or the kinds of vehicles found in the school parking lot over a week. Figure 7.17 shows how children place small paper rectangles on the graph to indicate preference in fruit. Figure 7.18 not only depicts kinds of vehicles but also involves more complex computation.

Graphs can plot frequency patterns, patterns of averages, percentages, etc. over time—for example, the number of vehicles observed over the different days of the week. Figure 7.19 (p. 308) illustrates such a graph.

See Baratta-Lorton (1995) for a good discussion of Graphing*

In sum, a range of graphs can be incorporated into the classroom across the curriculum. Planned graphs are considered as part of planning the WEB of a thematic unit; others can emerge spontaneously while children are engaged in activities or projects related to the theme.

Book Extensions*

Huck, Hepler, Hickman, & Kiefer (1997); Johnson & Louis (1987)

Young children learn by acting on their world, transforming it through play, art, drama, music, and language into something uniquely personal. Children can also enter into the world of the book and through these same avenues, remake and reshape their experiences with literature, making books memorable. It is through these transformations that the deepest response to books is possible.

Chapter 3 discussed ways to plan activities that would allow children to interact with the characters of books in the same ways they interact with people and events in real life. Activities such as these do not make workbooks out of children's literature. Instead, they represent experiences children are likely to have as language users in the real world. Children then transfer these possibilities to the world of the book. Most are designed to lead children back into the book, to refer to it for information, or to think more deeply about character motivation, themes, and ideas. Other activities can go beyond the book to help children compare and synthesize information, experiences, and ideas.

Huck, Hepler, Hickman, & Kiefer (1997)

A range of Book Extensions*—for example, Semantic Maps*, Comparison Charts*, and Sketch to Stretch* activities—has already been covered in this chapter, and many others have been mentioned and illustrated in other chapters. Three kinds of Book Extensions* suitable for fictional literature—Story Maps*, Plot Profiles*, and Character Sociograms*—are described in more detail in the following sections. Many others are possible. Figure 7.20 (p. 308) summarizes these possibilities.

Story Maps*

LeGuin (1968); Milne (1988)

Story Maps* help children visualize the physical geography that often undergirds stories. Think about the ways in which Ursula LeGuin's map of Earthsea helps the reader visualize Ged's voyage, or think what fun generations of children have had in tracing Pooh's adventures on A. A. Milne's maps. A Story Map* is particularly useful in visualizing created worlds in fantasy and science fiction, but think of how helpful a map can be in recreating a historic incident or following a mystery. Creating maps helps an author keep track of the relationships between setting and action. The reader who attempts to map a literary world must delve into a literary text deeply enough to recreate those relationships in ways that are true to both text and reader. As a result, mapping stories encourages frequent rereading as well as wrestling with spatial rela-

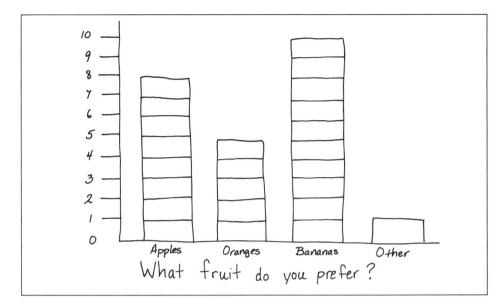

Figure 7.17

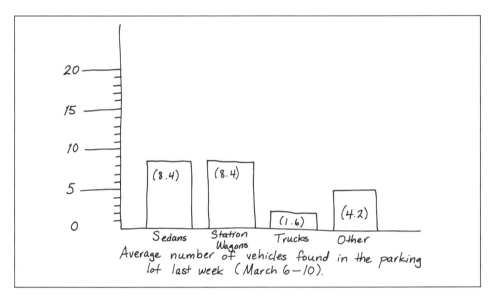

Figure 7.18

tionships. It also provides a glimpse of what might be called the reader's "mental geography" of a story.

A fifth-grader created a Story Map* of Terabithia, the secret place across the stream in Paterson's *The Bridge to Terabithia*. He struggled to represent both the magical nature of the kingdom in the woods and the menace that lay at the banks of the stream. He initially drew a map with a picture of the woods viewed from beyond the log that crossed the stream. This did not allow the student to represent Terabithia, however, and so he tried again, this time constructing a bird's-eye view of woods, stream, log, and field beyond. He added a key and a scale and labeled the map so that within Terabithia all labels were in green, the world outside was blue, and the log and stream that both protected Terabithia and took a life were red.

The final map may not have been particularly polished, but it represented a process through which this student came to grips with (1.) the ways in which maps represent physical features (e.g., bird's-eye view), (2.) the emotional geography of the story (i.e., safety in green, danger in red, emotional distance in blue), and (3.) the physical relationships between setting and action.

Younger children can also make Story Maps*, but they may need a more directed experience, at least initially. After a teacher has shared a favorite story with the class,

Paterson (1977)

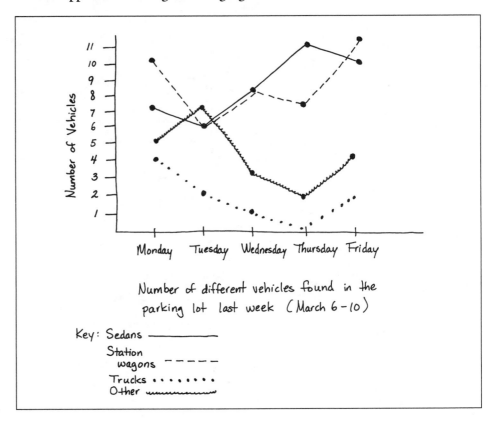

Figure 7.19

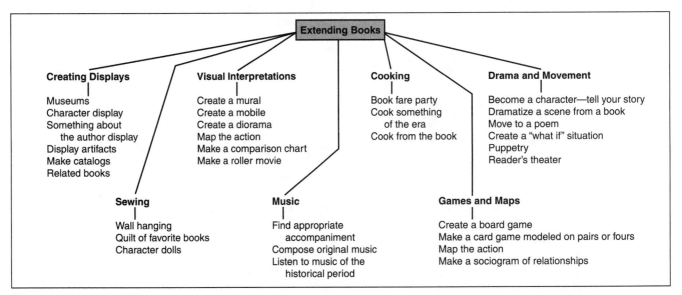

Figure 7.20

Source: *Huck, Hepler, Hickman, & Kiefer, 1997*

Lasky (1983)

children are led to contribute to a class list of all the features that a map of this story could contain. A Story Map* is then shown on the overhead, and the class discusses its major items, adding and labeling missing features. Afterward, they can work in pairs or small groups to construct maps of other stories. The teacher may want to share a story and discuss it with the whole class and then let small groups work on mapping it. Or children may prefer to pick their own stories and share these later as part of a book discussion.

Although children can learn a great deal from creating their own map, story mapping can also occur when children attach story features to an existing map. Historical fiction lends itself particularly well to this activity. Children reading Lasky's *Beyond the Divide*, for instance, used a large map of the United States and attached pictures, captions, and labels to show the progress of Meribah Simon's journey from Pennsylvania to California. Other children mapped folk- and fairy tales that were related to specific locales (e.g., Paul Bunyon, Pecos Bill, and John Henry).

However, the most challenging Story Maps* involve children in mapping stories that have only a literary geography. Sixth-graders, for example, found the mapping of Mary Q. Steele's *Journey Outside* particularly challenging because it moves across two planes—the underground river of the Raft People and the surface worlds through which Dilar travels after leaving the Raft People. One group constructed a two-layered map to graphically display the relationship between these planes. They found the river world relatively easy to visualize, as it flowed in a great circle below the surface. They went back to the book many times, however, in their attempts to locate the surface worlds in their relationship to one another. Where were the mountains relative to the sea? Were they the same mountains each time? How could they represent the different landscapes using a bird's-eye view? These students decided to use a relief map to better represent their story, depicting Dilar's wanderings with a dotted line across the map.

Steele (1969)

Younger children may need a fair amount of practice in drawing a bird's-eye view. One way to help them is to begin the mapping activity by using models rather than flat drawings. Like the group that made a relief map for their story, some younger children may be better able to visualize a view from above by first representing the story world in three dimensions. After the children have made a model of the story world, they can view it from the top, draw a map of what they see, and label it with story features and incidents. Some teachers also encourage children to include story quotations as part of a Story Map*.

A number of books lend themselves particularly well to story mapping. In general, any story about a journey has mapmaking potential. Hall's *Ox-Cart Man* provides an opportunity for children to use a map of New Hampshire to plot a journey to Portsmouth. Steig's *Caleb and Katie* lends itself to making a map of a journey that includes an encounter with a witch. Other books encourage mapping buildings (Norton's *The Borrowers*), imaginary worlds (Engdahl's *Enchantress from the Stars*), or the inside of a pyramid (Aliki's *Mummies Made in Egypt*).

Hall (1979)

Steig (1977)

Norton (1953); Engdahl (1970); Aliki (1979)

When children work on Story Maps*, they can develop a richer understanding in several areas relevant to both reading and geography. First, mapmaking involves sequencing physical features and events: Where does the map or story begin? Where does the map or story end? These facts are important in literary understanding and basic components of thinking in the social studies. Mapmaking also involves relative location and position, features that enrich literary understanding and also help children visualize spatial relationships outside of story worlds.

Mapping also requires that readers go back into the book to verify sequencing and relationships. One result of this close attention to the internal logic of a story is a richer understanding of the craft of the author. Mapmaking also helps the reader to understand the story in a way that is closer to the multidimensional illusion the author originally intended.

Johnson & Louis (1987)

Plot Profiles*

When children read and respond to literature, they become more informed about the structure of stories, recognizing certain clues to the kind of story they have begun (i.e., "Once upon a time" signals make-believe, whereas "It was a dark and stormy night" hints at mystery) and attending to the way in which a story rises to its climax or drops off into an ending that leaves the reader wishing for more. In integrated language classrooms, children are also authors. They write in a number of genres and so attend to literary elements from an author's as well as a reader's perspective. There are many ways to help children think about the elements of a piece of writing. Plot Profiles* are one way of calling attention to the way in which an author structures a story around a plot. Plot Profiles* also involve children in using time lines and rating scales and in plotting a graph, all of which can be used across the curriculum.

Johnson & Louis (1987)

Plot Profiles* can be constructed with children of various ages. In working with younger children, however, the story should be fairly simple and have a strong, clear plot line. Folk- and fairytales work particularly well because the plotline tends to be clear and uncluttered. The children take a story such as Goldilocks and the Three Bears and begin an incident summary. The teacher records the children's suggestions as follows:

1. Mama Bear makes the porridge.
2. The porridge is too hot.
3. The three Bears go for a walk to let the porridge cool.
4. Goldilocks wanders into the Bears' house.
5. She tries the chairs.
6. She tries the porridge.
7. She tries the beds.
8. Goldilocks falls asleep.
9. The Bears come home.
10. They find the broken chair.
11. They find the empty porridge bowl.
12. They find Goldilocks.
13. Goldilocks leaps from the bed and runs away.

The teacher then shows children a time and excitement chart such as the one in Figure 7.21. The horizontal axis represents time, with number 1 being the first incident (Mama Bear makes porridge) and number 13 being the last (Goldilocks runs away). Beginning with the most exciting point (perhaps number 12, the discovery of Goldilocks), the children plot where that incident would fall in terms of time and excitement. Next, they plot the least exciting part (perhaps number 1, Mama Bear making porridge), then all the points in between. After the chart is plotted, the points are connected showing the rhythm of the story's plot.

Discussion should be encouraged throughout the plotting procedure so that the plot represents some sort of consensus. When children try this technique on other stories, they may also want to make Plot Profiles* individually or in small groups. The profiles can be the basis of some interesting discussions when children explain why they made the decisions that led to differences between charts for the same stories.

Plot Profiles* for children reading more complex books can also be an interesting way to describe plot twists visually. A mystery, for instance, can have a number of rather sharp peaks as the author leads the reader from one clue to the next. These profiles can also be quite long. Sometimes a broader definition of "incident" is required to make the profile less cumbersome. A child plotting Yolen's *The Devil's Arithmetic* may deal with the entire first chapter, up to the point of opening the door into the past, as one incident. Entry into the past may be a second, shorter incident, and then the period from entry until the wedding trip may be a third.

Yolen (1988)

Illustrated Plot Profiles* can also be created on mural paper. At each point on the chart, an illustration represents the story incident. Children work in pairs to create the illustrations, selecting the medium that best exemplifies the incident being pictured. A sixth-grader illustrating an incident in the poem "The Highwayman" decided that the scene where the highwayman is shot "like a dog on the highway" needed special attention. On a piece of black construction paper, he used white chalk to sketch in the moonlit highway, with trees picked out of the darkness and shadowy figures standing over the body of the highwayman. The highwayman was all in white except for the scarlet color at his throat where his life bled away across the dark road. The mural that resulted from this and other pictures, including collages and simple line drawings, was a dramatic illustration of the students' emotional response to this piece of literature.

Noyes (1983)

Character Sociograms*

In responding to a book she had just finished reading, one child described the power of the story this way: "It sees through the eyes of this person." In a sense, Character Sociograms* are a way of representing the reader's understanding of what he or she

Levstik (1986)

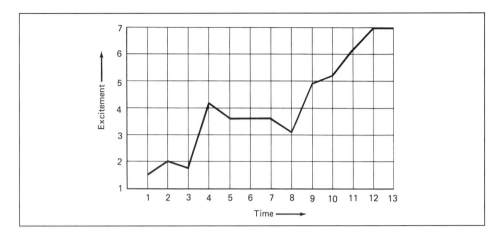

Figure 7.21

Time and Excitement Chart

saw through the eyes of a literary character. More than that, however, the sociograms are an opportunity to think and talk about the relationships between characters in stories and to think about the way in which the reader is drawn into these relationships.

It is not easy to clearly describe the processes involved in creating Character Sociograms*. It may be useful to think of a sociogram as a character WEB, similar to the thematic WEBs we have already talked about. The main character, then, is thought of as the center of the sociogram, just as the theme is the center of a WEB. The other characters in the story are arranged around the central character. Arrows connect the characters and show the direction and distance of the relationships. Figure 7.22 shows such a Character Sociogram* for Viorst's *Alexander and the Terrible, Horrible, No Good, Very Bad Day*.

Viorst (1972)

Some teachers have found that the initial steps in putting together a sociogram can be done by using movable objects and an overhead projector. For instance, the teacher sets out an array of small objects that can be used to represent each character in the story. Children identify an object with a character (this is an interesting part of the process, too!), and the teacher places each object on a transparency in relation to the main character. Pencils can be used as arrows and moved as discussion takes place.

Once the idea of the sociogram is generally understood, students work in pairs with either objects or paper shapes (circles, squares, etc.) and arrange their sociograms so that they can write brief statements on the connecting arrows. Figure 7.23 depicts an elaborated Character Sociogram* of the relationships in Viorst's book.

As with most other activities described in this book, there is no single way to do a sociogram. Their power lies in the quality of the thinking and conversing children do as they construct them. The following guidelines are helpful:

Johnson & Louis (1987)

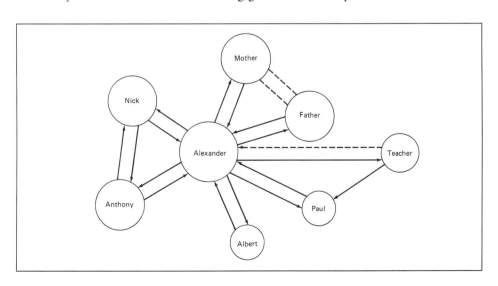

Figure 7.22

Character Sociogram for Alexander and the Terrible, Horrible, No Good, Very Bad Day*

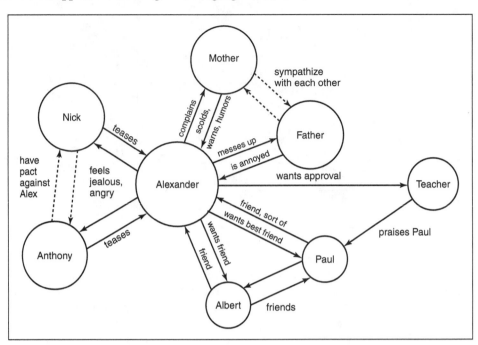

Figure 7.23

An Elaborated Character Sociogram for Alexander and the Terrible, Horrible, No Good, Very Bad Day*

Place the central character or characters at the center of the diagram.

Let the distance between characters reflect the perceived psychological distance between them.

Let the size of the shape representing a character vary with the importance or the power of the character.

Show the direction of a relationship by an arrow and its nature by a label.

Represent substantiated relationships with a solid line and inferred relationships with a broken line (a nice opportunity to discuss inferences).

Circle active characters with a solid line.

Circle significant absent characters with a broken line.

Place the characters who support the main character on one side of a dividing line and antagonistic characters on the other.

When Character Sociograms* are tried, teachers and children alike invent new conventions for dealing with new relationships. No single sociogram can ever entirely represent the relationships in a story, and no single interpretation of those relationships is necessary or possible. Instead, sociograms are successful to the degree that they involve children in thinking carefully about their reading and support their judgments. (See the earlier section on Observation and Inference* for further discussion.)

Drama Experiences*

Heathcote & Bolton (1995); McCaslin (1996); Siks (1977)

Creative dramatics, like the other arts, is a way of knowing. Drama can provide a rich vein of experiences that help children to find out about themselves and others. Such insights can shape and cement children's social growth and lead to a spirit of cooperation and trust within the classroom community. Drama also allows children from a variety of cultural backgrounds to develop communicative competence by taking on many additional registers through the characters they choose to become.

Way (1967)

O'Neill & Lambert (1982)

Process is emphasized in creative dramatics.

Creative dramatics exists on a continuum from interpretive to improvisational activities, but it is not the memorization of someone else's script performed before an audience. The true value of all forms of drama lies in the process, not the product (or production). Teachers play important roles in providing and suggesting opportunities for Drama Experiences* and in supporting the aspects of this process of drama. They offer ideas, situations, and problems to pursue in drama, and they encourage individual children to participate. Most of the time children share forms of drama with others, but they can just as well create imaginary worlds for no audience but themselves. Thus, any sets, props, or costumes should be kept simple. A drama corner could contain such general costumes as hats, old coats, cloaks, and paper bags that can serve many costume functions. A prop such as a yardstick can function as a sword, a scepter, or a magic wand. Several types of Drama Experiences* are discussed in the following pages.

Improvisation*

Improvisation*, one of the more difficult but rewarding types of drama, gives children a problem and asks them to solve it. Children can take situations from real life (past, present, or future) or rework situations they find in literature. They assume character roles and interact to solve problems confronting them as these characters. Negotiation between the participants occurs as a drama unfolds, and the finding of joint solutions is a dynamic process. The children create new situations rather than reenact previous scenarios, yet they rely on their own experience and judgment to orchestrate these make-believe worlds.

O'Neill (1985)

Improvisation* from a Book.   In *The Green Book*, Pattie and her family are forced to leave Earth to find a new home on another planet. They can take only a change of clothes, one or two small personal items, and one book. In a small group, children discuss what book they will take and explain their choices. A list of books that everyone agrees are important for survival on a new planet emerges.

Walsh (1982)

Improvisation* from the Past.   As a wagon train heads west to California in the 1800s, many disasters befall the travelers. Winter is fast approaching, and the wagons must make it through the mountains before the winter blizzards hit. The sick and starving are slowing the group down. Children assume the roles of the settlers, both sick and healthy, and find a solution.

Improvisation* for the Future.   A group of children becomes part of a community that values peace and has forbidden anyone to own or use weapons. A terrible warlike people are menacing the community's border and threaten to destroy the family. Children search for possible solutions.

Television News Broadcasts and Talk Shows*

Television provides children with models for presenting information, conducting interviews, reviewing, and editorializing. Children may assume roles of favorite news broadcasters to present the classroom news, to interview historical characters or to report on the latest information from a thematic unit. They may also give book reviews, like the children on PBS's *Reading Rainbow*. Sixth-graders who had read *Tuck Everlasting* developed an Oprah Winfrey-like host who interviewed Tuck, Ma, Jesse, Miles, Winnie and the Man in the Yellow Suit about their experiences. Class members took on the role of studio audience and asked their own questions. The children who played each of these characters had to recall events that took place in the book as they answered questions. They also had to immerse themselves in their character's personality to make the discussion more believable.

Babbitt (1975)

Reading Rainbow *is seen on Public Broadcasting System stations.*

Puppet Shows*

Puppetry is an ancient type of drama and is still enjoyed around the world in many forms. Puppet Shows* give children a comfortable vehicle for personal expression, and for writing scripts or improvising stories or other scenarios. Finger puppets, shadow puppets, and puppets made of socks, gloves, sticks, or even abstract shapes allow children to focus on the drama itself rather than on the manipulation of complex forms

Batchelder & Comer (1956); Champlin & Renfro (1985); Lynch-Watson (1980)

Carle (1969)

such as marionettes. Thus, although upper-elementary children may construct and use complicated puppets, most of the puppets younger children make or use should be kept simple. One first-grade teacher made a caterpillar out of an old brown sock and glued felt eyes to the top, then pulled it over her hand and had it "eat" through all the items of food in *The Very Hungry Caterpillar*. When she came to the part of the book where the caterpillar spins a cocoon, she pulled the bottom of the sock up over the caterpillar's head, then pulled the sock off entirely to reveal a felt "big, beautiful butterfly," which was wrapped around her hand and made to "fly away." The children were delighted and, of course, wanted to make their own caterpillars and read the story.

Choral Reading*

See Tierney, Readence, & Dishner (1995) and Wilner (1977) for more information on Choral Reading*.

Choral Reading* is an excellent way to share poetry and link it to musical performances. Poems are selected by the teacher or children. As a poem is read, everyone thinks about its mood and meaning to decide on ways to "orchestrate" its reading. The poem can be copied on an overhead transparency or a large piece of chart paper to identify the lines or refrains that are best suited to a single voice or small group interpretation and the lines that can be read by a larger group of voices. Directions such as fast/slow, loud/soft, or high/low can be incorporated, and sound effects or physical gestures can be added.

Reading materials other than poems can also be considered. Rhymes, patterned books, epics, or other books with lusciously lyrical or rhythmically sensitive language can be tried through Choral Reading*.

Readers' Theater*

Readers' Theater provides an opportunity for oral reading. Attention is aurally focused.*

Readers' Theater* is an interpretive reading activity that allows us to relive the radio broadcasts of past or present. Unlike plays that require costumes, movement, and stage sets, Readers' Theater* is mostly auditory although it is frequently complemented by facial expressions and a few gestures. It is therefore well suited to tape recording for later playback at listening posts. When different groups try the same passage (or the same group attempts repeated readings), children develop the notion of multiple interpretations. They come to see that reading is an active and open process of constructing meaning, not the accurate pronunciation of words. Because Readers' Theater* usually incorporates a practice before presentation, less proficient readers are able to be successful in oral reading.

Sloyer (1982)

A short story or a part of a book that has an exciting plot, compelling characters, and language that calls for visual images should be selected for Readers' Theater*. Some information books, such as Aliki's *A Medieval Feast* and Cole's *The Magic School Bus and the Electric Field Trip*, are also possible choices. Long descriptive passages or narration do not always work well and may need to be deleted or summarized; the "he saids" and "she saids" and other less essential passages can be omitted. A narrator and character roles are assigned, an introduction is prepared, and after careful rehearsal, the "play" is presented. Although commercial scripts are available, children can write their own scripts or work with photocopies of passages on which they can make changes and highlight individual parts.

Aliki (1983); Cole (1997)

Story Theater*

Moffett & Wagner (1992)

Like Readers' Theater*, Story Theater* involves children in interpreting written material. However, now a visual element is added. For younger children, the teacher frequently reads a story and has children pantomime the action as it unfolds. An alternative is to let several children read character dialogue and narrative while another group interprets the readings through pantomime, each child acting a particular character role. Written scripts or texts are not used, so pantomimists must listen carefully to the readers and interpret action and feelings nonverbally. Criteria for choosing material for Story Theater* are similar to those for Readers' Theater*, but now an element of character action is necessary. If a scene has characters sitting in chairs and

Story Theater provides an opportunity for movement interpretation.*

talking, it might work well as Readers' Theater* but not as Story Theater*. Although most teachers choose stories for Story Theater*, other nonstory genres can also be used. Children can pantomime information books written by Gibbons—*The Post Office Book: Mail and How It Moves* and *Department Store*—that describe the movement of mail and the activities occurring at a department store on a typical day. Children also enjoy acting out a description of a chemical reaction, a plant's growth, or a frog's or caterpillar's metamorphosis.

Some information books can also be used in Story Theater.*

Gibbons (1984, 1984)

Status of the Class*

Status of the Class* is a procedure developed by Atwell to keep track of students' daily status regarding writing. Each day the teacher quickly calls on each student to find out where he or she is in writing, and what the student is going to write about. Using a form that simply lists the names of the children down the left side with the rest of the paper separated into five columns, one column for each day of the week, the teacher notes what students will be doing. Besides the title of the piece, simple abbreviations are used to document the process: *PW* for prewriting activities (perhaps listing questions, making an outline or Semantic Map* to organize thoughts or ideas before attempting an initial draft); *D1, D2,* and so on for drafts; *PC* for peer conferencing (perhaps including the names of the peers with whom the student will conference); *SE* for self-editing, where a student goes through the last draft before publication; and *P* for publishing (the writing or typing of the final draft, along with any illustrations to be done). Content or Editing Conferences* to be scheduled with the teacher also might be determined and coded on the form. (See Chapter 6 as well as "Writing Activities and Experiences" in the present chapter for more details regarding writing.)

Status of the Class was initially used to keep track of students' status in writing.*

Atwell (1987)

The Status of the Class* procedure offers a way for teachers to track students' work so they can be most responsive to them. They can best decide how and when to share their expertise. Status of the Class* also provides accountability by helping teachers and students who are working at different stages on many different pieces not to get lost in the cracks. For example, if a student has been working for several days on some aspect of the writing process, perhaps prewriting or self-editing, the teacher knows that it will be important to talk to the student that day to see what problems he or she might have and how to help. Documentation gives a teacher grounds for a heart-to-heart talk about problems in using time during writing workshop, such as playing or off-task behavior, so that the teacher can help students become more responsible.

Some teachers modify the Status of the Class* to fit the needs of their children and the way in which they organize their work. Older elementary students may use their planning Journals* to track their work. While children are at work, the teacher can check the journals, which are kept open on the students' desks, and then fill in their Status of the Class* form. Many teachers find that it saves class time to do it this way, especially if class is large. By tracking their own work, the students have more opportunities to develop responsibility, commitment, and control in their writing and other work.

Johnston (1992)

The idea of the Status of the Class* procedure has also been modified by many teachers for use in other areas of the curriculum. For example, a similar form can be devised to keep track of students' reading. Here the book or books students are reading are noted with abbreviations to indicate which page or chapter students are on in their reading and other relevant information. Initials such as *PR* (personal reading), *IR* (reading related to a particular student inquiry), or *RLRG* (reading that is part of a Literature Response Group*) might be used. Book Extensions* that students are engaged in could also be noted with initials: *CC* (Comparison Chart) or *STS* (Sketch to Stretch*).

The idea of Status of the Class can be extended and modified for monitoring other areas.*

Status of the Class* procedures or checks are also especially useful in monitoring individual or small-group Student-Initiated Inquiries*. Resources at-hand or in-need, problems students have resolved or still have, and facets of the project that have been accomplished or are still in progress can be documented by such a form so that teachers can keep track of the process and progress of inquiry projects.

See Boyd (1985) for a good classroom example of the use of a Message Board*.

Message Board*

The Message Board* is usually a bulletin board where the teacher and children exchange messages. The board fosters functional communication by helping children learn the range of purposes that literacy serves. Also, because both the teacher and children use the Message Board*, it encourages a sense of community. The Message Board* is usually placed near the door so communications can't be missed. Paper and envelopes, writing implements, and thumbtacks are available nearby to facilitate its use. In the beginning of the year, the teacher introduces the Message Board* by putting a welcoming note on it, along with a short set of directions for using it: that it can be used for certain times, that it can be used for personal or general messages, that all exchanges must include the names of receivers and senders, and that messages can be sealed in an envelope.

See Short & Harste (1996) for another discussion of Message Boards*.

A range of teacher-children communications is possible on the Message Board*: Children may leave notes for the teacher regarding decisions they have made, or a small group may indicate that it is now ready to share the findings of its project. The teacher may suggest a book that a particular child may find useful for study or provide permission for a group of students to survey the third-graders on Tuesday on an issue related to some work they are doing in a thematic unit.

Most of the time, however, children use the Message Board* to communicate with one another. They leave a new math story problem they have written and challenge others to solve it, they announce the creation of a particular Literature Response Group*, or they ask their classmates to help locate a book they had been using for a report they are writing. They can also write more personal messages addressed to particular children in the class.

Focus Lessons*

Calkins (1986); Routman (1996)

The idea of Focus Lessons* (frequently called mini-lessons) was developed by Calkins to teach various aspects of the writing process. In integrated language classrooms, however, Focus Lessons* are much more broadly thought of; they can deal with any topic in the curriculum, not writing only.

Focus-Lessons grow out of needs of children, not an artificial scope and sequence of skills.*

A Focus Lesson* is a short meeting—usually five to twenty minutes—with the whole class (or a small group), during which the teacher addresses an issue that has arisen. While teachers observe children engaged in activities in various projects they have taken on, they focus on the needs of the children rather than an artificial scope and sequence of skills. They note problems or difficulties children may be having, or they recognize children's current understandings or strategies that they can build on or extend.

Focus Lessons* are specific occasions in which teachers share their knowledge or expertise by providing explicit instruction. Focus Lessons* usually deal with three major issues: presenting procedural information, demonstrating techniques, and teaching specific operations and conventions. Focus Lessons* have been illustrated throughout this book, although they may not always have been labeled as such. The following examples summarize and clarify the range of possibilities.

Presenting Procedural Information

Focus-Lessons address various procedural concerns.*

As one could expect, Focus Lessons* on procedures occur most frequently in the beginning of the year or at the beginning of a thematic unit. They are the ways through which teachers communicate what they expect from children and what children can expect from them. The lessons can cover the way each day will be structured and the activities that are available. They may include some of the choices for children in a particular thematic unit, how to keep a Learning Log*, or how to complete the forms in Authors' Folders*. Focus Lessons* can cover the rules for using the Message Board*, explain how to set up a particular scientific experiment, or tell how to use Jackdaws*.

Demonstrating Techniques

Focus-Lessons are opportunities for teacher demonstrations.*

Focus Lessons* also involve teacher modeling and demonstrations. Frequently, children don't revise because they don't know how to actually manipulate the page, use carets and arrows, delete information, or add information when there's no room between the lines or in the margins. Thus, using a composition of their own or a text written in a Group-Composed Writing* activity, teachers illustrate revision techniques. Focus Lessons* can consist of various brainstorming sessions to help children consider topics for their writing, problems they may want to pursue in individual or small group projects, and ways to go about tackling these questions in their inquiries. Focus Lessons* can demonstrate how to construct Semantic Maps* or Comparison Charts*, or how to do Story Maps*, Character Sociograms*, Book Talks*, or various Sketch to Stretch* activities. They can examine or compare certain authors' styles (and ideologies) or the structure or organization of a particular written genre, or they can evaluate ways several authors have dealt with the same topics or information.

Teaching Specific Operations and Conventions

Focus Lessons* can deal with teaching specific conventions and skills. They can cover ways to use the cotext to figure out or identify a word when reading (see strategies described under Teaching Phonics and Spelling in Context*). They can include how to structure a business letter and how to use quotation marks or other kinds of punctuation. Focus Lessons* can show how to write up scientific observations, how to do certain mathematical operations or computations for a graph, or how to label and design a graph.

Focus Lessons deal with specific conventions, strategies, and so on.*

In sum, Focus Lessons* offer help and instruction on many diverse issues. It is important to know that they are rarely on procedures, techniques, or specific conventions only. Many Focus Lessons* include aspects of all three. Teachers plan certain Focus Lessons* ahead of time because they know the areas in which most children need guidance and support. However, many Focus Lessons* cannot be preplanned because they result from careful observations. They are conducted in a more spontaneous fashion because they address the needs of specific children in specific circumstances. Teachers usually keep track of their Focus Lessons* so that they know when they covered a topic and evaluate the ways in which the ideas were taken up by students. After further observation, they might tackle the same topic from another angle to see if a new approach might be more useful for children. Some teachers keep their notes or transparencies they used for Focus Lessons* in a special folder or binder that is available for students to refer to at a later date—which is especially helpful for students who were absent for a particular Focus Lesson*.

Focus Lessons can be preplanned, or they can occur spontaneously.*

Conclusions

The activities and experiences described in this chapter are only suggestions. Teachers will make choices and draw on these strategies depending on the children with whom they work and the circumstances in which they find themselves. The activities presented here are based on teaching practices that we have seen in a variety of settings; other teachers who want to try them are free to modify or reshape them to meet their needs. They might serve as areas of teacher inquiry—see Guidelines for Teacher Inquiry at the end of the book.

References

Adams, M. J. (1990). *Beginning to read: Thinking and learning about print.* Cambridge, MA: MIT Press.

Alberti, D., Davitt, R. J., Ferguson, T. A., & Repass, S. O. (1974). *Teachers' guide for ice cubes: Melting rates of ice.* New York: McGraw-Hill.

Allington, R. L. (1994). The schools we have. The schools we need. *The Reading Teacher, 48,* 14–29.

Atwell, N. (1987). *In the middle: Writing, reading, and learning with adolescents.* Portsmouth, NH: Boynton/Cook.

Baratta-Lorton, M. (1995). *Mathematics their way.* Menlo Park, CA: Addison-Wesley.

Batchelder, M., & Comer, V. L. (1956). *Puppets and plays: A creative approach.* New York: Harper & Row.

Bauer, C. F. (1983). *This way to books.* New York: Wilson.

Bauer, C. F. (1993). *New handbook for storytellers.* Chicago: American Library Association.

Bayer, A. S. (1990). *Collaborative-apprenticeship learning: Language and thinking across the curriculum, K–12.* Mountain View, CA: Mayfield.

Bear, D. R., Invernizzi, M., Templeton, S., & Johnston, F. (1996). *Words their way: Word study for phonics, vocabulary and spelling instruction.* Columbus, OH: Merrill/Prentice Hall.

Beaver, J. (1982). Say it, over and over. *Language Arts, 59,* 143–147.

Boyd, R. (1985). The message board: Language comes alive. In J. M. Newman (Ed.), *Whole language: Theory in use* (pp. 91–98). Portsmouth, NH: Heinemann.

Brooks, J. G., & Brooks, M. G. (1993). *In search of understanding: The case for constructivist classrooms.* Alexandria, VA: Association for Supervision and Curriculum Development.

Butler, A., & Turbill, J. (1984). *Towards a reading-writing classroom.* Rozelle, Australia: Primary English Teaching Association.

Byrnes, D. A. (1988). Children and prejudice. *Social Education, 52,* 267–271.

Caine, R. N., & Caine, G. (1994). *Making connections: Teaching and the human brain.* NY: Addison-Wesley.

Calkins, L. M. (1986). *The art of teaching writing.* Portsmouth, NH: Heinemann.

Calkins, L. M. (1994). *The art of teaching writing.* Portsmouth, NH: Heinemann.

Calkins, L. M. with Harwayne, S. (1991). *Living between the lines.* Portsmouth, NH: Heinemann.

Chambers, A. (1986). *The practical guide to marbleizing paper.* New York: Thames & Hudson.

Chambers, A. (1996). *Tell me: children, reading and talk.* York, ME: Stenhouse.

Champlin, C., & Renfro, N. (1985). *Storytelling with puppets.* Chicago: American Library Association.

Clay, M. (1979). *Reading: The patterning of complex behavior.* Portsmouth, NH: Heinemann.

Cochrane, O., Cochrane, D., Scalena, S., & Buchanan, E. (1984). *Reading, writing and caring.* Winnipeg, Manitoba: Whole Language Consultants.

Cohen, D. (1968). The effect of literature on vocabulary and reading achievement. *Elementary English, 45,* 209–213.

Conference on College Composition and Communication. (1988). *The national policy* (position statement). Urbana, IL: National Council of Teachers of English.

Cunningham, P. E., & Cunningham, J. W. (1992). Making words: Enhancing the invented spelling-decoding connections. *The Reading Teacher, 46,* 106–115.

Dalton, J. (1985). *Adventures in thinking: Creative thinking and co-operative talk in small groups.* South Melbourne, Australia: Nelson (Distributed by Heinemann, Portsmouth, NH).

Delpit, L. (1995). *Other people's children: Cultural conflict in the classroom.* New York: The New Press.

Duthie, C. (1996). *True stories: Nonfiction literacy in the primary classroom.* York, ME: Stenhouse.

Ellis, A. (1986). *Teaching and learning elementary social studies.* Boston: Allyn & Bacon.

Fennimore, F. (1992). *The art of the handmade book.* Chicago, IL: Chicago Review Press.

Fisher, B. (1991). *Joyful learning: A whole language kindergarten.* Portsmouth, NH: Heinemann.

Fried, R. L. (1995). *The passionate teacher: A practical guide.* Boston: Beacon Press.

Fulwiler, T. (1980). Journals across the disciplines. *English Journal, 69,* 14–22.

Fulwiler, T. (1982). Writing: An act of cognition. In C. W. Griffin (Ed.), *New directions for teaching and learning: No. 12. Teaching writing in all disciplines* (pp. 15–26). San Francisco: Jossey-Bass.

Gee, J. P. (1996). *Social linguistics and literacies: Ideology in discourses.* London: Taylor & Francis.

Goodman, Y. M., & Burke, C. (1985). *Reading strategies: Focus on comprehension.* New York: Richard Owen.

Graves, D. H. (1983). *Writing: Teachers and children at work.* Portsmouth, NH: Heinemann.

Graves, D. H. (1994). *A fresh look at writing.* Portsmouth, NH: Heinemann.

Graves, D. H., & Hansen, J. (1982). The author's chair. *Language Arts, 60,* 176–183.

Hatano, G. (1988). Social and motivational bases for mathematical understanding. In G. B. Saxe & M. Gearhart (Eds.), *New directions for child development: No. 41. Children's mathematics* (pp. 55–70). San Francisco: Jossey-Bass.

Harste, J. C., & Short, K. G. (1988). *Creating classrooms for authors: The reading-writing connection.* Portsmouth, NH: Heinemann.

Heathcote, D., & Bolton, G. (1995). *Drama for learning: Dorothy Heathcote's mantle of the expert approach to education.* Portsmouth, NH: Heinemann.

Heimlich, J., & Pittelman, S. D. (1986). *Semantic mapping: Classroom applications.* Newark, DE: International Reading Association.

Hepler, S. (1991). Talking our way to literacy in the classroom community. *The New Advocate, 4,* 179–191.

Hepler, S. I., & Hickman, J. (1982). "The book was okay, I love you": Social aspects of response to literature. *Theory Into Practice, 21,* 278–283.

Hickman, J. (1981). A new perspective on response to literature: Research in an elementary school setting. *Research in the Teaching of English, 15,* 343–354.

Hill, B. C., Johnson, N. J., & Noe, K. L. S. (1995). *Literature circles and response.* Norwood, MA: Christopher-Gordon.

Hill, S., & Hill, T. (1990). *The collaborative classroom: A guide to co-operative learning.* Portsmouth, NH: Heinemann.

Hillocks, G. (1986). *Research on written composition: New directions for teaching.* Urbana, IL: ERIC Clearinghouse on Reading and Communication Skills.

Holdaway, D. (1979). *The foundations of literacy.* Sydney, Australia: Ashton Scholastic.

Hollins, E. R. (1996). *Culture in school learning: Revealing the deep meaning.* Mahwah, NJ: Lawrence Erlbaum.

Hornsby, D., & Sukarna, D. (1988). *Read-on: A conference approach to reading.* Portsmouth, NH: Heinemann.

Huck, C. S., Hepler, S., Hickman, J., & Kiefer, B. (1997). *Children's literature in the elementary school.* Madison, WI: Brown & Benchmark.

Hyde, A. A., & Bizar, M. (1989). *Thinking in context: Teaching cognitive processes across the elementary curriculum.* White Plains, NY: Longman.

Jackdaw. Grossman Publishers in association with Jackdaw Pub., Ltd., London, England.

Johnson, P. (1992). *A book of one's own.* Portsmouth, NH: Heinemann.

Johnson, P. (1993). *Literacy through the book arts.* Portsmouth, NH: Heinemann.

Johnson, T. D., & Louis, D. R. (1987). *Literacy through literature.* Portsmouth, NH: Heinemann.

Johnston, P. H. (1992). *Constructive evaluation of literate activity.* White Plains, NY: Longman.

Johnston, P. H. (1997). *Knowing literacy: Constructive literacy assessment*. York, ME: Stenhouse.

Krashen, S. (1993). *The power of reading: Insights from research*. Englewood, CO: Libraries Unlimited.

Krogness, M. M. (1995). *Just teach me, Mrs. K.* Portsmouth, NH: Heinemann.

Kwak, W., & Newman, J. M. (1985). Activity cards. In J. M. Newman (Ed.), *Whole language: Theory in use* (pp. 137–144). Portsmouth, NH: Heinemann.

Ladson-Billings, G. (1994). *The dreamkeepers: Successful teachers of African-American children*. San Francisco: Jossey-Bass.

Lave, J., & Wenger, W. (1991). *Situated learning: Legitimate peripheral participation*. New York: Cambridge University Press.

Lensmire, T. J. (1994). *When children write: Critical revisions of the writing workshop*. New York: Teachers College Press.

Levstik, L. S. (1986). The relationship between historical response and narrative in a sixth-grade classroom. *Theory and Research in Social Education, 14,* 1–15.

Levstik, L. S., & Barton, K. C. (1997). *Doing history: Investigating with children in elementary and middle schools*. Mahwah, NJ: Erlbaum.

Levstik, L. S., & Smith, D. (1996). "I've never done this before": Building a community of inquiry in a third grade classroom. In J. Brophy (Ed.), *Advances in Research on Teaching: Case Studies of Teaching and Learning in Elementary History*, Vol. 5., pp. 85–114. JAI.

Livdahl, B. S., Smart, K., Wallman, J., Herbert, T. K., Geiger, D. K., & Anderson, J. L. (1995). *Stories from response-centered classrooms: Speaking, questioning, and theorizing from the center of the action*. New York: Teachers College Press.

Lynch-Watson, J. (1980). *The shadow puppet book*. New York: Sterling.

Lytle, S. L., & Botel, M. (1988). *PCRP II: Reading, writing and talking across the curriculum*. Harrisburg, PA: Pennsylvania Department of Education.

Macrorie, K. (1988). *The I-search paper*. Portsmouth, NH: Boynton/Cook.

Manning, G. L., & Manning, M. (1984). What models of reading make a difference? *Reading World, 23,* 375–380.

McCaslin, N. (1996). *Creative drama in the classroom*. White Plains, NY: Longman.

McGinley, W., & Madigan, D. (1990). The "research" story: Forum for integration reading, writing and learning. *Language Arts, 67,* 474–483.

McKenzie, M. (1977). The beginnings of literacy. *Theory Into Practice, 16,* 315–324.

McKenzie, M. (1985). Shared writing: Apprenticeship in writing. *Language Matters, 1,* 1–5.

Moffett, J., & Wagner, B. J. (1992). *Student centered language arts, K–12*. Portsmouth, NH: Boynton/Cook.

Moll, L. (1992). Literacy research in community and classrooms. In R. Beach, J. L. Green, M. L. Kamil, & T. Shanahan (Eds.), *Multidisciplinary perspectives on literacy research* (pp. 211–244). Urbana, IL: National Conference on Research in English.

Moore, D. W., Moore, S. A., Cunningham, P. M., & Cunningham, J. W. (1998). *Developing readers and writers in the content areas K–12*. New York: Longman.

Morrow, L. M. (1988). Young children's response to one-to-one story readings in school settings. *Reading Research Quarterly, 23,* 89–107.

Mossip, J. (1985). It makes you feel needed: Students as teachers. In J. M. Newman (Ed.), *Whole language: Theory in use* (pp. 131–136). Portsmouth, NH: Heinemann.

Newmann, F., Sescada, W. G., & Wehlage, G. G. (1995). *A guide to authentic instruction and assessment: Vision, standards and scoring*. Madison: Wisconsin Center for Education Research.

O'Neill, C. (1985). Imagined worlds in theatre and drama. *Theory Into Practice, 24,* 158–165.

O'Neill, C., & Lambert, A. (1982). *Drama structures: A practical handbook for teachers*. Portsmouth, NH: Heinemann.

Ogle, D. (1986). K-W-L: A teaching model that develops active reading of expository text. *The Reading Teacher, 39,* 564–570.

Pappas, C. C. (in press). Becoming literate in the borderlands. In A. Goncu (Ed.), *Children's engagement in the world: Sociocultural perspectives*. Cambridge: Cambridge University Press.

Pappas, C. C., & Brown, E. (1989). Using turns at story "reading" as scaffolding for learning. *Theory Into Practice, 28,* 105–113.

Pierce, K. M., & Gilles, C. J. (Eds.). (1993). *Cycles of meaning: Exploring the potential of talk in learning communities*. Portsmouth, NH: Heinemann.

Raphael, T. E., & McMahon, S. I. (1994). Book club: An alternative framework for reading instruction. *The Reading Teacher, 48,* 102–116.

Reardon, S. J. (1988). The development of critical readers: A look into the classroom. *The New Advocate, 1,* 52–61.

Revel-Wood, M. (1988). Invitations to read, to write, to learn. In J. C. Harste & K. G. Short (Eds.). *Creating classrooms for authors: The reading-writing connection* (pp. 169–179). Portsmouth, NH: Heinemann.

Rief, L. (1992). *Seeking diversity: Language arts with adolescents*. Portsmouth, NH: Heinemann.

Rogoff, B. (1990). *Apprenticeship in thinking: Cognitive development in social context*. NY: Oxford University Press.

Routman, R. (1988). *Transitions: From literature to literacy*. Portsmouth, NH: Heinemann.

Routman, R. (1996). *Literacy at the crossroads: Crucial talk about reading, writing and other teaching dilemmas*. Portsmouth, NH: Heinemann.

Samway, K. D., & Whang, G. (1996). *Literature study circles in a multicultural classroom*. York, ME: Stenhouse.

Samway, K. D., Whang, G., & Pippitt, M. (1995). *Buddy reading: Cross-age tutoring in a multicultural school*. Portsmouth, NH: Heinemann.

Saul, W., Reardon, J, Schmidt, A., Pearce, C., Blackwood, D., & Bird, M. D. (1993). *Science workshop: A whole language approach*. Portsmouth, NH: Heinemann.

Short, K. G., & Harste, J. C. (1996). *Creating classrooms for authors and inquirers*. Portsmouth, NH: Heinemann.

Short, K. G., & Pierce, K. M. (1990). *Talking about books: Creating literate communities*. Portsmouth, NH: Heinemann.

Siks, G. B. (1977). *Drama with children*. New York: Harper & Row.

Sloyer, S. (1982). *Readers' theatre: Story dramatization in the classroom*. Urbana, IL: National Council of Teachers of English.

Sonnenschein, F. M. (1988). Countering prejudiced beliefs and behaviors: The role of the social studies professional. *Social Education, 52,* 262–266.

Stone, L. (1986). International and multicultural education. In V. Atwood (Ed.), *Elementary social studies: Research as a guide to practice* (pp. 34–54). Washington, DC: National Council for the Social Studies.

Strickland, D., & Cullinan, B. (1990). Afterword. In Adams, M. J. *Beginning to read: Thinking and learning about print.* (pp. 425–434) Cambridge, MA: MIT Press.

Takaki, R. (1993). *A different mirror: A history of multicultural America.* Boston: Little, Brown.

Temple, C., Nathan, R., Temple, F., & Burris, N. (1993). *The beginnings of writing.* Boston: Allyn & Bacon.

Tierney, R. J., Readence, J. E., & Dishner, E. K. (1995). *Reading strategies and practices: A compendium.* Boston: Allyn & Bacon.

Tompkins, G. E. (1998). *50 literacy strategies: Step-by-step.* Upper Saddle River, NJ: Merrill.

Tunnell, M. O., & Jacobs, J. (1989). Using "real" books: Research findings on literature-based reading in instruction. *The Reading Teacher, 42,* 470–477.

Unia, S. (1985). From sunny days and green onions: On journal writing. In J. M. Newman (Ed.), *Whole language: Theory in use* (pp. 65–72). Portsmouth, NH: Heinemann.

Vygotsky, L. (1978). *Mind in society: The development of higher psycological processes.* Cambridge, MA: Harvard University Press.

Waggstaff, J. M. (1997–1998). Building practical knowledge of letter-sound correspondences; A beginner's word wall and beyond. *The Reading Teacher, 51,* 298-306.

Wassermann, S., & Ivany, J. W. G. (1988). *Teaching elementary science: Who's afraid of spiders?* New York: Harper & Row.

Way, B. (1967). *Development through drama.* Atlantic Highlands, NJ: Humanities Press.

Weaver, C. (1996). *Teaching grammar in context.* Portsmouth, NH: Boynton/Cook.

Weber, L. (1989). Teachers using historical fiction. In J. Hickman & B. Cullinan (Eds.), *Weaving Charlotte's web: Children's literature in the elementary classroom* (pp. 147–156). Needham Heights, MA: Christopher-Gordon.

Wells, G. & Chang-Wells, G. L. (1992). *Constructing knowledge together: Classrooms as centers of inquiry and literacy.* Portsmouth, NH: Heinemann.

Wells, G. (1986). *The meaning makers: Children learning language and using language to learn.* Portsmouth, NH: Heinemann.

Wertsch, J. V. (1985). *Vygotsky and the social formation of mind.* Cambridge: Cambridge University Press.

Wertsch, J. V. (1991). *Voices of the mind: A sociocultural approach to mediated action.* Cambridge: Cambridge University Press.

Whitin, P., & Whitin, D. (1997). *Inquiry at the window: Pursuing the wonders of learners.* Portsmouth, NH: Heinemann.

Wilde, S.(1992). *You kan red this!: Spelling and punctuation for whole language classrooms, K-6.* Portsmouth NH: Heinemann.

Wilde, S. (1997). *What's a schwa sound anyway? A holistic guide to phonetics, phonics, and spelling.* Portsmouth, NH: Heinemann.

Wilner, I. (1977). *The poetry troupe: An anthology of poems to read aloud.* New York: Scribners.

Wilson, A. (1987). Cross-cultural experiential learning for teachers. *Theory Into Practice, 26,* 519–527.

Yopp, H. K. (1992). Developing phonemic awareness in young children. *The Reading Teacher, 48,* 538—542.

Young, K. A. (1994). *Constructing buildings, bridges, and minds: Building an integrated curriculum through social studies.* Portsmouth, NH: Heinemann.

CHILDREN'S LITERATURE

ABC I Like Me! by N. Carlson. Viking, 1997.

Alexander and the Terrible, Horrible, No Good, Very Bad Day by J. Viorst. Illustrated by R. Cruz. Atheneum, 1972.

Alligators All Around: An Alphabet by M. Sendak. HarperCollins, 1962.

Amelia's Road by L. J. Altman. Illustrated by E. O. Sanchez. Lee & Low Books, 1993.

Animalia by G. Base. Henry N. Abrams, 1986.

The Bee by S. Crewe. Raintree Steck-Vaughn, 1997.

Beyond the Divide by K. Lasky. Macmillan, 1983.

Big City Port by B. Maestro & E. DelVecchio. Illustrated by G. Maestro. Scholastic, 1983.

Bloomers! by R. Blumberg. Aladdin, 1996.

The Borrowers by M. Norton. Harcourt Brace Jovanovich, 1953.

The Bridge to Terabithia by K. Paterson. Crowell, 1977.

Brown Bear, Brown Bear, What Do You See? by B. Martin, Jr. Illustrated by E. Carle. Holt, 1983.

The Cabin Faced West by J. Fritz. Coward, McCann, 1958.

Caleb and Kate by W. Steig. Farrar, Straus, & Giroux, 1977.

Catherine, Called Birdy by K. Cushman. HarperTrophy, 1994.

The Cat's Purr by A. Bryan. Atheneum, 1985.

Chato's Kitchen by G. Soto. Illustrated by S. Guevara. G. P. Putman, 1995.

Child of the Owl by L. Yep. HarperTrophy, 1977.

Christmas in the Big House, Christmas in the Quarters by S. McKissack & F. L. McKissack. Illustrated by J. Thompson. Scholastic, 1994.

Circle of Gold by C. D. Boyd. Scholastic, 1984.

The Crane Maiden by M. Matsutani. Illustrated by C. Iwasaki. Parents Magazine Press, 1968.

The Crane Wife by S. Yagawa. Translated by K. Paterson. Illustrated by S. Akaba. Morrow, 1981.

Department Store by G. Gibbons. Harper & Row, 1984.

A Desert Scrapbook: Dawn to Dusk in the Sonoran Desert by V. Wright-Frierson. Simon & Schuster, 1996.

The Devil's Arithmetic by J. Yolen. Viking Kestrel, 1988.

Digging up Dinosaurs by Aliki. Crowell, 1988.

Enchantress from the Stars by S. L. Engdahl. Atheneum, 1973.

Evolution by J. Cole. Illustrated by Aliki. Crowell, 1987.

George Washington's Breakfast by J. Fritz. Illustrated by P. Galdone. Coward, McCann, & Geoghegan, 1969.

A Girl Called Boy by B. Hurmence. Clarion, 1982.

The Green Book by J. P. Walsh. Farrar, Straus, & Giroux, 1982.

Harlem by W. D. Myers. Illustrated by C. Myers. Scholastic Press, 1997.

Here Comes Henny by C. Pomerantz. Illustrated by N. W. Parker. Greenwillow, 1994.

The Highwayman by A. Noyes. Illustrated by C. Mikolaycak. Lothrop, 1983.

The Honey Makers by G. Gibbons. Morrow Junior Books, 1997.

How Do Bees Make Honey? by A. Claybourne. Illustrated by S. Allington & A. Spenceley. Usborne Publishing, 1994.

If I Had a Paka: Poems in Eleven Languages by C. Pomerantz. Illustrated by N. Tafuri. Greenwillow, 1993.

In Their Own Words by M. Meltzer. Crowell, 1977.

James and the Giant Peach by R. Dahl. Knopf, 1961.

Johnny Tremain by E. Forbes. Houghton Mifflin, 1943.

Journey Outside by M. Q. Steele. Viking, 1969.

Joyful Noise: Poems for Two Voices by P. Fleischman. Illustrated by E. Beddows. HarperTrophy, 1988.

The Ladybug and Other Insects by First Discovery Books. Translated from the French by C. Cramer. (American edition by L. Goldsen). Scholastic, 1991.

The Last Princess: The Story of Princess Ka'iulani of Hawai'i by F. Stanley. Illustrated by D. Stanley. Macmillan, 1994.

The Ledgerbook of Thomas Blue Eagle by G. Mattaei & J. Grutman. Illustrated by A. Cvijonvic. Lickie Publishing, 1994.

The Life and Times of the Honeybee by C. Micucci, Houghton Mifflin, 1996.

Lincoln: A Photobiography by R. Freedman. Clarion, 1987.

The Little Red Hen by B. Barton. HarperCollins, 1993.

The Magic Porridge Pot by P. Galdone. Houghton Mifflin, 1976.

The Magic School Bus and the Electric Field Trip by J. Cole. Illustrated by B. Degen. Scholastic, 1997

The Magic School Bus at the Waterworks by J. Cole. Illustrated by B. Degen. Scholastic, 1966.

The Magic School Bus inside a Beehive by J. Cole. Illustrated by B. Degen. Scholastic, 1996.

Many Luscious Lollipops: A Book about Adjectives by R. Heller. G. P. Putman, 1989.

A Medieval Feast by Aliki. Crowell, 1983.

Mojave by D. Siebert. Illustrated by W. Minor. Thomas Y. Crowell, 1988.

Mrs. Wishy Washy by J. Cowley. Illustrated by E. Fuller. Wright Group, 1981.

Mummies Made in Egypt by Aliki. Crowell, 1979.

My Brother Sam Is Dead by J. Collier & L. Collier. Four Winds, 1974.

On Market Street by A. Lobel. Illustrated by A. Lobel. Greenwillow, 1981.

The Owl and the Woodpecker by B. Wildsmith. Oxford University Press.

Owl Babies by M. Waddell. Illustrated by P. Benson. Candlewick Press, 1992.

Ox-Cart Man by D. Hall. Illustrated by B. Cooney. Viking, 1979.

Pearl Moscowitz's Last Stand by A. A. Levin. Tambourine, 1993.

People by P. Spier. Doubleday, 1980.

"The Pickety Fence" by D. McCord in *One at a Time* by D. McCord. Little, Brown, 1986.

A Picture Book of Frederick Douglass by D. A. Adler. Illustrated by S. Byrd. Holiday House, 1993.

Pioneer Women: Voices from the Kansas Frontier by J. L. Stratton. Simon & Schuster, 1981.

The Post Office Book: Mail and How It Moves by G. Gibbons. Harper & Row, 1982.

Questions and Answers about Bees by B. P. Reigot. Illustrated by K. Hendrickson. Scholastic, 1995.

Roar and More by K. Kuskin. HarperCollins, 1990.

The Rooster Crows: A Book of American Rymes and Jingles by M. Petersham & M. Petersham. Macmillan, 1945.

Rosie the Riveter by P. Colman. Crown, 1995.

The Secret Garden by F. H. Burnett. Lippincott, 1962.

Shoes from Grandpa by M. Fox. Illustrated by P. Mullins. Orchard Books, 1989.

Small Green Snake by L. M. Gray, Illustrated by H. Meade. Orchard, 1994.

The Squirrel by M. Lane. Illustrated by K. Lilly. Dial, 1981.

Squirrels by B. Wildsmith. Oxford University Press, 1974.

The Story of the Grateful Crane: A Japanese Folktale by J. Bartoli. Whitman, 1977.

Sylvester and the Magic Pebble by W. Steig. Windmill, 1979.

The Teeny Tiny Woman by P. Galdone. Clarion, 1984.

Thunder at Gettysburg by P. L. Gauch. Illustrated by S. Gammell. Coward, McCann & Geoghegan, 1975.

Time of Wonder by R. McClosky. Viking Penguin, 1957.

Tin Lizzie by P. Spier. Doubleday, 1978.

To Be a Slave by J. Lester. Dial, 1968.

Tuck Everlasting by N. Babbitt. Farrar, Straus, & Giroux, 1975.

Tunnels by G. Gibbons. Holiday House, 1984.

The Very Hungry Caterpillar by E. Carle. Philomel, 1969.

Uncle Jed's Barbershop by M. K. Mitchell. Illustrated by J. Ransome. Simon & Schuster, 1993.

Volcanoes by F. M. Branley. Illustrated by M. Simont. Crowell, 1985.

Wild and Woolly Mammoths by Aliki. Crowell, 1977.

Winnie the Pooh by A. A. Milne. Illustrated by E. Shepard. Dutton, 1988 (1926).

Wizard of Earthsea by U. LeGuin. Parnassus, 1968.

Women's Diaries of the Westward Journey by L. Schlissel. Schocken, 1982.

Working Cotton by S. A. Williams. Illustrated by C. Byard. Harcourt Brace Jovanovich, 1992.

Yo! Yes? by C. Rascha. Orchard Books, 1993.

Learning Kid-Watching Procedures and Techniques

This chapter describes certain procedures and techniques to help you become a good kid watcher. Teachers in integrated language classrooms have certain views regarding learners (and learning), language, and knowledge (see Chapters 1 and 2). They believe that children's language and concepts (knowledge) are related to the kinds of experiences they have in a range of contexts. Consequently, most traditional ways to assess or evaluate children's development or learning are rarely useful. For example, completed ditto sheets, besides not being examples of meaningful use of language, are frequently misleading because they cannot capture the *process* of what children are actually doing or learning. "Wrong" answers can reflect children's intelligent thinking or reasonable hypotheses, whereas "right" answers can be based on misunderstandings or misconceptions. There is no way for the teacher to know which is the case because these materials offer little reliable information for making appropriate teaching decisions.

The assessment of products without regard to process is usually unreliable.

Integrated language teachers need alternative means for assessment and evaluation of children's ways with words: how they learn to use a variety of language registers in a variety of contexts and apply what they know in a range of activities and projects. Teachers need assessment and evaluation strategies that are developmentally and culturally appropriate for gaining information about what children say (and/or write) and do so that they can understand how the children's schemas are being modified in various domains. This information is necessary to guide, extend, and support children's learning—to become an effective teacher. It is also critical for documenting teaching effectiveness; it provides a means for accountability. (See Chapter 9.)

Au (1993); Barrs, Ellis, Hester, & Thomas (1988, 1990); Harp (1993); Weiner & Cohen (1994)

This kid-watching chapter is organized into two major sections. The first section covers schemes for assessing and evaluating children's strategies and understandings in reading, writing, and producing certain oral language "compositions" (e.g., dictations and retellings). We call these kid-watching procedures *literacy assessments*. The second section describes several *general observation schemes* for gathering information about how language and concepts are developed across the curriculum. Both sets of observation systems may initially seem formal because they are new and unfamiliar. However, with practice, these kid-watching procedures or techniques become internalized by teachers so that they can use them to evaluate children's learning and language *informally* while children are actively engaged in a range of meaningful activities in the classroom. Classroom routines (indicated by an asterisk, *), which support and use techniques that follow, are described in Chapter 7.

Literacy Assessments

Three kinds of literacy procedures are covered: (1.) those that focus on reading and writing (Modified Miscue Analysis and Writing schemes); (2.) those that evaluate the literacy understandings of emergent learners (Concepts about Print, Approximations to Text, and Dictations); and (3.) those that evaluate children's retellings of a text.

Modified Miscue Analysis (MMA)

Miscue analysis was originally developed by Ken Goodman to provide a window on the reading process. A *miscue* is defined as a deviation or difference between a reader's production and the text when the reader is reading aloud. Miscue analysis is based on two major assumptions: (1.) Miscues are not random but have a variety of causes. Miscues are the result of readers' *constructions* of the linguistic message based on readers' present oral language development, their knowledge of the topic of the reading passage, their purpose for reading, and their familiarity with the register or genre of the text. Because reading is a constructive process, *everybody* makes miscues when they read aloud. (2.) Miscues reflect how readers are actually using the reading process. Besides pragmatic cues (e.g., reasons or purposes for reading), reading is the integration of three major cues: *graphic cues* (some people term these *graphophonemic cues*), which deal with the set of relationships between sounds and the written forms that represent them; *syntactic cues*, which deal with interrelationships of words, sentences, and paragraphs; and *semantic cues*, which deal with the meaning of a text.

There are many variations of miscue analysis. We present a Modified Miscue Analysis (MMA) that classroom teachers have found easy to use. Briefly, the MMA is a procedure by which a child's miscues (made while reading aloud) are qualitatively and quantitatively assessed to gain insights into the child's reading strategies. Part of the procedure is to ask the child to retell the text subsequent to the oral reading.

Selection of Material

It is best to use a piece of literature (not a basal passage) that is entirely new to the student but that incorporates concepts and situations that the reader can comprehend. It can be a story, an informational piece, a magazine article, or a chapter of a book—anything that can be read in ten to fifteen minutes. It is important that the student read an entire selection even if only a portion of the miscues are later coded and analyzed. The selection must be difficult or challenging enough for the student that miscues will be made, but not so difficult that the reader will not feel comfortable reading it. (If you do not know the child well—for example, at the beginning of a school year—a useful way to determine appropriate material is to bring several selections to the MMA session and ask the child to read silently a little of each. Ask the child after he or she reads some of each text if it seemed easy or hard to read. Don't use a text the child says is "easy" or "hard"; instead choose the text that the child describes as "sort of easy and sort of hard.") A selection must generate a minimum of twenty-five miscues to be used. A sample of fewer will be a less reliable indicator of the child's reading behavior.

Taping the Oral Reading and Retelling

The child reads from the printed text while the teacher marks on a specially prepared copy of the selection, called the MMA worksheet. The whole session is tape-recorded. The worksheet should retain the physical characteristics of the book from which the student reads. It should be an exact line-for-line copy, with sufficient space between the lines of the text so that all miscues can be clearly noted. However, many teachers use a clear photocopy of the text to save the time involved in typing a separate worksheet.

The taping should take place in a quiet atmosphere without distractions. (Frequently, teachers set up a small corner of the room where they can have conferences with individual students or small groups. This is an ideal place to do this part of the MMA.) Students are told (1.) that they are being asked to read because the teacher wants to understand how they read something they have never read or seen before; (2.) that they are to read the entire text aloud and that they will be asked to retell and talk about it at the end; and (3.) that they cannot be given any help during the reading. Consequently, if they come to a word that they don't know, they should do their best, as they would normally do while reading.

After the reading, students are simply asked to retell the text in their own words. If the retelling is a sparse one, the reader can be asked about a favorite or interesting

Goodman (1973, 1997); Goodman, Watson, & Burke (1987); Rhodes & Shaklin (1993); Watson & Henson (1993)

Miscues are constructions.

Miscues reflect the reading process in action.

The MMA taps readers' strategies.

part. (It is quite normal for a reader to give only a brief retelling here because the reader knows that the teacher knows the text. When retellings are short in this situation, it is important not to jump to the conclusion that the reader does not comprehend the text.) Follow-up questions can be prepared ahead of time as well (constructed perhaps to correspond to the types of transactions listed in Chapter 6) to complement the retelling, and more extemporaneous questions may be asked as appropriate.

Marking the MMA Worksheet

There are four categories of miscues.

While the reader is reading, the teacher identifies miscues and marks them on the MMA Worksheet according to the system described in Figure 8.1. Thus, the first decision to be made when a miscue occurs is what kind of deviation it represents. There are four kinds of miscues: substitutions, omissions, insertions, and reversals. These are mutually exclusive categories, and the teacher must decide *which one* more accurately categorizes each deviation. *Substitutions* involve replacing other words for those in the text. *Omissions* occur when words are dropped by the reader. There are two possibilities regarding omissions: Some omissions are fluent in that they are made without hesitation; others occur only after readers hesitate and inspect the text. Young children (e.g., kindergartners and first-graders) frequently make a lot of the second type; therefore, marking it may provide useful information regarding their reading development. For older elementary readers, this distinction may not be necessary. *Insertions* are words spoken by the reader that are not in the text. Finally, *reversals* occur when wordings are reversed during the reading. Figure 8.1 explains how these four types of miscues are marked and noted on the worksheet (i.e., the copy of the text that is read).

Reader *attempts to self-correct miscues* are also identified and marked on the worksheet. (Nothing is noted on the worksheet if the reader does not try corrections.) Attempts can be successful or unsuccessful and are noted accordingly. These notations are explained and illustrated on the bottom of Figure 8.1.

There are four other considerations to keep in mind in identifying miscues, as follows:

Miscues that are repeated throughout the text are coded the first time if the miscue is exactly the same each time (e.g., *Steve* for *Sven* miscued more than once). However, different miscues for the same word are each coded at their first occurrence (e.g., *Steve* for *Sven*, then *Seven* for *Sven*).

A related series of miscues can be coded as one miscue (e.g., *At first he saw* for *I first saw*). This can occur with a phrase or a clause.

Nonsense word substitutions are coded as miscues, but incomplete attempts are not (e.g., *glod* for *glad* is a miscue, but *gla-* then *glad* for *glad* is not).

See Goodman (1993) & Wilde (1997) on the issue of dialect and reading.

Slight dialectal differences (e.g., *pin* for *pen*) are not usually coded as miscues. Judgments of acceptability should depend on what is acceptable in that dialect.

Summary

Some teachers who have had a lot of experience in doing MMAs mark the worksheet as children read. Others (even those who are experienced) mark the worksheet later because they find it distracting to the reader to mark during the reading. Novices can also do the latter. Novices also find it useful simply to indicate by checks—with a pencil—places on the worksheet where there are deviations or possible miscues when they first hear the tape of the child's reading; they then listen to the tape a second time to mark the miscues with the appropriate designations.

Wilder (1953)

Figure 8.2 (see p. 326) shows the first eleven miscues made by a nine-year-old boy, Mike, while reading the beginning of Wilder's *Farmer Boy*. Most of his miscues are substitutions, but examples of the other three types of miscues (an omission, two insertions, and a reversal) are also present. In Mike's dialect, *bar* for *bare* is a miscue, but in some regional dialects, *bar* would be an acceptable pronunciation of *bare* and would not be considered a miscue. Note that *Elissa* for *Eliza* is counted as a miscue the first time, but the subsequent same renditions of the name are not.

1. *SUBSTITUTIONS:* Write the substitutions above the appropriate part of the text.

Example: He ran down the ~~street~~. [*road* written above]

2. *OMISSIONS:* Circle the *word(s)* left out. (If a reader reads "sing" for "singing," treat it as a substitution, not an omission of "ing.") Two types are possible:
   (a) *Omission without inspection (w/o I):* Just circle the omission. These are "fluent" omissions.

Example: John drank his milk, (too.) Then he left the table.

   (b) *Omission with inspection (I):* Circle the omission and place an "I" next to it. These are omissions where the reader hesitates and inspects a word in the text, and then omits it.

Example: He (usually) walked home alone. [*I* above]

3. *INSERTIONS:* Place an insertion sign (carat) at the point it occurs, and then write the insertion above the line.

Example: The hat blew ∧ into the tree. [*up* above the carat]

4. *REVERSALS:* Use the commonly used symbol (⌒⌣).

Example: "Hit the ball," yelled Pete.

ATTEMPTS AT CORRECTION:
   (a) *Attempted and Successful:* Mark © next to the miscue. Write each unsuccessful attempt above the word.

Example: He watched the ships in the harbor. [*shops* © above]

   (b) *Attempted but Unsuccessful:* Mark UC next to the miscue. Write each unsuccessful attempt above the word.

Example: Tommy never heard that noise before. [*hurt / hard* (uc) above]

   (c) *Changed Something Already Read Correctly* (rare): Mark AC next to the miscue. Write the change above the word.

Example: The hat blew into the tree. [*flew* (ac) above]

Figure 8.1

Instructions for Marking the MMA Worksheet

Completing the MMA Coding Sheet

After the miscues have been noted and numbered on the worksheet, they are transferred to the MMA Coding Sheet. For each miscue, certain judgments are made. Unlike errors, which are treated in an all-or-nothing fashion, miscues represent the predictions, confirmations, and disconfirmations of readers; thus, miscues must be examined qualitatively. Some miscues represent good, effective reading strategies, others may not. Figure 8.3 (p. 327) gives instructions for completing the MMA Coding Sheet shown in Figure 8.4 (p. 328).

On the coding sheet, each miscue is evaluated with respect to its acceptability—whether it is grammatically reasonable and makes sense. Substitution miscues are also judged by their graphic similarity to the text, and a reader's attempts to correct are examined. Finally, each uncorrected miscue is evaluated to see if it resulted in significantly changing the meaning of the author's message. Figure 8.5 illustrates how Mike's miscues would be transferred onto the coding sheet.

Notice that *maple* (for *maples*) and *sister* (for *sisters*) are treated as substitutions, not as omissions of the plural morpheme *s*. All but one of Mike's miscues are marked as being syntactically and semantically acceptable. *Boughts* for *boughs* is an interesting miscue. It is marked with a "?" under Column 9 because many teachers would mark this miscue as being syntactically acceptable in that it retains the plural morpheme. However, because *boughts* is a nonsense word, it cannot be semantically acceptable (hence, no check in Column 10) and the "meaning change" Column 13 is also checked. (In fact, a good rule of thumb is that when nonsense words are given, they are usually not semantically acceptable and they are likely to represent meaning changes.)

It is important to emphasize that although teachers try to be careful in doing MMAs to indicate what they think what a reader's strategies in the process of reading

Johnston (1997)

"School Days"

It was January in northern New York State, sixty–seven years ago. Snow lay very deep every–where. It loaded the bare limbs of oak and maples beeches, it bent the green boughs of cedars and spruces down into the drifts. Billows of snow covered the fields and the stone fences.

Down a long road through the woods a little boy trudged to school, with his big brother Roy–al and his two sisters, Eliza Jane and Alice. Royal was thirteen years old, Eliza was twelve, and Alice was ten. Almanzo was the youngest of all,

- -

and this was his first going–to–school, because he was not quite nine years old.

He had to walk fast to keep up with the oth–ers, and he had to carry the dinner–pail.

"Royal ought to carry it," he said. "He's big–ger than I be."

Royal strode ahead, big and manly in boots, and Eliza Jane said:

"No Manzo. It's your turn to carry it now, because you're the littlest."

Eliza Jane was bossy. She always knew what was best to do; and she made Almanzo and Alice do it.

Figure 8.2

Mike's Reading of "School Days," a Chapter in **Farmer Boy**

aloud, they are necessarily involved in interpretation. That is, deciding whether Mike was self-correcting a miscue or just figuring out a word (e.g., *bar* for *bare*), or deciding whether the miscue for *boughs* should be spelled *boughts* instead of *bots* are both instances of interpretation. Moreover, determinations as to whether particular miscues affect significant meaning changes of a text's message are sometimes hard ones to make. Two general principles frequently help teachers in their interpretations in doing MMAs: (1.) Consider the whole pattern of a reader's miscues when making decisions on particular miscues. For example, the teacher decided to spell the miscue *boughts* (and not *bots*) for *boughs* because Mike seemed to be sensitive to the graphic information of words in most of his substitution miscues (that is, all of his substitutions were graphically similar to the words in the text; all had checks in Column 5 in Figure 8.5). (2.) Try to be consistent and be true to your own criteria for making decisions about

Column	
1	*NO.* (1–25). The number of the miscue from the worksheet.
2	*TEXT.* Write the correct word or phrase that was miscued.
3	*READER.* Write the precise miscue that the reader made. If the reader makes more than one attempt at a word or phrase, code the *first* attempt.
4	*SUBS. (SUBSTITUTION).* Check (✓) if the miscue is a substitution.
5	GRAPHIC SIMILAR.. (GRAPHIC SIMILARITY). Coded only for substitutions. Check (✓) if the miscue is similar. A miscue is considered graphically similar to the text if: (1) both the first and last letters of the miscue match the first and last letters of the word(s) of the text, *OR* (2) either the first letter *or* the last letter *and* a majority of the remaining letters of the miscue match the letters and their position in the text.
6	*OMISSIONS w/o* I (without Inspection). Check (✓) if the reader maintains reading and fluency, reacting as if the word was not there.
7	*OMISSIONS w* I (with Inspection). Check (✓) if the reader obviously spends some time studying the word before omitting it.
8	*OTHER.* Check (✓) if the miscue is other than a substitution or an omission, namely, an insertion or a reversal.
9	*SYNTAC. ACCEPT. (SYNTACTIC ACCEPTABILITY).* Check (✓) if the miscue is syntactically acceptable. A miscue is considered semantically acceptable when the resulting sentence is acceptable according to its syntax (i.e., acceptable part of speech, acceptable word order, etc.) regardless of its meaning. Also, in evaluating the acceptability of a miscue, you must consider previous and subsequent miscues in the sentence (final attempts, successful or unsuccessful).
10	*SEMAN. ACCEPT. (SEMANTIC ACCEPTABILITY).* Check (✓) if the miscue is semantically acceptable. A miscue is considered semantically acceptable when the resulting sentence is acceptable according to its meaning (i.e., it makes sense) regardless of its syntax. However, because meaning and syntax are so closely related, it is unlikely that many syntactically unacceptable sentences will retain an acceptable meaning. Again, in evaluating the acceptability of a miscue, you must consider previous and subsequent miscues in the sentence (final attempts, successful or unsuccessful). Also, consider how the reader is making sense of previous text through the miscues.
11	*CORRECT.(ION): ATT. (ATTEMPTED).* Check (✓) if the reader made any attempt to correct.
12	*CORRECT.(ION): SUCC. (SUCCESSFUL).* Check (✓) if the reader's attempt to correct was successful.
13	*MEANING CHANGE.* Check (✓) if the miscue represents a *significantly* different meaning from that intended in the text *and* if the miscue was not successfully corrected.
TOTAL	Number of checks in each column on the coding sheet.

Figure 8.3

HOW TO COMPLETE THE MMA CODING SHEET

miscues. Talking with others about their explanations for why miscues are marked helps teachers, and especially those new to MMAs, cause their own criteria more explicit to them, thereby making these judgments easier.

Analyzing the Oral Reading Miscues

Using the data on the coding sheet, five major questions about oral reading miscues can be considered. Answers to these questions tell how a child is using the cuing systems. The result is quantitative data—percentages that reflect certain reading strategies. Figure 8.6 lists these questions and explains how to compute the percentages on the basis of counts taken from the coding sheet.

Remember, *no* percentage resulting from your computations on Figure 8.6 can be more than 100 percent. If you end up with something higher than 100 percent, you

If a percentage is over 100, you have not "read" the MMA Coding Sheet correctly.

Col.	1	2	3	4	5	6	7	8	9	10	11	12	13
	No.	Text	Reader	Subs.	Graphic Similar.	Omissions w/o I	w I	Other	Syntac. Accept.	Seman. Accept.	Correct. Att.	Correct. Succ.	Meaning Change
1													
2													
3													
4													
5													
⋮													
25													
TOTALS													

Figure 8.4
MMA CODING SHEET

Col.	1	2	3	4	5	6	7	8	9	10	11	12	13
	No.	Text	Reader	Subs.	Graphic Similar.	Omissions w/o I	w I	Other	Syntac. Accept.	Seman. Accept.	Correct. Att.	Correct. Succ.	Meaning Change
1	bare	bar	✓	✓				✓	✓	✓	✓	
2	maples	maple	✓	✓				✓	✓			
3	bent	went	✓	✓				✓	✓			
4	———	over					✓	✓	✓			
5	boughs	boughts	✓	✓				?				✓
6	sisters	sister	✓	✓				✓	✓	✓	✓	
7	Eliza	Elissa	✓	✓				✓	✓			
8	———	Jane					✓	✓	✓			
9	he had	had had	✓	✓				✓	✓	✓		
10	in	———			✓			✓	✓	✓	✓	
11	best to do	to do best					✓	✓	✓			
⋮												
25												
TOTALS												

Figure 8.5
MMA CODING SHEET FOR MIKE

1. The first question deals with *substitutions only* and has three parts:
   A. To what extent is the reader integrating all cueing systems (i.e., graphic, syntactic, and semantic) when making substitutions?

   $$\frac{\text{Number of miscues having a check in Cols. 5 \& 9 \& 10}}{\text{Total number of substitutions (Col. 4)}} \times 100 = \underline{\hspace{1cm}}$$

   B. To what extent is the reader using syntactic/semantic information only in making substitutions?

   $$\frac{\text{Number of miscues having a check in Col. 4, no check in Col. 5, but a check in Cols. 9 \& 13}}{\text{Total number of substitutions (Col. 4)}} \times 100 = \underline{\hspace{1cm}}$$

   C. To what extent is the reader using graphic information only in making substitutions?

   $$\frac{\text{Number of miscues having a check in Col. 5, and no check in Cols. 9 \& 10}}{\text{Total number of substitutions (Col. 4)}} \times 100 = \underline{\hspace{1cm}}$$

2. To what extent are the miscues syntactically and semantically acceptable?

   $$\frac{\text{Number of miscues having a check in Cols. 9 \& 10}}{\text{Total number of miscues (25)}} \times 100 = \underline{\hspace{1cm}}$$

3. To what extent is the reader successful in the corrections he or she attempts?

   $$\frac{\text{Total number of Col. 12 (succ. corr.)}}{\text{Total number of Col. 11 (att. corr.)}} \times 100 = \underline{\hspace{1cm}}$$

4. To what extent does the reader leave meaning changes?

   $$\frac{\text{Total number of Col. 13}}{\text{Total number of miscues (25)}} \times 100 = \underline{\hspace{1cm}}$$

5. To what extent is the reader stopping and inspecting text before it is omitted?

   $$\frac{\text{Total number in Col. 7 (w I)}}{\text{Total of Cols. 6 \& 7}} \times 100 = \underline{\hspace{1cm}}$$

Figure 8.6
QUESTIONS REGARDING PATTERNS OF MISCUES

have incorrectly counted the miscues on the Coding Sheet. A common mistake for computing Question 1A on Figure 8.6 (and thus ending up with a percentage over 100) is to take the totals of columns 5, 9, and 10 on the bottom Coding Sheet. Instead, use a ruler so you can look at each miscue line one at a time to determine if there is a check in each in these three columns. If there are three checks, one for each of these columns for a particular miscue, then count it. If one or more of the columns do not have a check, then don't include it in your count. Thus, six of the seven substitutions Mike made have the three checks—see MMA Coding Sheet for Mike in Figure 8.5— and would be figured in the calculation in Question 1A on Figure 8.6.

What Do These Percentages Mean?

These percentages (and the data on retelling to be described in the following section) provide useful information about readers' strategies.

Questions 1A, 1B, and 1C, regarding substitutions, tell us whether a reader is integrating all three cueing systems or overrelying on one or two of them. Consider first 1A: What percentage level would you expect from a hypothetical fluent reader? You would expect it to be high because effective reading integrates all sources of language cues—graphic, syntactical, and semantic. And you would expect that a hypothetical fluent reader's percentages of 1B and 1C to be low and about the same. Such a reader would not rely on one cue (e.g., graphics or letter-sound relationships) over the others (syntactic and semantic cues).

Consequently, by contrasting percentages of such a hypothetical reader with those of a particular reader, a teacher can decide on appropriate instruction. For example, if a child such as Mike has percentages in 1A, 1B, and 1C similar to our hypothetical fluent reader, it would indicate that the child is integrating all three cueing systems effectively. However, if a child has a low percentage in 1A and 1B but a relatively high percentage in 1C, it would suggest that the child is focusing too much on graphics or letter-sound relationships and is missing meaning altogether, especially if the percentage in Question 4 is high. The teacher might then conduct some CLOZE* Focus-

By contrasting your percentages with those of a hypothetical fluent reader, you can get a sense of your reader's strategies.

Lessons* to help the child consider using more of the context in identifying words, or other lessons that emphasize meaning over the accurate decoding of words (e.g., Say Something* and Readers' Theater* activities.)

Question 2 looks at the acceptability of all the miscues, not just substitutions. It tells whether the reading sounds like language and makes sense. Again, Mike's percentage (computations not included) is high, indicating that his reading is meaning driven. A low percentage for Question 2 indicates that the reader is not reading with meaning. Lessons (similar to those suggested earlier) can be created to give the reader that focus.

Question 3 gets at self-correction, an important feature of effective reading. Mike had a high percentage here. However, if a low percentage occurs here, lessons can be constructed to help the reader be more successful in correcting miscues. Or a teacher may note that the reader does not self-correct very much in general (even though there is a high percentage of meaning change) and may provide activities to motivate the reader to reread texts or self-evaluate initial responses in reading.

Question 4 involves significant meaning changes. Mike had a low percentage on this question, but if the percentage here is high for a particular reader, then again the teacher would try to get the child to focus more on meaning. For example, perhaps the teacher might include him or her in small Literature Response Groups* in which members share their interpretations of a book or text. Or the teacher might provide other experiences that require the reader to reevaluate and justify miscues (e.g., students in third grade and higher can usually profit from taping their own reading and then identifying and self-evaluating miscues).

Question 5 provides useful information for evaluating the reading progress of children who are in transition from emergent reading to more independent reading. Children in this stage do a lot of inspecting of text because they are beginning to integrate graphics with syntactical and semantic cuing systems. The results in this question can therefore document this development. The teacher can skip this last question for older elementary readers such as Mike.

Miscue patterns can provide important information for the teacher in two ways: in deciding on specific instructional activities to meet the needs of the reader, and in documenting a reader's strategies over time. Doing MMAs on children's reading of a variety of genres provides even more useful information for instruction and accountability. Once teachers have done one or two MMAs, they know how to "listen" for miscues and can take anecdotal records without *taping* children's reading.

Analyzing the Retelling

The retelling and discussion subsequent to the oral reading provide more information about the child's understanding of the text. Four general questions can be asked about this part of the MMA to complement the oral reading data analyzed in the preceding section:

1. What was the nature of the reader's retelling? Did the retelling include essential information expressed in the text? Did the reader adequately understand the major ideas, or the gist, of the message expressed in the text?
2. If the reader provided a sparse retelling (remember, it is normal to produce a brief response in such a social situation—i.e., when both the teacher and the reader know the text) and was asked to recount a favorite or interesting portion, did any aspects of this account indicate comprehension?
3. How did the reader respond to any questions asked about the selection?
4. Compare individual miscues when the reader had meaning changes (see column 13 on the MMA Coding Sheet, Figure 8.3) with the retelling (and other) responses. Were there cases when the reader left a meaning change miscue yet seemed to understand the author's message in subsequent responses? That is, are there miscues that might not have been overtly correct but might have been self-corrected in the reader's mind?

Summary

Miscue analysis must seem very complicated from the foregoing description, and indeed it *is complicated* until it is tried a few times formally by examining the miscues and retellings of real readers. However, it is only through doing MMAs that teachers can know how to observe by listening to the strategies and interpretations children use in oral reading in more informal contexts. Inherent in using this kid-watching technique is a new appreciation on the part of the teacher of the constructive nature of reading. Teachers learn to wait, or be more patient and not intervene too soon or too much when children do not read the actual words of the text with absolute accuracy. They learn that a reader may put in a reasonable substitution or may self-correct when something does not make sense. Thus, through these informal MMAs, teachers can collect useful on-going information to document children's progress in reading, and they can decide what instruction or intervention is appropriate to support and extend children's present understandings and efforts. (See the "Reading Activities and Experiences" section in Chapter 7 for more information regarding informal reading assessments.)

Writing

The view of writing described in Chapter 6 is sometimes termed a *process-conference approach*. It emphasizes the process of writing in which writers engage, and it uses teacher (and peer) conferences to evaluate and support this process. Teacher interactions and conferences occur while children are engaged in any of the types of writing experiences (prewriting, drafting, revising, editing, and publishing) described in Chapter 6. Here, however, we focus on conferences in which the teacher confers with children on drafts that children plan to revise or edit. An analysis scheme for evaluating children's writing is presented, and on the basis of that analysis, suggestions for ways teachers can conduct conferences to support revising and editing are covered.

Atwell (1987); Calkins (1986, 1991, 1994); Graves (1983); Routman (1991); Temple, Nathan, Temple, & Burris (1993); Turbill (1983)

This assessment assumes that the teacher has obtained a draft written by a child on a topic the child has chosen. If observation during the drafting process is also possible, the teacher can jot down notes about the ways children do the following:

Use space (how they start to write, the direction of writing, and whether they leave spaces between "words"), punctuation, capitalization, and paragraphing.
Form letters and words.
Correct or change what they write.
Comment on what they write.

It may be necessary for young children who use invented spellings—construct approximations on the basis of what they have learned about the orthographic system—to read their text right after they have finished so that it can be deciphered by the teacher (although experienced teachers, who have had lots of practice "cracking the code" of a range of young writers, usually can figure out these invented spelling patterns without having children read them). In integrated language classrooms, approximations are encouraged, so teachers need to know the general developmental changes in spelling. Figure 8.7 outlines general characteristics of these changes. We will go into these more when writing samples are reviewed.

Henderson & Beers (1980); Temple, Nathan, Temple, & Burris (1993); Wilde (1992, 1997)

Analyzing a Writing Sample

In analyzing a draft, consider both message, or content, aspects (listed under "Register/Genre" in Table 6.7) and medium aspects (listed under "Surface/Medium Features" in Table 6.7). Teachers usually have separate conferences regarding these two aspects of children's writing. That is, they have Content Conferences* with children to deal with the message of a text, and they have Editing Conferences* to address medium issues after children have revised their text. Chapter 7 discusses ways to implement these conferences in the classroom, but here we concentrate on the analysis scheme and review the types of questions teachers may ask by considering several

Content Conferences* deal with message aspects of a writer's text, Editing Conferences* with medium aspects.

Prephonemic Spelling

Characteristics: Prephonemic spellers know a lot about language; they know how letters are formed and that they somehow represent language. However, they string letters (mostly consonants) together in an unsystematic fashion because they have not as yet discovered the phonetic principle, that is, that letters represent the speech sounds, or phonemes, in words. Prephonemic spellers usually have not as yet learned to read.
Examples: BMKGTO (candy) MBRRDRGC (cat)

Early Phonemic Spelling

Characteristics: Early phonemic spellers have discovered the phonetic principle and attempt to represent phonemes in words with letters—they have begun to figure out how spelling works. Although they try to represent letters for sounds they hear in words, their products are sparse. That is, they usually just put down letters for only one or two sounds (and then may finish with random letters). This is because they usually do not have a stable concept of what a word is, so they can't keep words "in their minds" long enough to match sounds of words with letters. Early phonemic spellers are usually not reading as yet.
Examples: P (piano) N (engine)

Letter-Name Spelling

Characteristics: Letter-name spellers are able to break down a word into its phonemes and represent them with letters, but they work on a rule of one-to-one correspondence—one sound is represented by one letter. They are called letter-name spellers because they frequently use the sounds of the *names* of letters to stand for respective phonemes in words. Letter-name spelling is in many ways the most complex set of spelling approximations and is therefore the most challenging system for teachers to decipher. The examples below reflect some of the major rules children rely on in letter-name spelling. Letter-name spellers are often not readers, but they have a stable concept of word and are beginning to develop a slight vocabulary. When they begin to read, they will read conventional spelling but will write words in letter-name spelling (which sometimes leads to confusion when they try to read their own writing).
Examples: HARE (cherry). A good example of the use of letter-names and the one-to-one rule. Thus, consonant digraphs (e.g., *ch, sh, th, ph*) are represented by only one letter.
LAP (lamp) YET (went) Nasals (*n, m*) are dropped near medial vowels.
SOPR (supper) LETL (little). When vowels occur in syllables that are unstressed, they are said to be "reduced." In these cases, only the consonant (*R* and *L*, respectively) is provided by the child.
BAT (bet) PAT (pet) (front middle); FEH (fish) HEM (him) (front high), etc.
Lax, or "short," vowels are represented by letter-name vowels that have the same tongue positions when produced. That is, the tongue's position is in the front middle part of the mouth when the lax *e* in *bet* and the tense *a* in *bait* are made.

Transitional Spelling

Characteristics: Transitional spellers have gone beyond the one-to-one correspondence between sounds and letters. They have learned many features of conventional spelling; they include many conventional spellings—but these understandings are employed uncertainly or overextended. Transitional spelling *looks like* English and is easy to read. Frequently, transitional spellers may have all the correct letters of a word but not in the right order. Transitional spellers are readers.
Examples: NIHGT (night) DAER (dear). Correct letters but in the wrong order.
PUTT (put) DINNIGE (dining). Overextension of "double" consonants and "silent *e*" vowel pattern.

Derivational Spelling

Characteristics: Derivational spelling is very similar to transitional spelling. Derivational spellers rely on the *morphophonemic* nature of the English spelling system. That is, through their spellings, they demonstrate their awareness that the spelling of a particular word reflects, or is derived from, a "core" meaning.
Examples: EXPLAI NATION (explanation) JUDGEMENT (judgment). Spellings reflect the meaning of *explain* and *judge*, respectively.

Conventional Spelling

Characteristics: Correct spellings are used.

The best sources for learning about developmental changes of spelling are Temple, Nathan, Temple, & Burris (1993), Henderson & Beers (1980); Wilde (1992, 1997).

Figure 8.7
DEVELOPMENTAL CHANGES IN SPELLING

writing samples from a range of elementary-age children. We will thus be treating message and medium concerns together.

The analysis of children's writing consists of asking questions about the message and medium aspects of their texts. See Figure 8.8 for a list of these questions.

Use the following questions to evaluate children's texts:

Message Questions

1. What genre is the child attempting to write? How successful is the child? Are there certain beginnings, endings, and sequences used to indicate a certain genre?
2. Is the text complete according to the genre the child is attempting? If complete, is it sparse, or are relevant details and elaborations included?
3. Does the child use an interesting vocabulary? Is it appropriate to the genre attempted? Does the child use cohesive ties to knit the text together? Does the child use any words that are unclear or ambiguous (e.g., pronouns with uncertain antecedents)?
4. Are there any gaps of information or "missing links" in the text? Does the child order information to make sense?
5. Does the child appear to have audience or reader "sense"?
6. What ideologies or values (subtle or overt) are being expressed?

Medium Questions

1. Does the child show knowledge of the directionality principles of the writing system? How about the spacing principle? Layout features? Paragraphing?
2. Does the child show a stable concept of letter/word/sentence?
3. How does the child use punctuation, capitalization, and so on?
4. What does the child know about the orthographic (spelling) system? At what developmental level do you think the child is? (Give examples.)
5. How does the child control various grammatical structures (e.g., noun and verb agreement, parallel construction, and the like)?

Figure 8.8

ANALYSIS SCHEME FOR A WRITING SAMPLE

Facilitating the Revising and Editing of a Writing Sample

On the basis of this analysis, teachers then decide how to conference with children about their texts. As you may have noted, an important distinction is made between helping children learn to *edit* and to *revise* their writing. Editing involves medium changes, things that an editor, teacher, or someone else can change: spelling, punctuation, noun and verb agreement, for example. Most instruction and feedback in writing have traditionally emphasized editing. In the process-conference approach, these editing aspects are considered, but they are done differently.

Revising, on the other hand, has to do with changes of the message of a text. Only writers can revise, because only they know what they are intending to express. Although little instruction or feedback is given in the revision of writing in most traditional classrooms, it is the most important for it will help children be better writers. Facilitating revising helps children become readers of their own writing by sensitizing them to the requirements of other readers of their writing, so that their writing is comprehensible. Also, this is the area in which they can examine the underlying ideology of their texts—how their meanings might reflect certain values or biases they hold. (See Chapters 1 and 6 for a longer discussion on ideology.)

The reader-writer contract is emphasized.

The following general guidelines are useful in conferences:

1. Have children read their writing first and note any spontaneous changes they make.
2. Point out any changes children make in reading their texts aloud that they did not note on their actual text.
3. Address only one or two message issues and only one medium concern in each conference.
4. Be positive and show interest in what children are trying to express.
5. Start by responding to a strength or positive feature of the text.
6. Don't tell children what to do, but use questions to support them in finding their own answers.
7. Leave the pencil in children's hands. All changes or additions to the writing should be left under children's control and ownership.
8. When asking a question, be sure that children are given time to respond. Have a long "wait time."

9. Try to make your questions and responses as specific as possible.
10. End each conference by asking children what they will do next.

To get an idea of the kinds of specific questions teachers may ask, we'll consider the writing samples of grade K–6 children. For each child, we'll have a "conference," in which we pretend we're the teacher. Remember that we are addressing *both* message and medium aspects of students' writing here—typically these are dealt with by *separate* conferences.

Amber, Megan, and Mike: Kindergartners

Revising and editing concerns in very young emergent writers must be addressed with great caution.

We have to be careful in our conferences with such young writers as kindergartners Amber, Megan, and Mike to encourage them to see themselves as writers, to use their own approximations for conventional forms. If we stress revising or editing too much or too soon, we can give them the message that we do not value their efforts.

Amber's and Megan's texts were the result of a MONSTERS unit, and Mike's was a sign he wrote as the result of a classroom accident.

Amber

Amber's text (Figure 8.9) is short and is about the Cookie Monster of Sesame Street fame.

Message Analysis

The most prevalent issue in very young writers' texts involves trying to understand what genre they are attempting to tackle. (See Message Question 1, Figure 8.8.) This is partly because their texts are usually short; there isn't much information on which to base a reliable decision. This seems to be the case for Amber's text. What form is she trying? Is it a personal narrative? A story? And how does the last line fit with the rest of the text? Thus, a teacher might first ask a question to address this genre issue: "Amber, is this a pretend story about Cookie Monster, or are you writing about your actually seeing Cookie Monster?" Any subsequent questions would then depend on how Amber answers. If she says that it was a make-believe story, then the teacher may ask what Cookie Monster is going to do in the story and, perhaps, if Genna is going to do something with Cookie Monster. In contrast, if Amber indicates that her text is a personal narrative, then questions about what Cookie Monster did when she saw him would be appropriate. Frequently, revisions for young children like Amber are *talking* more about their texts. The teacher may not expect Amber actually to rewrite her text but may invite Amber to add those things she has related to her text, realizing that Amber may or may not be able to do so at this time.

Revising for young children consists of their talking about their texts.

Medium Analysis

Most of the spellings in this text indicate that Amber is an early phonemic speller. (Her last line consists entirely of conventional spellings, but she probably has learned these

Figure 8.9
AMBER'S TEXT

(Amber I saw Cookie Monster. I saw him again. I love Genna.)

words as "wholes.") "Genna" is Amber's friend; the first two letters of her text, "be," are part of Amber's name. Amber shows that she is aware of direction of print, but she does not seem to have a concept of a word (there is no spacing between words). She uses no capitalization or punctuation. At this point, the teacher would not say anything to Amber about editing. If the text is going to be published—perhaps typed up and then illustrated by Amber—then the teacher may edit it during the typing. Amber's progress in spelling will be facilitated by developing a stable concept of a word so that the teacher will engage her in many activities to facilitate this development (e.g., Dictations (discussed later in the chapter), Group-Composed Writing*, and Big Books*) as well as provide many other opportunities for her to write.

Figure 8.10 is Megan's text on dinosaurs in the form of a small, stapled, four-page booklet.

Megan

Message Analysis

It is not clear from Megan's short text what genre she is attempting. Is it an information book about dinosaurs? An attempt to write a story? The major issue to resolve is to help Megan decide which is the case. The teacher can begin by asking if this is a pretend story about dinosaurs or if it is an information book (notice that she uses present-tense verbs). If Megan says it is a story, then the teacher can ask her more about what exciting things the dinosaurs are doing or how they got to be friends. If Megan says it is an information book, then the teacher can get Megan to tell what else she has learned about dinosaurs that she could add to her book. Again, the teacher's expectations consist of encouraging only. Most revisions involve talking about revisions rather

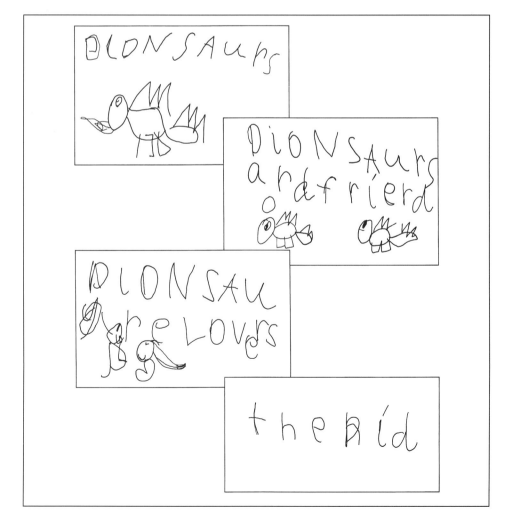

Figure 8.10
MEGAN'S TEXT

than actually more writing or rewriting. The teacher may suggest that Megan unstaple her booklet and add pages, which could be Megan's revision.

Medium Analysis

Although there is not much to work on in her short text, Megan does have a better grasp of the medium aspects of written language than Amber. She has a better sense of space and seems to know what a word is. Megan is a letter-name speller, although her text indicates that she may be more advanced than that. She incorrectly copied the word *dinosaurs* from a big display in the classroom, and her peers helped with *friends* (also incorrect) and *lovers*. Thus, the teacher would not do anything regarding editing.

Mike   Mike's text arose as the result of a classroom accident. The children were studying guppies and other fish, and the water tank was placed on a low shelf. One day a child lost her balance and accidentally sat down in the tank. At evaluation time at the end of the day, Mike argued that something should be done about the water tank so no one else would fall in it. The teacher asked him if he wanted to make a sign to put next to the tank. With her help, he wrote, "Dont pus," and then he finished it on his own. (See Figure 8.11).

Message Analysis

There is no doubt about Mike's genre. Notice how he has incorporated the grammatical structures appropriate to signs: "Don't push . . . ," "Be careful," "Read this. . ." It is an amusing sign, of course, as very few signs include the admonition to read it. The teacher did not suggest that Mike change the last line, because Mike was the youngest of several siblings and he was reluctant to use invented spelling at all because he was afraid he might be wrong. This was an important breakthrough for Mike, and the teacher merely confirmed and shared his delight of accomplishment. They published it by hanging it on the wall near the tank, and the teacher and the children frequently reread it as a reminder.

Medium Analysis

Mike has some early phonemic inclinations (his spelling for *careful*, perhaps), but he is mostly a letter-name speller with respect to this text. He relies on letter names to spell

Figure 8.11
MIKE'S TEXT

(Don't push anyone in the water tank. Be careful! Read this sign!)

any ("N E") and the beginning of *water* ("Y"). It's not clear whether he has a stable concept of a word; sometimes he has spaces between words and sometimes he runs his words together, as in the last line. The teacher does no editing because she doesn't want to risk harming his new confidence.

Annie and Robbie: First Graders

First graders Annie and Robbie are attempting to write stories. (See Figures 8.12 and 8.13.)

Message Analyses

Drawing is an important prewriting experience for Annie. She frequently draws (with lots of colors, which are lost in copying) on each page of her draft first, then writes what is going on in her picture. This is a complete but bare-bones story. Annie's story deals with everyday experiences—eating, going to bed, waking up, and getting dressed—but also incorporates the "fantastic" feature of having a snowman come back to life (perhaps influenced by "Frosty the Snowman" TV specials; she wrote her story in January of her first-grade year). The teacher would probably address this latter aspect of her text because it is not clear. For example, the teacher may ask, "I'm not sure about this part of your story. Did the girl's crying on the snowman *cause* him to come back to life? Tell me more about this." The teacher thus gives Annie an opportunity to clarify the reader's confusion and elaborate on her story to make it more comprehensible and credible.

Robbie is also attempting a story, but it seems to lack certain essential parts. Like Annie, Robbie is using information about everyday experiences. He includes what he knows about parents' having favorite chairs, and about visiting by including dialogue

Annie

Calkins (1986, 1994); Dyson (1987, 1989); Graves (1983); Newkirk (1989)

Robbie

Figure 8.12
Annie's Text

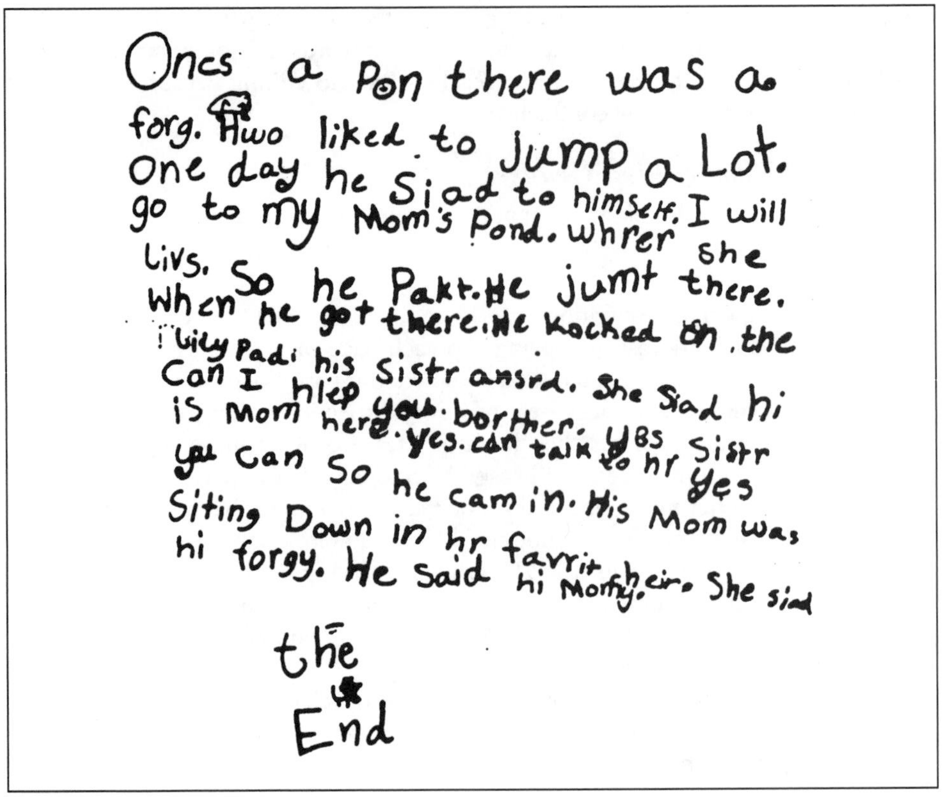

Figure 8.13
ROBBIE'S TEXT

with the frog's sister. However, we don't know what has happened that has caused the frog to go to his mom's house and live alone no longer, or how the fact that the frog liked to jump a lot is related to the storyline. Consequently, the teacher would address questions to these facets of the story: "Why is the frog living alone and now deciding to go back home? Does the fact that the frog jumps a lot have to do with his decision?" By thinking about the teacher's reaction to his story, Robbie can begin to think of ways to revise his text to fill in pertinent details, thereby clarifying his intentions.

Medium Analyses

Annie and Robbie

Both texts reflect letter-name and transitional spellings, but Annie seems to be more of a letter-name speller, whereas Robbie appears to be more of a transitional one. Words like "cam" (came), "bac" (back), and especially those words that incorporate the *ed* past-tense morpheme—"drest" (dressed), "meltid" (melted), and "pla" (played)—follow letter-name rules. However, Annie does have some spellings that reflect more transitional understandings: "ete" (eat), "gow" (go).

Robbie also uses letter-name spellings for *ed* words — "pakt" (packed), "jumt" (jumped), and "ansrd" (answered)—but he does include the conventional spelling of the morpheme in "kocked" (knocked) and "liked." Many of his words have all the correct letters, but they are in the wrong order, and there is evidence that he has gone beyond the letter-name one-to-one rule—"whrer" (where) and "cheir" (chair).

The teacher could address some spelling issue for each child: Both of them spelled a high-frequency word inconsistently. Annie spelled *then* conventionally and as "thin," and Robbie spelled *said* correctly once at the end of the story, but all the other times he used "siad." The teacher could point out the errors in an Editing Conference* or help Robbie understand the function of quotation marks without which it is hard to follow the dialogue. By having him mark those places (with his two index fingers) where someone is saying something, Robbie will begin to understand the role of quotation marks in a meaningful way.

My hamster

My hamster is so Pretty.
I say you are so cute
I go so crase becos he is cute.
One day we lost him and winwe fdd
him he was het.
Mom called the Vetinnren.
I said plese plese
Tell the Vetinnren we will bring him
to you. Mom said No. I said ok.
He had a brokin leg. Abot
13 days his leg was ok.
Win we pikt him up.
That mens he was all right.
The end.

my hamsters name is PeeWee

Figure 8.14
KATY'S TEXT

Katy and Russell: Second Graders

Katy's text (Figure 8.14) was some writing done as part of a ANIMALS—LARGE
AND SMALL unit in which children described their pets. (Children without pets described those they would like to have.)

Katy

Message Analysis

Katy doesn't really give much description of her hamster, focusing mostly on an event
in the hamster's life when he broke his leg. Two facets could be addressed. First, Katy
goes on about how cute her hamster is yet doesn't tell why she feels that way. Thus,
in conference the teacher could say, "You talk a lot about how cute your hamster is,
but you don't tell why. What can you add here to explain why it is so cute?" The second feature that could be discussed with Katy is the confusion involved in calling the
veterinarian: "Katy, I'm not clear about when your mom called the vet when your hamster was hurt. Is it important to include this telephone call, and what does this part—
'Mom said no. I said ok.'—mean?" Thus, the teacher's questions are posed both to
help Katy elaborate by giving reasons for her statements about her hamster and to get
her to think more about the relevance and clarity of part of her text.

Medium Analysis

Katy is in between being a transitional speller (she has many conventional spellings, plus
spellings like "plese" [please]) and a letter-name speller ("crase" [crazy], "win" [when],
"abot" [about], "pikt" [picked]). She has a better control of punctuation than most of
the children we have met so far, but the teacher could address the role of quotation marks
in the place where Annie asks her mom to call the vet. Of course, if Annie decides that

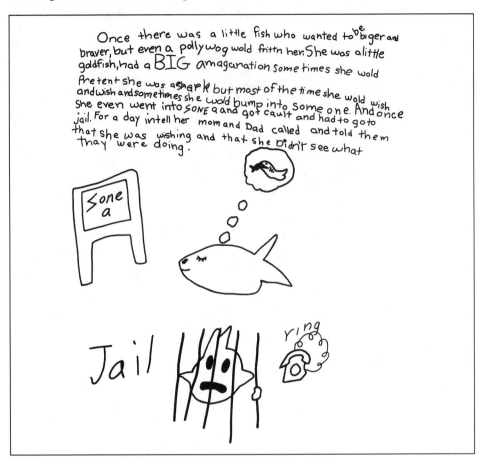

Figure 8.15
RUSSELL'S TEXT

the whole conversation about telephoning the vet is not necessary, then something else could be picked for Katy's attention—maybe the spelling of *when*, as that is a frequent word and would have a big payoff in editing in future pieces.

Russell

Russell's text (Figure 8.15) appears to be a story about the adventure of a little fish.

Message Analysis

Russell has a very elaborate Placement (see Chapter 6). In fact, it is more than half of his text. It is almost as if he spent so much energy on this first part that he had little left to include the other essential parts of his story. Thus, Russell's conference should try to help him sustain this good beginning. The teacher's comments could be: "Russell, I really liked the beginning of your story because I could really picture what the little goldfish was like, and I can sort of figure out the end where the fish ends up in the jail and her parents help her get out. But I don't understand the middle part—what is 'zone a'? I think your readers will want to know more about this part of the fish's adventure. This is the really exciting part, isn't it?" The teacher tries to point out how an important part of the story may be missing or not clear and encourages Russell to revise by mentioning that this is the part that readers will likely find most exciting. Then the teacher would have him talk more about what he might add, and this discussion will make his enacting this revision process on his text much easier.

Medium Analysis

Russell has mostly transitional (and conventional) spellings. Spellings like "cault" (caught), "intell" (until), and "thay" (they) show that he has gone beyond the one-to-one rule of letter-name spellers. He seems to have reasonably good control of the use of commas, but he is inconsistent in his use of periods. Because he does demonstrate that he has some sense of a sentence, the teacher may extend his understanding by reading through Russell's text, pausing only when periods are there and getting him to hear how it sounds that way. Then the teacher could have Russell go through the story again (with the teacher's help), reconsidering his use of periods.

Bryan and Carla: Third and Fourth Graders

Bryan, a third grader, has been studying kangaroos and has written a report (Figure 8.16) on what he has learned.

Bryan

Message Analysis

Bryan's text is a typical example of the information book genre. He does a good job in relating the typical behavior of kangaroos, where they live, and so on and is consistent in using the present tense of this genre. What Bryan seems to need help on is the organization of his information. Teacher comments could direct his attention to this issue: "You certainly have some useful information here, but I was somewhat confused about how you have ordered it. There seem to be three major subtopics here—do you agree? But sometimes you have mixed up this information, and that makes it not so clear." The teacher could then help Bryan identify these three subtopics: where kan-

Figure 8.16

BRYAN'S TEXT

Kangaroos live in Allstrailya. They are born alive. They fight for thier companyons. They use thier feet for fighting. Thier feet have sharp clows. Thier feet could tear open thier componets skin. When they fight they put thier heads back to pretect thier eyes. Kangaroos can jump very high. They use thier strengh to jump fast enouge to get away from prediters like the coyote, and the wolf. Theese animals eat meat. Kangaroos live where the gras is greene and on the lands where water is. Becaus They eat grass. They give live birth. The babies stay in a pouch for about 6 mounths in a row when geting bigger thier mothers pouch gets to littel and her musels have to loosen up for her babey

to get out. The babby gets bigger and its on its own. Meanwile the mother gives birth to a nouther Kungaroo and this repeats twice.

garoos live (in Australia and where there is green grass and water), how they protect themselves, and how they give birth. The teacher demonstrates the technique by using a Semantic Map* to help him organize his data, which might provide him with a framework on which to revise.

Medium Analysis

Bryan is a typical transitional speller. For example, look at his overextension of the terminal *e* in "greene" (green) and "enouge" (enough) and his understanding of vowel digraphs in "Allstrailya" (Australia) and "anouther" (another). However, in editing, the teacher would probably address the concept of paragraphs with him. Because Bryan is working on three major points about kangaroos, this is a good time for the teacher to show him how to use paragraphs to signal this organization of his information. He will get the idea of paragraphs more easily because in his writing it can be tied so nicely to function.

Carla

Figure 8.17 is the text written by Carla, a fourth grader, at the beginning of the year. As part of a HOUSES unit, Carla and some of her classmates had recently taken a tour through a house bus. Carla and her small group decided to come up with different versions of alternative housing and describe them to their classmates.

Message and Medium Analyses

Carla had told the teacher that she was having trouble describing her ideas on alternative housing in a poem. Both the message and medium aspects of Carla's text are being discussed together, because the structure or form of her poem and its physical layout were integrally linked. Both Carla and the teacher looked at a variety of poems, commenting on the possibilities. Then the teacher asked Carla to see if she could structure her individual sentences (find a pattern in her text that she could follow) and group her sentences as if they were sort of stanzas. Carla thought that she liked her first two sentences: "The first one sort of tells what my dream house is." She also liked the pattern she had in the second sentence: "for a light I would . . . when it's nighttime I would . . . " Carla noted that her third sentence began okay ("And for a special thing . . .") but that she wasn't consistent with the verb (she used *I'll* instead of *I would*). The teacher helped her go through several more sentences and then let her attempt a revision of the others on her own. The teacher suggested that the places where she wrote about water and food and so on could go together in a different stanza from the first set of sentences. The teacher also entered into a conversation with Carla about how her underlying values might be tied to the items she has included in her house. Thus, although Carla is writing about a "dream" house, she could think more about unacknowledged ideologies she might be expressing. Carla was given the job of evaluating

The teacher helped Carla consider her own values expressed in her text.

Figure 8.17
CARLA'S TEXT

MY DREAM HOUSE

I would like to live in a floating house on the beach. For a light I would cut some squares on the roof and when it's night time I would pin some square cloths on top of my roof windows and turn on my lamps. And for a special thing I'll cut a square on the floor in my bedroom and put a square glass between the cut wood and look at the fish before I go to bed. As for water, I'd open my back door and scoop up water from my pail and clean the water in my Water Cleaner machine that I invented. As for keeping my food cold I have two big Ice boxes. And for cooking food I have a electric stove. As for furniture there nailed to the ground. To keep me company I have a big television and some books to read. An when I need more food I climb into my little boat witch is tighten to my Boat House. An when I'm board of the same place I'm at, I have a Big motor in the end of my house and can go iney where I want.

THE END

the rest of her poem in light of that consideration. Thus, besides the ideological issue, grammatical structure and genre format were both incorporated into this conference.

David and Eileen: Fifth and Sixth Graders

David and Eileen are students in a fifth/sixth-grade classroom. Their texts were the result of a HEROES unit. Both wrote a biography of two heroes they had studied. These texts are quite long, so only excerpts can be provided here. Both texts were second drafts, as both David and Eileen had already had conferences with their teacher on their first drafts.

David, a fifth grader, wrote on Amelia Earhart. (See Figure 8.18.)

David

Message Analysis

David starts his text by describing the search for Amelia Earhart when she disappeared, and then he uses the flashback technique to talk about her life before then. The excerpt includes the first part of his text and the last few paragraphs. David attempted a sort of fictionalized biography. In relating the episode about the small girl on the sled, he was attempting to show the type of woman Earhart was: one who "thrived on excitement." Thus, he tried to provide a "story" about the girl/woman Earhart, based on the facts he discovered about her. Sometimes he was not consistent in his efforts to do this, and most of the teacher's initial conference addressed this issue. His second draft was much better, but he still had difficulty in expressing the transitions between the different

Figure 8.18
DAVID'S TEXT

AMELIA EARHART

8:45 A.M. Amelia Earhart's voice came over the microphone giving her position. Little did she know that this would be her last message. Somewhere around tiny Howland Island her plane would disappear.

A giant search party consisting of the battleship Itasca, four destroyers, a minesweeper and an aircraft carrier and all its planes began to embark on a sixteen day search . . . . .

A small girl on a boy's sled came whistling down an icy slope, her hair flying behind her. At the end of the slope the junk man and his old horse and buggy were slowly plowing through the snow. If she kept going on her present course she would surely collide with him! She held tight and hoped. She couldn't yell because the junk man was deaf, and the horse had blinders.

Closer and closer she came! She held her breath! She shot like a bullet right underneath the horse's belly, and out through the other side without a scratch!

Another time Amelia tried to build a contraption somewhat like a roller coaster. She fell off, almost breaking her leg, and rubbed her chin raw. To her this was fun.

She thrived on excitement.

-
-
-
-

March 17, 1937: the beginning of a journey from which she and her navigator, Fred Noonan would never return.

They had made many previous stops. Now, they were heading toward Howland Island.

Their plane was circling around Howland Island. They should have landed two hours ago. Then her last message was heard.

There is much speculation on what happened at 8:45 that day.

The teacher addressed ideologies/values around gender in the text.

episodes he chose to highlight. He chose times in Earhart's life that appeared to be significant in her decision to become a pilot, and the teacher helped him figure out how to express the chronological events so that they were coherent, not just a listing of isolated events. The teacher also asked David if he thought he might elaborate on the "speculation" about what happened to Earhart at the end of his text, that is, whether a discussion of the various hypotheses about her disappearance might be a useful addition. In addition, the teacher and David talked about whether he wanted to talk about how people might have treated the young girl or adult Earhart's desire for excitement.

Medium Analysis

Both David and Eileen helped each other with peer editing, so this second draft was very polished already. David was, for the most part, a conventional speller and had a good control of conventional grammar and punctuation. The teacher pointed out that there were two instances where David did not use commas appropriately regarding appositives, so he noted them for his final draft.

Eileen

Eileen's text was titled "Thurber Years." Figure 8.19 is an excerpt of the first part of her text (which consisted of five chapters). Eileen is a sixth grader.

Message Analysis

Eileen's text on James Thurber, a second draft, represented a more typical biography in one sense, but it was unusual in that she attempted to relate Thurber's life by "cloning" his style of writing. Her initial conference mostly addressed the difficulties she had in being consistent in doing this. This second conference reexamined places in which revisions had been made and where Eileen had rethought others. The teacher asked Eileen to consider places in which Eileen tells what she is doing in reporting on Thurber's life. Eileen begins her second chapter with: "Now I'm going to tell you

Figure 8.19
EILEEN'S TEXT

Thurber Years

CHAPTER ONE

In Which We Meet James

    Thurber Country, The Thurber Album, Lanterns and Lances, These and More.
Sound familiar? It should. Many has been the person who has recited these titles
"Who are they by?" asks the naive child. This is where I come in. I feel that it
is about time that someone else wrote about him, instead of him
doing all of the writing. "But who is he?" you ask. I reply with "I think that
everyone should be acquainted with James Thurber and his works." In this
biography, I will be telling why. Also, I will tell some of his escapades during
his career life.

    "What other books did he write?" you could probably be wondering. Well, you
asked for it. Is Sex Necessary, The Seal in the Bedroom, Arms and Diversions, and
Let Your Mind Alone, are all of his works. "Are they good?" you might ask. I'll
be contented to leave that to you.

about his Ohio life." The teacher asked, "Now, have you included this sentence because you think Thurber would have written it this way as part of his style or because you think this is appropriate for a biography?" The teacher attempted to help Eileen decide to distinguish style versus genre issues.

Medium Analysis

Eileen is also a conventional speller and has control of conventional grammar and punctuation. However, as with David, the teacher addressed a punctuation issue in the Editing Conference*. Eileen did not always put commas or periods within the quotation marks when she listed stories written by Thurber, so the teacher pointed out how to do this.

Summary

In conferences, teachers address message and medium issues of individual writers. The foregoing examples describe the kinds of problems children tackle in their developmental writing and the ways teachers can support and extend their efforts through their questions and comments in conferences. Writing Conferences* also are discussed in Chapter 7.

Kid-Watching Procedures for Emergent Learners

Before children are able to read in a conventional sense, that is, before they have acquired a sight word vocabulary or are able to figure out and use the graphic or graphophonemic cues in written language, they can engage in experiences that demonstrate their present literate understandings. Some of these were covered in the preceding section when children's invented spellings and other principles and concepts of writing were discussed. This section examines four other literacy activities involving emergent learners. When teachers know kid-watching techniques such as these, they are able to document and support the early stages of reading and writing more effectively. The first scheme involves examining what young children know about the medium aspects of written language as they help the teacher read a book. The second evaluates children's repeated reenactments of a book. The third focus on teachers' observations while taking down children's dictations. The fourth is the retelling assessment, which can be used for emergent learners, but is also appropriate for older students. Although these assessment schemes may at first seem difficult to use, teachers soon internalize them and begin using them informally in other classroom routines.

See also Avery (1993); Barrs, Ellis, Hester, & Thomas (1988, 1990); Fisher (1991, 1995); Johnston (1992, 1997); and Genishi & Dyson (1984) for other good ideas about assessment of emergent and primary-age learners.

Concepts about Print Assessment

The Concepts about Print (CAP) assessment was developed by Clay to find out what young children already know about medium aspects of written language (e.g., directional principles; concepts of first, last, word, and letter; and punctuation). Clay's two little books (*Sand* and *Stones*), created for teachers to share with children, contain various alterations. A picture is inverted, lines of print are reversed and upside down, and words or letters are switched around. Teachers read the book as if the book were normal, and as they do, they ask children to help them: "How should I put the book down to read it?" "Where should I start to read?" "Which way should I go?" "What's this for (pointing to a comma, period, etc.)?" "Show me the first part I should read on this page." Thus, this book-sharing experience represents an inquiry situation for children to show what they already know about the concepts and conventions of the medium aspects before they can read conventionally from print.

Clay (1979a)

Clay (1972, 1979b)

Many teachers use *Sand* in the beginning of the year and *Stones* at the end (or vice versa) to assess and document children's understandings. Others, following the format of these books, design and write their own books.

Another alternative is to apply the ideas in *Sand* and *Stones* in a regular book, which is what we illustrate here. Keep the following features in mind when choosing a book:

Before starting, thoroughly familiarize yourself with this test. Paginate the book (pencil in numbers in the corners of each page). Use instructions similar to the ones suggested below. Use the CAP scoring sheet (see Figure 8.21) to remind yourself of these instructions and to score the child's responses.

Begin by saying to the child: "I'm going to read you this book, but I want you to help me." (Note: You will read the whole text but will ask questions on only some of the pages.)

COVER

Item 1   Test: For orientation of book. Pass the book to the child holding the book vertically by the outside edge, spine toward the child.

          Say: "Show me the front of this book."

         Score: 1 point for each correct repsonse.

GO TO. . .
Pages 2/3

Item 2   Test: A left page is read before a right page.
          Say: "Where do I start reading?"
         Score: 1 point for left page indication.

GO TO. . .
Page 8

Item 3   Test: Capital and lowercase correspondence.
          Say: "Find a little letter like this." Point to the capital "S" and demonstrate by pointing to "Ss" if the child does not succeed. Then say, "Find a little letter like this." Point to capital "W" and "O" in turn.
         Score: 1 point if *both* "Ww" and "Oo" are located.
          Test: Three types of punctuation.
           Read the text.
          Say: "What's this for?"
Item 4   Point to the period or trace it with a pencil.
         Score: 1 point for a functional definition (e.g., "It tells you that it's done, or to stop).
Item 5   Point to the comma or trace it with a pencil.
         Score: 1 point for an acceptable functional definition.
Item 6   Point to the quotation marks or trace with a pencil.
         Score: 1 point for an acceptable functional definition.

GO TO. . .
Page 12   Test: For directional rules.
Item 7   Say: "Show me where to start."
         Score: 1 point for top left.
Item 8   Say: "Which way do I go?"
         Score: 1 point for left to right.
Item 9   Say: "Where do I go after that?"
         Score: 1 point for return sweep to left.
           (Score items 7–9 if all movements are demonstrated in one response.)
Item 10   Test: Word-by-word pointing on one page.
          Say: "Point to the words while I read." (Read slowly but fluently.)
         Score: 1 point for exact matching.

Figure 8.20

Instructions for the Concepts about Print (CAP) Test on Our Garage Sale *(Rockwell, 1984).*

1. Select a book in which some pages have print on both the left and right pages.
2. Select a book that has several types of punctuation.
3. Select a book that has one page with only one line of print (that is a complete sentence).
4. Select a book that has one page with three lines of print.

Rockwell (1984)

Figure 8.20 covers the instructions for sharing *Our Garage Sale* by Rockwell.

Pages 14/15

Item 11 Test: Word-by-word pointing on left and right pages.
          Say: "Point to the words while I read." (Read slowly, but fluently.)

        Score: 1 point for exact matching.

Pages 16/17

Item 12 Test: A left page is read before a right page. (This incorporates features of Item 2 and Items 7–9. However, here the lines of print on each page in this book are placed in the same place on the page, so it would be easy for the child to indicate to read the rest of the first line on page 16 and then to the first line of page 17, then to the second line of page 16, etc.)
          Say: "Where do I start reading?"
                "Which way do I go?"
                "Where do I go after that?"

        Score: 1 point for left page indication.

GO TO. . .
Page 20

Item 13 Test: Concept of first and last applied to text.
          Say: "Show me the first part to read on this page."
                "Show me the last part on this page."

        Score: 1 point if *both* are correctly indicated.

Read the rest of the book. Then go back to:

Page 18 Have two small index cards (3 x 5) that the child can hold and slide easily over the line of text to cover words and letters. To start, lay the cards on the page but leave all print exposed.

Item 14 Test: Letter concept.
          Say: "This page says, 'It didn't rain on Saturday.' I want you to push the cards across the page like this until all you can see is one letter." (Demonstrate the movement of the cards, but do not do the exercise.)
                "Now show me two letters."

        Score: 1 point if *both* are correct.

Item 15 Test: Word concept.
          Say: "Show me just one word."
                "Now show me two words."

        Score: 1 point if *both* are correct.

Item 16 Test: First and last letter concepts.
          Say: "Show me the first letter of a word."
                "Show me the last letter of a word."

        Score: 1 point if *both* are correct.

Item 17 Test: Capital letter concept.
          Say: "Show me a capital letter."

        Score: 1 point if letter is correctly located.

Back

Item 18 Test: Back of book.
          Say: "Show me the back of the book."

        Score: 1 point for correct response.

Top/Bottom

Item 19 Test: Top and bottom of book.
          Say: "Show me the top and the bottom of the book."

        Score: 1 point for correct responses.

Not all the concepts are included in Clay's books (they have twenty-four items, whereas the example in *Our Garage Sale* has only nineteen), mostly because in a real book there are no inverted pages and print. It is useful to develop a CAP Scoring Sheet to administer the assessment. Figure 8.21 (p. 349) has been developed for that purpose and illustrates how Amanda, a kindergartner, responded.

The first column indicates the page of the book involved, the second column lists the concept or principle involved, and the third column lists the items. The large column notes the behavior of the child that leads to a point for each item. The information in parentheses is a reminder for the teacher who administers the assessment. The last column reflects the score for each item. You will see that the teacher jotted down some extra information on some of Amanda's responses. Item 16 has children indicate the first and last letters of a word on the line of print found on page 18: "It didn't rain on Saturday." Amanda indicated these correctly by revealing the *I* (of *It*) and the *y* (of *Saturday*), but the fact that she showed only the beginning and end of the sentence indicates that she may be just beginning to understand the concepts of first and last. The teacher will note in subsequent observations whether she indicates first and last letters in the same word, which will suggest greater control of these concepts.

Thus, the CAP assessment gives a score, but more importantly it pinpoints those concepts that individual children already have and those that need to be fostered. Amanda, for example, knows orientational features of books, directional rules, and concepts of first and last. However, she does not have a stable concept of word—she could not locate one and two words (item 15) or indicate word-by-word pointing (items 10 and 11)—nor does she seem to know the functions of punctuation. Thus, the teacher will need to provide experiences to help her develop these concepts. Involving Amanda in Big Book* and Group-Composed Writing* activities and providing many opportunities for her to write her own texts will foster these concepts and extend Amanda's present understandings about written language.

Approximations to Text Assessment

Holdaway (1979); McKenzie (1977); Pappas (1993); Pappas & Brown (1989)

The Approximations to Text (ATT) assessment is also appropriate for emergent learners. It is based on research, as well as the observations of many parents and preschool teachers, that indicates that after young children are read to, they spontaneously "reenact" or roleplay "reading" on their own. As adults continue to share these books, children repeatedly "pretend read" their favorite texts, getting closer and closer to the actual wordings until they have learned them by heart. In the process, children develop an awareness of the nature of registers of written language. Their acquisition of "book language" is a gradual, constructive process. Subsequently, they begin to integrate the graphic cuing system with what they know about the syntactic/semantic or lexicogrammatical patterns of the message. Thus, ATT attempts to tap the reading process for children who cannot be evaluated through an MMA assessment.

The procedure consists of reading an unfamiliar book to a child three times, usually on consecutive days, and on each occasion inviting the child to take his or her turn to "read" or "pretend read" it. Each reading is audiotaped and then transcribed.

The teacher then compares the child's approximations to those of the book and to the ways the child's texts change across the three times. Analyses usually focus on the following four major areas:

1. *Children expand and elaborate on the message of the book across the three readings.* Children may initially give a bare-bones rendition of the text, but as they hear the text being read again and have opportunities to take their turns to read it again, they begin to fill in and add more of the author's message.
2. *Children acquire certain vocabulary used in the book.* They may provide a synonym or make up a word for certain vocabulary in early readings, but in subsequent readings they may incorporate the actual wordings of the author.
3. *Children incorporate the author's grammatical structures.* Written language uses various kinds of grammatical constructions (more use of relative clauses, passive voice, etc.) that are not as typical in oral language, so children frequently create their own versions of these structures and then gradually begin to include structures similar to those of the author in subsequent readings.

Child: _____ Date: _____ Score: _____

Concepts About Print Test for: OUR GARAGE SALE (by Anne Rockwell)
(Keep book jacket on book)

Page	Concept/Prin.	Item	Child's behavior for giving points (Remainder for admin.)	Score
cover	front	1	Indicates front of book (Show me the front of the book)	*l*
2/3	left page	2	Indicates that lft. page precedes rt. (Where do I start)	*l*
8	capital/lowercase	3	Locates two capital & lowercase letter pairs (Ww & Oo)	*l*
	punctuation	4	Indicates meaning of period (What's this for)	—
		5	Indicates meaning of comma (What's this for)	—
		6	Indicates meaning of quotation marks (What're these for)	—
12	direction	7	Points at top left page (Show me where to start)	*l*
		8	Indicates left to right (Which way do I go)	*l*
		9	Indicates return sweep to left (Where do I go next)	*l*
	one-to-one same pg.	10	Word by word pointing/matching (Point while I read) *almost*	—
14/15	one-to-one lft. to rt. pg.	11	Word by word pointing/matching (Point while I read) *almost*	—
16/17	all lft. pg.	12	Indicates all of lft. pg. read before rt. (Where do I, etc.)	*l*
20	first/last text	13	Indicates first & last of text (Show me the first/last)	*l*
GO BACK 18	letter/word	14	Locates one and two letters (Show me one/two letter(s))	*l*
C A		15	Locates one and two words (Show me one/two word(s))	—
R D	first/last ltr of word	16	Locates first & last letter of word (Show me first/last) *ends*	*l*
S	capital ltr	17	Locates a capital letter (Show me a capital letter) *Saturday d*	—
back	back	18	Indicates the back of book (Show me the back of book)	*l*
top/bottom	tp/bottom	19	Indicates the top & bottom of book (Show me tp/btm of bk)	*l*

Figure 8.21
CAP SCORING SHEET

4. *Children's elaborations based on the illustrations change across the readings.* In early readings, children rely on the illustrations of a book to construct and sustain the message, but these elaborations usually drop out or are somehow incorporated or expressed more in terms of the linguistic message in later readings.

Figure 8.22 (p. 350) shows an ATT Analysis Sheet, which can be used to document these four types of approximations.

Teachers respond to any child-initiated question about a book's message, pictures, or print during an ATT session. At the bottom of the form (Figure 8.22), the teacher might jot down interesting questions or comments the child might have had.

Children's questions, such as "What's this word?" or "Is this word ———?" are answered unless the child asks about every other word. If it is clear—after a page or so—that the child is unwilling to follow the "pretend route," then the teacher may consider an alternative procedure that consists of reading page by page, the teacher reading one page, then the child "reading" that page. The fact that some children are reluctant to "pretend read" is normal. It indicates that these children

Child's Name: _____	Date: _____		Book: _____	
	Reading #1	Reading #2	Reading #3	
Important message ideas and details included				
Strategies in learning vocabulary				
Strategies in learning grammatical constructions				
Changes in elaborations based on illustrations				
Interesting questions, comments made				

Figure 8.22
ATT ANALYSIS SHEET

See Pappas (1993) for examples of repeated pretending reading of stories and information books.

have acquired a lot about the graphic or medium aspects of written language and are more motivated to tackle the print realization of the message. An MMA scheme could be applied to the children's readings in these cases instead of the form illustrated in Figure 8.22.

Once learned, the ATT procedure helps teachers to appreciate children's constructive process of reading at the very early stages and to be aware of the kind of strategies children employ in learning "book language." Thus, it encourages teachers to provide opportunities in the classroom for children to reenact or "pretend read" books from a range of genres through Big Books*, Book Talks*, Buddy Reading*, and the like.

Dictation Assessment

Genishi & Dyson (1984); Routman (1991); Temple, Nathan, Temple, & Burris (1993)

Dictation and Retelling (described in the next section) are oral compositions. Although teachers are constantly encouraging children to write on their own, dictation experiences are also useful in fostering the composing process because they give children opportunities to concentrate more on creating their message. This leaves the scribing work to the teacher, who takes on the mechanical task of writing and the concerns about spelling and punctuation. Therefore, dictations provide important information about a child's potential in the composition process that is not available when only their own writings are considered. Figure 8.23, which provides examples of two stories composed around the same time (mid-October) by a first grader, illustrates this fact. Janet's dictation, which is on the top, is much more complex than her written story, which is on the bottom.

Dictation experiences provide a means to assess both the product and the process of children's composing. By means of the message criteria discussed earlier (see Figure 8.8), the dictation text as product can be evaluated. However, other information about children's participation in the process can also be assessed. What is the delivery style of the child's dictation? Does the child dictate the message at a pace that is easy for the teacher to take down? Or does the child seem to be unaware of constraints on the writing process, rattling on and on so that the teacher has to stop the child repeatedly to keep up? Does the child pay attention to what the teacher is scribing by seeming to read along? Does the child comment on or take notice of spelling or punctuation? Does the child initiate any repairs (or revisions) of the message during the

DICTATION:

Once upon a time there was a little boy. And he was trying to go to sleep, but he heard a noise in the closet. So he sat up in bed. He opened the door of the closet and he looked in. There was a monster. And so he says, "Are you a scary monster?" And the monster said, "No." And so he says, "Will you play with me?" The monster says, "Of course." And so the boy called in his sister, and he said, "Here, I have a friend. He is a monster." The little girl said, "You do?" because she liked monsters. So the little boy said, "Yes." "And so he asked the monster to play games with them. The monster won every game. And in London Bridges they couldn't fit their arms around him. In Hide-and-Go-Seek he had two heads so he could tell where they were going. Then the little boy asked him, "Why were you in the closest?" He said because he was looking for candy. The little girl said, "Well, I have some candy." The monster said, "You do?" And the little girl said, "Yes." And so she got him a piece, and he ate it up. But then he said, "Yuk!" He didn't like peppermint. And so he said, "Well, now I have to hunt in the closet for more candy." And so he did. And the little boy woke up and he found out that it was all a dream.

WRITING: (Note: spelling and punctuation have been corrected.)

Once there was a girl and a boy.
The girl said, "Let's play!"
So they played and played.
They turned and turned.
They got dizzy.
They stopped.
The room went around.

Figure 8.23
JANET'S DICTATION AND WRITTEN TEXTS

Child:	Date:
Questions	**Analysis/Observations**
How well does the child control the genre being attempted? Are there certain beginnings, endings, or sequences present to indicate a certain genre?	
Is the text complete? Are details or elaborations included?	
Interesting vocabulary used? Use of cohesive ties? Ambiguous terms?	
Any missing information? Is information ordered to make sense?	
Interesting repairs used?	
Attention to transcription of medium aspects of text?	
Delivery pace or dictating style?	

INSTRUCTIONAL IDEAS:

Figure 8.24
DICTATION ASSESSMENT SHEET

dictation process? Figure 8.24 summarizes the kinds of behaviors that can be assessed during dictation, based on the context in which a particular dictation occurred. (Janet's dictation came about because children were creating a classroom story anthology.) At the bottom of the Dictation Assessment Sheet are instructional ideas based on the dictation activity.

A more formal dictation assessment (usually audiotaped) has teachers keep their interactions with children to a minimum. Other than stopping children when unable to keep up with their dictation, teachers avoid commenting on or drawing the children's attention to message or medium aspects of the text being composed in order to have a clearer view of the children's understanding. Then, on the basis of the data gained in these formal contexts, teachers know what to focus on when they interact with children in subsequent dictations. They also know what other activities may be appropriate.

There are many reasons to use dictation in the early elementary grades. (Certain versions of dictation can be used with older elementary-age children, such as Group-Composed Writing* activities.) Children's sight vocabulary is fostered through dictation; children are very successful in identifying words when they are *theirs*. Moreover, many demonstrations of medium aspects of written language—directionality, spacing, spelling, use of punctuation, etc.—are available for children during the dictation process. Teachers can also demonstrate the revising and editing processes during dictation. Finally, once teachers have experience in assessing dictations formally, they know how to evaluate them informally. As Figure 8.24 shows, teachers can document the contexts in which dictations arise and note instructional ideas to foster and extend children's present efforts. Dictating can be important sources of evaluation and accountability, as explained in Chapter 9.

Retelling Assessment

See also Brown & Cambourne (1987) for other retelling procedures.

Like dictation, retelling is a type of oral composition in which children retell or reconstruct someone else's message, not their own. However, while dictations are usually used in the early primary grades, retellings can occur at any grade level. Retelling assessment procedures consist of either reading to children or having them read, then inviting them to retell it to someone who does not know it (usually other children in the class who haven't heard or read the text). The fact that children retell the text to naive listeners is a critical factor because it provides a social context that requires children to produce a complete linguistic message. The assessment thus addresses children's strategies to provide such a text. Such retellings are very different from those in the MMA assessment, where the listener has knowledge of the text being read.

Pappas & Pettegrew (1987)

Retellings are audiotaped and then transcribed formally. After the reading, most teachers have the children go through it again by letting them see the pictures (if the text is illustrated) or by discussing or commenting on any questions children might have beforehand. Because reading is a construction of meaning, retellings are viewed as "new" versions of the author's message. Retellings may be organized in ways that

Retellings are constructions of an author's message.

Figure 8.25
RETELLING ANALYSIS SHEET

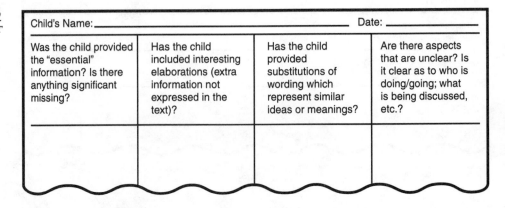

Child's Name: _____			Date: _____
Was the child provided the "essential" information? Is there anything significant missing?	Has the child included interesting elaborations (extra information not expressed in the text)?	Has the child provided substitutions of wording which represent similar ideas or meanings?	Are there aspects that are unclear? Is it clear as to who is doing/going; what is being discussed, etc.?

are different from the published text and may reflect interpretations different from those of the teacher. Figure 8.25 shows a Retelling Analysis Sheet, which could be used to document retellings from such a perspective.

In the first column, the teacher considers whether the essentials of the text have been included in the retelling and notes any significant information that seems missing. The second and third columns provide places to document the interesting elaborations and substitutions children may have used. In the last column, the teacher jots down any places where children may have been unclear, used ambiguous pronouns, or otherwise made the retelling incoherent. Thus, the analysis sheet can assess children's comprehension of a particular text and at the same time document the constructive nature of retelling by capturing various learners' "ways with words" or second language approximations in the retelling process. As an oral composition, the retelling provides a means to evaluate children's strategies in creating and organizing a text for others.

Cazden (1988); Heath (1983); Lindfors (1987); Michaels (1981); Nieto (1996); Perez & Torres-Guzman (1992)

When retelling analysis becomes second nature, teachers can evaluate children's retellings in more informal contexts, such as when they retell a story using props (flannel board characters), retell sections of a text in a Literature Response Group*, or share texts in Buddy Reading*.

General Observation Schemes

The schemes discussed in the preceding section focused specifically on certain literacy events, but teachers also need the means to evaluate how children are using language and developing concepts as they interact with others in a variety of activities across the curriculum. In the integrated language perspective, skills or strategies cannot be discerned in isolation from the culture or settings in which they appear. Valid kid-watching procedures and evaluation must include observation and documentation of children's understandings as they emerge in the natural and familiar settings of the classroom. We need to see how children are constructing concepts in particular domains, how they become experts in various topics, and how their learning develops over time in different patterns for different children. Because development is socially influenced, we need to discover how children act with partners and peers in small-group and whole-class interactions. Finally, we need to be able to find out how each child approaches, initiates, and sustains his or her work and inquiry. To meet these needs, three types of observation schemes or approaches are covered: target-child (or target children) observation, roving anecdotal observation, and other miscellaneous observation ideas.

Cambourne & Turbill (1994); Goodman, Goodman, & Hood (1989); Johnston (1987a, 1987b); Wexler-Sherman, Gardner, & Feldman (1988)

See Hindley (1996) and Power (1996) for useful ideas for improving your observational notetaking.
Sylva, Roy, & Painter (1980)

Target-Child(ren) Observation

The first observation approach is a modification of the kid-watching ideas developed by Bruner and his colleagues to document young children's sustained attention in activities in preschool playgroups and nursery schools. This scheme involves selecting a target child on whom to do repeated ten-minute observations. Teachers decide on a few children to follow each day, and using a recording sheet, they take notes on what these children do and say. See Figure 8.26 for an example of the Target-Child(ren) Observation Sheet.

At the top of the form, the teacher writes the name of the child, the date, and time of the observation. The procedure consists of making several ten-minute observations at different times of the day to capture a variety of experiences and interactions. The first half-minute of each minute is spent observing; the last half-minute is spent summarizing the child's activities and language (jotted down under the headings "Activity Record" and "Language Record," respectively). As Figure 8.26 shows, information about the context, activity, or task and any participants involved with the target child is also included on this form. At the bottom of the form, the teacher notes any instructional ideas that may come to mind and reminders for subsequent intervention. Teachers try to be unobtrusive during the observations, and most teachers use a signal

Name(s):		Date and Time Observed:	
ACTIVITY RECORD	LANGUAGE RECORD	CONTEXT/TASK	OTHER PARTICIPANTS
1			
2			
3			
4			
5			
. . .			
10			
Instructional Ideas:			

Source: Sylva, Roy & Painter (1980). Reprinted with permission.

Figure 8.26
TARGET CHILD(REN)
OBSERVATION SHEET

Describe, don't interpret yet.

Sylva, Roy, & Painter (1980)

system (e.g., wearing a certain hat or scarf) so that children know not to interrupt the teacher while the observations are occurring.

It is important to write down *what the child does* in the "Activity Record" column, not an interpretation of the behavior or what can be concluded about the child on the basis of what has been seen. Relevant information about materials or objects is also incorporated in the "Activity Record" column. Under the "Language Record" column, everything that the child says and what other children say to the child is noted. It is frequently impossible to write the exact words spoken, but the gist of comments can be recorded. Abbreviations can be used, as most teachers initially find it difficult to record observations. However, with practice the observations become second nature.

Part of observation is documenting how children sustain their attention in an activity or project, so after the writing is done, the record is reviewed for coherent themes in the child's behavior, that is, a continued stream of activity during which the child seems to be following a thread. The theme may be based on the materials the child is using or the children he or she is participating with, but it does not coincide with a shift of activity per se. A child—let's call him Joey—may finish reading a particular book and go over to the writing center for some paper and markers, glance over the book again as he chats with a peer about some of the illustrations, and then begin a Sketch to Stretch* activity. Joey tells his friend that he's going to finish the drawing later this afternoon, but before he joins everyone in a whole-class sharing session, Joey notes in his Learning Log* his ideas for the drawing so he doesn't forget them. Although the foregoing is only a summary of the child's behavior (i.e., it doesn't include the details of a real observation record), it illustrates the fact that a particular theme can integrate several activities and places over a brief period of time. Themes are noted on the observation sheet by drawing double lines to indicate where one theme ends and another begins.

The same form can be used to record observations of small-group activities. For example, when small groups are established to work on special projects in a thematic unit, teachers can document the course of their inquiries. Instead of one child, a target group of children is the focus. Afterward, teachers record relevant instructional ideas that could be helpful to support the group work, perhaps noting a question to ask the group, or a book or other resource to suggest.

Roving Anecdotal Observation

Roving anecdotal observation has many features of target-child(ren) observation but differs in focus. In the target-children observation scheme, teachers avoid interacting with children to concentrate on the ten-minute observations. In roving anecdotal observation, however, teachers move about the room to visit children as they engage in individual and small-group activities during integrated work time. Thus, teachers gather briefer, more specific "spot" information about children's particular strengths, needs, strategies, and interests in the natural social life of the classroom. There is a range of experiences to be recorded, so each observation must be focused to provide or generate appropriate instructional strategies. Categories of interesting behavior that such observations could concentrate on include, but are not limited to, the following:

Interactions with Peers

Strategies for joining and departing groups
Responses to initiations from others
Negotiation strategies
Examples of abilities to take the perspective of others
Instances of leadership or responsibility
Examples of peer support, empathy
Cooperation strategies
Examples of turn-taking abilities

Strategies and Processes

Process of problem-solving with people
Process of problem-solving with objects or materials
Creative use of resources to tackle problems
Strategies for accomplishing tasks
Unusual use of objects or materials beyond conventional roles
Unusual combination of objects, resources, or materials
Representational and imaginary object use

Oral Language Samples

Interesting quotations
Sophisticated vocabulary
Unusual working definitions of words
Examples of explanations and descriptions
Examples of metalinguistic awareness (using language as an object)
Instances of register or code switching
Comments indicating awareness or examination of ideologies or values

Literacy Samples

Use of books as a resource to help solve problems
Strategies used in reading aloud
Strategies used in various writing experiences (prewriting, drafting, revising, editing, publishing)
Creative Book Extensions*

Spontaneous use of reading and writing
Unusual or interesting use of reading and/or writing in projects

Miscellaneous

Examples of sustained attention and focusing
Self-correction strategies
Examples of reflective behavior
Examples of autonomous or self-management behavior
Examples of interesting working styles

More possibilities will become apparent as you learn more about specific curricular content (Chapter 5) and about how to implement a variety of activities and experiences in thematic units (Chapters 5 and 7). Some teachers write their observations on index cards. We like Post-it Notes because the teacher can easily transfer these notes to a separate page for each child (which can, in turn, be placed in the child's learning portfolio—see Chapter 9) at a later time. These sheets can then be easily copied to share with parents, who enjoy reading these "snapshots" of their child in the classroom.

The following guidelines are important to keep in mind while writing anecdotal observations:

Include the child's name (underlined), date, and perhaps where the child was observed, if relevant.
Try to confine one piece of anecdotal information to one Post-it page.
Try to confine information to *one* child's reactions or responses. If other children are involved, write additional notes for the other participants.
Confine comments to what is being observed that particular day; don't refer to behavior on previous days.
Include a description of problem-solving processes.

Teachers who are just beginning to write anecdotal observations sometimes find the last point the most difficult. However, it is critical that these notes include *how* a child accomplishes a task, rather than record *that* a child has done something. Figure 8.27 contrasts notes that provide helpful information with those that do not. As these examples illustrate, the more helpful, informative notes capture the process and strategies that children actually employed, not just a statement that something occurred or that a task was accomplished.

Describing the process of what the child is doing is emphasized.

The advantage of roving anecdotal observation is that teachers can easily interact with children while they are observing. Thus, if teachers ask a question or make a comment about children's behavior or activities, they are able to document the responses to suggestions or input. Children can also be encouraged to contribute their own observation notes when they think they have done something interesting that may have been missed by the teacher.

Miscellaneous Observation Ideas

Teachers can modify the ideas that we have discussed to come up with their own kid-watching systems of observation, such as schemes for particular purposes or checklists of various kinds. By using the same list several times over the year, teachers can document children's progress toward certain goals. Teachers can also construct checklists for certain types of activities that occur during the ongoing flow of the classroom. Checklists are timesavers and can provide useful information, but they cannot provide an adequate picture of progress unless they are complemented by more detailed observations, such as those described earlier in this chapter.

Vignettes are also useful for assessing progress. A vignette is an account of a particularly meaningful event of a child's classroom life that represents a significant milestone—or "aha" phenomenon—for a certain child. Vignettes are similar to roving

Less Helpful / Informative

More Helpful / Informative

9/7 Susan in the construction area counted up to 18.

→

9/7 Susan in construction area using inch cubes. Spontaneously sorted cubes by color, then regrouped them and systematically counted each w/one to one correspondence until she reached 18. Then her counting became random, losing one-to-one & skipping over several cubes.

2/19 Pedro & Janet had a huge argument in the science center. Fought over materials that they both wanted. Something broke & Janet left.

→

2/19 Pedro & Janet argued over a hand magnifier in science center. Pedro did not respond to Janet's repeated requests to have a turn or offer any substitutions in the center. Janet's frustration peaked and tried to grab the magnifier, and in the struggle knocked down one of the jars on the table. Janet left and Pedro picked up broken glass. Refused to verbalize the problem when I intervened.

2/19 Janet & Pedro argued over a hand magnifier in science center. Janet repeatedly asked, "When do I have a turn to use it? I need to use this one now." After 5 attempts w/same strategy, Janet attempted to grab magnifier in Pedro's hand. Pedro knocked down one of the jars when he tried to avoid Janet's grabbing. Janet left + told me that she tried to "ask for the magnifier 'nicely' but Pedro was 'too selfish.'"

Less Helpful / Informative

More Helpful / Informative

3/24 Christina helped Larry revise his book on rabbits.

→

3/24 Christina helped Larry figure out how to add new information on rabbits he has found for his draft. She first explained carats, but Larry said he didn't have room to just write it over the lines of his text. Then she took strips of paper on shelf & told him to staple them on the side. He began to write his info on the strips. Christina said, "I use spider legs all the time."

5/4 John read a part of his book in response group. He sometimes read haltingly but others didn't seem to notice and asked good questions. John answered them quite well.

→

5/4 John read a page (p26) from Fritz's Shh! We're Writing the Constitution. He paused four times, twice to re-run & twice to self-correct semantically unacceptable miscues. Others asked why he liked this part of the book. (It related the behavior of delegates during deliberation). John responded that it sounded just like the Senate hearings he heard on TV. He wondered how laws get enacted when some go on & on & others pay no attention to what people say.

Figure 8.27

Snail Study Center	Children involved:	Date:
① What are some of the hypotheses (or questions) Cs construct about snails?		
② What conclusions (or answers) about the snails do Cs come to?		
③ What are examples of Cs' using their "own language" to find out about snails?		
④ How does their language reflect their own feelings about snails?		
⑤ What are examples of joint action + cooperation in the learning process?		
⑥ How did books support Cs inquiries on snails?		
⑦ What writing resulted regarding Cs' study of snails?		
⑧ What other activities resulted from snails study (e.g. drawing, math, constructing, etc.)		

Figure 8.28
SPECIFIC OBSERVATION SHEET

Almy & Genishi (1979)

anecdotal observations and perhaps rely on them; however, vignettes are more detailed and are usually written up later by the teacher. Many teachers like to include at least one vignette per thematic unit or grading period to share with parents and to become part of the child's learning portfolio.

Specific observation sheets can be created to capture what is going on at a particular center and to document the kinds of hypotheses children are generating, the language they use to talk about what they see, and so forth. Figure 8.28 illustrates such an observation form for a classroom study of snails.

Using this form (a clean copy for each day), the teacher observes what is happening at the snail study center. In the first few days of the study, most of the teacher's notes probably center on questions 1 to 5, but as children's questions become better articulated, observations for questions 6 to 8 are filled in. By reviewing these forms during the course of the study, the teacher is able to document who was involved, the process by which children found their answers, what they produced as the result of their study, and how they relied on one another and written resources to support their inquiries.

Conclusions

We want children to continuously encounter novel and interesting problems. We want to encourage them to hypothesize and seek comprehension of their problems on the basis of what they presently know. We want them to use their interactions with others in the classroom community as sources for learning. Consequently, we need kid-watching techniques that are in-process assessments that let us evaluate what children are understanding about content as they are actually experiencing it. The kid-watching schemes presented in this chapter do this. The first set of procedures focused on ways to examine children's strategies in a range of literacy assessments; the last set provided more general schemes to capture the content and process of their ongoing experiences in individual and small-group activities and projects.

The approaches described here are not an exhaustive list but are offered as ways to learn how to become a kid watcher and acquire (and internalize) new ways of observing children's strategies as they go about using language and developing concepts or constructing their knowledge. In other chapters, we go into various curricular content in more detail. These chapters include examples of ways to integrate the disciplines into thematic units (Chapters 4 and 5), and they cover a variety of experiences and activities for putting an integrated language theory into action (Chapter 7). Thus, other kid-watching procedures and ideas emerge. Other issues related to kid watching and evaluation are addressed in Chapter 9. See also teacher researchers' descriptive and reflective writing and other observational ideas found in "Guidelines for Teacher Inquiry" at the end of the book.

Evaluation in context

REFERENCES

Almy, M., & Genishi, C. (1979). *Ways of studying children.* New York: Teachers College Press.

Atwell, N. (1987). *In the middle: Writing, reading, and learning with adolescents.* Portsmouth, NH: Boynton/Cook.

Au, K. H. (1993). *Literacy instruction in multicultural settings.* Fort Worth, TX: Harcourt Brace Jovanovich.

Avery, C. (1993). *And with a light touch: Learning about reading, writing and teaching with first graders.* Portsmouth, NH: Heinemann.

Barrs, M., Ellis, S., Hester, H., & Thomas, A. (1988). *The primary language record: Handbook for teachers.* London: Centre for Language in Primary Education.

Barrs, M., Ellis, S., Hester, H., & Thomas, A. (1990). *Patterns of learning: The primary language record and the National Curriculum.* London: Centre for Language in Primary Education.

Brown, H., & Cambourne, B. (1987). *Read and retell: A strategy for the whole-language/natural learning classroom.* Portsmouth, NH: Heinemann.

Calkins, L. M. (1986). *The art of teaching writing.* Portsmouth, NH: Heinemann.

Calkins, L. M., with Harwayne, S. (1991). *Living between the lines.* Portsmouth, NH: Heinemann.

Calkins, L. M. (1994). *The art of teaching writing.* Portsmouth, NH: Heinemann.

Cambourne, B., & Turbill, J. (1994). *Responsive evaluation.* Portsmouth, NH: Heinemann.

Cazden, C. B. (1988). *Classroom discourse: The learning of teaching and learning.* Portsmouth, NH: Heinemann.

Clay, M. (1972). *Sand—The concepts about print test.* Portsmouth, NH: Heinemann.

Clay, M. (1979a). *The early detection of reading difficulties: A diagnostic survey with recovery procedures.* Portsmouth, NH: Heinemann.

Clay, M. (1979b). *Stones—The concepts about print test.* Portsmouth, NH: Heinemann.

Clay, M. (1985). *The early detection of reading difficulties.* Portsmouth, NH: Heinemann.

Dyson, A. H. (1987). Individual differences in beginning composing: An orchestral vision of learning to write. *Written Communication, 4,* 411–442.

Dyson, A. H. (1989). *Multiple worlds of child writers: Friends learning to write.* New York: Teachers College Press.

Fisher, B. (1991). *Joyful learning: A whole language kindergarten.* Portsmouth, NH: Heinemann.

Fisher, B. (1995). *Thinking and learning together: Curriculum and community in a primary classroom.* Portsmouth, NH: Heinemann.

Genishi, C., & Dyson, D. H. (1984). *Language assessment in the early years.* Norwood, NJ: Ablex.

Goodman, K. S. (1973). Miscues: Windows on the reading process. In K. S. Goodman (Ed.), *Miscue analysis: Applications to reading instruction* (pp. 3–14). Urbana, IL: ERIC Clearinghouse on Reading and Communication Skills.

Goodman, K. S. (1993). *Phonics phacts.* Portsmouth, NH: Heinemann.

Goodman, K. S. (1997). Putting theory and research in the context of history. *Language Arts, 74,* 595–609.

Goodman, K. S., Goodman, Y. M., & Hood, W. J. (1989). *The whole language evaluation book.* Portsmouth, NH: Heinemann.

Goodman, Y. M., Watson, D. J., & Burke, C. L. (1987). *Reading miscue inventory: Alternative procedures.* New York: Richard C. Owen.

Graves, D. (1983). *Writing: Teachers and children at work.* Portsmouth, NH: Heinemann.

Harp, B. (1993). Principles of assessment and evaluation in whole language classrooms. In B. Harp (Ed.), *Assessment and evaluation in whole language programs* (pp. 37–52). Norwood, MA: Christopher-Gordon.

Heath, S. B. (1983). *Ways with words: Language, life, and work in communities and classrooms.* Cambridge: Cambridge University Press.

Henderson, E. H., & Beers, J. W. (Eds.). (1980). *Developmental and cognitive aspects of learning to tell.* Newark, DE: International Reading Association.

Hindley, J. (1996). *In the company of children*. York, ME: Stenhouse.

Holdaway, D. (1979). *The foundations of literacy*. Sydney, Australia: Ashton Scholastic.

Johnston, P. (1987a). Teachers as evaluation experts. *The Reading Teacher, 40,* 744–748.

Johnston, P. (1987b). Assessing the process, and the process of assessment, in the language arts. In J. R. Squire (Ed.), *The dynamics of language learning: Research in reading and English* (pp. 355–357). Urbana, IL: ERIC Clearinghouse on Reading and Communication Skills.

Johnston, P. H. (1992). *Constructive evaluation of literate activity*. White Plains, NY: Longman.

Johnston, P. H. (1997). *Knowing literacy: Constructive literacy assessment*. York, ME: Stenhouse.

Kemp, M. (1987). *Watching children read and write: Observational records for children with special needs*. Portsmouth, NH: Heinemann.

Lindfors, J. W. (1987). *Children's language and learning*. Englewood Cliffs, NJ: Prentice-Hall.

McKenzie, M. (1977). The beginnings of literacy. *Theory Into Practice, 16,* 315–324.

Michaels, S. (1981). "Sharing time": Children's narrative styles and differential access to literacy. *Language in Society, 10,* 423–442.

Newkirk, T. (1989). *More than stories: The range of children's writings*. Portsmouth, NH: Heinemann.

Nieto, S. (1996). *Affirming diversity: The sociopolitical context of multicultural education*. White Plains, NY: Longman.

Pappas, C. C. (1993). Is narrative "primary"? Some insights from kindergarteners' pretend readings of stories and information books. *Journal of Reading Behavior, 25,* 97-129.

Pappas, C. C., & Brown, E. (1989). Using turns at story "reading" as scaffolding for learning. *Theory Into Practice, 28,* 105–113.

Pappas, C. C., & Pettegrew, B. S. (1991). Learning to tell: Aspects of developing communicative competence in young children's story retellings. *Curriculum Inquiry, 21,* 439–454.

Perez, B., & Torres-Guzman, M. E. (1992). *Learning in two worlds: An integrated Spanish/English biliteracy approach*. White Plains, NY: Longman.

Power, B. M. (1996). *Taking notes: Improving your observational notetaking*. York, ME: Stenhouse.

Rhodes, L. K., & Shankler, N. L. (1993). *Windows into literacy: Assessing learners K–8*. Portsmouth, NH: Heinemann.

Routman, R. (1991). *Invitations: Changing as teachers and learners K–12*. Portsmouth, NH: Heinemann.

Sylva, K., Roy, C., & Painter, M. (1980). *Childwatching at playgroup and nursery school*. Ypsilanti, MI: The High/Scope Press.

Temple, C., Nathan, R., Temple, F., & Burris, N. A. (1993). *The beginnings of writing*. Boston: Allyn & Bacon.

Turbill, J. (1983). *Now, we want to write!* Rozelle, Australia: Primary English Teaching Association.

Watson, D., & Henson, J. (1993). Reading evaluation—Miscue analysis. In B. Harp (Ed.), *Assessment and evaluation in whole language programs* (pp. 53–75). Norwood, MA: Christopher-Gordon.

Wexler-Sherman, C., Gardner, H., & Feldman, D. H. (1988). A pluralistic view of early assessment: The project spectrum approach. *Theory Into Practice, 27,* 77–83.

Weiner, R. B., & Cohen, J. H. (1994). *Literacy portfolios: Using assessment to guide instruction*. Upper Saddle River, NJ: Merrill.

Wilde, S. (1992). *You kan red this! Spelling and punctuation for classrooms, K–6*. Portsmouth, NH: Heinemann.

Wilde, S. (1997). *What's a schwa sound anyway? A holistic guide to phonetics, phonics, and spelling*. Portsmouth, NH: Heinemann.

CHILDREN'S LITERATURE

Farmer Boy by L. I. Wilder. Illustrated by G. Williams. Harper & Row, 1953.

Our Garage Sale by A. Rockwell. Illustrated by H. Rockwell. Greenwillow, 1984.

Evaluation and Accountability

Imagine that, after completing the detergent-testing project described in Chapter 5, students took a test in which they filled in the blanks, listed formulas and matched results with products, defined terms, and ticked off a variety of true and false items. Although such an evaluation can tap some of what children learn, it also exaggerates the importance of specific bits of information and undercuts attention to the processes of science and the context within which information is important. As an assessment tool, this type of test ignores a wide range of significant learning activities and is incongruent with purposes and procedures in an integrated language classroom.

See Bussis & Chittenden (1987); Darling-Hammond & Falk, (1997); Goodman, Goodman, & Hood (1989); Hiebert & Hutchinson (1991); Shepherd (1991); and Valencia, Hiebert, & Afflerbach (1993) for other discussions of the necessity for rethinking assessment and evaluation in education.

Yet teachers in integrated language classrooms are just as accountable for the evaluation of pupil learning as their peers in more traditional classrooms. They, too, must find ways to evaluate and assess that are congruent with their educational purposes. They must become "constructive evaluators," able both to establish a context where children engage in a variety of learning activities and to recognize students' development in that classroom context. We have emphasized the ongoing interplay or reciprocal relationship of teachers' assessment of children's learning and teachers' decisions in instruction throughout this book. Assessment here is performance-based—it captures both the processes and the products of learning—while it documents worthwhile, valued inquiries, and learning outcomes. A critical feature of this kind of assessment involves students' self-evaluation of their learning. An integrated language classroom, then, requires evaluation and assessment that can reflect how children learn and think in context, how they connect what they have learned in various content domains, how they progress over time, and how they grow in their ability to self-evaluate.

See Johnston (1997) for further discussion of "constructive evaluators."

Johnston (1997); Routman (1991); Wexler-Sherman, Gardner, & Feldman (1988); Wolf (1988); Graves (1983)
A performance-based evaluation is an authentic way to assess both process and product of learning.

Au, Scheu, Kawakami, & Herman (1990)

The following four interrelated characteristics and challenges of assessment are important in developing such constructive evaluation techniques:

See King (1991) for a similar set of characteristics.

Comprehensive, Balanced, and Systematic Assessment. You want to have a broad picture of students' learning in various contexts, activities, and projects. Moreover, you want to be able to capture both the end products of student investigations—writing, art, reports, and presentations—and the processes or paths by which students produced a particular artifact. That is, student attempts, approximations, and risk taking are all important instances of their meaning making in action that need to be documented. Thus, authentic and valid assessment is systematic and multifaceted, not a single method or piece of information.

Assessment for Teaching. The major reason for assessment is to provide you with information to help you make informed decisions about your instruction and better understand your students' learning so that you can meet their needs. You want practical means to gather and record information that are part of everyday classroom activities. You want assessment that has both formative and summative characteristics. Assessment is formative in that it is used to help the teacher plan the kinds of topics, resources, activities, and organization children

Assessment has both formative and summative characteristics.

will need as they engage in thematic units. It helps you determine the Focus-Lessons*, conferences, and other interactions you have with your students. Assessment is summative in that you can use it to construct a history of learners' development. It enables you to interpret children's achievement and progress.

Assessment for Students. You want assessment that can help your students be self-monitoring, self-regulating, and independent in their learning. Such self-evaluation is an integral component of ownership in learning. As they learn, children need feedback so that they can evaluate their work and use it for their own purposes. Thus, you want children to know what is expected of them and what they have achieved, and to have some ideas about what is needed for future progress and achievement.

Assessment for Parents and Caregivers. You want to communicate with parents, caregivers, and other stakeholders about students' learning. Few parents have experienced the student-directed, collaborative approach to learning found in integrated language classrooms. They want to know what their children are doing and what things you believe are the indicators of progress. They want to know what their children have achieved and what they find difficult. Providing parents with detailed information about their children and finding ways to seek further information from them help parents be partners in students' progress and achievement.

Evaluation is collaborative.

In sum, meaningful and useful evaluation is thoughtful, ongoing, and multidimensional, and it takes place in authentic contexts. Because a teacher's style of teaching in an integrated language classroom is a collaborative one, evaluation is also collaborative. This type of performance-based assessment and evaluation has a functional orientation for it is an integral part of the ongoing processes of teaching and learning. It is developmentally and culturally responsive evaluation.

King (1994); Harp (1994)

Major Methods of Evaluation

Daly (1989); Reardon (1994); Routman (1991) Salinger & Chittenden (1994)

There are several major interrelated ways integrated language teachers assess and evaluate students' learning. Many are informal, but some teachers make more formal ones, too. In any case, assessment methods and techniques are tied to everyday classroom experiences, activities, and projects.

Ongoing Observations and Periodic Documentations

Evaluation is continuous and covers all aspects of an integrated language classroom.

In integrated language classrooms, teachers collaborate with children by supporting their choices of inquiries. As children pursue their investigations, teachers move around the room, interacting with individuals or small groups to find out what the children are doing and how the teachers can support their efforts. Teachers are continually evaluating and teaching; these acts are reciprocal processes. Evaluation is seen as part of a social interaction in which the teacher comes to understand the task or situation from the child's point of view, and the child is strengthened in self-evaluation. As a result, the teacher is better able to describe children through their strengths, and to put children in situations that encourage success. In Chapter 8, we discussed ways by which these reciprocal processes of evaluation and teaching can be made more explicit. Through roving anecdotal or periodic target-child observations, teachers know what kinds of experiences or resources certain children need now, when a particular Focus-Lesson* is necessary, how to evaluate children's strategies in tackling a problem, and whether a particular child needs to be encouraged to try something new.

Teachers keep journals, too.

Teachers can also keep journals of classroom events, perhaps one for each thematic unit studied during the year. These accounts review and highlight significant experiences or patterns occurring in the classroom. The journals include the teachers' own observation sheets developed to examine small-group inquiries (like the one quickly drawn up to document what was happening in the snails study described in Chapter 8). Journals can be complemented by incorporating concepts learned in a thematic unit, snapshots of the growth of a Graffiti Wall* or the artifacts constructed

Hull (1988)

by children in the course of a unit, and a review of the Activity Cards* children have used, modified, or written on their own during a unit. Such a journal helps teachers remember and reflect on how children participate in the culture or learning community of the classroom.

Keep "before" and "after" data.

Student/Teacher Conferences

Another part of ongoing evaluation is having one-on-one conversations with children. Reading and Writing Conferences* were discussed in Chapters 6, 7, and 8, but brief conferences need not be limited to literacy activities. Because literacy is integrated across the curriculum in this perspective, discussions always include specific content or a curricular domain or domains. But conferences can be planned to focus on a particular mathematical or scientific problem or a certain issue in social studies, for example, and not concentrate on reading or writing per se. Conferences provide an opportunity for joint assessment of student work, as teachers and children discuss student progress toward learning goals.

One-on-one conversations with children are important evaluative tools.

Teachers can have small-group conferences as well. Periodic documentation of the dynamics of group interactions when children collaborate to investigate a common topic is essential in this perspective that emphasizes the social, contextual influences in learning. Tape-recording or listening in on peer conferences (e.g., during Literature Response Groups*) provides still another way to document and evaluate learning and language in the classroom. Children can also take turns being "reporters" whose job is to summarize the discussion and decisions of a peer conference to share with the teacher.

Document group interactions, especially during collaborative investigations.

Student Self-Evaluation

A critical aspect of evaluation in an integrated language classroom is children's self-evaluation. This feature is usually incorporated into a child's learning portfolio, but it is such a critical factor in this perspective that we discuss it as a separate section. Self-evaluation can be seen as an extension of children's Learning Logs*, in which children jot down their own questions, pose possible answers, and organize (and reorganize) their own ideas. Thus, Learning Logs* are ways to make children's thinking more explicit. Self-evaluation is similar; children pause to consider what they have learned and what has been important from their own perspectives.

Self-evaluation encourages student reflection.

Hart (1994); Lenski, Riss, & Flickinger (1996)

As indicated below, an important time for children to explicitly self-evaluate their learning is at the end of a thematic unit, when they select the work to be included in their learning portfolios. As they choose some particular writing, they explain why they thought it was their best work or why it represented significant work on a particular project. Children can also be encouraged to review their Learning Logs* periodically (perhaps at the end of a thematic unit) and write a summary of what stood out for them. Or they can include an evaluation as part of any big project. Even younger elementary children can evaluate their own work. The teacher can take notes as children tell what was the best thing they have done or where they have done their hardest work. What children may think is significant in their learning may not be what teachers or parents or others deem valuable. Self-evaluation, therefore, is an important factor because it gives children opportunities to reflect on their learning, thereby helping them to be independent, autonomous, and confident learners.

Tests and Exams

Whether to give tests and exams is both an administrative and a teacher decision. Many schools adopting an integrated language perspective do not use tests because they believe that the children's work produced in various thematic units is sufficient, and provides more valid indicators of children's achievements and progress.

Others who have an integrated language perspective do not use teacher-made tests in the traditional sense. They conceive of tests in ways that make them more congruent with their instructional goals, rethinking the standard fill-in-the-blank and multiple-choice formats. For example, rather than have children give the answers to a list of math problems, teachers may ask them to analyze the problems they find the most difficult.

Hyde & Bizar (1989); Hart (1994)

These responses require that children identify the kind of problem and describe their approach to it. These analyses require the use of correct vocabulary, pattern recognition, and some knowledge of how to proceed. Another possibility is to have children identify five problems according to kind and then give a brief analysis of the approach to each, with no actual problem solving.

Social studies and science use laboratory-like tests.

Particularly in science and social studies, such tests have the flavor of "laboratory" assignments. They test for inquiry, one of the skills traditional tests fail to evaluate but that is critical in an integrated language perspective. It may seem difficult to construct a test that reflects inquiry skills, but it is possible. Observation and Inference*, two of the basic inquiry skills, can be tested by setting up a situation in which children are asked to observe carefully and then to make supported inferences. A test of these skills in science can include a demonstration in which children observe as the teacher places two cubes in a clear liquid. One cube floats; the other sinks to the bottom. Students are then required to list three observations and make two inferences that can be supported by their observations. Their responses are evaluated in terms of the accuracy of their observations (i.e., that they are not inferences), and the degree to which their inferences are supported by their observations.

A test in social studies can use a political cartoon relevant to the students' recent studies. The children are asked to interpret the symbols used in the cartoon to infer the cartoonist's "message." Their response is evaluated in terms of the way in which they draw on their recent study to interpret the cartoon and on the supportability of their inferences.

See also Ellis (1997); Hyde & Bizar (1989); Levstik & Barton (1997); Maxim (1987); and Wasserman & Ivany (1988) for further discussion of evaluation in science and social studies.

Another inquiry skill concerns children's ability to select and evaluate data. A test item following a unit on EXPLORATIONS can involve presenting children with a problem such as the following:

> You are considering inviting Mr. Erickson to speak to your class on early European explorations of the Americas. Which statements make Mr. Erickson most qualified to speak to your class? Explain your choices.
>
>   A. He is related to Leif Erickson.
>   B. He has written a book on the settlement of Greenland.
>   C. He conducted some of the first research on Viking settlements in Newfoundland.
>   D. He is director of the Viking museum in Oslo, Norway.

To answer this question, students need to know something about the Viking explorations in North America, but they also need to be able to explain why some of Mr. Erickson's qualifications are better than others for the stated purpose. The question is embedded in both content and process, and it evaluates children's ability to make connections between the methods of study and the content studied.

Communicating data is also an important skill in inquiry, and it can be evaluated on a written test, especially if the test is open book or note. This kind of test is, to some extent, individualized. The teacher must know what questions and content children have been grappling with and then give them an opportunity to write about that. The children who found different interpretations of a historic figure, for instance, can be asked to use their notes to write an argument for accepting one interpretation over another. Another child may be asked to compare the way the textbook interprets an event in history with the way in which that event was interpreted in a piece of historical fiction.

Kresse (1979)

Other possibilities are questions that ask children to construct a hypothesis to explain an observation in science or to select the most important thing they learned during a unit, and then to write a statement justifying their choice. One primary teacher uses a film on the first Thanksgiving as a test of her third graders' ability to compare and contrast sources after a study based on the MATCH unit "The Indians Who Met the Pilgrims" (see Chapter 4). The film is quite short, offers a number of contrasts to the MATCH unit, and contains several inaccuracies that have been pointed out in other contexts. The test includes, among other things, having children identify three ways in which the film supports what they have learned and three ways it contradicts what they have learned.

Another primary teacher uses a "Can you spot the errors?" format for some of his testing in social studies. He constructs pictures that include errors that children's studies should enable them to identify. After a study based on Turner's *Dakota Dugout,* he presents children with a picture of a prairie home and family. He asks students to draw first a red circle around anything in the picture that would not have been there during the time of *Dakota Dugout,* and then a blue circle around anything they think would not be there today. The children are thus required to use specific skills with a content they have been studying. The teacher does not assume that the children will know everything from the period, but he does know what the children have been studying and wants to evaluate the way in which they have been making sense of the time aspects of their study.

Turner (1986)

Thornton & Vukelich (1988)

A teacher could do a similar thing in science by drawing a series of pictures showing, say, plant growth under various conditions. The children circle the picture that ends a sequence (i.e., a plant bending in the direction of the sun after a series of pictures of a bean plant on a windowsill, or a long, white stem on a plant grown with little light). Some teachers give children a series of pictures representing a process they have observed to paste in order on their test paper. A similar format can be used in math. Teachers can use data children have been collecting in a unit and construct several problems and possible solutions. Children would be asked to identify those aspects of the approach that are correct and incorrect by circling them with different colored pens.

Children can also be asked to put what they have learned to more public use. Following a study of immigration patterns in North America, one teacher presented students with a problem that was very real in the local community and emblematic of larger issues for immigrants across the country:

> Given what you have learned about Americans' and Central and South Americans' images of each other and of the problems these stereotypes can cause, what suggestions would you give to the mayor to help your neighbors better understand the Central and South Americans who are moving into this community? To help the Central and South Americans better understand your community?
>
> As a class, we will be sending our suggestions to the mayor, so be as specific and practical as possible. Provide evidence of stereotyping and information on more accurate images. Remember that these are things we think the mayor should really do to prevent stereotyping and help people from different cultures better understand each other.

Note that the criteria for the task are made clear (identify stereotypes, identify characteristics of each culture that are more accurate, and suggest ways in which city government can alleviate some of the problems of cultural misconceptions) and provide a basis for the teacher's assessment and student self-evaluation.

Make sure criteria for an assessment task are clear to children.

Most tests in an integrated language classroom are not timed to test the speed of children's thinking. Instead, children are given time to think carefully about their answers and to go back and review their responses. Most tests also require students to develop ideas in writing and to justify or elaborate on responses. Many of these tests give students an opportunity to rehearse, refine, and revise and to communicate in a distinctive "voice" or style while solving the problem at hand. This helps students to better judge the effectiveness of their work and decisions. Such tests are also closer to the way in which adults operate when they are working and more congruent with the way in which the children have been working throughout the thematic units described in Chapters 3 and 4.

Hart (1994); Johnston (1997); Wiggins (1989)

Parent and Caregiver Input

Parental involvement is a significant factor in student success, and more and more schools are inviting parents and guardians to take an active role in the assessment process. Parents and guardians often feel frustrated in interpreting reports of students' progress and in supporting their children's intellectual development. Teachers, too, often feel that it would be helpful if they knew more about students' lives outside the classroom. Parental participation in assessment can help reduce some of the misconceptions

Fredericks & Rasinski (1990); Lenski, Riss, & Flickinger (1996)

and misinterpretations made by teachers and parents, and provide positive ways in which both can interact with children. There is no single best way to organize parental assessment procedures; rather, there is a continuum of efforts schools have made to better involve parents in this important aspect of their children's lives:

Record Parent/Caregiver Expectations. Ask parents and caregivers what kind of progress they would like to see for their child, then record parents' responses and refer to them on a regular basis. This can be most easily done early in the school year, then referred to throughout the rest of the year.

Keep a Read-at-Home Log. Ask children to read to someone outside of the school setting, such as a relative, neighbor, or babysitter. Children can read books, newspapers, or magazines. Whatever the child decides to read, the listener makes an entry in the child's reading log. The entries can range from a comment on strengths in the child's reading (the ease or difficulty of the selected reading) to suggestions for other things the child might like to read. An at-home observation guide that parents can fill out between reporting periods can also accompany the read-at-home log.

Use Homework/Project Assessment. Parents can also do periodic homework reviews. A simple questionnaire can be sent to parents along with an explanation of an assignment or project with which the child is involved. Parents are asked to evaluate the assignment in terms of its level of difficulty, how well the child understood the assignment, and the appropriateness of the assignment. This provides not only feedback on the parents' response to the assignment but also an opportunity for parents to discuss the assignment with their child and make suggestions so that the teacher might be able to improve the assignment.

Invite In-School Observations. Invite parents to come to the classroom and do structured observations. (See Figure 9.1.) These observations provide a framework for a conference between parents and caregivers and teachers. Introduce the observation/conference forms early in the year and provide samples of entries other parents have made. Following such focused observation, parents have a clearer picture of both the classroom situation and their child's performance.

Managing Authentic, Performance-Based Assessment

The Why, What, How, and When of Assessment

Although it is critical to have comprehensive assessment (review the four features listed in the beginning of the chapter) so that you have a full picture of growing learners, teachers can easily be overwhelmed—feel drowned—by too much detail. Thus, you have to be selective in your assessing, documenting, and data gathering. It is very easy to say that you need to observe all the time, but in practice you are going to have to make some choices. These decisions are easier if you keep in mind the *why, what, how,* and *when* of assessment.

Hart (1994); Turnbill (1989)

Why? The whys are tied to your beliefs and theories of how children develop language and learn in general—they are related to the principles of the integrated language perspective discussed in Chapter 1. For example, some of the general whys you would want to consider as you plan assessment techniques—encouraging risk taking and approximation; promoting collaborative, noncompetitive learning; and fostering self-evaluation and self-monitoring—are drawn from these principles. Other whys include those you had in mind in planning particular thematic units. (See Chapter 4.) Two of the performances Caitlin Cooper planned to assess in DIGGING UP THE PAST were students' progress in learning problem-solving techniques in various domains and their appropriate and accurate use of content in prob-

PARENT OBSERVATION GUIDE

Date: _____

Welcome to our classroom. While you are visiting, you might like to observe and make notes on some or all of the following:

When I watched my child as she/he was working, I expected to see:

_____
_____
_____
_____
_____

When I watched my child in the classroom, I was surprised to see:

_____
_____
_____

When I watched my child in the classroom, I was pleased to see:

_____
_____
_____

During my visit I wondered about:

_____
_____
_____

Figure 9.1

lem solving. As a result, she planned opportunities for students to write about process and content during small-group work related to different domains. In collaboration with her students, she established criteria for evaluating their work and provided regular opportunities for peer and teacher feedback about their progress. Dehea Munioz (JOURNEYS) was also interested in children's use of appropriate and accurate content, but she wanted to evaluate student progress in selecting and using genres appropriate for different audiences as well as different domains. Thus, one of her assessments was planned around a museum exhibit where students interpreted their studies in a variety of ways for particular audiences. As you look through the other prototypes in Chapter 4 you will see how assessment is tied to the particular agendas that concern the content of a thematic unit or a teacher's inquiry.

What? How? and When? These are frequently best thought of together. Sketching out a grid of possibilities is a useful way to begin. Such a plan can help your assessment be comprehensive and systematic and at the same time keep it manageable. See Figure 9.2 for the way one fifth-grade teacher began.

Janet listed under her "what" column six major categories that she wanted to assess or know about. Overall reading and writing development were the two top categories. Then came the understandings that were promoted by various inquiry projects in which different curricular areas were integrated and emphasized. The fourth category had to do with learning portfolios, and the fifth category with the teacher inquiry she planned to do during the thematic unit. Her last category was "other," a place to include any miscellaneous assessment that didn't really fit well under the other categories.

A grid of possibilities can help organize assessment.

EVALUATION POSSIBILITIES

What do I want to assess?	How am I going to assess?	
	Informal, ongoing assessment	More formal assessment
Reading development overall	(T) Anecdotal notes; (T) Status of Class R. Checks; (S) Daily planning journals; (S) Learning logs; (T) Status of Class project checks	(T) Conferences; (S) Literature response journals; (S) Comparison charts; (S) Various artifacts/extensions
Writing development overall	(T) Anecdotal notes; (T) Status of Class W. Checks; (S) Daily planning journals; (S) Learning logs; (T) Status of Class project checks; (S) writing drafts	(T) Content & editing conferences; (S) Published texts; (S) Various artifacts
Inquiry projects (individual/group)	(T) Anecdotal notes; (S) Daily planning journals; (S) Project proposals; (T) Status of class project checks; (S) Daily project evaluations; (S) Rough drafts on findings	(S) "Published" project findings; (TS) Inquiry project evaluation
Portfolio	(S) Friday portfolio review	(S) Final Portfolio evaluation & summary
My inquiry	My own journal; Student lit. response journals	Analysis of ongoing data and audiotaping of student-led lit. response groups
Other Written comm. w/students Math	(S) Dialogue journals (S) Math talk journals	(S) Excerpts from dialogue journals (S) Math story problems; (S) Math solvers

Figure 9.2

Janet's "how" section was divided into two columns—informal, ongoing assessment and more formal assessment. The "how" section encompassed her "when" considerations, too. Note that the informal, ongoing assessment column usually focused more on process; the more formal assessment column listed many of the "products" that were assessed. She typed this form with these categories ahead of time, but jotted down the details by hand. These handwritten notes provided specifics and changed over the course of a unit (and from unit to unit). Janet often added ideas that emerged as she and her students negotiated how project findings were to be determined. Sometimes she dropped a technique if she thought it was too cumbersome or was not really getting at what she wanted to know.

As you review Figure 9.2, two features are important to note. The first is that much of Janet's assessment "data" overlap. For example, during writing workshop, where student writing was emphasized, students were usually working on texts having to do with their individual and small-group collaborative inquiries, thus their writing during this workshop frequently included a curricular (usually an *integrated* curricular) focus. Another feature to notice is that she tried to note who had the main responsibility—student or teacher—for keeping the records of assessment. This latter feature, of course, not only helped to keep her students intimately involved in self-monitoring and self-evaluating their own learning, but it also helped her realize that she didn't have to, nor could she, collect all the records she wanted or needed for students' evaluation.

Assessment data overlap.

Teachers and students share responsibility for record keeping.

Some other things are useful to take note of in Figure 9.2. Janet took anecdotal records throughout the day on Post-it Notes (see Chapter 8). At the end of each day, she put them on sheets in a loose-leaf binder that had pages for each child. She also used three Status of the Class* versions to keep track of what her students were doing in reading and writing and in their inquiry projects. Janet also had more "formal" Reading and Writing Conferences* with students. The reading conferences included assessing a short sample of students' oral reading and, through discussion with them, noting their comprehension and interpretations. The writing conferences included focused interactions with students regarding content and editing issues. Students kept daily planning journals where they noted what they hoped to work on or accomplish each day. They also used three other journals: Dialogue Journals*, Learning Logs*, and Book Response Journals*. (These were put in one notebook for each thematic unit during the year with a section of the notebook for each journal. Another journal, called math talk journal, was a separate journal as noted below.)

Status of the Class* reports keep track of student projects and progress.

Janet had students develop proposals for their inquiry projects. Figure 9.3 provides an example of the simple form she developed to help students organize their proposals. Their daily evaluations of these projects and Janet's Status of the Class* records helped assess the progress of these research activities, while the final project findings and a separate evaluation by students and Janet represented more formal records.

Students develop inquiry proposals.

Janet also used learning portfolios (to be discussed in more depth below), one for each grading term, generally corresponding to a particular thematic unit. At the end of the unit, students collected their best work and evaluated their learning for that period. Janet had found, however, that this process was too important to wait until the end of the unit, so her students had what they called Friday portfolio folders where they went through their best work for the week to share with their parents over the weekend. These Friday folders provided important ongoing assessment.

Weekly portfolio review provides ongoing assessment.

For each thematic unit, Janet chose an inquiry for herself to conduct. During the term represented in Figure 9.2, she set aside time in the schedule for students to have student-led Literature Response Groups*. She kept her own journal to study how this new addition to her curriculum was working throughout the unit—evaluating problems and successes that might occur, considering how she might need to scaffold or intervene to support groups, reviewing students' Book Response Journals*, and analyzing audiotapes of groups' literature discussions. (See Chapter 4 and "Guidelines for Teacher Inquiry" for more information on teacher research.)

Under "Other" Janet included Dialogue Journals* that students kept and to which Janet responded. The Dialogue Journals* enabled students and teacher to have ongoing conversations about anything in their lives. These were not usually part of evaluation, but sometimes students chose excerpts from them for their learning portfolios, so she kept them in mind for a potential source of assessment. She also added math to the "Other" column. Although she tried to integrate math throughout the curriculum, Janet also had a special time to focus on math understandings. Last term (and unit), she had incorporated a math talk journal, which she studied in her own inquiry, to foster the idea that math is a different way to symbolize meanings—a different "language" or "talk." Thus, ongoing assessment involved students' work in this journal. More formal ways of assessment were the story problems students wrote for

Dialogue Journals* provide ongoing conversation.

MY INQUIRY PROPOSAL

My question for investigation is:

_____

_____

_____

The materials I will need are:

_____

_____

_____

I may need help with:

_____

_____

_____

Plan	Accomplishment	Date

I plan to share my results by: _____

We agree to the above plan: _____

_____   _____
Student signature & date   Teacher signature & date

_____
Parent signature & date

Figure 9.3

homework and "math solvers," which were their weekly "tests" on math. (See Chapter 5 for more details on math.)

As you can see, for performance-based assessment to be manageable in the classroom, teachers like Janet have to make choices. They have to keep in mind *why* they are assessing and constantly check it with the *what, how,* and *when* of assessment. Having an overall plan developed at the beginning of a thematic unit—as Figure 9.2 illustrates—helps teachers realize the possibilities and make decisions that they can deal with in practice.

An overall plan helps teachers make decisions about assessment.

Storing Record-Keeping Data in Assessment

Another integral aspect of managing performance-based assessment is figuring out how to store the records of learning that are created. Because ongoing evaluation is so important, this record-keeping data in the classroom has to be organized so that it can be easily accessible to both students and teacher alike. Thinking ahead about ways to store assessment data in the physical space available in a classroom requires selection and decisionmaking on the part of the teacher. Some ways to do this were mentioned above and throughout the book, but four categories of means of storage are summarized here:

Records have to be organized.

Index Cards, Post-it Notes, Labels

These are usually used to record periodic observational, anecdotal information gathered by teachers. They can be stored in index boxes or folders or attached to pages in the teacher's notebook or journal.

Notebooks

These can be used by both students and teacher alike to keep records. They can serve as various journals. Separate notebooks of different colors can distinguish the different journals that students might keep, or one larger notebook that has several sections, each used for a particular journal, might be used. Binder notebooks are also useful because teachers can easily set up and add pages for individual students. Notebooks can also store a particular unit's or term's records and then be placed in a more permanent folder after the unit is completed. New paper can then be added for the next unit. Students can make their own notebooks, too, by stapling or otherwise attaching some paper together with construction paper of different colors, again to note the types of journals being used (these usually work for one unit because of durability problems). Pocket folders that include paper can also be used as notebooks for journals. Usually, student notebooks or journals are stored in students' desks or cubbies, except when they are placed in a designated place for teacher response.

File Folders

Various folders can be used to store students' ongoing writing drafts, reading logs, and so forth. Teachers can also store their record-keeping data for each child in separate folders; these might serve as the source of the teacher's contributions to ongoing documentation of students' portfolio folders. Many teachers have students keep things they are presently working on in their folders in the desks and finished work in other folders. If finished work is being displayed in the classroom, or is of a size or nature that cannot be put in a folder, students (or teachers) include a short description (or even a photograph) of it as a reminder. Sturdier file folders with expandable bases can keep more permanent work done for a particular thematic unit or grading term.

Bins, Boxes, Etc.

Folders and journals that students use periodically can be placed in colorful bins or decorated boxes. Some schools also have classroom file cabinets or closets in which records, especially the more permanent ones from previous term or unit work, can be stored.

Learning Portfolios

An important part of assessment and evaluation from an integrated language perspective is keeping individual archives, or portfolios, on children. Some schools even keep portfolios of children's work over their years of attendance. Children's abilities and strategies are developed in meaningful, familiar contexts, and their expertise and talents grow gradually and in different patterns. Thus, gathering an extensive collection of their work and other information provides a profile that documents children's learning. The portfolio approach has long been evident in the area of the visual arts and is now suggested for reading and writing. Because reading and writing are integrated across the curriculum from an integrated language perspective, portfolios must be conceived of even more broadly as *learning* portfolios.

Anything can be included in students' learning portfolios: children's notes from their Learning Logs*, anecdotal or target-child observations, snapshots of artifacts children have constructed in the course of thematic units—topographical maps, dioramas, Comparison Charts*, Sketch to Stretch* productions, published texts in various genres, abandoned drafts, Semantic Maps*, MMA summaries (or ATT or CAP assessments), Evaluation Forms from Authors' Folders*, interviews, child-made Jackdaw* materials, graphs, and so on. Most teachers collaborate with children to decide what should be included in the portfolios, choosing what they think is indicative of children's best efforts and asking children to choose the work they feel best represents their work in a thematic unit or what reflects the most difficult tasks they accomplished, or something that they may not be satisfied with, along with comments about why they think so. Teachers respect their choices but also suggest other possibilities they think might be indicative of children's best efforts. Although it is important for teachers to find

See Tierney, Carter, & Desai (1991) and Valencia (1998) for more detailed discussions of literacy portfolios.

See Cohen (1969); Cole & Scribner (1974); Dyson (1987); Heath (1983); Heller, Holzman, & Messick (1982); and Jervis (1996) for discussion of children's various "ways with words" and working styles as they relate to assessment and evaluation.

Gitomer (1988); Wexler-Sherman, Gardner, & Feldman (1988)

Planning portfolios can be a collaborative effort between teacher and student.

ways to contribute and have a role in students' portfolios, it is critical to keep most of the control and ownership of them in the hands of the students.

It is critical to start the portfolio system in the beginning of the school year so that students will realize that there is a *process* to evaluation and take an active role in their own learning and evaluation. Giving students an overview of the system facilitates their control, organization, and responsibility in evaluation. This overview, perhaps in terms of a Focus-Lesson*, should cover (1.) the purpose of portfolios, (2.) where work will be kept, (3.) who determines the content in portfolios, (4.) any records related to the content in the portfolios that the students are going to be responsible for, and (5) the evaluation of the portfolios (e.g., how they will be used for grading).

Make sure students understand the portfolio system.

As Janet's evaluation system illustrated, many teachers do not wait until the end of a term or unit, but make portfolio assessment an ongoing process. Friday is a good day for student self-evaluation for several reasons: A week is a nice period for students to focus on in reflecting on what they have learned; it gives students a good opportunity to consider and plan what they might need to work on and try to accomplish in the week or weeks ahead; and it provides the weekend for students to share their work with parents or caregivers so that these important persons can have input on what should be included in students' portfolios.

Because self-evaluation is an essential ingredient in learning portfolios, why a student has chosen certain items in his or her portfolio is a critical facet of the process. Many teachers have students attach a short sheet of paper or index card to each item, on which students provide self-evaluation comments—why they chose it and what and how it documents what they have learned. Initially providing students with a list of possible "starters" helps them consider a range of reasons for including items in their portfolios—that an item is "something I am proud of because . . .," "an example of my best because . . .," "important to me because . . .," or "my first time doing this."

Besides these rationales, a summary sheet for the portfolio is usually also included. Figure 9.4 shows the items on such a summary form. (Note that this form would be much larger than depicted here so students would have more room to write.)

Students list all of the items in their portfolios and then list the major things they have felt they have learned in various curricular areas. At the end, students are asked what has emerged as important things to pursue as a result of their learning in the thematic unit. This information can be valuable for parents in supporting students' learning at home, and it provides teachers with good ideas for planning the next thematic unit.

Some teachers do not use a summary sheet but have children do their own summaries by creating a booklet describing the content of their portfolios and what they have learned during the course of the thematic unit.

Conclusions

Evaluation should interrelate process and content.

Practice produces higher quality self-analysis by students.

Assessment and evaluation must be consistent with principles of the integrated language perspective. Evaluation should interrelate process and content. It should also focus not on children's weaknesses but on those features of their behavior that demonstrate understanding and progress. Children are given many opportunities to monitor their own work, to revise and to evaluate it, and work with the teacher and peers to steadily improve it. Children review their work with a partner or the children, and questions are raised about it before a grade is attached. With practice, the children learn to be more self-analytical about the quality of their work. Because it is the children who have to do the learning, it makes sense first to teach them to be self-evaluative, and then to evaluate their progress toward that goal. Thus, evaluation should provide insights into children's evolving personal restructuring of knowledge—what they know, how they have come to know it, and what significance it has for them as members of the classroom community and the broader culture outside the classroom.

Teachers become researchers when they document children's progress.

This view of evaluation puts the teacher in a different role. Teachers are researchers in that they conduct their own inquiries about the language and learning constructed

```
┌─────────────────────────────────────────────────────────────────┐
│ PORTFOLIO SUMMARY FOR _____  Date _____      │
│ THEMATIC UNIT_____                            │
│ List and number the items you are including in your learning portfolio. │
│ (Be sure that you include your index card describing why you chose each item.) │
│                                                                   │
│                                                                   │
│ What are the major things you had hoped you would learn during the thematic unit? │
│                                                                   │
│ What are some of the major things you did learn? Which item or items in the portfolio │
│ show or reflect what you have learned:                            │
│                                                                   │
│     In reading?                                                   │
│                                                                   │
│     In writing?                                                   │
│                                                                   │
│     In math?                                                      │
│                                                                   │
│     In social studies?                                            │
│                                                                   │
│     In science?                                                   │
│                                                                   │
│     In art, music, or drama?                                      │
│                                                                   │
│ What would you like to find out about and learn as a result of what you learned in │
│ this thematic unit?                                               │
│                                                                   │
└─────────────────────────────────────────────────────────────────┘
```

Figure 9.4

by children in their classrooms. They are also reflective and self-analytical in that they document their own classroom practices and examine and reexamine their results and influences on children's learning. Thus, teachers are in a better position to document and interpret a wide range of student performance, and can therefore provide a more accurate picture of children's learning and achievement than so-called objective tests or other instruments that attempt to assess children's understandings in "decontextualized" situations. (See "Guidelines for Teacher Inquiry" at the end of this book for more information on teacher research.)

See Johnston (1987a, 1987b) and Moffett (1985) for more arguments for teachers as evaluators, and Cochran-Smith & Lytle (1993) and Goswami & Stillman (1987) regarding information on teachers as researchers.

REFERENCES

Au, K. H., Scheu, J. A., Kawakami, A. J., & Herman, P. A. (1990). Assessment and accountability in a whole literacy curriculum. *The Reading Teacher, 43,* 574–575.

Bussis, A. M., & Chittenden, E. A. (1987). Research currents: What the reading tests neglect. *Language Arts, 64,* 302–308.

Cochran-Smith, M., & Lytle, S. L. (1993). *Inside/Outside: Teacher research and knowledge.* New York: Teachers College Press.

Cohen, R. (1969). Conceptual styles, culture conflict, and non-verbal tests of intelligence. *American Anthropologist, 71,* 828–857.

Cole, M., & Schribner, S. (1974). *Culture and thought: A psychological introduction.* New York: Wiley.

Daly, E. (Ed). (1989). Monitoring children's language development: *Holistic assessment in the classroom.* Portsmouth, NH: Heinemann.

Darling-Hammond, L., & Falk, B. (1997). Using standards and assessments to support student learning. *Phi Delta Kappan, 79,* 190–199.

Dyson, A. H. (1987). Individual differences in beginning composing. *Written Communication, 4,* 411–342.

Ellis, A. (1997). *Teaching and learning elementary social studies.* Boston: Allyn & Bacon.

Flood, J., & Lapp, D. (1989). Reporting reading progress: A comparison portfolio for parents. *The Reading Teacher, 43,* 508–514.

Fredericks, A. D., & Rasinski, T. V. (1990). Involving parents in the assessment process. *The Reading Teacher, 44,* 346–349.

Gitomer, D. H. (1988, April). *Assessing artistic learning using domain projects.* Paper presented at the annual meeting of the American Educational Research Association, New Orleans, LA.

Goodman, K., Goodman, Y., & Hood, W. J. (Eds.). (1989). *The whole language evaluation book.* Portsmouth, NH: Heinemann.

Goodman, Y. (1989). Evaluation of students. In K. Goodman, Y. Goodman, & W. J. Hood (Eds.), *The whole language evaluation book* (pp. 3–14). Portsmouth, NH: Heinemann.

Goswami, D., & Stillman, P. R. (1987). *Reclaiming the classroom: Teacher research as an agency for change.* Portsmouth, NH: Boynton/Cook.

Graves, D. (1983). *Writing: Teachers and children at work.* Exeter, NH: Heinemann.

Harp, B. (1994). Principles of assessment and evaluation in whole language classrooms. In B. Harp (Ed.), *Assessment and evaluation in whole language programs* (pp. 37–52). Norwood, MA: Christopher-Gordon.

Hart, D. (1994). *Authentic assessment: A handbook for educators.* New York: Addison-Wesley.

Heath, S. B. (1983). *Ways with words: Language, life and work in communities and classrooms.* Cambridge: Cambridge University Press.

Hiebert, E. H., & Hutchinson, T. A. (1991). Research directions: The current state of alternative assessments for policy and instructional uses. *Language Arts, 68,* 662–668.

Heller, K. A., Holzman, W. H., & Messick, S. (1982). *Placing children in special education: A strategy for equity.* Washington, DC: National Academy Press.

Hull, O. (1988). Evaluation: The conventions of writing. In K. Goodman, Y. Goodman, & W. J. Hood (Eds.), *The whole language evaluation book* (pp. 77–83). Portsmouth, NH: Heinemann.

Hyde, A., & Bizar, M. (1989). *Thinking in context: Teaching cognitive processes across the elementary school curriculum.* White Plains, NY: Longman.

Jervis, K. (1996). *Eyes on the child: Three portfolio stories.* New York: Teachers College Press.

Johnston, P. (1987a). Teachers as evaluation experts. *The Reading Teacher, 40,* 744–748.

Johnston, P. (1987b). Assessing the process, and the process of assessment, in the language arts. In J. R. Squire (Ed.), *The dynamics of language learning: Research in reading and English* (pp. 335–357). Urbana, IL: ERIC Clearinghouse on Reading and Communication Skills.

Johnston, P. (1997). *Knowing literacy: Constructive literacy assessment.* York, ME: Stenhouse.

King, D. (1991). *Literacy assessment in practice.* South Australia: Education Department of South Australia.

King, D. (1994). Assessment and evaluation in bilingual and multicultural classrooms. In B. Harp (Ed.), *Assessment and evaluation in whole language programs* (pp. 37–52). Norwood, MA: Christopher-Gordon.

Kresse, F. H. (1979). *The Indians who met the Pilgrims, A MATCH unit. Materials and activities for teachers and children.* Boston: American Science and Engineering.

Lenski, S. D., Riss, M., & Flickinger, G. (1996). Honoring student self-evaluation in the classroom community. *Primary Voices, K–6, 4 (2),* 24–32.

Levstik, L. S., & Barton, K. C. (1997). *Doing history: Investigating with children in elementary and middle schools.* Mahwah, NJ: Erlbaum.

Maxim, G. W. (1987). *Social studies and the elementary school child.* Columbus, OH: Merrill.

Moffett, J. (1985). Hidden impediments to improving English teaching. *Phi Delta Kappan, 67,* 50–56.

Paulson, F. L., Paulson, P. R., & Meyer, C. A. (1991). What makes a portfolio a portfolio? *Educational Leadership, 48,* 60–63.

Reardon, S. J. (1994). A collage of assessment and evaluation from primary classrooms. In B. Harp (Ed.), *Assessment and evaluation in whole language programs* (pp. 37–52). Norwood, MA: Christopher-Gordon.

Routman, R. (1991). *Invitations: Changing as teachers and learners, K–12.* Portsmouth, NH: Heinemann.

Salinger, T., & Chittenden, E. Focus on research: Analysis of an early literacy portfolio: Consequences for instruction. *The Reading Teacher. 71,* 446–452.

Teale, W. H., Hiebert, E. H., & Chittenden, E. A. (1987). Assessing young children's literary development. *The Reading Teacher, 40,* 772–777.

Shepherd, L. A. (1991). Negative policies for dealing with diversity: When does assessment and diagnosis turn into sorting and segregation? In E. H. Hiebert (Ed.), *Literacy for a diverse society: Perspectives, practices, and policies* (pp. 279–298). New York: Teachers College Press.

Tierney, R. J., Carter, M. A., & Desai, L. E. (1991). *Portfolio assessment in the reading-writing classroom.* Norwood, MA: Christopher-Gordon.

Thornton, S. J., & Vukelich, R. (1988). Effects of children's understanding of time concepts on historical understanding. *Theory and Research in Social Education, 15,* 69–82.

Turnbill, J. (1989). Evaluation in a whole language classroom: The what, the why, the how, the when. In E. Daly (Ed.), *Monitoring children's language development: Holistic assessment in the classroom* (pp. 17–21). Portsmouth, NH: Heinemann.

Valencia, S. W. (1998). *Literacy portfolios in action.* Fort Worth, TX: Harcourt Brace.

Valencia, S., Hiebert, E., & Afflerbach, P. (1993). *Authentic reading assessment: Practices and possibilities.* Newark, DE: International Reading Association.

Wassermann, S., & Ivany, J. W. G. (1988). *Teaching elementary science: Who's afraid of spiders?* New York: Harper & Row.

Wexler-Sherman, C., Gardner, H., & Feldman, D. H. (1988). A pluralistic view of early assessment: The project spectrum approach. *Theory Into Practice, 27,* 77–83.

Wiggins, G. (1989). A true test: Toward authentic and equitable forms of assessment. *Phi Delta Kappan, 70,* 703–713.

Wolf, D. P. (1988). Opening up assessment. *Educational leadership, 45 (4),* 24–29.

Zach, K. (1990). *Classroom exercises to prepare for seeing Japan.* Lexington: University of Kentucky Art Museum.

CHILDREN'S LITERATURE

Dakota Dugout by A. Turner. Illustrated by R. Himler. Houghton Mifflin, 1986.

Developing an Antiracist, Multicultural Community

> We discover how we fit together . . . my piece of the puzzle is not like anyone else's . . . my face holds the history of my people and the feelings of my heart.
>
> *Teaching Tolerance*, Fall 1993, p. 1

An integrated language perspective classroom is grounded in the development of a learning community that is fundamentally democratic and inclusive. The learning community is consciously antiracist, drawing all students into full citizenship in the classroom and a multiracial/multicultural democracy and interdependent world. Multicultural and cross-cultural education must be at the heart of an integrated language curriculum, not just a marginal note slipped in during holidays or Black History Month. Culturally relevent teaching is a day-by-day enterprise. This means, as one teacher noted, having "antennas out" as you work with children, select resources and activities, put up displays, and so forth. As you think about the ways in which differences and commonalties are represented in your classroom and plan for an inclusive, integrated curriculum, consider the following:

The learning community is inclusive.

Multicultural learning is central, not marginal.

Bernard (1993); Ladson-Billings (1994); Mizell, Bennet, Bowman, & Morin (1993); Perry & Fraser (1993)

Does the classroom reflect sensitivity to and celebration of the cultural diversity of the students? Of the broader communities to which they belong? This means paying attention to the images displayed in your classroom—on the walls, in literature, in films and videos, as well as in the guests who work with your students. Images that affirm the cultures of diverse students can help build an antiracist community. (See the JOURNEYS and ROOTS prototypes in Chapter 4).

Richards (1993)

Celebrate and affirm cultural diversity.

Modify the structure of learning activities. There is evidence that different cultural environments encourage different patterns and preferred styles of learning. Varying the types of activities (e.g., incorporating activities that involve movement and multisensory stimulation) can help to keep children engaged. As you read through the prototypes in Chapter 4, you can see that teachers are "choreographing" their days so that task structures are varied and concepts are presented in multiple ways.

Gay (1991); Cohen, et al. (1994)

Vary structures of activities.

Organize heterogeneous cooperative groups that require multiple abilities. A variety of abilities are required in daily life, and should be required in the classroom. Group tasks should be *explicitly* organized so that students know that while no one person has all the abilities necessary for success, collectively they do. For instance, a teacher may explain that an upcoming task will require figuring out how something works, drawing a diagram, and constructing a new use for the system under investigation.

Cohen (1994); Cohen, et al. (1994)

Group tasks should involve multiple abilities.

Assign competence to all students. Too often race, class, gender, or ethnicity are related to status hierarchies in the classroom. Children's ideas of who is competent or incompetent can be difficult to dislodge. As a result, teachers must work to change those expectations by assigning competence *publicly*. This

Cohen (1994); Cohen, et al. (1994)

All students need to be seen as competent; teachers must publicly assign competence to low-status children.

means that the teacher specifies what a child does well that is relevant to a task at hand. This works best when used in conjunction with multiple ability tasks where a group *needs* particular skills and abilities. Thus a teacher may call attention to a child's ability to organize information in visual forms, or to analyze problems logically. This assignment of competence is reinforced as students demonstrate their skills and abilities in the context of group work.

Provide a wide variety of cultural examples and situations to illustrate major concepts and inquiries. These connect children to the topic of study and help provide models of real-world possibilities. Such examples should be carefully selected to avoid stereotyping. They should be comparable to examples taken from the "macroculture."

Provide many different cultural examples.

Gay (1991)

Build core values.

In the end, however, one of the most crucial aspects of developing a multicultural, antiracist classroom is developing a core of shared values and social relationships. These values include peaceful conflict resolution, respect for individual differences, and a concern for social justice. They are built into everything we do in the classroom, from content to process, from classroom discourse to playground games. Whether we are intentional or accidental in our attention to diversity, we nonetheless build an environment that speaks to children of their place in the classroom and the world. A basic step in developing an integrated language classroom is to become intentional in our efforts to honor diversity rather than perpetuate inequities. Particularly in the current political climate, teachers must think carefully about how they will organize and explain the kind of instruction that supports the development of antiracist and multicultural school communities.

Organize for Cooperative Learning

Implementing change

Cohen (1994); Sharan & Sharan (1992)

One of the characteristics of an integrated perspective, and of a more inclusive curriculum, is cooperative learning. This is so for several important reasons. As we explained earlier, one of the goals of an integrated perspective is the development of individuals who can live together in a democratic, multicultural, and nonracist manner. Cooperative learning *can* teach children important skills for living and working in such a manner. When organized in specific ways, cooperative learning increases student interest and engagement; students may also have greater opportunities for understanding than in more traditional, whole-class organizations. In addition, reflective, disciplined inquiry relies on group investigation to (1.) maximize student participation in identifying and investigating the kinds of questions discussed in earlier chapters, (2.) provide opportunities for extensive interaction and collaboration among group members, (3.) provide opportunities for the use of multiple abilities, and (4.) assign competence to all. Finally, cooperative learning is an authentic and important way of developing understanding in settings outside of schools. Cooperation is often necessary in order to bring different skills and abilities to bear in solving problems. Yet all of us have observed groups in which participation in and influence on tasks were unequal. Rather than reduce status hierarchies, these groups reinforce them. In order to transform *group work* into *cooperative learning* teachers must become *educational engineers*, applying the theories and principles we have talked about throughout this book to the crucial task of organizing for cooperative learning.

Cohen (1994); Cohen et al. (1994); Schaps & Solomon (1991); Sharan & Sharan (1992)

Cohen (1994)

Status Inequities

Status perceptions affect cooperative work.

We already mentioned that race, class, gender, and ethnicity are often related to status hierarchies—social rankings within a group. In addition, status may be related to perceived abilities—in reading, athletics, or music, for instance. These perceptions of unequal status affect cooperative work, just as they affect many other areas of children's lives because they influence teachers' and other students' expectations of competence. Altering status inequities is not easy but it *is* essential if all students are to benefit from cooperative learning. Reorienting children begins with attention to creating multiple ability tasks for heterogeneous groups and assigning competence to all (particularly low-status) students.

Begin by thinking about which of the essential questions in a theme best lend themselves to group rather than individual investigation. Consider whether a task:

Multiple abilities task
characteristics

Cohen (1994, p. 68)

- Has more than one answer or more than one way to solve a problem
- Is intrinsically interesting and rewarding
- Allows different students to make different contributions
- Uses multimedia
- Involves sight, sound, and touch
- Requires a variety of skills and behaviors
- Requires reading and writing
- Is challenging

Organize cooperative groups for maximum interaction. In a group of four or five it is most likely that all students will have an opportunity to interact; larger groups tend to discourage full participation while groups of three tend to pair off and leave one isolate. While there may be occasions when students select their own groups, overall this tends to reinforce rather than reduce status hierarchies. Instead, compose groups so that they are mixed in terms of status hierarchies (i.e. academic achievement, gender, race). Sometimes teachers organize these groups; other times students list several options and the teacher composes the groups to reflect these interests.

Radenich & McKay (1995); Sharan & Sharan (1992); Slavin (1995)

Delegate authority. Cooperative learning necessitates the redistribution of power and authority in a learning community. The teacher cannot be the sole arbiter and authority in the classroom when children are working at multiple tasks. Instead, children develop a set of *cooperative norms* with *procedural roles* for their group work. Basic cooperative norms include: "You have the right to ask anyone else in your group for assistance," and "You have the duty to assist anyone in your group who asks for help." Some teachers develop charts that present these norms with descriptions of "What it looks like" in practice, so that children have reminders in view during work times. These teachers also use some of the kid-watching procedures described earlier to monitor group behavior. In this way they can provide specific feedback, either to individuals or groups about the way they are working.

Cohen (1994)

Establish cooperative norms and procedural roles for group investigations.

Procedural roles—facilitator, recorder/reporter, materials manager—transfer authority to students. Instead of waiting for rescue by their teacher, students must manage their own work. The teacher intervenes when either the system has broken down, or students have exhausted other options. Specific procedural roles depend on the age and experience of the children involved, as well as on the nature of the task. Generally, however, groups need a facilitator whose task is to see that all group members get the help they need. It is important to note here that procedural roles do not mean that a task is divided among group members; rather, individuals must discuss their work with the group. Thus, the facilitator might ask the group to provide specific help to a member, or remind the group that certain tasks remain to be completed. The materials manager is not responsible for all the materials; rather, he or she is responsible for helping the group deal with materials responsibly. It is equally important to rotate procedural roles. As children practice different roles they grow in competence and confidence, and are perceived differently by their peers.

Procedural roles depend on age, experience, and the nature of the task.

Task descriptions are also an important feature of delegating authority. Traveling from group to group explaining tasks is not an efficient or effective use of teacher time. Instead, teachers in integrated language classrooms rely on written (sometimes with diagrams or visuals) or taped instructions and individual and group reports. Chapters 4, 5, 7, and 9 include examples of different types of reports. Often these tasks are developed in cooperation with students. At least initially, teachers usually need to help students design tasks that require multiple abilities.

Make a low-status student the group expert. As we mentioned earlier, one way to change status hierarchies is to assign competence to low-status students. Generally this

Cohen (1994)

means careful observation so that the teacher can take advantage of a student's display of competence and make it public. This can happen within the context of group work—the teacher notes that a student has a good idea but is not getting a hearing. The teacher steps into the group, calls attention to the idea, and then departs. Or it can happen as part of the debriefing when the teacher calls attention to the contributions of specific individuals in the class. It is important that these contributions be real, rather than contrived (i.e. "Jean does such *neat* work"), and that they are relevant to the work of the group. Sometimes it is difficult to capture such moments spontaneously. As a result, some teachers purposively arrange for a low-status student to develop expertise that will be needed by a group. One sixth-grade teacher, for instance, regularly asks students to become "class experts." Because she plans individual as well as group work times, children have time to develop their expertise. While all students are expected to become expert at something related to an ongoing theme, she is especially careful to give low-status students tasks where their expertise will be necessary to future group work. She asked one student, for instance, to become an expert on Golda Meir because the class was about to start a project on the Middle East. She asked another student if he would become "expert" on Middle Eastern architecture, and a third to work on music. In each case she provided appropriate materials and directions so that the children would be successful. Later, as cooperative groups developed, these students could make major contributions. In fact, their expertise was often solicited by other groups, as well. To facilitate this type of interaction, the teacher kept a chart of "class experts." Some students who had some facility with relevant languages (German, Arabic, Hebrew) were listed, along with children who had topical expertise (on different forms of Islam and Judaism, for instance), or specific technical skills (making maps to scale, using photoshop on the computer, editing for punctuation). Group facilitators were reminded to use the expert list when their group needed help. Remember that this technique only works if the students truly develop competence. Simply suggesting that a child become expert is not enough, especially when that child may not feel confident of his or her abilities, or when other children perceive him or her as incompetent. Instead, the teacher must support the development of expertise through the wise allocation of time, resources, and attention. It is the teacher's obligation to provide opportunities to develop expertise, and then to call that expertise to the attention of the class in ways that support its use in group interactions.

Redesigning the Physical Environment

Room arrangement signals teacher intention and expectations regarding the flow of talk and activity in the classroom. Straight rows facing the front of the room make cooperative student efforts more difficult and encourage children to direct activity toward the teacher rather than toward their peers. The teacher easily slips into the position of dispenser of information and sole arbiter of talk, and the traditional IRE-like classroom discourse pattern prevails. (See Chapter 2 for more on this type of classroom discourse.) Here a transmission-oriented model of education gets reinforced rather than a collaborative one. Think instead about some ways in which physical changes in the classroom environment foster peer interactions.

Exchange desks for tables, or rearrange desks into table groupings. This organizes children for group work by shifting their focus toward sharing materials, spreading out projects, and cooperating with peers. Children need not be assigned a particular seat; rather, shifting groups and activities dictates seating.

Arrange for personal space. Teachers often make "cubbies" for children's personal supplies and books by covering ice cream drums with contact paper and labeling each container with a child's name. This allows each child to have a place in the classroom that no one else may use, and it decreases problems with territoriality when seating patterns change. A child whose supplies are kept in

Brandt (1991); Pierce & Gilles (1993)

Teachers provide opportunities for children to develop expertise.

Goodman (1986); Routman (1988)

Cazden (1988); Wells & Chang-Wells (1992); Young (1992)

a desk that also doubles as part of a group work table may become upset when someone else handles his or her materials. If supplies are kept in a personal cubbie away from the work area, such upsets are less likely to occur.

If keeping individual desks seems necessary, use tables or some desks as centers where children can work on projects. This also refocuses attention toward peer interactions.

Establish a gathering or sharing area. As children become engaged in interesting and meaningful activities, they need to have a gathering place in the classroom separate from their work areas. A gathering place helps reorient children when the teacher needs to focus the attention of the whole class on a single event or activity. Children may gather to hear literature, talk over matters of group concern, observe a demonstration in science, or share the results of a group project in social studies. Some teachers set off an area with a rug and cushions on the floor. Others use a bookcase to separate this area from other work spaces. One teacher simply marks off a semicircle with masking tape, and her kindergartners bring "sit-upons" when they gather in this area.

Get rid of teacher-made and commercial room decorations. Let the classroom reflect children's work.

Display children's work aesthetically. When children see all the varieties of their work respected and beautifully displayed, they tend to treat their work as being worthy of respect. Simply trimming and mounting poems, pictures, and other work and inviting children to write captions can make very pleasing displays. Displays of student work also broaden the audience with whom children share their work.

Confront the Basics

One of the basic transitions from traditional to integrated language classrooms is rethinking the way in which reading, writing, and language learning occurs. Teachers must rethink the way in which basals, workbooks, and tests are used. If basal programs have been the focus of the reading program, there are several ways to move children toward more integrated approaches to reading.

Goodman (1986); Routman (1991)

Reorganize the way in which time is allocated in the reading program. Spend time each day sharing literature with students and letting children read material of their own choice (SSR*). The element of choice is crucial in developing lifelong readers. It is also important that children have the opportunity to read many books at a comfortable level so that they begin to perceive themselves as successful readers. Moving away from basals means moving away from the feeling that it is always "better" to read "harder" books. Most people read for a variety of purposes, rarely because they want to prove to someone else that they are "good" readers. Providing both choice and guidance is characteristic of integrated language classrooms.

Martinez & Teale (1989)

Choice and guidance are crucial features of an integrated setting.

Think of the basal as an anthology, not as a reading program, and use it accordingly. Carefully review the literature in the basal. Select texts that are good literature in their own right rather than adapted or abridged versions of stories that are much better in their original form. Try forming critique groups to read and discuss these selections, and talk about these texts in the ways suggested elsewhere in this book. Use Reader's Theater* instead of round-robin reading. Let the basal become one of many sources of literature, and provide opportunities for the same kinds of extensions suggested for use with trade books. If some of the basal selections are not good literature, label them as such and work with the children to rewrite a passage to make a story more interesting. Try Group-Composed Writing* to improve such selections. This activity not only encourages careful reading by children but also acknowledges their right to read good literature and make quality judgments on what they read.

Critique groups foster good book talk.

Chambers (1985)

See Harris (1992) and Huck, Hepler, Hickman, & Kiefer (1997) for excellent sources for multicultural literature.

Eeds & Wells (1989)

Organize Reading Buddies* and Literature Response Groups*.

Goodman (1986)

Apply reading skills in context.

Goodman (1986); Routman (1991)

Graves (1983)

Apply writing skills in context, too.

Atwell (1987, 1989); Calkins (1994)

Eliminate ability groups. Set up Buddy Reading*, pairing weaker readers with stronger ones, or older readers with younger ones. Look through the teacher's guide for additional reading selections, and collect other books that expand and complement the basal selection. Buddies can then read and discuss worthwhile basal stories while also sharing a variety of other literature. Including a range of multicultural literature is especially critical. Search out trade books or stories to contrast with, or complement, a basal selection. After children have read the basal story, organize Literature Response Circles* to read and discuss related literature. Select students or let them self-select so that a lively discussion will ensue. A sixth-grade class reading a basal selection on Jason and the Argonauts divided into groups that included analysis and comparison of other versions of the legend, a film of an excavation in Greece that appeared to confirm the historicity of another Greek legend that students then read, and a study of books of Greek mythology to learn more about some of the mythological characters Jason encountered.

Stop assigning workbook pages. Have children work on Book Extensions*, including the creation of Semantic Maps* and Sketch to Stretch* activities. Literature Response Circles* can work on extensions that can be shared to provide a backdrop for discussions of language use or literary interpretation. Recall, for example, the children involved in activities with Big Books* or CLOZE* activities described in Chapter 7. The children were applying skills listed in the scope and sequence of any basal program, but they were applying them in context rather than in isolation. They were using background knowledge, conventions of print, letter, and sound relationships, word endings, letter clusters, sight vocabulary, and both meaning and graphic cues. They were also searching for meaning, confirming predictions, and self-correcting. In another instance, children working on a Comparison Chart* of Asian folktales compared stories, read for details, made inferences, sequenced events, identified cause and effect, and analyzed story structure.

Generate thematic units from good basal passages. Most basal series include stories with particular themes (e.g., growing up, friendship, or mythology). Review the basal series to see how units may develop from the passages in the readers and incorporate books and activities from other content areas as you would in any thematic unit. Linking topics across the curriculum at this point may simply mean covering the units in content area texts out of the usual order.

Reduce the amount of time children spend in basal readers, and increase the time spent reading literature of their choice as well as literature related to theme studies. Confine work in the basals to one day, and use the rest of the week for integrated language work. If the school system requires that children complete the basal, send it home to be read and discussed with parents, or encourage its use as independent reading. During the time formerly allocated for reading groups, hold individual conferences and sit in on Literature Response Groups*.

Increase children's opportunities to write connected discourse. Instead of filling in the blanks in workbooks, have children write in Journals*, Learning Logs*, and the like.

Have children write on topics they have chosen, instead of those you have assigned so that they begin to see themselves as authors. Providing them with ways to share their writing with others in peer conferences and in the Author's Chair* gives them real audiences for their writing.

Try teaching writing skills in the context of children's writing rather than through separate, isolated grammar, spelling, or punctuation lessons and worksheets. Short Focus Lessons* and individual conferences with children are more meaningful ways for teachers to address writing issues and concerns. Children usually internalize and remember these written language conventions more readily when they are part of their ongoing written communication experiences.

Make reading and writing integral components of Student-Initiated Inquiries*. When children work on such activities, they have real reasons to read, and they have more to share both orally and in writing. In the No More Litter example in Chapter 5, many of the children in the second-grade class had already experienced school failures. Several were identified as having reading problems, some were receiving special education services, and a few had been detained several times in their short school careers. Most were reluctant readers and writers, yet they were excited about the prospect of working on a real problem in their community and were soon reading and writing extensively.

Wells & Chang-Wells (1992)

Set aside time when children share their work with one another—both work in progress and completed work.

Display children's original work rather than completed workbook pages, ditto sheets, or "100%" papers.

Send samples of work home so that parents have a sense of what their children are involved in learning.

Moulin (1988); Tierney, Carter, & Desai (1991)

Look to the Content Areas

The transition to an integrated language classroom is made across the curriculum, not only in the areas of reading and language arts. In traditional curriculums, reading, language arts, and mathematics have had the lion's share of the elementary day. Social studies and science have had little or no instruction, being generally relegated to the end of the day or interrupted and dismissed for assemblies, announcements, and so forth. While this is nothing to celebrate, it does mean that you are probably freer to experiment and take risks in these two areas than in any other part of the curriculum. The content in these areas also lends itself especially well to the development of thematic units, and most educators are more familiar with them, so they are a good place to begin making the transition to thematic units.

Goodlad (1984); Stodolsky (1988)

Gamberg, Kwak, Hutchings, & Altheim (1988); Wells & Chang-Wells (1992)

Content areas provide in-depth study and natural language use.

Begin with a mini-unit. (A mini-unit covers material in at least two content areas and can be extended through a wide variety of literature.) Perhaps the science text has a unit on the water cycle. A mini-unit on water could begin with science concepts, including information about areas of the world and how they are affected by rainfall patterns or water sources, then expand to include other cycles in nature.

Content textbooks can give you ideas for units.

Review your district's curriculum objectives in the content areas for potential themes. One sixth-grade teacher, who had initially thought he would try a mini-unit, ended up planning a much larger thematic unit when he realized how easily many of the district's objectives had to do with CHANGES. Several of the objectives in science (e.g., compare the interrelationships between living organisms and their adaptations to an environment; state basic properties of solids, liquids, and gases; describe the process of inheritance and transmission of physical traits from generation to generation; interpret physiological activities that help organisms to survive) and in social studies (e.g., describe how civilizations develop technology to meet their needs; outline the social, economic, and governmental conditions that lead to various political revolutions; trace the changing role of communism in the twentieth century) could be turned into interesting, worthwhile subthemes. Moreover, he was able to include related topics that were part of the CHANGES motif by having his predominantly Mexican-American students document and study their own family and community changes in both Mexico and the United States as well as the kinds of biological, social, and emotional changes they were going through as part of adolescence. He was also able to track down wonderful children's literature from a range of genres to support students' various inquiries.

District objectives also can be a useful source for units.

Learn how to present integrated activities to show how they meet state and local standards.

Plan activities to fit the structure or time constraints required by your school or system. In most cases, this is simply a matter of presenting integrated activities in a more linear fashion and knowing that although the state may have minimum time requirements for language arts or social studies, you will be teaching some language arts during the period set aside for social studies and some social studies during language arts time. One school calls this approach to the development of an integrated language curriculum "toe dipping" and has found it useful in introducing teachers to new ways of organizing instruction.

Organize the second half of the day—generally, the social studies and science portion of the curriculum—into long-term thematic units. Using some of the suggestions in this book, select topics that will have sustaining power for a four- to six-week period (or longer), and that integrate social studies and science. Although portions of this theme may be integrated into other parts of the day, afternoons can be devoted to the kind of thematic study characteristic of an integrated perspective. As teachers gain confidence in children's ability to work this way, and as they recognize that real learning is occurring, they broaden the type of inquiries children engage in. They begin to look for places where curricular areas overlap. If the third-grade science curriculum calls for a study of living systems and the social studies curriculum includes a unit on communities, why not combine these topics into a thematic unit? Set aside time in the afternoon for theme studies and make both science and social studies textbooks available, along with many trade books for student study.

Textbooks are one of many resources available to children.

Use textbooks as one of many sources in your room. Sometimes, teachers assume that an integrated language classroom does not use textbooks. Textbooks are often used, not as the class authority and arbiter of scope and sequence but as resources in the same way that trade books are used. This is particularly true as teachers make the transition from textbook-based to integrated language classrooms. One of the toe-dipping teachers began a thematic unit by using two conflicting textbook descriptions of the settlement of Jamestown and the role of Pocahontas. Which did students think might be correct? How could they check to find out? Soon students were checking a variety of other sources, including Fritz's biography of Pocahontas, high-school and college textbooks, material from Jamestown Historic Park, and a local historian. Their final assignment was to rewrite their textbook description of Pocahontas and the settlement of Jamestown. The students were engaged in an interesting inquiry into a historical topic and a careful, critical reading of their textbook. Although they did not integrate many other aspects of the curriculum into their inquiry, they did use a variety of language, from discussion to oral reports and debates, and from taking notes to organizing those notes into a written form. The assignment did not require reorganizing the entire class or the curriculum, but it did allow the teacher to test the waters and see what happened when children worked in an atmosphere of independent and small-group inquiry. It also allowed the children to see the textbook as one of many available sources rather than the single most important authority on a subject. This may seem a slight shift, but it is profoundly important in helping children become more independent thinkers.

Fritz (1983)

Shifts toward independent thinking are crucial.

Implement and Share Your Own Teacher Research

Cochran-Smith (1991)

Wells (1994); Wells & Chang-Wells (1992); Young (1992)

Collaborative teaching where power is shared with students is hard work—it is action research for social change.

Taking new steps toward an integrated language perspective frequently involves "learning to teach against the grain." It isn't just trying out new methods but taking to heart (and mind) the principles about learners, language, and knowledge upon which the perspective rests. Transmission-oriented teaching has deep roots, so it is likely that most of your educational experiences have been of that kind. Consequently, changing to a more collaborative approach that has teachers sharing power with their students is not easily pulled off. Reflective inquiry initiated and directed by students requires that teachers also have a reflective stance to their own teaching. Thus, teacher research—the systematic, intentional inquiry by teachers about their own school and classroom work—is a critical facet of the integrated language approach.

So far in this chapter (as well as throughout the whole book), we have covered many ideas or areas in which to toe-dip, or start to change your curriculum and teaching practices toward an integrated language perspective. These suggestions or possibilities can serve as initial topics for your own teacher research. Although most teaching could be seen as some kind of implicit inquiry, the notion of teacher research emphasizes explicitness and deliberateness of intention to study some aspect of teaching and learning. See "Guidelines for Teacher Inquiry" at the end of the book for tips to use for launching teacher inquiries.

Teaching can be a very lonely activity, especially if one is swimming against the mainstream. Therefore, it helps to build understanding among peers. One way to accomplish this is to share students' work with the rest of the school. Hang displays in the hall, or invite other classes to some performance aspects of your children's work. Think about the ways in which you can elicit recognition of your children's work by both your colleagues and school administrators. The children in the No More Litter example in Chapter 5 shared their videotape with other classes and the PTA. As a result, others recognized the quality of the children's work and encouraged their continued efforts. This can establish a climate in which the innovative teacher is viewed as a good and hard-working, if rather different, teacher. Such an attitude will make further changes less controversial and may even encourage a few peers to join in making changes.

Obviously sharing the results of your teacher research and your students' work helps validate your new steps in implementing an integrated language perspective. When colleagues see your openness and willingness to experiment and hear how you have approached resolving your questions about teaching and learning, they are often eager to hear what you have to say. They will appreciate the particulars and consequently may be willing to try out something new, especially if they have you as a resource.

Increasingly more teachers are also publishing their teacher inquiries in public ways for wider audiences—in school, district, or community newsletters as well as professional journals, books, and other publications. These writings provide another avenue to share your results.

Invite Parents to Participate

Do not stop at the schoolhouse door. Parents have a vested interest in quality education for their children, and there is strong evidence that high levels of parental involvement are related to positive student attitudes and achievement. Too often, parents' information about what is going on in a classroom is based on student reports and community gossip. This can create problems for a teacher trying to make changes that alter the kind of information going home to parents. Some teachers have reported that parents complained when fewer dittos came home because the parents felt that their children must not be "covering" as much material. It makes sense to create advocates rather than enemies by involving parents in your program at a variety of levels. Friday portfolios (see Chapter 9), where students bring home and share with parents the week's important work, can provide the kind of specific information parents want and need about these new ideas. Another way to communicate ongoing students' work with parents is through weekly reviews. Here, students briefly list some of the things they had done each week, three things they had learned, skills they worked on, what they had been reading, what they were proud of, and what they plan to work on the following week. At the end is a place for teacher comments, as well as family comments. Meeting with parents at open house or sending out letters or newsletters explaining what is going on in your class can help counter parental resistance. Remember, most

Cochran-Smith & Lytle (1993)

Let your first "steps" be topics for teacher research.

See GUIDELINES FOR TEACHER INQUIRY for more ideas on teacher research.

Cochran-Smith (1991); Hickman (1983)

Help to establish a climate supportive of innovation.

Sharing the details from teacher research is usually appreciated by colleagues.

See Dahl (1992) for an invaluable resource for teachers wanting to publish their findings.

Moulin (1988); Routman (1991, 1996)

Routman (1996)

See Fisher (1995), Rief (1992), Routman (1996), and Wilde (1992) for examples of letters to parents.

parents know only transmission-oriented curriculum teaching and learning. Thus, these letters, for example, can explain Literature Response Circles* where students are encouraged to read a book of choice in a thematic unit and talk about their responses to it with a small group of their peers; the writing process you have implemented in which students write drafts that might have areas that are unclear and might be filled with grammatical errors or misspellings, but will be addressed later during the revising and editing of texts; your explanation that invented spelling is not something that children do instead of learning to spell, but instead is the avenue they take to learning to spell that has the advantage of students writing all the time. In addition, sharing the results of your teacher research with parents can be an invaluable way to help parents understand the collaborative approach of an integrated language perspective.

Sharing teacher research with parents is critical to gaining support for an integrated language approach.

In any event, involve parents as supporters, service givers, and facilitators. Develop a cadre of parents who collect materials from scrap lumber to computer software, donate time to help put on a play, or organize a culminating activity for a unit. Provide parents with positive access to the school and opportunities to observe classroom activity. They want their children to feel good about school, excited about learning, and confident about themselves. An integrated language approach is often vigorously supported by parents once they understand its foundations and see its effects. Parents can be powerful advocates for teachers when they can speak on the basis of observation. (See Chapter 9 for more specific ideas on how teachers can support parents' classroom observations.)

Fisher (1995); Goodman (1989); Potter (1989); Huck (1980)

Parents can be learners. Those with younger children may especially want specific help in fostering their children's education. Some schools and classrooms have successfully organized discussion sessions where parents and teachers get together to talk about ways the home and school environments can support each other. The communication networks thus built between parents and teachers minimize misunderstandings. The teacher can show parents samples of student work and explain activities so that parents understand what is happening in the classroom and can offer constructive feedback based on their knowledge of their children. Local experts on language learning, children's literature, and child development can also be invited to parent meetings to provide additional background.

Parents have talents that can be valuable learning resources and encourage support for new programming. Some teachers ask parents ahead of time for ideas or topics that might be incorporated into the theme of the next unit. Others use parent volunteers on a weekly basis to work with children in individual or small-group situations, such as advising a special project that could use some expert assistance, sharing literature, or helping children organize their thoughts into writing. Parents work as partners with the teacher to develop a sound educational program for their children. (Examples of this partnership are given in the prototypes in Chapter 4.)

Work with Administrators

Teachers may be unaware of or confused by the plethora of guidelines and regulations for teaching and learning that exist at both local and state levels. School communities have their own share of myths about what is "required":

Myth 1. Teachers have to cover every unit of every textbook in the order in which they are written.
Myth 2. Teachers have to use the lesson plans in the textbooks.
Myth 3. Teachers have to use workbooks.
Myth 4. Children have to read every story and cover every lesson in every textbook.
Myth 5. Teachers teach reading for only one period a day.

Such regulations are neither good teaching practice nor mandated in most districts. When confronted by such myths, do not accept them without checking things out.

Talk with the principal or the district subject coordinators to find out what is required, what is encouraged, and what is open to change in your state or district.

Honig (1988); Stedman (1989)

Become familiar with the state curriculum guides and state laws governing curriculum. Many teachers have been surprised to find that state and local guidelines are very much in harmony with practices recommended for integrated language classrooms. If necessary, point out to the administration how the integrated language program matches state and local guidelines.

In some schools, it is possible for a teacher to share plans and explain their theoretical and research bases with administrators. Generally, teachers must be prepared to show how they will cover required skills and content in the context of the thematic unit approach. In schools where administrators are more willing to believe successful practice than plans and theory, inviting them in to see student activities or the products of student projects is more likely to garner their support.

Invite the Community in and Take Children into the Community

One of the most threatening aspects of an integrated language perspective is the feeling that the teacher must know so much and be able to draw on a vast array of resources beyond the confines of the textbook. When teachers make the transition to an integrated perspective, they quickly learn that they cannot be the source of all knowledge. They begin to shift their role from information giver to fellow constructor of meaning. To be most effective in this role, teachers need to think about the community resources waiting to be tapped.

Teachers cannot be the only source of knowledge in the classroom. The surrounding community is a rich resource.

Invite community people into the classroom. Begin with the students' parents and guardians. A kindergarten teacher invites parents or guardians individually to spend some time describing to students that adult's occupation or hobby. One full-time homemaker came to class with an apron stuffed full of symbols of all her jobs: a model car for her role as chauffeur, a tiny iron for her job as laundress, and so forth. Another parent who enjoyed woodworking taught children to make birdhouses. A grandfather taught the children dances popular in his youth.

Community officials are often willing to come and talk to school children, as are people involved in business, service, arts, and recreational areas. When children in one school became interested in machinery, a local factory worker helped children build models of various kinds of machines. A local artist came and taught puppetry. Inviting all sorts of people into the life of the classroom lessens the teacher's and children's isolation, lifts some of the burden teachers often feel in trying to be experts in everything, and models new ways of learning.

The community has a vested interest in schooling.

Take children into the community as much as possible. Try to lessen the barrier between school and the world by taking children to see people in nonschool environments. This visibility introduces the teacher and the class program to the community and builds a support group. These expeditions need not require schoolbus trips or expensive transportation arrangements. There are plenty of things to study in the immediate environment of most schools. Within a more urban community, students can use public transportation. A fourth-grade teacher arranged a bus trip to an art museum that was exhibiting African masks. As part of the class's study, students researched bus schedules, fares, distances, and transportation times in addition to developing charts of symbols and techniques used in making masks of different regions of Africa. They developed a trip book that contained necessary information for planning the trip and recording information about the uses of masks in various cultures.

Lessen the barriers between school and the "real" world.

Prepare children for responsible participation in the community.

Prepare your class for community contact. Well-prepared and well-behaved children are welcome in the community and are a pleasure to visit. Most people enjoy sharing their interest and respond well to children who have done some preparation before a visit. Work with children to establish ground rules for conduct and data gathering. Successful field trips and visits from community members reinforce new patterns of student responsibility for their own learning.

Find a Friend

Cochran-Smith (1991); McLaren (1989); McNeil (1988a, 1988b, 1988c)

Even two can be a critical mass for change in a school.

Change is not always welcomed. If a teacher is going to be a change agent in a school, some people will resent such activity and will work to encourage a return to tradition. It is easier to resist these pressures if the teacher finds a companion who shares a similar perspective. Sometimes even a "critical mass" of two can provide enough strength to make a difference, especially if both teachers are at the same grade level. In any case, it is good to have someone not only to share and plan with but also to commiserate with when things don't go as well as hoped. It is also good to have someone with whom to share your teacher research, maybe even developing joint inquiries. Good teaching is hard work. Finding someone who supports your efforts toward being a first-rate teacher can help you withstand pressures toward mediocrity.

Get Involved!

To continue teaching, teachers must continue learning. Most states require some form of continuing education, but that is not the only way to grow as a teacher. Teachers also need to grow in experiences outside the classroom. A number of professional organizations offer scholarships and other incentives that enable teachers to participate in a variety of special programs and travel for educational purposes. These programs provide opportunities to meet teachers from around the country (and sometimes, the world), to form a support group for innovative teaching, and to enrich the learning of your students. Some of the organizations that support this type of growth include the National Council of Teachers of English, the National Council for the Social Studies, the International Reading Association, the National Science Teachers Association, and the National Council of Teachers of Mathematics. These organizations and their local and state affiliates welcome teacher participation and leadership. Many teachers develop their own community or district networks through which to share teacher research, find out about new books or other resources, and discuss classroom practice. Individual enthusiasm coupled with continued education recharges intellectual batteries so that teaching remains a stimulating and mind-expanding activity.

Become Associated with a University or College

As teachers move toward a more integrated model, they sometimes take advantage of the resources in nearby colleges and universities.

See Miller (1990), Pappas & Zecker (in press a, in press b), Valencia (1998), and Weaver (1998) for examples of collaborative school-university work.

Collaborative efforts between college and university faculty and classroom teachers can be rewarding to all participants, so enlist the help of a sympathetic faculty member. You can get some expert assistance without the threat of administrative evaluation, and the university representative has an opportunity to observe and participate in an important "laboratory" setting. In fact, collaborative inquiry between university-based and school-based teacher researchers is becoming more prevalent, so many university professors are eager to consider the educational issues or questions you want to study together.

Let administrators know about these collaborations. An advocate from the university or college can sometimes encourage administrators to grant a classroom teacher a bit more leeway than might otherwise be allowed. The university person can also document the class's progress, provide feedback, and serve as a resource person.

Make presentations at professional conferences. Collaborative efforts can result in presentations that put teachers in contact with like-minded colleagues and extend the needed support network.

Incorporate Evaluation and Assessment Strategies

The performance-based procedures for evaluation discussed in Chapter 9 are appearing in a multitude of school settings. As more holistic measures of evaluation that may be relatively simple to implement are becoming acceptable even in settings where letter or number grades must be assigned for the report card, teachers can begin incorporating assessments that are more compatible with an integrated language perspective.

Keep good records. The kid-watching techniques discussed in Chapters 8 and 9 require good recordkeeping. They help teachers plan, of course, but they also help explain to parents and administrators what children are learning and doing. In a sense, good recordkeeping helps validate good teacher intuition—that sense of how children are doing and where they are ready to go next that comes from careful observation, good practice, and professional judgment.

Keep plenty of records. Especially in schools where single grades or standardized tests are the major means by which children's learning is measured and reported, it is important to accumulate other data as evidence of the kind of thinking and learning that more fully represent the progress of an individual child. One simple way to do this is to keep a learning portfolio that is periodically shared with parents. A child's story or poem, picture, or project can speak volumes about the kind of learning that is going on.

Goodman (1986)

Portfolios provide understandable feedback to parents.

Parents can also better understand the kind of documentation represented in a portfolio than the statistical interpretations required to make sense out of standardized measures. Even percentage scores on a teacher-made test do not tell a parent as much as a book their child has created during a thematic unit.

Teach children how to take tests. If standardized tests are used with children in integrated language classrooms, help prepare them for the format in which it will be given. Place a few practice sentences on the board periodically to accustom them to the test format. Practice working within time constraints, as young children often lack experience with timed tests. In most cases, however, children in integrated language classrooms do as well or better on standardized tests than those in more traditional classrooms.

Reardon (1990)

Huck (1980); Tunnell & Jacobs (1989)

Involve children in self-evaluation. Start by inviting them to put together their own portfolio of work. Initially, it helps to provide some guidelines about what types of work to include. Suggest that children include samples of the writing that they found the most interesting, that they enjoyed doing the most, or that they found the most difficult. They may include an outline of the work they have been involved in over a particular period and provide samples of things representative of that work. Children may also include samples that represent something brand new that they have learned, or an example of something they had trouble with but think they are beginning to understand or have mastered.

Gamberg, Kwak, Hutchings, & Altheim (1988)

Discuss evaluation with students. Some teachers provide check sheets for children to fill out that cover a child's activities for a particular period. The teacher fills out a similar sheet, and both meet to go over their evaluations. The child has an opportunity to provide feedback to the teacher, and the teacher can discuss areas of strength as well as areas of concern. In this way, even if the teacher must assign a number or letter grade, the child has a better understanding of where that grade came from and has an opportunity to provide evidence the teacher may not have considered. Thus, evaluation is collaborative, too.

Be patient. Good evaluative and assessment skills take time to acquire. They require continuous practice and careful reflection. Teachers have to be as patient with their own unfolding abilities as they are with children.

Conclusions

An integrated language perspective is accessible to many kinds of teachers in many kinds of situations. It is not a lockstep model but a belief about children and learning. No teacher enters the classroom with a perfect system in place; good teachers spend their entire careers building on decisions made as they confront the realities of life in classrooms.

Teachers share responsibility for building children's futures.

This book has emphasized the importance of choices and ownership for teachers and children. Teachers generally make their choices because they care about children. Teaching requires careful thinking about the future we want for children. The debate over that future and the ways to reach it have always been with us. We argue over whether it is enough to teach children to read and write or to achieve high scores on college entrance exams, or if there is some "cultural literacy" that will enable a diverse society to function as a democracy. We debate the impact of education on children's economic futures and on the political and economic future of our world. James Britton has said that "we want children, as a result of our teaching to *understand*, to be wise as well as well informed, able to solve fresh problems rather than have learnt the answers to old ones; indeed not only able to answer questions but also able to ask them" (p. 81). Choosing to teach from an integrated language perspective provides a context in which such goals are possible. Making the transition to that perspective can be an exciting and challenging experience.

Britton (1981)

REFERENCES

Atwell, N. (1987). *In the middle: Writing, learning and reading with adolescents.* Portsmouth, NH: Heinemann.

Atwell, N. (Ed.). (1989). *Coming to know: Writing to learn in the intermediate grades.* Portsmouth, NH: Heinemann.

Bernard, B. A. (1993). "If it's November, it must be Indians": Challenging Thanksgiving stereotypes. *Teaching Tolerance, 2 (2),* 54–56.

Brandt, R. S. (1991). *Readings from* Educational Leadership: *Cooperative learning and the collaborative school.* Alexandria, VA: ASCD.

Britton, J. (1981). Talking to learn. In D. Barnes, J. Britton, & H. Rosen (Eds.), *Language, the learner and the school* (pp. 81–115). New York: Penguin.

Calkins, L. (1994). *The art of teaching writing.* Portsmouth, NH: Heinemann.

Cazden, C. (1988). *Classroom discourse: The language of teaching and learning.* Portsmouth, NH: Heinemann.

Chambers, A. (1985). *Booktalk: Occasional writing on literature and children.* New York: Harper & Row.

Cochran-Smith, M. (1991). Learning to teach against the grain. *Harvard Educational Review, 61,* 279–310.

Cochran-Smith, M., & Lytle, S. L. (1993). *Inside/Outside: Teacher research and knowledge.* New York: Teachers College Press.

Cohen, E. G. (1994). *Designing groupwork: Strategies for the heterogeneous classroom.* New York: Teachers College Press.

Cohen, E. G., Lotan, R. A., Whitcomb, J. A., Balderrama, M. V., Cossey, R., & Swansom, P. E. (1994). Complex instruction: Higher order thinking in heterogeneous classrooms. In S. Sharan (Ed.). *Handbook of cooperative learning methods* (pp. 82–96). Westport, CN: Greenwillow Press.

Dahl, K. L. (Ed.). (1992). *Teacher as writer: Entering the professional conversation.* Urbana, IL: National Council of Teachers of English.

Eeds, M., & Wells, D. (1989). Grand conversations: An exploration of meaning construction in literature study groups. *Research in the Teaching of English, 23 (1),* 4–29.

Fisher, B. (1995). *Thinking and learning together: Curriculum and community in a primary classroom.* Portsmouth, NH: Heinemann.

Gamberg, R., Kwak, W., Hutchings, M., & Altheim, J. (1988). *Learning and loving it: Theme studies in the classroom.* Portsmouth, NH: Heinemann.

Gay, G. (1991). Culturally diverse students and social studies. In J. Shaver (Ed.), *Handbook of research on social studies teaching and learning* (pp. 144–156). New York: Macmillan.

Goodlad, J. (1984). *A place called school.* New York: McGraw-Hill.

Goodman, G. (1989). Worlds within worlds: Reflections on an encounter with parents. *Language Arts, 66 (1),* 14–20.

Goodman, K. (1986). *What's whole about whole language?* Portsmouth, NH: Heinemann.

Graves, D. H. (1983). *Writing: Teachers and children at work.* Portsmouth, NH: Heinemann.

Harris, V. J. (Ed.). (1992). *Teaching multicultural literature in grades K–8.* Norwood, MA: Christopher-Gordon.

Hickman, J. (1983). Moving toward a literature based approach. *The W.E.B.: Spring Weather, 7 (3),* 25–31.

Honig, B. (1988). The California reading initiative. *The New Advocate, 1 (4),* 135–140.

Huck, C. (1980). Teacher feature. *The W.E.B.: Learning to Read Naturally, 4 (4),* 14–17.

Huck, C. S., Hepler, S., Hickman, J., & Kiefer, B. (1997). *Children's literature in the elementary school.* Madison, WI: Brown & Benchmark.

Ladson-Billings, G. (1994). *The dreamkeepers: Successful teachers of African-American children.* San Francisco: Jossey-Bass.

Martinez, M. G., & Teale, W. H. (1989). Classroom storybook reading: The creation of texts and learning opportunities. *Theory Into Practice, 28 (2),* 126–135.

McLaren, P. (1989). *Life in schools.* White Plains, NY: Longman.

McNeil, L. A. (1988a). Contradictions of control: Part 1. Administrators and teachers. *Phi Delta Kappan, 69,* 333–339.

McNeil, L. A. (1988b). Contradictions of control: Part 2. Teachers, students, and curriculum. *Phi Delta Kappan, 69,* 432–438.

McNeil, L. A. (1988c). Contradictions of control: Part 3. Contradictions of reform. *Phi Delta Kappan, 69,* 478–485.

Miller, J. (1990). *Creating spaces and finding voices: Teachers collaborating for empowerment.* Albany: State University of New York Press.

Mizell, L., Benett, S., Bowman, B., & Morin, L. (1993). Different ways of seeing: Teaching in an anti-racist school. In T. Perry & J. W. Fraser (Eds.), *Freedom's plow: Teaching in the multicultural classroom* (pp. 27–46). New York: Routledge.

Moulin, N. (1988, April). *Effect of parent involvement in classroom activities on parents' and children's attitude toward school.* Paper presented at the annual meeting of the American Educational Research Association, New Orleans, LA.

Pappas, C. C., & Zecker, L. B. (Eds.). (in press a). *Teacher inquiries in literacy teaching-learning: Learning to collaborate in elementary urban classrooms.* Mahwah, NJ: Lawrence Erlbaum.

Pappas, C. C., & Zecker, L. B. (Eds.). (in press b). *Working with teacher researchers in urban classrooms: Transforming literacy curriculum genres.* Mahwah, NJ: Lawrence Erlbaum.

Perry, T., & Fraser, J. W. (1993). Reconstructing schools as multiracial/multicultural democracies: Toward a theoretical perspective. In T. Perry & J. W. Fraser (Eds.), *Freedom's plow: Teaching in the multicultural classroom* (pp. 3–24). New York: Routledge.

Pierce, K. M., & Gilles, C. J. (1993). *Cycles of meaning: Exploring the potential of talk in learning communities.* Portsmouth, NH: Heinemann.

Potter, G. (1989). Parent participation in the language arts program. *Language Arts, 66 (1),* 21–28.

Radencich, M. C., & McKay, L. J. (1995). *Flexible grouping for literacy in the elementary grades.* Boston: Allyn-Bacon.

Reardon, S. J. (1990). Putting reading tests in their place. *The New Advocate, 3,* 29–37.

Richards, J. J. (1993). Classroom tapestry: A practitioner's perspective on multicultural education. In T. Perry & J. W. Fraser (Eds.), *Freedom's plow: Teaching in the multicultural classroom* (pp. 47–63). New York: Routledge.

Rief, L. (1992). *Seeking diversity: Language arts with adolescents.* Portsmouth, NH: Heinemann.

Routman, R. (1988). *Transitions: From literature to literacy.* Portsmouth, NH: Heinemann.

Routman, R. (1991). *Invitations: Changing as teachers and learners, K–12.* Portsmouth, NH: Heinemann.

Routman, R. (1996). *Literacy at the crossroads: Crucial talk about reading, writing, and other teaching dilemmas.* Portsmouth, NH: Heinemann.

Schaps, E., & Solomon, D. (1991). Schools and classroom as caring communities. In R. Brandt (Ed.) Readings from *Educational Leadership: Cooperative learning and the collaborative school* (pp. 61–63). Alexandria, VA: ASCD.

Sharan, Y., & Sharan, S. (1992). *Expanding cooperative learning through group investigation.* New York: Teachers College Press.

Slavin, R. E. (1995). *Cooperative learning.* Boston: Allyn-Bacon.

Staff. (1993). People puzzle. *Teaching Tolerance, Fall,* p. 1.

Stedman, L. C. (1987). It's time we changed the effective schools formula. *Phi Delta Kappan, 63,* 216–224.

Stodolsky, S. S. (1988). *The subject matters: Classroom activity in math and social studies.* Chicago: University of Chicago Press.

Tierney, R. J., Carter, M. A., & Desai, L. E. (1991). *Portfolio assessment in the reading-writing classroom.* Norwood, MA: Christopher-Gordon.

Tunnell, M. O., & Jacobs, J. S. (1989). Using "real books": Research findings on literature-based reading instruction. *The Reading Teacher, 42,* 470–477.

Valencia, S. W. (1998). *Literacy portfolios in action.* Fort Worth, TX: Harcourt Brace.

Weaver, C. (Ed.). (1998). *Lessons to share on teaching grammar in context.* Portsmouth, NH: Boynton/Cook.

Wells, G. (1994). *Changing schools from within: Creating communities of inquiry.* Toronto: OISE Press. (Distributed by Portsmouth, NH: Heinemann.)

Wells, G., & Chang-Wells, G. L. (1992). *Constructing knowledge together: Classrooms as centers of inquiry and literacy.* Portsmouth, NH: Heinemann.

Wilde, S. (1992). *You kan red this! Spelling and punctuation for whole classrooms, K–6.* Portsmouth, NH: Heinemann.

Willinsky, J. (1990). *The new literacy: Redefining reading and writing in the schools.* New York: Routledge.

Young, R. (1992). *Critical theory and classroom talk.* Clevedon, England: Multilingual Matters.

CHILDREN'S LITERATURE

The Double Life of Pocahontas by J. Fritz. Illustrated by E. Young. Putnam, 1983.

GUIDELINES FOR TEACHER INQUIRY

Cochran-Smith & Lytle (1993)

Teacher inquiry is related to Student-Initiated Inquiry*.

Teacher inquiry fosters the idea of teacher-as-learner.

Teacher inquiry enables teachers to examine ideologies.

Bartolome (1994); Cummins (1994); Edelsky (1994); Gutierrez, Rymes, & Larson (1995); Pappas (in press)

We have argued throughout the book that teacher research—*the systematic, intentional inquiry by teachers* about their own school and classroom work—is a critical feature of the integrated language perspective. It goes along with our emphasis on student-directed inquiry where students tackle various dimensions of the essential questions of particular thematic units, do in-depth studies on them, then report their findings to the rest of the classroom participants (or even beyond to a school or community audience). Here, students are seen as knowers *and* teachers, and classroom teachers become learners. Teacher inquiry facilitates this move from teacher-as-information-transmitter to teacher-as-learner by encouraging teachers to take on a reflective stance towards teaching and learning. As they explicitly research their own practice and their students' learning, teachers become knowers—professionals who gain and generate knowledge about their own practice.

There is an important social activist agenda to teacher research as well. As we have argued throughout the book, developing multicultural curriculum that explores our underlying biases, values, and ideologies means that our pedagogy must always be critically examined. Teachers' local inquiries in their classrooms may be important sites of resistance regarding the broader power relations in the society at large. As we argued in the Introduction, teacher inquiry enables teachers to speak out as professionals.

Teacher Inquiry as Cycles of Action Research

Wells (1994)

Four components of action research

In their inquiries, students' understanding stems from their purposeful action. It is cumulatively constructed as they bring their current knowledge or schemas to new contexts, projects, and information to make sense of them. Once again there are parallels to teacher inquiry; namely, teachers engage in spirals of observation, reflection, and action for the purpose of developing their own understanding and improving their practice. Wells outlines the four major activities of this action research:

- *Observing* to make systematic observations of particular, relevant aspects of classroom life to determine what is actually happening.
- *Interpreting* these observations by reflecting on why things are happening as they are. For both those things that are working well and those that are not in the situation, they attempt to discover the factors that seem to be responsible.
- *Planning change* by constructing hypotheses for what changes might bring an improvement for the unsatisfactory aspects of the current situation. They consider how one or more of these changes might be undertaken and plan how to implement it.
- *Acting out* the planned change.

A teacher's own personal, interpretative theory is at the center of teacher inquiry.

Integrally related to these components of action research is the teachers' personal theory. This is the core of teacher inquiry—how a teacher's interpretative framework informs and is informed by the cycles of action research. By adopting the stance of reflectiveness, teacher researchers make the connections between theory and practice more explicit. Their theories are grounded by their practice and vice versa, and they are able to develop a more conscious understanding of the underlying basis of their actions.

Cochran-Smith & Lytle (1993); Hobson (1996); Wells (1994)

Similar to student-directed inquiry, two other important activities support teacher inquiry. First, reading about other work—both theoretical and practical—related to the inquiry topic is useful in that it can inform various facets of the action research. Second, having informal, collaborative talk with interested others at every stage of the process is critical for sustaining and extending teacher researchers' efforts.

Reading on the topic of inquiry and having conversations with others support teacher inquiry.

Altrichter, Posch, & Somekh (1993); Wells (1994); Zeichner & Liston (1996)

Whether you are a student teacher-researcher (STR) or an already practicing teacher-researcher (TR), any inquiry begins with *your own questions* about teaching and learning. Thus, we talk about questions first. Then we cover several other general topics that are involved in doing inquiry: the role of research journals and other methods of data collection; strategies for data analysis; and tips for publishing teacher inquiry. Subsequently, we suggest possible ways that student teachers might be engaged in teacher inquiry during their various fieldwork experiences, including student teaching.

Inquiries begin with questions.

Raising Questions about Teaching-Learning

Some teachers start out with a clear, formulated question, or at least a general question, "What's going on here?" or "What's the problem here?" However, many start with a very diffuse or vague interest in some aspect of the curriculum or content of a thematic unit, or a particular feature of student behavior that they have noted as interesting or problematic. Frequently, it is only through careful observation of the first cycle of the action research process that specific questions evolve.

See Altrichter, Posch, & Somekh (1993), Fischer (1996), and Hubbard & Power (1993) for more discussion on finding and framing inquiry questions.

Teaching-learning is a relationship, a reciprocal, dynamic connection that cannot be separated. This relationship also always involves *content*—the essential questions, important concepts, and worthwhile multicultural curriculum we have discussed throughout the book. Nevertheless, we have found that a useful way to begin to think about inquiry questions is to consider whether they focus mostly on the "teaching" side of the relationship, or whether they are directed more towards students' learning. That is, if you are interested in trying out how you might create Literature Response Groups* in your classroom—where students read the same book and then discuss it with peers in small groups—your questions would likely be concerned with questions on teaching. What books should I select for them? How can I set up a system where students could have choices? How do I help students learn their roles and responsibilities in their discussions? But notice that even though your emphasis is on questions about teaching, you cannot avoid issues of student learning. In fact, students' reactions or learning outcomes to what you implement will be your data to help you decide on the next steps you make, or what teaching strategies you might need to change or revise. Indeed, a question about students' learning—How can I facilitate their authentic responses to texts?—might have been the underlying impetus for your inquiry in the first place.

Decide which "side" of the teaching-learning relationship your inquiry emphasizes.

However, if you had kept that question in the foreground, you probably would have generated other questions stemming from it that would be more clearly related to students' learning. What kinds of responses do students develop in small-group discussions? In what ways do peer discussion enable them to evoke both personal and critical responses to texts? How are students' responses different depending upon the genre they are reading? Once again, although these questions rest more on the "learning" side of the relationship, the teaching influence cannot be denied. Students might begin with just retelling parts of text rather than responding to it, or they might offer only personal ones, when you had hoped that critical responses would be developed as well. Thus, you might have to create a series of Focus Lessons* to help students see the potential range of response that might be possible, or model ways of evoking critical responses during your teacher-led Reading Aloud* sessions with them.

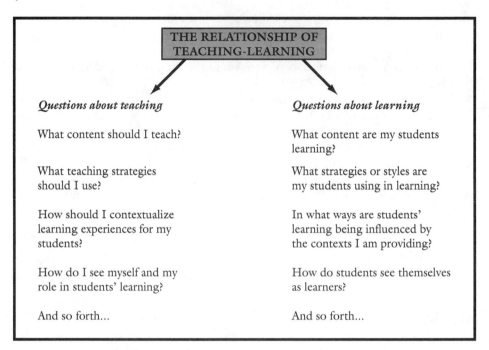

Figure G.1

Thus, it is impossible to separate teaching-learning; teaching influences learning and learning affects teaching. But in terms of raising questions, it usually helps to be more aware of *where* the underlying intent of your inquiry lies. Making this distinction—see Figure G.1—aids your being clearer in your own mind as to what questions you are generating, especially in the beginning of an inquiry. Whether your inquiry questions draw on either side or both sides, the process enables you to be more conscious of their source. This helps you create an initial framework for research, even though your questions are likely to become modified or even be replaced with new ones.

The Role of Research Journals in Teacher Inquiry

Research journals or diaries are a major means of recordkeeping in teacher research.

Altrichter, Posch, & Somekh (1993), Hobson (1996); Hubbard & Power (1993)

An integral aspect of any inquiry is recordkeeping. Most teacher researchers keep a small journal to record their observations and reflections for each inquiry. However, specifying ahead of time exactly when you plan to write in the journal during your daily schedule or everyday life leads to success in keeping journals. Many TRs take at least fifteen to twenty minutes at the end of the school day as a good time for journal writing, then think of other times, such as at the beginning of writing workshop or when students are writing in their own Journals*. Other teachers, because of after-school meetings or other commitments, schedule their journal time at home, after dinner, or before going to bed.

Frequently, or at least in the beginning of fieldwork, STRs have many opportunities for observation as they attempt to understand how mentor teachers and students interact in the classroom. As they take on more teaching responsibilities, however, they meet the same challenges as teachers in finding the right spots of the day to do journal writing. Thus, a first step in teacher inquiry is to determine the times that are best for you. (See below for more on the *when* of doing journal writing.)

The format of your journal is a personal choice, but there are three features that all journals should include.

Include descriptive and reflective writing.

Altrichter, Posch, & Somekh (1993); Hobson (1996)

1. You want to include *both* descriptive writing and reflective writing. The *descriptive writing* is the reporting of your observation in the action research cycle. Learning to be descriptive in recording what you have observed is hard to do in the beginning, but it gets easier and faster with practice. You

want details here—see the ideas provided under "General Observation Schemes" in Chapter 8. You want these descriptions to be useful at the time you wrote them, as well as later when you review, reread, and re-examine them. The *reflective writing* is the standing back, mulling over, searching for connections and possible meanings, considering various hypotheses or potential plans for action. Most TRs and STRs find ways to differentiate these two types of writing. For example, they make their journals have "double entries." That is, they have the right-hand pages of their journal be the place where they write down descriptive accounts, and the left-hand facing pages where they write down their reflections on those experiences. Or they might buy notebooks or paper (called "project planner" paper) that has a large margin. Another strategy—especially good for those who may want to take just brief notes on Post-it® Notes, index cards, or large address labels, and then write up these observations in more detail on the computer—is to use brackets to distinguish the reflections from descriptions.

Descriptive and reflective writing are sometimes called "raw" notes and "cooked" notes.

Hubbard & Power (1993)

Power (1996)

2. You want to be sure to note down the actions you take as part of your inquiry, with a short rationale for why you have undertaken this course of action. This documentation gives you an instructional trail of the various paths you have taken and helps you plan future action as you make sense of the themes or patterns that emerge in your inquiry.

Document the steps of your instructional trail.

3. Although it might seem obvious—sometimes it is easily forgotten—all of your journal entries should be dated. You want to have a record of when you observed something relevant in your inquiry or when you took action to implement a change.

Date all of your entries.

More on Journals and Other Ways to Collect Data

Just as format is a personal choice, so is the actual journal you can use. Some TRs and STRs like 8 ½ x 11 pages they can place in a binder. Pages can be removed, rearranged, and are large enough to tape or staple other notes, photographs, or other relevant information. Others prefer a smaller 6 x 9 notebook that can be easily slipped into a purse, book bag, or satchel. As already noted, there are lots of other ways to gather information for your inquiry that complement and extend the journal. Post-it® Notes, index cards, or large address labels are good for recording data for individual or group case studies. Audio- and videotaping are also useful means to gain information. However, although these ways for collecting data might seem easier, they will usually require that you do ongoing review and analysis. (Transcribing might be postponed to a later date, but taking notes on the tape recordings is almost always essential and is generally manageable.) Finally, of course, a lot of your documentation will also be your normal recordkeeping of students' work—the process and product of their reading, writing, and inquiries—as well as their recordkeeping of their own learning. See Chapters 4, 7, 8, and 9 for a range of other possibilities.

The physical size along with other characteristics of your research journal, is a personal choice.

Hobson (1996)

Preparing for Observation

Another important issue regarding inquiry is deciding what, why, when, and how to observe. You can't observe everything all the time, so it is important to prepare for observation. Of course, your initial questions may help you with direction—see also Figure G.1 on the teaching-learning relationship. However, the following may also be helpful:

Preparation for observation is critical.

Altrichter, Posch, & Somekh (1993)

Four questions about observation

What?

What are you going to observe? Are you going to observe a certain sequence of events in a particular routine, a student's behavior, or a certain aspect of your own behavior?

Why are you doing the observation? What assumptions or expectations are you bringing to the observation? You want to strive for objectivity in observation, but your prejudgments cannot be avoided. Thus, if you clarify ahead of time what your theories or preconceived ideas are about the context you are about to observe, you can more easily deal with them when you do your reflective writing.

Why?

When?

When will you do the observation and how long is it likely to take? Deciding the times when you will make your observations beforehand enables you to devote your energies to them and makes the inquiry manageable. Will it be during a particular time of the classroom day when a certain activity or routine occurs, such as during writing workshop, teacher-led Reading Aloud*, or Buddy Reading*? Or perhaps the focus might be on a particular child or group that requires that you note and record information during several times or even at specific intervals of the whole day.

Many TRs, such as Janet in Chapter 9, lay out the inquiry data possibilities along with their plans for the kinds of evaluative information they desire during a thematic unit so that they can envision what their inquiry will really involve and better decide what they can actually accomplish. This might lead to their cutting down on what they had initially considered or the amount of data they will gather by limiting the times, students, or groups they will concentrate on. Similarly, STRs will need to identify exactly when they think they will focus in on some aspect of teaching-learning so they can incorporate these inquiry facets in their planning of their lessons or activities. If not, they may be overwhelmed by the whole process.

How?

"In-the-midst" versus "after-the-fact" notes

Power (1996)

How are you going to do the observation? Are you going to take "in-the-midst" notes, perhaps while you sit back but near students who are having literature discussions? Or, will you take "after-the-fact" notes that are fleshed out later in your journal using the brief fragments you jotted down while you are actually interacting with students? Will you need Post-it® Notes or index cards, or a form you developed for the observation? Or will you briefly note the contextual features of an activity or routine that will be audio- or videotaped, and make your more detailed notes when you review the tapes at the end of the day?

Strategies for Analyzing Your Journal Entries and Other Data

Data analysis is a way of "seeing and then seeing again." It involves re-viewing to bring order, structure, and meaning to your data. Analyzing data is frequently a difficult part of the inquiry process so it is useful to view it as a puzzle that you can approach with playfulness and risk-taking. Remember that you are attempting to answer *your own questions*, so there are no correct answers here. It is these efforts that will lead you to the deep "seeing" of the underlying patterns that might be lurking under the surface. Going back to your initial inquiry questions—how they might have been modified, or how new ones have evolved—may all guide your first steps of analysis.

Take a problem-solving stance to data analysis.

Although it can be said that all teacher inquiry is ongoing, there is a time in an inquiry where there is a feeling of closure or a sense that it is "done." Perhaps it is the end of a particular thematic unit, as the ones that have been illustrated in Chapter 4. Or for STRs it might be the end of your fieldwork in a certain university quarter or semester. Or maybe there is a place where some classroom routine, for example, some way of doing Literature Response Groups*, seems to be going well for you and your students, at least for this year. Thus, it is at the end of this period that a major part of the data analysis usually occurs.

Ongoing cycles of data analysis are recommended.

Altrichter, Posch, & Somekh (1993)

However, we recommend that you do early cycles of analysis and do not postpone everything to the end. Of course, for every cycle of action research, data analysis has been employed in some sense. We are here referring to the more *overt* sitting back to see where you are so far. Two major approaches can be used in an ongoing fashion—developing categories and coding data, and making data summaries—and can help you both monitor and evaluate your inquiry and keep you from being completely overwhelmed by the whole process.

Developing Categories and Coding Data

Try to identify emerging themes and patterns in your data and give them particular codes.

At regular intervals of your inquiry, it is useful to try to identify emerging themes and patterns. Read through your journal. See if you can find similar issues or topics being covered. Create tentative categories to capture the patterns you are noting. List on a separate sheet these categories by giving each of them a short name or phrase that makes sense to you, along with an abbreviated code. Then write in the code next to your notes with a pencil. (You might also want to number instances of the same code.) You want to use a pencil in this initial coding because, as your inquiry progresses, you may further differentiate or collapse categories, or change your categories altogether, and the crossing out of ink-written codes usually makes a mess of your data notes.

Sometimes "counting" these categories can provide useful information about the status or shape of your inquiry so far. For example, perhaps your inquiry had to do with your understanding students' literature responses. Because you note that only some types are being made by your students, you might realize that it is time for a Focus Lesson* to help students consider other possible responses. If your inquiry is more related to your own teaching strategies, then the patterns of your interactions with students— say, in content conferences over their writing—might lead you to take stock and try another approach in talking to them.

An initial, tentative "count" of instances of particular categories sometimes helps to make instructional decisions.

Making Data Summaries

Data Summaries should be no more than two pages long. They might address the following questions:

Make your data summaries short.

Altrichter, Posch, & Somekh (1993)

1. What are the contexts in which the data were collected? What methods of collection (and why?) were used? Thus, these questions may be similar to the questions you posed for yourself in preparing for observation. However, these might have changed so it is important to reiterate them in your summaries.
2. What are the most important, surprising, and informative "facts" in the data?
3. In what ways do the data give rise to new questions, points-of-view, ideas, or suggestions?
4. In what ways do the data suggest your next steps, in terms of further data collection, analysis, or action?

It is also frequently useful to cross-reference the relevant journal sections (or categories or codes therein—see above), other notes you might have made on your reviews on audio- or videotapes, or students' work, etc. next to your answers to these questions listed above.

Tips for "Publishing" Teacher Inquiry

The major purpose of teacher inquiry is to promote teachers' development of their own explicit, principled basis for making changes to their own teaching in order to improve the learning opportunities for their students. Thus, it isn't the reporting of the findings for others per se that is so important, but the value of the experiences that the teacher researcher had in undertaking the inquiry.

The formats, or genres, of writing up teacher inquiry frequently have to do with the purposes you have for reporting or sharing your findings and the audience with whom you wish to communicate. Thus, just as student "publishing" might be seen as "sharing" and take on many forms (see Chapters 6 and 7), reporting the findings of the inquiry work of TRs and STRs can also be expressed in diverse ways. No matter how it is reported, the following ideas can be useful:

There are a range of formats or genres to publish or share the findings of teacher inquiry.

Cochran-Smith & Lytle (1993)

See Dahl (1992) for an invaluable resource for teachers wanting to publish their inquiry findings.

- Be sure that you explain the context of your inquiry: who the participants are, what was done, and why. This contextualization enables others to relate your account to their own experiences.

Explain the context of your inquiry.

- Tell about your own theory-in-action, interpretive framework, or your stance and ideologies or values regarding your inquiry and your interpretations and conclusions.

Describe your own personal theory or interpretive frame.

- Don't feel that you have to report on every single data "fact" of your inquiry. Choose the major themes and patterns as they relate to your inquiry questions and be sure that you organize them, perhaps with subheadings in your presentation or text.

Share major themes and patterns.

Give illustrative examples for your findings.

- Give examples and illustrations of your findings. Also, in presenting your examples, help readers understand your interpretation of these examples or why you think they are significant as evidence of the themes you found. Sometimes TRs and STRs just make examples "stand on their own" to tell the whole story. Instead they must explain to readers in the body of their report just *how* certain features of the examples are to be illustrative of their points.

Use your own voice when you relate others' work on your inquiry topic.

- When relevant, weave the ideas of the other work you might have read that you think is related to your inquiry topic—*but* be sure that you explicate these ideas through *your voice.* Sometimes TRs and STRs fill their reports with so many quotes from others that their stance on the ideas gets muffled or even lost.

Include descriptions about the difficulties of the research process and any remaining concerns you have.

- Try to be honest in telling the difficulties and vulnerabilities that arose for you in your inquiry. Include any findings that didn't seem to fit that you might still be concerned about. Sometimes TRs' and STRs' inquiry reports sound so rosy that others reading them either do not find the account credible enough to try out the ideas and benefit from them, or if they do attempt them and end up with unsatisfactory results, they blame themselves, or worse, their students.

Tell about new questions that have emerged.

- Because teacher inquiry is such an ongoing enterprise, tell about new questions or ideas that you plan to pursue in future inquiries and why.

Inquiry Possibilities for Student Teacher Researchers

The settings for STRs and TRs are different.

STRs find themselves in different contexts than TRs. They are often in a cultural context where a classroom mentor teacher and his or her students have already developed norms, some of which are very subtle and hard to recognize. Also, much of what is done in terms of their teaching usually has to be okayed or is directed by the mentor teacher and the university or college instructor. This makes many student teachers reluctant to "step on someone's toes" in *their* steps in teaching and doing inquiry.

In contrast, TRs often need to "step on their *own* toes"—that is, to make the everyday or normal classroom activities and experiences *become* strange. Frequently, teacher research isn't gathering new information about teaching and learning as much as it is reconsidering or "REsearching" information you already have. Thus, a major goal of teacher inquiry is to make your tacit, implicit assumptions and interpretative frameworks more explicit so you can examine and evaluate them.

Student teachers find *everything* strange in a fieldwork setting and they are sometimes even frightened about how they might get through a day of teaching. As a result, they are often eager to find the right methods to teach a particular content or reading or writing and may see inquiry as some "extra" activity rather than seeing it as an integral feature of teaching. However, we think inquiry for student teachers is also important for three major reasons. First, although they find a classroom initially strange, they very easily get caught up with how things are done in their fieldwork setting and try to do exactly what they see mentor teachers doing. They quickly become socialized into certain approaches without thinking about or evaluating whether or why they should be done. Second, they may take on the methods that are being stressed in the university classroom without examining how they might or might not be related to their own developing core principles or beliefs about teaching and learning. Also, they may not consider the theoretical underpinnings that inform these methods or examine what the implications might be if these methods are uncritically replicated with classroom students' whose status may be different in terms of cultural, class, gender, and linguistic background. Third, they can learn with the help of their peers, mentor teachers, and university instructors, strategies for teacher inquiry as they are becoming teachers. Many of these skills involve ways to do careful kid-watching, thereby also enabling them to acquire useful assessment techniques.

Inquiry conducted by STRs is important because it enables them to better examine familiar classroom activities and interactions, explore how methods are related to their developing personal theories about teaching-learning, and develop useful kid-watching strategies.

Teacher education programs at universities or colleges usually include several fieldwork or practicum experiences. Early ones may involve mostly observation, or teaching one student or a small group. Subsequently, they may begin to develop and implement various lessons with the whole class, or complete a project with students for part of the school day for several days or weeks. They then graduate to the final experience where a student teacher takes on the teaching responsibilities for several weeks (most of the quarter or semester). Thus, the teaching experiences for STRs will vary and the contexts in which they are placed for their teaching efforts will also be quite different. Below, we suggest five possible ways that STRs might be engaged in inquiry, which might be chosen and modified depending on the various factors noted previously.

The possibilities for inquiry by student teacher researchers will vary.

Having a collaborative group to share ideas throughout the inquiry process is useful for all of the possibilities. Moreover, reports or presentations of inquiries could and should be shared with a range of audience (including university classmates and instructors, mentor teachers, fieldwork setting teachers, and so forth).

Class Inquiry

Class inquiries may be useful during early field experiences. Here, your particular university or college class might choose a specific topic to investigate. For example, you might study how reading, writing, or a specific content area is taught in your respective fieldwork settings. Or you may decide to collect data on how girls and boys are treated differently in the classroom in general or during certain particular content area instruction. Another inquiry might center around examining the various interactions that occur between the teacher and the students along the teacher-directed to collaborative continuum (see Chapter 2) and how these result in different patterns of classroom discourse.

The entire university class studies the same topic in their respective field settings.

These inquiries would begin in broad brush strokes, which individual STRs would narrow down, as you meet regularly to report on your data and the methods and strategies you have employed to do your descriptive and reflective writing. It is especially useful for those of you who are working in the same grade to meet to discuss your ongoing findings. By sharing your data, you can begin to discover common patterns found in 1st or 4th grade teaching-learning, for example, but also begin to see how different instructional routines are done in your respective settings. As these various grade-level groups report to the university class as a whole, another facet of your inquiry could be facilitated, namely, trying to tease out which classroom student behaviors in your fieldwork settings may be developmental and which may be influenced by instructional patterns.

These class inquiries may occur throughout the semester or quarter or for a specified number of weeks. Towards the end, they may also include your own inquiry of your own efforts in teaching that has to do with the topic of the class study. These action plans would be based on the themes or patterns your group had discovered so far in your findings.

Individual STR reports may be written, which would include data analysis of the respective grade-level group data as well their own individual teaching. Or each group-level group might write up its findings that would be part of a whole-class report.

Focus Inquiry Lesson

As you begin to have more experience in the fieldwork setting and mentor teachers begin to give you more teaching responsibilities, you may be asked to plan specific lessons for groups of students or the whole class, all of which can be occasions for inquiry. Typical lesson plans have student teachers describing their plans for the lesson ahead of time, which are frequently checked by the mentor or university instructor. These lesson plans include the purpose or rationale of the lesson, materials, and steps the STR plans to use and take in implementing the lesson. The idea of Focus Inquiry Lessons transforms these typical lesson formats to ones where you also create questions of inquiry for yourself, as well as how you might collect data during the lesson. For example, say you are thinking of reading a story picture book on a topic or theme of the current curriculum. You might have already taken journal notes on how the mentor teacher does Read-Alouds* and/or how you might have read-aloud a book to students previously. That is, you may have already completed several cycles of action-research

Focus Inquiry Lessons transform the traditional lesson plans.

on this classroom routine and are now ready to develop a new action plan based on these findings. As described previously, you may generate questions that are related on either side of the teaching-learning relationship. Perhaps this time the concern is around teaching issues because you have noticed that you, and maybe even your mentor teacher, seem to be asking all of the questions in the read-aloud sessions, thereby controlling most of the talk in the discussions. Thus, you might consider the following kinds of questions: In what ways can I encourage *students'* responses to the book? Also, in what ways can I promote more cross-discussions—where students talk to each other about what they think about the book instead of directing all of their remarks to me? You decide to try out at least three strategies: (1) pause frequently while you read the book and look to students with an expectant manner; (2) use some very open questions, such as "What do think so far?" or "Any comments?", and to promote cross-discussion specifically; (3) try to have students address their remarks to others by saying frequently, "What's your ideas on that? Could you turn around to tell [child's name] your thoughts?"

You might take very abbreviated "in-the-midst" descriptive notes on Post-it® Notes during the session, which you would expand and elaborate on in your research journal afterwards. (You might also audiotape the session and transcribe sections that reflect the major features of the discourse—that is, identify where your strategies were or were not successful.)

The value of Focus Inquiry Lessons is that it helps you avoid trying to teach "perfect" lessons or worry about using the "right" teaching methods. It makes you think about your own core principles that you are developing about teaching-learning.

Case Study Inquiry

Case study inquiry focuses on a particular child (or group) in the classroom setting.

See Rust (1994) for more information on a case study inquiry from the child's point of view.

As the term implies, this is an inquiry that focuses on one case, a particular student, in the fieldwork setting, which can be done at any level of your fieldwork experiences. Here, you attempt to understand what the curriculum or instructional routines of the classroom might be like from the perspective of this child. You "shadow" the child's behavior in various activities, his or her reactions to them, his or her interactions with peers and the mentor and yourself (and the gym or art teacher). You might find out other background information from your mentor teacher or other teachers your case student might have had in previous years. You may also implement various kid-watching activities with him or her—e.g., do a miscue analysis, take a dictation, collect and analyze writing samples written across the curriculum (see Chapter 8 for other possibilities.)

In this inquiry you are raising questions mostly about student learning, but throughout you are also reflecting upon how that learning and how his or her attitudes as a learner might have been influenced by instructional techniques and strategies. Thus, this inquiry enables you to clarify and make explicit your own connections between teaching and learning.

Mini-Thematic Project Inquiry

Mini-thematic unit inquiries focus on classroom student-directed inquiry projects around a "node" or subtopic of a thematic unit.

This inquiry is a possibility usually after STRs have already have had some teaching experiences in fieldwork settings. In the university classroom, you might have worked on developing thematic units similar to the ones illustrated in Chapter 4, perhaps with a buddy or in small groups. However, you might not have implemented any of them yet. Here you attempt to collaborate and negotiate with the mentor teacher to develop a mini-thematic unit—one perhaps that would go for a three- or four-week period. A major characteristic of this small unit would be student-directed inquiry projects to teach certain curricular content that the mentor would identify as important to be taught later in the school term and towards the last few weeks of your university quarter or semester. You would develop small WEBs for the content topic, think of the essential questions that would guide the activities and inquiry invitations for classroom students, collect the books and other materials you will need, and plan and outline the specific activities and times during the school day you would implement the mini-unit project during the three-week period. In other words, you don't take on a large thematic unit, such as the ones depicted in Chapter 4, but instead only some portions or "nodes" of one. Usually these projects involve a particular subject-area focus, but include the integration of talking, reading, and writing.

As you create your WEB and plans, you begin to think about a specific aspect of your implementation for your inquiry. Because this is likely to be a big step in your teaching and orchestrating of curriculum, it is important to be selective on your inquiry topic. You will have to decide whether you want to raise questions about your own teaching strategies or whether you will focus more on students' learning (see Figure G.1). Perhaps, because the classroom students have never conducted student inquiries in social studies (maybe the mentor teacher relies on the social studies textbook), you might focus on questions around how you will scaffold their first experience in the inquiry process. Using the ideas in Chapter 7 (Organizing/Monitoring Student-Initiated Inquiry Projects*), you set up the times and methods you will use to study your efforts in this area. You will have to keep track of the larger picture in order to manage the whole project, but as you begin several cycles of the action research, you may narrow its focus to how you will try to provide feedback to students in the course of their inquiries and their reactions to any Focus Lessons* you end up having as a result of what you observe. To make the inquiry even more manageable, you might decide to take *detailed notes* only on a small group of students or several case students from several groups. (Asking your mentor teacher to take notes on particular students is also a good idea.)

If you decide to have your inquiry emphasize students' learning, you might examine how students' strategies in finding the answers to their own inquiry questions as they read various children's literature books or other resources (including the textbook) you have brought in for their use have worked. Again, you might concentrate on several students' approaches to document in greater detail to understand their difficulties and successes in finding the data they need for their projects.

As you decide on the specific contexts that you will observe, and specify your inquiry questions, you will also consider how you will collect your data. Besides your research journal in which you will keep track of issues of the whole project, you might decide to fashion a Status of the Class* Sheet that lists your case students. Here you will jot down in-the-midst notes of what you say to them during their research, or if you focus on students' learning, what these students employed as strategies during their research. You will also go over students' inquiry logs (see Chapter 7) as other data for your inquiry. In addition, you think that after several cycles of observation, you might be able to identify some useful categories to use for the rest of the inquiry. These categories, then, might be included on the status sheet, enabling you to make your notes more organized and easier to write down.

Thematic-Unit Inquiry During Student Teaching

Usually STRs do their last fieldwork experience during a quarter or semester of student teaching. And for a large part of this term, they are responsible for developing a curricular unit. Here then is the opportunity for you to create and implement a larger version of a thematic unit. And in many ways you might try to develop inquiries similar to the ones that are depicted in Chapter 4.

Or, drawing on the ideas described above, you may fashion a series of smaller inquiries—perhaps a case student (or group) inquiry, several focus inquiry lessons, and a mini-thematic unit inquiry.

Because several STRs usually meet weekly with a supervisory university or college instructor, it may be possible to have a class inquiry as well. That is, you and your fellow STRs might choose several inquiries on common topics in your respective classroom settings. For example, you could examine the classroom discourse of various settings (see the Activity 2 in Chapter 2). Or you might all try to implement some particular routine—e.g., students' doing Book Talks*, peer conferencing, or math journals. Another might be analyzing students' writing of a particular genre—informational texts, realistic fiction, or historical fiction.

Thematic-unit inquiries usually occur during the student teaching experience where full-fledged units are developed and implemented.

Summary

Teacher research represents many things. First, of course, it is an important way in which teachers make sense of, and become reflective about, teaching and learning in their classrooms and schools. Just as inquiry empowers students, it also empowers teachers to be active learners, to construct their own knowledge, and to take a more authoritative stance toward their practice. The knowledge generated by teachers—sometimes called "teacher lore"—is fundamentally particular, which is also its major contribution, for it is embedded in the various social contexts of everyday teaching and learning. Thus, teachers' theories reflect certain ways of knowing because they are grounded in practice. Teacher research can also be cumulative and accessible to others, thereby playing an important role in the formation of the knowledge base of teaching in the larger educational community.

Teacher inquiry empowers teachers.

See Schubert & Ayers (1992) for more on "teacher lore."

See the online journal for teacher research (NETWORKS website at: http://www.oise.utoronto.ca/~ctd/networks).

REFERENCES

Altrichter, H., Posch, P., & Somekh, B. (1993). *Teachers investigate their work: An introduction to the methods of action research.* London: Routledge.

Bartolome, L. I. (1994). Beyond the methods fetish: Toward a humanizing pedagogy. *Harvard Educational Review, 64,* 173–194.

Cochran-Smith, M., & Lytle, S. (1993). *Inside/Outside: Teacher research and knowledge.* New York: Teachers College Press.

Cummins, J. (1994). From coercive to collaborative relations of power in the teaching of literacy. In B. M. Ferdman, R. M. Weber, & A. G. Ramirez (Eds.), *Literacy across languages and cultures* (pp. 295–331). Albany: State University of New York Press.

Dahl, K. L. (Ed.). (1992). *Teacher as writer: Entering the professional conversation.* Urbana, IL: National Council of Teachers of English.

Edelesky, C. (1994). Education for democracy. *Language Arts, 71,* 252–257.

Fischer, J. (1996). Open to ideas: Developing a framework for your research. In G. Burnaford, J. Fischer, & D. Hobson (Eds.), *Teachers doing research: Practical possibilities* (pp. 33–55). Mahwah, NJ: Lawrence Erlbaum.

Gutierrez, K., Rymes, B., & Larson, J. (1995). Script, counterscript, and the underlife in the classroom: James Brown versus *Brown v. Board of Education. Harvard Educational Review, 65,* 445–471.

Hobson, D. (1996). Beginning with the self: Using autobiography and journal writing in teacher research. In G. Burnaford, J. Fischer, & D. Hobson (Eds.), *Teachers doing research: Practical possibilities* (pp. 1–17). Mahwah, NJ: Lawrence Erlbaum.

Hubbard, R. S., & Power, B. M. (1993). *The art of classroom inquiry: A handbook for teacher-researchers.* Portsmouth, NH: Heinemann.

Pappas, C. C. (in press). Becoming literate in the borderlands. In A. Goncu (Ed.), *Children's engagement in the world: A sociocultural perspective.* Cambridge: Cambridge University Press.

Power, B. M. (1996). *Taking note: Improving your observational notetaking.* York, ME: Stenhouse.

Rust, F. O. (1994). From the child's point of view: A preliminary report on an assignment designed to promote critical reflection in teacher education. *Journal of Early Childhood Teacher Education, 15,* 3–6.

Schubert, W. H., & Ayers, W. C. (Eds.). (1992). *Teacher lore: Learning from our own experience.* White Plains, NY: Longman.

Wells, G. (1994). *Changing schools from within: Creating communities of inquiry.* Toronto, Canada: Ontario Institute for Studies in Education Press. (Distributed by Heinemann Press.)

Zeichner, K. M., & Liston, D. P. (1996). *Reflective teaching: An introduction.* Mahwah, NJ: Lawrence Erlbaum.

Index